Configuring CallManager and Unity:
A Step-by-Step Guide

David Bateman

Cisco Press

800 East 96th Street
Indianapolis, Indiana 46240 USA

Configuring CallManager and Unity: A Step-by-Step Guide

David Bateman

Copyright © 2005 Cisco Systems, Inc.

Cisco Press logo is a trademark of Cisco Systems, Inc.

Published by:
Cisco Press
800 East 96th Street
Indianapolis, IN 46240 USA

Printed in the United States of America   4 5 6 7 8 9 0

Fourth Printing November 2006

Library of Congress Cataloging-in-Publication Number: 2004100283

ISBN: 1-58705-196-6

Warning and Disclaimer

This book is designed to provide information about configuration and administrative tasks related to CallManager and Unity. Every effort has been made to make this book as complete and as accurate as possible, but no warranty or fitness is implied.

The information is provided on an "as is" basis. The authors, Cisco Press, and Cisco Systems, Inc. shall have neither liability nor responsibility to any person or entity with respect to any loss or damages arising from the information contained in this book or from the use of the discs or programs that may accompany it.

The opinions expressed in this book belong to the author and are not necessarily those of Cisco Systems, Inc.

Trademark Acknowledgments

All terms mentioned in this book that are known to be trademarks or service marks have been appropriately capitalized. Cisco Press or Cisco Systems, Inc. cannot attest to the accuracy of this information. Use of a term in this book should not be regarded as affecting the validity of any trademark or service mark.

Corporate and Government Sales

Cisco Press offers excellent discounts on this book when ordered in quantity for bulk purchases or special sales.

For more information please contact: **U.S. Corporate and Government Sales**   1-800-382-3419
corpsales@pearsontechgroup.com

For sales outside the U.S. please contact: **International Sales**   international@pearsoned.com

Feedback Information

At Cisco Press, our goal is to create in-depth technical books of the highest quality and value. Each book is crafted with care and precision, undergoing rigorous development that involves the unique expertise of members from the professional technical community.

Readers' feedback is a natural continuation of this process. If you have any comments regarding how we could improve the quality of this book, or otherwise alter it to better suit your needs, you can contact us through e-mail at feedback@ciscopress.com. Please make sure to include the book title and ISBN in your message.

We greatly appreciate your assistance.

Publisher	John Wait
Editor-in-Chief	John Kane
Executive Editor	Brett Bartow
Cisco Representative	Anthony Wolfenden
Cisco Press Program Manager	Jeff Brady
Production Manager	Patrick Kanouse
Development Editor	Betsey Henkels
Project Editor	Sheila Schroeder
Copy Editor	Michelle Kidd
Technical Editor	Mick Buchanan, Roger Robert, Todd Stone
Editorial Assistant	Tammi Barnett
Cover Designer	Louisa Adair
Composition	Interactive Composition Corporation
Indexer	Tim Wright

CISCO SYSTEMS

Corporate Headquarters
Cisco Systems, Inc.
170 West Tasman Drive
San Jose, CA 95134-1706
USA
www.cisco.com
Tel: 408 526-4000
    800 553-NETS (6387)
Fax: 408 526-4100

European Headquarters
Cisco Systems International BV
Haarlerbergpark
Haarlerbergweg 13-19
1101 CH Amsterdam
The Netherlands
www-europe.cisco.com
Tel: 31 0 20 357 1000
Fax: 31 0 20 357 1100

Americas Headquarters
Cisco Systems, Inc.
170 West Tasman Drive
San Jose, CA 95134-1706
USA
www.cisco.com
Tel: 408 526-7660
Fax: 408 527-0883

Asia Pacific Headquarters
Cisco Systems, Inc.
Capital Tower
168 Robinson Road
#22-01 to #29-01
Singapore 068912
www.cisco.com
Tel: +65 6317 7777
Fax: +65 6317 7799

Cisco Systems has more than 200 offices in the following countries and regions. Addresses, phone numbers, and fax numbers are listed on the
Cisco.com Web site at www.cisco.com/go/offices.

Argentina • Australia • Austria • Belgium • Brazil • Bulgaria • Canada • Chile • China PRC • Colombia • Costa Rica • Croatia • Czech Republic
Denmark • Dubai, UAE • Finland • France • Germany • Greece • Hong Kong SAR • Hungary • India • Indonesia • Ireland • Israel • Italy
Japan • Korea • Luxembourg • Malaysia • Mexico • The Netherlands • New Zealand • Norway • Peru • Philippines • Poland • Portugal
Puerto Rico • Romania • Russia • Saudi Arabia • Scotland • Singapore • Slovakia • Slovenia • South Africa • Spain • Sweden
Switzerland • Taiwan • Thailand • Turkey • Ukraine • United Kingdom • United States • Venezuela • Vietnam • Zimbabwe

Printed in the USA

About the Author

David J. Bateman is a certified Cisco Systems instructor and CCNA with more than 16 years of internetworking experience. For more than 10 years, David was a Senior LAN/WAN Engineer, working on networks with up to 5000 users. Later in his career, he took on the responsibility of running the business operations of a technical services company, while maintaining his existing client base. David has always enjoyed sharing his knowledge, and in 1999, he added to his list of accomplishments by becoming a technical seminar leader. After many successful seminars, he decided to become a full-time Cisco instructor for Skyline Advanced Technology Systems. He has been teaching and implementing Cisco voice technologies since 2000. David's years of real world technical and business knowledge allow him to bring a unique perspective to the classroom, where he not only delivers critical technical knowledge but can also explain how technologies can be used to address various business issues.

About the Technical Reviewers

Mick Buchanan began working with CallManager in 1998 as one of the original Selsius Systems customer support engineers. He currently works as a technical resource and consultant to large named accounts using the Cisco AVVID solution.

Roger G. Robert is an instructor and consultant for Skyline-ATS. His professional responsibilities include teaching Cisco certified routing, switching, and IP Telephony classes to Cisco employees, Cisco Value Added Resellers (VARs), and Cisco customers. Roger also develops and delivers custom curriculum and deploys IP Telephony solutions under Skyline's consulting umbrella. During the course of the last 30 years, Roger has worked as an installation and maintenance technician, project manager, and instructor in virtually every aspect of Telecommunications from radio and satellite communications to legacy PBX/Voice Mail/Call Center applications. For the past four years, he has focused his efforts on Cisco IP Telephony.

Todd Stone is a technical marketing engineer at the ECS business unit of Cisco, the makers of Unity. Todd's career spans more than 18 years in the computer industry including an initial stint in the US Army as a tech controller at a fixed communications station near Washington, DC. Todd attended Northern Kentucky University and has also held various technical certifications. His background includes telecommunications, voice systems, data communications management and design, and large-scale server and infrastructure deployment projects, in addition to administration and management with various directories and messaging systems. He has also been heavily engaged in various other design and deployment-oriented activities. Todd and his wife have three children and live in a small town located on the Kitsap Peninsula on the western side of Puget Sound in the state of Washington.

Dedications

I dedicate this book to a man who has taught me more through deeds and actions than through words. A man who worked for 32 years on the Chrysler assembly line, not because he loved his job but because he loved his family. A man who never wanted more than for his children to have it better than he had. My Dad, William A. Bateman.

Acknowledgments

There are a number of people that I would like to thank in helping me complete this book. Often the greatest help that can be received is when someone is willing to sacrifice so that you may succeed. With this in mind I would like to thank my girlfriend, Nikki. She has sacrificed many beautiful summer days that we could have spent out on the motorcycle so that I could work on this book. She sacrificed hours each week reading what I had written in order that I might deliver a more readable copy to the editors. I know it was not always fun for her, but it helped me complete this book. Without her sacrifice this book would not have been possible.

I would also like to thank all of the technical editors. Their keen insight and willingness to ask me what the heck I was thinking on some subjects has helped make this a much better book than it was when I first wrote it. I also need to send a special thanks to one particular technical editor, Roger Robert. Roger has been with me through this entire project. During the beginning, before he had officially joined the project as a technical editor, he was always there when I needed to bounce a concept or two off someone. Even beyond his role as a technical editor his contributions to this book are great.

Of course I'd like to thank those at Skyline-ATS, where I work, for allowing me to write this book. I would especially like to thank them for the skill they showed in increasing my workload as deadlines for the book drew near. I guess they figured I would do better under pressure. But seriously, I would like to thank Mike Maudlin and Mike Zanatto for their understanding and cooperation during this project. And of course my boss, Andy DeMaria. No matter how much work I had, he was always able to find me more! Where would I have been without him. On a serious note, I'd like to thank him for his encouragement when I told him about the book and for listening to me throughout the year when I needed to vent and do a little more complaining than normal. I also need to thank all the others that I worked with at Skyline, the awesome amount of knowledge that we hold as a team is incredible, and to have such a resource at my disposal has been invaluable.

A big thank you to the following folks at Cisco Press: Jim Schachterle, who assisted from the beginning of this project and believed in it enough to make it happen. Raina Han, who was always there to remind me of upcoming deadlines long enough in advance so that I had time to either meet the deadline or come up with a really good excuse. Dayna Isley who helped me with the formatting when I began this project and Betsey Henkels who acted as my development editor and was always helpful and encouraging.

One last thanks. One night I was sitting at dinner talking with Wendell Odom, and I told him about a book that I thought Cisco Press should write. Because he has written a number of books for Cisco Press I thought he could pass the idea along, and then one day maybe I would see it in the bookstore. Little did I know then that I would be the one writing it. As they say, "Be careful what you wish for." No matter how busy Wendell is, and trust me he is a busy person, he always makes time for me and offers whatever help he can.

Thanks one and all for all you've done.

This Book Is Safari Enabled

The Safari® Enabled icon on the cover of your favorite technology book means the book is available through Safari Bookshelf. When you buy this book, you get free access to the online edition for 45 days.

Safari Bookshelf is an electronic reference library that lets you easily search thousands of technical books, find code samples, download chapters, and access technical information whenever and wherever you need it.

To gain 45-day Safari Enabled access to this book:

- Go to http://www.ciscopress.com/safarienabled
- Complete the brief registration form
- Enter the coupon code LPON-C51P-0OEM-IFPX-J4DU

If you have difficulty registering on Safari Bookshelf or accessing the online edition, please e-mail customer-service@safaribooksonline.com.

Contents at a Glance

Table of Contents

Icons Used in This Book

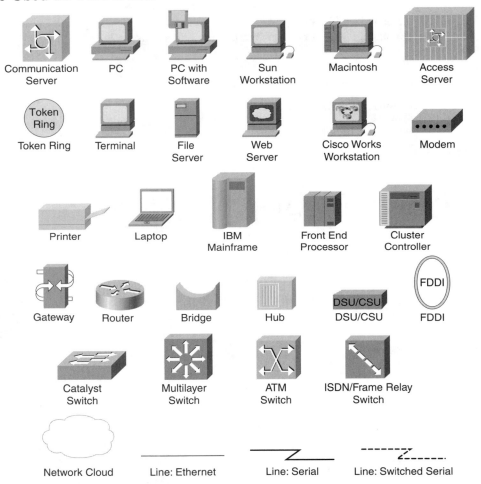

Command Syntax Conventions

The conventions used to present command syntax in this book are the same conventions used in the IOS Command Reference. The Command Reference describes these conventions as follows:

- **Boldface** indicates commands and keywords that are entered literally as shown. In actual configuration examples and output (not general command syntax), boldface indicates commands that are manually input by the user (such as a **show** command).

- *Italics* indicate arguments for which you supply actual values.

- Vertical bars (|) separate alternative, mutually exclusive elements.

- Square brackets [ ] indicate optional elements.

- Braces { } indicate a required choice.

- Braces within brackets [{ }] indicate a required choice within an optional element.

Introduction

On March 10, 1876, Alexander Graham Bell made the first successful telephone call. As with many things, the test was purely accidental; Graham spilled acid on his leg, and Watson, his assistant, heard his call for help through the telephone. So, what has changed over the last 129 years? It would be easier to discuss what hasn't changed. The world of telephony has undergone some significant changes, but none as exciting as Voice over IP (VoIP) solutions from Cisco. There are still those who believe we were all a lot better off in an analog world, but you can't stop progress, and the Cisco IP Telephony solutions are starting to grow faster than many had believed. Just look at a few of the interesting trends:

- AT&T has announced that it plans to offer Voice over Internet Services that will interconnect with CallManager from Cisco.

- Foster and Sullivan expect the annual compound growth rate for the Asia Pacific IP-PBX market to reach 65.1 percent by 2008.

- According to Phillips InfoTech, in the near future IP-PBXs are expected to exceed half of all PBXs shipped.

This new technology brings with it the need for individuals to learn how it works. While there are many fine Cisco Press books on this technology, I noticed many of my students requesting a task-oriented book. They were looking for a book in which they could look up a specific task and be walked through it. This was the initial goal of the book. Through the writing process, the book evolved from offering only a step-by-step guide into also offering easy to understand explanations for many of the Cisco IP Telephony concepts and components.

Goals and Methods

New technologies bring new opportunities and challenges. One of the challenges that we are faced with in the Cisco IP telephony world is the ability to easily understand the many facets of the configuration and integration process. Because this platform can be deployed in so many different configurations and environments, system administrators and system engineers need a resource that offers quick access to step-by-step solutions. In an environment such as this, it is nearly impossible to keep track of the exact steps for each configuration task. Those tasks that you do on a daily basis are easy to perform, but when you are called upon to perform unfamiliar tasks, you don't always have the time to learn the proper steps. *Configuring CallManager and Unity* shows readers how to complete many of the common tasks, and some not-so-common tasks, performed within a Cisco IP telephony solution.

Who Should Read This Book?

The book is aimed at individuals who are required to configure CallManger and Unity solutions as a primary part of their jobs. The book is unique because it covers both CallManager and Unity.

Although this book focuses on the tasks that must be performed, it also offers easy-to-understand explanations for many of the technologies that are commonly found with Cisco IP telephony environments, which makes it an excellent resource for individuals who are new to this technology.

How This Book Is Organized

Within the book, tasks are organized in the same order in which they would naturally be performed. Some tasks include cross-references to prerequisite tasks. Whenever possible, however, all tasks are presented within the same section.

Different people, depending on their knowledge and background, will use this book in different ways. Many will find it a useful reference tool when completing an unfamiliar task, and those new to this technology will find that reading this book from cover to cover will help them gain a solid understanding of this technology. Although the step-by-step guides were written with the assumption that the reader has access to a CallManager while reading the steps, this is not required. This book includes numerous screen shots, which allow the reader to see what is happening in the administration interface even if they do not have access to a CallManager.

Chapter 1 offers the reader a high-level overview of most of the concepts and components that are found within CallManager and Unity. Basically, the information found in two weeks of classes has been compressed in order to quickly bring the reader up to speed. This by no means is a replacement for these classes—just a quick overview.

Chapters 2 through 6 cover CallManager configuration, while Chapters 7 through 11 discuss Unity configuration. The last chapter speaks to more advanced features of both technologies and offers a few ways to leverage the strengths of both to create a more feature-rich environment.

The following is a brief description of each chapter.

Chapter 1: Cisco CallManager and Unity Overview

This chapter offers a broad overview of the Cisco IP telephony solutions to ensure that the reader is comfortable with what is to follow in the book. The intent of this chapter is to offer the reader an overview of the various components of a Cisco Voice over IP solution. The reader is strongly encouraged to refer to suggested reference material for additional information on any topic with which they may be unfamiliar. This material can be found in the appendix.

Chapter 2: Preparing CallManager for Deployment

In order to ensure a smooth deployment, tasks must be performed in a certain order. In this chapter, you learn what tasks must be completed before adding devices. As with most things, if you fail to create a solid foundation, you will encounter problems in the future. This chapter ensures that the proper foundation is created and future problems are avoided. Topics covered include services configuration, enterprise parameters, and device registration tasks. Additionally, this chapter includes step-by-step instructions for each task.

Chapter 3: Deploying Devices

After the predeployment tasks are completed, you are ready to add devices. This chapter focuses on the tasks required to add various devices to your CallManager environment. Devices have been divided into two major categories: clients (IP phones, softphones, etc.) and gateways. The chapter includes step-by-step instructions for adding each device.

Chapter 4: Implementing a Dial Plan

Before you can place calls to destinations that are not directly connected to your CallManager environment, you must configure a dial plan. This chapter discusses all the components of a dial plan, such as route patterns, route lists and route groups and the tasks that are needed to implement an efficient dial plan. The step-by-step tasks show how to create and configure route patterns, route lists and route groups and more advanced components, such as CTI route points, translation patterns and route filters.

Chapter 5: Configuring Class of Service and Call Admission Control

After a dial plan is created you may want to limit what destinations certain devices can reach. This chapter discusses how to do this by configuring Calling Search Spaces and Partitions. It is also necessary that some types of call admission control be deployed on WAN links so that the quality of voice is maintained. To this end, Call Admission Control features are covered. Finally, this chapter discusses the importance of special services, such as 911 and how to properly configure the dial plan to handle these types of calls.

Chapter 6: Configuring CallManager Features and Services

After basic call processing functions are configured and working properly, you need to add new features, and monitor the health of the system. This chapter explores a number of the features that can be implemented, including IP phone service, media resources and Extension Mobility. The need for, and the functions of, SRST is also covered in this chapter. Furthermore, this chapter examines some of the monitoring services that are included in CallManager. Step-by-step instructions that explain how to add each feature and service are included.

Chapter 7: Unity Predeployment Tasks

The first step to proper configuration is verifying that the integration is correct and that all predeployment tasks are complete. This chapter includes step-by-step instructions for completing predeployment tasks, such as verifying integration, defining system parameters, and creating templates, distribution lists, and CoS.

Chapter 8: Subscriber Reference

After a proper integration between Unity and CallManager is achieved and the predeployment tasks discussed in the previous chapter are completed, subscribers can be added. In this chapter, the different types of subscribers are examined. Then, the process for adding, importing, and managing subscribers is explored. Within the Managing Subscriber section, various administrative tasks are discussed, which range from "How to reset a subscriber password" to "How to properly remove subscribers." Each task includes step-by-step instructions.

Chapter 9: Call Management

One of Unity's most useful and often under-utilized features is Call Management. This chapter ensures that the reader understands the way Unity processes a call. The most basic object of the call management system is a call handler. A brief review of how call handlers work is included in the beginning of this chapter. Additionally, a common use of Unity's call management feature is to deploy Unity as a basic auto-attendant, which is described within this text. The chapter also addresses some of the more advanced call management features, such as call routing rules and audio-text applications. Complete step-by-step instructions are included within this chapter.

Chapter 10: Implementing Unity Networking

Because many organizations are migrating to Unity from a voice-mail system or have other voice-mail systems deployed at other locations, Unity must be able to communicate with them. Unity can be integrated with these systems through a number of industry-standard protocols. This chapter discusses the different types of networking that can be deployed and looks at how to determine the proper one to use.

Chapter 11: Exploring Unity Tools

Although most day-to-day tasks can be accomplished using the System administrative interface, it is often more efficient to use one of the many tools that are included with Unity. The tools help accomplish tasks that range from making bulk subscriber changes to migrating users to another server. This chapter introduces the reader to these tools and includes step-by-step details on how to use each of them.

Chapter 12: Maximizing the Capabilities of Unity and CallManager

As CallManager and Unity evolve, more and more advanced features are added. This chapter looks at a few of these more advanced features, such as IPMA, Time of day routing and call queuing. In addition, the chapter offers a few examples of features that can be created by taking existing features of each application and adding a new twist to them, such as using Unity as a conference manager.

Target Version

This book was written to CallManager version 4.1 and Unity version 4.04. This is not to say that you must be running these versions for this book to be of value to you. It does, however, mean that some of the step-by-step guides may be slightly different. With each new version, the menus are sometimes moved or changed slightly, or there may be a field in the new version that is not in an older version. However, none of these issues should cause you great concern. If the field isn't there, don't worry about it. If a menu isn't exactly where you expect it, just look above or below, and you are sure to find it. Including the exact steps for every version of these applications would have made the book larger than you would care to lift let alone read. Remember that the value of this book goes beyond the step-by-step guides, as it also provides easy-to-understand explanations of many Cisco IP telephony concepts.

CallManager Configuration

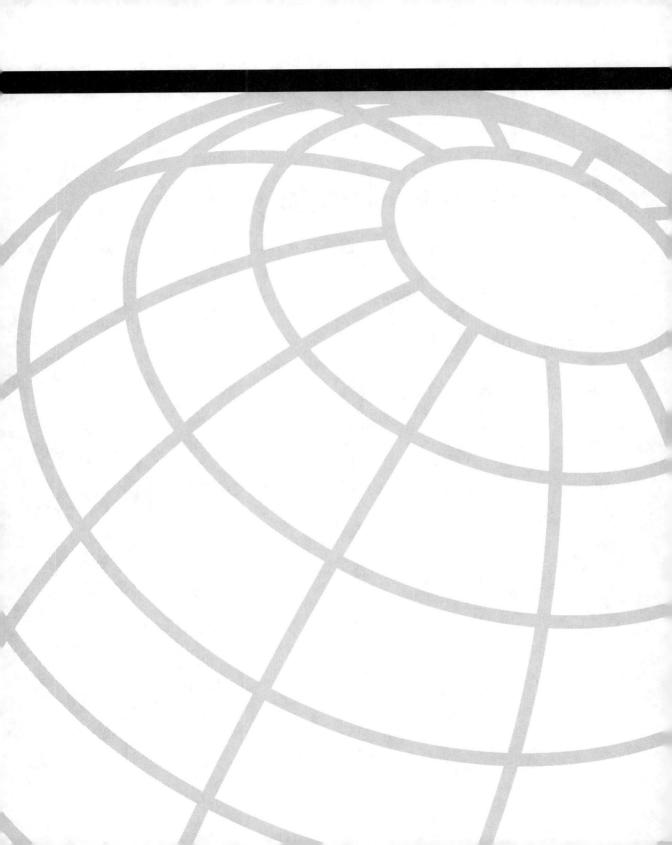

CHAPTER 1

Cisco CallManager and Unity Overview

Before embarking on any worthwhile adventure it is important that you have a good map and a solid understanding of the purpose of your trip. This chapter provides just that—an introduction to some of the many components that make up a Cisco Voice over IP (VoIP) environment.

Technical books can be divided into one of two categories, "why books" and "how to books." Why books provide the reader with a solid understanding of the technology and explain why you would want to deploy it. How to books tell the reader how to deploy a given technology. This is a how to book. The main purpose of this book is that of a configuration reference. However, it is important that you have a solid understanding of the technology. This chapter provides you with a broad overview of this technology and references to further information. If you are new to this technology, you are strongly encouraged to pursue more in depth information than is presented in this chapter before deploying this technology. If you haven't been involved in this technology for a while, you may be thinking of skipping this chapter and moving on to the meat of the book. This, of course, is your decision, but reading this chapter will give you a better understanding of the specific technologies that are discussed later in this book.

After reading this chapter, you should have a high-level understanding of the CallManager and Unity components and how they fit into a Cisco VoIP solution. This chapter has been divided into the following sections:

- Reliable Foundation
- CallManager Overview
- Unity Overview
- Security Concerns

Because this technology is really a mixture of two pre-existing technologies, traditional telcom and traditional data, it is very likely that you started out solely in one of these disciplines. Often when we start to learn a new technology, we try to compare it to technologies we've learned. This sometimes causes learners to miss an important point because they were preoccupied with trying to make this new information fit in with previous learning. If you are new to this technology, I would encourage you to take any current knowledge you have and place it aside while reading. After you have read this chapter and feel that you understand it, you should then integrate it with your current knowledge base. At first, this will be difficult because we all seem to want to fall back on what we already know. So each time you find yourself doing this, just stop reading for a moment and refocus on acquiring new information, knowing that later you can integrate it with what you already know. Also, try not to make judgments while reading. Many times people have made up their minds about a product or technology before they have even seen it. Even if you are learning this technology because "you have to," be as open to it as possible. Regardless of any man's resistance, technology will not stop or even slow down.

Ensuring a Reliable Foundation

Whether you are building a house or a network, a solid foundation is crucial. In a VoIP network, the foundation is even more crucial because both data and voice will be using the same network. This means that you need to implement an even higher level of redundancy than you feel is necessary in a traditional data network. The term five 9s is used a lot in the traditional telcom world; this stands for 99.999 percent uptime. The expectation is that any network that carries voice should be up 99.999 percent of the time. This calculates to just a little more than five minutes a year, not including planned down time for upgrades and maintenance. You may be saying, "That's impossible," but actually it is possible. With the proper planning and design, you can expect to see nearly no downtime. Make note that I said with the proper planning and design. There have been a number of VoIP deployments that failed solely because a proper infrastructure was not implemented. Typically, a VoIP environment is broken into four layers. Each layer plays a vital role. An example of the devices that are in each layer follows.

- Clients—IP phones
- Applications—Unity
- Call Processing—CallManager
- Infrastructure—switches and gateways

The foundation of the network is at the infrastructure level where components such as switches, routers and gateways reside. A solid understanding of these components is needed to design a solution that will withstand common day-to-day problems that arise on most networks. The discussion begins with a look at these components.

Infrastructure Overview

A properly deployed infrastructure is the key to a reliable network. This section begins by examining the foundation of the infrastructure. The cable is one of the most often overlooked components of the network. This is often due to the fact that it rarely causes problems after it is installed. Cabling problems normally don't appear until some new type of technology is added to the network. I remember one client that was running a four megabit network with no trouble at all. When they upgraded to 16 megabit, the network started failing and they had to rewire the whole network.

Nowadays, twisted pair Ethernet is installed in most environments. The Cisco VoIP solution is designed with the assumption that twisted pair Ethernet is installed at each desktop.

One of the common issues that arises with cabling is when the installer takes a few shortcuts. A common shortcut is failing to terminate all the pairs of the cable. The installer figures that because Ethernet only uses pins 1,2, 3 and 6, there is no need to terminate the others. In most cases, the network will function when cabled this way. The problem is, however, that such a network is not installed to industry standards, and all of Cisco's solutions are based on the assumption that the existing infrastructure is installed according to industry standards. In an environment such as this, you cannot use the Cisco power patch panel because it relies on pins 4, 5, 7 and 8 to deliver power to the phone. Ensure that you have all cabling tested and certified before the deployment begins. As the saying goes, "An ounce of prevention is worth a pound of dropped calls" (or something like that).

After you have the cabling under control, you need to look at the equipment to which the cabling connects. On the one end of the cable you have phones, which is pretty straightforward. On the other end, you have the phone plugged into a switch.

NOTE	Please note that this discussion assumes that the phone is plugged into a switch, not a hub. Plugging phones into hubs is not advised because all devices on a hub share the same bandwidth and this can lead to poor voice quality. In addition, do not daisy-chain phones (plug one phone into another).

When deciding which switch to use, a few things must be considered. First, it is recommended that all switches you plan to use within the Cisco VoIP solution are Cisco switches. This is not simply because Cisco wants to sell more switches, but because certain Cisco switches include special features that allow greater functionality within your network. These features include: Inline power, Voice virtual LANs (VLANs), and Cisco Discovery Protocol (CDP) support. This does not mean that switches from other manufacturers cannot be used. It simply means that some features discussed in the following sections may not be supported.

Inline Power

This is the ability to provide power to the phones through the Ethernet cable. There are two inline power schemes; the first is the Cisco inline power convention, which uses pins 1, 2, 3 and 6 to provide power. These same wires are used for the transfer of data. The other method for providing the power of Ethernet (PoE) is the IEEE standard 802.3af. This is an approved industry standard that differs from Cisco's inline power scheme in a number of ways. Since its approval, Cisco has begun to produce phones that support this new standard. The net effect of either standard is the same—power is supplied to the phone through the Ethernet cable. The switches that support either of these conventions are able to detect if the attached device requires inline power, and if the device does require inline power, the switch provides it. Having two methods of supplying inline power can be confusing, so it is important that the phones and switches you purchase use the same method.

Voice VLANs

This allows the use of a single switch port to simultaneously support both a phone and a PC by allowing a single port to recognize two VLANs. The PC is plugged into the back of the phone, and the phone is plugged into the switch. The switch then advertises both VLANs. The phone can recognize the voice VLAN and use it. PCs cannot recognize voice VLANs and use the native VLAN.

CDP Support

CDP is a Cisco proprietary protocol that allows Cisco equipment to share certain information with other Cisco equipment. The phones use CDP to determine if a voice VLAN is present on that port. It also shares other information such as port power information, and quality of service (QoS) information with the Cisco Catalyst switch.

Make sure the switch you choose supports these features. Currently, some of the 6500, 4000, and 3500 series switches are capable of supporting all these features.

After you ensure that the cabling and switches are adequate for a VoIP solution, you are ready to deploy the endpoints. Endpoints can be any of the following: phones, CallManager servers, or gateways. Of these devices, only gateways are considered to reside at the infrastructure level. Phones and CallManagers are covered later in this chapter.

In its simplest form, a gateway is a device that allows connectivity of dissimilar networks. In the VoIP world, a gateway is used to connect the CallManager voice network to another network. The Public Switched Telephone Network (PSTN) is the most popular network with which the CallManager must be able to communicate. The job of the gateway is to convert the data traveling through it to a format the other side understands. Just as a translator is needed when a person speaks German to someone who understands only Spanish, a gateway is needed to convert VoIP to a signal the PSTN understands.

The hardware that acts as a gateway varies, depending on what type of network you connect to and what features you require. When choosing a gateway it's important to ensure that it supports the following four core gateway requirements:

- **DTMF Relay**—Dual Tone Multi Frequency (DTMF) are the tones that are played when you press the dial pad on a phone. Many people refer to this as touch-tones. Because voice is often compressed, the DTMF can become distorted. The DTMF relay feature allows the DTMF to be sent out-of-band, which resolves the distortion problem.

- **Supplementary Services**—Includes hold, transfer, and conferencing.

- **Cisco CallManager (CCM) Redundancy**—Supports the ability to fail over to a secondary CallManager if the primary CallManager fails.
- **Call Survivability**—Ensures that the call will not drop if the CallManager, to which either endpoint is registered, fails.

Later, the various types of gateways are discussed. For now, understand the purpose of a gateway and the required features.

Creating a Reliable VoIP Infrastructure

In the summer of 2003, the northeastern portion of the United States experienced a widespread power outage. The power outage lasted from six hours to three days depending upon the area. One of the most impressive and yet understated events that occurred during this time is what didn't happen. For the most part, the PSTN didn't fail and nobody even noticed. The fact that no one really noticed shows us how much people expect the phones always to work. The power was completely out and yet most people didn't think for a second that the PSTN might fail. The system didn't fail because of the highly reliable and redundant infrastructure that has been developed over the years. This is the type of reliability people have come to expect from the phone system. It has been stated that many people view dial tone as a God-given right, or even one of the inalienable rights in the constitution. (I doubt anyone thinks that, but you get the idea.) With this in mind, you must make every effort to ensure that nothing short of a natural disaster prevents your customer from having dial tone.

The most important thing to keep in mind is that individual components of the system will fail. It is not a question of if something will fail, but when. Since components will fail, it is up to you to determine how to prevent the failure from affecting dial tone. This is done during the design phase of the project.

NOTE   The design phase is perhaps the single most important part of any deployment. Countless times I've had panicked customers, whom I inherited from other integrators, calling me with problems that could have been averted if dealt with during the design phase. Often when I ask clients how this problem was dealt with during the design phase, they answer, "What design phase?" Make certain that you cover as many foreseen and unforeseen eventualities as possible during the design phase. Although your customers may never see how good you are at fixing a system when it fails, they will know how good you are because it doesn't fail.

Redundancy is the core component in a reliable infrastructure. The system design should include redundancy at every level. This starts in the wiring closet.

Reducing the cable infrastructure and allowing for ease of cable management is one of the motivating factors for migrating to a VoIP solution. Therefore, it does not make sense that redundancy is extended to the cable level. Remember, our goal is to achieve the same level of reliability that people expect from a phone system. People understand that if there is a cabling problem, the phone won't work. This is one of the few acceptable reasons for a phone system to fail. So, as far as the cabling goes, you just need to ensure that the existing network cabling infrastructure is certified as previously mentioned.

Switches are the next piece of the infrastructure that need to be considered. Redundancy at the switch level is nothing new. Although redundancy has always been encouraged in data networks, it is no longer just a good idea, it is required in order to achieve the expected level of reliability. In smaller environments that may have only a single switch, redundancy at the switch level doesn't apply; however, in large networks make sure that you design a highly available network by building redundancy in at the switch level. This means that there will be multiple paths a packet may take to get to its destination. Due to a protocol called STP (Spanning Tree Protocol), only one path is available at any given time. STP ensures that if a link fails, an alternate path will be opened. To find out more about STP, see the additional references listed in the Appendix, "Additional Reference Resources."

A redundant path can ensure that a packet reaches its destination, but it is also important that it gets there in a timely manner. Voice traffic does not handle delay very well. If too much delay is introduced, the quality of the conversation tends to degrade rapidly. You have probably noticed the effect delay can have on a conversation when watching a TV news reporter via satellite link. It seems to take the reporter a few seconds to respond to a news anchor's question. This is because there is a several second delay between the time the question is asked and when it reaches the reporter's destination.

Many things can affect the delay that is introduced into a conversation. One of the most common is the competition between voice and other traffic for bandwidth. To help alleviate this, QoS must be implemented within the network. QoS gives certain traffic priority over other traffic. The proper configuration of QoS is essential for any network that will have both voice and data on the same wire. A detailed discussion on QoS is really out of the scope of this book. Please refer to Appendix A for suggested references on this subject.

Before leaving the wiring closet, one more thing requires attention: power. Remember that a power failure is not an acceptable reason to lose dial tone. As a matter of fact, a power outage is not necessarily an acceptable reason for data networks to fail anymore. There was a time when people expected and accepted the loss of data during a power outage. They were never happy about it, but they weren't surprised either. Nowadays with the reasonable price of uninterruptible power supply (UPS), data networks are no longer as susceptible to power outages as they were in the past. It is nearly unheard of not to have a UPS on file servers, and in many cases, throughout the network. Switches are no exception. As with any equipment, you need to do some research to determine the proper size of the UPS you need. To do this, determine the amount of power that the switch will draw and then determine the amount of time you want the switch to be able to run without power. You don't need to worry about redundant power at the phone if you are using inline power. Keep in mind that the more phones drawing power from the switch, the larger UPS you need.

As mentioned previously, gateways are also considered part of the infrastructure. Therefore, whenever possible, redundancy should be included at the gateway level. In some cases, such as an environment that only has a single trunk from the PSTN, redundancy is not feasible. If the environment has other Cisco routers, try to use the same model router for your PSTN gateway. This way, if the PSTN gateway does fail, you may be able to swap equipment for a short-term solution or, at the very least, use the other router for testing purposes after hours. If you do have multiple trunks, it is a good idea to have at least two physical gateways connecting the network to the PSTN. A level of redundancy can be added by using multiple service providers. For example, if you have two trunks use a different service provider for each. This way if either of the service providers has a wide-spread outage the other trunk will still be functional.

This section dealt with the reliability of the infrastructure. This is only a portion of the solution that must be considered when implementing a reliable system. A system is only as good as its weakest link, so you need to ensure that the entire system is designed with the same goal in mind—"Don't affect dial tone." In the next section, you look at the call-processing layer, more specifically, the CallManager.

CallManager Overview

In the previous section, the infrastructure was discussed and you learned what was necessary to create a solid foundation on which to build the rest of the system. As when building a house, you can move to the heart of the project once the foundation is set.

The CallManager is considered the heart of the Cisco VoIP solution. It is responsible for device registrations and call control. CallManager is an application that runs on a Media Convergence Server (MCS). Often the term CallManager is used to refer to the physical device that the application is running on, but the hardware should be referred to as MCS. CallManager is the software running on the hardware.

NOTE   Cisco has certified certain servers for use as MCSs. Currently only certain HP and IBM servers are certified. These servers may be purchased from Cisco or directly from IBM or HP. The different platforms offer various features, such as redundant hard drives and power supplies. Be sure to take this into consideration when choosing a server. Keep in mind that not all IBM and HP servers are approved, so be certain to check with Cisco to be certain the server you choose is approved. Many integrators choose to purchase the MCS from Cisco in order to have a single vendor solution.

Every system should have at least two CallManagers, and the two are referred to as a CallManager cluster. Later in this chapter, you learn why a minimum of two CallManagers is strongly recommended. Based on the previous section you might be able to guess for yourself. Does the word redundancy come to mind?

Defining CallManager Components

CallManager is responsible for all device registration and call control. Much of the configuration is performed through the CallManager interface. This section introduces you to the various components of CallManager and the devices that it controls.

Most configuration is performed through CallManager's web browser interface. Using this interface, one can configure phones, add users to CallManager's directory, define the dial plan, and perform various other tasks. The majority of the tasks that you will learn how to perform later in this book will be done using this interface. Because this interface is actually a series of web pages, Internet Information Services (IIS) must be running on the CallManager. IIS is installed during the automated install process. The interface is fairly simple to navigate and, after a short time, most people are quite comfortable using it. It is important to remember that it is a web-based interface and, hence, may not be as responsive as you would expect. Each evolution of this interface is improving the end-user experience, and, nowadays, it is much more enjoyable to use than in years past.

All the information that you enter through the web interface must be stored. CallManager uses Structured Query Language (SQL) 2000 to store this information. Nearly everything you enter into the CallManager is stored in the SQL database. The user information is one exception; it is stored in a Lightweight Directory Access Protocol (LDAP) directory. CallManager installs DC directories, which is an LDAP directory. You may use DC directories or another LDAP directory such as Netscape or Microsoft AD (active directory) to store the user information.

As mentioned earlier, each CallManager cluster should have at least two CallManagers. The reason for this is redundancy. Remember, the system needs to deliver the same level of reliability that people are used to with a traditional phone system. Having multiple CallManagers also provides for a more scalable system, which will be explained shortly. For now, the focus is on the role that the various CallManagers play in regards to SQL. A CallManager is referred to as either a Publisher or a Subscriber. Each CallManager cluster has only one Publisher. All other CallManagers within that cluster are referred to as Subscribers.

The job of the Publisher is to maintain the most current copy of the SQL database. Whenever anything is added to the database, the information is sent from the Publisher to all of the Subscribers. The data is never written to the Subscribers first and then transferred to the Publisher. The Subscriber, however, acts as if it does not have a copy of the database, and each time it needs to read from the database, it sends a request for the information to the Publisher. At first glance, this may seem odd. Because the Subscriber has a copy of the database, one would think that it would just look to itself for the requested information. Keep in mind that the Publisher always has the most current copy of the database. This is why the Subscriber always looks to the Publisher for the information. If the Subscriber is unable to reach the Publisher, then and only then, does it look to itself for the requested information.

So, the life of a Subscriber is a pretty simple one, because it never has to depend on itself; however, although the Subscriber doesn't have to do much work for the database, it does serve a very useful purpose, which is explored next.

So far, we have discussed only the roles the CallManagers play in regards to SQL. The other job of the CallManager is device control. All devices register to a CallManager. This CallManager is known as that device's primary CallManager. Each device also has a secondary CallManager that it can register to if the primary fails. Configure devices use a Subscriber as their primary CallManager. This leaves the Publisher alone so that it can take care of its main responsibility, which is to maintain the database. In some cases a device may have a tertiary server, to which it can fail over if both the primary and secondary are not available. Just as with the secondary, the tertiary server should be a Subscriber.

If the primary CallManager fails, the device registers to the secondary. The device registers with the secondary CallManager only if it is not on a call when the CallManager fails. If the device is active when the CallManager fails, it registers with the secondary CallManager when the call ends. In most cases, a call stays up even if the CallManager that is controlling devices participating in the call fails. The reason being that during a call the communication is point to point, meaning that the CallManager is not involved with the actual voice stream. The device has no idea that the CallManager has failed because it does not communicate with the device again until either the call is over, or a feature, which requires CallManager, is invoked, such as hold or transfer. If a device, whose CallManager has failed, tries to invoke such a feature, the phone display indicates a CallManager failure and the feature either fails or is unavailable (grayed out), depending on phone type. The call itself is not affected. A message also appears on the phone stating that the CallManager is down and the feature is not available.

In small environments where there are only two CallManagers, it is acceptable to use the Publisher as a secondary CallManager. If you have more than 1000 users, it is not recommended to use the Publisher as a secondary CallManager. Figure 1-1 shows a typical CallManager environment that can support up to 5000 phones. This figure is an example of what is referred to as one-to-one redundancy. In this configuration, 2500 phones register to CallManagers B and C. CallManagers D and E are secondary servers for these phones. CallManager A is the Publisher and no phones register to it. This example is based on the assumption that all the servers on which the CallManager is loaded are MCS-7835s or equivalent. Other server models support a different number of phones per server.

Figure 1-1 *One-to-One Redundancy CallManager Cluster*

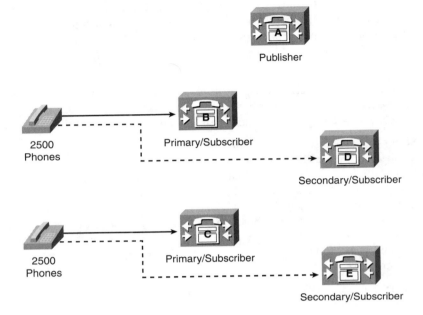

CallManager Devices

A large number of devices register with a CallManager, but they typically fall into one of the following categories:

- Phones
- Gateways
- Gatekeeper
- Media resources

Each of these devices has its own unique role within the CallManager environment and this section briefly describes each. For more information on these devices, please refer to Appendix A.

Phones

A number of different model phones can be used in a CallManager environment. This section briefly describes some of the more popular models.

Model 7902

The 7902 is the entry-level phone and is best suited for environments such as a lobbies or other high-traffic areas. It is a singe line IP phone and offers the most basic features.

Models 7905/7912

The 7905/7912 are nearly the same phone, except the 7912 offers a switch port in the back to which you can attach a PC. Both phones offer single line capability as well as eXtensible Markup Language (XML) support.

NOTE   One of the advanced features of many Cisco IP phones is their ability to parse XML. These phones have an LCD screen on which the user can look up others in the directory, receive messages, log in and out of services, and perform many other functions. Through the use of XML programming, many companies have applications developed such as time clocks, inventory look up, and a variety of others.

Model 7940

The 7940 has the capability to support two lines and XML applications. This phone is considered a mid-range phone and is typically used in environments where two lines are adequate. It also has a switch port in the back for attaching a PC.

Model 7960

The 7960 has the ability to handle up to six lines. It has six buttons that can be configured as lines or speed dial buttons. For instance, a user may have the phone configured so that the first three buttons are used as lines and the other three are configured as speed dial. Besides the additional four buttons, it is essentially the same phone as the 7940 except for the fact that only the 7960 can support a 7914, a 14-button attachable sidecar. Up to two 7914s can be attached, which adds 28 buttons, and gives the phone a total of 34 buttons.

Model 7970

The 7970 is the first color display IP phone from Cisco. It has the same abilities as the 7960 with two additional buttons that may be used as lines or speed dials. This phone includes the new Cisco IP phone feature of a touch screen.

Model 7920

The 7920 is a wireless phone that connects to the network via an 802.11b wireless access point. The phone's shape and size are similar to a cell phone, but it only works in a CallManager environment.

Softphone

Softphone is an application that runs on a PC, and allows the PC to be used as a phone. Typically, a headset is attached to the PC, and the user can make and receive calls using the PC. A new software client that is replacing the Softphone is called the IP communicator. It offers the same functions as softphone as well as most features found on the 7970 phone.

Gateways

As mentioned earlier, gateways are used to connect dissimilar systems together, such as connecting CallManager to the Public Switched Telephone Network (PSTN). The core requirements were discussed earlier, so this section examines the different types of gateways and how they communicate, that is, the protocol they use. There are two main protocols that are used today for communicating between CallManager and gateways; they are Media Gateway Control Protocol (MGCP) and H.323. Both are industry standard protocols and offer similar features.

The type and number of trunks that a customer has also affects the type of gateway you select. CallManager is connected to the PSTN using either an analog or a digital trunk. The trunk used also affects the type of equipment you use for the gateway. Gateways differ in interface types and capacities. If analog trunks are used, then an Foreign Exchange Office (FXO) port is required for each line. With analog lines, each call takes up a port on a gateway, not always a practical solution in a large environment. Typically, a T1 or E1 is used to connect to the PSTN if a company needs more than a few lines. These types of trunks are normally more cost-effective if more than eight simultaneous connections to the PSTN are required.

So far we have only discussed using gateways as a way to connect to the PSTN. Gateways are also needed to connect CallManager to traditional phones systems. In many cases, customers choose to integrate the CallManager into their existing voice solution and slowly replace the traditional PBX. This is done by connecting the CallManager to the traditional PBX through either analog or digital interfaces. The interface used depends on the volume of traffic expected to travel between the two phone systems and the interface available. For environments that expect large volumes of calls to travel between the phone systems, a T1 or E1 is used. Figure 1-2 shows how this integration might look.

NOTE   To connect a traditional PBX with CallManager using T1 interfaces, simply connect a crossover T1 cable from the T1 interface of the traditional PBX to the T1 interface on the CallManager gateway.

Gateways are used not only to connect CallManager to traditional PBXs but also to connect multiple CallManager environments together. As mentioned earlier, two or more CallManagers are known as a CallManager cluster. All the IP devices within a cluster can communicate with each other without a gateway. However, when two CallManager clusters need to be connected, a gateway must be configured. The connection between the two CallManager clusters is called an ICT (Intercluster Trunk). In earlier versions of CallManager, these were configured under gateways. Now they are referred to as trunks in the configuration menu. These are, in fact, H.323 gateways. Chapter 3, "Deploying Devices," discusses these gateways more fully.

Figure 1-2   *CallManager to PBX Integration*

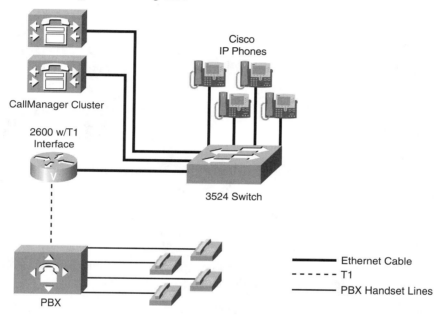

Gateways are also used to provide analog connectivity within a CallManager environment. Although the goal of VoIP is to use IP to transport voice whenever possible, there are times when an analog connection is required; modems and fax machines are examples. To connect an analog device such as a fax machine, an Foreign Exchange Station (FXS) port is required. A gateway with FXS ports allows analog devices to operate within a VoIP network.

Gatekeepers

Now that you understand how to connect CallManager to the other systems, you need to make sure that the path used to connect to another system does not become congested. It is not possible to allow more calls than a connection can handle when connecting to the PSTN or a traditional PBX using analog lines or voice T1s. However, when connecting devices using an IP connection, oversubscribing is possible. Oversubscribing occurs when more calls connect across a link than the link can adequately handle. When connecting multiple CallManager clusters together, you can use gatekeepers to prevent oversubscribing. This is referred to as CAC (Call Admission Control).

A gatekeeper typically runs on a router such as a 2600, an H.323 device. Hence, CallManager communicates with it using H.323. A typical deployment is shown in Figure 1-3. This diagram shows two CallManager clusters connected through an Inter-cluster Trunk. The gatekeeper manages the available bandwidth between the sites. The total allowable bandwidth for voice calls is configured in the gatekeeper.

Figure 1-3   *Gatekeeper*

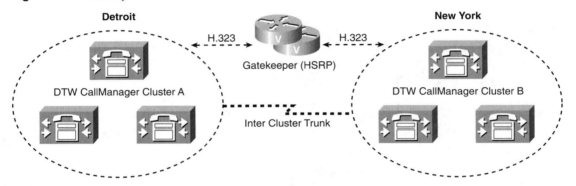

An example call flow would go something like this:

1   Joe, who resides in Detroit, attempts to place a call to Fred, who resides in New York. The CallManager in Detroit sends a request to the gatekeeper to see if there is enough bandwidth to place the call.

2   The gatekeeper replies with either a confirmation (bandwidth is available) or a rejection (bandwidth is not available).

3   If the bandwidth is available, the call setup proceeds and the CallManager in New York is informed that a call is being placed to Fred.

4   The CallManager in New York then sends a request to the gatekeeper to see if there is enough bandwidth for its side of the call.

5   If the gatekeeper sends a confirmation, the call setup is complete and Joe and Fred can talk about how the Lions actually won a game that weekend.

Much more occurs during setup. The previous example was presented to help you understand how a gatekeeper enforces CAC.

Assume for a moment the gatekeeper in the previous example failed. What happens when the Detroit CallManager sends a request to the gatekeeper? Because the gatekeeper isn't working, the CallManager does not receive a confirmation and the call does not go through. How do you prevent a failed gatekeeper from negatively affecting call setup? Have two of them. Once again, the theme running throughout this chapter is redundancy. It is recommended that a second router running HSRP (Hot Stand-by Routing Protocol) be configured as a fail-over gatekeeper.

Not only can the gatekeeper be used for CAC purposes, but he/she can also determine the location of a requested device. This feature is discussed more fully in the CAC sections of Chapter 5, "Configuring Class of Service and Call Admission Control."

There are times when CAC is needed within a cluster. Because the gatekeeper is used when communicating outside a cluster, some other type of CAC must be implemented. For example, some type of CAC is needed within a cluster when a number of offices use the same CallManager at a central site.

NOTE   The configuration in the previous example—of CAC within a cluster—is referred to as Internet Protocol Wide Area Network (IP WAN) with a Centralized Call Processing Deployment model and is discussed in greater detail in the next section.

CAC is accomplished in an IP WAN with centralized call processing deployment by configuring what are known as locations in CallManager. When configuring locations, the amount of bandwidth that is available for voice calls is entered in each location. When calls are placed between locations, bandwidth is deducted from the available bandwidth and calls are allowed or disallowed based on the available bandwidth. Locations are configured within CallManager and no additional hardware is required. Often people ask if they can use locations instead of a gatekeeper to save money. Remember that locations work only when the call is placed between two devices within the same cluster. Because a gatekeeper is used for calls placed between separate networks, locations cannot be used.

Media Resources

In order to accomplish certain tasks such as conferencing and MOH (Music on Hold), CallManager needs to call upon additional resources. The core CallManager application does not have the ability to perform these tasks, so it relies on other resources, which are either hardware or software. Some resources reside on the same server as CallManager, and others require additional hardware. A list and brief description of the various resources follows.

Conference Bridge (CFB)

CFBs are required for a caller to have a conference call with at least two other callers. CFBs can be either software or hardware, however, hardware is recommended. Software CFBs run as a process on CallManager, whereas hardware CFBs require additional equipment. Hardware CFBs require Digital Signal Processors (DSPs). Not all devices that have DSPs can be configured as a CFB. The following devices can be configured as CFBs:

- Catalyst 6000 T1/E1 ports
- Catalyst 4000 Access Gateway Modules
- Supported Cisco routers with DSP farms

Transcoders

A transcoder allows devices that are using different codecs to communicate. Transcoders are able to change an incoming codec to another codec that the destination device can understand.

NOTE　A codec (which stands for compression/decompression) is used to express the format used to compress voice. An algorithm is used to compress voice so that it requires less bandwidth. The two most common codecs used in a CallManager environment are G.711 and G.729a.

MOH

MOH allows an audio source to be streamed to devices that are on hold. It is a process that runs on a CallManager. The audio can be streamed either multicast or unicast, and the codec can be configured. Up to 51 audio sources can be configured, including live audio that is plugged into a sound card installed in the CallManager.

Now that you have an overview of the components required in a CallManager environment, you should review various deployment models. As this technology matures, the way it is deployed continues to evolve. It is essential that it be deployed only in a supported fashion. The next section discusses the various supported deployment models.

Understanding CallManager Deployment Models

There are essentially three main CallManager deployment models currently supported by Cisco. Although during the past few years these models have evolved to create what appear to be new deployment models, all support models fit into one of the following three categories of sites: Single Site, Multisite WAN with Centralized Call Processing, and Multisite WAN with Distributed Call Processing.

Single Site

In this model a CallManager is deployed within a single building or perhaps in a campus area. However, some would argue a campus area would typically fall into the centralized model. The core theme behind this model is that there is no VoIP connectivity to any system outside its own. Any call placed to a destination outside its own is sent to the PSTN.

Multisite WAN with Centralized Call Processing

A centralized deployment includes remote locations that have IP phones registering to the CallManager at the main site. Normally, there is only one CallManager cluster in a deployment such as this. Remote phones send all requests across the WAN to the

CallManager. If the WAN fails and the phones have no local device to which to register, the phones are unusable.

NOTE   A technology called Survivable Remote Site Telephony (SRST) has been developed that allows remote offices to have dial tone and make calls across the PSTN if the WAN or remote network fails. SRST runs on a router such as a 3600. The number of phones that can register to an SRST system depends on the hardware on which it is running. SRST is discussed in Chapter 6, "Configuring CallManager Features and Services."

Multisite WAN with Distributed Call Processing

There are multiple sites in this model, each having its own CallManager cluster. There is IP connectivity between them, and ICTs are configured to send the voice across. A gatekeeper is required in this deployment to prevent oversubscribing and assist in call routing.

Often companies that need distributed deployment also have remote sites with just a few phones. A CallManager cannot be justified for the remote site, so the phones register to a remote CallManager just as they would in a centralized deployment. When centralized and distributed deployments are merged together like this, it is referred to as a Hybrid deployment.

Another form of this deployment is referred to as a Clustering Over the IP WAN. In this scenario a single CallManager cluster is split among multiple sites. For example, a Publisher and a Subscriber are in the Detroit office and a Subscriber at the New York office. The phones within the respective offices register with the local CallManager.

One of the major requirements in a deployment such as this is that the round-trip delay be no greater than 40 ms. The standard one-way delay allowed for voice is 150 ms, so the requirements in this type of deployment are much more stringent. Figure 1-4 shows an example of a Clustering Over the IP WAN deployment.

Figure 1-4   *Distributed Single-Cluster*

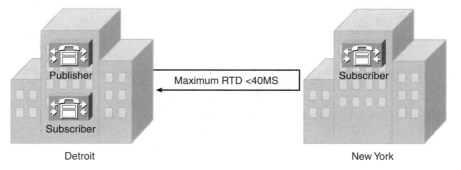

The environment in which you deploy CallManager typically dictates which deployment model you choose. Regardless of which model is being deployed, it will most likely connect to an outside system such as the PSTN. When a call is placed outside the local system, the CallManager must know where to send the call based on the numbers dialed. The next section discusses how these call routing decisions are made.

Dial Plan Overview

CallManager knows about all devices that are registered within the cluster and knows how to route calls to any destination within the cluster. However, if a call is placed to a destination outside the cluster, CallManager needs to know where to send the call. This is the purpose of a dial plan. A dial plan is configured with CallManager to determine where to send calls based on the number that is dialed.

A dial plan consists of a number of components, which are discussed in this section. Here is a brief description of each of the components that make up a dial plan. The list is in the order in which these devices must be configured. Later, the actual flow will be discussed.

- **Device (Gateway)**—Gateways were explained earlier as devices that connect dissimilar systems. The gateway is the last component in a dial plan because it sends the call to an outside system. As mentioned before, the gateway connects the CallManager system to the PSTN as well as to other destinations.

- **Route Group**—A route group is used to route the call to a gateway. Each route group includes at least one gateway, but because there is often more than one gateway, a call can be routed through a route group that can point to multiple gateways. The order in which the gateways appear in the route group determines which gateway the call is routed to first. If the gateway the call is sent to is not available, the route group sends the call to the next gateway in its list.

- **Route List**—A route list is used to route the call to a route group. Each route list must have at least one route group in it. Just as a route group can point to multiple gateways, a route list can point to multiple route groups. The order in which the route groups appear in the route list determines which route group the call is routed to first. If all the devices in the first route group are unavailable, then the route list routes the call to the next route group in the list. If all gateways in the route groups within the list are unavailable, the call fails.

- **Route Pattern**—When a user dials a number, CallManager compares the digits dialed against all the route patterns it knows. As mentioned earlier, CallManager knows about all devices within the cluster. If the number dialed matches the number assigned to a device in the cluster, CallManager sends the call to that device. If the call is placed to a device outside the cluster, a matching pattern must be configured in the CallManager. Because it is impossible to enter every possible number that might ever be dialed, wildcards are used to allow a single route to pattern match multiple numbers. An example of one of the wildcards used in CallManager is an X. In a route pattern, an X matches any single digit 0-9. For example, a route pattern of 5XXX would match all numbers between 5000 to 5999.

Typical Call Flow

Now that you understand the basic components of a dial plan, examining a typical call flow is in order. CallManager in this example has the following route pattern 9.1248547XXXX:

1 A user dials 912485479000.

2 CallManager analyzes the dialed digits and determines that the closest match it knows of is 91248547XXXX.

3 CallManager routes the call to the route list that has been configured for the route pattern 91248547XXXX.

4 The call is then routed to the first route group in the route list.

5 If there is more than one gateway in the route group, the call is sent to the first gateway in the list. If the gateway is available, the call is sent out that gateway.

At times, a dialed number matches more than one pattern. When this occurs, CallManager selects the closest match. For example, if a user dials 5010 and CallManager has 5XXX and 50XX as route patterns, 50XX is selected because there are only 100 possible matches, whereas there are 1000 matches with the route pattern 5XXX.

Wildcards

Up to this point the only route pattern wildcard that has been discussed is the X. Chapter 4, "Implementing a Dial Plan," discusses wildcards further. For now, the following is a list of wildcards that can be used in route patterns:

The Wildcard @

This wildcard matches any phone number that is part of the North American Numbering Plan (NANP). The easiest way to understand what numbers are part of NANP is that any number you can dial from a home phone in North America would be part of the NANP. This includes numbers such as 911 and all international numbers.

The Wildcard !

This wildcard represents any digit and any number of digits. At first people think that "!" is the same thing as the X wildcard, but remember that the "X" represents only a single digit. The "!" can represent any number of digits.

The Wildcard [x-y]

This wildcard represents a single digit range. For example,

5[3-5] would match 53, 54 or 55. The numbers inside the brackets always represent a range and match only a single digit.

NOTE   In a pattern such as 5[25-7], the only matches are 52, 55, 56 and 57. When people first look at this pattern, they think it matches 525, 526 and 527, but remember that the brackets can only represent a single digit.

The Wildcard [^x-y]

This wildcard represents an exclusion range. That is, any single digit that is not included in the range matches. For example, the pattern 5[^3-8] matches 50, 51, 52 and 59.

Class of Service (CoS)

While creating a dial plan you will find that some individuals within the company are allowed to place calls that others are not. For instance, some companies do not allow all employees to make long distance calls. Also, it is highly unlikely that you would want to allow international calls to be placed from a lobby phone. These issues are addressed by assigning a telephony Class of Service (CoS) to devices.

NOTE   Those of you that come from a data background should not confuse this with the QoS component known as CoS. Although it stands for the same thing, Class of Service, it does not mean the same thing. Think of it this way: CoS, in the data world, is about prioritizing; CoS in the IP telephony world involves rights and restrictions. When CoS is mentioned in this section, it refers to the telephone CoS.

CoS is essentially a way to determine what destinations a given device may reach. For instance, if you want to call someone in Germany, your CoS would have to allow international calls. In the same regard, if you want to prevent a device from being able to call Germany, you would assign a CoS that does not allow international dialing.

A CoS comprises two components, a Calling Search Space (CSS) and Partitions. A solid understanding of these two components is essential in order to create an effective CoS. These two components seem to cause some confusion for those who are new to the concept, but at the core they are very simple concepts.

The simplest way to view this concept is to imagine a partition as a lock and a CSS as a key chain. If a number has a lock on it, you need the key on your key chain to reach that number. Simple, right? Well, as with anything, as things grow they can become more complex.

Partitions are assigned to anything that has a pattern, such as a directory number or a route pattern. Calling search spaces are assigned to devices such as phones and gateways. The configuration of these components is discussed in Chapter 5, "Configuring Class of Service and Call Admission Control." Taking a closer look at how the components are configured can help clarify the concept.

Figure 1-5 shows how assigning partitions to a pattern and CSS to phones affect dialing privileges.

Figure 1-5   *CoS Example*

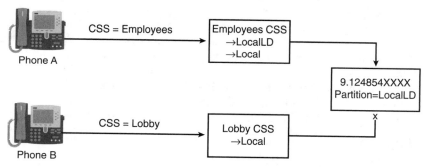

The two phones in Figure 1-5, Phone A and Phone B, each have a different CSS that determines where they can call. They both dial 912485479000. Based on the CSS of the phone, a match is determined. The only pattern that the dialed digits match is the 9.1248547XXXX pattern, which has the LocalLD partition. Because phone A's CSS allows access to the LocalLD partition, its call goes through. However, Phone B's CSS does not allow access to the LocalLD partition so that call fails.

NOTE	If you feel a little uncertain on this concept, fear not. I have had many students who worked with CSS and partitions for years and still didn't have a handle on it. The best advice is to start small, such as the example in Figure 1-5, and build on that. Although the design may become complex, the way CSS and partitions work does not change and is really very simple.

As you can see, the components that are required to implement a Cisco CallManager solution are quite extensive. This section has presented only a very high-level overview. By now you should understand the importance of a solid infrastructure and be able to describe the role redundancy plays in providing reliable service. Furthermore, you should be comfortable with the various devices that may register to CallManager and the various deployment models of CallManager. Finally, you should understand the basics behind dial plans and how CoS can affect a device's ability to reach certain destinations.

Unified Messaging Overview

Unity is the recommended messaging solution for CallManager environments. Many people view Unity as a voice-mail solution, and although it does handle all the functions of a voice-mail system, it is much more than that. Unity is a completely unified communication system. That is, it not only handles voice-mail functions for a company, but is also able to integrate into an existing e-mail and faxing infrastructure. Because the voice mail, e-mail and faxing systems can be integrated with one another, they are able to use a single message store. This means end users can now retrieve all of their voice mail, e-mail and faxes from one location. In the past, users would have to use the phone to get their voice mail, the PC to get their e-mail, and a fax machine to retrieve their faxes. With unified messaging all of these messages can be retrieved from a single device, be it a PC or a phone. Using a PC, users can read their e-mail and faxes or listen to their voice mail over the PC speakers. The users can also use a phone to retrieve their voice mail and e-mail, as Unity's text-to-speech engine converts the e-mail to a synthesized voice and streams it over the phone.

These features, although useful, are only examples of unified messaging, not unified communications. The plan is to add features to Unity that will turn it into a unified communication solution. Features from a Cisco product called Personal Assistant may be added to Unity. These features will allow users to manage their messages, and their incoming and outgoing phone calls. The following is a list of features that are currently part of Personal Assistant, but may one day be found in Unity:

- **Rules-based routing**—Rules-based routing allows a user to determine where a call is forwarded, based on the Call ID and other factors, such as time of day. When CallManager receives a call destined for that user phone, it diverts the call so that it can be checked against the rules that the user created and forwarded to the desired destination. An example of a rule a user might set up would be if a client called between 5PM and 8PM, to send that client's call to the user's home office and send all other calls to voice mail.

- **Follow me**—The Follow me feature allows callers to dial in from the outside and enable all calls to be forwarded to a destination of the caller's choosing.

- **Conferencing**—A user can dial into the system and start a conference call by simply telling the system to start a conference and then speaking the names of other users in the system.

- **Voice-mail browsing**—This feature allows users to browse their voice mail by issuing spoken commands such as "Check voice mail." This enables the user to bypass using the dial pad of the phone to navigate through voice mail.

You can see how these features, combined with the messaging features of Unity, make Unity a truly unified communications system, not just voice mail.

Unity is a very powerful application that requires a variety of components to accomplish its tasks. The topics covered in this section will provide you with a good understanding of the components within Unity and how these components fit into the Unity solution. The areas covered in this section are:

- Unity Software Architecture
- Call flow
- Call handlers
- Subscribers
- Unity networking

Unity Software Architecture

Unlike some applications, Unity is not a stand-alone application. That is, in and of itself, it cannot provide voice-mail services. Unity depends on a number of other applications to provide its array of services. If Unity were merely a voice-mail system, it could have been designed not to require other applications. However, the fact that it is a unified communications solution requires that it integrate with a company's e-mail server. Because both a voice-mail system and an e-mail server have to be able to send, receive, and store messages, Unity simply uses the existing e-mail server to handle these functions. This is not to say that Unity does not handle the messages. This is discussed later. The various software components with which Unity interfaces include a mail store, a directory, such as AD, SQL, and IIS. A closer look at the software architecture will help you understand the need for each component.

The discussion begins at the lowest level of the software architecture. The first layer of any software architecture is the OS (Operating System). Unity requires Windows 2000 Server OS. Unity integrates very tightly with Microsoft's AD when using Exchange 2000. As of version 4.04 Unity, Windows 2003 server is supported, but not recommended, for most installations.

NOTE   Much like CallManager, Unity is supported only on Cisco-approved servers. Currently there are a number of models approved by Cisco. These servers may be purchased from Cisco or directly from HP or IBM. You can find the most current list of approved servers by searching for "Cisco Unity supported platforms list" at Cisco.com.

After the OS is on the server, other supporting applications have to be available before Unity can be configured. Unity depends on an outside message store to store messages. Currently you can use Microsoft Exchange or Lotus Notes as the message store. If Exchange is used, it can run on the same server as Unity, but this should be done only if you are using Unity as a voice mail-only solution. If Unity is used as a unified communications solution, then Exchange should be loaded on a separate server. If Notes is the message store, it must be running on a separate server.

NOTE   If Notes is the message store, an additional piece of software is required. It is called Domino Unified Communication Services (DUCS). This can be purchased from IBM and is used to allow the transfer of information between Unity and the Domino environment.

All the information entered into Unity must be stored. As with CallManager, Unity uses SQL as its database, and most of the information you enter, such as user names and phone passwords, are stored in SQL. Hence, SQL must be running on the Unity server.

As mentioned earlier, Unity integrates with AD when using Exchange 2000 or Exchange 2003, so the server must be part of an AD. If the Unity server is a stand-alone computer, that is, it is not part of an existing AD, then it must be configured with AD and act as its own domain controller. Some of the information, for example, name, telephone number, and alias that is stored in SQL, is replicated to the AD.

Unity is similar to CallManager in that most of the configuration of Unity is done through a web browser interface. This requires that IIS be running on the Unity server. During the installation process, IIS is installed. Additional tools perform many of the same tasks that are accomplished using the web browser interface. These tools are discussed in Chapter 11, "Exploring Unity Tools." The main advantage to using the browser interface is that no additional software has to be loaded on a PC to administer Unity. This is a very useful feature when you find yourself away from your desk needing to change something in Unity.

Following the Call Flow

Before discussing the actual components that determine the path a call takes, let's take a high-level look at the various ways a call can enter Unity and how Unity deals with each type.

Typically, calls are forwarded to voice-mail systems because the phone that was called is either busy or is not answered. When Unity receives a call, it examines the reason that it is receiving the call. The phone system that forwarded the call includes a call forwarded reason to Unity. In this case, it was forwarded because the called party was busy or did not answer. If the call is forwarded because the caller did not answer, Unity plays the called party's standard greeting. If the call was forwarded because the called party was on the phone, Unity plays the called party's busy greeting.

Each user on the Unity system is known as a Subscriber, and each Subscriber can have five different greetings, which are:

- Standard—Played during open hours when the Subscriber does not answer the phone
- Busy—Played when the Subscriber is on another call
- Closed—Played after hours
- Internal—Played when another Subscriber reaches voice mail
- Alternate—If enabled, always plays regardless of the forwarded reason or time of day. This greeting may be used as a vacation greeting

Unity is often used as an Auto-Attendant, which allows all incoming calls to be answered by Unity, then forwarded to the desired destination. In this instance, the call is not forwarded to Unity and is considered a direct call. Unity handles direct calls differently than forwarded calls. The first thing Unity does is to try to determine if the caller is a Subscriber. It does this by seeing if the caller ID matches any phone number that is associated with a Subscriber. If it finds a match, it assumes that the Subscriber is calling and asks for the Subscriber's password.

NOTE   All Subscribers have at least one phone number associated with them; this is their phone extension. Additional numbers can be assigned to Subscribers; these are referred to as alternate extensions. A common use for alternate extensions is to associate a Subscriber's cell phone or home number so that when they call in to check messages they are taken directly to the login prompt.

If Unity determines that the caller ID is not associated with a Subscriber, the call is sent to Unity's opening greeting. An opening greeting is the main greeting that outside callers hear when they reach the auto attendant. It may say something like "Thank you for calling Bailey, Inc. If you know your party's extension, you may dial it anytime during this greeting ..." The options offered to the caller are determined by the system administrator based on the company's needs.

Exploring Call Handlers

Often companies that use Unity as an auto-attendant create a menu that can lead outside callers to the proper department. We have all experienced memorably frustrating menus. To create menus in Unity, objects titled call handlers are created. As a matter of fact, one call handler was mentioned in the previous section. The opening greeting is a call handler. The easiest way to think of a call handler is as an object that can be used to help route calls. You can also think of call handlers as the building blocks that make up the menu system.

There are primarily three types of call handlers that can be used within Unity:

- General Call handlers
- Interview handlers
- Directory handlers

The first type is the kind we have been discussing, General call handlers. These are used to build the menu system and typically contain a recorded prompt and ask the caller for input, such as "Press 1 for sales, press 2 for technical support, or hold on the line for further assistance." These types of call handlers have no special classification and can be referred to as general call handlers. They are simply known as call handlers and have a number of configurable parameters. Table 1-1 shows the five sets of configurable parameters of a call handler and the information that each contains. This table gives you a good idea of the number of parameters that need to be configured for each call handler. More detail is given to these parameters in the "Configuring Call Handlers" section found in Chapter 9, "Call Management."

Table 1-1 *Call Handler Parameters*

Parameter	Description
Profile	Name, Creation date, Owner, Recorded voice, Schedule, Extension, Language, Switch (PBX)
Transfer	Status, Transfer incoming call, Transfer type, Rings to wait, If Busy, Announce, Introduce, Confirm, Ask Caller's Name,
Greeting	Greeting, Status, Source, Allow Caller Input, After Greeting Action, Reprompt, Number of Reprompts
Caller Input	Allow Extension Dialing During Greeting, Milliseconds to wait, Lock Key, Action
Message	Message Recipient, Max Message Length, After message Action, Caller Edit, Urgent Marking.

The next type of call handler is called an interview handler. It is used to extract information for the caller that requires asking more than one question. An interview handler can contain up to 20 questions. It allows the user time to answer between the questions. Unlike the call handler described previously, there are only two sets of parameters that need to be configured for the interview handler. Table 1-2 shows these parameters in the "Creating Advanced Call Routing Systems" section found in Chapter 9, "Call Management."

Table 1-2 *Interview Handler Parameters*

Parameter	Description
Profile	Name, Creation date, Owner, Recorded voice, Extension, Language, Deliver Response to, Response Urgency, After interview Action.
Question	Questions Number, Question Text, Maximum Length in Seconds (for response). Recorded Question.

NOTE An example used for an interview handler would be a class survey hotline. After students take a class, they are able to call a number and answer five questions. The answers are later transcribed and entered into the school's database.

The third type of call handler is known as a directory handler. The directory handler allows callers to dial by name. As the caller spells the person's name using the dial pad, Unity searches to find all matching names. Unity then offers the caller name choices and allows the caller to choose the party to which they would like to be forwarded. Unity allows for multiple directory handlers so that each department could have a separate one if desired. Directory Handlers have four sets of configurable parameters as shown in Table 1-3. More detail is given to these parameters later in the "Configuring Directory handlers" section found in Chapter 9, "Call Management."

Table 1-3   *Directory Handler Parameters*

Parameter	Description
Profile	Name, Creation date, Owner, Recorded voice, Extension, Language, Play All Names
Search Options	Search In, Search By
Match List Options	On Unique, Announce Matched using, Announce Extension
Caller Input	No Input Timeout, Last Input Timeout, Repeat Prompt, Send On To Exit.

Figure 1-6 shows a typical Unity menu system flow chart. The various types of call handlers that have been discussed are shown in this figure. Each of the boxes represents a call handler.

TIP It is a good idea to draw your menu system in flow chart form before creating it on the system. This helps ensure that all the call handlers are linked and the flow makes sense.

Typically call handlers are used to route a call through the system, however, they can be configured to take messages. If a call handler is configured to take a message, the message must be sent to a Subscriber, because call handlers are simply SQL objects and do not have mailboxes.

As you can see, call handlers are a very fundamental part of Unity. Even the most basic Unity system contains a number of call handlers, so a solid understanding of how they are configured and work is essential. This section has only touched the surface of the power and flexibility of call handlers. Once again, you are encouraged to review the listed references in Appendix A for further study of this technology.

Figure 1-6   *Example Menu System Flow Chart*

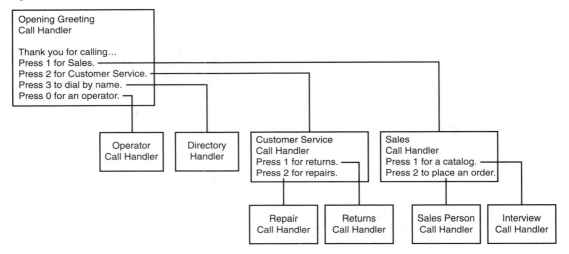

Defining Various Types of Subscribers

Now that you have a good understanding of how calls are routed through a system, let's take a look at the Subscribers. A Subscriber is anyone who has an account on the Unity system. Typically a Unity Subscriber's messages are stored on the message store that is associated with Unity. However, Subscribers are sometimes created where the mailbox actually resides on a different voice-mail system. This section explores all the types of users who can be configured in Unity and appropriate uses for each.

When creating and configuring Subscribers, you will notice that a number of the parameters are similar to those found in a call handler. This is because each Subscriber has an associated call handler. When you create a Subscriber, a call handler is also created. So, when you are configuring certain Subscriber parameters, you are actually configuring the call handler associated with that Subscriber. Table 1-4 shows all the parameter sets. Those marked with an asterisk (*) are the parameters used to create the call handler.

NOTE   Not all Subscribers have all the parameters listed in Table 1-4. The parameters available depend on the type of Subscriber you are creating. As a matter of fact, in some cases there are some parameters that are not listed in the table. Only the most common parameters are listed.

Table 1-4   *Subscriber Parameters*

Parameter	Description
*Profile	Name, Display Name, CoS, Extension, FAX ID, Recorded voice, Schedule, Time Zone, Self Enrollment Setting, Directory, Language, Switch (PBX)
Account	Account Status, GUI Access Status, Creation Date, Last Phone contact, Billing ID, Call Handlers Owned, Windows NT Account Status
Phone Password	User Cannot Change Password, Must Change on Next Login, Never Expires, Password, Date of Last Change.
Private Lists	Private List Number, Name of List, Recorded Name, Current Members,
Conversation	Menu Style, Volume, Language, Time Format, Send To, Identify By, Play Recorded Name, Message Counts, Message Type Menus, Sort By, Message Number, Time Message was Sent.
*Call Transfer	Transfer to, Transfer type, Rings to wait, If Busy, Announce, Introduce, Confirm, Ask Caller's Name,
*Greetings	Greeting, Status, Source, Allow Caller Input, After Greeting Action, Reprompt, Number of Reprompts
*Caller Input	Allow Extension Dialing During Greeting, Milliseconds to wait, Lock Key, Action
*Messages	Max Message Length, After message Action, Caller Edit, Urgent Marking. Language, MWI
Message Notification	Device, Phone Number, Extra Digits, Dialing Options, Status, Schedule
Alternate Extensions	Alternate Extensions

*Parameters used to create the call handler

A Subscriber is more than just a call handler, as you can see by the additional parameters that need to be configured. A Subscriber can be seen as a collection of objects, one being the call handler. It is the call handler's job to offer the caller any available choices and play the greeting. Another piece of a Subscriber is the mailbox where the voice messages are stored. For a standard Subscriber the mailbox resides on either an Exchange or Notes server. There are also additional Subscriber settings. These are settings that are not part of the mailbox or the call handler. These attributes deal with things such as phone passwords, message notification, and CoS. These settings, much like the call handlers, are stored in SQL.

As you can see, many parameters need to be configured for each Subscriber. If you had to configure each parameter for every Subscriber, it would take far too long. To simplify this task, objects known as Subscriber templates are used when creating Subscribers. A Subscriber template defines how the parameters should be set by default. Typically there are large groups of Subscribers that need very similar settings. A Subscriber template is created for each such group, and after creation, a Subscriber can be edited as needed.

NOTE   It is important to understand that Subscriber templates are significant only at the point of Subscriber creation. Changing a template after a Subscriber is created has no affect on that Subscriber.

As previously stated, not all Subscribers have all the parameters listed in Table 1-4. Parameters depend on what type of Subscriber is being created. Six different types of Subscribers can be configured as follows: Exchange, Dominos, Internet, AMIS-a, VPIM, and Bridge.

Exchange Subscriber

An Exchange Subscriber is the most common type Subscriber. This Subscriber, as the name implies, has its messages stored on an Exchange server. Exchange Subscribers have access to voice mail using the phone, also called the telephone user interface (TUI). If licensed, they may also have access to voice mail using a PC. This is referred to as the graphical user interface (GUI).

NOTE   Exchange Subscribers can be divided into two subtypes of Subscribers. One type is referred to as voice mail only, and these Subscribers use the Exchange server only as a place to store their voice-mail messages. Furthermore, they cannot retrieve their e-mail through Unity or their voice mail through a PC. The other type is known as unified messaging. These Subscribers have both their e-mail and voice mail stored on the Exchange server and can access both from either a phone or a PC.

Dominos Subscriber

A Domino Subscriber is similar to an Exchange Subscriber except that it uses Domino as the message store, not Exchange. Unlike Exchange Subscribers, a Domino Subscriber must be a unified messaging user. Domino is not supported as a voice mail-only solution.

Internet Subscriber

An Internet Subscriber does not have a mailbox on the message store associated with Unity. The mailbox is an Internet e-mail account. This type of account allows outside workers to be listed in the directory and receive voice mail without being given any type of access to Unity. One use for this type of Subscriber is to provide voice mail for contract employees who work from their homes. When messages are left for Internet Subscribers, they are delivered to the Internet e-mail account as WAV file attachments, and the Subscribers retrieve them when they download their mail.

The following three types of Subscribers are used only when you are networking with another voice-mail system. Networking options are discussed in the next section.

AMIS-a (Audio Messaging Interchange Specification—Analog) Subscriber

This type of Subscriber is used when Unity is connected to a non-Unity voice-mail system using the AMIS protocol. The Subscriber's mailbox is located on the non-Unity voice-mail system. This type of Subscriber has no direct access to Unity.

Voice Profile for Internet Mail (VPIM) Subscriber

This type of Subscriber is used when Unity is connected to a non-Unity voice-mail system using the VPIM protocol. The Subscriber's mailbox is located on the non-Unity voice-mail system. This type of Subscriber has no direct access to Unity.

Bridge Subscriber

This type of Subscriber is used when Unity is connected to an Octel voice-mail system using Bridge networking. The Subscriber's mailbox is located on the Octel voice-mail system. This type of Subscriber has no direct access to Unity.

Normally, a company wants to have the ability to send messages to a number of people at one time. To do this, public distribution lists are created. A public distribution list can contain a select group of Subscribers or all Subscribers. By default, there are three public distribution lists. One of these lists is called "All Subscribers." As the name implies, this list is used when a message needs to be sent to everyone on the system. Typically companies set up other lists based on their business needs. Quite often a public distribution list is created for each department within the company.

There are a number of ways to add Subscribers to public distribution lists. One way is to add Subscribers at the point of creation. This is done by assigning the public distribution list to the Subscriber template. The other way to add users to a public distribution list is to manually enter them one at a time using the public distribution list configuration page. This is much more time consuming than adding them at the point of creation. Other ways to add Subscribers to public distribution lists are discussed in Chapter 7, "Unity Predeployment Tasks."

Unity Networking Overview

Unity has the ability to network with other types of voice-mail systems. This feature allows employees of large companies that have multiple voice-mail systems to efficiently exchange voice mails regardless of the system on which they are homed. Cisco understands that companies have a substantial investment in current solutions and may not be ready to do a total cut over. Often Unity is deployed for a portion of the users as a pilot. It is easier to convince the client to start with a pilot because Unity can talk with other systems and allow the end user to use the most common features.

There are five types of Unity networking:

- Digital
- SMTP
- VPIM
- AMIS
- Bridge

Typically people think of networking as plugging two PCs into an Ethernet jack and having them communicate. Unity networking is not just plugging an Ethernet cable into the Unity server. Unity networking refers to connecting Unity to another voice-mail system. This can be done in a variety of ways, which are described in this section. The overall goal is to have Unity interface with another voice-mail system as seamlessly as possible.

Digital Networking

The first type of networking is called Digital Networking. Digital Networking allows multiple Unity systems within the same directory, such as AD, to seamlessly interact with one another. When using Digital Networking, the Unity systems have the ability to share the directory of each other, allowing outside callers to search for any Subscriber regardless of with which Unity server they are associated. This type of networking offers many other features, which will be discussed in Chapter 10, "Implementing Unity Networking."

Simple Mail Transfer Protocol (SMTP) Networking

SMTP networking allows Unity systems that are in separate directories to communicate with one another. Because they do not share the same AD, the directory is not shared. It is still possible to allow outside callers to search all Subscribers regardless with which Unity servers they are associated. This is done by creating Internet Subscribers.

In the future, a move is expected away from SMTP networking toward VPIM networking to connect these types of Unity servers.

VPIM Networking

VPIM networking allows Unity to interface with non-Unity voice-mail servers via a TCP/IP link. This link can be an Internet connection or a private network. The non-Unity voice-mail system must support VPIM, which is often an add-on that requires an additional investment.

AMIS Networking

AMIS networking allows Unity to interface with a non-Unity voice-mail system across analog lines. This is typically done across the PSTN, but might also be used for in-house migration. AMIS is not as efficient as VPIM, because it uses analog lines, and transmissions can therefore be more time consuming. For instance, a five-minute message being sent to five people through AMIS takes 25 minutes plus setup and teardown time. With VPIM this transmission is much shorter (actual transmission time depends on the speed of the connection). The non-Unity voice-mail system must support AMIS, which is often an add-on that requires an additional investment.

BRIDGE Networking

Bridge networking is used to connect a Unity system with an Octel voice-mail system. Bridge networking is unique in that it requires an additional server. This is called the Unity bridge server. The bridge server communicates with the Unity server through a TCP/IP connection and with the Octel server across analog lines. The bridge server acts as a translator between the Octel analog protocol and Unity's Digital Networking protocol. The overall message delivery can experience the same type of delay that is common with AMIS because they both use analog connectivity. Octel networking adds features that are not found in VPIM or AMIS and creates a more feature-rich environment. Bridge networking is recommended if a company is going to gradually migrate from Octel to Unity.

So which one should you use? The voice-mail solution with which you choose to integrate will often dictate the answer. If you have a choice between AMIS and VPIM, most often VPIM is recommended. As mentioned previously, when integrating with Octel, bridge networking should be used. When connecting multiple Unity systems, Digital Networking is the solution if the Unity systems share the same AD, and SMTP networking (VPIM in the future), if they do not.

Securing CallManager and Unity Environments

With the proliferation of viruses and malicious attacks on computer systems today, it is not just wise, but mandatory, to protect your systems. Many network administrators remember Nimda and Blaster all too well. Even some that thought they were fairly well protected got hit. Sometimes it seems that just when one type of attack can be defended, another begins. To make matters worse, in an IP telephony environment you need to protect the system not only from computer-related attacks, but also from the types of attacks common to voice systems, such as toll fraud. You might as well face it now; there is no silver bullet that completely and forever protects you. But there are steps you can take to make sure you are not an easy mark. This section examines some of the current security concerns of which you should be aware. When possible, solutions are offered, but remember, this is an on-going battle. The goal of this section is to make you aware of a few of the security issues and encourage you to be vigilant in protecting your system.

Both CallManager and Unity use Windows as their operating system, so they are both vulnerable to the security issues that exist for Windows. Because Microsoft is undeniably the most commonly installed OS, it is a very large target. For various reasons, some people hold grudges against Microsoft and hence find it fun to attack systems running on a Microsoft OS. Whether they are valid grudges or not is not important when it comes to protecting your systems. What is important is that the attacks do occur and you need to protect your system.

Typically an attack is virus driven. The damage viruses cause can range from something very benign to data corruption and destruction. All viruses should be considered dangerous. For this reason virus protection software should be installed on all systems. Cisco has qualified the following list of antivirus software for use with Unity 4.0:

- Computer Associates InoculateIT for Microsoft Windows NT and Windows 2000, version 4.53, build 627 and later
- McAfee GroupShield Domino, version 5.0 and later
- McAfee NetShield for Microsoft Windows NT and Windows 2000, version 4.5 and later
- Norton AntiVirus for Lotus Notes/Domino, version 2.5 and later
- Norton AntiVirus for Microsoft Exchange, version 2.13 and later
- Norton AntiVirus for Microsoft Windows NT and Windows 2000, version 5.02 and later
- Trend Micro ScanMail for Lotus Notes, version 2.5 and later
- Trend Micro ScanMail for Microsoft Exchange 2000, version 5 and later
- Trend Micro ScanMail for Microsoft Exchange 5.5, version 3.x and later

At the time this was written Cisco did not formally approve antivirus software for CallManager. However McAfee VirusScan, Norton Antivirus and Trend Mirco's ServerProtect have been tested and are supported by TAC. Search "third party platform agents running with Cisco CallManager" at Cisco.com for a current list of supported antivirus software.

Another commonality of CallManager and Unity is that both use SQL. In the past, SQL has been the target of attacks, so attention should be given to this. The best way to secure any SQL installation is to ensure that the latest approved security patches are applied.

NOTE   Before applying any patch, make sure it has been tested and approved by Cisco. In some cases there are special instructions on how to load certain patches. It could even be required that you load only patches available directly from Cisco. Don't assume that all Microsoft patches can be loaded on CallManager or Unity.

CallManager and Unity have some common vulnerabilities because they both use the same OS and SQL. However, they each also have unique vulnerabilities due to other applications and the way each is accessed. The next sections look at a few areas of concern for each. There are a number of other areas of concern, which are discussed in various white papers listed in the appendix.

CallManager Security Issues

Protecting the system from outside threats is only half the battle. There are also internal threats that exist. Ever since a telephone system has existed, people have tried to exploit it. These exploitations range from illegal wiretapping to toll fraud.

Earlier in this chapter it was mentioned that a PC can be connected to the back of the phone, allowing both devices to share a single Ethernet port. Although this is an efficient use of ports, if not properly configured, both devices could be using the same VLAN. When both devices are on the same VLAN, it is possible for a PC to capture voice traffic. A tool called Voice Over Misconfigured Internet Telephones (VOMIT) can then reassemble the captured data into a WAV file. The conversation could then be played back on a PC. By ensuring that the voice traffic is on a separate VLAN, you help prevent this from occurring, but that alone is not enough. You also need to prevent data and voice networks from communicating with each other as much as possible. It is understood that there are times when the networks may need to send packets to each other, but this traffic should be managed by a firewall to ensure that only the desired traffic is allowed through. Earlier it was recommended that voice and data traffic be separated on different VLANs so that the voice could be prioritized. Now you see that it can protect not only the quality of the voice but also protect the voice from prying ears.

PC-based phones, such as the SoftPhone or Cisco IP communicator, introduce the same problem that having voice and data on the same VLAN produces. Because a PC is being used as phone, the voice traffic is sent on the data VLAN. This allows prying ears on the data network to capture the conversation.

Another often overlooked area that can be exploited is allowing rogue phones to auto-register. This occurs when auto-registration is used during deployment and not turned off or restricted later. Auto-registration is a useful tool during some deployments. It allows a phone to be plugged into the system and register without having to configure it in CallManager first. It is most often used in greenfield deployments. However if auto-registration is not disabled after the initial deployment, rogue phones could register to CallManager. In and of itself, this seems like a minor issue until you factor in that if the dial plan has not been secured, a user on a rogue phone could place a call anywhere in the world without detection until the bill arrives.

The administration of CallManager should also be considered when securing the voice system. If people get access to CallManager administration, they can do anything from changing users CoS, to shutting down gateways, or even the entire system. Security is often a double-edged sword, too little and anyone can do anything, too much and no one can do anything. Often you find that you want to allow limited access to the administration interface. An example might be to allow someone to add users to the CallManager directory. You do not want this person to be able to change the dial plan. A CallManager add-on, called Multi-Level Access (MLA), allows you to do this by granting limited administration access to individuals. An even higher level of security can be implemented by restricting which physical system can access the CallManager through the use of an access list.

The preceding few paragraphs discussed only a few security issues that you need to address. The task of completely securing a CallManager environment may seem daunting at times, but all possible efforts must be taken to ensure the system is protected from both external and internal threats.

Unity Security Issues

Unity offers a new way of looking at message management. It is now possible to store all voice mail, e-mail, and faxes in a single location. In addition, it is possible to retrieve them from nearly anywhere in the world. Of course to do this, there must be a way to access the system. Although this comes as no surprise, remember, at every entry point there are people trying to exploit that point of entry. Because of the many features Unity offers, there are many points of entry. By default, Unity allows access through the phone, web browser, and e-mail client. All of these entry points add to the task of securing the system. Securing Unity is not a trivial task and sufficient attention must be given to this task. Following are just a few examples of areas that must be secured.

Unity uses a third-party message store, and currently this is either Microsoft Exchange or Lotus Notes. Both of these systems are subjected to the same types of attacks as any e-mail systems. There are, in fact, attacks aimed specifically at these systems. Securing these systems requires that you stay current on all security-related patches.

NOTE   Make sure that before applying any patch you check to see if it has been tested and approved by Cisco. In some cases there are special instructions on how to load certain patches. It could even be required that you only load patches available directly from Cisco. When a patch is related to a high-level security issue, Cisco is very quick to test and report these patches on Cisco.com. You can find available patches in the software download section of Cisco.com. You can also set up to have alerts e-mailed to you automatically. Search "Product Alert Tool" at Cisco.com to set this up.

Just as with CallManager, administration access has to be secured. By default, the administrator selected when configuring Unity has full administrative access. Often you need to allow others access for limited administrative tasks. You can do this by creating a CoS that allows them only the access that you wish them to have.

NOTE   Both CallManager and Unity use the term CoS. It is important to remember that although they are similar, they are separate. The CoS in CallManager has no association with the CoS in Unity. The CoS you assign a Unity Subscriber determines things such as the maximum length of a greeting, whether they have access to their messages through the Internet, and whether they have any administrative privileges.

Unity has the ability to track all administrative access and create reports showing this access. This can prove very useful when troubleshooting to determine if changes were made and who made them. For this reason, it is necessary for every person accessing the administration interface to use individuallogin credentials. Don't just create one administrative login and allow everyone to use the same one, because there is no way to determine who made what changes.

When you create Subscribers, you determine which features they can access. A few of these features can affect the security of your system. One of these features is the user's ability to define one-key transfer options that can be performed during their greeting. This allows the outside caller to be transferred to another extension or number by pressing a single key. However, this also opens up the possibility of toll fraud. A Subscriber could set up a one-key transfer that transfers the call to a long distance number, perhaps a friend who lives out of state. This option, of course, would not be announced during the greeting, but the Subscribers could dial into their voice mail from home at night and be transferred to their friend's number all on the company's dime. The configuration of such features should be restricted to administrative personnel only. Even then, you may want to take further action to ensure that individuals with the ability to configure this feature do not exploit the privilege. To prevent possible exploitation, you can restrict the numbers to which Unity can transfer for these users. Chapter 7, "Unity Predeployment Tasks," discusses how to perform these tasks.

Each Subscriber in Unity has two passwords. The first is the phone password. This is the password that is used when accessing Unity through the phone. This password is only numeric because it is entered using the digits on a phone. Unity should be configured to require minimum length passwords for each Subscriber. The longer the minimum length, the harder it is for someone to figure out. It is important that you don't take Unity phone passwords lightly. Often people don't think that their voice-mail password is as important as their e-mail password, but with unified message, if you can access one, you can access the other. The second password Subscribers use to access Unity is their AD or NT account password. This password is used when Unity is accessed using a PC, such as when checking messages over the Internet. This password should contain both letters and numbers and a minimum length of more than five should be used.

NOTE   All accounts have default passwords. Make sure that these are changed the first time an account is accessed. There are a few default accounts that are created when Unity is installed. Make certain that the default password on these accounts is changed immediately following the installation. On more than one occasion, I have logged into systems at clients' sites and retrieved messages, unknowingly sent to these accounts, simply by using the default extension and password. This, of course, was done with the full knowledge of the customer and only to show them that their system was not secured by the installer.

This section has touched on only a few security concerns to bring attention to the fact that these are valid concerns that must be addressed. Additional reference material is listed in Appendix A.

Summary

A Cisco IP telephony deployment comprises a number of technologies and platforms. Before beginning to deploy such a solution, much thought must be given to the proper design. It all begins with a reliable, solid infrastructure. A proper infrastructure begins with a redundant physical topology as well as proper backup power. To allow access to outside systems, gateways are used and methods of call admissions control must be implemented.

At the call processing layer, redundant CallManagers should be deployed. These systems must run on Cisco approved hardware called MCSs. Devices such as phones, gateways, and conference bridges register to CallManager. When a call is placed or a resource is requested, the request is sent to the CallManager to which the device is registered. The

CallManager uses the configured dial plan to determine how to route the call to the desired location. Once the call is complete, CallManager ensures that it is properly torn down.

Unity is a unified communications server that allows individuals to have all their voice mail, e-mails, and faxes stored in a single location. This allows more efficient access to all messages. Unity has the ability to function as an auto-attendant and have outside callers routed through the system when they make selections from the available menu. In the future, unified communications will allow calls to be routed based on predefined rules that individual users can configure.

The advances being made in IP telephony are very exciting. As with most new technologies, there are those who find ways to exploit them. It is critical that sufficient attention be given to securing all IP telephony deployments.

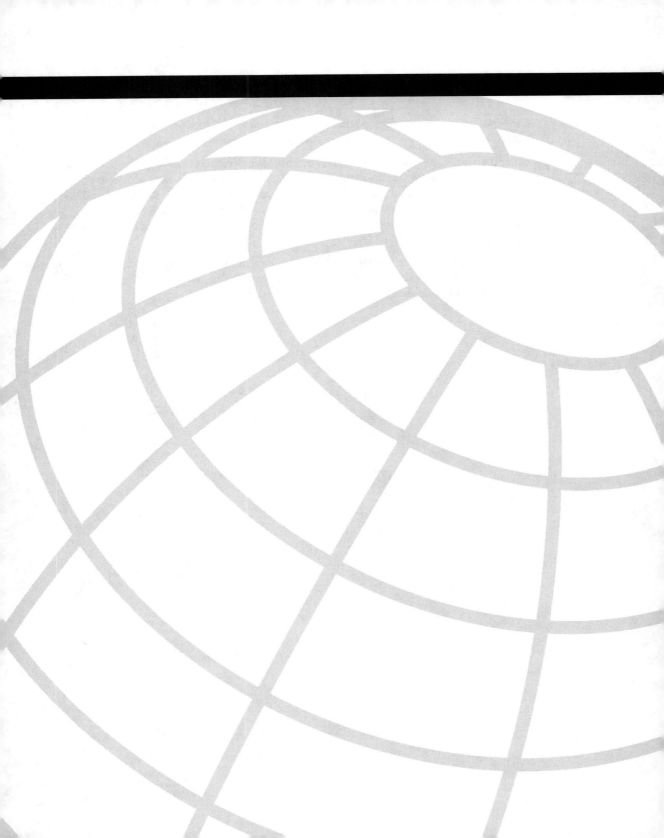

CHAPTER 2

Preparing CallManager for Deployment

In order to ensure a smooth deployment, certain tasks must be performed in a certain order. In this chapter, you will learn what tasks need to be completed before adding devices. As with most things, if you fail to create a solid foundation, you will encounter problems. The topics covered in this chapter give you that firm foundation.

Before adding any devices to the system, ensure that a number of predeployment tasks are accomplished. Because this book assumes that CallManager is already installed, most settings discussed in this chapter should already be properly configured.

The goal of this chapter is to help you understand these settings and how changing them may affect your system. This chapter covers services configuration, enterprise parameters, and device registration tasks. In addition, this chapter includes step-by-step instructions for many of these tasks. It is worth the time to review these settings and make sure they are configured properly for your system. Although the system may seem to function fine even if some of these tasks are overlooked, it is recommended that all are verified before adding devices.

Configuring CallManager for Maximum Performance

CallManager is the heart of the call processing system, and it is important to ensure that it is running at peak performance. A number of processes are capable of running on the CallManager, but not all of them are always necessary. This section explores the various processes that may be running on a CallManager and discusses which may be safely disabled to preserve more processing power for other CallManager functions.

This section looks primarily at two types of processes that may affect CallManager: CallManager-specific services and Windows services, which may be automatically enabled on the CallManager system. The section describes these two sets of processes and which can be disabled.

Deactivating Unnecessary Services

A large number of Windows services are loaded when CallManager is installed. Although a number of these services are required, most of them can be disabled, regardless of whether the CallManager is a Publisher or a Subscriber. There are, however, a few services that can be disabled only on the Subscriber. In more recent versions of CallManager, many of these services have been disabled during the installation and will not need to be changed.

You can see the services that are currently running on the system by opening up the services viewer as follows:

Step 1   From the console of the CallManager, click the **Start** button.

Step 2   Navigate to **Programs>Administrative Tools>Services**.

Step 3   The services viewer displays, listing all the services currently loaded on the system.

You can see in Figure 2-1 that this interface lists all the services along with brief descriptions. Also included on this screen is the current status of the service, how the service starts up, and the account the service uses to log onto the system.

Figure 2-1   *Windows Services Window*

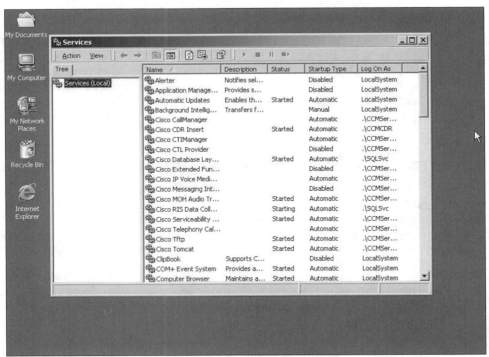

This chapter deals with the Status and the Startup Type.

The Status column shows three types of status: Started, Starting, or Paused. If there is nothing in the Status field this means the service is stopped.

There are two Startup Types shown in the Startup Types column:

- **Automatic**—The service automatically starts when needed.
- **Manual**—The service must be manually started or disabled, which means the service never starts unless it is re-enabled.

Because some services that may be running are unneeded, they should be disabled. The following is a list and brief description of each service that can be disabled on both the Subscriber and Publisher. Remember that based on the version of OS that CallManager is running, some of these services may already be disabled.

Alerter Service—Used to alert users of certain administrative alerts

Computer browser—Keeps track of other computers on the network

DCHP Client—Used to dynamically obtain an IP address

Distributed file system—Is responsible for managing logical volumes split across a network

Fax Service—Used for sending and receiving faxes

FTP Publishing—Allows FTP connectivity

License Logging Service—Tracks usage of various Microsoft services

Smartcard—Provides support for SmartCard readers

Note   There is an exception to the Smartcard service. If you plan to install the Cisco Certificate Trust List (CTL) Client on the CallManager, you must make sure the Smartcard service is set to automatic, not manual or disable. The Cisco CTL client offers added security authentication services. For additional information on this feature search "Cisco CallManager Security Guide" at Cisco.com.

Smartcard Helper—Allows support for earlier non–plug-and-play Smartcard readers

To disable these services follow these steps from the console of each CallManager:

Step 1   Click the **Start** button.

Step 2   Navigate to Programs>Administrative Tools>Services.

Step 3   The Services window displays the services loaded on this system.

Step 4   Using the list of services presented earlier in this section, disable each by following these steps.

- Double click the **desired service**.

- If the service is started, stop it by clicking the **Stop** button.

— Change the startup type to **Manual**.

— Click **OK**.

— Repeat these steps for each service you need to disable.

Step 5   Close the services window.

In addition to the services mentioned, you can disable the additional service on the Subscribers. Do not disable these services on the Publisher, if you do, you cannot access the administrative interface. The following are the services that you may disable on the Subscribers:

- **Internet Information Server Admin Service**—Allows administration of the IIS services.

- **World Wide Web Publishing Service**—Allows the server to act as a web server.

Not only does disabling these services save resources on the CallManager server, it also helps reduce access points for possible malicious attacks. As you may know, IIS is often the target of hackers, and disabling it, on servers where it is not needed, can reduce this concern.

After these services are disabled, you can move on to the CallManager-specific services. The next section explores how to activate these services and the function of each one.

Activating CallManager Services

As of CallManager 3.3, all CallManager services are deactivated by default. Before CallManager 3.3, the user determined which services would be running by choosing to install them during the installation process. In the current versions of CallManager, all services are loaded, but none are activated. This section discusses each of these services and explores the proper way to activate them.

Although the CallManager services are listed in the Window's services window, they cannot be activated from that interface. If these services are enabled from Widows Service pages, unexpected and unstable results could occur. You must activate them using the Service Activation screen within the CallManager Serviceability interface. You can access this screen in two ways. The simplest is to navigate to **Start>Programs>Cisco CallManager X.X** (the CallManager version shows in place of the X.X) and select Cisco Service configuration. You may also access this screen from within the CallManager Serviceability interface. Access to this interface is discussed in greater detail later. Although these services can be stopped from the Window's services page, this should never be done. You should only stop these services from **Cisco CallManager Serviceablity>Tools> Control Center**.

Figure 2-2 shows the Service Activation screen as it appears the first time it is accessed.

Figure 2-2   *Service Activation Screen*

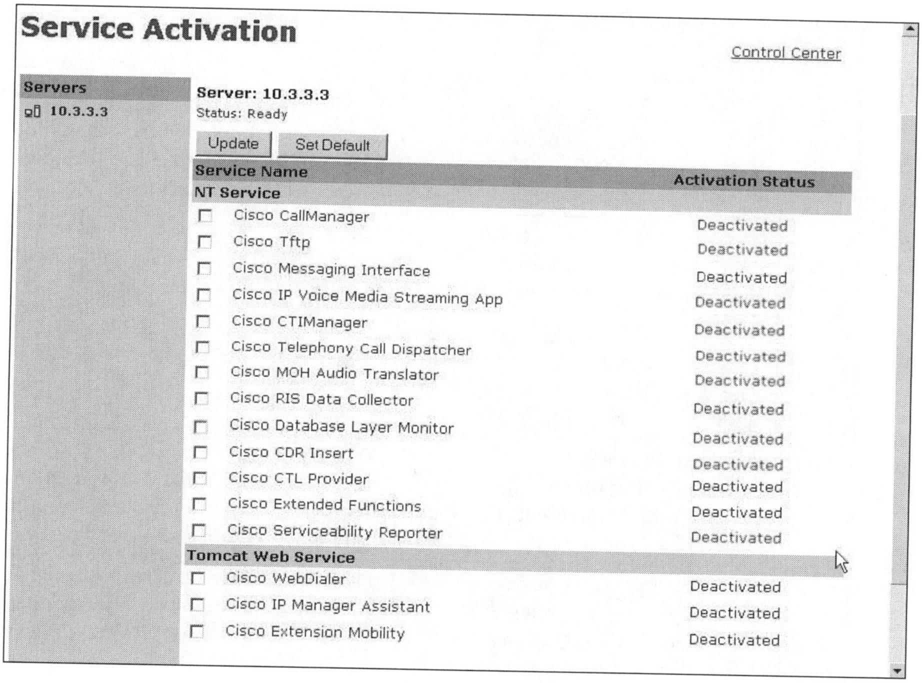

To activate the services screen simply follow these steps:

Step 1   From the console of the CallManager, navigate to **Start>Programs>Cisco CallManager X.X**. (The CallManager version displays in place of the X.X)

Step 2   Select **Cisco Service Configuration**.

Step 3   You are prompted for a user name and password. Enter the administrative **username** and **password** and click **OK**.

Step 4   Select the server you wish to activate services on from the list on the left side of the screen.

Step 5   Check the box next to each service you wish to activate and click the **Update** button.

NOTE   The Set Default button is next to the Update button. If this button is selected, all the services that are required for the functioning of CallManager will be activated. In most cases you do not activate all the same services on all the servers. Only use this button in a single server environment. The reason you shouldn't select all services on all the CallManager servers is because doing so would activate services that may not be needed, thereby consuming CPU cycles that could be used for other functions.

Table 2-1 lists all CallManager services with a brief explanation of their functions and activation recommendations.

Table 2-1 *CallManager Services*

Service	Function	Recommendations and Dependencies
Cisco CallManager	Provides call processing, signaling, and call control functions.	Servers with this service activated should also have the Cisco Database Lay Monitor and Cisco RIS Data Collector services activated.
Cisco Trivial File Transfer Protocol (TFTP)	Provides TFTP services for device configuration files. It is also responsible for building the configuration files.	This service should be activated on at least one CallManager. This server is responsible for servicing TFTP requests.
Cisco Messaging Interface	Provides Simplified Message Desk Interface (SMDI) connectivity for traditional voice-mail systems.	This does not need to be activated if Unity is the voicemail solution.
Cisco IP Voice Media Streaming App	Provides service such as Music on Hold (MoH), conferencing, and Media Termination Points (MTP).	You do not need to activate this service on all CallManagers. Activate it only on CallManagers that you want to provide these services. This should not be activated in the Publisher.
Cisco CTIManager	Provides support for devices requiring Computer Telephony Integration such as Call Back and Cisco Web Dialer.	This service must be activated on at least one server in a cluster in which Real-Time Information Server (RIS) Data Collector is running.
Cisco Telephony Call Dispatcher	Provides support for hunt groups and Attendant Console.	Should be activated on every server on which the CallManager service is running.
Cisco MOH Audio Translator	Converts audio files so that they may be used as MoH sources.	This service should be activated on the same server that is running the TFTP server. Do not run this on the Publisher.
Cisco RIS Data Collector	Gathers real time information such as IP addresses and distributes this information as needed.	This service should be activated on all servers.
Cisco Database Layer Monitor	Provides services for the database during failover and fallback operations. Also logs off phones that use extension mobility.	This service should be activated on all servers.
Cisco Call Detail Record (CDR) Insert	Inserts CDR records from the Subscriber into the database on the Publisher.	CDR database should be on the Publisher, hence this service should be activated on the Publisher.
Cisco CTL Provider	If enabled, turns the security mode from unsecured to mixmode. This service works in concert with the Cisco CTL Client.	This service should be activated on all servers on which TFTP and CallManager services are activated.

Table 2-1 *CallManager Services (Continued)*

Service	Function	Recommendations and Dependencies
Cisco Extended Functions	Enables features such as Call Back and Quality Report Tool.	The Cisco RIS Data Collector must be running on servers that are running this service. The CTI manager service must be loaded on at least one server.
Cisco Serviceability Reporter	Generates a report once daily. The generated reports include statistics on server, devices, services, call activities, and alerts. These reports can be accessed from the CallManager Serviceability Tools menu.	This service is activated on the Publisher. Be careful when running reports, because the service can impact call processing. It is best to run reports after hours.
Cisco WebDialer	Allows users to dial from a web page or desktop application.	This service requires the CTI Manger service be activated on the same sever on which it is running. Typically this service is loaded on one server in the cluster.
Cisco IP Manager Assistant	Is required to enable the IPMA feature. This feature allows managers additional features such as divert and DND.	This service should be active on servers that service these features.
Cisco Extension Mobility	Used to define time limits for Extension Mobility.	This service should be active in environments for which Extension Mobility is planned.

After these services are activated, they may be deactivated if desired. To deactivate any of these services, follow these steps.

Step 1 From the console of the CallManager, navigate to **Start>Programs>Cisco CallManager X.X**. (The CallManager version displays in place of the X.X)

Step 2 Select **Cisco Service Configuration**.

Step 3 You are prompted for a username and password. Enter the **administrative username** and **password** and click **OK**.

Step 4 From the list on the left side of the screen, select the server on which you wish to deactivate service.

Step 5 Uncheck the box next to each service you wish to deactivate and click the **Update** button.

After all the services are configured properly on all the servers in the cluster, you can move on to defining CallManager enterprise settings. The next section explores the various parameters that should be defined before devices are deployed.

Configuring CallManager's Enterprise Settings

Once services are active, CallManager is functioning. However, before devices are added, a few more tasks must be accomplished. This section examines the importance of removing Domain Name System (DNS) reliance and the system's enterprise parameters.

Removing DNS Dependencies

It is recommended that CallManager be configured so that the devices that register to it do not have to rely on DNS to resolve the CallManager. This is accomplished quite easily as you will see in the steps that are provided later. You may be wondering why is it recommended to remove DNS reliance. Primarily there are three reasons for this. First, it allows devices to be able to register without querying a DNS server. Second, a DNS server failure will not cause devices such as phones to fail registering. Third, because the device makes a call directly to the IP address of the CallManager, it can register faster. This is because an IP address can be resolved at Layer 3 of the Open System Interconnect (OSI) model, whereas a DNS request has to go up to Layer 7. Don't assume this means that DNS is not needed anywhere in the system. This is only done to allow devices to register without having to use DNS to resolve the CallManager. Other processes may still need to be able to resolve the CallManager's name. For instance, SQL replication between CallManager servers depends on NetBIOS name resolution. This can be accomplished by adding all CallManager names and IP addresses to the LMHOST files on each CallManager.

NOTE   You are removing the DNS reliance from the devices, not DNS from your network. Removing DNS from your network may cause your network to stop functioning properly.

Removing DNS reliance simply requires that you change the name of each CallManager server to the IP address. This is done within the web-based CallManager administration tool. Throughout the CallManager chapters within this book, this interface is referred to as CCMAdmin. To access CCMAdmin from the CallManager's console navigate to **Start>Programs>Cisco CallManager X.X** (the CallManager version displays in place of the X.X) and select CallManager Administration.

NOTE   Keep in mind that it is recommended that the World Wide Web Publishing Service and IIS be disabled on all servers in the CallManager cluster except the Publisher. Because the World Wide Web Publishing Service is not running on the Subscribers, you cannot access CCMAdmin from these servers. All CCMAdmin access must be done from the Publisher.

NOTE	Accessing CCMAdmin from a remote computer is quite simple. Just point your web browser to the IP address of the server followed by "/ccmadmin." For example, if the IP address of the CallManager is 10.3.3.3 the address you enter is http://10.3.3.3/ccmadmin. In some cases, you may need to use https: instead of http:.

To change the names of the servers follow these steps:

Step 1 From within CCMAdmin, open the System dropdown menu by clicking on **System** at the top of the screen.

Step 2 **Select Server** from the dropdown menu.

Step 3 A search criteria screen appears. You may search based on the name or the description of the CallManager. You may also leave the search criteria blank, and all servers will be listed. If you wish, enter the criteria to narrow down the search and click the **Find** button.

Step 4 A list of servers that matched the criteria appears. Select the first server in the list.

Step 5 A screen similar to that shown in Figure 2-3 appears. In the field labeled Host Name/IP Address, the current name of the server appears. In Figure 2-3 you see that the name is being changed from DTW-CCM to 10.3.3.3.

Figure 2-3 *Server Configuration Screen*

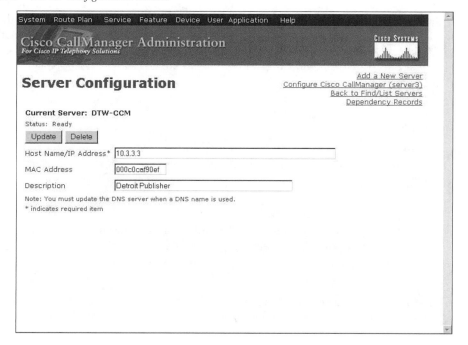

Step 6   The next field is labeled MAC Address. This field needs to be populated only if you plan to move the server from time-to-time. Entering the MAC address aids in helping the other devices identify the server. Enter the MAC address of the server in this field if you plan to move the server.

Step 7   The last field on this page is the Description field. Enter a description that will aid in determining the location and function of this server.

Step 8   Click the **Update** button to save the changes.

Step 9   Repeat Steps 1–8 for all CallManagers in the cluster.

Now that the reliance on DNS has been removed, the enterprise parameters should be defined. The next section discusses the function and proper settings for each of these parameters.

Defining Enterprise Parameters

Enterprise parameters are settings that apply to the entire cluster. As of CallManager 4.1, there are more than 40 enterprise parameters. These are divided into 10 categories. This section explores the recommended settings for these parameters and examines how these settings are configured. In some cases the recommended setting depends on your environment, and in these cases an explanation of the setting is offered to help you determine the proper setting for your environment. It is important to understand that although some of these settings may be left alone, others (such as the path entries) should be changed in most environments. Path entries are settings that point to a path that includes the server name. Because it is recommended that the server name be changed to the IP address, any field that points to the old name must be changed to point to the new name (the IP address). One example of such a field is the Call Detail Record (CDR) path. Because there are such a large number of parameters, they are tackled one category at a time in this chapter.

General Parameters

The first category you find within enterprise parameters is labeled General Parameters. The following steps show how these parameters are configured and explain the function of each of them.

NOTE   Some of these parameters require that the CallManager be restarted before changes will take effect. You will be informed if you change a parameter that requires a restart.

Step 1   From within CCMAdmin, open the System dropdown menu by clicking on **System** at the top of the screen.

Step 2   Select **Enterprise Parameters** from the dropdown menu.

Step 3   Figure 2-4 shows the six fields that appear under General Parameters on this page. The first field is called Synchronization Between Auto Device Profile and Phone Configuration. The setting in this field determines if changes that are made to a device are updated to the auto device profile of that device. An auto device profile is created when the Log Out Profile of a phone configured to allow extension mobility has been set to Use Current Device Settings. The default setting for this field is True. So that the both profiles are kept in sync, leave this set to True.

Figure 2-4   *Enterprise Parameters Configuration*

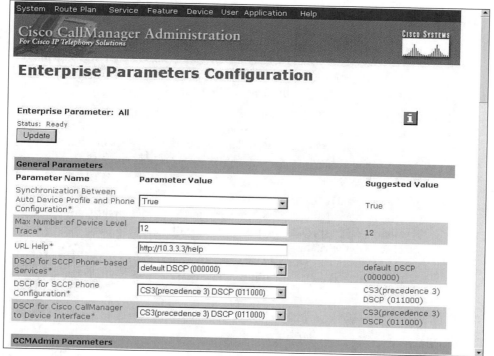

Step 4   The second setting in this category is Max Number of Device Level Trace. This setting determines the maximum number of devices that can be traced at one time when a device name-based trace is run. The default is 12. Valid ranges are 0 to 256. In most cases this setting can remain at the default. If you ever need to trace more than 12 devices when performing a device name-based trace, you must increase this setting to match the number of devices you are tracing.

Step 5   The third field found under this category is URL Help. This field contains the help hyperlink used from within some device configuration pages. You can change the name of the server in this field to the IP address, which will eliminate the need to resolve the name. In most cases you can enter the IP address of the Publisher followed by "/help" in this field. For example, if the server's IP address is 10.3.3.3 you enter http://10.3.3.3/help.

Step 6 The next three fields determine the Differentiated Service Code Point (DSCP) value for various communications. This value determines the priority of this type of packet. The first of these three, which is labeled DSCP for SCCP Phone-based Services deals with the DSCP that is assigned to IP phone services. Certain IP phones are capable of providing services such as weather, stock quotes, or whatever the administrator makes available. To ensure these services do not affect the quality of voice, and because this type of data should have the lowest priority, the default value is set to all zeros. This field can be left at the default.

Step 7 The next field is the DSCP for SCCP Phone Configuration traffic. This determines the priority of any traffic related to phone configuration. This includes TFTP, DNS, and DSCP traffic. The default of CS3 will grant higher priority than services traffic, but lower priority than voice, which is set to CS5. This field can be left at the default.

Step 8 The next field in this category, which is labeled DSCP for Cisco CallManager to Device Interface, determines the priority of CallManager to device traffic. The default of CS3 gives this traffic priority over services, but not over voice. This field can be left at the default.

Step 9 The last field is "Connection Monitor Duration." This setting defines how long a phone that is in SRST mode waits to fail back to the CallManager after it detects that CallManager is back online. This can help prevent the phone from switching back and fourth between the SRST server and the CallManager when a CallManager connection is going up and down (also know as "flapping"). The default value of 120 should be adequate.

CCMAdmin Parameters

The second category in enterprise parameters is CCMAdmin Parameters. These parameters affect the CCMAdmin web-based interface. The following steps show how these parameters are configured and explain the function of each of them.

Step 1 Navigate to the enterprise parameters page in CCMAdmin.

Step 2 The first field under the CCMAdmin Parameters is labeled Max List Box Items. It determines the maximum number of items that a list box can contain. The default value is 250. This setting can be set in the range of

50 to 9999. The larger the number, the longer it takes for the page to load. It is best to leave this value set to default. If the number of items is larger than the value set, only the current value appears in the list. A button labeled "..." appears next to the list. By clicking on this button you can search for the item you wish to select.

Note	A list box is the list of items that appears when you click on the down arrow at the end of a field. In Figure 2-5 you see that a list box appears when the down arrow is clicked in the Partition field.

Figure 2-5   *List Box Example*

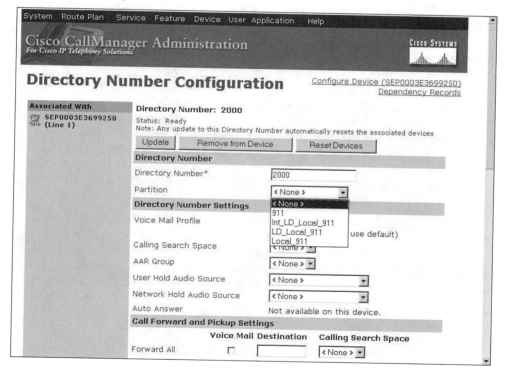

Step 3   The next field, the Max Lookup Items field, determines how many items will be returned to the browser when a lookup is done. The default for this setting is 1000, which should be adequate for most installations. This field can be set from 250 to 99999. Keep in mind that the higher this value is set, the longer it takes to load the page.

Step 4 The final field in this category, the Enable Dependency Records, field determines whether dependency records can be retrieved or not. Because this feature can be tasking on the CPU, it is set to False (off) by default. It is best to leave this value set to False. However, there are times when this feature can save hours. For instance, if you are trying to delete a CSS, you can only delete it once you have removed it from all devices to which it is assigned. When you try to remove the CSS, a message displays stating that the CSS cannot be deleted because it is assigned to one or more devices. If dependencies are not enabled, you must manually search to find to which devices the CSS is assigned. You save time if dependencies is enabled, because you can find out exactly the number and type of devices to which the CSS is assigned. When this feature is needed, it is best to enable it (set the value to True) after hours only and then disable it (set the value to False) when you are finished using it.

CCMUser Parameters

The third enterprise parameters category is called CCMUser Parameters. These settings determine what options are available to a user from the user web pages. The user web pages allow users to change many of their phone settings. Often you may not want the user to be able to change certain settings from the web pages, such as the Message Wait Indication (MWI) policy. Each setting has two valid values, either True or False. If an option is set to True, it is available through the user web pages. If it is set to False, it is not available. This section simply explains what action the user can take from the user web page if the option is set to True. If you do not want one or several of these features available from the user web page, set the value to False.

- **Show Ring Settings**—Allows the user to set when and how a line rings, based on the state of the line. This means that if the phone is idle, the user can choose to have the phone ring normally and when the phone is in use, the user can choose to have it only flash the light. Each line can be configured to act differently. The ring options available while the phone is idle are to ring normally, ring once, flash only, or do nothing. The options available while the phone is in use are to ring normally, ring once, flash only, beep only, or do nothing.

- **Show Call Forwarding**—Allows users to see if call forwarding is currently set on their phones and change it.

- **Show Speed Dial Settings**—Allows users to see the current speed dial settings for their phones and change them.

- **Show Cisco IP Phone Services Settings**—Allows users to view the services to which the phone is currently subscribed. Also allows users to subscribe to new services.

- **Show Personal Address Book Settings**—Allows users to view, edit, and add the entries in their personal address books.

- **Show Message Waiting Lamp Policy Settings**—Allows users to edit if and how each line indicates that a new voice mail message has arrived for that line. They may choose to have the light shine, have an icon appear next to the line number, both of these options, or have no indication at all.

- **Show Locale for Phone Settings**—Allows users to set the language on the phone.

- **Show Locale for Web Pages Settings**—Allows users to set the language for the user web pages.

- **Show Change Password Option**—Allows users to change their passwords.

- **Show Change PIN Option**—Allows users to change their PINs

- **Show Online Guide Option**—Adds a link to the user guide for the type of phone that is associated with the user. The guide is in PDF format. In some cases the guide may not be available for certain model phones. This is normally the case if the phone model is relatively new.

CDR Parameters

The fourth enterprise parameters category is called CDR Parameters and deals with Call Detail Record (CDR) settings. These setting determine the location and format of CDRs. The following steps explain the function of each setting as well as recommended settings.

Step 1 Navigate to the enterprise parameters page in CCMAdmin.

Step 2 The first field under the CDR Parameters is labeled CDR File Time Interval and determines the length of time CDR information is written to a local file before being sent to the CDR database. The default value is 1, which means the data is written every minute to the CDR database. You may increase this value, but the higher you set the value, the longer it will take before the data is written to the CDR database.

Step 3 The next field is labeled CDR Format and determines whether the data is inserted into the database. The choice for this setting is to insert CDRs into the database or keep them in a flat file. The suggested value for this field is CDRs will be inserted into database. This value causes the CDR files to be deleted as they are inserted. If you change this setting to CDRs will be kept in flat files, the files are not deleted, which could cause the drive on the CallManager to fill up.

Step 4 The next field, labeled CDR UNC Path is used to specify to what location the CDR files that are created within the cluster are moved. This is typically the Publisher. It is a good idea to change the name of the server that appears in this field to the IP address of the Publisher.

Step 5 The next field is labeled Cluster ID and is used to identify this cluster when multiple clusters exist. The default value is StandAloneCluster. If you have multiple clusters, it is recommended that you change this value to one that aids in identifying this cluster. The value cannot exceed 50 characters.

Step 6 In the next field labeled Local CDR Path you specify where the CDR files are stored locally until they are transferred to the CDR Universal Naming Convention (UNC) path that you specified earlier. It is best to leave this field at the default.

Step 7 The last field in this category, which is called Off Cluster CDR Connection String, is used if you choose to store the CDRs in a database other than the CallManager Publisher. The value entered into this field must point to an Open Database Connectivity (ODBC) data machine that has a matching CDR database schema. In most environments this field is left empty.

Localization Parameters

The fifth category within the enterprise parameters is called Localization Parameters and deals with languages and tones. What language is used depends on where the CallManager solution is deployed. Just as there are different languages around the world, there are also different tones and cadences for phones. For instance, when placing a call in England, the caller hears a double ring back instead of the single ring back that is heard in the U.S. The following steps show how to edit these parameters and explain each of them.

Step 1 Navigate to the enterprise parameters page in CCMAdmin.

Step 2 The first field under the Localization parameters is the Default Network Locale field. This parameter is used to determine what types of tones and cadences are used by the system. The default is United States. If needed, this parameter may be changed by clicking the down arrow at the end of the field. A list of valid choices displays in the drop down list. Choose the desired language from the list.

Step 3 The last field in this category is the Default User Locale field. This parameter determines the default language used for the devices in the system. English United States is the default value for this field. If additional languages are installed on the CallManager, they display in the dropdown list in this field. Choose the appropriate language for your environment.

Multi-Level Precedence and Pre-Emption (MLPP) Parameters

The sixth category of enterprise parameters is the MLPP parameters. MLPP adds the ability to grant higher priority to calls. This is useful in many government and military situations where it may be imperative that a call is successful. A call of a higher priority can actually cause a call of a lower priority to be terminated so that the resources can be used to complete the higher priority call. The MLPP parameters deal with this feature. The following steps include explanation of each parameter and recommended settings.

Step 1   Navigate to the enterprise parameters page in CCMAdmin.

Step 2   The first field under the MLPP Parameters is the MLPP Domain Identifier. MLPP grants higher priority only from calls within the same MLPP domain. For this reason an MLPP identifier must be chosen. The default value is 0.

Step 3   The second field in this category, which is called MLPP Indication Status, determines whether tones and indications are presented when a precedence call is made. The precedence indication may be a special ring back or a display notification, if the caller's phone supports it, and a special ringer on the called party's side. By default, this parameter is set to MLPP Indication turned off. To enable this feature set this parameter to **MLPP Indication turned on**.

Step 4   The next field is MLPP Preemption Setting. This parameter determines whether a higher precedence call preempts a lower precedence call. The default value of No Preemption allowed does not allow this to happen. To cause a lower precedence call to be terminated if a higher precedence call requires the resources, set this parameter to **Forceful Preemption**.

Step 5   The next field, which is called Precedence Alternate Party Timeout, determines how long the system will wait before sending a precedence call to the alternate party. The default is 30 seconds. Valid values for this field are 4 to 60. Enter the desired value in the field.

Note   This parameter is used when the called party has set an alternate party diversion. This is separate from a standard call forward setting.

Step 6   The last parameter in this category is labeled Use Standard VM Handling For Precedence Calls and determines whether precedence calls are forwarded to voicemail in the same manner as all normal calls. It is recommended that precedence calls not be forwarded to voicemail, so the default value is False. For a configuration that forwards precedence calls to voicemail, set the value to **True**. It is recommended that the value be left at False.

Security Parameters

The seventh category within enterprise parameters is Security parameters. These parameters are defined if security is enabled within the cluster and set as default security behavior for phones. There are four fields in this category. The first, called Device Security Mode, determines how devices register that are set up to use system default for their device security modes. The default is Non Secure, which means it does not use any type of authentication. The other two values are Authenticated and Encrypted. When set to Authentication, the device and signaling authentication take place. When set to Encrypted, device and signaling authentication takes place in addition to the encryption.

The second security parameter is Cluster Security Mode. This is the setting that displays whether the cluster is operating in a nonsecure or mixed mode fashion. This field is read only and can only be affected by running the CTL client plugin. The valid values for this field are 0, which indicates a nonsecure mode, and 1, which indicates a mixed mode.

The third parameter is CAPF Phone Port. This defines a port that listens for Cisco Authority Proxy Function Service (CAPF) requests from a phone for a Certificate. The valid values for this field are 1023 through 55556. The default is 3804. Leave this set to 3804 unless the default port is not used.

The final security parameter is CAPF Operation Expires in (days). This parameter determines how many days a CAPF operation has to complete. The valid values are 1 to 365. The default is 10.

Phone URL Parameters

The eighth category of enterprise parameters is the Phone URL Parameters. These parameters deal with URLs phones use for various purposes. One example is the URL for services; this is the address that the phones point to when the services button is pressed. The following steps explain each parameter and its recommended configuration.

Step 1 Navigate to the enterprise parameters page in CCMAdmin.

Step 2 The first field under the Phone URL parameters is called URL Authentication. This parameter specifies the URL that certain phones use for authentication proxy services between them and the LDAP directory. This value is set during the installation and in most cases should not be changed. However, if you change the name of the server to the IP address, make sure you change that portion of the URL. For example, if the URL is http://DTW_CCM/CCMCIP/authenticate.asp and you have changed the name of the server to its IP address, which is 10.3.3.3, make sure you change the URL to http://10.3.3.3/CCMCIP/authenticate.asp.

Step 3 The next field, which is called URL Directories, contains the URL that phones use to access directory functions. This occurs when the "directory" button on the phone is pressed. Once again, if you changed the name of the server to the IP address, make sure to change it in this URL.

Step 4   The next field is labeled URL Idle. Some Cisco IP phones have the ability to display information on the screen after the phone is idle for a certain amount of time. This parameter specifies the URL the phone should call to retrieve this information. A common use for this feature is to display the company's logo on the phone. By default this field is empty. Enter the URL you wish to use if you have configured one.

Tip	For more information on how to create a graphic that can be used for this purpose, refer to the document titled "Creating Idle URL Using Graphics on Cisco IP Phone" at Cisco.com. Document ID: 42573

Step 5   The fourth Phone URL parameter is URL Idle Time. This parameter determines how long a phone must be idle before the Idle URL is displayed. The default is 0, which means the URL is not displayed. Set the desired value in seconds.

Step 6   The next parameter is URL Information. This parameter specifies the URL the phone requests when the help function is invoked by pressing the **i** or **?** button on the phone. Make sure that if you change the name of the server to the IP address, you change it in this URL.

Step 7   The next parameter, which is called URL Messages, contains the URL the phone requests when the Messages button is pressed. By default this field is empty.

Step 8   The next field, which is labeled IP Phone Proxy Address, specifies the address of the proxy server all phone URL requests use. If this field is blank, the phone tries to make a direct request for URLs. By default this field is empty. If this field is used, the address must contain the server name or IP address and the port number.

Step 9   The last parameter in this category is URL Services. This parameter contains the URL that the phone requests when the Services button is pressed. Again, if you change the name of the server to the IP address, make sure to change it in this URL.

User Search Parameters

The ninth enterprise parameter category is User Search Parameters. Certain Cisco IP phones enable the user to search the phone directory from the LCD screen on the phone. This feature is activated by pressing the Directories button on the phone. The newer model phones have an icon that looks like an open book instead of the word "directories."

This gives the phones a more global look. These two parameters define the breadth of a directory search and its results. These parameters also apply to searches that are made from within the CallManager User Options web page.

The first parameter, which is labeled Enable All User Search, determines whether a search, in which the user left all the fields blank, is allowed. By default, the value is True, which means that a search of this nature would attempt to return all the names in the directory. To disable this type of search, set the value to False.

The other parameter in this category determines the maximum number of results a search can return. This parameter is called User Search Limit. The default value is 64, which means that no more than 64 results are returned. The valid values for this parameter range from 1 to 500. Keep in mind that the higher this value is, the longer it can take to return the results. A number more than 64 can have a negative effect on the performance of the CallManager.

CCM Web Services Parameters

The tenth category of enterprise parameters is CCM Web Services Parameters. These parameters limit the number of performance counters and device queries that can be made. If too many requests are made, it can negatively affect performance. Other applications such as the Voice Health Monitoring and Gateway Statistic Utility may receive delayed responses. The following are the three parameters with brief descriptions.

The first parameter in this category is labeled Allowed Performance Queries Per Minute. This parameter determines the maximum AVVID XML Layer (AXL) performance counter queries that are allowed per minute. The default value is 50. Valid values for this parameter are 1 to 80.

The next parameter in this category is labeled Allowed Device Queries Per Minute. This parameter determines the maximum AXL device queries that are allowed per minute. The default value is 15. Valid values for this parameter are 1 to 18.

The third parameter in this category is labeled Performance Queue Limit and determines the size of the queue for performance counter queries. If a query is made and the queue is full, the query is dropped. The default is 100. Valid values for this parameter are 20 to 1000.

The last parameter in this category is Maximum Performance Counters Per Session. This parameter sets the maximum number of performance counters allowed per session.

The last set of parameters is the Trace Parameters. The first parameter is called File Close Thread Flag. This parameter is set to False by default. If set to True, it enables separate threads to be used to close trace files. This may improve performance when traces are run.

The last trace parameter is called FileCloseThreadQueueWatermark. This parameter defines how many trace files the separate thread accepts before refusing trace files. The trace file is then closed without the use of a separate thread. The default is 100. The valid values are 0 through 500.

As you can see, there are a number of enterprise parameters. Most of them can be left at default, but others, such as those that contain the name of the CallManager, may need to be changed. In most cases the integrator makes these changes at the time of installation. It is still a good idea to know the function of each parameter so that if one ever needs to be adjusted you know where to find it, how to change it, and what the impact of the change is.

At this point, the system is now almost ready for the attachment and configuration of devices. There are, however, a few more tasks that should be completed before device attachment and configuration. The next section examines the core tasks that should be accomplished before devices are allowed to register to the system.

Preparing CallManager for Device Registration

When a device registers with CallManager a number of things need to be known about that device, such as the type of device and the IP address and MAC address. However, determining other information is also necessary, including what time zone the phone is in, and with which CallManager the device should register. Instead of defining this information at every device, a component known as a device pool is used. Because most often a large number of devices require the same information, the needed information is assigned to a device pool, and then the device pool is assigned to those devices. This way, instead of defining more than ten configuration values for each device, you assign the values once in the device pool.

As of CallManager 4.1, the device pool contains 16 fields. Eight of these fields are required to be configured when creating a new device pool. Although configuring the others is not required, it is recommended. This section briefly explains each field and explores how to configure the fields that are crucial to a proper deployment. The following is a list of fields found in a device pool.

- **Device Pool Name (Required)**—No doubt you can figure out what this is without any description. It is simply the name of the device pool. The name you choose should enable you to easily identify the function of this device pool. For example, you might name the device pool EST-DTW1-DTW2 for a device pool that is used by devices that are in the Eastern Time Zone and use CallManager DTW1 as a primary CallManager and CallManager DTW2 as a secondary server.

- **Cisco CallManager Group (Required)**—A CallManager group defines which CallManager is used as the primary server, which as the secondary server, and which as the tertiary server. The next section discusses how to create these servers.

- **Date/Time Group (Required)**—Because it is possible that devices belonging to the same cluster may be in different time zones, it is necessary to define the correct time zone for each device. The Date/Time Group is used to specify to which time zone a device belongs. The date and time format is also defined by the Date/Time group. The configuration of Date/Time Groups is covered later in this chapter.

- **Region (Required)**—Because VoIP calls may traverse links of different bandwidth, it is often necessary to use a codec that requires less bandwidth to make most efficient use of the link. A codec converts voice signals from their analog form to digital signals that are acceptable to modern digital transmission systems. Some codecs use algorithms that compress the voice stream so that less bandwidth is required. Using regions, you can define what codec one device should use when talking to another device. Further discussion and the configuration of region are covered later in this chapter.

- **Softkey Template (Required)**—Most Cisco IP phones have keys called *softkeys* that allow the user to access certain functions such as hold, transfer, and call park. The function of each key changes depending on the state of the call. In addition, because there are often more available functions than softkeys, the user must sometimes scroll through the available options. The softkey template allows you to determine what functions are available on the phone and in what order they appear.

- **Survivable Remote Site Telephony (SRST) Reference (Required)**—SRST is a feature that allows phones that are remote to the CallManager to continue functioning even if they are unable to communicate with the CallManager. This is done by having the phones register with a local router that is acting as an SRST box. The SRST Reference is used to define which device the phone should try to register with if it is unable to communicate with the CallManager.

  Another use for SRST is when a small office has only a single CallManager. Although it is always recommended to have two CallManagers for redundancy purposes, it is possible to use SRST for redundancy when only one CallManager is installed.

- **Calling Search Space for Auto-Registration**—When using auto-registration, it is a good idea to restrict where the device can call until its legitimacy is confirmed. This field allows you to specify a calling search space for all devices that auto-register.

- **Media Resource Group List**—Media Resources provide features such as Music on Hold (MOH) and conferencing. A device Media Resource Group List defines to which media resource the device has access.

- **Network Hold MOH Audio Source**—There are two kinds of hold, user hold and network hold. A user hold occurs when the hold button on the phone is pressed. Any other time a call is placed on hold, for instance if the call is being transferred, it is considered a network hold.

  The Network Hold MOH audio source determines what audio stream a caller hears when placed on a network hold.

- **User Hold MOH Audio Source**—The User Hold MOH audio source determines what audio stream a caller hears when placed on a user hold.

- **Network Locale**—This field determines what locale is used for the devices. The field impacts the tones and cadences used. The default Network Locale was defined in the enterprise parameters. If a different value is selected here, this value takes precedence. Make sure that you select only a locale that has been loaded in the system; otherwise, the device associated with this device pool fails. If this field is set to None, the enterprise parameter setting is used.

- **User Locale**—This parameter determines the language and fonts used for the devices in this device pool. The default User Locale, which is set in the enterprise parameters, will be used if this field is left set to None.

- **Connection Monitor Duration**—This setting defines how long a phone, which is in SRST mode, waits to fail back to the CallManager after it detects that CallManager is back online. This can help prevent the phone from switching back and forth between the SRST server and the CallManager when a CallManager connection is going up and down (also know as flapping).

- **MLPP Indication (Required)**—This field determines whether tones and indications are presented when a precedence call is made to or from a device in this device pool. If this field is set to Default, the MLPP Indication setting in the enterprise parameters is used.

- **MLPP Preemption (Required)**—This parameter determines whether a higher precedence call preempts a lower precedence call. If this field is Default, the MLPP Indication setting in the enterprise parameters is used.

- **MLPP Domain**—This field determines to which MLPP domain the devices in this device pool belong. If this field is left blank, the MLPP Domain Identifier defined in the enterprise parameters is used.

A number of these fields point to other objects that may not have been configured yet. Throughout this book many of these components are discussed in more detail. From this point on, we are going to focus on the required components that most often need to be defined before devices are deployed.

Creating CallManager Groups

A CallManager group defines which CallManagers a given device points to as its primary, secondary, and tertiary CallManager. The concept is really quite simple. The CallManager group contains a list of CallManagers; the order in which they appear determines their function (that of either a primary, secondary, or tertiary CallManager). A CallManager may be in more than one group and its function may be different in each group. For example, Table 2-2 shows two CallManager groups. Each group contains the same three servers, but they appear in a different order. The result is that the DTWA CallManager is the primary in Group DTWABC, but it is the tertiary in group DTWCBA. The only thing that defines the CallManager's function in regards to primary/secondary/tertiary is the order in which they appear in the CallManager Group.

Table 2-2   *Two CallManager Groups*

CallManager Group DTWABC	CallManager Group DTWCBA
DTWA	DTWC
DTWB	DTWB
DTWC	DTWA

Creating CallManager groups is a simple task, but before creating them you need to spend some time determining how many CallManager groups you need. The number of CallManagers you have impacts the number of CallManager groups you have. For instance, if you have only two CallManagers, you have only two CallManager groups at most. However, having six CallManagers by no means indicates that there will be six CallManager groups. When determining the number of CallManager groups you will have, keep two goals in mind, redundancy and load balancing. By keeping these two goals in mind and using common sense, you can easily figure out the proper number of CallManager groups for your environment. For further information on CallManager groups and cluster sizes, refer to the "Cisco IP Telephony Network Design Guide," which can be found on Cisco.com by searching for **Cisco IP Telephony Network Design Guide**.

CallManager Groups are configured using CCMAdmin. The process is quite simple, as you will see in the provided steps. Before you start, make sure that all CallManagers are running and able to communicate with each other. To add CallManager Groups follow these steps.

Step 1   From within CCMAdmin, open the System menu by clicking **System** on the top of the window and selecting **Cisco CallManager Group**.

Step 2   Select the link **Add a New Cisco CallManager Group** in the upper-right portion of the screen.

| Note | A default CallManager Group already exists. If you choose to use the default, make sure that all the desired CallManagers appear in this group in the desired order. This can be done using the steps listed here as well as by choosing the **Find** button and then selecting the **Default group** instead of selecting **Add a New CallManager Group**. |

Step 3   A screen similar to that shown in Figure 2-6 displays. Enter the desired name for this CallManager group. Give it a name that it is easily identified. For instance, in the example shown in Figure 2-6, the name CMGAB is used to show that CallManagers DTWA and DTWB belong to that group in that order.

Figure 2-6   *CallManager Group Configuration*

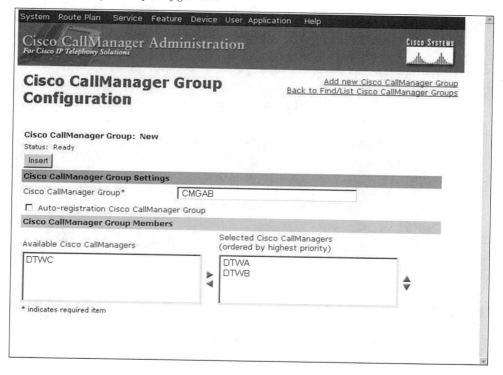

Step 4   All the available CallManagers display in the box labeled Available Cisco CallManagers. Highlight the CallManager you want to act as the primary CallManager in this group. Between the two boxes on the screen are two arrows. To move the selected server, click the arrow that points to the **Selected Cisco CallManagers** box.

Step 5   Repeat this step to move the remainder of the desired CallManagers into the **Selected Cisco CallManagers** box.

Step 6   The order in which the CallManagers appear in the Selected Cisco CallManagers box determines whether they are considered primary, secondary or tertiary. You can change the order in which they appear by highlighting a CallManager and clicking the up and down arrows to the right of the box.

Step 7   After all the CallManagers have been added and display in the desired order, click the **Insert** button.

Use these steps to configure all CallManager Groups that you need. After that is accomplished, you need to define Data/Time Groups.

Defining Date/Time Groups

Imagine that you have asked someone to call you at 10:00 a.m. and they call at 11:00 a.m. You answer the phone frustrated from the wait only to find that your friend is calling from a different time zone and thinks she's on time. Just as we need be aware of time zones in our daily lives, we need to make sure that CallManager knows the time zone of its registered devices. This is accomplished by configuring a Date/Time group for each time zone that devices will be in.

The default Date/Time group, called CMLocal, is created when CallManager is installed, and it is set to the zone selected during the installation. If all the devices are in the same time zone, you can use the CMLocal Date/Time group without adding any others. However, if your devices are in different time zones, you can use these steps to guide you through the process of creating a Date/Time group for each time zone.

Step 1   From within CCMAdmin, open the System menu by clicking on **System** at the top of the window and selecting **Date/Time Group**.

Step 2   From the screen that displays, you either search for an existing Date/Time Group or add a new one. Select the **Add a New Date/Time Group** link in the upper-right portion of the screen.

Step 3   A screen similar to that shown in Figure 2-7 appears. All fields on this screen are required. The first field is Group Name. Give the group a name that is easily identified. For example, the Date/Time group that is being created in Figure 2-7 is for the devices that are in Chicago, and Chicago is in the Central Time zone so it has been named Chicago-CST. Enter an appropriate name for this Date/Time Group.

Figure 2-7 *Date/Time Group Configuration*

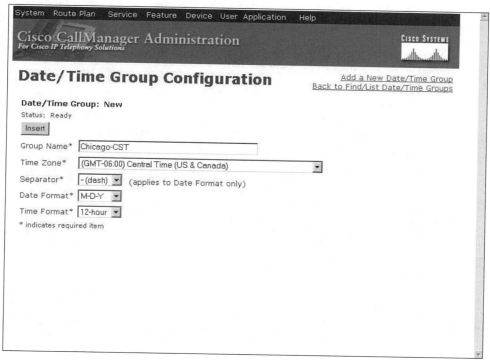

Step 4 In the Time Zone field, select the correct time zone from the drop down list that is displayed when you click the down arrow at the end of the field.

Step 5 The next field, called Separator, is used to define the symbol that is used as a separator when the date is displayed. The valid values for this field are a dash (-), forward slash (/) or a dot (.). Choose the desired value from the drop down list.

Step 6 The Date Format field determines how the date is presented. The choices are month-day-year, day-month-year, or year-month-day. Choose the desired format from the drop-down list.

Step 7 The last field, labeled Time Format determines whether the time will be displayed in 12-hour or 24-hour format. Choose the desired format.

Step 8 Click the **Insert** button.

Repeat these steps for each Date/Time group needed.

Configuring Regions

When calls traverse lower bandwidth IP links, such as a WAN link between offices, it may be necessary to compress the audio stream so that the link is used efficiently. The compression is accomplished by using a codec that has a lower bandwidth requirement, such as G729, for the call. When using a codec that requires lower bandwidth, the quality of the call is affected. For this reason, it is recommended that these codecs are used only when bandwidth is at a premium. With this in mind, you can understand that the codec used should depend on the call destination, rather than what device is placing the call. Regions allow for this.

The two most often used codecs in a Cisco VoIP environment are G.711 and G.729. G.711 requires approximately 80 kps when overhead is included. G.729 requires only 24 kps including overhead. Because most of the newer generation Cisco IP phones support both codecs, G.729 is often used when traversing a WAN link.

By creating and assigning regions, you define which codec is used between regions. Figure 2-8 shows three regions and the codecs that are used when calls are placed within the region and to other regions. As you can see, if someone from Detroit calls another party in Detroit, the G.711 codec is used, but when a party in Detroit calls someone in Chicago, the G.729 codec is used.

Figure 2-8 *Use of Codec Regions Example*

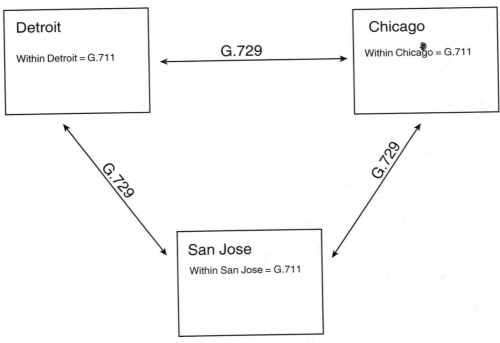

A default region named Default is created during the installation of CallManager. If calls in your environment never traverse lower bandwidth links, additional regions may not be needed. Regions are created from within CCMAdmin. You can create the required regions by following these steps.

Step 1 From within CCMAdmin, open the System menu by clicking **System** at the top of the window and selecting **Region**.

Step 2 From the screen that displays, you can either search for an existing region or add a new one. Select the **Add a New Region** link in the upper-right portion of the screen.

Step 3 A figure similar to that shown in Figure 2-9 displays. Enter the name of the region in the field labeled Region Name. It is recommended that you enter a name that is easily identified. In this example, because the region will be used for devices that are in Detroit, the region is named Detroit.

Figure 2-9 *Adding a Region*

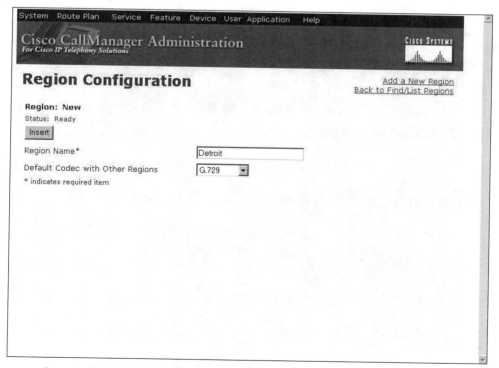

Step 4 In the **Default Codec with Other Regions** field, select the codec that you will want to use for all other regions by selecting it from the drop down list. If you know that you do not want to use the same codec between all other regions, select the codec you want to use between most

other regions. Later, you can define more particularly the codec used between regions.

Step 5   Click **Insert**. A screen displays that shows the region you just created as the active region, and all other regions listed below. If you have more regions to add, select the **Add a New Region** link in the upper-right portion of the screen. Using steps 3–5, add all other regions.

After all the regions are added, you can use the following steps to change the codec that is used between them.

Step 1   From within CCMAdmin, open the System menu by clicking **System** at the top of the window and selecting **Region**.

Step 2   From the screen that appears, you either search for an existing Region or add a new one. In the box just to the left of the **Find** button, enter the name, or part of the name, of the region you wish to edit and click **Find**.

Step 3   Select the desired region from the list that displays. A screen similar to that shown in Figure 2-10 appears.

Figure 2-10   *Region Configuration*

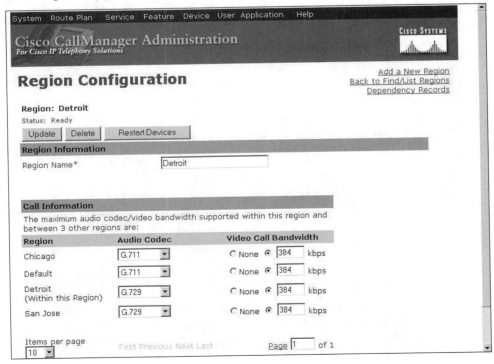

Step 4 Find the other region for which you want to define the codec and select the codec from the drop-down list. For example, Figure 2-10 shows the calls between Detroit and Chicago are set for G.711. This should be set to G.729, so G.729 should be selected from the drop-down list next to the word Chicago.

Step 5 From this screen, you can also define the amount of bandwidth to be allotted for video calls between regions. If this feature is to be used, enter the desired value in this field.

Step 6 After all desired changes have been made, click the **Update** button. Repeat these steps for all other regions.

You may want to configure a few more things before creating device pools. One is softkey templates. There is a default softkey template, so if you plan on using just that one, you can move on to creating device pools. Because softkey templates are specific to phones, they are covered in the next chapter with phone button templates. For the purpose of the next section, which is configuring Device Pools, we will use the defaults values available for all other required objects.

Building Device Pools

Now that the Device Pool's required components have been configured, you can create the device pools. The first thing you have to determine is how many device pools are needed. This is determined by looking at the number of device pool components you have created and how they tie together. Let's take a look at a very simple example.

Imagine that you have configured two CallManager groups, three regions, and two date/time groups as shown in Table 2-3.

Table 2-3 *Determining the Number of Device Pools Needed*

CallManager Groups	DTWABC DTWCBA
Regions	Detroit
	Grand Rapids
	Chicago
Date/Time Groups	Eastern
	Central

Right away you can tell that because you have three regions, there will have to be at least three device pools. If the devices in each region are part of the same date/time groups, and use the same CallManager group, then only three device pools will be needed. However, in this example, you want half the phones in each region to use CallManager group DTWABC and the other half to use CallManager group DTWCBA, so three device pools won't be enough. It would take six device pools to accomplish this as shown in Table 2-4.

Table 2-4   *Device Pool Example*

Device Pool	CallManager Group	Region	Date/Time Group
DTWABC_DP	DTWABC	Detroit	Eastern
DTWCBA_DP	DTWCBA	Detroit	Eastern
GRRABC_DP	DTWABC	Grand Rapids	Eastern
GRRCBA_DP	DTWCBA	Grand Rapids	Eastern
ORDABC_DP	DTWABC	Chicago	Central
ORDCBA_DP	DTWCBA	Chicago	Central

From this simple example, you can see how the number of device pools could easily grow if not managed properly. So what is the right number of device pools? There is no definitive answer. That really depends on your specific requirements, but make sure you take the time to properly plan the number of device pools that your environment will require.

After all the components that belong in a device pool are created, you have planned out how many device pools you need, and planned what components will belong to each pool, creating the device pools is quite simple. The following steps show how to create a device pool. The steps will not detail each component because each was discussed previously in this chapter.

Step 1   From within CCMAdmin, open the System menu by clicking **System** at the top of the window and selecting **Device Pool**.

Step 2   From the screen that displays, you can either search for an existing Device Pool or add a new one. Select the **Add a New Device Pool** link in the upper-right portion of the screen.

Step 3   A screen similar to that is shown in Figure 2-11 displays. In the **Device Pool Name** field, enter the name of the new device pool. Remember to give the device pool an easily identifiable name.

Step 4   Now simply select the desired object for each of the remaining fields. If you are uncertain of the function of any object, refer to the earlier section in this chapter that discussed each field. The fields that are marked with an asterisk (*) are required, so you must select a value. The other fields are not required, but it is recommended that a value be set. Many of these values are discussed in more detail in future chapters.

Step 5   After you have selected an object for all required and desired fields, click the **Insert** button.

Figure 2-11 *Device Pool Configuration*

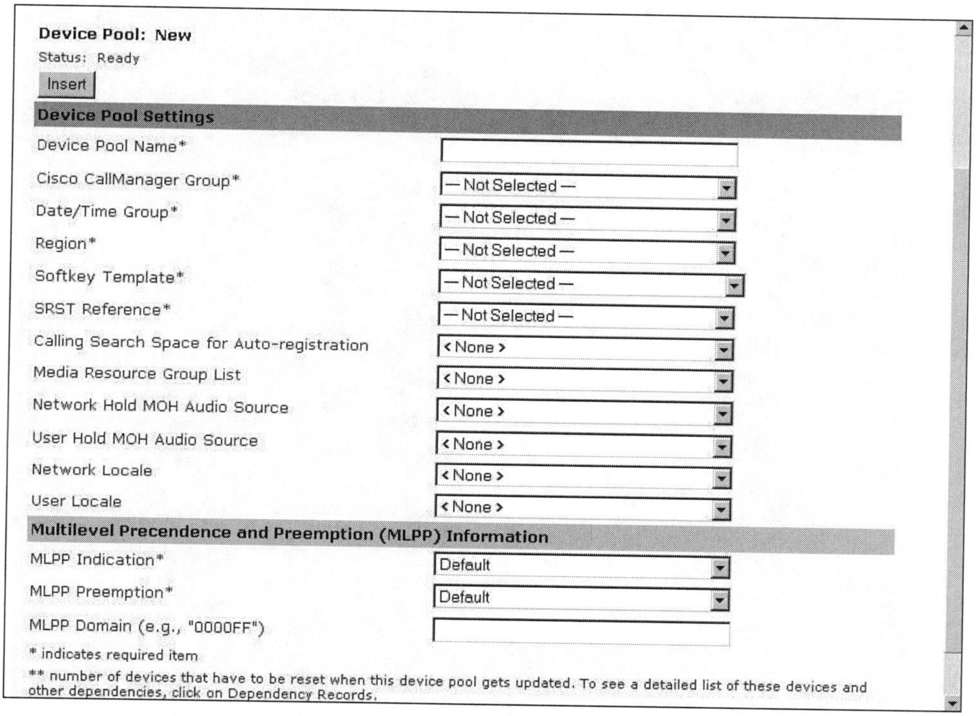

Device Pool: New
Status: Ready
[Insert]

Device Pool Settings

Device Pool Name*	
Cisco CallManager Group*	— Not Selected —
Date/Time Group*	— Not Selected —
Region*	— Not Selected —
Softkey Template*	— Not Selected —
SRST Reference*	— Not Selected —
Calling Search Space for Auto-registration	< None >
Media Resource Group List	< None >
Network Hold MOH Audio Source	< None >
User Hold MOH Audio Source	< None >
Network Locale	< None >
User Locale	< None >

Multilevel Precendence and Preemption (MLPP) Information

MLPP Indication*	Default
MLPP Preemption*	Default
MLPP Domain (e.g., "0000FF")	

* indicates required item
** number of devices that have to be reset when this device pool gets updated. To see a detailed list of these devices and other dependencies, click on Dependency Records.

Step 6 That's all there is to creating a device pool. Creating a device pool is simple because its only function is to point to other objects. The real work, as you learned in this chapter, is making sure all the objects that are contained in the device pool have been created.

Summary

This chapter examined various CallManager predeployment tasks. First, the Windows and CallManager services that are required were discussed, in addition to those that can be disabled in order to increase the performance of the server. Next, the DNS requirements and enterprise parameters were covered, and finally the device pools and components of the device pools were explored. At this point, you are ready to start adding devices to the system. The next chapter discusses what tasks must be performed in order to add phones and gateways and the various ways these devices may be added.

CHAPTER 3

Deploying Devices

After all predeployment tasks are completed, devices can be added to the system. This chapter discusses the tasks required to add certain devices to the CallManager cluster.

A number of types of devices can be added to the CallManager. The devices discussed in this chapter fall into one of two categories, clients or gateways. Other devices, such as gatekeepers, are discussed in future chapters.

We start by looking at clients, more specifically phones. There are a number of different models of Cisco IP phones, but the task of adding each is very similar. Next, gateways are covered. Gateways allow connectivity to another system such as the Public Switch Telephone Network (PSTN) or another private branch exchange (PBX). In CallManager 4.0 there are over 30 different types of gateways, and although the function of each is similar, the configuration of each varies. It is not possible to provide a step-by-step guide for the configuration of each, but this chapter does include detailed steps on how to configure the most popular types.

NOTE   In all the steps in this book, I have tried to cover all the parameters that appear on the screen. Because each version of CallManager adds fields, all the fields you see in these steps may not appear on your screen, or additional fields may be present, due to the version of CallManager you are running. Regardless of the version you are running, the steps in this chapter will help you walk through the process. Not all the parameters must be configured. Some can remain at default, whereas others are not required at all. The end of the names of required parameters are marked with an asterisk (*). In some cases you may need to configure only the required parameters for a device to function. It is a good idea, however, to review each parameter so that you can be certain the device is configured exactly the way you want it.

Adding Clients

Depending on the environment, adding a phone can be as simple as plugging it into a port that has connectivity to the CallManager. Although it is possible to configure a CallManager to allow phones to be automatically added simply by connecting them to the network, it is not always wise or desired. This section explores four ways phones can be added to the system, but before adding phones to a system, there are a few more components to configure.

You are probably thinking, "Wait a minute, the last chapter discussed predeployment tasks." That's right, it did, but those were the general or global settings that should be configured. This section looks at settings that are specific to phones.

NOTE   Which came first the chicken or the egg? This is a question that has plagued the minds of great thinkers from the beginning of time. Okay, maybe it hasn't, but a similar issue sometimes occurs when teaching new technologies. When two separate concepts are interdependent, it may be difficult to grasp either concept until you understand both of them. This being said, you will notice throughout this chapter that new concepts and components are mentioned that are not discussed in detail until later in this book. In these cases, a brief description is offered for each new concept, as is a reference to the chapter that lends greater detail. You may choose to jump ahead to gain a better understanding or just accept the brief description, knowing more detail is offered later.

Defining Device Settings

Before adding phones, it is recommended, but not required, that some device settings be configured. Configuring the device setting first will most likely save time. These settings include Phone Button Templates, Softkey Templates, and Device Defaults. The following section explains the function of each of these and how to configure them.

Phone Button Templates

Some Cisco IP phones have buttons that can be configured for various functions. The most popular functions these buttons support are lines and speed dials. When configured as lines, extension numbers can be assigned to the buttons. Each phone must have at least one button configured as a line. When a button is configured as speed dial, administrators or users can assign a speed dial number to it, and because most Cisco phones have only a few of these buttons (one to eight), the number of speed dials that can be defined in this way is limited. The user can access additional speed dials by using a feature known as abbreviated dial, which is discussed later in this chapter.

In addition to lines and speed dial functions, these buttons may be able to be configured for other functions, depending on the phone model. There are also phones on which the buttons are not configurable. Table 3-1 shows which phones have configurable buttons and which do not.

Table 3-1   *Configurable/Non-Configurable Phone Buttons*

Configurable Button Phones	Fixed Button Phones
30 VIP	7902
12 SP(+)	7905
7910	7912
7920	7935
7940	7936
7960	ATA 186–188
7970	VCG

The exact function that can be assigned to buttons varies depending on the model of the phone. The 7940, 7960, and 7970 buttons can be configured as Service URL, privacy, speed dial, or line buttons. By configuring a button as a Service URL, a user may access a phone service by simply pressing the button. A button that is configured as a privacy button allows a user to make a call private. This feature is used on shared lines and prevents the other shared-line phone from entering the call. It is also possible that a button has no function assigned to it. When a button serves no function, it is labeled as "none."

NOTE   The 7920 buttons can be configured only as lines or speed dials.

When a phone is added to the system, a phone button template is associated to the phone. The template is used to determine the function each button will serve. If the phone is added via auto-registration, it uses the template defined under device defaults. Device defaults settings are discussed later in this chapter. The creation of these templates is simple because, on most phones, there are only two functions for these buttons.

To create phone button templates follow these steps:

Step 1   From within CCMAdmin, select **Device>Device Settings>Phone Button Template**.

Step 2   Select the **Add a New Phone Button Template** link.

Step 3   On the next page you must select an existing phone button template to copy. This is because a new phone button template must be based on an existing template. From the drop-down list in the field labeled Phone Button Template, select the standard template for the correct model of phone. For example, if you are creating a phone button template for a 7960, select the Standard 7960 Template.

Step 4   Then click the **Copy** button.

Step 5   A screen like that shown in Figure 3-1 displays. At first glance you may think that you have selected the wrong phone type because it shows 34 buttons instead of the six you were expecting. Because the 7960 can support two 7914 expansion modules, which support 14 buttons apiece, 34 total buttons are possible. In the Button Template Name field enter a descriptive name.

Figure 3-1   *Phone Button Template Configuration*

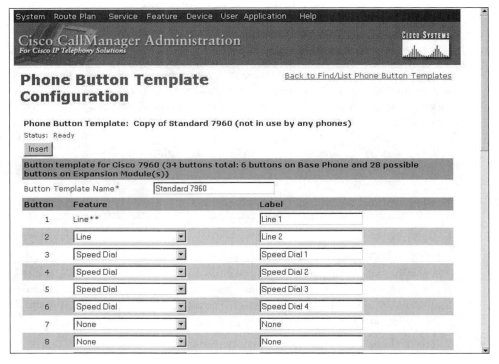

Note   It is recommended that the Button Template Name identify the configuration of this template. For example, if the template is configured with two lines, three speed dials, and a privacy button, a good name would be "7960 2-3 w/Privacy."

Step 6   Assign the proper function to each line by selecting Service URL, Privacy, Line or Speed Dial, or None from the drop-down list next to the button number.

Step 7   Next to the feature field is a label field. Enter a descriptive label in this field such as Speed Dial 2 or Line 3.

Step 8   Click the **Insert** button to save the new template.

Softkey Template

In addition to the buttons that can be used for lines and speed dials, Cisco IP phones have buttons that are referred to as *softkeys*. These buttons (keys) allow the user to access features of the phone such as hold, transfer, conference as well as many others. The function of each key changes depending on the state of the call. Because there are often more available functions configured than physical softkeys, the last softkey functions as a toggle key allowing the user to scroll through all the available options. The softkey template allows you to determine what functions are available on the phone and in what order they display. Much like phone button templates, the softkey templates can be associated directly with a phone. However, as you saw in the last chapter, the softkeys templates are also associated to device pools, which are in turn associated with phones. By associating the softkey template to a device pool, you can easily and quickly assign the softkey template to a large number of phones. If different softkey templates are associated with a phone at both the phone level and the device pool, the one at the phone level takes precedence.

The following steps take you through the process of creating a softkey template.

Step 1   From within CCMAdmin, select **Device>Device Settings>Softkey Template**.

Step 2   Click the **Add a New Softkey Template** link.

Step 3   On the next page you must select an existing softkey template on which to base the new template. Select a template from the drop-down list in the **Create a softkey template based on** field.

Step 4   Then click the **Copy** button.

Step 5   On the next screen, enter name and description for the new template. The description should help identify the features associated with the template.

The Application field lists the applications that are available in this template and cannot be changed in this screen.

Step 6   Click the **Insert** button to add the new template.

Step 7   After the template is added, you must configure it. If you want to add applications that are found on other softkey templates, click the **Add Application** button. If you do not wish to add applications from an existing template, skip this and the next step. For example, you would not add an application if you are simply moving or adding standard softkeys to the template.

Step 8 If you selected Add Application in the new window that displays, select the standard softkey template that contains the application you want to add to the new template and click **Insert and Close**.

Step 9 Click the **Configure Softkey Layout** link to modify the current layout.

A screen similar to that found in Figure 3-2 displays. On the left side of the screen, all of the states of the phone are listed. Because the softkeys change depending on the state of the phone, each state must be configured separately. In Figure 3-2 the new template allows access to the call-back feature. In this example the call-back softkey must be configured for all states from which it might be accessed which are On Hook and Ring Out.

Figure 3-2 *Softkey Layout Configuration*

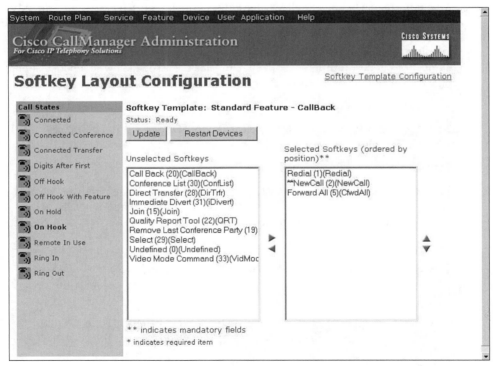

Step 10 Determine which call state you want to modify and select it from the list. For instance, if you wanted to add a softkey that would appear on the phone while you were on a call, you would select **Connected**.

Step 11 The softkey currently assigned displays in the box on the right side of the screen labeled Selected Softkey. The softkeys that may be added display in the box on the left side labeled Unselected Softkeys. To add unselected softkeys, click once on the **softkey** and then click on the **top arrow** of the two arrows that display between the two boxes.

Note	Because there are a limited number of softkeys on the phone, it is common to have more softkeys assigned than buttons on the phone. In this case the last button becomes a "more" button that acts as a toggling mechanism to allow users to access the other features. It is important to understand that the more button will automatically appear on the phone and is not something you configure on the template.

Step 12 To remove a current softkey, click on the softkey you wish to remove and click the **bottom arrow** of the two arrows that display between the boxes.

Step 13 The softkeys display on the phone in the same order that they display in the Selected Softkeys box. To change the order in which they display, highlight the desired softkey and click the **up or down arrow** that displays on the left side of the Selected Softkey Box.

Note	If softkeys are used in more than one call state, for instance the callback softkey is available in the On Hook and Ring Out call states, pay attention to the position of the softkey in each of the call states. It's a good idea to keep the softkey in the same position for each call state if possible. If it is desirable to leave a softkey position unused, the Undefined softkey can be used as a placeholder.

Step 14 After you have modified all the desired call states, click the **Update** button.

NOTE	When modifying an existing softkey template, you need to reset the devices that are associated with the templates. To do this, click the Restart Devices button on this page. Take care when resetting devices, because resetting causes the phones to be unusable while they reset. This will not affect phones that are currently on a call. The reset will occur once the phone is idle. It is always recommended that whenever a reset must be performed on a large number of phones, it be done off hours to minimize the impact on the end user.

Device Defaults

When a phone boots, it requests a configuration file from the CallManager Trivial File Transfer Protocol (TFTP) server. The file that it requests is associated with the phone's Media Access Control (MAC) address. If the phone has not previously been registered with a CallManager on the system and has not been manually added, no configuration file exists. When auto-registration is being used, a phone uses a default configuration file that defines how it is to attach to the system and register. The Device Defaults settings define the values used.

Three settings are defined under the Device Defaults settings as follows:

Load Information

This is the ID of the firmware load that the device should be running. When CallManager is shipped, it includes a current version of the firmware loaded for each device. From time-to-time the firmware is upgraded to offer additional features or patches. By editing this field you can specify the ID of the new load. The next time the device boots, it downloads the new firmware load.

Device Pool

This field allows you to define which device pool is used when auto-registration takes place.

Phone Template

This field allows you to define what phone button template devices use when auto-registration takes place.

The following steps show how the device defaults are configured.

Step 1   From within CCMAdmin, select **System>Device Defaults**.

Step 2   A screen similar to that shown in Figure 3-3 displays. Most often the Load Information can remain at default. However, from time-to-time new loads need to be deployed. In this case, locate the name of the device for which you are updating the load and enter the new load ID in the Load Information field. Make sure you enter the ID correctly and that the ID is for the correct device. Entering an invalid or incorrect ID in this field can cause the device to fail.

Note   When a new load is to be used, it must first be copied to the TFTP server so that the device will be able to download it.

Figure 3-3 *Device Defaults Configuration*

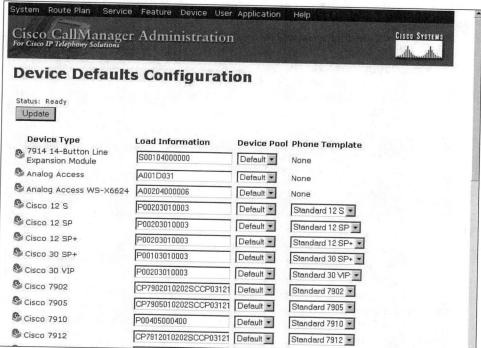

Step 3   Next, you edit the Device Pool. To change the default device pool for a device, simply click the **down arrow** in the Device Pool field associated with the device and select the desired device pool from the list that displays.

Step 4   The last item that can be selected on this page is the phone button template. To change this item for a device, click the **down arrow** in the Phone Template field associated with the device and select a template from the list that displays.

Adding Phones

When a phone is added to the system, information about the phone is entered into the SQL database. This information defines nearly every aspect of the device. Phones can be added to the system in a number of ways, but the net effect is the same.

Four methods for adding phones are explored in this chapter starting with the method known as auto-registration. Before delving too deeply into this method, let's take a quick look at all four.

1 Auto-Registration—allows phones to be plugged into the system and automatically register. An extension is assigned to the phone from a range defined by the administrator.

2 Manual—all information for the phones manually entered before the phone is plugged in.

3 Bulk Administration Tool (BAT)—information for a large number of phones inserted using BAT. This is done by entering the information into a Comma Separated Value (CSV) file and then using BAT to insert the information into the CallManager database.

4 Tools for Auto-Registration Phone Support (TAPS)—Similar to BAT except that the MAC address is not entered in the CSV file and additional steps are required when the phone is plugged into the network. However, even with the additional steps, it is quicker than just using BAT when performing a large installation.

Auto-Registration

As the name implies, using this method allows phones to register to the system by merely being plugged into the CallManager network. Although this method has the advantage of allowing you to quickly add phones, it has its disadvantages as well. When a phone is added this way, it is assigned an extension number from a range of numbers that you define. It assigns these extensions in a first-come-first-served fashion. For instance, if you defined the range to be from 2000 to 2100, the first phone to register would receive the extension 2000, the second 2001, and so on. You can see how this may not be desirable. If you are fortunate enough to be performing a deployment in which you can assign extensions as you wish, then this may not be a concern. However, in situations such as when you are replacing an existing PBX, you will most likely want to reuse the existing extensions, hence the auto assignment of extensions may not be desirable. Auto-registration may still be used in these environments; you will just need to modify the extensions that were automatically assigned.

Rogue phones are another anomaly that can arise when auto-registration is used. If improperly configured, it is possible for a phone to be added to the system without your knowledge. The addition would, of course, have to be made by someone who has a Cisco IP phone and is able to plug it into your network. Although this may seem less than likely, it is still important to ensure that the dialing capabilities be restricted for any rogue phones that may find their way onto your system. This is done by defining a Calling Search Space (CSS) for auto-registration in the device pool. CSS defines a device's calling privileges. This concept is discussed in greater detail in Chapter 5: Configuring Class of Service and Call Admission Control. Choose a CSS that has limited access, perhaps only internal or local access. This, however, also has a drawback. Limiting the CSS of auto-registered phones means that all phones that are added using auto-registration will have a limited CSS. This means for a phone that was added through auto-registration to have greater calling privileges, the CSS must be changed. Often auto-registration is used during the initial deployment and then turned off.

As you can see, using auto-registration has both benefits and drawbacks. The choice of whether to use it depends on the environment and is ultimately up to you.

If all the previously discussed predeployment tasks have been completed, very little additional configuration is required to implement auto-registration. All that needs to be done is to assign an extension range and enable auto-registration at the CallManager Group. If you choose to use auto-registration, the steps that follow help walk you through these tasks.

Step 1   From within CCMAdmin, select **System>Cisco CallManager**.

Step 2   Enter search criteria in the search field, and click **Find**. You may also leave the search field blank and click **Find**. This results in all CallManagers being displayed.

Step 3   From the list that displays, select the **CallManager** on which you want to enable auto-registration.

Step 4   A screen similar to that shown in Figure 3-4 displays. Enter the starting extension number in the **Starting Directory Number** field and the ending extension in the **Ending Directory Number** field.

Figure 3-4   *CallManager Configuration for Auto-Registration*

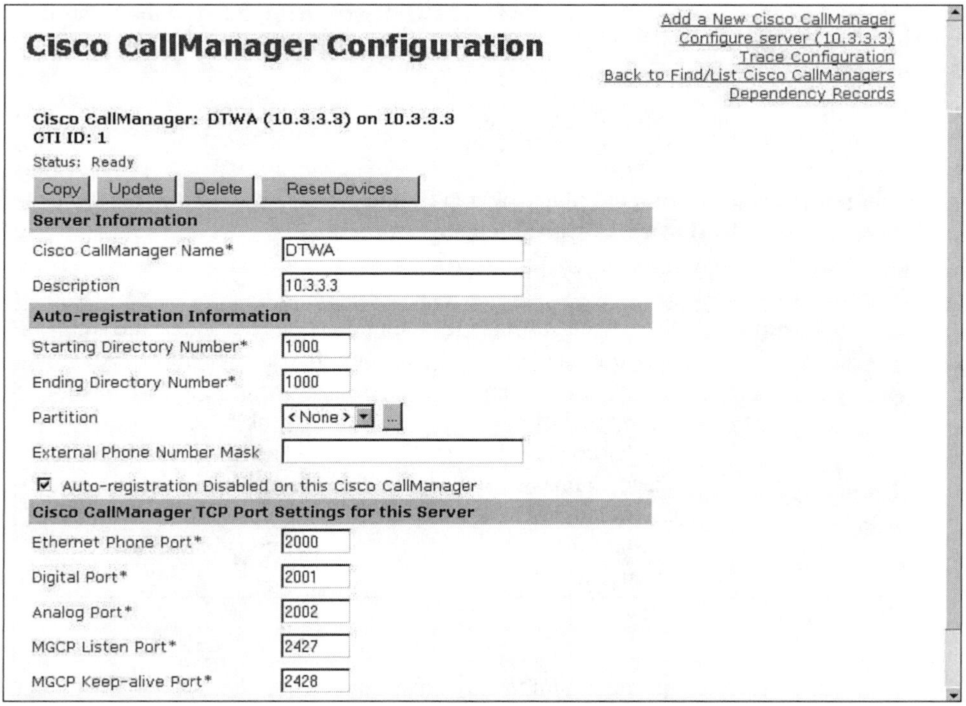

Step 5   You should notice that in the Auto-Registration Information field the Auto-Registration Disabled checkbox is unchecked at this point. This checkbox automatically becomes unchecked when you enter a starting and ending extension number. DO NOT check this box. Checking this box resets the starting and ending extension numbers.

Step 6   Click the **Update** button to save settings.

NOTE   In the next section, you will be selecting a CallManager Group for auto-registration. If the CallManager Group that you select contains more than one CallManager, you should enter the starting and ending extension numbers for each of the CallManagers in the group.

After an extension range is defined, you need to enable auto-registration for the CallManager group. The steps that follow show how this is done.

Step 1   From within CCMAdmin, select **System>Cisco CallManager Group**.

Step 2   Enter search criteria in the search field and click **Find**. You may also leave the search field blank and click **Find**. This results in displaying all CallManager Groups.

Step 3   From the list that displays, select the CallManager Group on which you want to enable auto-registration.

Step 4   A screen similar to that shown in Figure 3-5 displays. Check the **Auto-registration Cisco CallManager Group** box.

Note   Only one CallManager Group may be selected as the Auto-registration CallManager Group. If you check this box and there is already an existing Auto-registration CallManager Group, a window displays stating, "You have selected this Cisco CallManager Group to be the Auto-registration Cisco CallManager Group. The old Auto-registration Cisco CallManager Group will be deselected." Only check that box for the CallManager Group that is responsible for auto-registration.

Step 5   Click the **Update** button to save changes.

Figure 3-5   *CallManager Group Configuration for Auto-registration*

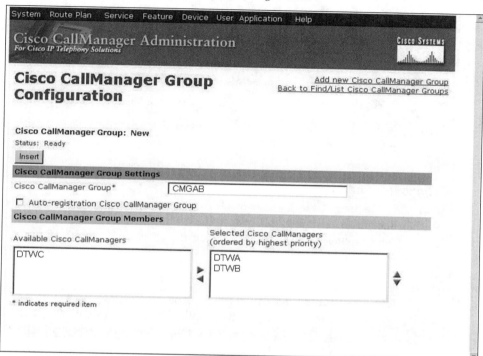

Manually Adding Phones

In addition to using auto-registration to add phones, you can manually add them. You often add phones manually for a small number of phones (such as 20). If all the predeployment tasks have been completed, the manual adding of phones is quite simple. This section takes you through the steps of the process of manually adding phones.

Manually adding phones has very few drawbacks, aside from the fact that it can be somewhat time consuming. You must enter the MAC address and other information, such as device pool and directory numbers, when you add each phone. Because CCMAdmin is a web-based interface, you must wait for the page to reload when you update information. Although a second or two may not seem too long, when you have to wait for multiple page reloads, it can start to add up. That is just the nature of this type of interface and little can be done about it.

The steps that follow take you through the process of manually adding a phone and explore each field that can be populated for each phone. A brief description is included for any field that has not yet been discussed in this book. The phone used in these steps is a 7960, but the process is very similar for most of the more popular Cisco IP Phone models. When you add other phone models, a field may not display. This simply means that the model does not require or support that particular field. Because there are a number of steps to this process, section headings are used to mark the point at which each new set of parameters begins. These same headings display on the configuration screen as well, which should help you keep track of where you are.

Step 1 From within CCMAdmin, select **Device>Add a New Device**.

Step 2 Select **Phone** from the drop-down list and click **Next**.

Step 3 A new page displays. From the drop-down list, select the type of phone you want to add. Click Next.

Device Information

Step 4 A screen similar to that shown in Figure 3-6 should display. The first field that must be entered is the MAC Address of the phone. The MAC address can be found on the back of the phone as well as the box in which the phone was packaged.

Note	It seems that over the years the numbers on the back of the phone have been getting smaller. Then again it seems everything I am reading nowadays is getting smaller, so maybe it's not the phone. If you find the same to be true for you, you can also get the MAC address to display on the LCD of the phone. The method for this differs among the various models. On the 7960 and 7940, press the settings and then the 3 on the keypad. Of course, power must first be supplied to the phone.

Step 5 The next field is the Description field. Enter a description that will help you quickly identify the phone later.

Note	If you do not enter anything in the Description field, a default description that is the MAC address preceded by SEP is entered automatically. SEP stands for Selsius Ethernet Phone. Selsius was the name of the company that made CallManager before Cisco bought the company and the product. A description I like to use follows the following format: Last Name, First Name Extension Number (for example, Smith, John 2012). This format allows me to search by name and easily see the extension number from the search page.

Figure 3-6   *Phone Configuration*

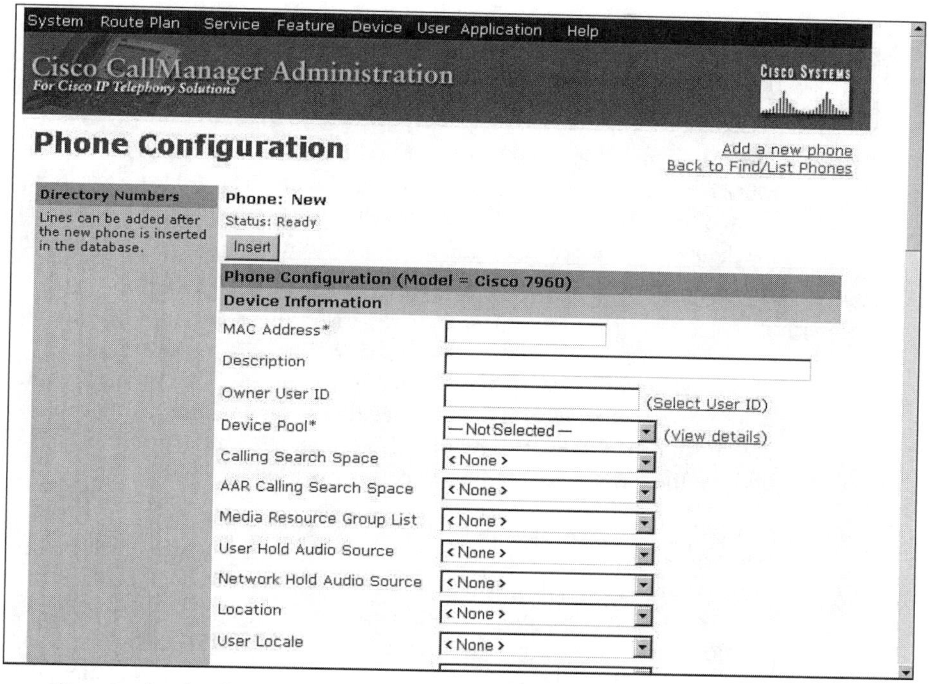

Step 6   In the **Owner User ID** field, enter the user ID of the primary user of the phone. The user must already exist in the directory that is used with CallManager, which by default is DC directories. Creating users is covered in Chapter 6: Configuring CallManager Features and Services. An easy way to assign a user is to click the **Select User ID** link to the left of the field and then search for the desired user. This information is included in Call Detail Records (CDRs). Leave this field blank if extension mobility is going to be used.

Step 7   From the Device Pool drop-down list, select the device pool the phone will use.

Note   The device pool, MAC address, and phone button template are the only required fields, aside from product-specific information that can be found at the bottom of the configuration screen. Because the product-specific information is automatically set to default values, you could add the phone at this point without configuring any other parameters. This is useful if you need to quickly add phones and you are certain that the default system values, and those set in the device pool, are adequate for this phone.

Step 8 The CSS determines the destinations that can be dialed from the phone. CSS are discussed in Chapter 5: Configuring Class of Service and Call Admission Control. Choose a CSS from the Calling Search Space drop-down list. If this field is left at None, the dial privileges of this phone could be limited.

Step 9 The Automated Alternate Routing (AAR) is used to provide an alternate route if a call fails due to insufficient bandwidth. The AAR CSS can be used to limit the paths a call may use when it is rerouted. ARR is covered in Chapter 6: Configuring CallManager Features and Services. Select an AAR CSS from the AAR Calling Search Space drop-down list.

Step 10 The next field is Media Resource Group List. This determines to which media resources this phone will have access. Media resources are discussed in further detail in Chapter 5: Configuring Class of Service and Call Admission Control. From the Media Resource Group List drop-down list, select the desired group. If no media resource group list is chosen, the list defined in the device pool is used.

Step 11 The next two fields allow you to configure what audio source is heard when a call is placed on hold. The first of the two, which is labeled User Hold Audio Source, determines what is heard when the call is placed on hold by pressing the hold button. The second of the two, Network Hold Audio Source, determines what audio is heard when the call is placed on hold by pressing the transfer, call park, or conference button. Select the desired audio source from the drop-down list for each field. If no audio source is chosen, the source defined in the enterprise parameters is used.

Step 12 Information entered in the Location field is used to prevent WAN links from becoming oversubscribed in centralized deployments. These locations are discussed more in Chapter 5, "Configuring Class of Service and Call Admission Control." If you have defined locations, select the appropriate one for this phone from the drop-down list.

Step 13 The User Locale field determines the language and fonts used for the phone. The default user locale, which is set in the enterprise parameters, is used if this field is left set to None. If this phone needs to use a different locale than is defined by its device pools, or the enterprise parameters, select the proper one from the drop-down list.

Step 14 The Network Locale field determines what locale is used for this phone. This impacts the tones and cadences used. The default network locale was defined in the enterprise parameters. If a different value is selected here this value takes precedence. If this field is set to None, the enterprise parameter setting is used. If this phone needs to use a different locale than is defined by its device pools, or the enterprise parameters, select the proper locale from the drop-down list.

Step 15 The next field labeled Device Security Mode is used to determine if any security is used for calls placed from this phone and, if so, what type. Select the desired security mode or leave it set as Use System defaults.

Step 16 The next field is the Signal Packet Capture Mode. This field is for trouble shooting purposes only and should not be configured when adding a new phone.

Step 17 The Packet capture duration field is for trouble shooting purposes only and should not be configured when adding a new phone.

Step 18 The Built-In Bridge field is used to enable and disable the built-in bridge. This bridge can be used when the barge feature is invoked. Select the desired state of the built-in bridge from the drop-down list.

Note   Barge is a feature that allows a phone to join an active call on another phone if the two phones have a shared line.

Step 19 If the Retry Video Call as Audio checkbox is checked, a video call will try to connect as an audio call if it cannot connect as a video call.

Step 20 If the Ignore Presentation Indicators (internal calls only) check box is checked, internal caller ID restrictions are ignored. This means that if an internal call is configured to block caller ID, the caller ID will still show up on this device.

Step 21 The Privacy field is used to determine if the phone can enable privacy for calls on a shared line. Select the desired state for this field from the drop-down list.

Phone Button Template Information

Step 22 In the next field, a phone button template is selected for this phone. From the drop-down list in the Phone Button Template field, select the desired template.

Note   Not all the templates will display in this field, only those will that apply to the model of phone you are adding.

Softkey Template Information

Step 23 From the drop-down list in the Softkey Template field, select a softkey template for this phone.

Expansion Module Information

Step 24 The next two fields labeled Module 1 and Module 2 are used when expansion modules (7914) are used with the phone being added. If the phone has expansion modules, select the modules from the drop-down list.

Firmware Load Information

Step 25 The next three fields are used to define which firmware load ID the phone and its expansion modules use. In most cases, these fields should be left blank. When left blank, the Load ID specified on the Device Defaults Configuration page is used for this phone. If the need ever arises to set a specific phone to a specific load ID, the load ID should be entered in this field.

Cisco IP Phone—External Data Locations

Step 26 The next set of fields is used to define data locations for the phone. This information is used to determine where the phone should search for certain data, such as help screens and phone services. In most cases these fields can be left blank and the system defaults will be used. Table 3-2 lists these fields and a brief description of each. If values other than the system defaults need to be used by this phone, enter them in the appropriate fields. Any values entered in these fields will be used for this device and will override the values found in the enterprise parameters page.

Table 3-2   *Cisco IP Phone—External Data Locations Parameters*

Parameter	Description
Information	The URL the phone uses when the (i) is pressed on the phone
Directory	The location of the directory the phone uses
Messages	The URL that is used when the Messages button is pressed. Because you normally want a number dialed when this button is pressed, this field should be left blank.
Services	The URL where services can be found
Authentication Server	URL of the authentication server for requests made to the phone web server
Proxy Server	The proxy server used by the phone
Idle	The URL that is displayed on the phone after the Idle Timer expires
Idle Timer	The amount of time in seconds that the phone must remain idle before the Idle URL is displayed

Certificate Authority Proxy Function (CAPF) Information

Step 27 The next set of parameters deals with Certificate Authority Proxy Function (CAPF). These settings are used to configure certificate specific information. Certificates are used to help prevent the tampering of call signaling and media streams. For more information on CAPF refer to the "Cisco IP Phone Authentication and Encryption for Cisco CallManager" guide at Cisco.com. This guide can be found by searching **Cisco IP Phone Authentication and Encryption** at Cisco.com. If CAPF is not being used, these fields do not need to be configured. The Certificate Operation field is used to install, upgrade, or delete a certificate. The available options are:

- No Pending Action—Displays when no certificate operation is currently active.

- Install/Upgrade—Select this when you want to install or upgrade a certificate.

- Delete—When selected the current certificate will be deleted.

- Troubleshoot—Allows certificate information to be viewed in a CAPF trace file.

Step 28 The Authentication Mode field determines the method that will be used by the phone to authenticate with CAPF. Choose one of the following:

- By Authentication String

- By Null String

- By Existing Certificate (Precedence to LSC)

- By Existing Certificate (Precedence to MIC)

Step 29 The Authentication String is used only when the By Authentication String is chosen in the previous step. Enter the string you wish to use. It must be between 4 to 10 digits.

Step 30 The Key String field determines the key size for the certificate. The valid choices are 512, 1024 and 2048. Select the desired value.

Step 31 The Operation Completes By field specifies when the install, upgrade, or delete must be complete. Enter the desired date and time in this field.

Step 32 The Certificate Operation Status field displays the progress of the certificate operation. Nothing is entered in this field; it is read only.

Multilevel Precedence and Preemption Information

Step 33 The next three fields define Multilevel Precedence and Preemption (MLPP) characteristics of the phone. If these fields are left blank or set to default, the values set in the device pool are used. If MLPP is not being used, these fields may be left blank. The first MLPP field is the MLPP Domain. MLPP grants only higher priority from calls within the same MLPP domain. For this reason a MLPP domain is needed.

Step 34 The second field in this category, which is called MLPP Indication, determines whether tones and indications are presented when a precedence call is made. The precedence indication may be a special ring back or a display if the caller's phone supports it, and a special ringer on the called parties' side.

Step 35 The third MLPP field is MLPP Preemption. This parameter determines whether a higher precedence call preempts a lower precedence call. The value of Disabled does not allow this to happen. To cause a lower precedence call to be terminated if a higher precedence call requires the resources, set this parameter to Forceful.

Product Specific Information

Step 36 The last set of fields labeled Product Specific Configuration are specific to the model of phone you are configuring. To see an explanation of each of these fields click the [i] icon located to the right of the category title.

Step 37 After all settings have been defined, click the **Insert** button at the top of the screen. A message displays informing you that the phone has been added and asking you if you would like to add extensions. Press **OK** and continue using the steps outlined in the following sections to add and configure a line on a phone.

Add a Line to a Phone

After a phone is added, a line must be configured for it. The following steps show how to add a line to a phone. Because there are a number of steps to this process, section headings are used to mark the point at which a new set of parameters begins. These same headings also display on the configuration screen, which should help you keep track of where you are.

Step 1 If you are adding a new phone and have used the steps in the preceding section, you should see a screen similar to that shown in Figure 3-7. To add a line to an existing phone, follow steps 2 though 4 to reach this screen. If you are already at this screen, skip to step 5.

Figure 3-7   *Directory Number Configuration*

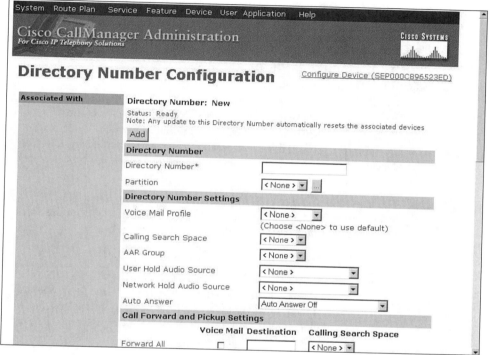

Step 2   From within CCMAdmin, select **Device>Phone**.

Step 3   Enter search criteria in the search field to limit the results, and click the **Find** button.

Step 4   From the list that is generated, select the phone to which you want to add a line. On the left side of the Phone Configuration screen the available lines are listed. Choose a line that has the label Add new DN.

NOTE   If all lines have an extension number already assigned, no more lines can be added to this device. If the phone button template assigned to this phone has some of the buttons defined as speed dial, you may be able to add more lines by changing the phone button template.

Directory Number

Step 5   The first and only required field is the Directory Number. Enter the extension number in this field.

Step 6 The Partition field defines the partition to which this directory number is assigned. The partition is used to determine what devices may call this extension. Partitions are discussed in more detail in Chapter 5: Configuring Class of Service and Call Admission Control.

Directory Number Settings

Step 7 The Voice Mail Profile field determines which voice mail profile the directory number uses. The voice mail profile defines the number that is dialed when the messages button on the phone is pressed. Voice mail profiles are discussed in further detail in Chapter 5: Configuring Class of Service and Call Admission Control. Select the voice mail profile from the drop-down list.

Step 8 The next field allows a CSS to be assigned as the line level. This determines what destinations can be reached when calling from this line. Select the Calling Search Space from the drop-down list.

Note	It is important to understand what happens when a CSS is assigned to the line and the device. In short, the two CSSs are combined, however there is a little more to it than this. For a detailed explanation, refer to Chapter 5: Configuring Class of Service and Call Admission Control.

Step 9 The AAR Group field determines the AAR group with which the line is associated. An AAR group defines the prefix that is assigned when a call fails due to insufficient bandwidth. AAR is discussed in further detail in Chapter 6: Configuring CallManager Features and Services. Select an AAR group if AAR is being used. If this field is set to None, AAR is, in effect, disabled on the line.

Step 10 The next two fields allow you to configure what audio source is heard when a call is placed on hold. The first of the two, which is labeled User Hold Audio Source, determines what is heard when the call is placed on hold by pressing the hold button. The second of the two, Network Hold Audio Source, determines what audio is heard when the call is placed on hold by pressing the transfer, call park, or conference button. Select the desired audio source from the drop-down list for each field. If no audio source is chosen, the source defined at the device level is used, and if None is chosen there, the source set in the device pool is used.

Step 11 The Auto Answer field determines if the line automatically answers incoming calls without the handset being lifted. This parameter can be set to auto answer using the speakerphone or headset. If you want the line to auto answer, select either **Auto Answer with Headset** or **Auto Answer with Speakerphone** from the drop-down list. If auto answer is not desired on the line, leave this field set to **Auto Answer Off**.

Call Forward and Pickup Settings

Step 12 The next seven fields deal with call forwarding. These fields determine the forwarding destination, which depends on the reason for the forward. The seven types of forwards are:

— Forward All—forwards all incoming calls

— Forward Busy Internal—forwards calls from internal callers when the line is busy

— Forward Busy External—forwards calls from external callers when the line is busy

— Forward No Answer Internal—forwards calls from internal callers that are not answered

— Forward No Answer External—forwards calls from external callers that are not answered

— Forward No Coverage Internal—forwards calls from internal callers when a CTI route point has no coverage

— Forward No Coverage External—forwards calls from external callers when a CTI route point has no coverage

---

Note   The no coverage forwards are needed only when configuring a line for a computer telephony integration (CTI) route point.

You may configure each type of "forward" to forward calls to voicemail or a specific extension. To forward to voice mail, check the Voice Mail box. For this to work, a voice mail profile must be defined for the line. To forward calls to another extension, enter the extension number in the Destination field. When a destination is entered into any of the internal forwards, the number is automatically entered into the corresponding external forward. If you wish the external calls to be forwarded to a different destination, simply enter the desired destination in the appropriate external forward field. A calling search space can be applied to each forward type, which limits the destinations to which a call can be forwarded. This is useful when you want to restrict a line from forwarding calls to numbers that are long distance, but still want long distance calls to be placed from the line.

Step 13 Enter the appropriate destinations and calling search spaces for each forward type.

Step 14 In the No Answer Ring Duration field, enter the number of seconds that the line will ring before forwarding to the Forward No Answer destination. If this field is left blank, the value configured in CallManager service parameter is used.

Step 15 The Call Pickup Group field determines which call pickup group this directory number belongs to. Call pickup groups allow a user to redirect an incoming call on another phone to the user's phone. Select the desired call pickup group from the drop-down list. Call pickup groups are covered in more detail in Chapter 6: Configuring CallManager Features and Services.

MLPP Alternate Party Settings

Step 16 The next set of parameters deals with MLPP alternate party settings. These settings allow you to configure an alternate destination for precedence calls that are not answered on this line or the forwarded number assigned to this line. If MLPP is not being used, these parameters can be left empty. In the first field, which is labeled Target (Destination), enter the number to which unanswered precedence calls should be forwarded.

Step 17 In the MLPP alternate party Calling Search Space field, select the appropriate search space from the drop-down list. This calling search space limits the destinations to which precedence calls can be forwarded.

Step 18 In the MLPP alternate party No Answer Ring Duration field, enter the number of seconds that the phone will ring when it receives a precedence call before forwarding to the Forward No Answer destination if unanswered.

Line Settings for all Devices

Step 19 In the Alerting Name field, enter the name that should be displayed on the caller's phone.

Line Settings for these Devices

Step 20 The set of parameters under Line Settings for this Device define Caller ID, Message Waiting Indicator (MWI) and ring settings. The settings configured here only affect the line on this phone even if it is a shared line appearance. If you want these settings to apply to all phones that have this directory number as a shared line appearance, check the **Update Shared Device Settings** button next to the setting. The Update Shared Device Settings button is displayed only if the line is shared. The first of these fields, labeled Display (Internal Call ID), is used to configure which caller ID is displayed when calls are placed to other internal callers. Enter up to 30 characters in this field. Both letters and numbers are allowed. If this field is left blank, the lines directory number will be used.

Step 21 The next field, which is labeled Line Text Label, is used to define how the line displays on the phone. If you want the extension number to display next to the line button, leave this field blank. To display a label other than the directory number next to the line button, enter that label in this field.

Step 22 The External Phone Number Mask field may be used to modify the external caller ID for calls placed from this line. An example mask might be 408370XXXX. The extension number is used to fill in the XXXX portion. In this example, if the directory number is 1401, the external phone mask would cause the external caller ID number to be 4083701401. The External Phone Mask on the first line creates the fully qualified directory number that is displayed above the first extension on certain IP Phones. Masks are explored in further detail in Chapter 4: Implementing a Dial Plan.

Step 23 The Message Waiting Lamp Policy field which determines if the light on the phone is turned on when a new message is left for this extension. In most cases, this value should be left at Use System Policy. The available choices are as follows:

— Light and Prompt—The light turns on and the envelope icon next to the line displays.

— Prompt Only—Only the envelope icon next to the line displays.

— Light Only—Only the light is turned on.

— None—No indication is used.

— Use System Policy—Uses the setting selected in CCM services parameters.

Step 24 The next two settings determine if the phone rings when incoming calls are being received on this directory number. In most cases this value should be left at Use System Default. The available choices are as follows:

— Disable—Phone does not ring.

— Flash Only—The light flashes—No ring.

— Ring Once—Rings once and then stops.

— Ring—Normal Ringing.

— Beep Only—A beep is played (only valid for the Phone Active setting).

— Use System Policy—Uses the setting selected under services parameters.

Step 25 Select the desired value for Ring Setting (Phone Idle) and Ring Setting (Phone Active).

Multiple Call / Call Waiting Settings

Step 26 The next field, which is labeled Maximum Number of Calls, determines how many active calls can be on the line. The maximum is 200 active calls per phone. Enter the maximum number of calls in this field. The default of four should be adequate for most phones.

Step 27 The field labeled Busy Trigger determines how many active calls are required before the line is considered busy. The default is two. This means that if the maximum number of calls on the line is four and the busy trigger is two, the third call will receive a busy indication. However, two more calls could be placed from this phone because the maximum number of calls is four.

Forwarded Call Information Display

Step 28 The Forwarded Call Information Display section determines what information is sent when a call is forwarded. Select the information to be sent by checking the box next to each desired field.

Step 29 The last field on this page is the Character Set. Select the character set that is to be used on the display setting for the line from the drop-down list.

Step 30 If this is a new directory number that you have added to the phone, click the **Add** button at the top of the screen. If you are modifying an existing directory number, click the **Update** button at the top of the screen.

That's all there is to it! It really is a pretty simple task once you are familiar with all of the parameters that need to be configured. However, if you are new to CallManager, a number of these parameters may seem confusing. Rest assured that these parameters will be explained in greater detail throughout the remainder of this book.

Using BAT to Add Devices

Imagine having to add more than a hundred phones and you must choose between adding them manually or adding them using auto-registration. At first glance you would most likely choose to add them using auto-registration. Normally, this would be a good choice; however, you discover that each phone needs to have a specific directory number. Then, to make things more complicated, a number of the phones need to use different phone button templates. You could still use auto-registration, but after the phones were added you would have to change the directory numbers and phone button templates of each phone. It would be more efficient to add these phones and not have to go back and touch each one. This is where a utility called Bulk Administration Tool (BAT) comes in. BAT allows you to pre-populate CallManager with all the information for the phones before they are connected to the system. By adding the phones' information, a configuration file is created that the phones download from the TFPT server when it boots up.

BAT adds devices to CallManager by importing a Comma Separated Value (CSV) file that contains the required information about the phones. The CSV contains a number of fields that must be populated. The easiest way to create this CSV file is to use an Excel template that is included with BAT. The template offers an easy, well-formatted interface to add all the required and optional information. However, before this template can be used to create a CSV file, BAT must first be installed. BAT is included with CallManager, but is not installed by default. BAT must be installed on the publisher and will cause Internet Information Services (IIS), World Wide Web (WWW) publishing, and File Transfer Protocol (FTP) publishing services to stop during the installation. It is recommended that you install BAT during nonproduction hours, due to the impact that this can have on the server.

Installing BAT

The following steps guide you through the installation process.

Step 1   From within CCMAdmin, select **Applications>Install Plugins**.

Step 2   From the list of plug-ins on the Install Plug-ins page, click the icon to the left of Cisco Bulk Administration Tool.

Step 3   A window displays asking, "Would you like to open the file or save it to your computer?" Select **Open**. Depending on the version of Internet Explorer you are using, this message may vary. It may give you the choice, "Run this program from its current location." If it does, select this option and click **OK**.

Step 4   The install preparation process begins automatically. During this time you may receive a security warning. If you do, select **Yes**.

Step 5   A Welcome window displays. Click **Next** to start the installation.

Step 6   When the installation is complete, a window displays informing you that it is complete. Click the **Finish** button.

After BAT is installed, the CSV files need to be created. To do this, use the Excel template that was mentioned previously in this section. The number of available fields in the template depends on the model of phone you are importing. For example, the 7960 can contain more than 30 fields. The top row displays what information should be entered into the field and whether it is a required field. The fields include, but are not limited to, information such as the user's name, MAC address of the phone, directory numbers, and speed dial numbers. When you first open the template, it displays only a few fields. The template then lets you add other fields, as you desire. This feature enables you to avoid dealing with unneeded fields. After the information is added to the template, a CSV file is created and must be placed in the C:\BATFiles\Phones\Insert\directory on the publisher. The necessary steps are presented later in this section.

NOTE   Although Excel may be used as part of the overall BAT process, it should never be installed on the CallManager. Excel should be loaded on another PC and the file copied to the CallManager after the export to a CSV is completed.

NOTE   On a large deployment, a Universal Serial Bus (USB) thumb drive may prove useful to transport these files.

It may appear that the hardest part of creating the CSV file is the entry of all the information. However, often what is harder is acquiring the information that must be entered into the template. Make sure you take the proper amount of time beforehand to ensure you have obtained all the required information. The best way to get this information is to perform station reviews. A station review is a formal process that is used to record information about each phone that is to be added to the system. The information acquired during this process includes the number of lines (and directory numbers assigned to each), number of speeds, required features (conference calls, voicemail, and so on) and the type of calls that may be placed by the phone (local, national, international, and so on). This, of course, is only a sample of the information that is gathered during the station review process. It is important that you gather as much information as possible during station reviews. After this information is collected, the creation of the CSV files can begin.

In addition to the CSV file that is created, templates within the BAT application must also be created. These templates define the characteristics of the phones that you are going to add. These templates contain parameters for things such as phone type, phone button template, softkey templates, calling search spaces, number of lines, and partitions just to name a few. After these templates are configured, they are used in concert with the CSV file that has been created to insert phones into the system. Because these templates contain many parameters, it may be necessary to create a number of templates depending upon your environment. For each set of phones that require different settings on any parameter defined within a template, a new template must be created. Let's look at a simple example so you can see how easily the number of these templates can grow.

Let's say you have 70 7940s and 50 7960s to deploy. Right off the bat (no pun intended), you know you need at least two templates because there are two types of phones. For this example, let's assume half the 7940s are going to be two-line phones and the other half are going to be one-line phones. This means that at least two templates are needed for the 7940s alone. As for the 7960s, let's assume that through the station review process, you determine that you need two-, three-, and four-line phones, which means that at least three templates are needed for the 7960s. If all the phones with the same number of lines do not differ in any other way, five templates in all are needed. However, just to make things interesting, let's say that half the three-line phones and half of the four-line phones require different calling search spaces. This adds the need for two more templates, bringing the total to seven. You can see how minor changes can cause the number of required templates to grow quite quickly. It is important to understand that because each template is used with a CSV file, you need to create the same number of CSV files as there are templates.

NOTE   Make sure you take time to determine the number of templates that will be needed. Sometimes after determining how many templates are needed, you may feel it is not worth the effort. I can remember an installation of 3000 phones that required more than 230 templates. Although this was a large number of templates, days if not weeks of time was saved on that deployment by creating the templates and CSV files. Keep in mind that this is an extreme example. Another deployment of 300 phones required only one template.

Before you can determine how many templates you need, you must be familiar with all of the parameters that are set in the BAT templates. Each model of phone has unique parameters, but there are also a number of parameters that are common among all models. The following is a list of parameters that can be defined in the template for most models of phones.

- Device Pool
- Calling Search Space
- AAR Calling Search Space
- User and Network Hold Audio Source
- Location
- User Locale
- Network Locale
- Phone Button Template
- Phone Load Name

- External Data Locations
- Multilevel Precedence and Preemption Information
- Number of Lines

By taking the number of different models of phone that will be deployed and determining how many of the parameters defined in the template will be different among like models, you can determine approximately how many templates and CSV files that must be created.

NOTE   After you have set up a template, you can often reuse it over and over with only minor modifications.

Now that you have a good overview of what is required for BAT to work, let's take a look at the steps required to add phones to the system using BAT.

After BAT is installed, you can begin the process of creating the CSV files and the templates. Before creating the templates and CSV files you should have conducted a detailed analysis of the phones that are to be deployed. Based on the disparity of the phones in your system, you should have a good idea of how many templates and CSV files you need. The analysis should also have supplied the information that will be needed to create the templates and files.

You can create either the template or the CSV first. In the steps that follow the creation of the CSV is described first.

NOTE   It's a good idea to use same naming convention for both the template and the CSV file that will be used together. This way, when you are selecting the CSV file, it is easy to determine which file goes with which template.

Creating a CSV File for BAT

Step 1   Copy the Excel BAT template to a PC on which Excel is installed. The Excel BAT template can be found in C:\CiscoWebs\BAT\ExcelTemplate on the publisher. The name of this file is bat.xlt.

Step 2   Open the BAT template in Excel. You may get a security warning about macros. Macros must be enabled for this template to function properly, so you may need to change Excel's settings to allow this.

Step 3   A template like that shown in Figure 3-8 displays. As you can see, by default, only three fields display in the template. Click the **Create File Format** button to add fields.

Figure 3-8   *Excel BAT Template*

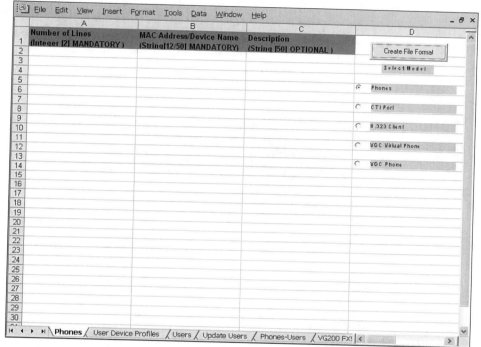

Step 4   A screen similar to that shown in Figure 3-9 should display. Select the device and line fields you want added to the template by highlighting the field in the box on the left side and clicking the **>>** arrows.

Step 5   To remove device and line fields from the template, highlight the field in the box on the right side and click the **<<** arrows.

Step 6   After you move all the desired fields to the box on the right side, click the **Create** button. When asked if you want to overwrite the existing CSV format, click **Yes**.

Step 7   Go to the far right of the template and in the appropriately labeled fields, enter the number of lines and speed dials these phones will have. When you enter information in these fields, the template adds the appropriate fields.

Step 8   At this point the template is ready for the data to be entered.

Step 9   After all the data is entered, click the **Export to BAT Format** button, which is located at the top far-right portion of the template.

Step 10   You are prompted for a place to store this file. BAT creates a default location and file name. An example is c:\XlsDataFiles\Phones#09072004193840. BAT always selects c:\XlsDataFiles as the default file location. The file name is based in part on the tab you have selected to export, such as Phones, PhonesUsers, and UserDeviceProfiles, followed by the number symbol (#). The second part of the filename is the date and time that the file was exported. Note that in the preceding example, 09072004193840 represents September 7th, 2004 at 19:38 and 40 seconds. If you prefer a different file location or name, you can change it before clicking **OK**.

Figure 3-9   *Excel BAT Template File Format*

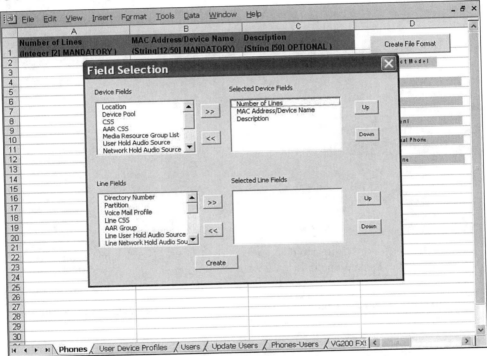

Step 11   Copy this file to the C:\BATFiles\Phones\Insert\ directory on the publisher.

Adding Phones Using BAT

The process of inserting phones using BAT is actually a four-stage process, and each stage has its own set of steps. The first stage of adding phones in BAT is creating the templates. The following steps walk you through this stage. A 7960 template is created in this example.

Step 1   At the console of the Publisher, navigate to **Start>Programs>CallManager 4.x>Bulk Admin Tool>BAT x.x** (x.x is the version number).

Step 2   From within the Bulk Administration Tool select **Configure>Phones**.

Step 3   From the Phone Options screen, make sure the **Insert Phones** radio button is selected and click the **Next** button at the bottom of the screen.

Step 4   The Steps to Insert Phones page appears and shows all the steps that must be completed to insert phones. In all, there are four steps, but each step includes additional substeps. Make sure the radio button labeled Step 1: Add, view, or modify phone templates is checked and click the **Next** button.

Step 5   A screen similar to that shown in Figure 3-10 displays. On this screen you define the parameters for this template. In the Phone Template Name field, enter a name for this template. Remember to try to keep the naming convention the same as the CSV file that will be used with this template.

Figure 3-10 *BAT Phone Template Configuration*

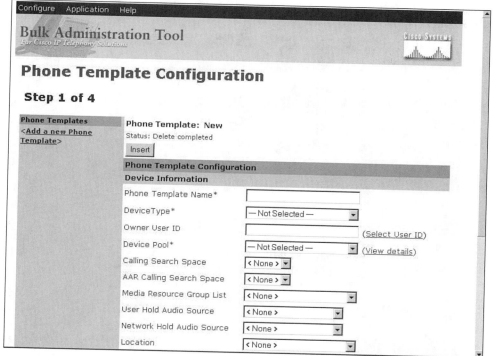

Step 6   From the drop-down list in the Device Type field, select the type of phone for this template. When a phone is selected, the page refreshes so that all applicable fields are displayed.

Step 7   The remainder of this page contains all the parameters that can be configured for this device. Because all these parameters are covered earlier in this chapter, they are not discussed in this section. If necessary, refer back to steps 6–26 in the *Manually Adding Phones* section in this chapter for details of each parameter. Enter the appropriate information in each field.

Step 8 After the parameters have been configured, click the **Insert** button at the top of the screen. An alert window informs you if the operation is successful. Click the **OK** button in the alert window.

Step 9 After the template is inserted, a Line Details section is added at bottom of the screen. Find this section and click **Add Line 1** to define the parameters for this line.

Step 10 A screen similar to that shown in Figure 3-11 displays. This screen is used to define all the parameters for this line. Because all these parameters are covered earlier in this chapter, they are not discussed in this section. If necessary, refer back to steps 6–25 in the *Add a line to a Phone* section in this chapter for details on each parameter. Enter the appropriate information in each field.

Figure 3-11 *BAT Phone Line Configuration*

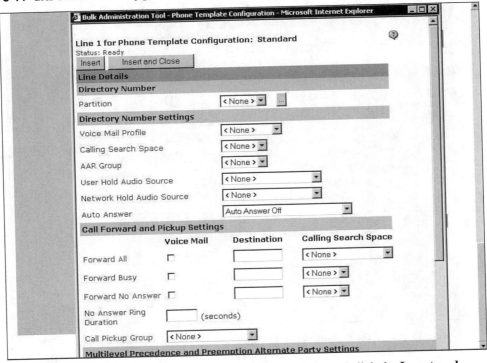

Step 11 Enter the desired information in these fields and click the **Insert and Close** button. Repeat steps 9–10 for each additional line.

Step 12 When configuring templates for certain models of phones, you may also add speed dial, and services, to the template. To add speed dials to the template, click the **Add/Update Speed Dials** link in the upper-right corner on the Phone Template Configuration page.

Step 13 A screen displays that allows you to add two types of speed dials. The first type is associated with a button on the phones. The user accesses the second type by pressing the two-digit speed dial number, which has the number they want to reach assigned to it, and by pressing the **AbbrDial** softkey. Enter the desired speed dials and click **Update and Close**.

Step 14 To add services to the template, click the **Subscribe/Unsubscribe Services** link in the upper-right corner on the Phone Template Configuration page. Services are cover in more detail in Chapter 6: Configuring CallManager Features and Services.

Step 15 A window displays that allows you to select the available services. Select the desired service and click **Continue**. Enter any additional information the service may require.

Step 16 After all services have been added, the template is complete. Click the **Back** button at the bottom of the page to return to the Steps to Insert Phones page.

The previous stage left you at the page labeled Steps to Insert Phones, on which you should see four options. Step 1: Add, view, or modify phone templates has just been completed, and if you created the CSV data file using the Excel template Step 2: Create the CSV file is also completed. This brings you to Step 3: Validate phone records. This part of the process checks the CSV file that you created to make sure it is formatted properly.

Step 1 On the Step to Insert Phones page, select the radio button that is labeled Step 3: Validate phone records and click the **Next** button.

Step 2 From the File Name drop-down list, select the CSV file that you created using the Excel template. Only CSV files that you placed in C:\BATFiles\Phones\Insert\ on the publisher display in this list.

Step 3 Select the corresponding template that you created from the Phone Template Name drop-down list.

Step 4 Click the **Validate** button.

Step 5 After the file has been validated, the status line should state Validate Completed. Click the **View Latest Log File** link next to the Validate button to view the log.

Step 6 If no errors are reported, close the log window, click the **Back** button, and move on to the next set of steps.

The last stage is to actually insert the phones into the CallManager database.

Step 1 On the Step to Insert Phones page, select the radio button labeled Step 4: Insert Phones, and click the **Next** button.

Step 2   From the File Name drop-down list, select the CSV file that you created using the Excel template. Only CSV files that you placed in C:\BATFiles\ Phones\Insert\ on the publisher display in this list.

Step 3   Select the corresponding template that you created from the Phone Template Name drop-down list.

Step 4   Click the **Insert** button.

Step 5   A warning message displays informing you that you are about to insert records. Click **OK** to continue.

Step 6   While the insertion is being made, a status window displays. After the insertion is completed, the status line should state "Insert Completed." Click the **View Latest Log File** link next to the Insert button to view the log.

Step 7   If no errors are reported, close the log window and exit BAT.

Adding Phones Using TAPS

A more advanced method of adding phones called Tool for Auto-registered Phone Support (TAPS) is also available. This tool allows you to pre-populate CallManager's database with all the information about the phones, except for the MAC address. After the information is entered, the phones are plugged into the system and auto-registered. Because the MAC addresses have not been entered into the system, the TFTP server cannot deliver a con-figuration file to the phone based on the MAC address. This causes a default configuration to be issued and the phone to be registered with basic configuration. After the phone is registered, a predetermined number is dialed that routes the call to an Interactive Voice Response (IVR) server. The IVR server asks what language you would like to use and the extension number that should be assigned to the phone. After this is completed, the MAC address of the phone is associated with the configuration that matches the extension number entered, and a configuration file is created. The phone gets this file from the TFTP server when it reboots.

Integrators often use this method of adding phones during large deployments. Because this method allows the integrator to populate the system without having to add MAC addresses, the deployment of the phones is simpler. Integrators don't have to make sure a certain phone with a certain MAC address is plugged into a certain jack. The integrator need only be concerned that the proper model is placed in each location. Previous to the introduction of this tool, the MAC addresses had to be entered before the phones were deployed, and this required the integrator to label the box of each phone with the extension number for which it was configured. This also meant that no information could be added to the system until the phones where in hand.

The detailed steps for TAPS are outside of the scope of this book, but further information can be found in Cisco's Bulk Administration Tool documentation on the Cisco website. You can find the latest copy of this by searching "bulk administration tool guide" at Cisco.com.

Adding Gateways

After phones are configured, calls may be placed to other phones within the cluster. Although this is useful, it is also quite limiting. Imagine if the phone system were allowed to reach only other phones within the cluster. I have a feeling not too many of these systems would be sold. Therefore, you need to consider how you will go about allowing calls outside the cluster. This is accomplished by configuring gateways that connect the cluster to other systems. The function of a gateway is to allow connectivity between dissimilar systems. Basically, the job of the gateway is to allow your phone system to make calls to other phone systems.

In most cases, the first system to which you should connect your system is the Public Switched Telephone Network (PSTN). This allows callers on your system to call nearly any other phone in the world. In addition to connecting to the PSTN, you may also want to connect your system to other systems in your company and bypass the PSTN. In either case the steps are very similar.

This section explores four types of gateways. The main difference in these gateways is the protocol they use to communicate with the CallManager. Their functions are the same—to provide connectivity to another system.

The following is a list of the four types of gateways and a brief description of each:

- **H.323**—Typically used to connect to the PSTN and requires its own dial plan configuration. Requires a significant amount of configuration on the gateway.
- **MCG**—Typically used to connect to the PSTN and does not require its own dial plan configuration. Requires minimal configuration on the gateway.
- **Non-IOS MCGP**—Typically used to connect to the PSTN and does not require its own dial plan configuration. Requires almost no configuration on the gateway itself.
- **Inter-cluster Trunk**—Connects CallManager clusters together. Runs on the CallManager server and does not require additional hardware.

Adding H.323 Gateways

The first type of gateway to be discussed is an H.323 gateway. H.323 is best described as a suite of protocols. It is also often referred to as an umbrella under which a number of other protocols exist. The specifics of what H.323 is and how it works are far beyond the scope of this book. This section focuses on the process of configuring an H.323 gateway.

The configuration steps required for an H.323 gateway are somewhat more advanced than those of other types of gateways. This is because much of the configuration has to be done using the command-line interface (CLI) of the gateway itself. For example, when configuring a Media Gateway Control Protocol (MGCP) gateway, only a few commands must be entered in the CLI, and CallManager handles all the call routing. An H.323 gateway does not depend on the CallManager for call routing; it contains a dial plan of its own. This means that the dial plan must be entered using the CLI, which increases the difficulty of configuring an H.323 gateway. In order to properly configure an H.323 gateway, you must have a high level of experience in configuring IOS devices for VoIP deployments. Because it is not possible to provide you with all the required knowledge to configure the CLI portion of an H.323 gateway in a book of this size, we focus on the steps required in CCMAdmin. The CLI configuration varies in each environment and can sometimes become quite complex. For more information on the CLI configuration for an H.323 gateway, refer to the Cisco IOS Voice, Video, and Fax Configuration Guide, which can be found at Cisco.com by searching "Cisco IOS Voice, Video, and Fax Configuration Guide."

After the entire CLI configuration of the gateway is completed, it can be configured in CallManager. There are a number of Cisco devices that can be configured as H.323 gateways. Because the list of supported devices is always evolving, it is best to check at Cisco's website to see what gateways currently support H.323. You can find a list of supported gateways by searching "Understanding Voice Gateways" at Cisco.com. You can further refine the search by including the CallManager version with this search. For example, by searching "Understanding Voice Gateways 4.1(2)" the very first result is a link to the correct page. Because there are a variety of devices that can be configured as an H.323 gateway, it is not possible to include a step-by-step guide on how to configure each of them. However, because the configurations are similar, you should be able to use the following steps, which show how to configure a Cisco 3620 as an H.323 gateway, as a guide to install the H.323 gateway you choose.

The following steps are required to configure a Cisco 3620 as an H.323 gateway. Because there are a number of steps to this process, section headings are used to mark the point at which each new set of parameters begins. These same headings display on the configuration screen as well, which should help you keep track of where you are.

Step 1 From within CCMAdmin select **Device>Add a New Device**.

Step 2 On the Add a New Device page, select **Gateway** from the Device type drop-down list and click **Next**.

Step 3 On the next page, select the **H.323 Gateway** from the Gateway type drop-down list.

Step 4 The Device Protocol field remains at H.225; this is the only option. Click the **Next** button.

Device Information

Step 5 The Gateway Configuration screen, as shown in Figure 3-12, displays. Enter the DNS Name or IP address of the gateway in the Device Name field.

Step 6 In the Description field, enter a description that will help make this device easily identifiable.

Step 7 From the Device Pool drop-down list, select the desired CallManager group for this gateway.

Figure 3-12 *H.323 Gateway Configuration*

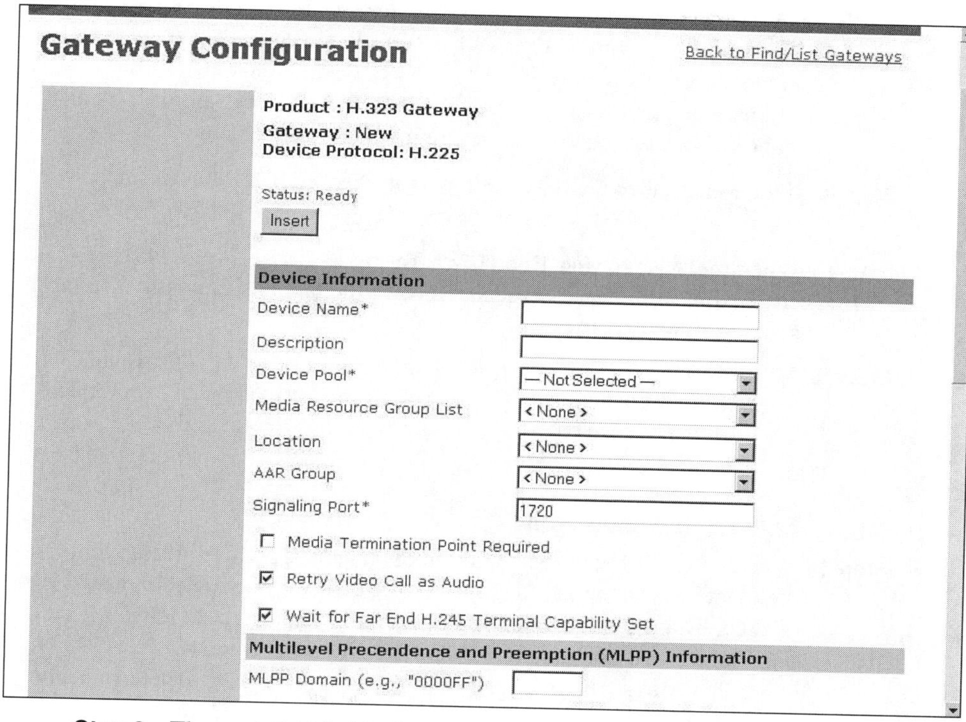

Step 8   The next field is Media Resource Group List. This determines to which media resources this phone will have access. Media resources are discussed in further detail in Chapter 6: Configuring CallManager Features and Services. From the Media Resource Group List drop-down list, select the desired group. If no Media Resource Group List is chosen, the one defined in the device pool is used.

Step 9   Information entered in the Location field is used to prevent WAN links from becoming oversubscribed in centralized deployments. These locations are discussed more in Chapter 5: Configuring Class of Service and Call Admission Control. If you have defined locations, select the appropriate one for this phone from the drop-down list.

Step 10   The AAR Group field determines the AAR group with which this device is associated. An AAR group provides the prefix that is assigned when a call fails due to insufficient bandwidth. AAR is discussed in further detail in Chapter 6: Configuring CallManager Features and Services. Select an AAR group if AAR is being used. If this field is set to None, AAR is, in effect, disabled on this device.

Step 11   The Signaling Port field defines the H.225 signaling the gateway uses. The default of 1720 can be used in most cases.

Step 12 The Media Termination Point Required check box needs to be checked if the H.323 device does not support features such as hold and transfers. This is the case with H.323 version 1 gateways. These gateways cannot support such features because H.323v1 does not have the ability to modify a channel, which means it cannot transfer a call or place a call on hold, because this would require modifying the channel.

Step 13 If the Retry Video Calls as Audio box is checked, CallManager sets up a voice call if a video calls fails to set up.

Step 14 When the Wait for Far End H.245 Terminal Capability Set box is checked, CallManager expects to receive the far ends capabilities before sending its own.

Step 15 The only MLPP setting that can be configured is the MLPP Domain. Enter the domain in this field. If left blank the settings found in enterprise parameters are used.

Call Routing Information—Inbound Calls

Step 16 The next set of fields deals with inbound calls. The Significant Digits field determines the number of digits of an incoming dialed number that CallManager uses. CallManager counts from right to left, so if the number entered in this field is 4 and the digits received are 8105559090, 810555 would be removed and only 9090 would be used to determine the destination of this call.

Step 17 A Calling Search Space (CSS) determines what destination inbound calls to this gateway will be able to reach. CSS is discussed in Chapter 5: Configuring Class of Service and Call Admission Control. Choose a CSS from the Calling Search Space drop-down list. If this field is left at None, the dial privileges of this device could be limited.

Step 18 The Automated Alternate Routing (AAR) is used to provide an alternate route if a call fails due to insufficient bandwidth. The AAR CSS can be used to limit the paths a call may use when it is rerouted. Select an AAR CSS from the AAR Calling Search Space drop-down list.

Step 19 The Prefix DN field defines what digits will be added to the front of the incoming destination number. This is applied to the number, after CallManager truncates the number based on the Significant Digits setting.

Step 20 If your voicemail system supports Redirecting Number IE, check the Redirecting Number IE Delivery–Inbound box. Otherwise, leave this box unchecked.

Step 21 Check the Enable Inbound Faststart box if you wish to support H.323 FastStart. H.323 FastStart requires only two message exchanges to open logical channels, whereas normal setup requires 12. However, if FastStart is selected, both ends must support and be configured for FastStart.

Call Routing Information—Outbound Calls

Step 22 The next set of fields deals with outbound calls. The Calling Party Selection field determines what number is sent to outbound calls. The choices are:

- Originator—the directory number of the device that placed the call

- First Redirect Number—the directory number of the first device to forward the call

- Last Redirect Number—the directory number of the last device to forward the call

- First Redirect Number (External)—the external directory number of the first device to forward the call

- Last Redirect Number (External)—the external directory number of the last device to forward the call

Select the desired value for this field.

Step 23 The Calling Party Presentation field determines if CallManager sends Caller ID information. To send caller ID information, select **Allowed** from the drop-down list. To block caller ID, select **Restricted** from the drop-down list.

Step 24 Cisco recommends that the next four fields remain set to the default of Cisco CallManager:

- Called party IE number type unknown

- Calling party IE number type unknown

- Called Numbering Plan

- Calling Numbering Plan

These fields deal with dial plan issues and should be changed only when advised to do so by Cisco or an experienced dial plan expert. The need to change these usually occurs when installing CallManager internationally.

Step 25 The Caller ID DN field is used to determine what caller ID is sent out this gateway. A mask or a complete number can be entered in this field. For example, if the mask 55536XX is entered in this field, CallManager sends 55536 and the last two digits of the directory number (DN) that is placing the call.

Step 26 If the Display IE Delivery check box is checked, then the calling and called party name information is included in messages.

Step 27 The Redirecting Number IE Delivery–Outbound check box should be checked when integrating with a voicemail system that supports Redirecting Number IE. Otherwise, leave it unchecked.

Adding MGCP Gateways

Cisco recommends that you use a Media Gateway Control Protocol (MGCP) gateway whenever possible. MGCP is a protocol that, as its name implies, is used to control gateways. Unlike H.323, MGCP does not handle the routing of calls; it depends on CallManager for this. Therefore, very little needs to be configured at the CLI.

MGCP gateways that are used in a Cisco CallManager solution are separated into two categories: Internetworking Operating System (IOS) and NON-IOS MGCP gateways. The difference is whether the device that is acting as the gateway is running IOS or not. For instance, a 3725, which runs IOS, is considered an IOS gateway; whereas, a Catalyst 6500 running native IOS is considered a NON-IOS gateway. This section focuses on ISO MGCP Gateways. NON-IOS gateways are discussed in the next section.

Adding ISO MGCP Gateways

As with an H.323 gateway, some configuration must be done from the CLI of the gateway. Figure 3-13 shows a sample of the commands that must be entered in the CLI in order to configure the gateway to communicate through MGCP. As you can see, the CLI configuration is quite simple. This is because it relies on CallManager for all call routing functions. For this reason, it is recommended that an MGCP gateway be used whenever possible.

For more information on the CLI configuration for a MCGP gateway, refer to the Cisco IOS Voice, Video, and Fax Configuration Guide, which can be found at Cisco.com by searching "Cisco IOS Voice, Video, and Fax Configuration Guide."

After the CLI configuration is completed, the MGCP gateway must be configured in CCMAdmin. There are a number of Cisco routers that can act as MGCP gateways, and it is not possible to include a step-by-step guide for each type in this section. However, because their configuration is similar, you should be able to use the following steps that show how to configure a Cisco 3620 as a MGCP gateway. You can use these steps as a guide to help you install the MGCP gateway you are using.

Figure 3-13 *MGCP Gateway CLI Configuration Example*

```
mgcp
mgcp call-agent 172.10.10.1
mgcp dtmf-relay  codec all mode out-of-band
mgcp sdp simple
!
ccm-manager  switchback graceful
ccm-manager  redundant-host 172.10.10.10
ccm-manager mgcp
!
voice-port 1/1/1
!
dial-peer voice 4 pots
 application MGCPAPP
 port 1/1/1
```

The following steps are required to configure a Cisco 3620 as a MGCP gateway. Because there are a number of steps to this process, section headings are used to mark the point at which each new set of parameters begins. These same headings display on the configuration screen as well, which should help you keep track of where you are.

Step 1   From within CCMAdmin, select **Device>Add a New Device**.

Step 2   On the Add a New Device page, select Gateway from the Device Type drop-down list and click **Next**.

Step 3   On the next page, select the desired gateway from the Gateway Type drop-down list. In this example, the 362X is selected. Click **Next**.

Step 4   A page similar to that shown in Figure 3-14 displays. In the first field, enter the DNS name of the gateway in the Domain Name field, if DNS is configured to resolve this name. If DNS is not used, enter the host name of the gateway. It is important to note that if an IP Domain Name is configured on the router, it must be included in the Domain Name field. For instance, if the hostname is MGCPGateway and the IP Domain Name is configured as cisco.com, the Domain Name field should read MGCPGateway.cisco.com. The name is case sensitive. The gateway will not register to CallManager if the name is not entered correctly.

Step 5   In the Description field, enter a description that will help make this device easily identifiable.

Figure 3-14 *MGCP Gateway Configuration*

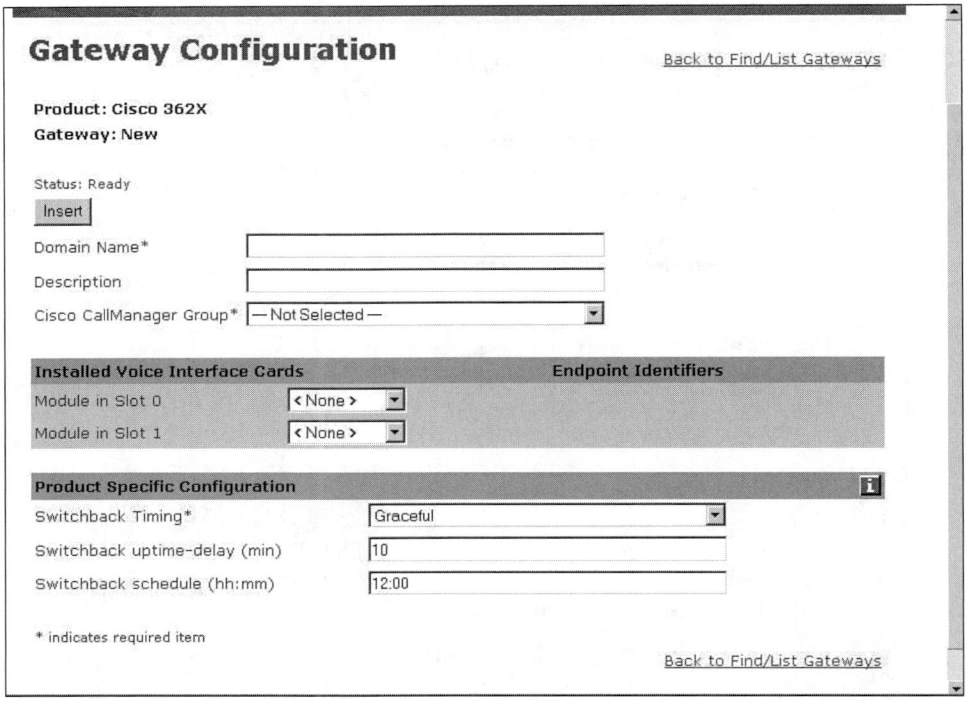

Step 6   From the Cisco CallManager Group drop-down list, select the desired
CallManager group for this gateway.

Installed Voice Cards

Step 7   The next set of fields defines what type of voice ports are installed in
the gateway. This example assumes two FXS and two FXO ports are
installed. Select the voice module(s) from the drop-down list next to each
slot. For this example the NW-1V is selected.

Step 8   Click the **Insert** button. New fields display next to each configured slot.
From the Subunit drop-down list, select the device that is installed in
this slot. In this example VIC-2FXS was selected for subunit 0 and a
VIC-2FXO was selected for subunit 1.

Step 9   Click the **Update** button. Endpoint Identifiers display next to each
configured subunit as seen in Figure 3-15.

Figure 3-15   *MCGP Gateway Configuration with Endpoints*

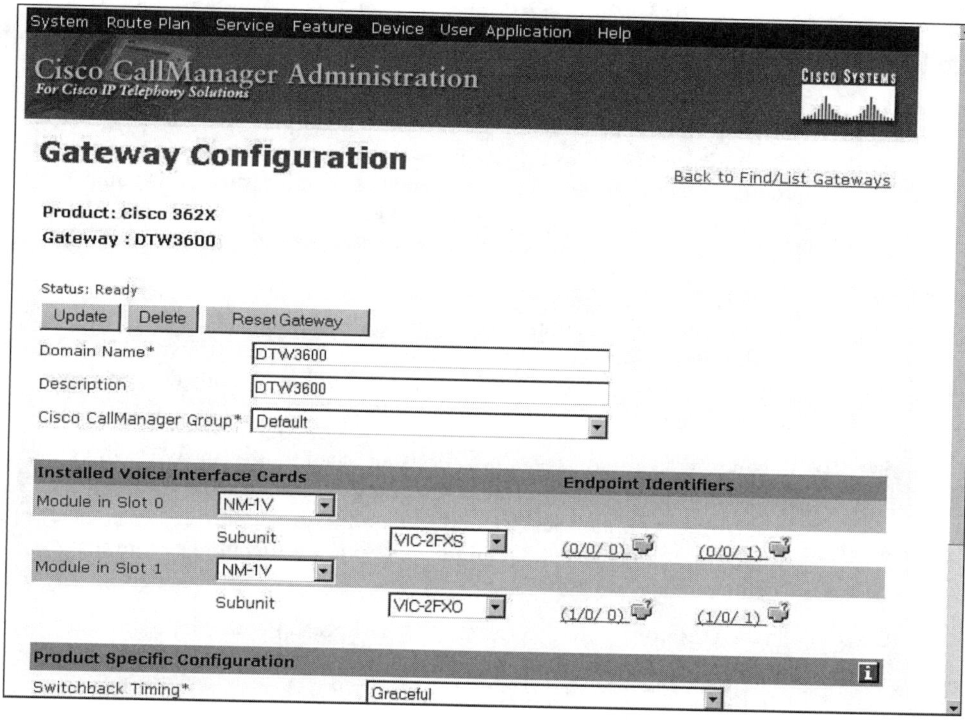

Gateway Information

Step 10 The endpoint identifiers must be configured. Select an endpoint to display the Endpoint Configuration page. In this example an FXS port is used. Depending on the type of port selected, the fields you will work with may differ. A description for this endpoint is pre-populated in the Description field. You may modify it if you like.

Step 11 From the Device Pool drop-down list, select the device pool this endpoint will use.

Step 12 The Calling Search Space (CSS) determines where the device (in this case the gateway) will be able to dial. The CSS affects only incoming calls through the gateway. CSSs are discussed in Chapter 5: Configuring Class of Service and Call Admission Control. Choose a CSS from the Calling Search Space drop-down list. If this field is left at None, the dial privileges of this device could be limited.

Step 13 The Automated Alternate Routing (AAR) is used to provide an alternate route if a call fails due to insufficient bandwidth. The AAR CSS can be used to limit the paths a call may use when it is rerouted. Select an AAR CSS from the AAR Calling Search Space drop-down list.

Step 14 The next field is the Media Resource Group List, that determines to which media resources this phone will have access. Media resources are discussed in further detail in Chapter 6: Configuring CallManager Features and Services. From the Media Resource Group List drop-down list, select the desired group. If no Media Resource Group List is chosen, the one defined in the device pool is used.

Step 15 The next field allows you to configure what audio source is heard when a call is placed on hold. Select the desired audio source from the Network Hold drop-down list. If no audio source is chosen, the one defined in the device pool is used.

Step 16 In centralized deployments, locations are used to prevent WAN links from becoming oversubscribed. These are discussed more in Chapter 5: Configuring Class of Service and Call Admission Control. If you have defined locations, select the appropriate one for this phone from the Location drop-down list.

Step 17 The AAR Group field determines the AAR group with which this device is associated. An AAR group provides the prefix that is assigned when a call fails due to insufficient bandwidth. AAR is discussed in further detail in Chapter 6: Configuring CallManager Features and Services. If AAR is being used, select an AAR group. If this field is set to None, AAR is, in effect, disabled on this endpoint.

Step 18 The Network Locale field determines what locale is used for this endpoint. This impacts the tones and cadences used. The default Network Locale was defined in the enterprise parameters. If a different value is selected here, this value takes precedence. If this field is set to None, the enterprise parameter setting is used. If this phone needs to use a different locale than is defined by its device pools, or the enterprise parameters, select the proper one from the drop-down list.

Multilevel Precedence and Preemption (MLPP) Information

Step 19 The next three fields define the Multilevel Precedence and Preemption (MLPP) characteristics of the endpoint. The only field that applies to the device in this example is the MLPP Domain. MLPP grants higher priority only from calls with the same MLPP domain. For this reason a MLPP domain is needed if MLPP is being used.

Port Information

Step 20 The Prefix DN field defines what digits will be added to the front of an incoming destination number. This is applied to the number after CallManager truncates the number based on the Num Digits setting.

Step 21 The Num Digits field determines the number of digits of an incoming dialed number that CallManager will use. CallManager counts from right to left, so if the number entered in this field is four and the digits received are 8105559090, 810555 would be removed and only 9090 would be used to determine the destination of this call.

Step 22 The Expected Digits field defines how many digits are expected on inbound calls. This field is rarely used and can be left at the default of 0 in most cases.

Step 23 The last field, which is the SMDI Port Number, is used only when integrating with a traditional voicemail system. The port number should be set to the same port number as on the voicemail system.

Step 24 Click **Insert**. The endpoints now display on the left side of the page. After you have configured all the endpoints, directory numbers may be assigned.

Step 25 To add a directory number to an endpoint, click on the **Add DN** link next to the endpoint on the left side of the screen.

Step 26 The Directory Number Configuration page displays, which is just like the page used when adding a line to a phone. For detailed information on how to configure this page, refer back to steps 6-25 in the *Add a Line to a Phone* section in this chapter.

Step 27 Click the **Back to Main Gateway Configuration Link** and repeat steps 10 through 25 to configure all other endpoints.

Step 28 After all information has been entered click the **Add** button.

Step 29 After all configuration is completed, click the **Reset Gateway** button.

Adding Non-IOS MGCP Gateways

As mentioned in the previous section, some non-IOS devices can be configured as MGCP Gateways. Just as with the IOS MGCP gateway, these devices do not handle call routing tasks. They depend on CallManager to handle all call routing needs. Unlike the IOS MGCP gateway, there is virtually no configuration required on the gateway itself.

The most widely used non-IOS gateways are the Catalyst 6000 T1/E1 blades. The T1 blades are Cisco 6608s and have eight T1 ports. These ports must be configured in the Catalyst switch with the appropriate IP configuration, including the TFTP server address, and VLAN information. To complete the configuration of the T1 port in CCMAdmin, you need to know the MAC address of the port.

The following steps take you through the configuration of a single T1 port of a 6608 as a non-IOS MGCP Gateway. Because there are a number of steps to this process, section headings are used to mark the point at which each new set of parameters begins. These same headings also display on the configuration screen, which should help you keep track of where you are.

Step 1   From within CCMAdmin, select **Device>Add a New Device**.

Step 2   On the Add a New Device page, select **Gateway** from the Device Type drop-down list and click **Next**.

Step 3   On the next page, select the desired gateway from the Gateway Type drop-down list. In this example the Cisco Catalyst 6000 T1 VoIP Gateway is selected.

Device Information

Step 4   From the Device Protocol drop-down list, select the appropriate protocol. For this example Digital Access PRI is used. Click **Next**.

Step 5   The Gateway Configuration page displays. Enter the MAC address of the T1 port in the field labeled MAC Address. The MAC address can be found by using the show port command at the CLI of the Catalyst 6000.

Step 6   In the description field, enter a description that will help make this device easily identifiable.

Step 7   From the Device Pool drop-down list, select the device pool this gateway or device will use.

Step 8   The Device Destination field determines if calls on this trunk will be considered OnNet (on network) or OffNet (off network) calls. Different alerting tones are used for OnNet and OffNet calls. By default this is set to OnNet. If you are unsure of the value to assign, leave it at the default.

Step 9   From the Network Locale drop-down list, select the locale for this gateway. If it remains set to None, the locale selected in the device pool is used.

Step 10   The next field is Media Resource Group List. This determines to which media resources this gateway will have access. Media resources are discussed in further detail in Chapter 6: Configuring CallManager Features and Services. From the Media Resource Group List drop-down list, select the desired group. If no Media Resource Group List is chosen, the one defined in the device pool is used.

Step 11   Locations are used to prevent WAN links from becoming oversubscribed in centralized deployments. These are discussed more in Chapter 5: Configuring Class of Service and Call Admission Control. If you have defined locations, select the appropriate one for this device from the drop-down list.

Step 12 The AAR Group field determines with which AAR group this gateway is associated. An AAR group defines the prefix that is assigned when a call fails due to insufficient bandwidth. AAR is discussed in further detail in Chapter 6: Configuring CallManager Features and Services. If AAR is being used, select an AAR group. If this field is set to None, AAR is, in effect, disabled on this gateway.

Step 13 The next field is used to define which firmware load ID the gateway uses. In most cases this field should be left blank. When left blank, the Load ID specified on the device defaults configuration page is used for this gateway. If the need ever arises to set a specific gateway to a specific load ID, the load ID should be entered in this field.

Multilevel Precedence and Preemption (MLPP) Information

Step 14 The next three fields define the Multilevel Precedence and Preemption (MLPP) characteristics of this gateway. If these fields are left blank or set to default, the values set in the device pool are used. The first MLPP field is the MLPP Domain. MLPP grants higher priority only from calls with the same MLPP domain. For this reason a MLPP domain is needed.

Step 15 The second field in this category, which is called MLPP Indication, determines whether tones and indications will be presented when a precedence call is made. If the is field set to Off, no precedence indication is presented. If this field is set to On, indication is used for a precedence call.

Step 16 The third MLPP field is MLPP Preemption. This parameter determines whether a higher precedence call preempts a lower precedence call. The value of Disabled does not allow this to happen. To cause a lower precedence call to be terminated if a higher precedence call requires the resources, set this parameter to Forceful.

Interface Information

Step 17 The next set of fields defines characteristics of the interface. The first of these fields, labeled PRI Protocol Type, defines the protocol used. The value placed in this field depends on the type of equipment the T1 is connected to on the other side. Your T1 provider should be able to supply this information. Select the appropriate protocol from the drop-down list.

Step 18 The field labeled Protocol Side, determines if the T1 connects to a Network Device or a User device. The simplest way to look at this is that one side must be User and the other side Network. If connecting to the phone company's Central Office (CO) you will most likely choose User. Select the appropriate protocol side from the drop-down list.

Step 19   The Channel Selection Order field determines in what order the ports are used, either starting at the first, which is referred to as TOP_DOWN, or starting at the last, which is referred to as BOTTOM_UP. In most cases, TOP_DOWN is used. Select the desired value from the drop-down list.

Step 20   The next field, which is labeled Channel IE Type, determines the channel selection method. The selection in this field depends on the connection on the other side.

Step 21   The PCM Type determines the type encoding format that is being used. For the United States, Japan, Taiwan, and Hong Kong select "μ-law" (mu-law). In the rest of the world, select "a-law."

Step 22   The Delay for first restart (1/8 sec ticks) field determines how long this port waits before restarting when instructed. This allows you to stagger the restart times when a large number of PRIs are installed.

Step 23   The next field, labeled Delay between restarts (1/8 sec ticks), determines the length of time between restarts of the PRI when PRI RESTART is sent.

Step 24   The Inhibit restarts at PRI initialization check box determines if a RESTART message is sent when the D-channel successfully connects. The default is to leave this box checked, which does not cause a RESTART message to be sent.

Step 25   When the Enable status poll check box is checked, the Change B-Channel Maintenance Status is enabled, which allows individual B-Channels to be taken out of service. The default is to leave this box unchecked.

Call Routing Information—Inbound Calls

Step 26   The next set of fields deals with inbound calls. The Significant Digits field determines the number of digits, of an incoming dialed number, that will be used by CallManager. CallManager counts from right to left, so if the number entered in this field is four and the digits received are 8105559090, 810555 will be removed and only 9090 will be used to determine the destination of this call.

Step 27   A Calling Search Space (CSS) determines what destination inbound calls to this gateway will be able reach. CSS is discussed in Chapter 5: Configuring Class of Service and Call Admission Control. Choose a CSS from the Calling Search Space drop-down list. If this field is left at None, the dial privileges of the calls coming in to the gateway could be limited.

Step 28   The Automated Alternate Routing (AAR) is used to provide an alternate route if a call fails due to insufficient bandwidth. The AAR CSS can be used to limit the paths a call may use when it is rerouted. Select an AAR CSS from the AAR Calling Search Space drop-down list.

Step 29 The Prefix DN field defines what digits are added to the front of an incoming destination number. This is applied to the number, after CallManager truncates the number, based on the Significant Digits setting.

Call Routing Information—Outbound Calls

Step 30 The next set of fields deals with outbound calls. The Calling Line ID Presentation field determines if CallManager sends Caller ID information. To send caller ID information, select **Allowed** from the drop-down list. To block caller ID, select **Restricted** from the drop-down list.

Step 31 The Calling Party Selection field determines what number is sent to outbound calls. The choices are:

— Originator—the directory number of the device that placed the call

— First Redirect Number—the directory number of the first device to forward the call

— Last Redirect Number—the directory number of the last device to forward the call

— First Redirect Number (External)—the number of the first device to forward the call using the external phone mask

— Last Redirect Number (External)—the number of the last device to forward the call using the external phone mask

Select the desired value for this field.

Step 32 Cisco recommends that the following four fields remain set to the default of Cisco CallManager:

— Called party IE number type unknown

— Calling party IE number type unknown

— Called Numbering Plan

— Calling Numbering Plan

These fields deal with dial plan issues and should be changed only when advised to do so by Cisco or an experienced dial plan expert. The need to change these usually occurs when installing CallManager internationally.

Step 33 The next field, which is labeled Number of digits to strip, determines how many digits should be stripped for outbound calls. For example, if this value is set to two and the number 995551001 is dialed, the 99 is stripped before the call is sent.

Step 34 The Caller ID DN field is used to determine what caller ID is sent out this gateway. A mask or a complete number can be entered in this field. For example, if the mask 55536XX is entered in this field, CallManager sends 55536 and the last two digits of the calling number.

Step 35 The last field, which is the SMDI Base Port, is used only when integrating with a traditional voicemail system. Enter the first T1 port being used for voicemail functions.

PRI Protocol Type Specific Information

Step 36 The PRI Protocol Type Specific Information fields determine what Information Elements are sent in messages. For most installations this field can remain at default.

UUIE Configuration

Step 37 The Passing Precedence Level Through UUIE check box determines if the MLPP precedence is sent through the use of the User-to-User Information Element (UUIE). To enable this check the box.

Product Specific Configuration

Step 38 The last set of fields, which is labeled Product Specific Configuration, is specific to the gateway you are configuring. To see an explanation of each of these fields, click the [i] icon located to the right of the category title. The information needed to determine the settings of these fields comes from the T1 carrier. Enter the information provided by your carrier in the appropriate fields. Table 3-3 lists these fields and supplies a brief description of each field.

Step 39 After the required and desired parameters have been entered, click the **Insert** button at the top of the page. After the gateway is added, an alert window informs you that the gateway needs to be reset. Press the **OK** button.

Table 3-3   *Product Specific Configuration Detail*

Parameter	Description
Clock Reference	This parameter specifies the location from which the master clock is derived. Required field. Default: Network.
TX-Level CSU	This parameter specifies the transmit level based on the distance between the gateway and the nearest repeater. The default is full power (0dB). Required field. Default: 0dB.

Table 3-3   *Product Specific Configuration Detail (Continued)*

Parameter	Description
FDL Channel	This parameter specifies what kind of facility data link (FDL), if any, is supported by the span. The FDL is a maintenance channel that allows remote troubleshooting of link-layer problems and remote monitoring of performance statistics of the link. Required field. Default: ATT 54016.
Framing	This parameter specifies the multiframe format of the span. Required field. Default: ESF.
Audio Signal Adjustment into IP Network	This parameter specifies the gain or loss applied to the received audio signal relative to the port application type. Required field. Default: NoDbPadding.
Audio Signal Adjustment from IP Network	This parameter specifies the gain or loss applied to the transmitted audio signal relative to the port application type. Required field. Default: NoDbPadding.
Yellow Alarm	This parameter specifies how a remote alarm indication is coded on a T1 span. A yellow alarm indicates that the other end of the link has lost frame synchronization on the signal being transmitted by this end. Required field. Default: Bit2.
Zero Suppression	This parameter specifies how the T1 or E1 span electrically codes binary 1s and 0s on the wire (line coding selection). Required field. Default: B8ZS.
Digit On Duration (50–500ms)	This parameter specifies the duration in milliseconds of Dual Tone Multi-Frequency (DTMF) digits generated by the gateway. Valid durations range from 50–500ms. Required field. Default: 100. Minimum: 50. Maximum: 500.
Interdigit Duration (50–500ms)	This parameter specifies the duration to pause between digits when sequences of DTMF digits are generated by the gateway. This parameter is in milliseconds. Valid durations range from 50–500ms. Required field. Default: 100. Minimum: 50. Maximum: 500.

continues

Table 3-3   *Product Specific Configuration Detail (Continued)*

Parameter	Description
SNMP Community String	This parameter specifies the community string to be used for accessing the Simple Network Management Protocol (SNMP) agent for this interface. Default: public.
Disable SNMP Set Operations	This parameter specifies whether all SNMP set operations are disabled. Required field. Default: false.
Debug Port Enable	This parameter specifies whether the developer (debug) port should be enabled. Required field. Default: true.
Hold Tone Silence Duration	This parameter specifies, in milliseconds, the inter-tone (off) duration of the hold tone. If this value is set to zero, the default duration of 10 seconds is used. Required field. Default: 0. Minimum: 0. Maximum: 65535.
Port Used for Voice Calls	This parameter should be selected if this port is used for voice calls. If this port is used only for fax or modem calls, do not select this option. Required field. Default: true.
Port Used for Modem Calls	This parameter should be selected if this port is used for modem calls. If this port is used only for fax or voice calls, do not select this option. Required field. Default: true.
Port Used for Fax Calls	This parameter should be selected if this port is used for fax calls. If this port is used only for voice or modem calls, do not select this option. Required field. Default: true.
Fax and Modem Parameters	
Parameter	Description
Fax Relay Enable	This parameter specifies whether Cisco fax relay encoding should be negotiated when a fax tone is detected. Required field. Default: true.
Fax Error Correction Mode Override	This parameter specifies whether error correction mode (ECM) should be disabled for fax transmissions using Cisco fax relay. Required field. Default: true.

Table 3-3   *Product Specific Configuration Detail (Continued)*

Parameter	Description
Maximum Fax Rate	This parameter specifies the maximum fax rate to negotiate. This parameter applies only to fax transmissions using Cisco fax relay. Required field. Default: 14400bps.
Fax Payload Size	This parameter specifies the fax payload size. The default is 20 bytes. Required field. Default: 20. Minimum: 20. Maximum: 48.
Non-Standard Facilities Country Code	This parameter specifies the non-standard facilities country code. A value of 65535 will leave this field unused. This parameter applies only to fax transmissions using Cisco fax relay. Required field. Default: 65535. Minimum: 0. Maximum: 65535.
Non-Standard Facilities Vendor Code	This parameter specifies the non-standard facilities vendor code. A value of 65535 will leave this field unused. This parameter applies only to fax transmissions using Cisco fax relay. Required field. Default: 65535. Minimum: 0. Maximum: 65535.
Fax/Modem Packet Redundancy	This parameter specifies whether packet redundancy (RFC2198) should be enabled for modem calls and fax calls not using Cisco fax relay. Required field. Default: false.
Named Service Event (NSE) Type	This parameter specifies the NSE type to be used for peer-to-peer messaging. Required field. Default: Non-IOS Gateways.

Playout Delay Parameters

Parameter	Description
Initial Playout Delay	This parameter specifies the initial delay introduced by the jitter buffer in milliseconds. Required field. Default: 40. Minimum: 20. Maximum: 150.

continues

Table 3-3   *Product Specific Configuration Detail (Continued)*

Parameter	Description
Minimum Playout Delay	This parameter specifies the minimum delay introduced by the jitter buffer in milliseconds. Required field. Default: 20. Minimum: 20. Maximum: 150.
Maximum Playout Delay	This parameter specifies the maximum delay introduced by the jitter buffer in milliseconds. Required field. Default: 150. Minimum: 20. Maximum: 150.
Echo Canceller Configuration	
Parameter	Description
Echo TailLength (ms)	This parameter defines the tail length duration (in ms) to be used by the echo canceller. Supported values are 24, 32, 48 and 64ms. Required field. Default: 32ms.
Minimum Echo Return Loss (ERL) (db)	This parameter defines the minimum ERL value that can be handled by the Echo Canceller. Available options are 0db, 3db and 6db. Required field. Default: 6db.

Adding Inter-Cluster Trunks

The last type of gateway to be covered in this section is what is known an Inter-Cluster Trunk. This type of gateway is configured to allow calls to be placed between CallManager clusters across some type of IP connectivity. Inter-cluster trunks are normally used to connect clusters, within the same organization, together across an exiting WAN link, thus utilizing the WAN link for both data and voice.

The concept is very simple—in each cluster a gateway is configured that points to the IP address(es) of the CallManager in the other cluster. One thing that often causes confusion at first, is that there is no real gateway "device" that is used, unlike with other types of gateways. The easiest way to think of it is that an inter-cluster trunk is a process that runs on the CallManager cluster.

The following steps show how to configure an inter-cluster trunk and explain the various settings of one. Because there are a number of steps to this process, section headings are used to mark the point at which each new set of parameters begins. These same headings display on the configuration screen as well, which should help you keep track of where you are.

Step 1   From within CCMAdmin, select **Device>Add a New Device**.

Step 2   On the Add a New Device page, select **Trunk** from the Device Type drop-down list and click **Next**.

Step 3   On the next page, select the Inter-Cluster Trunk (Non-Gatekeeper Controlled) from the Trunk Type drop-down list.

Note	Typically non-gatekeeper controlled inter-cluster trunks are used only when bandwidth is not an issue. Gatekeepers and gatekeeper-controlled inter-cluster trunks are discussed in Chapter 5: Configuring Class of Service and Call Admission Control. The configuration of inter-cluster trunks is very similar for both types.

Step 4   The Device Protocol field can be left at Inter-Cluster Trunk. No other option is available. Click the **Next** button.

Device Information

Step 5   The Trunk Configuration screen, as shown in Figure 3-16, displays. Enter a functional name for the gateway in the Device Name field.

Figure 3-16 *Trunk Configuration*

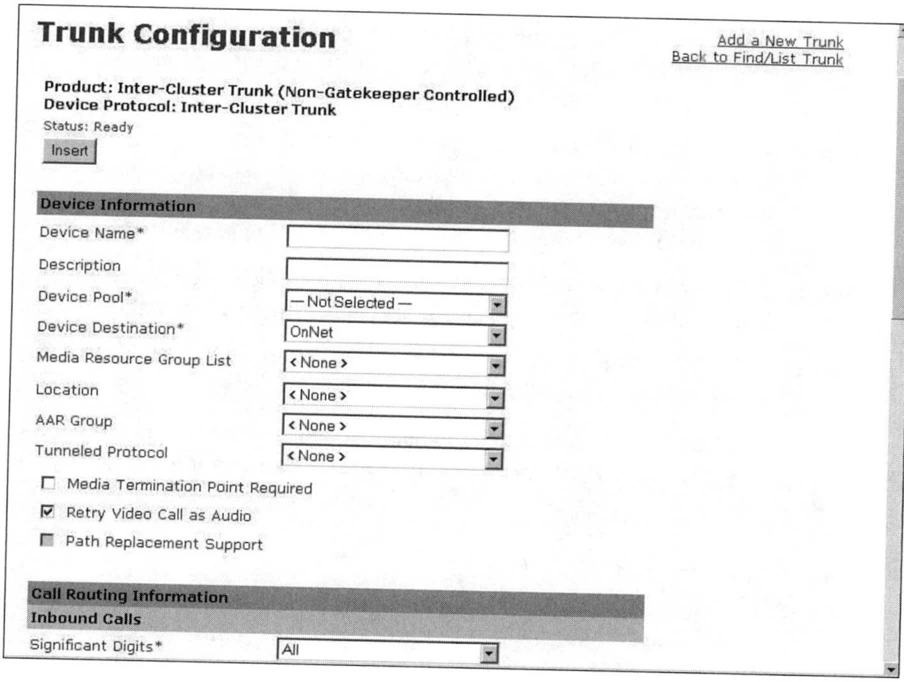

Step 6 In the Description field, enter a description that makes this device easily identifiable.

Step 7 From the Device Pool drop-down list, select the desired device pool for this gateway.

Step 8 The Device Destination is used to determine if calls on this trunk will be considered an OnNet (on network) or OffNet (off network) call. Different alerting tones are used for OnNet and OffNet calls. By default, this is set to OnNet. If you are unsure of the value to assign, leave it at the default.

Step 9 The next field is the Media Resource Group List. This determines to which media resources the gateway and device have access. Media resources group list determines to which media resources a device has access. These are discussed further in Chapter 6: Configuring CallManager Features and Services.

Step 10 Information entered in the Location field is used to prevent WAN links from becoming oversubscribed in centralized deployments. These are discussed more in Chapter 5: Configuring Class of Service and Call Admission Control. If you have defined locations, select the appropriate one for this device from the drop-down list.

Step 11 The AAR Group field determines with which AAR group this device is associated. An AAR group provides the prefix that is assigned when a call fails due to insufficient bandwidth. AAR is discussed in further detail in Chapter 6: Configuring CallManager Features and Services. Select an AAR group if AAR is being used. If this field is set to None, AAR is, in effect, disabled on this device.

Step 12 The Tunneled Protocol drop-down list allows you to select Q Signaling (QSIG), which enables inter-cluster trunk (ICT) to transport non-H.323 protocol information by tunneling it through H.323. Leave this set to None, unless you know that this type of tunneling is required.

Step 13 The Media Termination Point Required check box needs to be checked if the H.323 device does not support features such as hold and transfers.

Step 14 If the Retry Video Call as Audio box is checked, CallManager sets up a voice call if a video calls fails to set up.

Step 15 The Path Replacement Support is automatically checked if you select QSIG from the Tunneled Protocol drop-down list. Otherwise it is left unchecked.

Call Routing Information—Inbound Calls

Step 16 The next set of fields deals with inbound calls. The Significant Digits field determines the number of digits of an incoming dialed number that CallManager uses. CallManager counts from right to left, so if the number entered in this field is four and the digits received are 8105559090, 810555 would be removed and only 9090 would be used to determine the destination of this call.

Step 17 A Calling Search Space (CSS) determines what destinations inbound calls to this gateway will be able to reach. CSS is discussed in Chapter 5: Configuring Class of Service and Call Admission Control. Choose a CSS from the Calling Search Space drop-down list. If this field is left at None, the dialing privileges of this gateway could be limited.

Step 18 The Automated Alternate Routing (AAR) is used to provide an alternate route if a call fails due to insufficient bandwidth. The AAR CSS can be used to limit the paths a call may use when it is rerouted. Select an AAR CSS from the AAR Calling Search Space drop-down list.

Step 19 The Prefix DN field defines what digits are added to the front of an incoming destination number. This is applied to the number, after CallManager truncates the number, based on the Significant Digits setting.

Step 20 The Redirecting Number IE Delivery–Inbound should be used if your voicemail system supports Redirecting Number IE. Otherwise, leave this box unchecked.

Step 21 If the Enable Inbound Faststart check box is checked, FastStart will be used. H.323 FastStart requires only two message exchanges to open logical channels, whereas normal setup requires 12. However, if FastStart is selected, both ends must support and be configured for FastStart.

Call Routing Information—Outbound Calls

Step 22 The next set of fields deals with outbound calls. The Calling Party Selection field determines what number is sent for outbound calls. The choices are:

— Originator—the directory number of the device that placed the call

— First Redirect Number—the directory number of the first device to redirect the call

— Last Redirect Number—the directory number of the last device to redirect the call

— First Redirect Number (External)—the external directory number of the first device to redirect the call

— Last Redirect Number (External)—the external directory number of the last device to redirect the call

Select the desired value for this field.

Step 23 The Calling Line ID Presentation field determines if CallManager sends Caller ID information. To send caller ID information, select **Allowed** from the drop-down list. To block caller ID, select **Restricted** from the drop-down list.

Step 24 Cisco recommends that the next four fields remain set to the default of Cisco CallManager. The four fields are:

— Called party IE number type unknown

— Calling party IE number type unknown

— Called Numbering Plan

— Calling Numbering Plan

These fields deal with dial plan issues and should be changed only when advised to do so by Cisco or an experienced dial plan expert. The need to change these usually occurs when installing CallManager internationally.

Step 25 The Caller ID DN field is used to determine what caller ID is sent out this gateway. A mask or a complete number can be entered in this field. For example, if the mask 55536XX is entered in this field, CallManager sends 55536 and the last two digits of the calling number.

Step 26 If the Display IE Delivery check box is checked, the calling and called party name information is included in messages.

Step 27 The Redirecting Number IE Delivery–Outbound check box should be checked when integrating with a voicemail system that supports Redirecting Number IE. Otherwise, leave it unchecked.

Step 28 If the Enable Outbound Faststart check box is checked, FastStart will be used. H.323 FastStart requires only two message exchanges to open logical channels, whereas normal setup requires 12. However, if FastStart is selected, both ends must support and be configured for FastStart.

Step 29 If the Enable Outbound Faststart check box is checked, you must select the codec that is to be used. This is selected from the Codec For Outbound FastStart drop-down list.

Remote Cisco CallManager Information

Step 30 In the next three fields, the IP addresses of the CallManager in the destination cluster are entered. Enter the IP addresses of the remote CallManager group. Enter the remote primary CallManager IP address in the Server 1 field, the remote backup CallManager IP address in the Server 2 field and, if remote tertiary CallManager exists, enter its IP address in the Server 3 field. If there are more than three CallManagers in the remote cluster, additional inter-cluster trunks may need to be configured.

Multilevel Precedence and Preemption (MLPP) Information

Step 31 The next three fields define the Multilevel Precedence and Preemption (MLPP) characteristics of this trunk. If these fields are left blank or set to default, the values set in the device pool are used. The first MLPP field is the MLPP Domain. MLPP grants higher priority only from calls with the same MLPP domain. For this reason an MLPP domain is needed.

Step 32 The second field in this category, which is called MLPP Indication, determines whether tones and indications will be presented when a precedence call is made. If the is field set to Off, no precedence indication is presented. If this field is set to On, indication is used for a precedence call.

Step 33 The third MLPP field is MLPP Preemption. This parameter determines whether a higher precedence call preempts a lower precedence call. The value is not available for this device.

Step 34 After all the fields are configured, click the **Insert** button at the top of the screen to add this ICT.

Summary

This chapter covered all the required tasks needed to add phones and gateways to a CallManager system. Four methods to add phones to the system were discussed: manual registration, Auto-registration, BAT, and TAPS.

After phones were added, the addition of four types of gateways was discussed. A description and an installation example of H.323, MGCP, Non-MGCP, and Inter-Cluster Trunk gateways were provided.

The chapter should help you feel comfortable with the task of adding phones and gateways. Because it is not possible to include step-by-step instructions for every possible type of phone and gateway in this book, the examples given were based on widely deployed models. These instructions should serve as a good guide to help you deploy most other models as well.

Now that the phones and gateways are deployed, a dial plan is needed. A dial plan is used to determine how calls are routed. Let's move onto the next chapter and explore dial plans.

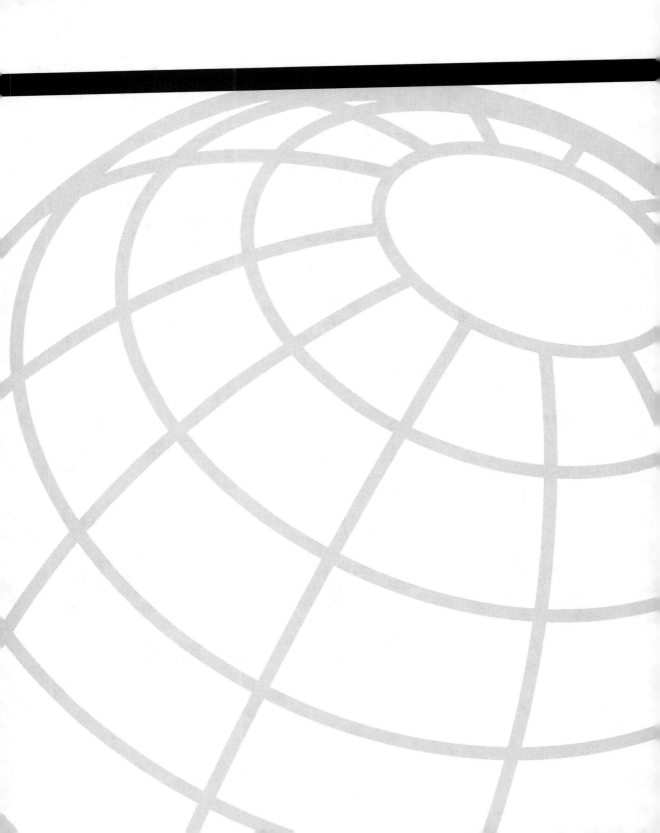

CHAPTER 4

Implementing a Dial Plan

After phones and gateways have been added to the cluster, a dial plan must be created to allow calls to reach destinations outside the cluster. As soon as the first directory number is entered in CallManager, the creation of a dial plan begins. By default, calls that are placed to destinations within the same cluster can be successfully routed. This is because all directory numbers that are registered to the CallManager cluster become part of that cluster's dial plan. However, for CallManager to route a call to a destination that is outside its cluster, additional information must be programmed that will make up CallManager's external dial plan. Although directory numbers do belong to the dial plan, it is common to refer to the external dial plan as "the dial plan."

A dial plan can become quite complex and many unforeseen issues can arise, so you should outline the plan on paper before any devices are deployed. Someone that has proven experience in this field should create the dial plan. After the dial plan is created on paper, configuring it in the CallManager can begin. If you are new to dial plans, seek out an individual with dial plan experience for assistance.

Before discussing how to configure a dial plan, let's take a closer look at the components required to make a call. The next section provides an overview of the flow of a typical call.

NOTE   Because the components within a dial plan have to be created in the opposite order of the call flow, it is recommended that you read the entire chapter before trying to implement any of the specific tasks covered. This will help you achieve a higher understanding of each component and its role in the call flow process.

Understanding Call Flow

A call begins when someone picks up the handset and dials a number. Although this seems rather simple, much more is happening than the entry of numbers on one end and the magical ring of the phone on the other end. For the purposes of this chapter, we are only concerned with how the call is routed within the cluster. After the call is handed off to a device outside the cluster, the CallManager has no control on the path the call takes.

Before examining an example call flow, you need to be familiar with a dial plan's required components. The following is a list of components that are used to make up a dial plan along with a brief description of each. Later, sections of the chapter supply more detail on each component.

- **Pattern**—Patterns are made up of numbers, wildcards, and special characters. Wildcards allow a single pattern to match multiple-dialed numbers. The most popular wildcard is the "X." This wildcard matches any single digit 0–9. For example, a pattern of 91248XXXXXXX matches any dialed number that begins with 91248 and is followed by seven more digits, such as 912485554123. Wildcards are covered in detail later in this chapter.

- **Device**—A gateway that connects the CallManager system to another system such as the Public Switched Telephone Network (PSTN). In some documentation these are also referred to as route group devices.

- **Route Group**—An ordered list of gateways to which a call can be sent. The call is sent to the first device in the group, and if the call is unable to use that gateway for any reason, the route group sends the call to the next device in its list.

- **Route List**—A prioritized list of route groups used to determine to which route groups an outbound call is sent. The call is sent to the first route group in the list. If that route group refuses the call for any reason, the route list sends the call to the next route group in its list.

The following steps outline what happens within the cluster when a call is placed to a destination outside the cluster. For example, let's assume the call is being placed to the pizza place down the street.

Step 1   The caller dials the phone number of the pizza place.

Step 2   CallManager looks at those digits and finds a pattern that matches it. If it finds multiple patterns that match, it uses the closest (the one with the fewest possible matches).

Step 3   The pattern that the dialed number matches points to a route list that in turn points to one or more route groups.

Step 4   The route list sends the call to the first route group in its list.

Step 5   The route group points to one or more gateways and sends the call to the first gateway in the group.

Step 6 If the gateway is unable to handle the call, the route group sends the call to the next gateway in its list if there is one.

Step 7 If no other gateway exists in the group or if the last gateway in the group is unable to route the call, the call is returned to the route list and the route list sends the call to the next route group in the list.

Step 8 The next route group sends the call to the first gateway in the group.

Step 9 After the call reaches a gateway that is able to handle the call, the call is sent out of the system using that gateway.

Step 10 If no gateway is available, the call fails.

Figure 4-1 offers an example of the preceding steps. This simple example shows that the processing of a single call can be quite complicated. For calls to be delivered to the proper destination, each of the components discussed in this example, such as patterns, route list, route groups and gateways, must be configured in CallManager. This section has offered a broad overview of these components. The following sections build on what you have learned here, offers more detail on each component, and explain how each component is configured.

Figure 4-1 *Call Flow*

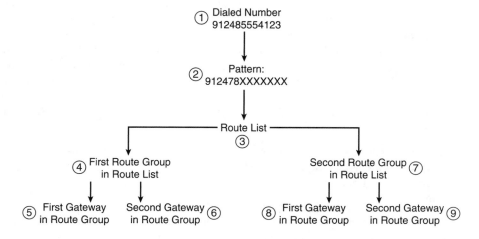

NOTE	The flow of the call starts at the pattern and ends at the gateway. However, the creation of the required components is in the opposite order. This is because when a route group points to a gateway, the gateway pointed to must exist. Therefore, the gateway must be configured first, followed by the route group, then the route list, and last, but not least, the pattern. Because gateway configuration is discussed in the last chapter, we look at the route groups and lists first.

Understanding Route Groups and Route Lists

The job of a route group is to send the call to the gateway or gateways to which it points. The route group sends the call to the first gateway in the group, and if that gateway is unable to handle the call, the route group sends the call to the next gateway in the group. This process is repeated until a gateway in the list is identified that is able to handle the call, or there are no more gateways in the group. If the route group is unable to find an available gateway, the call is returned to the route list.

The job of a route list is to send the call to a route group, which in turn sends the call to a gateway. In the example shown in Figure 4-2, the call is first routed across the wide-area network (WAN). If that path is unable to accommodate the call, it is routed to the PSTN. As you can see, depending on which path the call takes, a different number of digits need to be sent. If the call is sent across the Inter-Cluster Trunk (ICT), only five digits are needed, assuming that the remote cluster is using five digit directory numbers. However, if the call goes across the PSTN, 11 digits are needed. To accomplish this, digit manipulation must take place. Digit manipulation occurs when a called (dialed) or calling (Caller ID) number is changed. In this case, the digit translation strips the required number of digits from the called number so that the call can be routed across the chosen path. Because the path the call takes is not known until it reaches the route group, the digit manipulation should take place there.

Digit manipulation can be accomplished a number of ways. Each of the various methods used for digit manipulation is covered in this chapter, as are examples of when each type might be used. Let's first look at what type of digit manipulation can take place at the route group level.

After the call is sent to a route group and an available gateway is found, six types of digit manipulation can be performed. Three affect the calling number (caller ID) and three affect the called party number. Digit manipulation can be performed by applying a mask to digits. CallManager applies the mask to digits by right justifying both the digits and the mask, placing the mask directly under the digits, so to speak. Where there are X's in the mask, CallManager will pass the digits. Where there are numbers in the mask, CallManager will replace the digits with the number in the mask. For instance, a mask of 612555X2XX applied to the digits 4321 would look like this:

```
    4321 - Digits
612555X2XX - Mask

6125554221 - End Result
```

Figure 4-2   *Digit Manipulation Required*

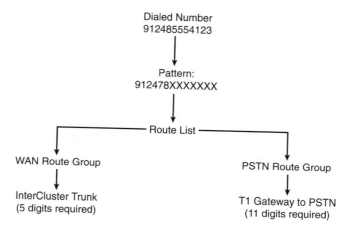

The following is a list of the six methods of digit manipulation and a brief explanation for each.

- **Calling Party's External Phone Mask**— If configured under the directory number, this mask changes the caller ID information. When adding a route group to a route list, you can choose to enable or disable this mask. For instance this mask can be used to send a phone's Direct Inward Dial (DID) number for caller ID. If you apply an External Phone Mask of 408370XXXX to a 4-digit extension number and you choose to enable this mask, CallManager can pass the DID number for caller ID. For instance:

```
    4112 - Extension number
408370XXXX - External Phone Mask

4083704112 - Caller ID
```

  With this type of mask, CallManager passes the actual fully qualified directory number as caller ID.

- **Calling Party Transform Mask**—Sometimes it is not desirable to pass the phone's DID number as caller ID, or the phone DN is not a DID number. The Calling Party Transformation Mask can be used to further manipulate digits passed for caller ID. It can also be used to pass a DID number for caller ID if the External Phone Mask is not used. The actual digits supplied depend on whether the external phone number mask is applied or not. If the External Phone Mask is not used, the Calling Party Transformation Mask is applied to the extension number as follows:

```
4112 - Extension Number
408370XXXX - Calling Party Transformation Mask

4083704112 - End Result
```

If the External Phone Mask is used, the Calling Party Transformation Mask is applied to the end result of the External Phone Mask transformation as follows:

```
4083704112 - Result of External Phone Mask transformation
4083701200 - Calling Party Transformation Mask

4083701200 - End Result (perhaps the company's main number)
```

As you can see, transformation masks are powerful tools.

- **Prefix Digits**—These digits prepend the digits to which they are applied. An example might be to use 40837 as Prefix Digits in a 5-digit internal dial plan. For example, if the extension number is 58321, CallManager adds 40837 in front of 58321, which results in 4083758321.

- **Discard Digits**—This determines if any dialed digits are discarded. Discard Digits are often used to remove the 9 from the front of outbound calls. The specific options of this field are covered later in this chapter.

- **Called Party Transform Mask**—This mask changes the called number (dialed digits). This could be used in an environment that requires callers to dial only five digits to reach a phone via an ICT. However, if the ICT is unable to accommodate the call, it is routed to the PSTN. The PSTN needs the full phone number, so a transformation mask is used. A mask of 1408370XXXX could be used in this example. This mask tells CallManager to apply 1408370XXXX to the dialed number of 58321 as follows:

```
       58321 - Dialed number
1408370XXXX - Called Party Transformation Mask

14083708321 - Digits passed to the PSTN
```

The assumption in this example is that 14083708321 is the called party's phone number.

- **Prefix Digits**—These digits are added to the front of a called number (dial digits). An example might be 140837. This mask tells CallManager to place 140837 in front of the extension. For example, if the extension number is 58321, CallManager adds 140837 in front of 58321, which results in 14083758321.

Even though digit manipulation can be done at the group level, it is applied to the group at the route list level. This may sound confusing at first, but it makes more sense after you have seen it applied. This is examined in the Creating a Route List section of this chapter.

Now that you understand the task of the route list and the route groups, let's take a look at how they are created. Because they must be created in the opposite order of the call flow, the route groups must be created first.

Creating Route Groups

Because route groups point to gateways, the gateways must be configured before creating route groups. For information on gateway configuration, refer to Chapter 3, "Deploying Devices." The steps presented in this section assume that gateways already exist and that you have a written dial plan, which you can refer to while configuring the route groups.

The following steps show how to create a route group that can point to multiple gateways.

Step 1   From within CCMAdmin, select **Route Plan>Route/Hunt>Route Group**.

Note   In earlier versions of CallManager, the path to reach route groups is slightly different, such as Route Plan>Route Group.

Step 2   Click the **Add a New Route Group** link.

Step 3   A screen similar to that shown in Figure 4-3 displays. Enter a descriptive name in the Route Group Name field.

Figure 4-3   *Route Group Configuration*

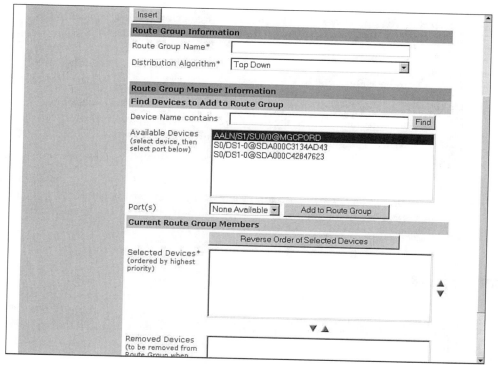

Step 4 From the drop-down box labeled Distribution Algorithm, choose how CallManager will distribute the calls. If you want CallManager to send the call to the first available gateway in the list, choose **Top Down**. When **Circular** is chosen, the call is routed to the gateway that is listed below the gateway to which that call was most recently extended. For example, using the list that is shown in Figure 4-3, if the last call was extended to the gateway labeled S0/DS1-0@SDA000C3134AD43, the next call would be sent to S0/DS1-0@SDA000C42847623, regardless of the availability of the other gateways.

Step 5 From the Available Devices box, highlight the gateway you want to add to this route group. If there are many gateways, you can limit the ones that appear in this box by entering search criteria in the Device Name contains field.

Step 6 Certain gateways allow you to choose which ports on the gateway you want to use for this route group. In the Port(s) field, select the ports on this gateway that should be added to this route group. If the gateway you are configuring does not allow the selection of ports, leave this field set to default.

Step 7 Click the **Add to Route Group** button. Repeat steps 5 through 7 for gateways you want to add to this group.

Step 8 After you have selected all of the desired gateways, they appear in the Selected Devices box. The order in which they appear in this box determines the order in which calls are distributed. To change the order, highlight the gateway you wish to move and click the up or down arrow to the right of the box.

Step 9 You may remove a gateway from the route group by highlighting the gateway and clicking the down arrow below the Selected Devices box. The gateway then appears in the Removed Devices box.

Step 10 Click the **Insert** button to complete the configuration of this route group.

After the route group is created, it must be added to a route list. As mentioned previously, digit manipulation can be done at the route group level, but is configured when route groups are added to a route list. The next section discusses how to create and configure route lists.

Creating Route a List

Before proceeding, ensure that you have created all required route groups. Because a route list points to route groups, the route groups must exist. The steps provided in this section guide you through the creation and configuration of a route list, in addition to configuring route group level digit manipulation.

Step 1   From within CCMAdmin, select **Route Plan>Route/Hunt>Route List**.

Note	In earlier versions of CallManager, the path to reach route groups is slightly different, such as Route Plan>Route List.

Step 2   Click the **Add a New Route List** link.

Step 3   A screen similar to that shown in Figure 4-4 displays. Enter a descriptive name in the field labeled Route List Name.

Figure 4-4   *Route List Configuration*

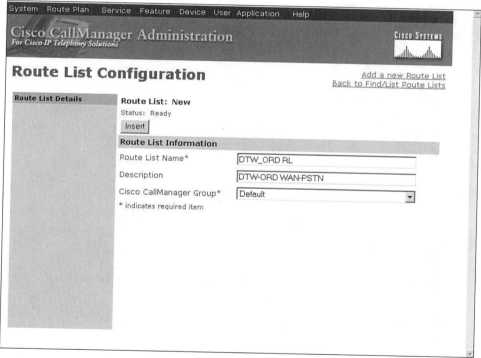

Step 4   In the Description field, enter a description that helps to easily identify this route list.

Step 5   From the drop-down list labeled Cisco CallManager Group, select the CallManager group that will be used to determine to which CallManager this route list will register.

Step 6   Click the **Insert** button. An informational window informs you that you must add at least one route group to this route list. Click **OK**.

Step 7   A screen similar to that shown in Figure 4-5 displays. Notice that below the CallManager group is a check box labeled Enable this Route List. By default this is checked, which means that the route group is active. If during testing or troubleshooting you need to disable this route group, uncheck this box. For now leave it at default.

Figure 4-5   *Route List Configuration—Adding Route Groups*

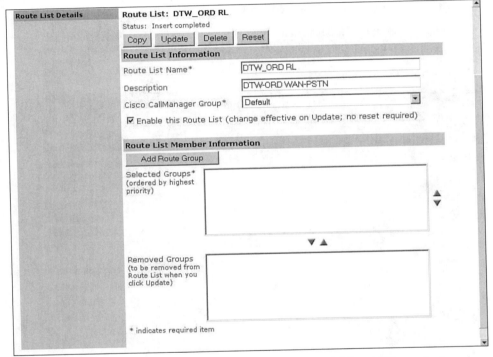

Step 8   To add a route group to this list, click the **Add Route Group** button.

Step 9   A screen similar to that shown in Figure 4-6 displays. From the Route Group drop-down menu, select the desired route group.

Step 10   This is the point at which you can configure digit manipulation. If you wish to affect caller ID information, configure the three fields found under the Calling Party Transformations heading. These fields are discussed earlier in this chapter. The first field is labeled Use Calling Party's External Phone Number Mask. This field determines if the mask configured on the directory number is used for calls that are routed through this route group.

Step 11   In the Calling Party Transform Mask field, enter any mask you want to affect the caller ID.

Figure 4-6   *Adding Route Groups to Route List*

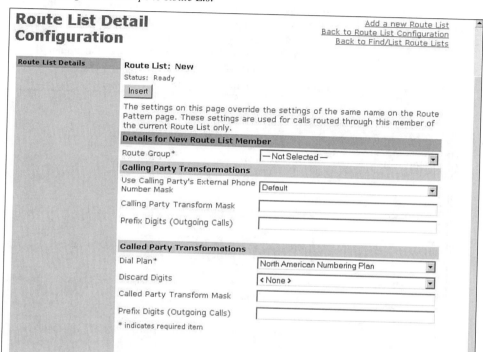

Step 12 In the Prefix Digits (Outgoing Calls) field, enter any digits that you want added to the front of the caller ID.

Step 13 The fields under the Called Party Transformations heading affect the dialed number. This is where you can manipulate the number that is sent to the gateway. An example of how this might be used was shown in Figure 4-2. When the call goes across the WAN, only five digits are needed, but if the WAN cannot handle the call and it is sent to the PSTN, 11 digits are needed in order for the PSTN to properly route the call. The first field in this category is Dial Plan. Currently there is no choice other than the default.

Step 14 From the drop-down list labeled Discard Digits, select the digit discard instructions that should apply to calls that are sent out this gateway. A discard instruction determines which digits are removed from the dialed digits before the call is sent out the gateway. There are more than 30 different discard instructions for this field. However, most of them are combinations of one another. Table 4.1 lists of the seven core discard instructions.

Note	Some of the discard instructions depend on the pattern that is matched when the number is dialed. The following examples make reference to these patterns, and the next section explains these patterns in more detail. So, if you are unfamiliar with patterns shown in these examples, fear not—you will find explanations for them very soon.

Table 4-1 *Digit Discard Instructions*

Discard Instruction	Description	Example
10-10-Dialing	Removes 1010 and the carrier code	1010-321-585-555-5555 becomes 585-555-5555
11/10D->7D	Changes 11 and 10 digits to 7	1-246-555-1212 or 246-555-1212 becomes 555-1212
11D->10D	Changes 11 digits to 10	1-246-555-1212 becomes 246-555-1212
Intl TollBypass	Removes international access and country codes	011-64-3214322 becomes 3214322
PreAt	Removes all numbers before the @ in the matching pattern	When 912485551212 matches the pattern 9@, the 9 is stripped resulting in 12485551212
PreDot	Removes all digits before the dot (.) in the matching pattern	When 912485551212 matches the pattern 9.@, the 9 is stripped resulting in 12485551212
Trailing-#	Removes the # from the end of the dialed digits	12465551212# becomes 12465551212

These instruction are combined to create the more than 30 instructions you find in the list. Let's look at an example. The discard instruction PreDot 10-10-Dialing removes any number before the dot in the pattern, the 10-10 and carrier code. So when the number 910103215835551212 is dialed and matches the 9.@ pattern, the 9 is removed, because of the PreDot portion of the instruction, and the 10-10 and carrier code of 321 are removed because of the 10-10 Dialing instruction, which results in 5835551212. Applying what you learned here, you can quite easily determine what effect the other discard instruction will have on a dialed number.

NOTE	If the @ wildcard is not used, the only valid discard digit instructions are PreDot or None.

Step 15 In the Called Party Transform Mask field, enter the mask you want to use for calls going out this gateway.

Step 16 In the Prefix Digits (Outgoing Calls) field, enter any digits that you want added to the front of the dialed number before the call is sent out the gateway.

Note	Because a number of transformations can be applied, it is important to understand the order in which the transformations take place. The order for calling party transforms is external phone mask first, followed by calling party transform mask, and finally prefix digits. The order for called party transforms is discard instructions first, followed by called party transform mask, and finally prefix digits.

Step 17 Click the **Insert** button.

Step 18 An informational window displays stating that the route group has been added and that the route list must be reset for the changes to take effect. Click **OK**.

Step 19 The page shown in Figure 4-5 redisplays with the addition of the route group you just added. Repeat steps 7 through 16 for any additional route groups you wish to enter.

Step 20 After all route groups are added, they display in the Selected Groups box. The order in which they display in this box determines the order in which calls are distributed. To change the order, highlight the route group you wish to move and click the up or down arrow to the right of the box.

Step 21 You may remove a route group from the route list by highlighting the route group and clicking the down arrow below the Selected Groups box. This route group displays in the Removed Groups box.

Step 22 Click the **Update** button to complete the configuration of this route list.

Step 23 Depending on the version of CallManager, the route list may need to be reset before the change takes effect. Later versions of CallManager include a note that states "change effective on Update; no reset required." Click the "Reset" button if required.

Step 24 An informational window displays stating that you are about to reset the route list. Click **OK**.

Step 25 An informational window displays stating the route list is being reset. Click **OK**.

After all route groups and route lists are created, patterns need to be configured so that when someone dials a number, there is something to match it against and route it to the proper route list.

Understanding Patterns

When dialed digits are sent to the CallManager, that CallManager must be able to match those digits with a pattern. A pattern is simply a set of numbers or wildcards that CallManager matches against a dialed number. If there is no pattern configured in CallManager that matches the dialed digits, the call fails. You have already seen some examples of patterns in previous sections. However, this section supplies more detail, and the configuration process on patterns. Now that you know that every dialed number must have a matching pattern configured in CallManager, you might be thinking that it is impossible to enter a pattern for every number that might ever be dialed. If it were not for what are called wildcards, you would be correct.

Patterns are made up of numbers, wildcards and special characters. Wildcards allow a single pattern to match multiple-dialed numbers. The most popular wildcard is the "X." This wildcard matches any single digits of 0 through 9. You could use it, for example, if you want to configure a pattern that matches the five digits extensions of another cluster. Let's say the extension range of the other cluster is 52000 through 52999. In this case a pattern of 52XXX can be used because it matches all numbers within this range.

The "X" is only one of a number of useful wildcards that are listed as follows:

- X—This wildcard matches any single digit 0-9.

  Example—52XXX matches 52000 through 52999.

- @—The 'at' sign matches any number in the North America Numbering Plan (NANP). A simple way to think of this pattern is that it matches any number that can be dialed from a phone in North America.

  Example—9.@ matches a number that can be dialed from North America and is proceeded by a 9.

- !—The exclamation point matches any digit, or any number of digits.

  Example—55! matches any number that begins with a 55. The possible matches that results from using the (!) are almost limitless.

- [ ]—The digits found within the bracket represent a range of numbers that a single digit can match.

  Example—55[2-5] matches 552, 553, 554 and 555.

- [^]—The digits found within brackets that include a (^) represent a range of numbers that are to be excluded when matching a single digit.

  Example—55[^2-5] matches 550, 551, 556, 557, 558, 559, 55* and 55#.

- **+** —The (+) matches one or more instances of the preceding character or range in the pattern.

  Example —572+1 matches 5721, 57221, 572221, 5722221 and so on.

- **?** —The (?) matches zero or more instances of the preceding character in the pattern.

  Example —57?2 matches 572, 5772, 5772, 577772, 5777772, in short it matches any pattern that begins with a 5 followed by any number of 7s which is followed by a 2 as the last number.

NOTE

You can extend the power of patterns by using multiple wildcards in the same pattern. This can also lead to unexpected behavior. For example, the pattern 532X? results in matching nearly any dialed number that begins with 532. Take time to test the patterns that you create to make sure they behave as expected.

In addition to wildcards there are other characters that can be part of a pattern. These are sometimes referred to as Special Characters and are listed as follow:

- **.** —The dot (.) is used with digit manipulation. It is used to determine what digits are to be stripped.

  Example —If the discard instruction of PreDot is used with the pattern 9.@, the 9 is stripped because it is in front of (pre) the dot (.). If the number 912485551212 is dialed the 9 is striped leaving 12485551212.

- ***** —The asterisk (*) is a valid digit that can be dialed from a phone so it can be part of a pattern. It is important to realize that this is not a wildcard. The asterisk is used as a wildcard in many applications, but not when it is part of a CallManager pattern.

  Example —543* only matches 543*

- **#** —The octothorpe (#), which is often referred to as the pound sign or hash mark, is also a valid digit that can be dialed. However, it is most often used to signify the caller has finished dialing. The octothorpe should only be used as the last digit of a pattern. Discard instructions can be used with this pattern to remove the (#) before sending the call out.

  Example —542342# matches only 542342# and routes the call as soon as the (#) is pressed. This is useful when the (!) is used in a pattern. Typically the (#) is used after the (!) in a pattern.

Now that you know what a pattern does and what characters can be used to make up a pattern, let's create some. The following section takes you though the steps that are required to add a basic route pattern, and to point that pattern to a route list.

Creating Basic Route Patterns

Before creating any route patterns, route lists should be created. This is because route patterns point to route lists and can't point to something that doesn't exist. The following steps show how to create a route pattern and point the route pattern to a route list. For example, let's create a route pattern that matches all 11-digit calls and use 9 as the PSTN access code.

A number of route patterns are needed to create an efficient dial plan. The exact number of route patterns needed varies. There are many things to be considered when creating dial plans such as how many digits must be dialed for each type of call.

NOTE	While configuring a route pattern, keep in mind that, as with many components which are configured in CallManager, not all the parameters need to be configured. In some cases, you may need to configure only a few parameters. In order to allow you to fully understand the purpose of each, these steps cover each parameter.

Step 1 From within CCMAdmin, select **Route Plan>Route/Hunt>Route Pattern**.

Step 2 Click the Add a New Route Pattern link in the upper-right corner.

A screen similar to that shown in Figure 4-7 displays. Enter the route pattern in the Route Pattern field. In this example, we want to match 11 digits; this includes the 9 that is used as a PSTN access code, the route pattern is 9[2-9]XX[2-9}XXXXXX. The [2-9] is used instead of an (X) because area codes and exchanges never start with a 1.

Step 3 The Partition field determines what devices can access this route pattern. Partitions are discussed in more detail in Chapter 5:, Configuring Class of Service and Call Admission Control. Select the desired partition from the Partition drop-down list.

Step 4 In the Description field, enter a description that helps identify the purpose of this route pattern.

Step 5 In the Numbering Plan field, choose the appropriate numbering plan.

Step 6 From the Route Filter drop-down list, select the route filter that is to be applied to this route pattern. Route filters are used to limit what digits match the route pattern. These are explained in more detail in Chapter 5, "Configuring Class of Service and Call Admission Control."

Figure 4-7   *Route Pattern Configuration*

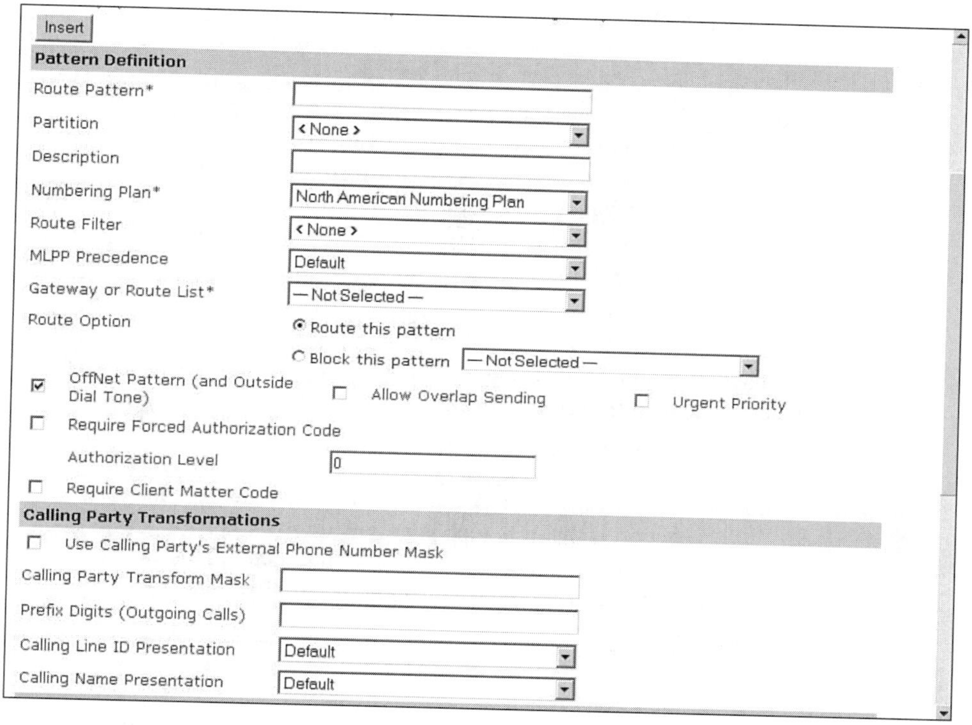

Step 7   Determine the precedence level to be assigned to this route pattern from the MLPP Precedence drop-down list (MLPP stands for multilevel precedence and preemption). Table 4-2 shows the available options.

Table 4-2   *MLPP Precedence Levels*

Precedence	Description
Flash Override	Highest level of precedence, also known as level 0
Flash	Second highest level of precedence, also known as level 1
Immediate	Third highest level of precedence, also known as level 2
Priority	Fourth highest level of precedence, also known as level 3
Routine	Lowest level of precedence, also known as level 4
Default	Leaves the incoming precedence unchanged.

Step 8   From the **Gateway or Route List** drop-down list, select the route list to which calls that match this route pattern are sent.

Step 9 To allow calls that match this route pattern to be routed, select the **Route this pattern** radio button.

Note	So far we have discussed only using route patterns to route calls, however, route patterns can also be used to block calls, by selecting the **Block this pattern** radio button. For instance, if you want to block all 900 calls, you can add a route pattern of 91900[2-9]XXXXXX and then select the **Block this pattern** radio button.

Step 10 To have a secondary dial tone played after the first digit is dialed, check **OffNet Pattern (and Outside Dial Tone)**.

Note	One caveat to the OffNet Pattern (and Outside Dial Tone) option is that dial tone is provided only when all possible matching patterns have this option selected. This can result in a dial tone being provided after multiple digits have been dialed.

Step 11 If the device you are connecting to requires that each digit is sent to it one at a time, check the **Allow Overlap Sending** box. In most cases this box is left unchecked.

Step 12 To route a call as soon as it matches this route pattern, check the **Urgent Priority** box. Typically, a call is not routed if there are other patterns that may also match; for example, if there is a 911 route pattern and a 91XXXXXXXXXX route pattern. When a caller dials 911, CallManager matches the 911 route pattern, but could also match the 91XXXXXXXXXX route pattern. If Urgent Priority is not checked, CallManager waits for the Interdigit time out to expire (15 seconds by default) before routing the call. You can see how this is undesirable in many cases. By checking the Urgent Priority, you ensure that CallManager does not wait for any other digits to be dialed and instead routes the call immediately.

Step 13 In some versions of CallManager you have the ability to choose the Require Forced Authorization Codes (FAC) and Client Matter Codes (CMC) fields. FAC forces the user to dial a code in order to be able to place the call. CMC allows the user to enter a code so that the call can later be billed back to a client. If you are implementing these features, check the appropriate checkboxes. If you are implementing FAC, enter an authorization level. FAC and CMC are discussed in greater detail in Chapter 6: Configuring CallManager Features and Services.

Step 14 If you wish to affect caller ID information, configure the fields found under the Calling Party Transformations heading. These fields are discussed earlier in this chapter. The first field is labeled Use Calling Party's External Phone Number Mask. This field determines if the mask configured on the directory number is used for calls that are routed through this route group.

Step 15 In the Calling Party Transform Mask field, enter any mask you wish to affect the caller ID.

Step 16 In the Prefix Digits (Outgoing Calls) field enter any digits that you want added to the front of the caller ID.

Step 17 The Calling Line ID Presentation field determines if caller ID information is to be blocked for outbound calls that match this route pattern. To block caller ID, select **Restricted** from the drop-down list. To allow caller ID select, **Allowed** from the drop-down list.

Step 18 The Calling Name Presentation field determines if caller name information is to be blocked for outbound calls that match this route pattern. To block calling name ID, select **Restricted** from the drop-down list. To allow calling name ID, select **Allowed** from the drop-down list.

Step 19 The Connected Line ID Presentation field determines if the connected party's ID information is to display on the calling party's phone. To block connected party's ID, select **Restricted** from the drop-down list. To allow connected party's ID, select **Allowed** from the drop-down list.

Step 20 The Connected Name Presentation field determines if the connected party's name information is displayed on the calling party's phone. To block connected party's name, select **Restricted** from the drop-down list. To allow connected party's name, select **Allowed** from the drop-down list.

Step 21 From the Discard Digits drop-down list, select the digit discard instruction that should be applied to calls that match this route pattern. These instructions are explained earlier in this chapter. Refer to Table 4-1 for additional information.

Step 22 In the Called Party Transform Mask, enter the mask you want to use for calls that match this route pattern. If no mask is to be used, leave this field empty.

Step 23 In the Prefix Digits (Outgoing Calls) field, enter any digits that you want added to the front of a dialed number before it is sent to the route list.

Step 24 ISDN network service can be invoked by configuring the ISDN Network-Specific Facilities Information Element fields. To do this, first enter the carrier code in the Carrier Identification Code field. Your carrier provides this information

Step 25 From the Network Service drop-down list labeled Protocol select the appropriate protocol. Your carrier provides this information

Step 26 Based on the protocol being used, various services can be selected and configured using the last three fields, which are the Network Service, Service Parameter Name, and the Service Parameter Value.

Step 27 Click the **Insert** Button at the top of the screen to save this route pattern.

Now that you know how to add route patterns, let's move on and take a look at what a basic dial plan might look like.

Using Pattern Wildcards to Create a Basic Dial Plan

Many factors have to be taken into consideration when implementing a dial plan such as types of calls that will be allowed, the path each type of call will take, and the dialing characteristics of your local carrier. To help explain these factors in more detail, let's take a look at a mockcompany. This illustration touches on the different factors to consider and offers a sample dial plan for the company.

Figure 4-8 shows an overview of what must be accomplished for this company.

Figure 4-8 *Example Company Overview*

Dialing Rules for Chicago
• Calls to San Jose use 7 as a leading digit followed by an extension number.
• Most 10-digit calls and all 7-digit calls are local.
• Toll charges apply to area codes 249 and 348.
• All long-distance calls are allowed.
• International calls are allowed.
• 900 numbers are to be blocked.
• 911 calls are to be given priority.
• Must dial 9 to access the PSTN.

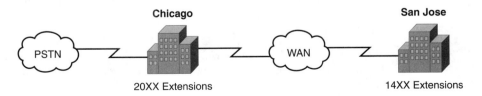

The goal is to create a dial plan for the Chicago office that satisfies the following dialing rules:

- To reach the San Jose office, callers should dial 7 followed by the extension number.
- All calls routed to the PSTN should be preceded by a 9.
- The user should be able to dial all local calls.
- Ten-digit calls that are not local should be allowed. These numbers require a pattern different from the one that matches ten-digit calls that are local. This is done so that when calling search spaces and partitions are added, these calls can be restricted.
- Long distance calls should be allowed.
- International calls should be allowed.
- 900 calls should be blocked.
- 911 calls should be routed immediately

At first glance, one might think that the 9.@ pattern can accomplish these goals. However, it will not because it does not allow for calls to the San Jose office, and it does not block 900 calls. So, as you can see, a single pattern will not suffice. As a matter of fact, using the 9.@ could allow calls that you had not intended. 9.@ matches any number that can be dialed from North America as long as a 9 is dialed first. The (@) wildcard is equal to adding hundreds of patterns. Because you often want to restrict the destinations that can be reached from certain devices, it is sometimes desirable to use patterns more specific than 9.@.

Let's look at the requirements one at a time to determine what patterns need to be created. Table 4-3 lists the goals and the patterns needed to accomplish this goal.

Table 4-3   *Example Dial Plan*

Goal	Pattern	Notes
To reach the San Jose office, callers should be able to dial 7 followed by the extension number.	7.14XX	PreDot Discard
All calls routed to the PSTN should be preceded by a 9.		Add 9. to the front of all patterns that point to the PSTN
Ensure local calls can be dialed.	9.[2-9]XXXXXX 9.[2-9]XX[2-9]XXXXXX	PreDot Discard PreDot Discard
Allow nonlocal 10-digit calls that use a pattern different from that used for 10-digit calls that are local.	9.249[2-9]XXXXXX 9.348[2-9]XXXXX	PreDot Discard PreDot Discard

continues

Table 4-3 *Example Dial Plan (Continued)*

Goal	Pattern	Notes
Allow long distance calls.	9.1[2-9]XX[2-9]XXXXXX	PreDot Discard
Allow International calls.	9.011!	PreDot Discard
	9.011!#	PreDot Trailing-# Discard
Block 900 calls.	9.1900[2-9]XXXXXX	Block Pattern
Route 911 calls immediately.	911	Urgent Priority
	9.911	PreDot Discard and Urgent Priority

NOTE Note that there is a 911 and a 9911 pattern. This is done to ensure that all attempts to reach emergency services are successful. It is not possible to know if people dialing 911 will know or remember that they must first dial a 9 and then 911. By having both patterns, the call will be successful regardless of which pattern is used.

This example offers you a small sample of the types of patterns that need to be created for an efficient and effective dial plan. This is only an example and should by no means be interpreted as a recommended dial plan. Remember that dial plans vary based on the environment. It is up to you to design a proper dial plan from scratch and thoroughly test it before using it in a production environment. Chapter 5, "Configuring Class of Service and Call Admission Control," builds on this example to show how to restrict certain devices from dialing certain numbers.

Now that you understand what a dial plan is and how to create one, let's move on and take a look at some additional components that can be used when creating complex dial plans.

Advanced Dial Plan Components and Behavior

This section examines the function and configuration steps for three additional components that are found in dial plans. These components are used when creating a more complex dial plan.

Let's start with a brief overview of each component and then a more detailed exploration of the configuration of each. The first component is a Route Filter. Route filters are applied to route patterns to limit the matches the pattern will have. As mentioned before, the (@) wildcard is equal to hundreds of different patterns. Route filters allow you to reduce the number of patterns that will match the (@). For example, you can create a pattern of 9.@ and apply a route filter that disallows 900 numbers from matching this pattern. The Creating Route Filters section takes a look at how these are configured.

The next component that is discussed is the Translation Pattern. Translation patterns allow a dialed number to be changed to another number. This is another place that digit manipulation can be accomplished. You might be wondering why you would need another place for digit manipulation because it can be done at both the route group and the route pattern. There are times when digit manipulation may need to be done before matching a route pattern and for incoming calls. Translation patterns allow the manipulation of both the dialed number and the caller ID of the calling party. In addition, translation patterns can be used to grant a different Calling Search Space and MLPP Precedence. In the Creating Translation Patterns section these are explored in greater detail.

The last dial plan component examined in this chapter is Computer Telephony Integration (CTI) Route Points. CTI route points are used to route calls to external service or devices. For example, CTI route points are used to direct calls to a Cisco IP Interactive Voice Response (IVR) system and Cisco's Personal Assistant system. After a CTI route point is created, a device or service registers with it, and CallManager learns its IP address. All calls that match the CTI route point are then sent to the registered IP address. More discussion and configuration examples are offered in the Creating CTI Route Points section.

Creating Route Filters

Route filters can make the (@) wildcard much more manageable. It is often tempting to just add the (@) pattern to your dial plan to make sure that all calls are allowed to be placed, and if your company is unconcerned with whom is calling where, you might be able to get away with this. However, most companies today want to make sure their resources are not being misused. By applying route filters to route patterns, you can limit what calls match the pattern. Route filters allow you to use the (@) and still ensure that only intended types of calls are successful. Route filters are only used with route patterns that contain the (@).

NOTE   It is important to ensure calls that should not be placed cannot be placed. "When is doubt, don't let it out." This simply means that it is better for a dial plan to be too restrictive than too liberal. If callers are unable to place calls that normally get placed, they will be sure to let you know. However, if they discover they are able to place calls, which they normally cannot place, don't expect them to tell you. This being said, remember above all else, you *MUST* ensure that certain types of calls, such as 911, can be placed from ALL phones.

To make route filters work, you create one or more mandatory conditions in order for the filter to allow the call to match the pattern. Figure 4-9 shows how a filter can affect which calls match a pattern. As you see, the pattern used in this example is 9.@, and the condition in the filter is that the area code matches 248. All the dialed digits match the pattern, but only 912485559093 match the filter conditions. You may think the 92485559090 should match because the area code is 248, but if it is not preceded by a 1, it is considered a local area code and does not meet the conditions of the filter. There is a condition that can be set on a route filter matching local area codes, but it is not included in this example.

Figure 4-9   *Route Filter Example*

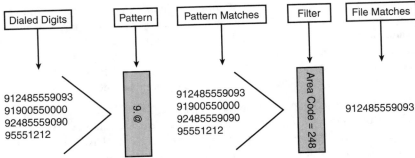

Let's look at creating a route filter and applying it to a pattern. The following steps show how to create a route filter.

Step 1   From within CCMAdmin, select **Route Plan>Route Filter**.

Step 2   Click the **Add a New Route Filter** link found in the upper-right portion of the screen.

Step 3   A page similar to that shown in Figure 4-10 displays. Select the appropriate Dial Plan from the Choose a Dial Plan drop-down list.

Figure 4-10   *Adding a Route Filter*

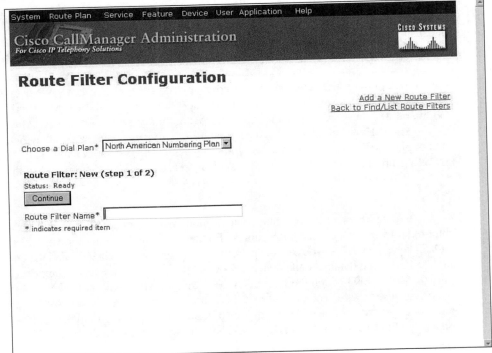

Step 4 In the Route Filter Name field, enter a descriptive name for this filter. For instance, if this filter is going to match on area code 248, you may want to name it AC248. Whatever naming convention you choose, make sure it helps you recognize the function of the route filter.

Step 5 Click the **Continue** button.

Step 6 A page similar to that shown in Figure 4-11 displays. On this screen you choose what condition(s) must be met.

Figure 4-11 *Configuring a Route Filter*

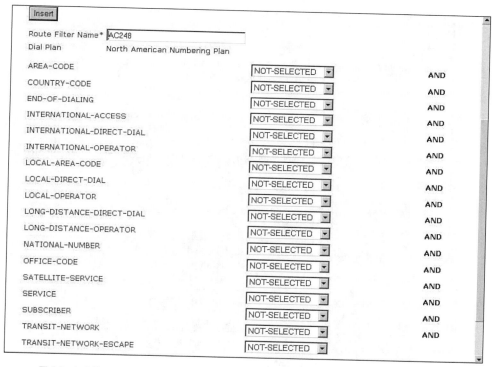

Table 4-4 lists each tag and gives a brief description. The example in the description shows the portion of the number to which the tag is referring in bold.

Table 4-4 *Route Filter Tags*

Tag	Description
Area-Code	Three digits that follow the 1 when dialing 11 digit numbers. [1-**248**-555-9093]
Country-Code	Each country has a one-, two-, or three-digit country code. [011-**63**-2-475983#]

continues

Table 4-4   *Route Filter Tags (Continued)*

Tag	Description
End-of-Dialing	Character used to signify the end of a dialing string. The # in the NANP. [011-62-2-475983#]
International-Access	Two digits that signify an international number is being dialed. 01 is used in the U.S. [**01**1-62-2-475983#]
International-Direct-Dial	The digit that follows the International-Access code. 1 is used in the U.S. [01**1**-62-2-475983#]
International-Operator	The digit that is used when accessing the international operator. 0 is used in the U.S. [**00**]
Local-Area-Code	The first three digits of a 10-digit call. [**248-555**-9093]
Local-Direct-Dial	The single digit code dialed when dialing a local call directly. 1 is used in the NANP. [**1**-555-9093]
Local-Operator	The digits used to reach the operator. 0 is used in the NANP. [**0**]
Long-Distance-Direct-Dial	The single digit code dialed when dialing a long distance call directly. 1 is used in the NANP. [**1**-248-555-9093]
Long-Distance-Operator	One or two digit code that requests operator assistance for the call.
National-Number	The nation-specific portion of an international call.
Office-Code	The first three digits of a 7-digit call. [**555**-9093]
Satellite-Service	Single digit used to access satellites for international calls.
Service	Three digit codes used for services. [**911**]
Subscriber	The last four digits of a 7-digit number. [555-**9093**]
Transit-Network	The 4-digit carrier code. [101**0321**-1-248-555-9093]
Transit-Network-Escape	The 3-digit code entered before the carrier code. [**101**0321-1-248-555-9093]

Step 7   To enable any of these tags, you have to select an operator from the drop-down list to the right of the tag. The available operators are:

NOT-SELECTED—Ignores this tag.

EXISTS—Requires that this portion of the number exist.

DOES-NOT-EXIST—Requires that this portion of the number does not exist.

==—Requires that this portion of the number match the value entered in the box that appears to the right of this operator. The value box does not appear unless this operator is selected.

Step 8   Select the operator for each tag you wish to enable and enter the value for any tag you select (==) as the operator.

Step 9   Click the **Insert** button.

Figure 4-12 shows what a page looks like for a filter that matches on a number that does not include a country or area code and has 248 as the local area code. The filter would allow the number 248-555-9093 through, but not 1-248-555-9093.

Figure 4-12   *Route Filter Configuration Example*

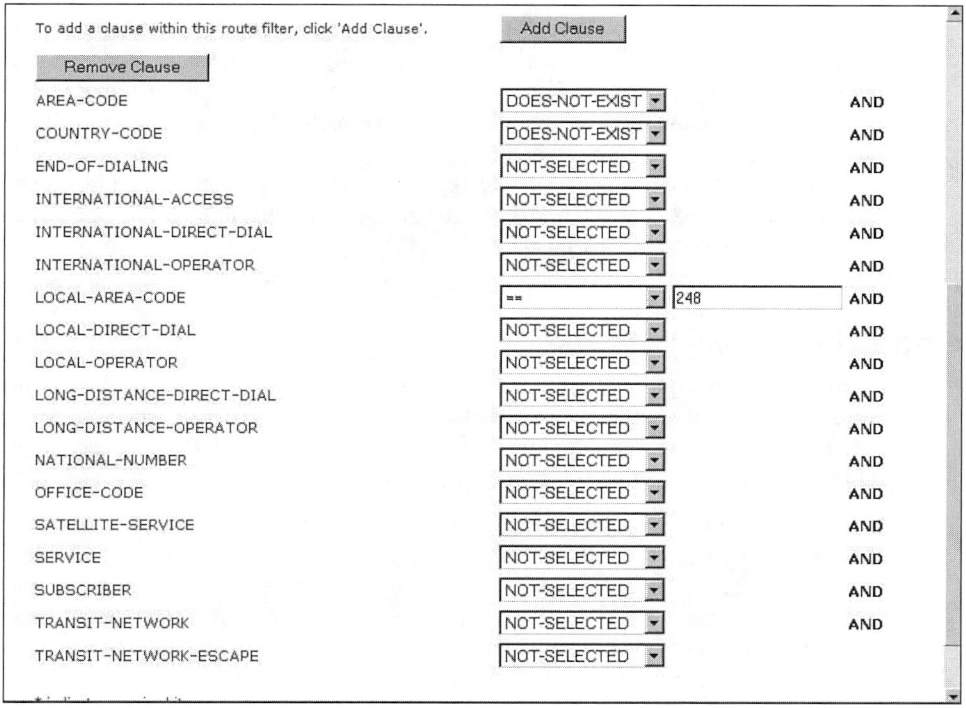

To add a clause within this route filter, click 'Add Clause'.	Add Clause	
Remove Clause		
AREA-CODE	DOES-NOT-EXIST ▾	AND
COUNTRY-CODE	DOES-NOT-EXIST ▾	AND
END-OF-DIALING	NOT-SELECTED ▾	AND
INTERNATIONAL-ACCESS	NOT-SELECTED ▾	AND
INTERNATIONAL-DIRECT-DIAL	NOT-SELECTED ▾	AND
INTERNATIONAL-OPERATOR	NOT-SELECTED ▾	AND
LOCAL-AREA-CODE	== ▾ 248	AND
LOCAL-DIRECT-DIAL	NOT-SELECTED ▾	AND
LOCAL-OPERATOR	NOT-SELECTED ▾	AND
LONG-DISTANCE-DIRECT-DIAL	NOT-SELECTED ▾	AND
LONG-DISTANCE-OPERATOR	NOT-SELECTED ▾	AND
NATIONAL-NUMBER	NOT-SELECTED ▾	AND
OFFICE-CODE	NOT-SELECTED ▾	AND
SATELLITE-SERVICE	NOT-SELECTED ▾	AND
SERVICE	NOT-SELECTED ▾	AND
SUBSCRIBER	NOT-SELECTED ▾	AND
TRANSIT-NETWORK	NOT-SELECTED ▾	AND
TRANSIT-NETWORK-ESCAPE	NOT-SELECTED ▾	

Now that the route filter is created, it must be applied to a route pattern. Typically route filters are applied when the route pattern is created. The steps for creating a route pattern showed how to apply a route filter. The following steps show how to add a route filter to a route pattern that already exists.

Step 1   From within CCMAdmin, select **Route Plann>Route/Hunt>Route Pattern**

Step 2   Search for the route pattern to which you want to add the route filter. You can search by Pattern, Description, or Partition by selecting one of these from the first drop-down list. In the next drop-down list, select the Search Match Operator and enter the search criteria in the field to the left of the Find button. Click the **Find** button. Leaving the search criteria empty results in returning all route patterns. You can use the drop-down list to the left of Items Per Page to select how many results you want returned on a page.

Step 3   From the results that display, select the route pattern to which you want to add the route filter.

Step 4   The next page that displays shows the properties of the route pattern you selected. From the Route Filter drop-down list, select the route filter you wish to apply to this pattern.

Step 5   Click the **Update** button to save the changes.

As you can see, route filters have a significant effect on the route patterns to which they are applied. Make sure that once you have created and applied route filters to route patterns, the pattern behaves as you expect. The Dialed Number Analyzer is a good tool for verifying the results. This tool can be found on, and installed from, the Install Plugins page. The Dialed Number Analyzer allows you to enter an origination and destination number, and shows you how the call will be handled based on the current dial plan. For more information on this tool, refer to the Dialed Number Analyzer guide which can be found at Cisco.com by searching "Dialed Number Analyzer."

Creating Translation Patterns

At times, digit manipulation might be necessary, other than at the route pattern or route group level. This is where translation patterns can be used. Translation patterns allow caller and calling digit manipulation to be performed. Translation patterns can also change the calling search space and MLPP Precedence of a call.

The issues that one can address using translation patterns are limited only by one's imagination. Often, I come across interesting problems that are resolved using translation patterns. The change in extension numbers represents one of the more common issues that translation patterns can help resolve. Often when a company moves, it is forced to get a new range of DID numbers from the phone company. More times than not, the new range is completely different than the old range. When the last few digits of a person's DID is also his or her extension number (which is normal), the person ends up with a new extension number after the move. Employees are used to dialing the old extensions, which are no longer valid, so the call fails. By creating a translation pattern that matches the old extension and transforms it to the new extension, frustration is reduced while the users get used to the new extension range.

Let's take a closer look at how this would work. Assume that the old extension range was 5000-5999, but the new DID range is 7000-7999. The only part of the extension number that changes is the first digit, so a translation pattern of 5XXX is created that changes 5XXX to 7XXX. When a user dialed 5050, it matches the 5XXX translation pattern and changes the called number to 7050. Because 7050 is the new extension, the call is extended to the phone.

Another use for a translation pattern is changing the calling search space of a call. An example of this is used with Cisco Personal Assistant (PA). PA has the ability to intercept calls on behalf of a PA user and route the call based on rules that the user creates. This is done by creating a CTI Route Point that matches the extension of all PA users' phones. The phones are then placed in a partition to which only PA has access. This works wonderfully until PA is not functioning; at this point, all calls to PA users' phones fail. By creating a translation pattern that also matches the PA users' phones and assigning a calling search space that has access to the PA users' phones, calls are allowed directly to the phone if PA fails. More complete information on the configuration can be found in the PA installation guide, but the previous summary gives you an idea of how a translation pattern can help resolve this issue by granting a call in the required calling search space.

The following steps show how to create and configure a translation pattern.

Step 1   From within CCMAdmin, select **Route Plan>Translation Pattern.**

Step 2   Click the **Add a New Translation Pattern** link.

Step 3   A screen similar to that shown in Figure 4-13 displays. In the Translation Pattern field, enter the pattern that you want to match. For example, if you are trying to match all calls to the extensions from 2000 to 2999, enter 2XXX.

Step 4   The Partition field determines what devices are able to access this pattern. Partitions are discussed in more detail in Chapter 5, "Configuring Class of Service and Call Admission Control." Select the desired partition from the drop-down Partition list.

Step 5   In the Description field, enter a description that helps identify the purpose of this pattern.

Step 6   In the Numbering Plan field, choose the appropriate numbering plan.

Step 7   From the Route Filter drop-down list, select the route filter that is to be applied to this pattern. Route filters are used to limit what digits match the pattern and are only used when the pattern contains the (@).

Step 8   From the Calling Search Space drop-down list, select the calling search space for this translation pattern.

Figure 4-13 *Translation Pattern Configuration*

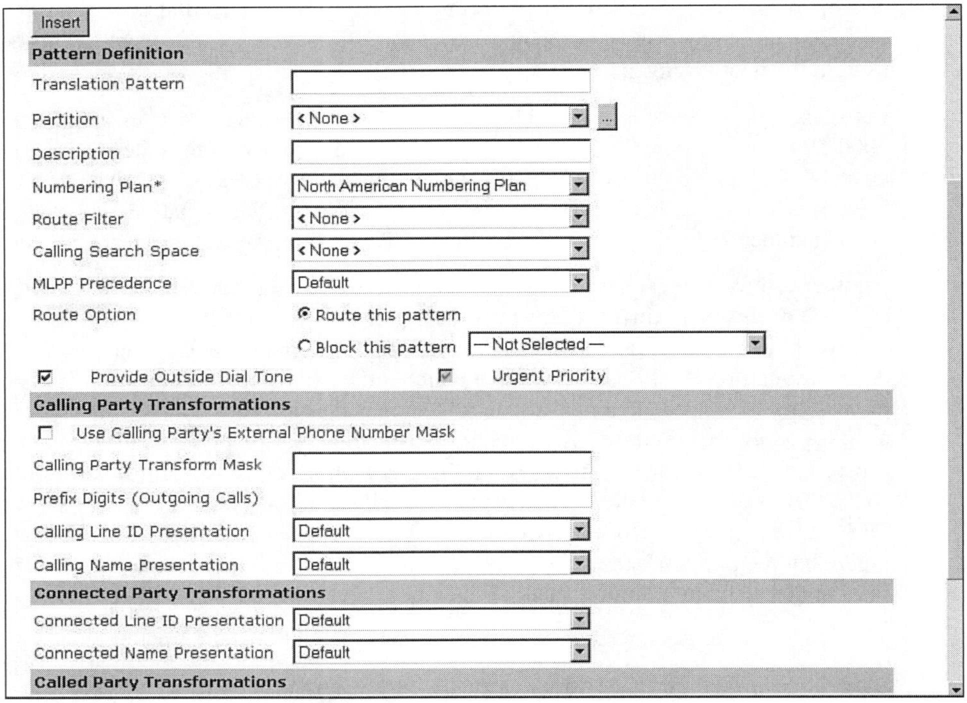

Step 9 Determine the precedence level that will be assigned to this pattern from the MLPP Precedence drop-down list. Refer to Table 4-2 earlier in this chapter for the available options.

Step 10 To allow calls to be routed that match this pattern, select the **Route this pattern** radio button. To disallow calls that match this pattern select the **Block this pattern** radio button. When you select the button that blocks the pattern, you must select a reason from the drop-down list to the right of the radio button.

Step 11 To provide a secondary dial tone, check the Provide Outside Dial Tone checkbox.

Note Take note that the Urgent Priority box is checked and cannot be unchecked. This means that as soon as a pattern matches a translation pattern the call is sent through the translation pattern; CallManager does not wait for additional digits even if other possible matches exist.

Step 12 The field labeled Use Calling Party's External Phone Number Mask determines if the mask configured on the directory number is used for calls that are routed through this route group.

Step 13 In the Calling Party Transform Mask field, enter any mask you wish to affect the caller ID.

Note	This is where most people make mistakes. Often administrators enter the pattern here to which they want the number changed. This is not correct. This field affects caller ID, not the number dialed. To affect a change on the dialed number, change the Called Party Transform Mask. This is a common mistake because the Called Party Transform Mask field cannot be seen on the screen unless you scroll down.

Step 14 In the Prefix Digits (Outgoing Calls) field, enter any digits that you want added to the front of the caller ID.

Step 15 The Calling Line ID Presentation field determines if caller ID information is to be blocked for outbound calls that match this pattern. To block caller ID, select **Restricted** from the drop-down list. To allow caller ID, select **Allowed** from the drop-down list.

Step 16 The Calling Name Presentation field determines if caller name information is to be blocked for outbound calls that match this pattern. To block calling name ID, select **Restricted** from the drop-down list. To allow calling name ID, select **Allowed** from the drop-down list.

Step 17 The Connected Line ID Presentation field determines if the connected party's ID information is to be displayed on the calling party's phone. To block the connected party's ID, select **Restricted** from the drop-down list. To allow the connected party's ID, select **Allowed** from the drop-down list.

Step 18 The Connected Name Presentation field determines if the connected party's name information is displayed on the calling party's phone. To block a connected party's name, select **Restricted** from the drop-down list. To allow a connected party's name, select **Allowed** from the drop-down list.

Step 19 The next set of fields determines if digit manipulation is performed on the dial digits. From the Discard Digits drop-down list, select the digit discard instruction that should be applied to calls that match this pattern. These instructions are explained in Table 4-1.

Step 20 In the Called Party Transform Mask field, enter the mask you want to use for calls that match this pattern. This field determines how the dialed digits will be transformed.

Step 21 In the Prefix Digits (Outgoing Calls) field, enter any digits that you want added to the front of the dialed number before it is sent to the route list.

Step 22 Click the **Insert** button at the top of the page to add this translation pattern.

At this point you should feel comfortable with translation patterns and understand how to create them. When trying to create custom solutions, make sure you keep translation patterns in mind because they can be used in a limitless number of ways.

Creating CTI Route Points

The last dial plan component that is covered in this chapter is CTI Route Points. CTI Route Points can be viewed as virtual ports that allow connectivity to other services and devices. CTI Route Points are also sometimes used as "dummy" phones when you have a DID that is associated with a voicemail box, but not assigned to a physical phone. A CTI Route Point can be created that matches the DID number. This number is then configured to forward all calls directly to the voicemail system.

The creation and configuration of CTI Route Points is very similar to that of a phone. The following steps show how to create and configure a CTI route point:

Step 1 From within CCMAdmin, **select Device>CTI Route Point.**

Step 2 Click the **Add a New CTI Route Point Route Point** link.

Step 3 A screen similar to that shown in Figure 4-14 displays. The first field that must be configured is the Device Name for this route point. Use a name that helps identify the function of this route point. For instance, if this route point is to be used with PA, a name such as "PA_Route_Point" would be a good choice.

Step 4 The next field is the Description field. Enter a description that helps you quickly identify the CTI route point.

Step 5 From the **Device Pool** drop-down list, select the device pool this CTI route point will use.

Step 6 A Calling Search Space (CSS) determines what destination the CTI Route Point will be able to reach. CSS is discussed in Chapter 5: Configuring Class of Service and Call Admission Control. Choose a CSS from the Calling Search Space drop-down list. If this field is left at None, the dial privileges of this CTI route point could be limited.

Step 7 Locations are used to prevent WAN links from becoming oversubscribed in centralized deployments. These are discussed more in Chapter 5: Configuring Class of Service and Call Admission Control. If you have defined locations, select the appropriate one for this CTI route point from the Location drop-down list.

Figure 4-14 *CTI Route Point Configuration*

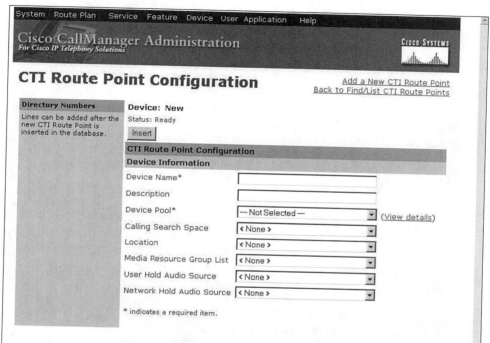

Step 8   The Media Resource Group List field determines to which media resources this CTI Route Point will have access. Media resources are discussed in further detail in Chapter 6: Configuring CallManager Features and Services. From the Media Resource Group List drop-down list, select the desired group. If no media resource group list is chosen, the one defined in the device pool is used.

Step 9   The next two fields allow you to configure what audio source is heard when a call is placed on hold. The first of the two, which is labeled User Hold Audio Source, determines what is heard when the call is placed on hold by the application. The Network Hold Audio Source determines what audio is heard when network initiates the hold. Select the desired audio source from the drop-down list for each field. If no audio source is chosen, the one defined in the device pool is used.

Step 10 Click the **Insert** button to create the CTI Route Point. An informational window displays informing you that the CTI Route Point has been added and that a line needs to be configured. Click **OK**.

Adding a Line to a CTI Route Point

Step 1   If you are adding a new CTI Route Point and have used the previous steps, you should see a screen similar to that shown in Figure 4-15. To add a line to an existing CTI Route Point, follow steps 2 through 5 to reach this screen. If you are already at this screen skip to step 6.

Figure 4-15   *CTI Route Point Directory Number Configuration*

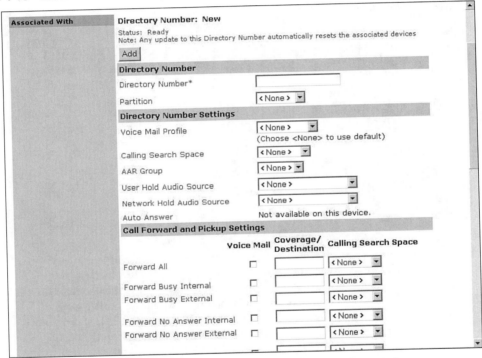

Step 2   From within CCMAdmin, select **Device>CTI Route Point**.

Step 3   Enter search criteria in the search field to limit the results and click the **Find** button.

Step 4   Select the CTI Route Point to which you want to add a line from the list that is generated.

Step 5   On the left side of the CTI Route Point Configuration screen, the available lines are listed. Choose a line that has the label **Add new DN**.

Step 6   The first required field is the Directory Number. Enter the extension number in this field.

Step 7   The Partition field defines the partition to which this directory number is assigned. The partition is used to determine what devices may call this extension. Partitions are discussed in more detail in Chapter 5, "Configuring Class of Service and Call Admission Control." Select the partition for this extension from the drop-down list.

Step 8   The field labeled Voice Mail Profile determines which voice mail profile this directory number uses. Voice mail profiles are discussed in further detail in Chapter 6, "Configure CallManager Features and Services." Select the voice mail profile from the drop-down list.

Step 9   The next field allows a Calling Search Space to be assigned at the line level. This determines what destinations can be reached by this CTI Route Point. Select the Calling Search Space from the drop down menu.

Step 10 The AAR Group field determines the AAR group with which this line is associated. An AAR group defines the prefix that is assigned when a call fails due to insufficient bandwidth. AAR is discussed in further detail in Chapter 6, "Configuring CallManager Features and Services." Select an AAR group if AAR is being used. If this field is set to None AAR, is, in effect, disabled on this line.

Step 11 The next two fields allow you to configure what audio source is heard when a call is placed on hold. The first of the two, which is labeled User Hold Audio Source, determines what is heard when the call is placed on hold by the application. The Network Hold Audio Source determines what audio is heard when network initiates the hold. Select the desired audio source from the drop-down list for each field. If no audio source is chosen, the one defined in the device pool is used.

Step 12 The Auto Answer field is not a configurable field for CTI Route Points.

Step 13 The next eight fields deal with call forwarding. These fields determine the destination of a forwarded call depending on the reason for the forward. The eight types of forwards are:

- Forward All—Forwards all incoming calls

- Forward Busy Internal—Forwards calls from internal callers when the line is busy

- Forward Busy External—Forwards calls from external callers when the line is busy

- Forward No Answer Internal—Forwards calls from internal callers that are not answered

- Forward No Answer External—Forwards calls from external callers that are not answered

- Forward No Coverage Internal—Forwards calls from internal callers when a CTI route point has no coverage

— Forward No Coverage External—Forwards calls from external callers when a CTI route point has no coverage

— Forward On Failure Ext/Int—Forwards both internal and external calls when the controlling application fails

You may configure each type of Call Forward field to forward calls to voice mail or a specific extension. To forward to voice mail, check the box under the Voice Mail label. For this to work, a voice mail profile must be defined for this line. To forward calls to another extension, enter the extension number in the Destination field. A calling search space can be applied to each forward type, which limits where a call can be forwarded. Enter the appropriate destinations and calling search spaces for each forward type.

Step 14 In the No Answer Ring Duration field, enter the number of seconds that the CTI Route Point will ring before forwarding to the Forward No Answer destination.

Step 15 The Call Pickup Group field determines to which call pickup group this directory number belongs. Call pickup groups allow users to redirect an incoming call on another device to their phones. Select the desired call pickup group from the drop-down list. Call pickup groups are covered in more detail in Chapter 6, "Configuring CallManager Features and Services."

Step 16 The next set of parameters deals with MLPP alternate party settings. These settings allow you to configure an alternate destination for precedence calls that are not answered on this line, or the forwarded number assigned to this line. If MLPP is not being used, these parameters can be left empty. In the first field, which is labeled Target (Destination), enter the number to which unanswered precedence calls should be forwarded.

Step 17 In the MLPP alternate party Calling Search Space field, select the appropriate search space from the drop-down list. This calling search space limits the destinations to which precedence calls can be forwarded.

Step 18 In the MLPP alternate party No Answer Ring Duration field, enter the number of seconds that the phone will ring when it receives a precedence call before forwarding to the "Forward No Answer" destination if unanswered.

Step 19 In the Alerting Name field, enter the name that should be displayed on the caller's phone.

Step 20 The Display (Internal Caller ID) field is used to configure what caller ID is displayed when calls are placed to other internal callers. Enter up to 30 characters. Both letters and numbers can be used in this field. If this field is left blank, the lines directory numbers are used.

Step 21 The next field, labeled Line Text Label, is not used for CTI Route Points.

Step 22 The External Phone Number Mask field is used to modify the external caller ID for calls placed from this line.

Step 23 The next field, labeled Message Waiting Lamp Policy, is not used for CTI Route Points.

Step 24 The next two settings, which determine if the device rings when incoming calls are being received on this directory number, are not used for CTI Route Points.

Step 25 The Maximum Number of Calls field, determines how many active calls can be on this line. The maximum is 10,000 active calls per CTI route point. Enter the maximum number of calls in this field.

Step 26 The Busy Trigger field determines how many active calls are required before the line is considered busy.

Step 27 The Forwarded Call Information Display section determines what information is sent when a call is forwarded. Select the information to be sent by checking the box next to each desired field.

Step 28 The last field on this page is the Character Set. Select the character set that is to be used on the display setting for this line from the drop-down list.

Step 29 Click the **Add** button at the top of the screen to add this line.

Step 30 An informational message appears stating that the directory number has been added. Press **OK**.

The number of CTI Route Points you need depends on how many applications you need to connect to and their individual requirements. Be sure to refer to the specific application installation guide when configuring CTI Route Points to ensure that you set all the parameters correctly.

Summary

This chapter has covered the tasks required to implement a basic dial plan. The call flow was explored to give the reader a good overview of the components that make up a dial plan. After that, each individual component was discussed including route groups, route lists and route patterns, and step-by-step configuration. Additional components that are used in more advanced dial plans such as route filters, translation patterns, and CTI Route Point were also covered. After completing this chapter, the reader should feel comfortable with how a basic dial plan works and how to configure one. The next chapter covers components that can be added to a dial plan to restrict certain devices from placing calls to certain destinations, and ways to ensure that WAN links are not over-subscribed, which in turn helps maintain good voice quality.

Configuring Class of Service and Call Admission Control

Now that you have created a basic dial plan, it is time to build on that and create a more complete dial plan. Often you will want to allow and disallow access to certain destinations. For example, you may want only a certain group of callers to be able to dial international numbers. This is done by creating a telephony Class of Service (CoS). In addition, if there are calls traversing limited bandwidth links, some type of Call Admission Control (CAC) should be deployed to help ensure voice quality. This chapter examines the various concepts associated with CoS and CAC and how to configure the required components for each.

Rights and Restrictions

After the dial plan is created and users are able to place calls to destinations outside the cluster, you may think that you are all set and can sit back and relax. Not quite. After the system is configured to allow calls to be placed outside of the system, you need to start working on how to prevent certain calls from being placed. We touched on how you can use route patterns to block certain destinations, and now we need to move beyond that and discuss how certain destinations will be reachable by some devices, but not by others. To accomplish this you need to configure what are known as Calling Search Spaces (CSS) and partitions. This section explains what these are and how they work.

Understanding Call Search Spaces and Partitions

Of all the concepts within a CallManager environment, I believe the CSS and partitions cause the most confusion. This is rather odd because they are quite simple. Simply put, the partition assigned to the destination affects what devices can reach it, and the CSS determines which destinations can be reached. Locks and key rings are good analogies. Think of the partition as a lock and the CSS as the key ring. To place a call to a destination, you must have a key that matches up with the device's lock. The key ring contains all the keys and therefore determines which destinations you can reach.

Of course, there is more to it than just locks and keys, but by using this analogy you begin to understand how they work. Let's take a closer look at this analogy. Figure 5-1 shows five phones. The first four phones have partitions (locks). It is important to point out the partitions (locks) are not assigned to devices, but rather to patterns and Directory Numbers (DNs). For this example, assume that each phone has only a single line and the partition (lock) is assigned to that line. Below each phone is a CSS (key ring), which shows to which partitions (locks) the phone has access. CSS (key rings) can be assigned to the device or the line. In this example, assume they are assigned to the device.

Figure 5-1 *Calling Search Spaces and Partitions Analogy*

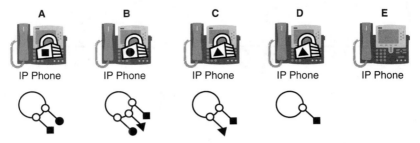

The locks in this example have differently shaped keyholes, which means that to open a lock you must have a key ring that has the correct shape key. Keeping in mind that the locks represent partitions and the key rings represent CSS answer the following questions:

- What phones can phone A reach?
- What phones can phone D reach?
- What phone can reach all other phones?
- What phones can reach phone E?
- What phones can phone E reach?

Let's take a look at the answer to these questions.

Q. What phones can phone A reach?

A. To determine what phones phone A can reach, we need to look at its CSS (key ring). Phone A has a circular key and a square key on its key ring, which means it can call itself and phone B. However, because phone E has no lock (partition) assigned to it, any phone can reach it, just as a door with no lock can be opened by anyone.

Q. What phones can phone D reach?

A. Because phone D has only a square key, it can dial phone A and, of course, phone E because it has no lock (partition.)

Q. What phone can reach all other phones?

A. Because phone B has a key ring (CSS) that contains all the keys, it can reach all the devices.

Q. What phones can reach phone E?

A. Because phone E has no lock (partition) all phones can reach it.

Q. What phones can phone E reach?

A. Because phone E has no keys, it can only reach devices that have no locks. In this example phone E can only dial itself.

Figure 5-1, along with these questions and answers, should help you begin to understand how partitions and CSS work. Of course, as with any simple concept, it has the potential to become more complicated as the number of CSS and partitions grows. This is where some people begin to become confused, due to an inaccurate base understanding of the concepts. Let's look at some of the more interesting aspects of CSS and partitions.

The first misconception that should be dispelled is this: if two devices have the same partition, they can call each other. Having the same partition alone is not enough. Going back to the lock and key ring analogy, if two people have the same locks, keyed the same way on their houses, but they have no keys, can they access each other's houses? Of course they can't, and as a matter of fact, they cannot even access their own houses. This demonstrates that a device's partition (lock) has no effect on where the device can call. However, if two devices that have the same partition also have a CSS that allows them access to their partitions, they can dial each other.

The next important point is the order of CSS. As demonstrated in the earlier example, CSS can allow access to more than one partition. Now, imagine that a device has a CSS that allows it to match two devices with the same number, but in different partitions. Figure 5-2 offers an example of this situation.

Figure 5-2   *CSS Matches Multiple Destinations*

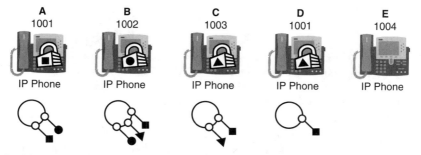

In this example phones A and D have the same extension of 1001. Phones B and C can reach both phones because their CSS allows access to both the square and triangle partition. So the question is, which phone rings when phone C dials 1001? Often people answer this question with, "It takes the closer match." Because 1001 matches 1001 exactly, both phones are the closest matches. Others assume both phones ring because phone C has access to both partitions. What actually happens is that when a search for a match is conducted, multiple closest matches are found. Because there are multiple closest matches, the order in which objects appear in the CSS comes into play. When you create a CSS, you prioritize the order in which partitions should be searched. This order determines which partition is used if there are two closest matches. In the example, Figure 5-2 shows that the order of the keys for phone C is square followed by triangle, meaning that when phone C dials 1001, it would first match the 1001 that has the square partition, which is phone A.

To add a little more complexity to this, it is possible to have a CSS on both the device and the line. For instance, the phone can have a CSS that grants access to the square partition and a line on the phone can have a CSS that grants access to the triangle partition. In such a case, the line CSS takes priority. Figure 5-3 shows an example of this. This example moves away from the locks and keys analogy to focus more on the actual terms.

Figure 5-3   *Line/Device CSS Example*

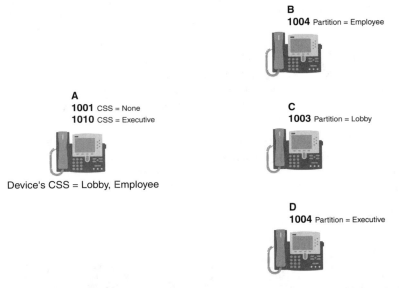

In the example illustrated by Figure 5-3, phone A has two lines, 1001 and 1010. 1001 has no CSS, and line 1010 has a CSS that grants access to devices in the Exec partition. Phone A also has a CSS at the device level, which allows access to devices in the lobby and employee partitions. Because the 1001 line does not have a CSS of its own, it has access only to devices that can be reached using the device's CSS. Because line 1010 has a CSS of its own, it has access to devices that can be reached using its CSS and the device's CSS. This means that when dialing from line 1001, only devices in the lobby and employee partitions are accessible; but when dialing from line 1010, devices in the lobby, employee, and exec partitions are accessible.

Now, take a look at the other three phones. Phone B has the extension of 1004, and that line is in the employee partition. Phone C has the extension of 1003, and that line is in the lobby partition. Phone D has the extension of 1004, and that line is in the exec partition.

Using what you have learned, answer the following three questions:

- What is the result if 1004 is dialed from line 1001?

- What is the result if 1004 is dialed from line 1010?
- Can line 1010 reach line 1003?

Let's take a look at the answers to these questions.

What is the result if 1004 is dialed from line 1001?

Because line 1001 has no CSS of its own, it relies solely on the device's CSS. The device's CSS has access to the employee and lobby partitions, so line 1001 can reach only the 1004 on phone B because it is in the employee partition.

What is the result if 1004 is dialed from line 1010?

Because line 1010 has a CSS, it has access to all devices to which the line and device's CSS grants access. Because it can reach both phone B and D and both of them match 1004, the line's CSS takes priority and phone D rings.

Can line 1010 reach line 1003?

Line 1010 can reach any device to which the line and/or the device's CSS grants access. Because the device's CSS has access to the lobby partition, which is the partition that 1003 is in, it can reach it.

At this point, you should have a good idea of how partitions and CSS work. Let's take a look at a real-world, practical example of how CSS and partitions can be used.

The BGD Company has deployed a CallManager solution and has configured the route patterns that are shown in Table 5-1. As you can see, the route patterns allow callers to reach anywhere they may need to dial with the exceptions of 1-900 numbers, which are blocked. The problem is that these patterns also let some callers make calls that the company disapproves. For example, if a person's job does not require the placement of international calls, the dial plan should not allow the employee's phone to place them.

Table 5-1   *BGD's Route Patterns*

Pattern	Notes	Matches
9.[2-9]XXXXXX	PreDot Discard	Local 7 and 10 digit calls
9.810[2-9]XXXXXX	PreDot Discard	
9.810586XXXX	PreDot Discard	10 digit calls that are not local
9.810587XXXX	PreDot Discard	
9.1[2-9]XX[2-9]XXXXXX	PreDot Discard	Long distance calls
9.011!	PreDot Discard	International calls
9.011!#	PreDot Trailing-# Discard	
9.1900[2-9]XXXXXX	Block Pattern	1-900 numbers
911	Urgent Priority	Emergency Service calls
9.911	PreDot Discard and Urgent Priority	

In this example, BGD has decided that it really has four classes of users. The first class, the executives, are able to make any calls they want, other than 1-900 calls. The second class, the administrative assistants, are not allowed to make 1-900 calls or international calls. The third class, standard users, can only reach internal, local numbers, and emergency services. The fourth class, lobby phones, for example, can only make calls internally and to emergency services. To accomplish this, partitions and CSS must be configured and assigned to patterns and devices.

A common practice when creating partitions is to name them so that the name describes to what the partition is assigned. For instance, a partition that is going to be assigned to a pattern that matches a local number may be called Local_PT.

TIP   The PT at the end of the name helps identify this object as a partition. Because it is possible to have partitions and CSS with the same name, it is recommended that you add a PT to the end of partition names and CSS to the end of CSS names.

In this example, five types of calls are allowed: internal, local, long distance, international and emergency. The following is the list of partitions that are needed, and to which patterns they are assigned.

- Internal_PT–patterns that match internal numbers
- Local_PT–patterns that match local numbers
- Long_Distance_PT–patterns that match long distance numbers
- International_PT–patterns that match international numbers
- Emergency_PT–patterns that match emergency service numbers

After the partitions are created, CSS are needed. Because BGD has defined four classes of users, four CSS are needed. Just as with partitions, it is recommended that CSS are named so that the name helps identify to which partitions the CSS have access. Table 5-2 shows the CSS and the partitions to which each has access and that are needed for BGD.

Table 5-2   *CSS and Associated Partitions*

CSS	Partitions
Internal_CSS	Internal_PT
	Emergency_PT
Internal_Local_CSS	Internal_PT
	Local_PT
	Emergency_PT

Table 5-2   *CSS and Associated Partitions (Continued)*

CSS	Partitions
Internal_Local_LD_CSS	Internal_PT Local_PT Long_Distance_PT Emergency_PT
Unlimited_CSS	Internal_PT Local_PT Long_Distance_PT International_PT Emergency_PT

Now that partitions and CSS are defined, let's take a look at to what each is assigned. First, let's examine the partitions. It is important to understand that partitions are assigned to patterns of DNs, not devices. This means that if you want to prevent a device from making long distance calls, you assign a partition to the patterns that match long distance numbers, and make sure that the device's CSS does not have access to the partition. Table 5-3 shows the five partitions that have been created and the patterns to which each is assigned.

Table 5-3   *Partitions and Patterns*

Partitions	Patterns
Internal_PT	DNs of the phones
Local_PT	9.[2-9]XXXXXX 9.810[2-9]XXXXXX
Long_Distance_PT	9.810586XXXX 9.810587XXXX 9.1[2-9]XX[2-9]XXXXXX
International_PT	9.011! 9.011!#
Emergency_PT	911 9.911

You may notice that the 9.1900[2-9]XXXXXX pattern has not been assigned to a partition, but this will still work. Remember, if a pattern does not have a partition explicitly assigned, it falls into the null partition, and all devices have access to the null partition. Because the 9.1900[2-9]XXXXXX pattern is set up so that it blocks all calls that match it, we want all devices to have access to it, so that no one is able to place these types of calls. However it is recommended to apply partitions to all patterns to ensure that no calls can be placed by phones that do not have the proper CSS. With this is mind, the Internal_PT partition can be applied to the 9.1900[2-9]XXXXXX pattern because all devices can reach that partition.

Now let's look at how the CSS should be assigned. Remember that CSS can be assigned at both the device and line. For this example they are assigned at the device level only. Table 5-4 shows the CSS and the types of device to which each is assigned.

Table 5-4   *CSS and Assigned Devices*

CSS	Devices
Unlimited_CSS	Executive phones
Internal_Local_LD_CSS	Administrative assistant phones
Internal_Local_CSS	Standard users
Internal_CSS	Lobby phones

Now that you understand what CSS and partitions are needed for BGD, and where each is applied, let's take a look at the big picture. Table 5-5 shows which CSS is assigned to each of the four different classes of phones. Under each CSS the partitions it can access are listed, and under each partition the patterns that have the partitions that are listed. Using this table, it is easy to see what destinations various phones can reach.

Table 5-5   *CSS Assigned To Phones and The Patterns They Can Reach*

Devices	CSS>Partition>Patterns
Executive Phones	Unlimited_CSS
	Internal_PT
	All Internal Phones
	Local_PT
	9.[2-9]XXXXXX
	9.810[2-9]XXXXXX
	Long_Distance_PT
	9.810586XXXX
	9.810587XXXX
	9.1[2-9]XX[2-9]XXXXXX
	International_PT
	9.011!
	9.011!#
	Emergency_PT
	911
	9.911

Table 5-5 *CSS Assigned To Phones and The Patterns They Can Reach (Continued)*

Devices	CSS>Partition>Patterns
Administrative Assistant Phones	Internal_Local_LD_CSS
	Internal_PT
	All Internal Phones
	Local_PT
	9.[2-9]XXXXXX
	9.810[2-9]XXXXXX
	Long_Distance_PT
	9.810586XXXX
	9.810587XXXX
	9.1[2-9]XX[2-9]XXXXXX
	Emergency_PT
	911
	9.911
Standard User Phones	Internal_Local_CSS
	Internal_PT
	All Internal Phones
	Local_PT
	9.[2-9]XXXXXX
	9.810[2-9]XXXXXX
	Emergency_PT
	911
	9.911
Lobby Phones	Internal_CSS
	Internal_PT
	All Internal Phones
	Emergency_PT
	911
	9.911

Up to this point, only the assigning of CSS to phones and lines has been discussed. CSS are assigned to devices, which include gateways. A CSS is assigned to a gateway so that inbound calls can reach internal destinations. In the example of BGD, all the internal phones are placed in the Internal_PT partition. If the gateways do not have access to this partition, no incoming calls are allowed. So you can see that not only must phones have

CSS, but gateways require them as well. In the case of BGD, the Internal_CSS can be assigned to the gateways, which would grant outside calls access to all internal phones.

NOTE	Keep in mind that CSS and partitions are only locally significant. This means, for all intents and purposes, that after a call leaves the local system, the CSS and partitions no longer exist.

In the BGD example, all internal phones were in the Internal_PT partition, meaning that because all devices had a CSS that granted access to the Internal_PT partition, all phones could be reached. In some cases, this may not be desired. Sometimes there are certain numbers that should be reached only by certain devices. An example often used is that of an executive's phone. Often it is desired that only the executive's assistant be able to reach the executive. To accomplish this, the executive's phone is placed in a separate partition, to which only the assistant's phone has access.

Now that you have a good idea of what CSS and partitions are, let's move on to how they are created and configured.

Creating Calling Search Spaces and Partitions

Creating CSS and partitions is much easier than understanding and properly applying them. Before you move on to the process of creating them, you should make sure that you have taken the time to determine the different classes of users your environment has, and what destinations each user will be allowed to call. After you have done this, create a list of the partitions that are required. Next, create a CSS that defines what partitions are accessible. After you have created this, you can begin to create the partitions and CSS. Because CSS are created by choosing partitions to which they will have access, the partitions must be created first. The following steps show how to create partitions.

Step 1 From within CCMAdmin, select **Route Plan>Class of Control > Partitions**.

Step 2 Click the **Add a New Partition** link.

Step 3 A screen displays that offers an area in which you can enter the name of the partition followed by a description. You must place a **comma** (,) between the name and description. You may create as many partitions as you would like on this screen by placing each on a new line. Figure 5-4 shows an example of adding five partitions at one time.

Step 4 After you have entered all the desired partitions, click the **Insert** button.

Step 5 A window displays informing you that the partitions were added. Click **OK** in this window.

Figure 5-4   *Creating Partition Configurations*

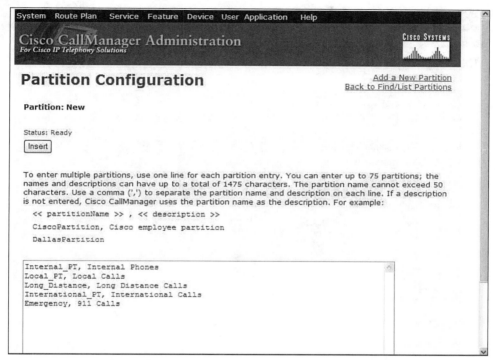

As you can see, the creation of partitions is a very simple task. Now that partitions are added, you can start to create CSS by working through the following steps.

Step 1   From within CCMAdmin, select **Route Plan> Class of Control>Calling Search Space**.

Step 2   Click the Add a New Calling Search Space link.

Step 3   A screen similar to that shown in Figure 5-5 displays.

Step 4   Enter a name in the Calling Search Space Name field. Remember that the name should help identify the purpose of this CSS.

Step 5   Enter a description in the Description field.

Step 6   A list of partitions displays in the Available Partitions box. If you have a large number of partitions, you can limit the partitions that display in this box by entering part of the partition's name in the Find Partitions containing field and clicking the **Find** button.

Step 7   Highlight the first partition to which you want the CSS to have access and click the **down arrow** below this box. This causes that partition to display in the Selected Partitions box.

Figure 5-5 *Creating CSS*

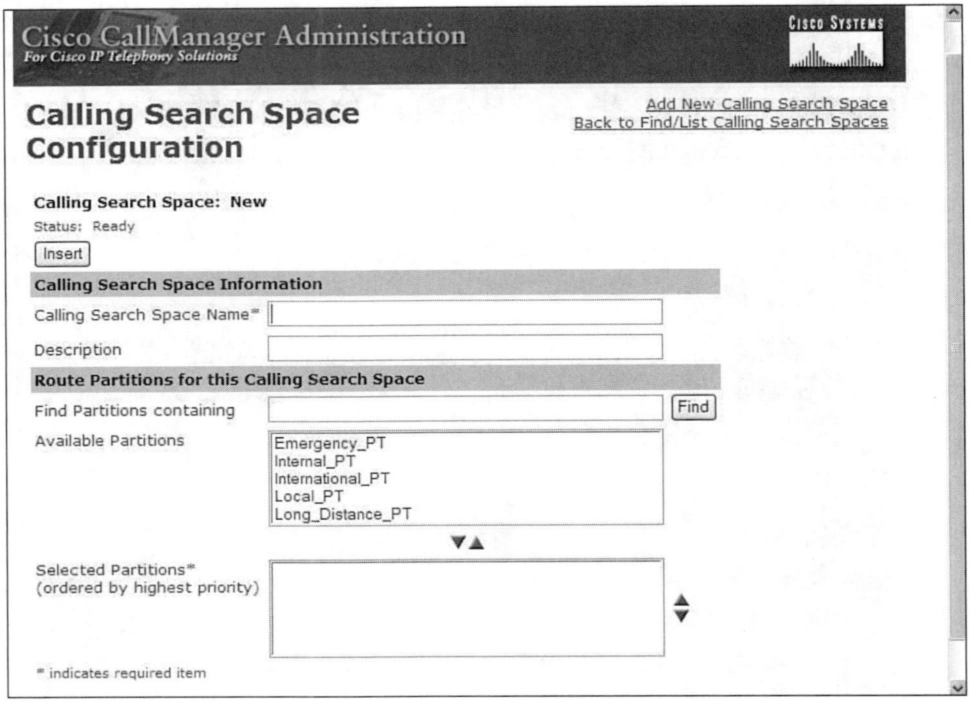

Step 8 Repeat step 7 for each partition to which you want the CSS to have access. These should be added in the order you want them searched.

Step 9 After all the partitions have been added, you can change the order in which they display. Remember, the order in which they display determines which partition is used if multiple partitions within the same CSS contain exact matches for a dialed number. To change the order, highlight the partition you want to move and click the **up** or **down arrow** to the right of the box. Figure 5-6 shows what the screen looks like when adding the Internal_Local_CSS, which was used in the previous example.

Step 10 After all desired partitions are listed in the correct order in the Selected Partitions box, click the **Insert** button.

Step 11 After the CSS is added, you are returned to the CSS configuration screen. You know that the CSS was added because the Status line reads Insert completed.

You need to repeat these steps to add all the CSS your environment requires. After all of the partitions and CSS are added, it is time to apply them. Adding partitions and CSS have absolutely no affect on call processing until they are applied to patterns and devices.

Figure 5-6   *Example CSS*

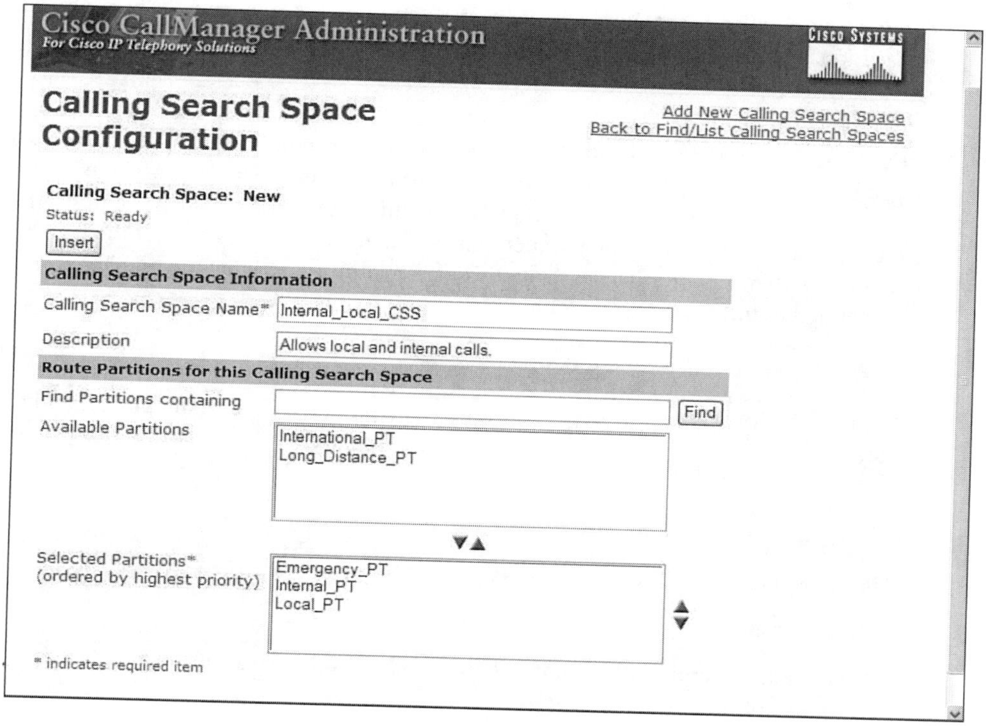

Applying Calling Search Spaces and Partitions

You are now ready to start applying the partitions and CSS to devices and patterns. After a partition is added to a pattern, only devices that have the correct CSS can reach that pattern. For this reason, you may want to assign CSS to the devices before assigning partitions. Assigning partitions before assigning CSS is similar to putting a lock on a door and not giving anyone a key. Until the keys are handed out no one can get in.

NOTE	When adding partitions and CSS to a system, it is best to apply them during nonproduction times. Once added, thorough testing should be done. If it is not possible to add them off-hours, then be certain to apply CSS before applying partitions. A good tool that can be used to verify the results is called the Dialed Number Analyzer. This tool can be installed from the Install Plugins page. This tool allows you to enter an origination and destination number and shows you how the call will be handled, based on the current dial plan. For more information on this tool, refer to the Dialed Number Analyzer guide, which can be found at Cisco.com by searching "Dialed Number Analyzer."

CSS are applied to devices and lines. When applied to both, the line's CSS has priority, but does not nullify the devices. This means a line that has its own CSS has access to partitions that both the line's CSS and the device's CSS allows.

NOTE   Often people want their assistants to be able to answer their lines for them. To do this, you must put the directory number on the assistant's phone. The CSS assigned to the line stays with the line, no matter which phone the line is on. This means if the boss's line has the rights to call international numbers, the assistant can do so as well, if the boss's line is on the assistant's phone. To deal with this, it is recommended that the more generous CSS be applied to the device, not the line.

Let's take a look at how a CSS is assigned to a phone, a line on the phone, and a gateway.

Assigning a CSS to a Phone

The steps that follow show how to assign a CSS to a phone.

Step 1   From within CCMAdmin, Select **Device>Phone**.

Step 2   Enter search criteria in the search field to limit the results and click the **Find** button.

Step 3   Select the phone to which you want to assign a CSS from the list that is generated.

Step 4   The Phone Configuration screen displays. To assign a CSS to the phone, select a CSS from the Calling Search Space drop-down list as shown in Figure 5-7.

Step 5   Click the **Update** button.

Step 6   A window displays informing you that you must reset the phone for the change to take affect. Click **OK**.

Step 7   Click the **Reset Phone** button.

Step 8   A window displays allowing you to reset or restart the phone. Click the **Reset** button.

Step 9   A window displays informing you that the reset has been initiated. Click **OK**.

Figure 5-7   *Assigning a CSS to a Phone*

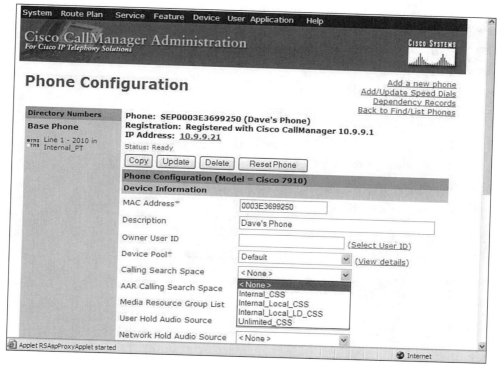

Assigning a CSS to a Line

The steps that follow show how to assign a CSS to a line on a phone.

Step 1   From within CCMAdmin, select **Device>Phone**.

Step 2   Enter search criteria in the search field to limit the results and click the **Find** button.

Step 3   Select the phone that contains the desired line from the list of phones that is generated.

Step 4   Click the desired line on the left side of the screen.

Step 5   On the Directory Number Configuration page, select the desired CSS from the Calling Search Space drop-down list as shown in Figure 5-8.

Step 6   Click the **Update** button.

Figure 5-8 *Assigning a CSS to a Line*

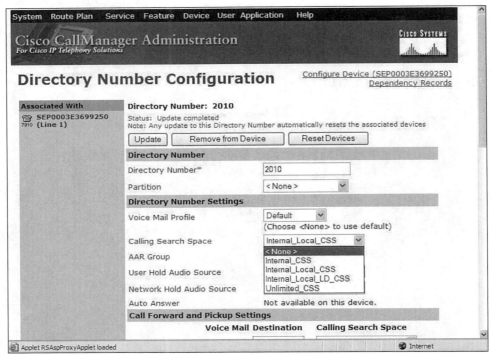

NOTE When you make a change to the directory number configuration and click Update, the line will be reset on all the phones that appear on this line. If a caller is currently on a call, the line resets after the call is ended.

Assigning a CSS to a Gateway or Inter-Cluster Trunk

The steps that follow show how to assign a CSS to a gateway or an intercluster trunk. Because the steps are so similar for both components, they have been combined.

Step 1 From within CCMAdmin, select **Device>Gateway** or **Device>Trunk**.

Step 2 Enter search criteria in the search field to limit the results and click the **Find** button.

Step 3 From the list that is generated, select the Gateway/Trunk to which you want to assign a CSS.

Step 4 Select the CSS from the Calling Search Space drop-down list.

Note	For some gateways such as MGCP, you need to navigate to the subunit configuration page to assign a CSS.

Step 5   Click the **Update** button.

Step 6   A window displays informing you that you must reset the gateway/trunk for the change to occur. Click **OK**.

Step 7   Click the **Reset Gateway** or **Reset Trunk** button.

Step 8   A window displays allowing you to reset or restart the gateway/trunk. Click the **Reset** button.

Step 9   A window displays informing you that the reset has been initiated. Click **OK**.

Now that you have assigned CSS, you can assign partitions. Partitions are assigned to patterns of directory numbers. Examples of how to assign them to CSS and partitions follow.

Assigning a Partition to a Line (Directory Number)

The following steps show how to assign a partition to a line.

Step 1   From within CCMAdmin, select **Device>Phone**.

Step 2   Enter search criteria in the search field to limit the results and click the **Find** button.

Step 3   Select the phone that contains the desired line from the list of phones that is generated.

Step 4   Click the desired line on the left side of the screen.

Step 5   On the Directory Number Configuration page, select the desired partition from the Partition drop-down list as shown in Figure 5-9.

Warning	When you make a change to the directory number configuration and click **Update**, the line will be reset on all the phones that have an appearance of this line. If a caller is currently on a call, the line will reset after the call is ended.

Step 6   Click the **Update** button.

Figure 5-9 *Assigning a Partition to a Line*

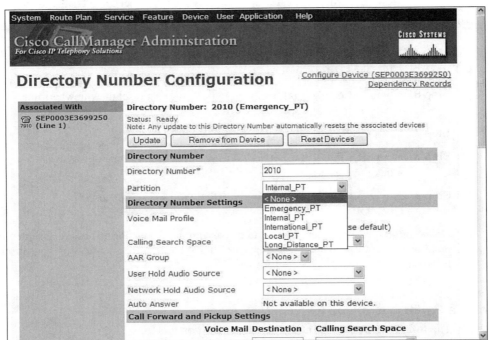

Assigning a Partition to a Pattern

Step 1 From within CCMAdmin, select **Route Plan>Route/Hunt>Route Pattern**.

Step 2 To limit the results, enter search criteria in the search field and click the **Find** button.

Step 3 Select the route pattern from the list that displays.

Step 4 Select the partition from the Partition drop-down list as shown in Figure 5-10.

Step 5 Click the **Update** button. When the update is complete, the status line of the page reads Update completed.

After the partitions are applied, you can begin testing the system to ensure that calls that are allowed can be placed, and those that are not allowed cannot be placed.

Adding CSS and partitions after the system is in place can require a lot of work. Remember that you can use BAT (the Bulk Admin Tool) to quickly apply or change a CSS or partition on a large number of objects.

Figure 5-10 *Assigning a Partition to a Route Pattern*

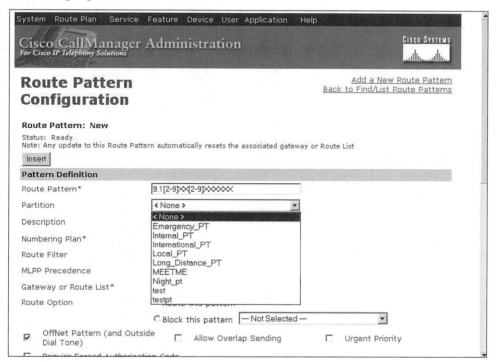

Implementing Call Admission Control

After you have set up your system to allow calls to be placed to outside destinations and have applied CSS and partitions to restrict access, you need to configure the system to ensure the quality of the calls. Although there are many things that can affect the quality of the call, this book deals only with things that can be configured directly in CallManager. This section discusses what must be configured to ensure the Voice over Internet Protocol (VoIP) link is not over subscribed.

When calls are placed between sites using an IP link as the transport, the quality of the call can be affected if more calls are allowed than what the link can support. To prevent this, some type of Call Admission Control must be deployed. How this is accomplished depends on the environment. If the calls are being sent across intercluster trunks, a gatekeeper is required, but if calls are being placed to remote sites that are part of the same cluster, Locations are used. If both types of calls are taking place, both solutions must be deployed.

Locations are objects that are configured within CallManager. A location for each site is created that contains available bandwidth for calls. A closer look at the configuration of locations is offered later in this chapter, but before looking at locations, gatekeepers are examined.

Configuring CAC for a Distributed Deployment

A gatekeeper is a process that runs on a Cisco IOS router. It keeps track of the active calls between clusters and determines if a call can be placed across an intercluster trunk. In most cases, only one gatekeeper is needed because each can support more than a 100 sites. It is recommended, however, to have a redundant gatekeeper. This can be accomplished by having a second router running Hot Standby Routing Protocol (HSRP). The only requirement for the physical location of a gatekeeper is that all clusters must be able to reach it via an IP path.

When a call is placed across a gatekeeper-controlled intercluster trunk, the CallManager on the originating side asks the gatekeeper if the call can be placed. If there is enough bandwidth, the gatekeeper grants admission. If admission is granted, call setup begins and the CallManager on the other side of the call must request admission. If the gatekeeper determines that there is enough bandwidth, admission is granted and the call setup can complete.

A gatekeeper grants admission based upon availability of configured bandwidth. The gatekeeper is configured with the amount of bandwidth that may be used for calls. Each time a call is placed, the gatekeeper removes a certain amount from the available bandwidth. When the call is over, it returns the bandwidth to the available pool.

The amount of bandwidth required for each call depends on which codec is being used. The gatekeeper has the preconfigured amount of bandwidth that each codec requires, and this number cannot be changed. This figure may not be the actual bandwidth the call needs, but is used to ensure that enough bandwidth is available. A gatekeeper running IOS 12.2(2)XA or later assumes 128 kbps is needed for G7.11 calls and 16 kbps for G.729 calls. A gatekeeper running IOS earlier than 12.2(2)XA assumes 64 kbps is needed for G7.11 calls and 64 kbps for G.729 calls. Although it may seem odd that the gatekeeper may request more or less bandwidth than it really needs, it isn't really a problem because the amount of available bandwidth is a setting that you configure in the gatekeeper. The gateway does not have the ability to monitor the link and decide for itself if there is available bandwidth. It relies totally on the number that is configured. It is best to determine how many calls you want to allow on the link and the codec that will be used. Then simply multiply the amount of bandwidth the gatekeeper uses for that codec by the number of calls. The result is the amount of bandwidth that should be configured. For example, if the gatekeeper is running IOS version 12.2(2)XA or later and you want to allow ten calls all using the G.729 codec, the formula is 10x16 (10 calls x 16 kbps) which means 160 kbps will be needed.

The gatekeeper can also be configured to provide the destination IP address to which the call should be sent. This feature is sometimes referred to as an anonymous device. An anonymous device is preferred in many environments, especially those with multiple inter-cluster trunks. When more than two clusters are connected, an intercluster trunk must be created between each cluster if anonymous device is not used. Figure 5-11 shows that when connecting four clusters, 12 intercluster trunks are required.

Figure 5-11 *Inter-cluster trunks*

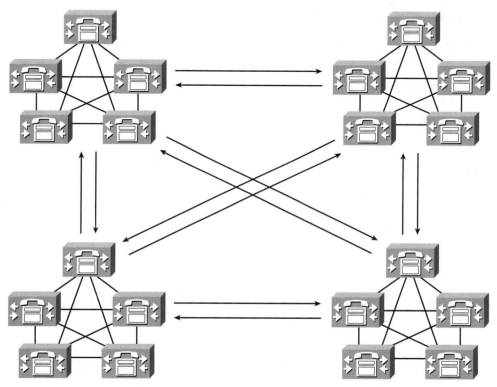

The formula used to determine how many intercluster trunks are required is Nx(N-1). That is the number of clusters times the number of clusters minus 1. In Figure 5-11 there are four clusters. This means that the total number of intercluster trunks is 4x(4-1) or 4x3, which equals 12. As the number of clusters increases, the number of required trunks does as well. For example, with four clusters, 12 intercluster trunks are needed, but with eight clusters, 56 intercluster trunks are needed. This is where an anonymous device becomes extremely useful. Instead of creating all of the intercluster trunks, just one gatekeeper controlled intercluster trunk is created and all calls destined to any of the other clusters are sent to this trunk. When the gatekeeper responds to an admission request, it also provides the IP address of the destination.

Because the gatekeeper is going to provide destination information, it has to know the destination IP address. This is part of the configuration that must be done on the gatekeeper itself. The bandwidth allowed for calls must also be configured in the gatekeeper and to give you an idea of what needs to be configured. The following example is presented that shows a partial configuration.

```
gatekeeper
zone local DTW bgd.com 10.10.12.28
zone prefix DTW 4… 10.10.12.21
gw-type-prefix 1#* default-technology
bandwidth total zone DTW 256
no shutdown
```

A complete explanation of this configuration can be found in the "Configuring an Anonymous Device Gatekeeper with Cisco CallManager Versions 3.3 and 4.1" on Cisco.com. However, to give you an idea of what this is doing, the third command, "zone prefix DTW 4… 10.10.12.21," denotes that calls in the 4000 range should be routed to IP address 10.10.12.21. The fifth command, "bandwidth total zone DTW 256" means that the total amount of bandwidth available for calls to and from DTW is 256kbs.

WARNING The gatekeeper should be configured only by an individual who is extremely knowledgeable of IOS configurations and commands and who thoroughly understands VoIP technologies. Because the gatekeeper may also be serving other routing functions, incorrect configuration could negatively affect the network as a whole.

Configuring a GateKeeper

In addition to the required configuration on the gatekeeper itself, the gatekeeper must also be configured in the CallManager. Adding a gatekeeper in CallManager is quite simple. The following steps show how this is done.

Step 1   From within CCMAdmin, select **Device>Gatekeeper**.

Step 2   Click the **Add a New Gatekeeper** link.

Step 3   A screen similar to that shown in Figure 5-12 displays. Enter the IP address of the gatekeeper in the Host Name/IP Address field.

Step 4   In the Description field, enter a description that helps to identify this gatekeeper.

Step 5   The Registration Request Time to Live field should be left at default. Change this field only if TAC tells you to do so. This field determines how often the CallManager must send a registration keep-alive to the gatekeeper.

Step 6   The Registration Retry Timeout field should be left at default. Change this field only if TAC tells you to do so. This value determines how long CallManager waits before trying to register after a registration attempt fails.

Figure 5-12 *Gatekeeper Configuration*

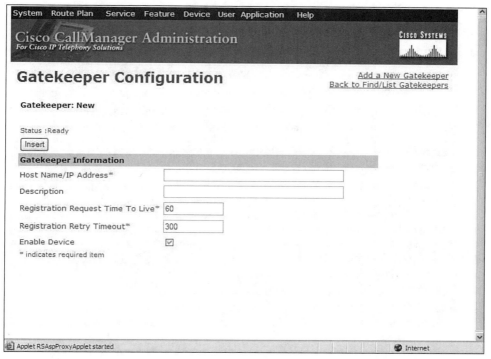

Step 7   Typically, the Enable Device check box should be left checked. This allows the gatekeeper to register with CallManager. When you need to gracefully unregister the gatekeeper, uncheck this box.

Step 8   Click the **Insert** button.

Step 9   A window displays informing you that the gatekeeper must be reset. Click **OK**.

Step 10   Click the **Reset Gatekeeper**.

Step 11   A window displays allowing you to reset or restart the gatekeeper. Click the **Reset** button.

Step 12   A window displays informing you that the reset has been initiated. Click **OK**.

After a gatekeeper is configured, you must create a Gatekeeper Controlled Intercluster Trunk so that the calls placed across the intercluster trunk request admission from the gatekeeper. This also allows you to take advantage of the anonymous device features if the gatekeeper is configured to provide call routing information. Creating a gatekeeper-controlled intercluster trunk is very similar to creating a nongatekeeper controlled intercluster trunk.

Configuring a Gatekeeper Controlled Intercluster Trunk

The following steps show how to configure a Gatekeeper Controlled Intercluster Trunk and explain its various settings.

Step 1   From within CCMAdmin, select **Device>Add a New Device>**.

Step 2   On the Add a New Device page, select **Trunk** from the Device Type drop-down list and click **Next**.

Step 3   On the next page, select the **Inter-Cluster Trunk (Gatekeeper Controlled)** from the Trunk Type drop-down list.

Step 4   The Device Protocol field can be left at Inter-Cluster Trunk. No other option is available. Click the **Next** button.

Step 5   The Trunk Configuration screen, as shown in Figure 5-13, displays. Enter a functional name for the gateway in the Device Name field.

Figure 5-13 *Trunk Configuration*

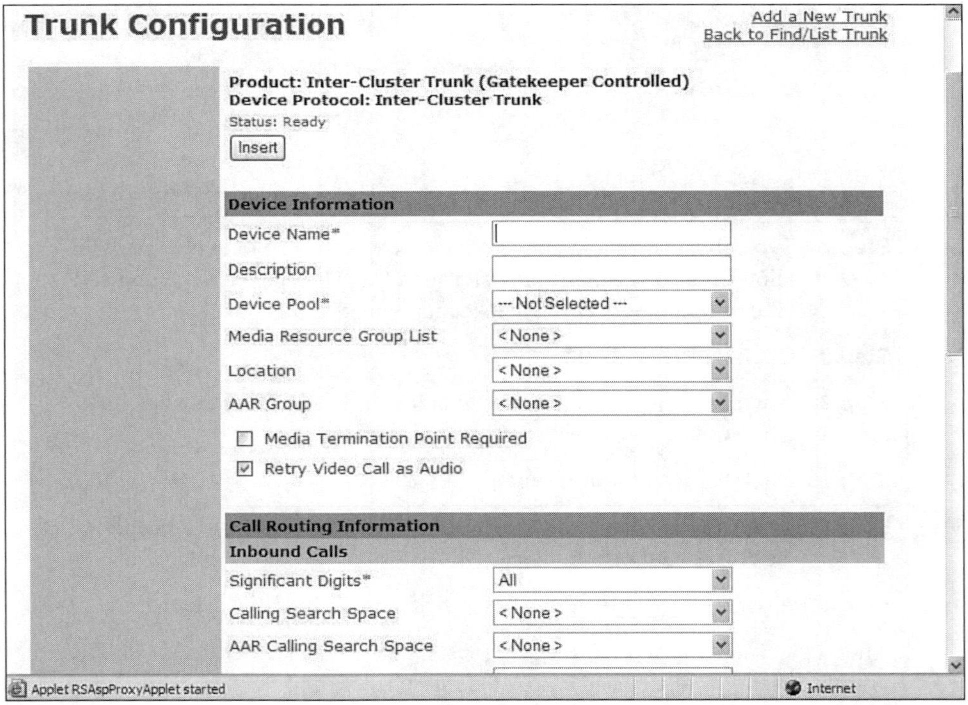

Step 6   In the Description field, enter a description that makes this device easily identifiable.

Step 7   From the Device Pool drop-down list, select the desired device pool for this gateway.

Step 8   The Device Destination is used to determine if calls on this trunk will be considered an OnNet (on network) or OffNet (off network) call. Different alerting tones are used for OnNet and OffNet calls. By default, this is set to OnNet. If you are unsure of the value to assign, leave it at the default.

Step 9   The next field is the Media Resource Group List. This determines to what media resources this gateway will have access.

Step 10   Locations are used to prevent wide-area network (WAN) links from becoming oversubscribed in centralized deployments. These are discussed later in this chapter. If you have defined locations, select the appropriate one for this trunk from the drop-down list.

Step 11   The Automated Alternate Routing (AAR) Group field determines the AAR group with which this trunk is associated. An AAR group defines the prefix that is assigned when a call fails due to insufficient bandwidth. AAR is discussed in further detail in Chapter 6, "Configuring CallManager Features and Services." Select an AAR group if AAR is being used. If this field is set to **None** AAR is, in effect, disabled on this trunk.

Step 12   The Tunneled Protocol drop-down list allows you to select Q Signaling (QSIG), which enables ICT to transport non-H.323 protocol information by tunneling it through H.323. Leave this set to None unless you know that this type of tunneling is required.

Step 13   The Media Termination Point Required check box needs to be checked if the H.323 device does not support features such as hold and transfers.

Step 14   If the Retry Video Calls as Audio box is checked, CallManager sets up a voice call if a video call fails to setup.

Step 15   The Path Replacement Support is automatically checked if you select QSIG from the Tunneled Protocol drop-down list. Otherwise it is left unchecked.

Step 16   The next set of fields deals with inbound calls. The Significant Digits field determines the number of digits of an incoming dialed number that will be used by CallManager. CallManager counts from right to left, so if the number entered in this field is four and the digits received are 8105559090, 810555 is removed and only 9090 is used to determine the destination of the call.

Step 17 A Calling Search Space (CSS) determines what destinations inbound calls to this trunk will be able to reach. Choose a CSS from the Calling Search Space drop-down list. If this field is left at None, the dial privileges of this trunk could be limited.

Step 18 AAR is used to provide an alternative route if a call fails due to insufficient bandwidth. The AAR CSS can be used to limit the paths a call may use when it is rerouted. Select an AAR CSS from the AAR Calling Search Space drop-down list.

Step 19 The Prefix DN field defines what digits will be added to the front of an incoming destination number. This is applied to the number after CallManager truncates the number based on the Significant Digits setting.

Step 20 The Redirecting Number IE Delivery–Inbound should be used if your voice-mail system supports Redirecting Number IE. Otherwise, leave this box unchecked.

Step 21 If the Enable Inbound Faststart check box is checked, FastStart will be used. The H.323 FastStart requires only two message exchanges to open logical channels, whereas normal setup requires 12. However, if FastStart is selected, both ends must support and be configured for FastStart.

Step 22 The next set of fields deals with outbound calls. The field labeled Calling Party Selection determines what number is sent for outbound calls. The choices are:

   — Originator—The directory number of the device that placed the call

   — First Redirect Number—The first directory number that forwarded the call

   — Last Redirect Number—The directory number of the last device to forward the call

   — First Redirect Number (External)—The number of the first device to forward the call using the external phone mask

   — Last Redirect Number (External)—The number of the last device to forward the call using the external phone mask

Step 23 The Calling Line ID Presentation field determines if CallManager sends Caller ID information. To send caller ID information, select **Allowed** from the drop-down list. To block caller ID, select **Restricted** from the drop-down list.

Step 24 Cisco recommends that the next four fields remain set to the default of Cisco CallManager. These fields are Called party IE number type unknown, Calling party IE number type unknown, Called Numbering Plan, and Calling Numbering Plan. These fields deal with dial plan issues and should be changed only when advised to do so by Cisco or an experienced dial plan expert. The need to change these usually occurs when installing CallManager internationally.

Step 25 The Caller ID DN field is used to determine what caller ID is sent out this gateway. A mask or a complete number can be entered in this field. For example, if the mask 55536XX is entered in this field, CallManager sends 55536 and the last two digits of the calling number.

Step 26 If the Display IE Delivery check box is checked, the calling and called party name information is included in messages.

Step 27 The Redirecting Number IE Delivery–Outbound check box should be checked when integrating with a voice-mail system that supports Redirecting Number IE. Otherwise, leave it unchecked.

Step 28 If the Enable Outbound Faststart check box is checked, FastStart will be used. The H.323 FastStart requires only two message exchanges to open logical channels, whereas normal setup requires 12. However, if FastStart is selected, both ends must support and be configured for FastStart.

Step 29 If the Enable Outbound Faststart check box is checked, you must select the codec that is to be used. This is selected from the Codec For Outbound FastStart drop-down list.

Step 30 In the field labeled Gatekeeper Name, enter the name or IP address of the gatekeeper that will control this trunk.

Step 31 The Terminal Type field specifies the type of devices this trunk controls. Choose **Gateway** for normal trunks.

Step 32 The Technology Prefix field allows you to assign a prefix that matches the prefix in the gatekeeper. By assigning a matching prefix, you can avoid having to add the IP address of each CallManager in the gatekeeper on the gw-type-prefix line. It is recommended that you use 1#* in both this field and the gatekeeper configuration. The value entered in this field must exactly match what is configured in the gatekeeper.

Step 33 The Zone field determines with which zone this CallManager registers on the gatekeeper. If this field is left blank, the gatekeeper's zone subnet command is used to determine to what zone the CallManager registers. If you enter a zone name in this field, it must match exactly with what is configured in the gatekeeper (this includes capitalization).

Step 34   The next three fields define the MultiLevel Precedence and Preemption (MLPP) characteristics of this trunk. If these fields are left blank or set to default, the values set in the device pool are used. The first MLPP field is the MLPP Domain. MLPP grants higher priority only from calls with the same MLPP domain. For this reason, an MLPP domain is needed when MLPP is to be used.

Step 35   The second field in this category, called MLPP Indication, determines whether tones and indications will be presented when a precedence call is made. If this field is set to Off, no precedence indication is presented. If this field is set to On, indication is used for a precedence call.

Step 36   The third MLPP field is MLPP Preemption. This parameter determines whether a higher precedence call preempts a lower precedence call. The value is not available for this device.

Step 37   Click the **Insert** button at the top of the page.

Step 38   A window displays informing you that the trunk must be reset. Click **OK**.

Step 39   Click **Reset Trunk**.

Step 40   A window displays allowing you to reset or restart the trunk. Click the **Reset** button.

Step 41   A window displays informing you that the reset has been initiated. Click **OK**.

After the gatekeeper controlled intercluster trunk is configured, you can add it to a route group. Then configure a pattern that matches calls that should be routed over this trunk. The pattern should point to a route list that contains the route group of which this trunk is a member.

Configuring CAC for a Centralized Deployment

To accomplish CAC for environments that have remote sites, locations are configured in CallManager. Locations define the amount of bandwidth that can be used to place calls to and from the remote sites. After locations are configured, they must be assigned to phones. When a call is placed across the IP WAN, CallManager uses the location information to determine if there is enough available bandwidth for the call. By deducing available bandwidth for each call that is active on the WAN, CallManager can determine how much is available. When using locations, CallManager assumes the following bandwidth is required for each codec.

- G.711 call uses 80 kbps.
- G.722 call uses 80 kbps.

- G.723 call uses 24 kbps.
- G.728 call uses 16 kbps.
- G.729 call uses 24 kbps.
- GSM call uses 29 kbps.
- Wideband call uses 272 kbps.

To better understand locations, let's look at the steps required to create and apply them.

Creating Locations

The following steps show how to create a location.

Step 1   From within CCMAdmin, select **System>Location**.

Step 2   Click the **Add a New Location link**.

Step 3   A screen similar to that shown in Figure 5-14 displays. Enter the name of the location in the Location Name field.

Figure 5-14   *Location Configuration*

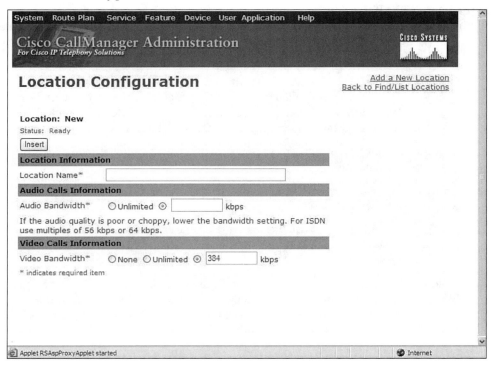

Step 4 In the field labeled Audio Bandwidth, enter the amount of bandwidth available for voice calls to and from this location. If you select the radio button labeled Unlimited, no limit is placed on voice calls. To determine the value to enter here, take the bandwidth CallManager uses for each call based on the codec that is being used, and multiply it by the number of calls you know can safely traverse the link. For instance, if you are using G.729 and you know that 10 calls can traverse the link, multiply 24 kbps by 10. This tells you that 240 should be entered in this field. The bandwidth CallManager assumes for each codec is listed earlier in this section.

Step 5 In the field labeled Video Bandwidth, enter the amount of bandwidth available for video calls to and from this location. If you select the radio button labeled **Unlimited**, no limit is placed on video calls. You may also select the radio button labeled **None**, which disallows video calls.

Step 6 Click the **Insert** button. The location has been added when the status line reads Insert completed.

Assigning a Location to Devices

After locations are added, you must assign them to devices. To assign a location to a device, follow these steps. Because the steps to add a location to a phone, ICT or gateway are all very similar, the following steps can be used to add a location to any of these devices.

Step 1 The path you will select from within CCMAdmin depends on which type of device you are assigning a location. To assign a location to a phone, select **Device>Phone**. To assign a location to an ICT, select **Device>Trunk**. To assign a location to a gateway, select **Device>Gateway**.

Step 2 To limit the results, enter search criteria in the search field and click the **Find** button.

Step 3 Select the device to which you want to assign a location from the list that is generated.

Step 4 If configuring a MGCP gateway, select the end point to which you want to assign a location. If you are not configuring an MGCP gateway, skip this step.

Step 5 The device configuration screen displays. Select a location from the Location drop-down list as shown in Figure 5-15. Figure 5-15 shows a phone configuration screen, but the screen should be similar regardless of the device you are configuring.

Figure 5-15 *Assigning a location to a Device*

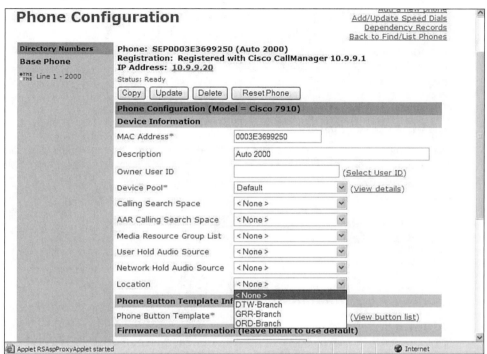

Step 6 Click the **Update** button.

Step 7 A window displays informing you that you must reset the device for the change to occur. Click **OK**.

Step 8 Click the device reset button. The label of this button varies depending upon what type of device you are configuring. It will be labeled **Reset Phone**, **Reset Gateway** or **Reset Trunk**.

Step 9 A window displays allowing you to reset or restart the device. Click the **Reset** button.

Step 10 A window displays informing you that the reset has been initiated. Click **OK**.

That's all there is to it. Unlike with gatekeeper, no additional configuration is required outside of CallManager because CallManager handles all the CAC functions itself when locations are used for remote sites.

Special Services Configuration

There are certain types of calls that should always be given priority and should be able to be dialed from all phones. The first call of this type is 911. When a 911 call is placed, it is important that the call gets through. Not only is it necessary to make the call possible, you need to ensure it goes to the right destination. This section discusses some of the issues that may arise with these services.

Special Services Overview

Depending on your local service, various special services may be available. The following is a list of special service numbers that may be available. You need to check with your local phone company to see which of these are valid in your area.

- 311—nonemergency police services
- 411—directory assistance
- 511—travel information
- 611—phone equipment repair
- 711—Telecommunications Device for the Deaf (TDD) operator
- 911—emergency

After you have determined which services are available, you must configure route patterns that will match these calls. The most important of these calls is 911. Because in an emergency a person might not think to dial 9 before dialing 911, patterns should be created that allow the call out regardless of whether 9 is dialed first. This means two patterns need to be created, 911 and 9.911. PreDot discard instructions must be applied to the 9.911 pattern so that only 911 is sent out the Public Switching Telephone Network (PSTN).

When there are remote locations, things become a little more complicated. Imagine you have an office in San Jose and a remote office in San Francisco. When callers dial 911 from San Francisco, the call must be routed to the local emergency service, not the service in San Jose. Although this seems obvious, it is sometimes overlooked. To accomplish this, multiple 911 and 9.911 patterns must be created. Partitions and CSS are used to allow phones in each location to match only the pattern that routes the call to the correct location.

For all other special services, the 9.X11 pattern should be sufficient. However, once again, be sure to create patterns for each remote location so that the call is routed to the local PSTN.

Another concern when dealing with 911 calls is that some local legislation requires that more detailed location information be sent than just the street address. These laws normally apply to buildings that are over a certain size. Typically the floor and room number is required in addition to the street address. This requirement is referred to as an E911 or enhanced 911. Imagine that someone dialed 911 from a 20-story building and all that was sent is the street address. This would make it difficult to determine which floor, let alone which office, it came from. The solution is to have a database that contains the detailed address information for each phone number in your company. This database is typically maintained by an outside company and is accessible by the emergency service.

Another issue that arises with CallManager is that because a phone can be moved so easily, the information in the database can become outdated rather quickly. In addition to this, a feature known as extension mobility makes the CallManager system even more nomadic. To deal with these issues, Cisco offers a product known as Emergency Responder. This product is used to ensure that the correct detailed information is sent when a 911 call is placed. For more details on this product, refer to the "Cisco Emergency Responder Administration Guide" that can be found on Cisco.com.

Configuring Special Services Route Patterns

To ensure that special services numbers are accessible, you must create route patterns for them. As mentioned previously, it is recommended that you create at least three patterns for each location. The first two are for 911 services and should be 911 and 9.911. If your location does not use a leading 9 for PSTN access, the first 9 in the 9.911 pattern should be replaced with whatever number is used for PSTN access. The third pattern is 9.X11. This pattern will match all other special services numbers.

The 9.911 and 911 patterns should be marked Urgent Priority so that as soon as the number is dialed, it is sent. If this pattern is not marked Urgent Priority, delays could occur before the call is sent, and this should never happen.

As often happens, one solution creates another problem. I have heard people say that they do not use the 911 pattern because people often dial it by mistake. What happens is that a person dials 9 for an outside line, then presses one to begin a long distance call, and then mistakenly presses one again. This, of course, matches 911 and routes the call to emergency services. It is NEVER recommended that you not include the 911 pattern. Although people misdialing 911 is problematic, it is gravely problematic if 911 cannot be dialed during an emergency. I have heard of many ways people have fixed this problem, but would not recommend any of them because they all result in either the failure or delay of the call.

An overview of the tasks required to create patterns to allow access to special services numbers follows. Refer to Chapter 4, Implementing a Dial Plan, for detailed steps on how to create route patterns.

Step 1   Create a 911 route pattern.

Step 2   Assign a partition to this pattern that all phones in the location can dial.
If there are remote locations, a separate pattern must be created and
placed in a partition that only phones in that location can reach. This
pattern must then point to a route list that will send the call out the local
PSTN. Figure 5-16 shows an example of this.

Figure 5-16 *Routing 911 Calls For Multiple Locations*

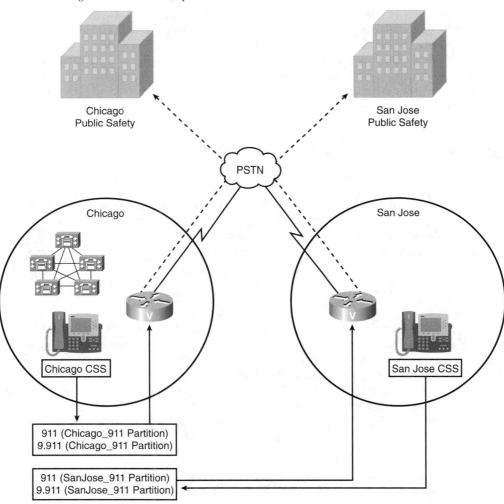

Warning   When configuring 911 patterns in environments that include remote locations, it is imperative that you create a route plan that will send the call to the proper 911 operator. For instance, if the CallManager cluster is in Chicago and a remote location is in San Jose, you must make certain that when a user in San Jose dials 911 it reaches the San Jose 911 operator, not the Chicago 911 operator. The responsibility to ensure this works properly is solely upon you. If you are uncertain as to how to properly implement this, you should seek additional help from an individual with proven experience in this field.

Step 3   Select a gateway or route list that will send this pattern out the local PSTN gateway.

Step 4   Check the **Urgent Priority** and **OffNet Pattern** (and **Outside Dial Tone**) check box.

Note   Although it is not necessary to provide an outside dial tone for this pattern, if you do not, the outside dial tone will not be played for any number that begins with 9, until enough digits are dialed so that the number does not match 911. That means, in most cases, when dialing a long distance number, the outside dial tone is not heard until three digits are dialed. For this reason, it is recommended that you check the OffNet Pattern (and Outside Dial Tone) check box.

Step 5   Create a 9.911 route pattern. If your location does not use a leading 9 for PSTN access, then the first 9 in the 9.911 pattern should be replaced with whatever number is used for PSTN access.

Step 6   Assign a partition to this pattern that all phones in the location can dial. If there are remote locations, a separate pattern must be created and placed in a partition that only phones in that location can reach. The pattern must then point to a route list that will send the call out the local PSTN. Figure 5-16 shows an example of this.

Warning	When configuring 9.911 patterns in environments that include remote locations, it is imperative that you properly create a route plan that will send the call to the proper 911 operator. For instance, if the CallManager cluster is in Chicago and a remote location is in San Jose, you must make certain that when a user in San Jose dials 9.911 it reaches the San Jose 911 operator, not the Chicago 911 operator. The responsibility to ensure this works properly is solely upon you. If you are uncertain as to how to properly implement this, you should seek additional help from an individual with proven experience in this field.

Step 7 Select a gateway or route list that will send the pattern out the local PSTN gateway.

Step 8 Check the **Urgent Priority** and **OffNet Pattern (and Outside Dial Tone)** check box.

Step 9 Set the discard digits to **PreDot**.

Step 10 Create a 9.X11 route pattern.

Step 11 Assign a partition to the pattern that all phones in the location can dial. If there are remote locations, a separate pattern must be created and placed in a partition that only phones in that location can reach. The pattern must then point to a route list that will send the call out the local PSTN.

Step 12 Select a gateway or route list that will send the pattern out the local PSTN gateway.

Step 13 Set the discard digits to **PreDot**.

Step 14 Check the **OffNet Pattern (and Outside Dial Tone)** check box.

It is essential that after you have created patterns for these services, you make test calls to ensure that the call is routed properly. The steps provided previously are only general practices; additional configuration may be required. There is no guarantee that the previous steps will work in each situation. It is your responsibility to make sure you test these services thoroughly before the system goes live.

Summary

This chapter explored how certain calls can be restricted by applying CSS and partitions to devices and patterns. Because it is often required that different devices have access to various destinations, the steps for creating and applying CSS and partitions are provided.

When deploying VoIP solutions, ensuring the quality of the call is essential. To accomplish this, CAC was discussed. Detailed steps were provided that show how to configure a gatekeeper that provides CAC for calls between clusters. Steps were also included to show how to configure locations for CAC, for calls to and from remote sites.

Finally, special services, such as 911, were discussed in this chapter. An overview of the required steps for the proper configuration of these services was reviewed.

Configuring CallManager Features and Services

CallManager provides a number of features that users have come to expect, and each new version of CallManager adds new features. Many features add needed functionality, such as conference calls, whereas others simply help to make the phone system more enjoyable, such as Music On Hold (MoH). Years ago CallManager was not as feature rich as other traditional systems. However, lately CallManager has begun to provide not only the most frequently used features but also go beyond the features offered by traditional systems. This chapter examines a wide range of features and the configuration tasks required to implement them.

Configuring Features

Let's start by looking at some of the basic features that are most often implemented. These are features that offer users extended functionality and are found on most modern phone systems.

As one may expect, all of these features are listed under the Features menu in CCMAdmin and are simple to configure. Each of the following six sections will introduce you to a feature, explain its function, and show you how to configure these features.

Many of the features available to the users do not require any additional configuration. Because no configuration is required, these features are not discussed in detail in this chapter. The features that require no configuration include Hold, Call Waiting, Mute, Transfer, On-Hook Dialing and Redial.

Creating Call Pickup Groups

Call Pickup Groups allow people to answer a line that is ringing on another phone from their phone. For example, if extension 1005 is ringing, the call can be answered from a phone that does not have 1005 as an extension. There are two ways this can happen. The first is called Call Pickup. Call Pickup allows a call to be picked up from another phone if both phones are in the same pickup group. The second type of call pickup is called Group Call Pickup. Group Call Pickup allows a call to be picked up from another phone if both phones are not in the same pickup group. To help clarify this, Figure 6-1 shows three phones. Phones A and B are in the same call pickup group, while Phone C is in a separate call pickup group.

Figure 6-1 *Call Pickup Example*

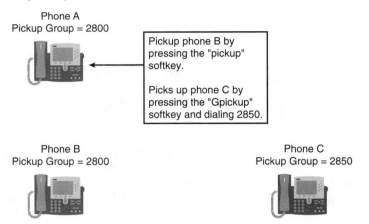

If phone B is ringing, the call can be answered from phone A by going off hook and pressing the **pickup** softkey. After the softkey is pressed, phone A will start ringing and the call can be answered. However, if phone C is ringing and a user wishes to answer the call from phone A, he would have to go off hook and press the **Gpickup** softkey and enter phone C's group pickup number. After this is done, Phone A starts to ring and the call can be answered.

There are a couple of things to be aware of when deploying the call pick up feature. First, a phone must be a member of a call pickup group in order to use this feature. If a phone has not been assigned a call pickup group, that phone cannot answer another phone's incoming call. Second, in order for a user to answer a call ringing on a phone that is not in the same call pickup group, the user must know the number. In addition, if the call pick up number has a partition assigned to it, the phone or line must have a Calling Search Space (CSS) with access to that partition.

To implement the call pickup feature, call pickup groups must be created and then assigned to the phones. The following steps show how to perform both of these tasks.

Add a Call Pickup Number

Step 1   From within CCMAdmin, select **Feature>Call Pickup**.

Step 2   Click **Add a New Call Pickup Number**.

Step 3   A screen similar to that shown in Figure 6-2 displays. In the **Call Pickup Number** field, enter the desired number. This number must be unique, in that it is not assigned to any other function or device.

Step 4   Enter a description that helps identify the purpose of this call pickup group in the **Description** field.

Figure 6-2   *Call Pickup Group Configuration*

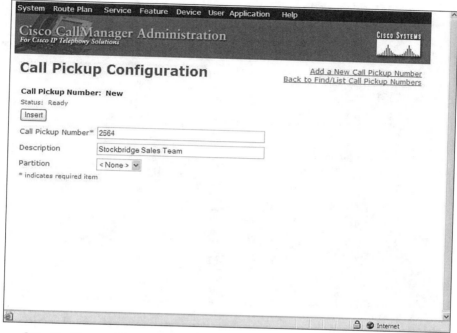

Step 5   If you wish to assign a partition to this call pickup group, select one from the **Partition** drop-down list.

Step 6   Click the **Insert** button to add this call pickup group.

Assign a Call Pickup Group to a Line

Step 1   From within CCMAdmin, Select **Device>Phone**.

Step 2   Enter search criteria in the search field to limit the results and click the **Find** button.

Step 3   Select the desired phone from the list that displays.

Step 4   Click the desired line on the left side of the screen.

Step 5   On the **Directory Number Configuration** page, select the desired Call Pickup Group from the **Call Pickup Group** drop-down list as seen in Figure 6-3.

Step 6   Click the **Update** button at the top of the screen.

WARNING   When you make a change to the directory number configuration and click **Update**, the phone will be reset. If a caller is currently on a call, the phone will reset after the call has ended.

Figure 6-3 *Assigning a Call Pickup Group to a Line*

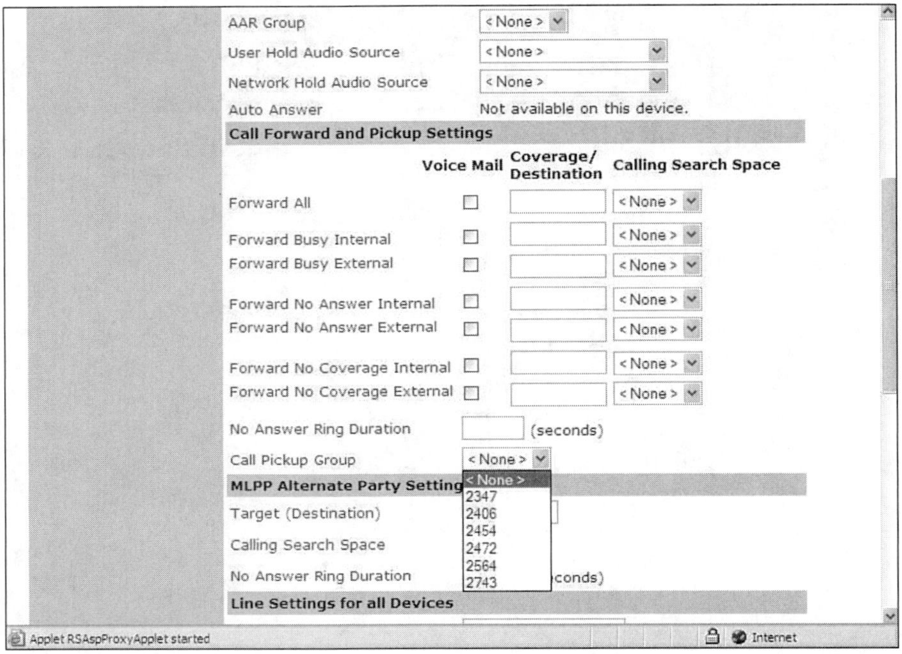

After call pickup groups are created and assigned to lines, this feature is ready to be used. One common mistake that users make when trying to use this feature is that they want to press the pickup softkey without going off hook. This softkey is not available until the phone is off hook. After off hook, the pickup softkey can be pressed and the call starts to ring on the phone.

NOTE   Because call pickup groups are assigned to lines, a different call pickup group can be assigned to line 1 than to line 2 and so on. One variation that has worked well for some customers is to have different pickup groups assigned to different lines instead of using group call pickup (Gpickup softkey). That way the user need only remember which line belongs to which pickup group instead of having to memorize the pickup group number.

Creating Meet-Me Patterns

CallManager supports two types of conference calls. The first is called an ad-hoc conference call. An ad-hoc conference call is the type that takes place when two people who are having a phone conversation decide to conference in another person. One of the active callers initiates the conference call by pressing the conference button, which is the softkey labeled Confrn on the phone, and calling the third party.

The other type of conference call is called a Meet-Me. A Meet-Me conference call is scheduled ahead of time and all participants are told to call a certain number to join the conference.

Both types of conference calls require some type of conference resources, which are referred to as conference bridges. CallManager supports two types of conference bridges: hardware and software. When CallManager is installed, a software conference bridge is installed on CallManager when the Cisco IP Voice Media Streaming Application is activated. Configuring hardware conference bridges is discussed later in this chapter.

Ad-hoc conference calls require no configuration if a conference bridge is available. By default the conference button is available on each of the standard softkey templates. By pressing this key, an ad-hoc conference can be established. Limits to the number of participants that are allowed in a conference can be set in CallManager services parameters.

Meet-Me conferences require more configuration than just having a conference bridge available. A Meet-Me pattern must also be created, which is the number into which participants of the conference will call. Each active Meet-Me conference requires a unique number. This means the Meet-Me patterns you create will determine the maximum amount of Meet-Me conferences that can take place at one time.

Meet-Me patterns allow the use of wildcards, which means that you can create one pattern that will result in multiple Meet-Me numbers. For example, if the pattern 523X is used, it defines 10 numbers as Meet-Me conference numbers, 5230 through 5239.

Creating Meet-Me patterns is done through CCMAdmin. The following steps take you through this process.

Step 1   From within CCMAdmin, select **Feature>Meet-Me Number/Pattern**.

Step 2   Click the **Add a New Meet-Me Number** link.

Step 3   A screen similar that shown in Figure 6-4 displays. In the **Directory Number or Pattern** field enter the number or pattern that you want to use as a Meet-Me number.

Step 4   In the **Description** field, enter a description that helps identify the purpose of this Meet-Me pattern.

Step 5   To allow only certain people to join a conference, you can assign partitions to the pattern. This prevents callers who do not have access to this partition from establishing or joining a conference using this number. This is often done to ensure that unauthorized callers do not accidentally join a conference call. If you wish to restrict the callers who can reach this Meet-Me number, select the desired partition from the **Partition** drop-down list. To allow all devices access to this Meet-Me number select **None** for the partition.

Step 6   Click the **Insert** button to create the Meet-Me number. After the number is created, the status line displays "Insert completed."

Figure 6-4   *Creating a Meet-Me Pattern*

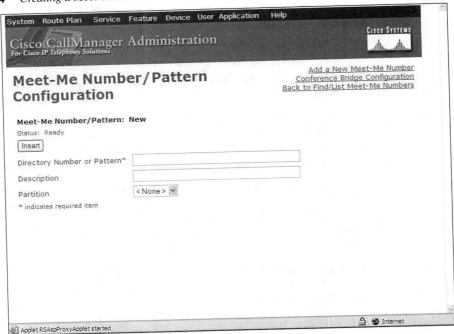

Once the Meet-Me numbers are created, users can start to use this feature. To initiate a Meet-Me conference, the Meet-Me button must be pressed. All standard softkey templates include the Meet-Me softkey. Limiting access to specific Meet-Me numbers by using a partition was discussed previously. One way to restrict a device from initiating Meet-Me conferences is by assigning their phones a softkey template that does not have a Meet-Me softkey. Phones without a Meet-Me softkey can still join a Meet-Me conference by simply dialing the Meet-Me number once the Meet-Me conference is active.

NOTE   The most common error users make with Meet-Me conference calls is that they press the Meet-Me button when they are trying to join an active conference call. Make sure users understand that the Meet-Me button is only used to initiate conference calls.

Creating Call Park Numbers

Calls can be placed on hold by pressing the hold button; however, the call can only be picked up from the same line. This means that when a call is placed on hold, it can only be retrieved from a phone with the same directory number from which it was placed on hold. Often, a call placed on hold needs to be retrieved on a different phone. To accomplish this, the call park feature is used.

Call park places the call on hold and parks it on a virtual directory number. By dialing that number, you can retrieve the call from a different phone. A common use for call park is to have an attendant or operator park the call, then announce the call using an overhead paging system.

For call park to work, call park numbers must be configured. Just as with Meet-Me numbers, wild cards are allowed. This means a single pattern can result in multiple call park numbers.

Call park patterns are created through CCMAdmin. The following steps take you through this process.

Step 1   From within CCMAdmin, select **Feature>Call Park**.

Step 2   Click the **Add a New Call Park Number** link.

Step 3   A screen similar to that shown in Figure 6-5 displays. In the **Call Park Number/Range** field enter the number or pattern that you want to use as a call park number.

Figure 6-5   *Creating a Call Park Pattern*

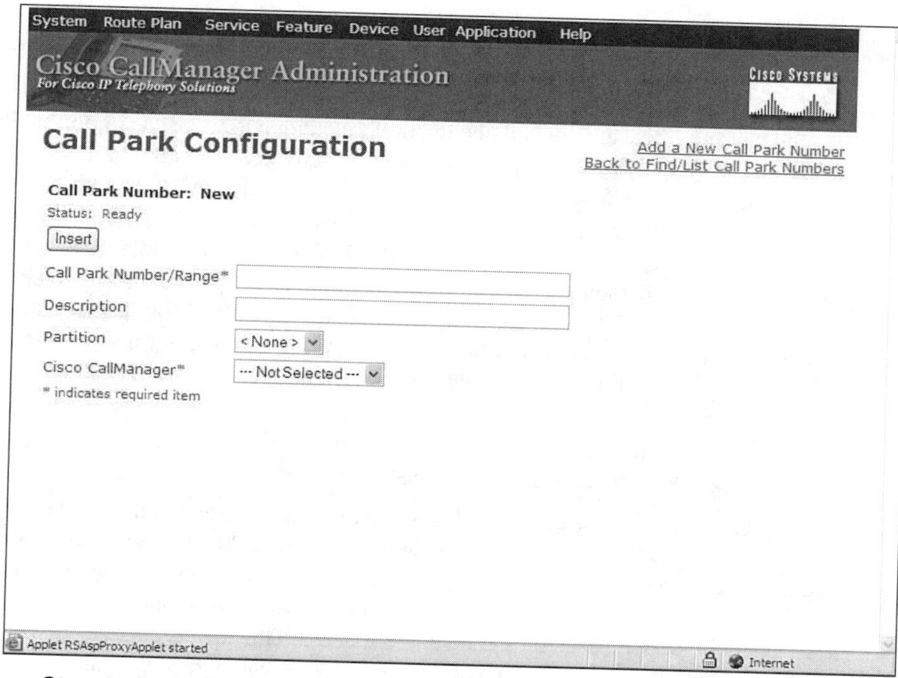

Step 4   In the **Description** field, enter a description that helps identify the purpose of this call park pattern.

Step 5 To restrict who can retrieve a parked call, a partition can be assigned to the call park number. Only devices that have access to the assigned partition can then retrieve the parked call. To restrict access to this call park number, select the desired partition from the **Partition** drop-down list. To allow all devices access to this call park number, select **None** for the partition.

Step 6 From the **CallManager** drop-down list, select the CallManager with which this call park pattern registers.

Note	For a call to be placed on hold, the CallManager with which the phone is registered must have call park numbers configured. For this reason it is recommended that all CallManagers with which phones may register have call park numbers configured. This means you must also configure call park numbers for backup CallManagers, so that the call park feature is available if the primary CallManager fails.

Step 7 Click the **Insert** button to create the call park number. After the number is created, the status line displays "Insert completed."

After call park numbers are created, the feature is available for use. It is important that users understand how this feature works. This feature is activated when the Park softkey is pressed. The call is then automatically parked. The phone displays the number at which the call is parked. Often users think they choose where the call is to be parked, but actually CallManager chooses the number automatically based on the available call park numbers. This means that the person parking the call must look at the phone display to see at what number the call is parked. By default, a call only stays "parked" for 60 seconds before it reverts to the phone that originated the park. This value can be modified via the Call Park Reversion Timer found in the CallManager Service parameters.

Creating Forced Authorization Codes

Earlier in this book, you learned how CSS and partitions are used to allow and restrict calls from being placed to certain destinations. The problem with CSS and partitions is that they are based on the device from which the call is being placed, not from the person who is making the call. In new versions of CallManager, you can use Forced Authorization Codes (FACs) to allow calls to be placed based on a code that is entered. This means that the call is permitted or prohibited based on who is calling and not the device from which they are calling.

It works this way: when a call is placed that requires an authorization code, a double beep is heard that alerts the caller to enter the code. After the code is entered, the call is completed.

Enabling FACs requires that FACs exist and that the route patterns that are to be restricted are configured to require an FAC. The following steps show how to accomplish both of these tasks.

Create a Forced Authorization Code

Step 1 From within CCMAdmin, select **Feature>Forced Authorization Code**.

Step 2 Click the **Add a New Forced Authorization Code** link.

Step 3 A screen similar to that shown in Figure 6-6 displays. In the **Authorization Code Name** field, enter a name for this code. Choose a name that helps identify the code. This name displays in authorization code reports that can be produced.

Figure 6-6 *Creating Forced Authorization Codes*

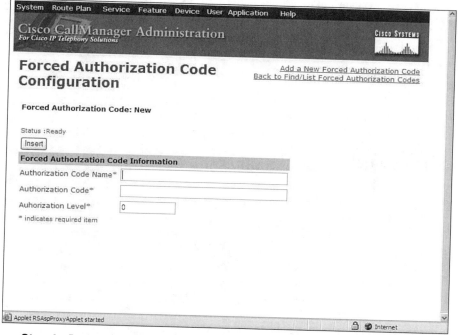

Step 4 In the **Authorization Code** field, enter a numeric code. This is the code a caller will have to enter to place calls that require authorization.

Step 5 In the **Authorization Level** field, enter a numeric value between 0 and 255. This value determines the authorization level of this code. In order for the code to allow a call, the value in this field must be equal to or greater than the value assigned to the pattern.

Step 6   Click the **Insert** button to add this code. After the code is created, the status line displays "Insert completed."

Assign a Forced Authorization Code to a Route Pattern

Step 1   From within CCMAdmin, select **Route Plan>Route/Hunt>Route Pattern**.

Step 2   Enter search criteria in the search field to limit the results and click the **Find** button.

Step 3   From the list that displays, select the route pattern to which you wish to add an FAC.

Step 4   A screen similar to that shown in Figure 6-7 displays. Check the **Require Forced Authorization Code** box and enter a numeric value in the **Authorization Level** field. This value is used to determine which FACs have the right to use this pattern. An FAC must have a value equal to or greater than this value in order to be granted access.

Figure 6-7   *Require a Forced Authorization Code for a Route Pattern*

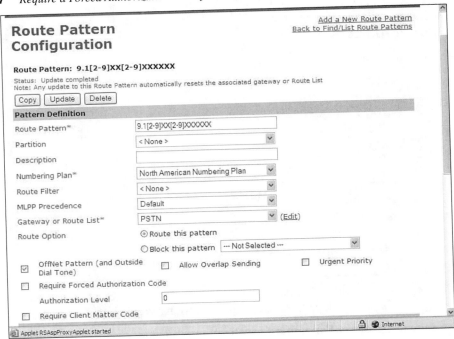

Step 5   Click the **Update** button to apply FAC to this pattern.

Step 6   Repeat these steps for all other route patterns on which you wish to enable FAC.

After completing these two tasks, FAC is enabled. Make sure you take the time to properly plan the implementation of FAC. If improperly implemented, it can cause adverse effects. Make certain that FAC is never applied to a pattern that allows access to emergency services such as 911.

Configuring Client Matter Codes

Another commonly requested feature is Client Matter Codes (CMC). This allows a caller to enter a client code while placing a call, so the call is associated with a client. Companies that bill customers for time spent on projects, such as lawyers, require this feature.

The process to enable CMCs is very similar to that of configuring FACs. First CMCs must be created and then route patterns need to be configured to require CMCs. The following steps walk you through both processes.

Create a Client Matter Code

Step 1   From within CCMAdmin, select **Feature>Client Matter Code**.

Step 2   Click the **Add a New Client Matter Code** link.

Step 3   A screen similar to that shown in Figure 6-8 displays. In the **Client Matter Code** field, enter the desired code.

Figure 6-8   *Creating Client Matter Codes*

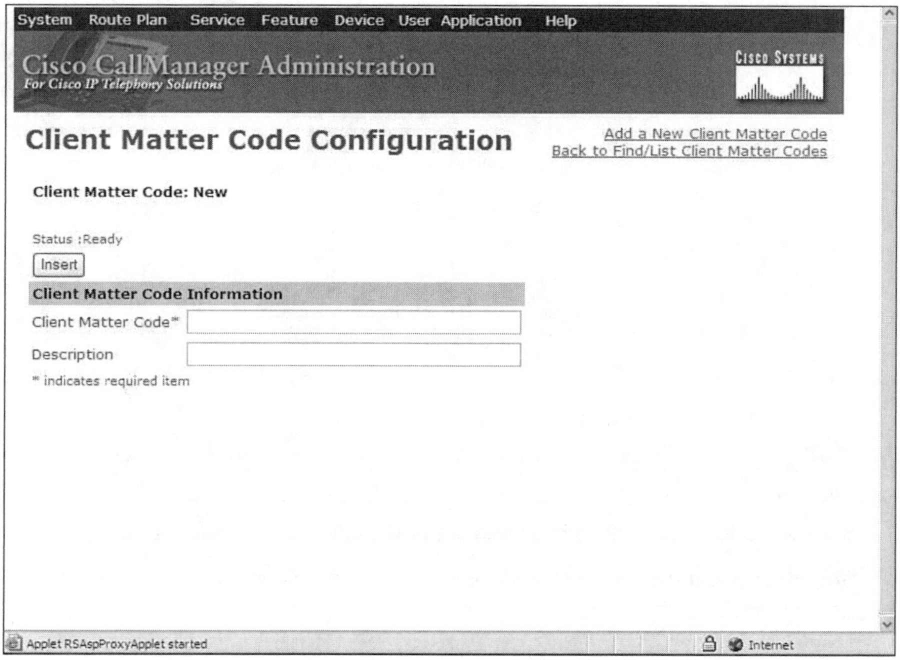

Step 4 In the **Description** field, enter a description that identifies the client or project with which this code is associated.

Step 5 Click the **Insert** button to add this code. After the code is created, the status line displays "**Insert completed**."

Assign a Client Matter Code to a Route Pattern

Step 1 From within CCMAdmin, select **Route Plan>Route/Hunt>Route Pattern**.

Step 2 Enter search criteria in the search field to limit the results and click the **Find** button.

Step 3 From the list that displays, select the route pattern to which you wish to add a CMC.

Step 4 A screen similar to that shown in Figure 6-9 displays. Check the **Require Client Matter Code** box.

Figure 6-9 *Require Client Matter Codes on a Route Pattern*

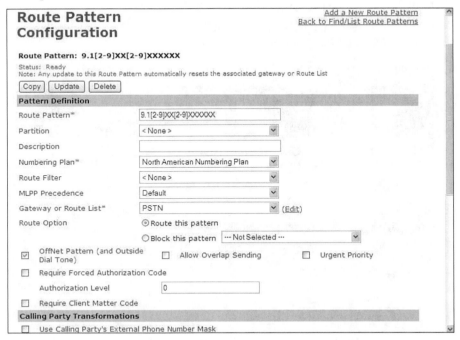

Step 5 Click the **Update** button to apply the CMC requirement to this pattern.

Step 6 Repeat these steps for all other route patterns on which you wish to require CMC.

After these two tasks are completed, CMC is enabled. Make certain that CMC is never applied to a pattern that allows access to emergency services such as 911.

Configuring Voice Ports and Profiles

Another feature—voice mail—is covered in great detail in the second half of this book. To integrate with a voice-mail system, a number of feature configurations must be completed. The voice-mail feature menu has five different submenus. This section examines the function of each of these and how each is configured.

Table 6-1 lists the five voice-mail submenu items with a brief explanation of each.

Table 6-1 *Voice Mail Submenu Items*

Item	Description
Cisco Voice Mail Port	A virtual port that allows communications between CallManager and Unity
Cisco Voice Mail Port Wizard	A wizard for creating voice-mail ports
Message Waiting	Directory numbers that are used for MWI activation
Voice Mail Pilot	A directory number used to define voice-mail pilot number
Voice Mail Profile	A profile that defines voice-mail parameters for devices

The first thing that must be configured is the voice-mail ports. Voice-mail ports can be created manually or by using the wizard. It is recommended that you use the wizard because it walks you through the process. The following steps walk you through this wizard.

Step 1 From within CCMAdmin, select **Feature>Voice Mail>Cisco Voice Mail Port Wizard**.

Step 2 On the next page, enter the name on the voice-mail port name in the **Add ports to a new Cisco Voice Mail Server using this name** field. In most cases you can leave it at CiscoUM1. This field needs to be changed only if CiscoUM1 is already being used for another voice-mail integration. Click **Next**.

Step 3 On the next field, select from the drop-down list the number of voice-mail ports to create. Click **Next**.

Step 4 A screen similar to that shown in Figure 6-10 displays. Enter a description that helps identify the purpose of these voice-mail ports in the **Description** field.

Step 5 From the **Device Pool** drop-down list, select the device pool these voice-mail ports will use.

Step 6 A CSS determines where the voice-mail port will be able to dial. Choose a CSS from the **Calling Search Space** drop-down list. If this field is left at None, the dial privileges of this voice-mail port could be limited. This can affect message notification and call transfers.

Figure 6-10 *Voice Mail Port Wizard Device Configuration*

Step 7 The Automated Alternate Routing (AAR) is used to provide an alternate route if a call fails due to insufficient bandwidth. The AAR CSS can be used to limit the paths a call may use when it is rerouted. Select an **AAR CSS** from the **AAR Calling Search Space** drop-down list.

Step 8 Locations are used to help wide-area network (WAN) links from becoming oversubscribed in centralized deployments. If you have defined locations, select the appropriate one for these voice-mail ports from the **Location** drop-down list.

Step 9 Click **Next**.

Step 10 A screen similar to that shown in Figure 6-11 displays. In the **Beginning Directory Number** field, enter the directory number to be assigned to the first voice-mail port.

Tip On the previous configuration page, the parameters for the device were configured. In this section you are configuring the parameters for the line. This is why you see some of the same fields as you did on the previous configuration page.

Figure 6-11 *Voice Mail Port Wizard Directory Number Configuration*

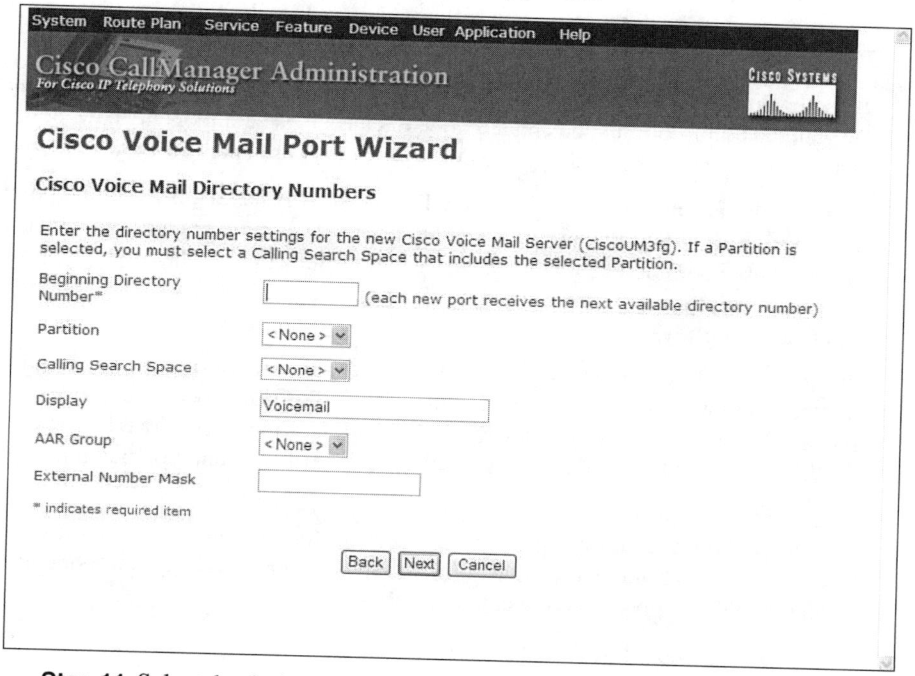

Step 11 Select the desired partition for the voice-mail port line from the **Partition** drop-down list.

Step 12 Select the desired CSS for the line from the **Calling Search Space** drop-down list.

Step 13 In the **Display** field, enter the name that is displayed on a phone when connected to voice mail.

Step 14 Select the AAR group for the line from the **AAR Group** drop-down list.

Step 15 In the **External Number Mask** field, enter the mask that should be applied to the voice-mail port line number when it places outside calls.

Step 16 Click **Next**.

Step 17 You are now asked if these lines should be assigned to a line group. Think of a line group as a group of lines through which a call can be forwarded. If the first line doesn't answer, it is sent to the next number, and so on. In most new installations, you choose **Yes. Add directory numbers to a new Line Group**. Click **Next**.

Step 18 Enter a name that helps identify this line group, perhaps **VoiceMailLG**. Click **Next**.

Step 19 A summary screen displays listing the configuration of the voice-mail ports. If all the information is correct, click **Finish**. A progress meter displays. When the meter disappears, the voice-mail ports are created.

A screen displays informing you that the voice-mail ports have been created and that a Hunt List and a Hunt Pilot must be created now. Because these components have not been discussed yet, let's take a moment to define what they are and how they work.

A Hunt Pilot is a number that points to a Hunt List. A Hunt List is a list that points to one or more line groups. A line group is a group of directory numbers through which a call can travel. These combined components create hunt groups in CallManager. The flow is very similar to how a route pattern points to a Route List, which points to a route group, which points to a gateway.

Because Unity has a number of ports on which a call can enter, a hunt group has to be created to allow the call to try the first number and, if it is not available, move onto the first available port. The voice-mail port wizard first creates the lines. Next, the wizard creates the line group. Unfortunately, this is where the wizard ends and you begin the rest of the setup manually.

Because the voice-mail line and line group are configured, the Hunt List must be created next. Just as with route patterns, list, and groups and devices, these components must be created in a flow opposite to the call travel flow.

The following steps show how to create a Hunt List.

Step 1 From within CCMAdmin, select **Route Plan>Route/Hunt>Hunt List**.

Step 2 Click the **Add a new Hunt List** link.

Step 3 On the screen that displays, enter the name of the Hunt List in the **Hunt List Name** field.

Step 4 In the **Description** field, enter a description that helps identify this Hunt List, such as VoiceMailHL.

Step 5 Select the CallManager group that this hunt group will use from the **Cisco CallManager Group** drop-down list.

Step 6 Click the **Insert** button. An informational window displays informing you that at least one line group must be assigned to the Hunt List. Click **OK**.

Step 7 From the screen similar to that shown in Figure 6-12, click the **Add Line Group** button.

Step 8 A new screen displays. Select the desired line group from the **Line Group** drop-down list. Click **Insert**.

Step 9 An informational window displays telling you that the Hunt List must be reset before changes will take effect. Click **OK**.

Figure 6-12 *Hunt List Configuration*

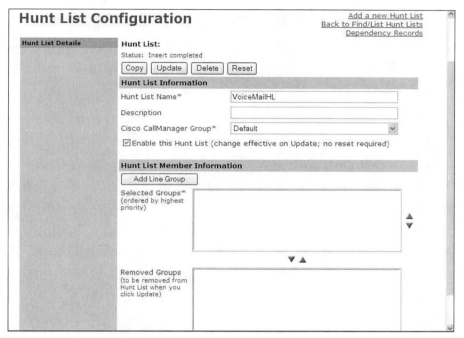

Step 10 The hunt list configuration screen returns. Click the **Reset** button. An informational window informs you that calls to this Hunt List will be refused while the list is being reset. Click **OK**.

Step 11 Another informational window informs you that the Hunt List is being reset. Click **OK**.

Now that the hunt list is configured, a hunt pilot needs to be created. The hunt pilot is the number users will dial to reach the voice-mail system. The steps that follow show how to complete this process.

Step 1 From within CCMAdmin, select **Route Plan>Route/Hunt>Hunt Pilot**.

Step 2 Click the **Add a New Hunt Pilot** link.

Step 3 A screen similar to that shown in Figure 6-13 displays. Enter the route pattern in the **Hunt Pilot** field.

Step 4 The partition field determines what devices can access this hunt pilot. Select the desired partition from the **Partition** drop-down list.

Step 5 Enter a description that helps identify the purpose of this hunt pilot in the **Description** field.

Step 6 In the **Numbering Plan** field, choose the appropriate numbering plan.

Figure 6-13 *Hunt Pilot Configuration*

Step 7 From the **Route Filter** drop-down list, select the route filter that is to be applied to this hunt pilot. This field is left to None in most cases.

Step 8 Determine the precedence level that will be assigned to this hunt pilot by selecting it from the **MLPP Precedence** drop-down list.

Step 9 From the **Hunt List** drop-down list, select the hunt list to which calls to this hunt pilot are sent.

Step 10 Select the **Route this pattern** radio button.

Step 11 To have a secondary dial tone played after the first digit is dialed, check **Provide Outside Dial Tone**. In most cases this box should be unchecked.

Step 12 To route a call as soon as it matches this route pattern, check the **Urgent Priority** box. In most cases this box should be unchecked.

Step 13 The next two fields determine where a call is sent if the call is never answered or if all ports are busy. The fields are Forward Hunt No Answer and Forward Hunt Busy. Enter the appropriate destination number in the **Destination** field. A separate CSS can be defined for calls that are forwarded if desired.

Step 14 In the **Maximum Hunt Timer** field enter the maximum number of seconds that a call is allowed to remain in the hunt group before being classified as unanswered.

Tip	In most cases the remaining fields can be left at default. The following steps are provided to help you understand the purpose of each.

Step 15 If you wish to affect caller ID information, configure the fields found under the **Calling Party Transformation** heading. These fields are discussed earlier in this chapter. **Use Calling Party's External Phone Number Mask** is the first field.

Step 16 In the **Calling Party Transform Mask** field, enter any mask you wish to affect the caller ID.

Step 17 In the **Prefix Digits (Outgoing Calls)** field, enter any digits that you want added to the front of the caller ID.

Step 18 The **Calling Line ID Presentation** field determines if caller ID information is to be blocked for outbound calls from this hunt pilot. To block caller ID, select **Restricted** from the drop-down list. To allow caller ID select **Allowed** from the drop-down list.

Step 19 The **Calling Name Presentation** field determines if caller name information is to be blocked for outbound calls from this hunt pilot. To block calling name ID, select **Restricted** from the drop-down list. To allow calling ID name, select **Allowed** from the drop-down list.

Step 20 The **Connected Line ID Presentation** field determines if the connected party's ID information is displayed on the calling party's phone. To block connected party's ID, select **Restricted** from the drop-down list. To allow connected party's ID select **Allowed** from the drop-down list.

Step 21 The **Connected Name Presentation** field determines if the connected party's name information is displayed on the calling party's phone. To block the connected party's name, select **Restricted** from the drop-down list. To allow the connected party's name, select **Allowed** from the drop-down list.

Step 22 From the **Discard Digits** drop-down list, select the digit discard instruction that is applied to calls that match this route pattern.

Step 23 In the **Called Party Transform Mask** field, enter the mask you want to use for calls that match this route pattern.

Step 24 In the **Prefix Digits (Outgoing Calls)** field, enter any digits that you want added to the dialed number before it is sent to the route list.

Step 25 Click the **Insert** button at the top of the screen to save this route pattern.

A hunt pilot is now configured that points to a hunt list, which routes the call to the line group of the voice-mail port lines.

By dialing the hunt pilot number, users can access Unity. This is, of course, assuming Unity is running and properly integrated with CallManager. The Unity side of the integration is covered in the Unity portion of this book.

Now the MWI settings must be configured so that the MWI on the phone will activate when a new message is received. The MWI setting is simply a directory number that is configured to act as either MWI on or MWI off. The following steps show how to create MWI directory numbers in CallManager.

Step 1 From within CCMAdmin, select **Feature>Voice Mail>Message Waiting**.

Step 2 On the next page, select the **Add a New Message Waiting Number** radio button.

Step 3 A screen similar to that shown in Figure 6-14 displays. In the **Message Waiting Number** field, enter the directory number that you want to use to activate MWI on or MWI off.

Figure 6-14 *MWI Configuration*

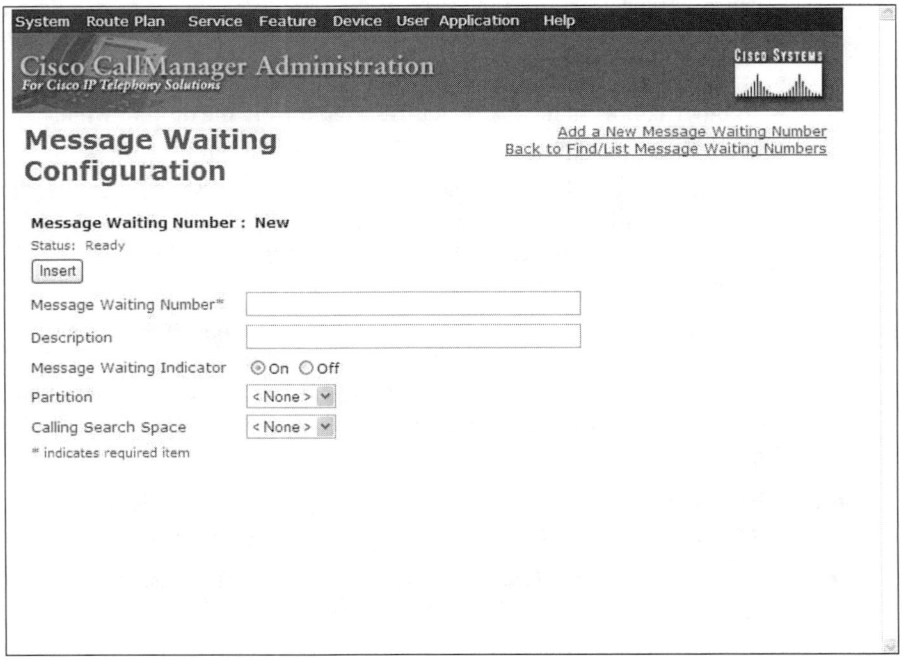

Step 4 In the **Description** field, enter a description that helps identify the purpose of this MWI number.

Step 5 Select either the **On** or **Off** radio button to define whether this number will be used to turn MWI on or off.

Step 6 If you want to assign a partition to the MWI number, select the desired one from the **Partition** drop-down list. To allow unrestricted access to this number select **None**.

Step 7 Assign a CSS that has access to all the phones on which the MWI will activate the MWI. Select the appropriate CSS from the **Calling Search Space** drop-down list.

Step 8 Click **Insert** to create this MWI number.

After you have created an MWI on and off number, you can test them by dialing each number from a Cisco IP phone. When the MWI on number is dialed, the light should come on. When the MWI off number is dialed, the light should go off.

Now a voice-mail pilot must be created. A voice-mail pilot is used to determine the number that is dialed when users press the messages button on their phones. This number is normally the same as the hunt pilot number you defined for the voice-mail hunt list. After the voice-mail pilot number is created, it is assigned to a voice-mail profile. Voice-mail profiles are associated with lines on phones and are used to define voice-mail related attributes. Voice-mail profiles will be discussed shortly, but first, let's create a voice-mail pilot.

Step 1 From within CCMAdmin, select **Feature>Voice Mail>Voice Mail Pilot>**.

Step 2 On the next page, select the **Add a New Voice Mail Pilot** radio button.

Step 3 In the **Voice Mail Pilot Number** field, enter the hunt pilot number that points to the voice-mail hunt list.

Step 4 In the **Description** field, enter a description that will help identify this voice-mail pilot. For example, if there are multiple Unity servers connected to this CallManager, use the name of the Unity server to which this pilot points as part of the description.

Step 5 Select the CSS for this voice-mail pilot from the **Calling Search Space** drop-down menu.

Step 6 If you want this number to be the default voice-mail number for phones on the system, check the **Make this the default Voice Mail Pilot for the system** box.

Step 7 Click the **Insert** button to add the voice-mail pilot.

The last thing that must be configured is a voice-mail profile. Voice-mail profiles are assigned to lines and determine what voice-mail pilot the line uses. A voice-mail profile also applies a voice mailbox mask, if one is defined. A voice mailbox mask is used to change the extension number that is sent to Unity. This may be needed if the extension number in Unity is different than the one assigned to the phone. However, some similarity is needed. For instance, if the extension on the phone is 2001 and the extension in Unity is 52001, a mask of 5XXXX could be used. This mask changes 2001 to 52001.

To create a voice-mail profile, follow these steps.

Step 1   From within CCMAdmin, select **Feature>Voice Mail>Voice Mail Profile**.

Step 2   On the next page, select the **Add a New Voice Mail Profile** radio button.

Step 3   In the **Voice Mail Profile Name** field, enter a name for this voicemail profile.

Step 4   In the **Description** field, enter a description that helps identify this voice-mail profile. For example, if there are multiple Unity servers connected to this CallManager, use the name of the Unity server to which this profile points as part of the description.

Step 5   Select the voice-mail pilot from the **Voice Mail Pilot** drop-down list.

Step 6   In the **Voice Mail Box Mask** field, enter a mask if there is a need to change the extension number that is sent to Unity.

Step 7   If you want this profile to be the default voice-mail profile for phones on the system, check the **Make this the default Voice Mail Profile for the system** box.

Step 8   Click the **Insert** button to add the voice-mail pilot.

All of the configuration required within CallManager for a Unity integration should now be complete. By default all the phones on the system will use the default voice-mail profile that is defined as shown in Step 7 of the previous steps.

Creating Users

Some CallManager features require that users be defined on CallManager. The users added to CallManager are stored in a Lightweight Directory Access Protocol (LDAP) directory on CallManager by default. CallManager offers the option of using Active Directory and Netscape's LDAP directory but by default uses DC Directory, which is loaded on the CallManager during the install process.

Some of the features covered later in this chapter require that users be created, so let's take a look at how this is done. This section demonstrates only how to create a user. Later in the chapter, advanced user configuration is discussed. This section is also limited to covering how to add a user when using DC directory, which is installed on the CallManager, not AD or Netscape.

The following steps show how to create a user on CallManager.

Step 1   From within CCMAdmin, select **User>Add a New User**.

Step 2   A screen similar to that shown in Figure 6-15 displays.

Figure 6-15   *User Configuration*

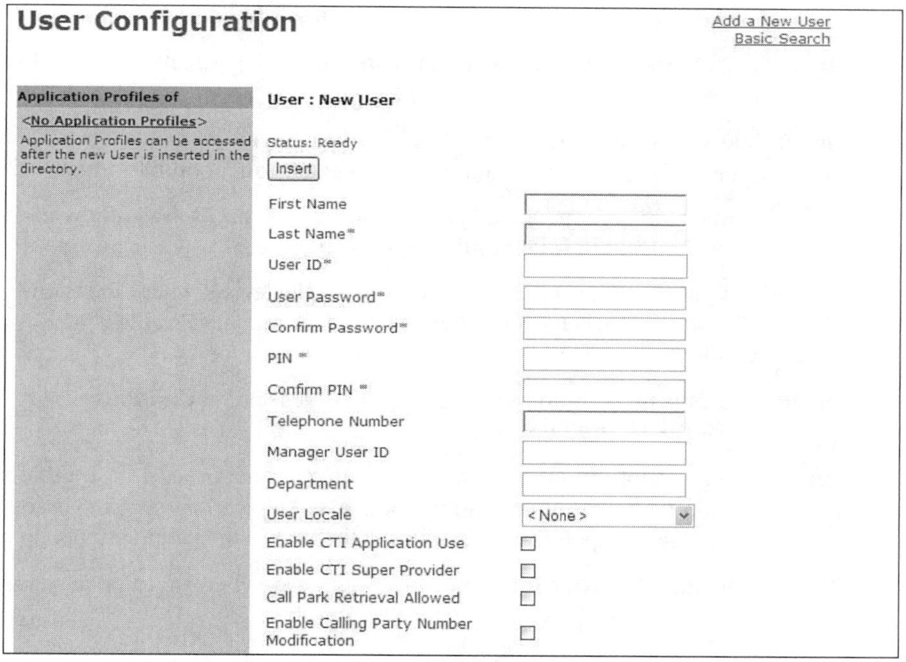

Step 3   Enter the first and last name in the appropriate fields.

Step 4   In the **User ID** field, enter a username. This name is used when the user logs into CallManager's user web pages. After the user is added, this field cannot be changed.

Note   If extension mobility is going to be used, you may want to make the user ID all numeric. Extension mobility can be configured to accept only digits for user IDs. This makes the login process a little faster for the users because they don't have to spell out user IDs.

Step 5   Enter the password for this user in the **User Password** field and confirm it in the **Confirm Password** field. The user password is the same one that is used when the user logs in to the user web pages.

Step 6   Enter a PIN in the **PIN** field and confirm it by entering it again in the **Confirm PIN** field. The PIN can only be numeric and is used to log into services on the phone.

Step 7   Enter the telephone number of the user in the **Telephone Number** field.

Step 8   Enter the manager of this user in the **Manager User ID** field. The user you enter in this field must already exist in the directory.

Step 9   In the **Department** field, enter the name of the department in which this user works.

Step 10   Select the locale for this user from the **User Locale** drop-down list. This information is used for features such as extension mobility.

Step 11   To allow this user to use CTI applications, such as Cisco's softphone, check the **Enable CTI Application Use** box.

Step 12   To allow the CTI application to control all CTI devices, check the **Enable CTI Super Provider** box. If this box is checked, the **Enable CTI Application Use** box should also be checked.

Step 13   To enable this user to retrieve parked calls, check the **Call Park Retrieval Allowed** box.

Step 14   To allow applications to modify the calling number, check the **Enable Calling Party Number Modification** box. Applications such as Cisco's Emergency Responder need to be able to modify the calling number.

Step 15   From the **View page in** drop-down list, select the language that this user phone should display.

Step 16   Click the **Insert** button to add this user.

After users are added, the user can log into CallManager's user web pages and change items, such as passwords and PINs. The user web pages also allow users to subscribe to phone services, configure speed dials, and configure various other features on the phone, but this can only be done once a device is associated with the user. The following steps show how to associate a device to a user.

Step 1   From within CCMAdmin, select **User>Global Directory.**

Step 2   Enter the user's last name in the **Search** field and click **Search**.

Step 3   Select the user you want to associate to the profile from the list that displays.

Step 4   Select the **Device Association** link.

Step 5   Enter search criteria to limit the results returned and click **Select Devices**.

Step 6   A list of devices displays. Check the box next to the device(s) you want to associate with this user and click **Update Selected**.

Configuring Advanced Services

In addition to the standard features that users expect a phone system to offer, CallManager offers a number of advanced features. The first part of this section explores a number of CallManager features that offer additional flexibility. These features allow users to do things such as log into phones other than their own and have those phones take on all the attributes of their own phones including directory numbers. There are a number of other features that can be configured which are accessible from a Cisco IP phone by pressing the Services button. This section examines a few of these.

The second part of this section looks at what are referred to as media resources. Media resources are required for many standard features, such as conferencing and MoH. A number of media resources are automatically installed when certain services are activated, such as the software conference bridge that was discussed earlier in this chapter. A closer look at these and at hardware media resources is offered later in this section.

Implementing Advanced Features

All users expect a phone to allow them to place a call on hold, transfer a call, and possibly initiate a conference call from time to time. These types of features are considered standard on most systems; but how about being able to look up stock quotes or check the status of an airline flight on the display of your phone? Although many would not consider this a standard feature, it is just one of the many advanced features that can be performed on many Cisco IP phones. As cool and useful as some of these features are, not all phones need them, so they can be made available only to certain phones if you wish. However, before any of these features can be used, they must first be configured on the CallManager. Let's take a look at some of these features and the configuration each requires.

Configuring IP Phone Services

Most Cisco IP phones have the ability to run services. These services allow them to perform functions that range from checking the weather to serving as a time clock. The services available are too numerous to mention. Each service is an XML script that the phone downloads from a server. If you have programming experience, you may choose to create your own services or purchase services from a variety of companies that sell prepackaged phone services.

Before any phone can use a service, the system administrator must make the service available by configuring it on the CallManager. The steps to configure the services are similar for all services, but many services require specific parameters. Each service will include instructions that are unique for that particular service.

Two of the services that come with CallManager are personal address book and fastdials. Personal address book allows a user to search an address book. The address book can be created using the user web pages. Fastdials allows users to create up to 50 speed dials that they can access from this service.

To give you an idea of how these services are configured on CallManager, the following steps are presented to take you through the process of adding the Personal Directory service.

Step 1 From within CCMAdmin, select **Feature>Cisco IP Phone Services**.

Step 2 On the next page, select the **Add a New IP Phone Service** radio button.

Step 3 A screen similar to that shown in Figure 6-16 displays. In the **Service Name** field, enter **My Personal Directory**. This field determines the name of this service. This name will display on the phone under services.

Figure 6-16 *IP Phone Service Configuration*

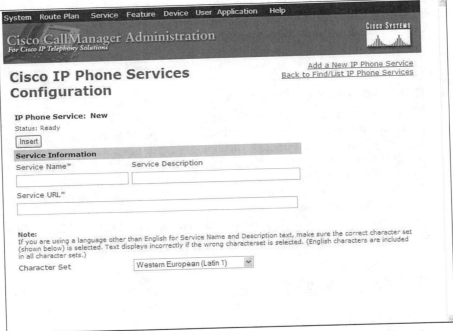

Step 4 In the **Service Description** field, enter a description for the service. In this example use **Personal Address Book**.

Step 5 In the **Service URL** field, enter the location where this service is located. In this example use "**http://x.x.x.x/ccmpd/xmlAddressBookInput.asp**" where x.x.x.x is the IP address of the CallManager and the quotes are not used. Before entering the URL, you can always check to make sure it is correct by entering the URL in your browser address box and pressing **Enter**. A good URL gives you a line-by-line display of the code; a bad URL gives you the following message: "This page cannot be displayed."

Step 6 Click **Insert**.

Note	The URL may be case sensitive, so be sure to enter it exactly as the installation notes state.

Step 7 After the service is added, additional parameters display at the bottom of the page. Click **New**.

Step 8 A new window displays. This window allows you to add parameters for this service. This service requires three parameters. To add these parameters, use the required information for each parameter that is listed in Table 6-2. The parameter name must be entered exactly as it displays in the table. After adding the first parameter, click **Insert**. After the parameter is added, click the **New** button to add the next one. Figure 6-17 shows how this screen looks with the values for the first parameters entered.

Table 6-2 *Personal Address Book IP Phone Service Parameters*

Parameter Name	UserID	UserPIN	Predial
Parameter Display Name	User Identification	PIN	Outside Access Code
Default Value	None	None	None
Parameter Description	User ID used with the Cisco IP Phone User Options window	PIN used with the Cisco IP Phone User Options window	Code used to make outside calls
Parameter is Required	Yes	Yes	No
Parameter is a Password (mask contents)	No	No	No

Step 9 After adding the third parameter, click **Insert and Close**. An informational message displays telling you to update the subscription. Click **OK**.

Step 10 Click the **Update Subscriptions** button. An informational window displays stating that, depending on how many devices subscribe to this service, the reset could take a while. Click **OK**.

Step 11 A message displays stating that the update was successful. Click **OK**.

The personal directory service is now configured, but it is not available on any phone. Users must log into the user web pages and subscribe to the service. An administrator can also subscribe a phone to the service from the phone configuration page.

Extension Mobility

Extension mobility is another feature of CallManager. This allows users to log into other phones and have those phones take on all of the attributes of their own phones or user profiles. A user device profile includes all the required phone attributes including extension numbers. This can be useful in environments where users are often working in different locations.

Figure 6-17 *Cisco IP Phone Service Parameters*

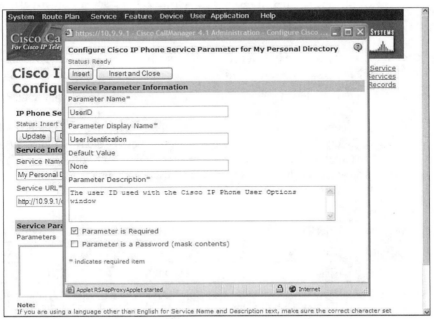

A number of items must be configured to implement extension mobility, and because certain tasks depend on other tasks already having been completed, the order in which these tasks are done is important. Let's start by configuring the extension mobility service parameters and adding the extension mobility IP phone service.

To configure the extension mobility services on the CallManager, follow these steps.

Step 1 From within CCMAdmin, select **Service>Service Parameters**.

Note As this is not one of the more common services, it may need to be enabled before it shows up in the service parameters drop-down list. If it is not present, you will need to activate the service from the Serviceability>Service Activation window.

Step 2 Select the CallManager name from the **Server** drop-down list.

Step 3 Select **Cisco Extension Mobility** from the **Service** drop-down list.

Step 4 A screen similar to that shown in Figure 6-18 displays. The Enforce Maximum Login Time field determines if the value in the Maximum Login Time field is enforced. If set to True, phones automatically log out when the time entered in the Maximum Login Time field has expired. To not logout phones after this time has expired, select **False**.

Figure 6-18 *Extension Mobility Service Parameters*

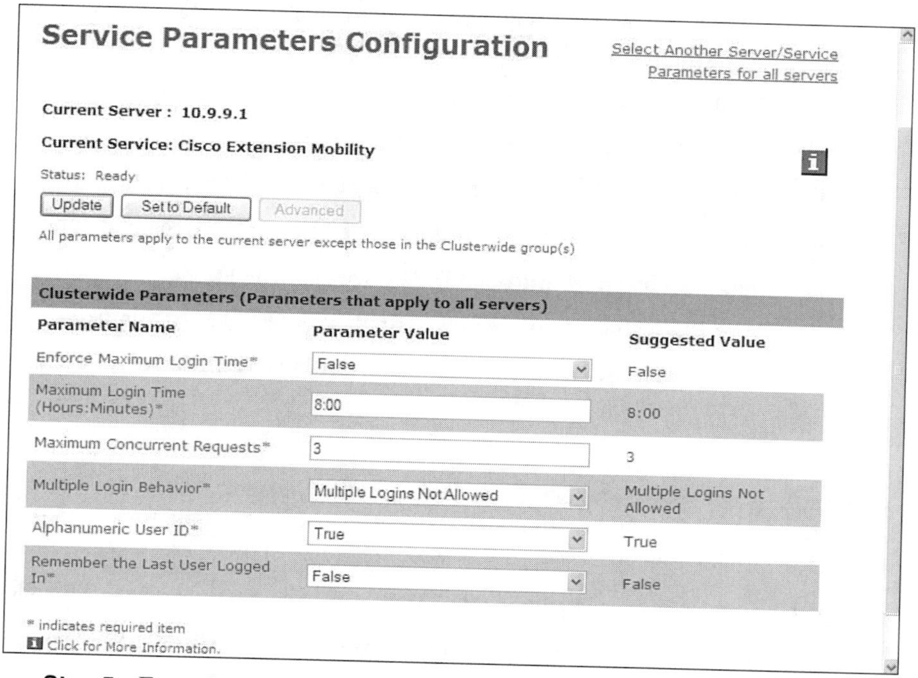

Step 5   Enter the amount of time after which phones will automatically log out. This value is used only if the Enforce Maximum Login Time is set to True.

Step 6   In the Maximum Concurrent Requests field, enter the number of concurrent login or logout requests that this service will allow. This number prevents the service from consuming too many system resources.

Step 7   From the **Multiple Login Behavior** drop-down list, select if the multiple logins will be allowed and if so how. The choices are:

— **Multiple Logins Allowed**—A user can log into multiple devices at the same time.

— **Multiple Logins Not Allowed**—A user can log into only one device at a time.

— **Auto Logout**—If a user who is already logged into one device logs into another device, she will be automatically logged out of the first device.

Step 8   The Alphanumeric User ID drop-down list defines whether user IDs will contain letters and numbers or numbers only. Selecting **True** means that the ID contains letters and numbers, and **False** means the ID contains only numbers.

Step 9 The Remember the Last User Logged In field determines if the phone will remember the ID of the last user who logged in. For security reasons it is recommended that this be set to **False**.

Step 10 If you have changed any of the values on this page, click **Update**.

Now let's look at the steps required to add the extension mobility IP phone service.

Step 1 From within CCMAdmin, select **Feature>Cisco IP Phone Services.**

Step 2 On the next page, select the **Add a New IP Phone Service** radio button.

Step 3 Enter **Extension Mobility** in the Service Name field.

Step 4 Enter **Extension Mobility Service** in the Service Description field.

Step 5 Enter "**http://x.x.x.x/emapp/EMAppServlet?device=#DEVICENAME#**" where x.x.x.x is the IP address of the CallManager.

Step 6 Click **Insert**.

After these tasks are completed, user device profiles must be created for users who will be using extension mobility. In most cases, the user device profile should have the same attributes as the user's phone. The following steps show how to create a user device profile.

Step 1 From within CCMAdmin, select **Device>Device Settings>Device Profile.**

Step 2 On the next page, select the **Add a New User Device Profile** radio button.

Step 3 A screen similar to that shown in Figure 6-19 displays. From the **Device Type** drop-down list, select the type of phone on which this profile is based.

Step 4 In the **User Device Profile Name** field, enter a name for this profile.

Step 5 In the **Description** field, enter a description that helps identify this profile.

Step 6 From the **User Hold Audio Source** field, select the audio source to be played when a call is placed on hold by pressing the Hold button.

Step 7 The **User Locale** field determines the language and fonts used for the phone. The default user locale, which is set in the enterprise parameters, is used if this field is left set to None. If this phone needs to use a different locale than is defined by its device pools or the enterprise parameters, select the proper one from the drop-down list.

Step 8 If the **Ignore Presentation Indicators (internal calls only)** check box is checked, internal caller ID restrictions are ignored. This means that if an internal call is configured to block caller ID, the caller ID will still show up on this device.

Step 9 From the drop-down list in the **Phone Button Template** field, select the desired template for this profile.

Figure 6-19 *Device Profile Configuration*

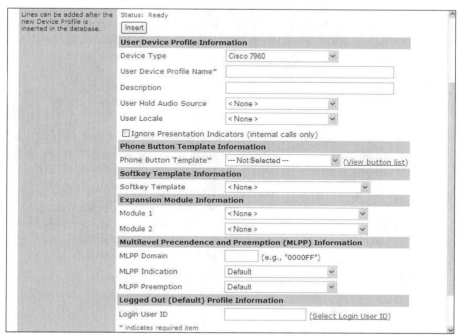

Step 10 From the drop-down list in the **Softkey Template** field, select a softkey template for this phone.

Step 11 The next two fields, **Module 1** and **Module 2** are used when expansion modules (7914) are used with this profile. If this profile is going to use expansion modules, select the modules from the drop-down list.

Step 12 The next three fields define MultiLevel Precedence and Preemption (MLPP) characteristics of this phone. If these fields are left blank or set to default, the values set in the device pool are used. The first MLPP field is the MLPP Domain. MLPP only grants higher priority from calls with the same MLPP domain. For this reason a MLPP domain is needed.

Step 13 The MLPP Indication field determines whether tones and indications are presented when a precedence call is made. The precedence indication may be a special ring back or a display, if the caller's phone supports it, and a special ringer on the called parties' side.

Step 14 The MLPP Preemption field determines whether a higher precedence call preempts a lower precedence call. The value of Disabled does not allow this to happen. To cause a lower precedence call to be terminated if a higher precedence call requires the resources, set this parameter to Forceful.

Step 15   In the **Login User ID** field, enter the user ID of the user with which this profile is associated. If the user device profile is used as a logout profile, specify the login user ID that is associated with the phone. After the user logs out from this user device profile, the phone will automatically log into this login user ID.

Step 16   Click the **Insert** button to add this profile.

Step 17   A message displays informing you that the profile has been added and that lines must now be configured. Click **OK**.

Step 18   A screen that allows you to configure the parameters for the line displays. In the **Directory Number** field, enter the extension number to be used for this line.

Step 19   The remainder of the settings on this page are the same as those found on the directory line configuration of a phone. Because you should be familiar with those settings already, individual steps are not included for each. However, if you do desire individual steps, refer to the "Adding a Line to a Phone" section in Chapter 3, "Deploying Devices."

Step 20   After you have completed filling in the remaining fields, click **Insert** to add the line. A message displays stating that the changes have been made and that any device using this profile must log out and back in before the changes will take effect. Click **OK**.

Step 21   Click the **Configure Device Profile (name)** link and add additional lines as needed.

Step 22   After all lines are configured, you must add the extension mobility service to this profile. Click the **Subscribe/Unsubscribe Services** link.

Step 23   A screen similar to that shown in Figure 6-20 displays. Select **Extension Mobility** from the Select a Service drop-down list. Click **Continue**.

Step 24   Click the **Subscribe** button.

Step 25   After the window refreshes, close it.

Now the profile must be associated with a user as shown in the steps that follow. These steps assume that the user already exists in the directory.

Step 1   From within CCMAdmin, select **User>Global Directory**.

Step 2   Enter the user's last name in the **Search** field and click **Search**.

Step 3   Select the user you want to associate with the profile from the list that displays.

Step 4   Make sure that the **Enable CTI Application** box is checked. If it isn't, check the box and click **Update**.

Step 5   Select the **Extension Mobility** link.

Figure 6-20 *Add Extension Mobility Service to a Profile*

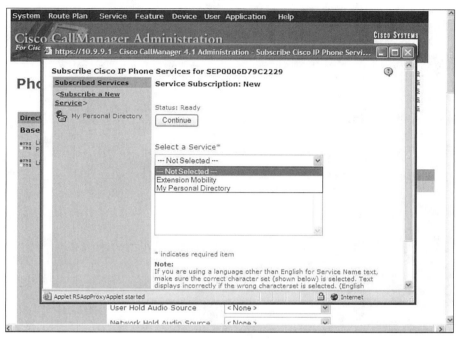

Step 6 Enter search criteria to limit the results returned and click **Select Profiles**.

Step 7 A list of profiles displays below. Check the box next to the profile you want to associate with this user and click **Update Selected**.

After device profiles are configured and associated with a user, extension mobility must be enabled on the phones. This requires that the phone is subscribed to the extension mobility service and that the extension mobility parameters are configured on the phone. The following steps show how to complete the tasks.

Step 1 From within CCMAdmin, select **Device>Phone**.

Step 2 Enter search criteria in the **Search** field to limit the results and click the **Find** button.

Step 3 Select the phone on which you want to enable extension mobility from the list that is generated.

Step 4 Figure 6-21 shows the extension mobility parameters that display on the phone configuration page. To enable this feature, check the **Enable Extension Mobility Feature** box.

Step 5 The Log Out Profile determines what profile the phone uses when no one is logged into it. To have the phone keep its current settings, select **Use Current Device Settings**.

Figure 6-21 *Phone Configuration Page–Extension Mobility*

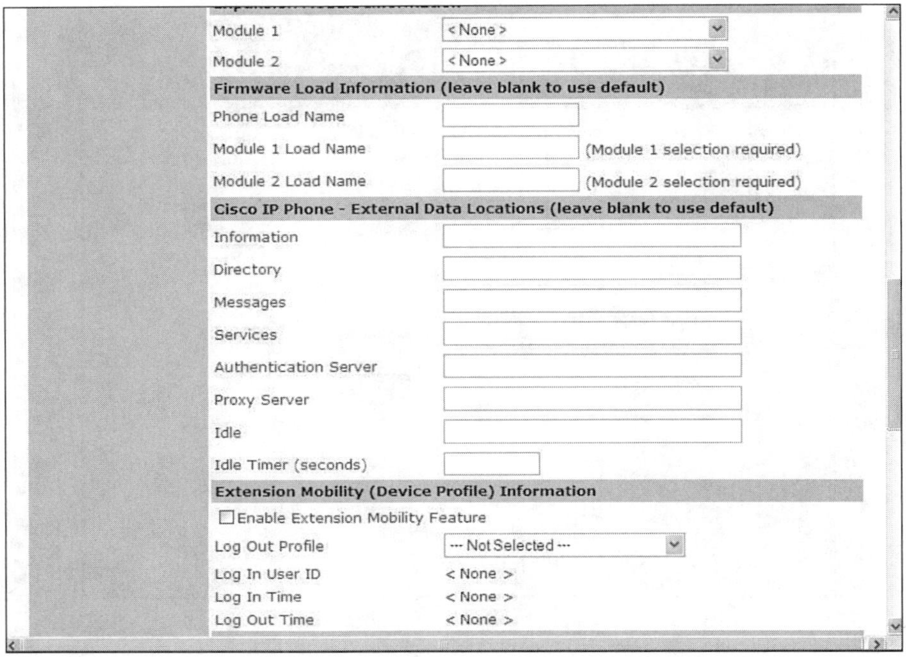

Step 6 Click **Update** to save the changes. A message displays stating that the phone must be reset before the changes take effect. Click **OK**.

Step 7 Click the **Reset Phone** button and then the **Reset** button on the page that displays next. A message displays informing you that the phone has been reset. Click **OK**.

Note If reset is requested for a phone that is currently on a call, the reset will not occur until the call has ended.

Step 8 Click the **Subscribe/Unsubscribe Services** link.

Step 9 A screen similar to that shown when adding the extension mobility server to a device profile displays. Select **Extension Mobility** from the **Select a Service** drop-down list. Click **Continue**.

Step 10 Click the **Subscribe** button.

Step 11 After the window refreshes, close it.

At this point users should be able to start to use the extension mobility feature.

Creating and Managing Media Resources

Some of the features that are available on CallManager require what are known as media resources in order to function. These resources may be processes that run on the CallManager or separate hardware devices. This section explores various media resources and how each is configured. A few of these are created automatically when certain CallManager services are activated, such as Annunciators, MoH servers, software MTPs and software conference bridges. For these types, the section focuses more on the function than the creation because these media resources are automatically created.

Configuring an MOH Server

MoH requires an MoH server. This is a service that runs on CallManager, and it is created when the IP Voice Media Streaming Application is activated. This service provides the resources needed to play an audio source while a call is on hold. Because this resource is automatically created, detailed configuration steps are not provided here. However, certain parameters that are unique to this service are explained. Figure 6-22 shows the configuration screen for an MoH server. Navigate to **Service>Media Resource>Music On Hold Server**, click **Find** and select the desired MoH server to reach this page.

Figure 6-22 *Music On Hold Server Configuration*

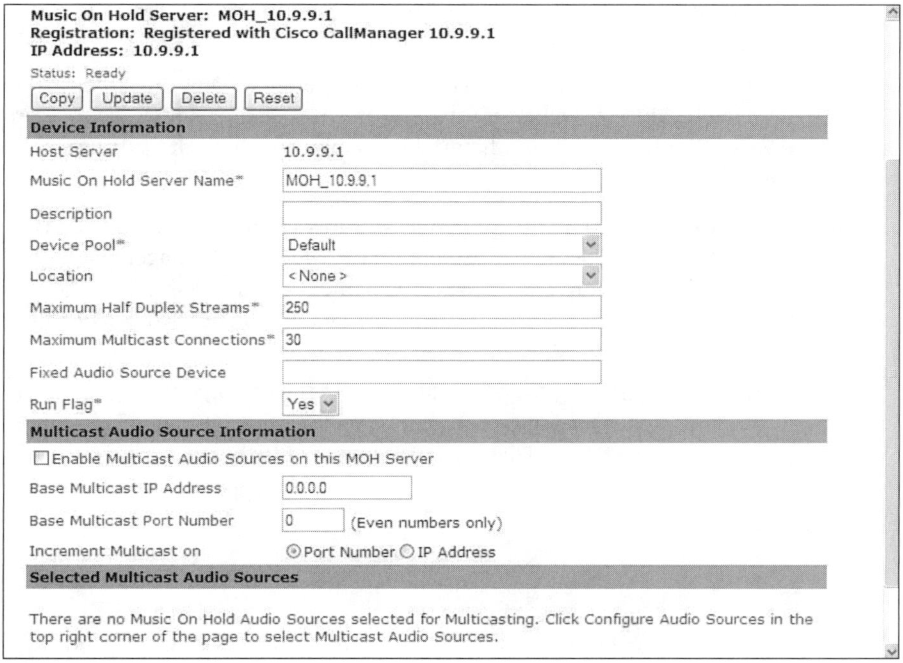

The following parameters are unique to the MoH server:

- **Maximum Half Duplex Streams**—Determines the number of devices to which the server can provide a unicast audio stream at one time.

- **Maximum Multicast Connections**—Defines the maximum number of devices to which the server can provide a multicast music audio stream at one time.

- **Fixed Audio Source Device**—Allows you to use a live audio source for MoH if a sound card is installed in the CallManager that is acting as the MoH server. Enter the name of the sound card in this field. The name of the sound card must be the same as the name that displays in the **Sound Recording** field found in Windows **Control Panel>Sounds and Multimedia> Audio** tab.

- **Run Flag**—When set to No the MoH server does not provide music on hold. Set to **Yes** to have the MoH server provide music.

- **Base Multicast IP Address**—This is the base address that multicast uses if multicast is enabled. To enable multicast, the **Enable Multicast Audio Sources on this MOH Server** check box must be selected, and the MoH server must be assigned to a multicast media resource group. Media resource groups are discussed later in this section.

- **Base Multicast Port Number**—Determines the base port number that the multicast stream uses.

The multicast stream can increase, based on port number or IP address. This is configured by choosing the appropriate radio button on this page.

Additional audio files can be added to the MoH server. After they are added, devices can be configured to play different audio sources. Adding new audio sources is fairly simple. MP3 and WAV files can be used. The following steps take you through the process of adding an audio source file.

Step 1   Copy the desired file to the **Program Files\Cisco\MOH\DropMOH AudioSourceFilesHere** directory on the MoH CallManager. No, I am not making this up. That is really the name of the directory. After the files are placed there, they are formatted so that they can be used as MoH files.

Note	If the **C:\Program Files\Cisco\MOH\DropMOHAudioSource FilesHere** directory cannot be found, make sure that the MoH Audio Translator service has been activated. If this service is not activated, the directory may not appear.

Note	While the CallManager is processing the audio files, the CPU utilizations may reach high levels. This could negatively impact call processing. It is best to add files during low peak hours. Also, adding a large number of files at one time can cause the CPU utilization to remain high until all files are processed.

Step 2   You know that the files have been processed when they no longer display in the Program Files\Cisco\MOH\DropMOHAudioSourceFilesHere directory. After the audio files are copied onto the MoH server, you need to configure the MoH to serve them as audio sources. From within CCMAdmin, select **Service>Media Resource>Music On Hold Audio Source**.

Step 3   Up to 51 audio sources can be configured. Using the **MOH Audio Stream Number** drop-down list, select the number that determines where this audio source displays in the list of audio sources.

Step 4   From the **MOH Audio Source File** drop-down list, select the desired audio. The files you copied to the Program Files\Cisco\MOH\DropMOH AudioSourceFilesHere directory should display in this list. After you select a file, the detail of the file displays in the MOH Audio Source File Status box.

Step 5   Enter a name in the **MOH Audio Source Name** field that helps identify this audio source later.

Step 6   To have the audio source repeat when it reaches the end, check the **Play Continuously** check box.

Step 7   If you have enabled multicast for the MoH server the **Allow Multicast** box must be checked for audio sources that you wish to be used as a multicast stream.

Step 8   Click the **Insert** button to add this audio source.

The audio source is now available to be added to a device. Throughout this book you have seen that an MoH audio source file can be placed at the line level, the device level, or the device pool level. If an audio source is not specified on any of these levels, the default level defined on the Cisco CallManager service parameters configuration page is used. The steps that follow show how to assign the user hold and network hold audio source fields at the device level for a phone.

Assign an MOH Audio Source to a Phone

The steps that follow show how to assign an MoH audio source to a phone.

Step 1   From within CCMAdmin, select **Device>Phone**.

Step 2   Enter search criteria in the **Search** field to limit the results and click the **Find** button.

Step 3   From the list that is generated, select the phone to which you want to assign an MoH audio source.

Step 4   The phone configuration screen displays. To assign a user hold audio source to the phone, select an audio source from the **User Hold Audio Source** drop-down list.

Step 5 To assign a network hold audio source to the phone, select an audio source from the **Network Hold Audio Source** drop-down list.

Step 6 Click the **Update** button.

Step 7 A window displays informing you that you must reset the phone for the change to take effect. Click **OK**.

Step 8 Click the **Reset Phone** button.

Step 9 A window displays allowing you to reset or restart the phone. Click the **Reset** button.

Step 10 A window displays informing you that the reset has been initiated. Click **OK**.

After all audio sources are added, assign them as desired. In most cases audio source files can be added at the device-pool level. If there is a need to have phones within the same device pool use different audio sources, you can configure the audio sources at the device level, which will override the device pool settings.

It is important to understand that a device's audio source determines what the held party hears when a call is placed on hold. A device's audio source does not determine what that device hears when it is placed on hold. To determine what outside callers hear, configure the audio sources on the PSTN gateway.

Creating Conference Bridges

As discussed earlier, CallManager has the ability to accommodate conference calls. In order to do this, a conference bridge is required. Conference bridges come in two types: hardware and software. The software bridge runs on the CallManager and is created when the IP Voice Media Streaming Application is activated. Because the software conference bridge is a process that runs on CallManager, it takes available cycles away for other functions of the CallManager. To avoid this, hardware conference bridges are recommended.

Hardware conference bridges run on a number of Cisco devices. These devices have Digital Signal Processors (DSPs) that can be used for conferencing purposes. The devices that support hardware conference bridges are continuing to expand. It is recommended that you check Cisco.com for the most current list of hardware. The Catalyst 6000, 6608, T1 blade, and a Cisco 2600 with a DSP farm are examples of the range of equipment that can serve as a conference bridge.

Depending on the hardware that is being used, the configuration of a conference bridge varies. To give you an idea of the configuration process, the following steps show how to configure a T1 port on a catalyst 6000 as a hardware conference bridge.

Step 1 From within CCMAdmin, select **Service>Media Resource>Conference Bridge**.

Step 2   On the next page, select the **Add a New Conference Bridge** link.

Step 3   From the **Conference Bridge Type** drop-down list, select **Cisco Conference Bridge Hardware**.

Six different types of conference bridges can be configured. Table 6-3 provides a brief explanation of each bridge and examples of the type of hardware required.

Table 6-3   *Conference Bridges*

Bridge Type	Features	Hardware
Cisco Conference Bridge (WS-SVC-CMM)	Up to 64 Conference resources depending on codec. Codecs supported are G7.11 and G7.29.	WS-SVC-CMM-ACT
Cisco Conference Bridge Hardware	Up to 32 Conference resources depending on codec. Codecs supported are G7.11, G7.29, G7.23, GSM FR and GSM EFR.	WS-X6608-T1 WS-X6608-E1
Cisco Conference Bridge Software	Up to 64 Ad-Hoc or 128 Meet-Me conference resources. Supports G7.11 codec.	Runs on CallManager. The Cisco IP Voice Media Stream App must be activated.
Cisco IOS Conference Bridge	Total supported number of participants per conference is 6. Codecs supported are G7.11 and G7.29.	NM-HDV NM-HDV-FARM
Cisco IOS Enhanced Conference Bridge	Total supported number of participants per conference is 8. Codecs supported are G7.11, G7.29, GSM FR and GSM EFR.	NM-HD NM-HDV2
Cisco Video Conference Bridge (IPVC-35xx)	The number of conferencing resources varies based on hardware and the type of conferencing. Supports a wide variety of audio and video codecs.	IP/VC 3511 IP/VC 3540

Step 4   Enter the MAC address of the T1 port in the **MAC Address** field. The MAC address can be found by entering the **show port (slot number)** command on the Catalyst.

Step 5   In the **Description** field enter a description that helps identify the purpose of this conference bridge. In the description, you may want to include on which Catalyst it is installed.

Step 6 From the **Device Pool** drop-down list, select the device pool for this conference bridge.

Step 7 From the **Location** drop-down list, select a location for this conference bridge if one is required.

Step 8 The **Special Load** field allows you to enter special load information. In most cases this field is left blank.

Step 9 Click the **Insert** button to add this bridge.

After the conference bridge is created, it is available for use. Sometimes it may be necessary to reset the T1 port in the Catalyst 6000 in order for it to register to CallManager before this bridge can be used.

Configuring MTPs

Media Termination Points (MTPs) are typically thought of as a software process that runs on the CallManager. Although MTPs can also be hardware devices, this section focuses on the function and configuration tasks for software MTPs. Hardware MTPs are discussed in the next section.

MTPs serve two different functions. First, they provide what are called supplementary services for calls coming from an H.323 (version 1) gateway. Supplementary services are features such as hold, transfer, conferencing, and park. Each of these features requires that the connection be modified, and H.323 (version 1) does not have the ability to modify connections. So, the MTPs serve as a termination point between the end point and the gateway. This allows modification of the connection to take place between the MTP and the end point while the connection between the MTP and the gateway remains intact.

MTPs are also required for (Session Initiation Protocol) SIP calls. SIP sends dual tone multifrequency (DTMF) tones in-band, whereas Skinny Client Control Protocol (SCCP) uses out of band. This means that DTMF tones need to be translated between the two. MTPs can provide this function.

Software MTPs are created when the Cisco IP Voice Media Streaming Application service is activated. No other configuration is needed other than perhaps to change the MTPs device pool. To change the MTPs device pool follow these steps.

Step 1 From within CCMAdmin, select **Service>Media Resource>Media Termination Point**.

Step 2 On the next page, enter search criteria to limit the results and click **Find**.

Step 3 Select the MTP from the list that displays.

Step 4 Select the desired device pool from the **Device Pool** drop-down list.

Step 5 Click **Update**. A message displays stating that the change will take effect when the streaming is idle. Click **OK**.

Because the activation of Cisco IP Voice Media Streaming Application service causes MTPs to be created, nothing else needs to be done other than assigning MTPs to media resource groups and lists, which will be discussed later in this chapter.

Creating Transcoders

Transcoders are hardware devices that convert calls from one codec to another. This needs to be done when a call is placed between two devices that cannot communicate using the same codec. For example, if a device that could only use G7.29 called a device that could only use G7.11, a transcoder would be needed to convert the codec so that the call could take place. Here is a real world example. A phone in a remote branch, which is configured to use G.729 when placing calls across the WAN, wants to participate in a conference call that originated on the other side of the WAN, and a software conference bridge is being used. Because software conference bridges support only G7.11, and the remote can only support G7.29 across the WAN, a transcoder is needed to convert 7.29 to 7.11 and vice versa.

Transcoders can run on a number of Cisco devices. These devices have Digital Signal Processors (DSPs) that can be used for transcoding purposes. The devices that support hardware transcoding continue to expand. It is recommended that you check Cisco.com for the most current list of hardware. The Catalyst 6000, 6608, T1 blade, and a Cisco 2600 with a DSP farm are examples of the wide range of equipment that can serve as transcoders.

Depending on the hardware that is being used, the configuration of a transcoder will vary. To give you an idea of the configuration process the following steps show how to configure a Cisco 2600XM with a NM-HDV as a transcoder.

Step 1 From within CCMAdmin, select **Service>Media Resource>Transcoder**.

Step 2 On the next page, select the **Add a New Transcoder** link.

Step 3 From the **Transcoder Type** drop-down list, select **Cisco Conference IOS Media Termination Point**.

Four different types of transcoders can be configured. Table 6-4 provides a brief explanation of each and examples of the type of hardware required.

Table 6-4   *Transcoders*

Transcoder Type	Features	Hardware
Cisco Media Termination Point (WS-SVC-CMM)	Transcodes G7.11, G7.29, G7.23, GSM FR and GSM EFR.	WS-SVC-CMM-ACT
Cisco Media Termination Point Hardware	Transcodes G7.11, G7.29, G7.23, GSM FR and GSM EFR.	WS-X6608-T1 WS-X6608-E1
Cisco IOS Media Termination Point	Transcodes G7.11, G7.29, GSM FR and GSM EFR.	NM-HDV NM-HDV-FARM
Cisco IOS Enhanced Media Termination Point	Transcodes G7.11, G7.29, GSM FR and GSM EFR.	NM-HD NM-HDV2

Step 4   In the **Description** field, enter a description that helps identify the purpose of this conference bridge. In that description, you may want to include on which Catalyst it is installed.

Step 5   Enter name of the IOS device in which the transcoding resource is installed in the **Device Name** field.

Step 6   From the **Device Pool** drop-down list, select the device pool for this conference bridge.

Step 7   The **Special Load** field allows you to enter special load information. In most cases this field is left blank.

Step 8   Click the **Insert** button to add this transcoder.

After the transcoder is created, it is available for use. Later in this chapter, you will see how to assign transcoders to media resource groups and lists.

Configuring Annunciators

Annunciator is a process that runs on a CallManager that plays recorded announcements to devices. These announcements are triggered by specific events. An example is when a user dials a number that is not valid. In the past, the user would receive what is called a reorder tone, which sounds like a fast busy signal. With the annunciator, a message plays that states "Your call cannot be completed as dialed. Please consult your directory and call again or ask your operator for assistance. This is a recording."

The annuncitor is also used to play other messages to inform the caller of events, such as service disruption, or the MLPP causing a call to fail.

An annunciator is created when the Cisco IP Voice Media Streaming Application service is activated. No other configuration is needed other than perhaps to change the device pool. To change the device pool of an annunciator, follow these steps.

Step 1   From within CCMAdmin, select **Service>Media Resource>Annunciator**.

Step 2   On the next page, enter search criteria to limit the results and click **Find**.

Step 3   Select the Annunciator from the list that displays.

Step 4   Select the desired device pool from the **Device Pool** drop-down list.

Step 5   Click **Update**. A message displays stating that the change will take effect when the streaming is idle. Click **OK**.

Step 6   Another message displays stating that the annunciator must be reset before the changes will take effect. Click **OK**.

Step 7   Click the **Reset** button. A message displays stating that this action will reset the annunciator. Click **OK**. Another message displays stating that the annunciator is being reset, click **OK**.

Because an annunciator is created when the Cisco IP Voice Media Streaming Application service is activated, the only other configuration that you may want to make is to add the annunciator to a media resource group. Media resource groups and lists are discussed next.

Media Resource Management

After all of the media resources are configured, they can be used. To make the most effective use of the resources, however, CallManager allows you to manage how resources are used and what devices are allowed to use them. In addition, media resource management allows the resource to be shared throughout the cluster.

Media resource management is accomplished by creating Media Resource Groups (MRGs) and Media Resource Group Lists (MRGLs). Media resource groups are groups that contain various media resources. A media resource group list contains one or more media resource groups. A device is then assigned a media resource group list that determines the media resource groups to which the device has access. The order in which the groups display in the list determine which group is queried first for a requested resource. Resources that are assigned to an MRG are shared in a round-robin fashion with exception of conference bridges. Consequently, the first conference resource listed in an MRG wouldn't necessarily be the one that is used. In the case of conference resources, CallManager checks each conference bridge in the MRG to see how many resources are available and selects the bridge with the greatest number available, which gives the user the greatest chance of successfully adding the number of audio streams to the conference. The order in which the media resources appear in the group determines the order in which requested resources are used. Figure 6-23 shows an example of this.

Figure 6-23 *Media Resource Group List Example*

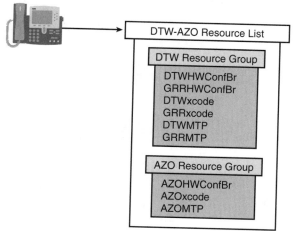

In this example, the phone is assigned the DTW-AZO Resource List. When the phone needs a conference bridge resource, all conferences in the MRG are queried to see which one has the most available resources. When all resources are available on all conference bridges, the first one is used. In this example, that would be the DTWHWConfBr because it is the first one listed in the first group. If all the conference resources in the first group were unavailable, then the AZOHWConfBr would be used because it is in the second group. In the event that a device requests a resource that is not in any of its resource groups, an attempt is made to use a resource allocated to the default group. Any device that is not associated with a specific group is part of the default group.

You will see that the creation and configuration of media resource groups and lists is very similar to that of route groups and lists. Let's take a look at how a media resource group is configured.

The following steps show how to create a media resource group.

Step 1   From within CCMAdmin, select **Service>Media Resource>Media Resource Group**.

Step 2   Click the **Add a New Media Resource Group** link.

Step 3   A screen similar to that shown in Figure 6-24 displays. In the **Media Resource Group Name** field, enter a name for this group.

Step 4   In the **Description** field, enter a description that helps identify this group.

Figure 6-24   *Media Resource Group Configuration*

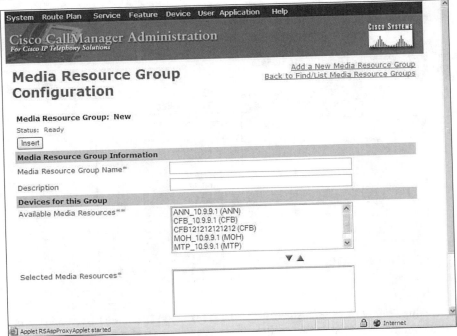

Step 5   From the **Available Media Resources** box, select the resource you want to add to this group. Click the **down arrow** below this box.

Note	You can select more than one resource at a time by holding down the **Ctrl** key when selecting them.

Step 6   The selected resources now display in the Selected Media Resources box. You may remove a resource by selecting it and clicking the up arrow.

Step 7   After all the desired resources are in the Selected Media Resources box, click the **Insert** button to add this group.

Now the groups need to be assigned to a media resource list. The following steps show how to assign MRG to MRGL.

Step 1   From within CCMAdmin, select **Service>Media Resource>Media Resource Group List**.

Step 2   Click the **Add a New Media Resource Group List** link.

Step 3   A screen similar to that shown in Figure 6-25 displays. Enter a descriptive name in the **Media Resource Group List Name** field.

Figure 6-25   *Media Resource Group List Configuration*

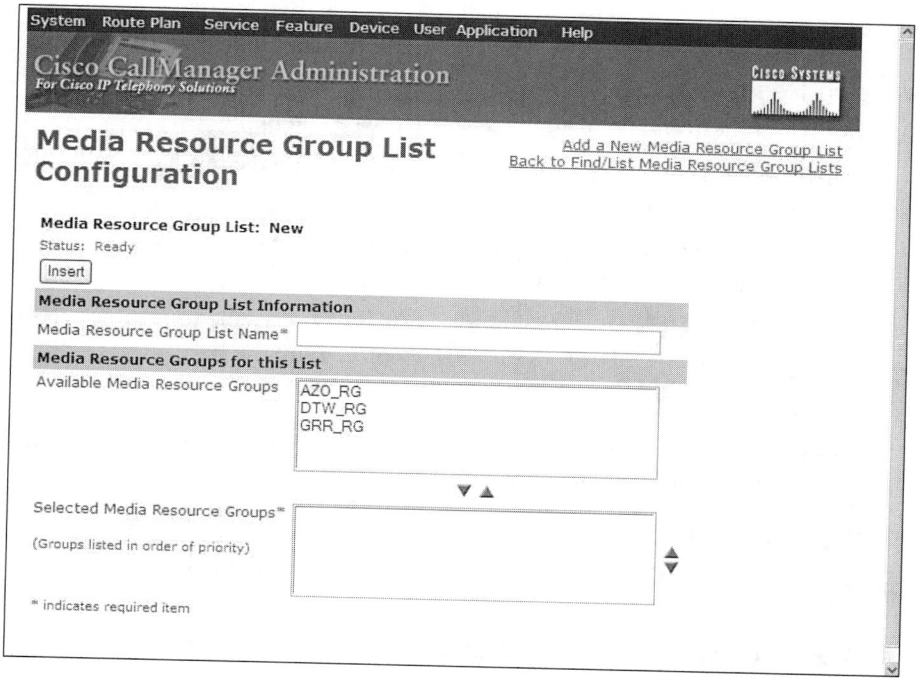

Step 4   From the **Available Media Resource Groups** box, select the groups you want to add to this list. Click the **down** arrow below this box.

Note   You can select more than one group at a time by holding down the **Ctrl** key when selecting them.

Step 5   The selected resources now display in the **Selected Media Resource Groups** box. You can change the order a group displays in the list by highlighting the name and clicking the **up** and **down** arrows located to the right of the Selected Media Resource Groups box. You may also remove a group by selecting it and clicking the **up** arrow located above this box.

Step 6   After all of the desired groups are in the Selected Media Resource Groups box, click the **Insert** button to add this group.

After the resource lists are created you must assign them to devices. This can be done at the device level or at the device pool level. If a media resource list is not assigned to a device, the device will use the one assigned to its device pool.

The following steps show how to assign a media resource group list to a phone and a device pool.

Assign a Media Resource Group List to a Phone

Step 1   From within CCMAdmin, select **Device>Phone**.

Step 2   Enter search criteria in the **Search** field to limit the results and click the **Find** button.

Step 3   From the list that is generated, select the phone to which you want to assign a media resource group list.

Step 4   The phone configuration screen displays. Select a media resource group list from the **Media Resource Group List** drop-down list.

Step 5   Click the **Update** button.

Step 6   A window displays informing you that you must reset the phone for the change to take effect. Click **OK**.

Step 7   Click the **Reset Phone** button.

Step 8   A window displays allowing you to reset or restart the phone. Click the **Reset** button.

Step 9   A window displays informing you that the reset has been initiated. Click **OK**.

Assign a Media Resource Group List to a Device Pool

Step 1   From within CCMAdmin, select **System>Device Pool**.

Step 2   To limit the results, enter search criteria in the **Search** field and click the **Find** button.

Step 3   From the list that is generated, select the device pool to which you want to assign a media resource group list.

Step 4   The device pool configuration screen displays. Select a media resource group list from the **Media Resource Group List** drop-down list.

Step 5   Click the **Update** button.

Step 6   A window displays informing you that all the devices in this device pool must be reset for the change to take effect. Click **OK**.

Step 7   Click the **Reset Devices** button.

Step 8   A message warns you that you are about to reset all the devices in this pool. This could cause some calls to be dropped, so it is recommended that this action only be performed during off hours. Click **OK**.

Step 9   A window displays informing you that the reset has been initiated. Click **OK**.

In most cases it is recommended to assign the media resource group list at the device pool level. This makes it easier to manage. If a device requires a unique media resource, it should be assigned at the device level.

Configuring Remote Site Failover

When deploying CallManager with remote sites, it is necessary to deploy some type of remote site redundancy in the event that the link with the central site is lost. Because every time a phone places a call it must be able to talk to CallManager. No call can be placed if the phone is unable to communicate with a CallManager. As mentioned earlier in this book, as soon as the phone goes off hook, it sends a request to CallManager. If the primary CallManager fails, the secondary can respond to all requests. What happens in a remote environment when the link to the CallManager fails? Because the phone can't reach the CallManager, the phone doesn't even know to provide dial tone. The solution is to deploy a Survivable Remote Site Telephony (SRST) solution at the remote site.

Another issue that can occur with remote sites is that the link can be operating properly but all the available bandwidth is in use and additional calls cannot be sent across this link. So, when a phone on the remote site tries to call a phone at the central site, the call is rejected due to insufficient bandwidth. This means that until bandwidth is available, the only way to reach the central site is by sending the call over a different path such as the Public

Switched Telephone Network (PSTN). This requires the caller to hang up and dial a number that will use the PSTN instead of the WAN link. The solution for this issue is to configure AAR Groups.

This section examines how SRST and AAR work and how each is configured.

SRST Overview

SRST is a service that can run on a number of Cisco devices such as the 1760, 26000XM, and 2821, just to name a few. The SRST device is located at the remote site and is typically the same device that is used for the remote site PSTN gateway.

When phones are unable to communicate with any of the CallManagers at the central site, they register with the SRST device. This device then accepts and responds to SCCP requests. All calls that are not destined for devices at the remote site are then routed out to the PSTN.

Because the SRST device is responsible for routing calls, it has to have some type of route plan programmed in it, just like a normal H.323 gateway.

The majority of the configuration is done on the SRST device itself. This part of the configuration requires some IOS telephony programming experience.

Configuring SRST

The configuration of an SRST solution is done in two places. The first is on the SRST device itself and the second is in the CallManager. Let's first take a look at a sample of the configuration on the SRST device itself.

```
access-code fxo 9
default-destination pattern 2002
dialplan-pattern 1 547....
ip source-address 10.1.1.2 port 2000
keepalive 30
max-ephones 24
max-dn 48
transfer-pattern 5472....
voicemail 5479100
```

Let's take a closer look at each of these commands and what they mean.

- access-code fxo 9

  Signifies that when a 9 is the first digit, the call is routed out an FXO port.

- default-destination pattern 2002

  Causes all inbound calls that do not match a registered directory number to be routed to extension 2002.

- dialplan-pattern 1 547 . . .

For inbound calls (calls to an IP phone in a Cisco SRST system) where the calling party number matches the dial-plan pattern, the call is considered a local call and has a distinctive ring that identifies the call as internal. Any calling party number that does not match the dial-plan pattern is considered an external call and has a distinctive ring that is different from the internal ringing. For outbound calls, the **dialplan-pattern** command converts the calling party's extension number to an E.164 calling party number. Outbound calls that do not use an E.164 number and go through a Primary Rate Interface (PRI) connection to the PSTN, may be rejected by the PRI link as the calling party identifier.

- ip source-address 10.1.1.2 port 2000

  Specifies the IP address of the interface that services all SCCP requests.

- keepalive 30

  Defines the keepalive interval in seconds.

- max-ephones 24

  Determines the maximum number of phones that are allowed to register to this device.

- max-dn 48

  Determines the maximum number of directory numbers that are allowed to register to this device.

- transfer-pattern 5472 . . .

  Determines to what numbers calls can be transferred. In this case, calls can only be forwarded to seven digit numbers that begin with 5472. IP Phone directory numbers that have registered to SRST can also be transferred to without additional configuration.

- voice mail 5479100

  Defines the number that is dialed when users press the voice-mail button on their phones.

In addition to these commands, additional dial plan and port configuration is required. It is recommended that only those familiar with IOS devices and telephony configuration of such devices perform this portion of the configuration.

After the SRST device is configured, you must configure CallManager so that phones can use this service. If the SRST device is the phone's default gateway at the remote site, fewer configurations are required. However, if the SRST device is not the default gateway for the phone, an SRST reference must be created.

An SRST reference is used to tell the phone to what device it should register if it cannot communicate with a CallManager. The following steps show how to create an SRST reference. If the SRST device is the phone's default gateway, you may skip to the Assign an SRST Reference to a Device Pool section.

Creating an SRST Reference to a Device Pool

Step 1 From within CCMAdmin, select **System>SRST>**.

Step 2 Click the **Add a New SRST Reference** link.

Step 3 A screen similar to that shown in Figure 6-26 displays. In the **SRST Reference Name** field, enter a name for this SRST Reference.

Figure 6-26 *SRST Reference Configuration*

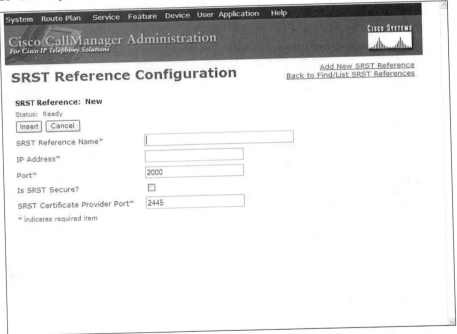

Step 4 In the **IP Address** field, enter the IP address in the interface of the SRST device that is going to service SCCP requests.

Step 5 Enter the port number that is used for SCCP in the **Port** field. In most cases this should be left at 2000.

Step 6 If the SRST device contains a self-signed or certificate-authority issued certificate, check the **Is SRST Secure?** box.

Step 7 In the **SRST Certificate Provider Port** field, enter the port number the CallManager uses to retrieve the certificate from the SRST device.

Step 8 Click **Insert** to add this SRST reference.

After you have configured all the SRST references needed, you must define which will be used by which devices. This is done by assigning an SRST reference to the device pools. The following steps show how this is done.

Assign an SRST Reference to a Device Pool

Step 1 From within CCMAdmin, select **System>Device Pool**.

Step 2 To limit the results, enter search criteria in the search field and click the **Find** button.

Step 3 From the list that is generated, select the device pool on which you want to define an SRST reference.

Step 4 The device pool configuration screen displays. Select an SRST reference from the **SRST reference** drop-down list. You will notice that, in addition to the SRST reference you created, the option **Use Default Gateway** is provided. If the SRST device is the phone's default gateway, select this option. To disallow phones from using SRST leave the SRST reference set to **Disable**.

Step 5 Click the **Update** button.

Step 6 A window displays informing you that all the devices in this device pool must be reset for the change to take effect. Click **OK**.

Step 7 Click the **Reset Devices** button.

Step 8 A message warns you that you are about to reset all the devices in this pool. This could cause some calls to be dropped, so it is recommended that this action only be performed during off hours. Click **OK**.

Step 9 A window displays informing you that the reset has been initiated. Click **OK**.

After all device pools have been configured, the SRST configuration process is complete.

Configuring AAR

AAR is used to reroute a call over an alternate path when the call fails due to lack of bandwidth. This is accomplished by creating AAR groups that define a prefix that should be assigned to a number if the call fails due to inadequate bandwidth. Figure 6-27 shows an example.

The user at the remote office only needs to dial 4201 to reach the phone in the central office. If there is enough bandwidth, the call will be successful. However, if there is not enough bandwidth, the call needs to be rerouted over the PSTN. Because 9 is used as the outside access code, the number that needs to be dialed to reach extension 4201 via the PSTN is

95484201. With AAR properly configured, the dialed digits of 4201 are automatically changed to 95484201 and the call is sent out the PSTN.

Figure 6-27 *AAR Group Example*

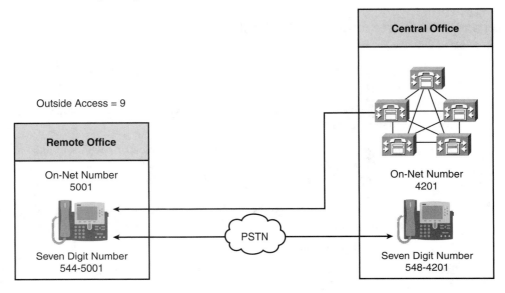

NOTE	If an external phone number mask is assigned (for example 612548XXXX) then the Prefix Digits are added to the end result of the mask's transformation. Hence in this example 916125484201 would be the end result.

To configure AAR you simply need to create AAR groups and assign them to directory numbers. The following steps show how to create an AAR Group.

Creating an AAR Group

Step 1   From within CCMAdmin, select **Route Plan>AAR group**.

Step 2   Click the **Add a New AAR Group** link.

Step 3   Enter a name for the group in the **AAR Group Name** field and click **Insert**.

Step 4   A screen like that shown in Figure 6-28 displays. Because this is the first group, there is only one field to populate. In the **Prefix Digits** field, enter the digits that will be added to the beginning of the dialed number when a device from within this group dials another device within this group.

Figure 6-28 *AAR Group Configuration*

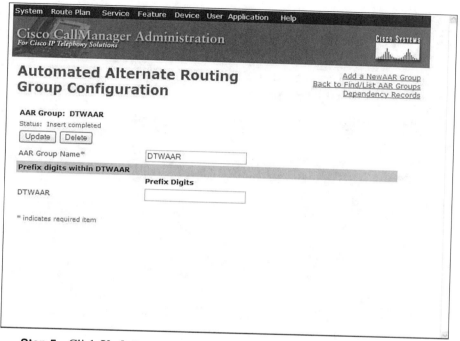

Step 5 Click **Update**.

Step 6 To see how the configuration changes when more than one group exists, create another group by clicking on the **Add a New AAR Group** link.

Step 7 Enter a name for the group in the **AAR Group Name** field and click **Insert**.

Step 8 A screen like that shown in Figure 6-29 displays. In the **Prefix Digits** field, enter the digits that will be added to the beginning of the dialed number when a device from within this group dials another device within this group.

Step 9 On this screen, there are additional fields that do not exist when only one AAR group is created. In the **Prefix Digits (From <AAR GROUP NAME>)** field, enter the digits that will be added to the beginning of the dialed number when a device from within this group dials a device within the other group.

Step 10 In the **Prefix Digits (To <AAR GROUP NAME>)**, enter the digits that will be added to the beginning of the dialed number when a device in the other group dials a device within this group.

Step 11 Click **Update**.

Figure 6-29 *AAR Group Configuration (Multiple Groups)*

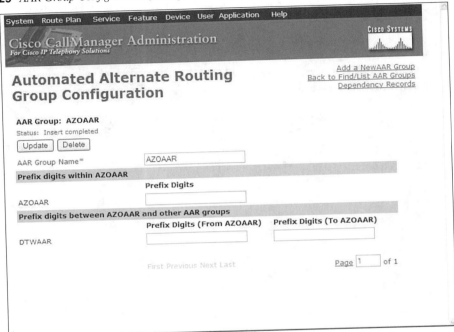

Now the AAR groups must be assigned to lines. The following steps show how to assign an AAR group to a line on a phone.

Assign an AAR Group to a Line

Step 1 From within CCMAdmin, select **Device>Phone**.

Step 2 Enter search criteria in the **Search** field to limit the results and click the **Find** button.

Step 3 Select the desired phone from the list that displays.

Step 4 Click the desired line on the left side of the screen.

Step 5 On the **Directory Number Configuration** page, select the desired AAR group from the **AAR Group** drop-down list as shown in Figure 6-30.

Step 6 Click the **Update** button at the top of the screen.

NOTE When you make a change to the directory number configuration and click **Update**, the phone will be reset. If a caller is currently on a call, the phone will reset after the call is ended.

Figure 6-30 *Assigning an AAR Group to a Line*

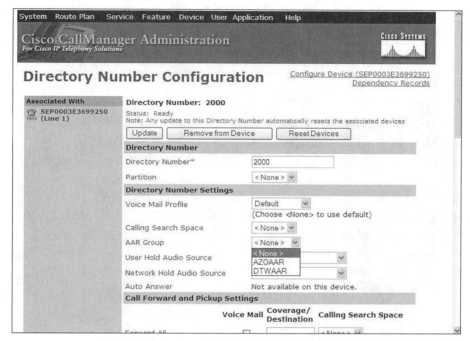

Exploring CallManager Serviceability

CallManager provides an administrative interface that allows administrators to perform common monitoring tasks. Through this interface you can perform tasks such as restarting services and running intensive diagnostic traces.

The tasks that can be performed here are useful when troubleshooting issues. Some of these tasks can cause negative performance issues on the CallManager, so extreme caution should be taken. In most cases many of these tasks should be performed only by a certified VoIP specialist or at the direction of Cisco TAC.

This section provides a brief overview of some of the tasks that can be performed through this interface.

The interface is called Cisco CallManager Serviceability and is accessed through the CCMAdmin interface. To access this interface, navigate to **Application> Cisco CallManager Serviceability** in CCMAdmin. Figure 6-31 offers an example of this interface.

As you can see, this interface has five menus heading across the top. Each of these is discussed in the following sections with the exceptions of the Help and Application menus. The Help menu offers links to the help contents and a link to a page on which the version of each component is displayed. The application menu offers a link to take you back to CCMAdmin, as well as a link that takes you to the plugins installation interface. The plugins installation interface is the same interface that is used when installing the Bulk Administration Tool (BAT). The following sections explore each area of this interface.

Figure 6-31 *Cisco CallManager Serviceability Interface*

Exploring Alarms

Alarms are used to define which events should be reported when they occur. Alarms for the various CallManager services are predefined. You can configure the destination to which this information should be sent when an alarm is triggered.

The first option of the Alarm menu is Configuration. From here you can configure where the information should be sent when an alarm is triggered. The available destinations are the Windows event viewer, syslog, SDI trace, or SDL trace.

From the Alarms menu option, Definitions, you can search all the predefined alarms and view the configuration of each.

Configuring and Collecting Traces

The next menu is the Trace menu. Traces are configured to record information of various transactions that take place with the CallManager. These traces can then be used to help troubleshoot issues that may arise. Typically, Terminal Access Controller (TAC) requests that traces be sent to them for analysis. Care should be taken whenever configuring and enabling traces because active traces can cause performance issues for the CallManager.

The first trace menu option is Configuration. For this screen you can configure a trace for the various CallManager services. Figures 6-32 and 6-33 show the configuration screen for the CallManager service.

Figure 6-32 *Trace Configuration*

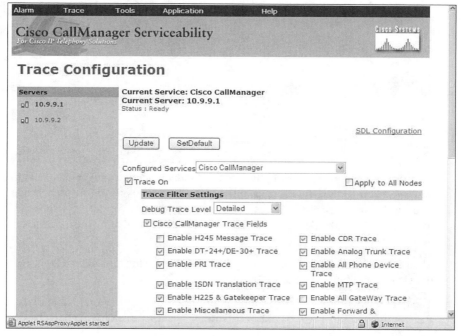

To configure a trace, you must first enable tracing by checking the **Trace On** box. Then, using the Trace Filter Settings, select the specific attributes to be traced and the debug level. The Debug Trace Level ranges from Error to Detailed. Selecting the Error level causes only errors to be recorded. Each level between Error and Detailed records a greater amount of information. When the Detailed debug trace level is selected, nearly all transitions of the selected attributes are recorded. Traces can be run on specific devices by checking the **Device Name Based Trace Monitoring** box and then selecting the desired device. Finally, file parameters should be configured to define the attributes of the file to which the trace information will be written. If you plan to use the Trace Analysis, which is discussed next, you must check the Enable XML Formatted Output for "Trace Analysis" box.

Figure 6-33 *Trace Configuration (Continued)*

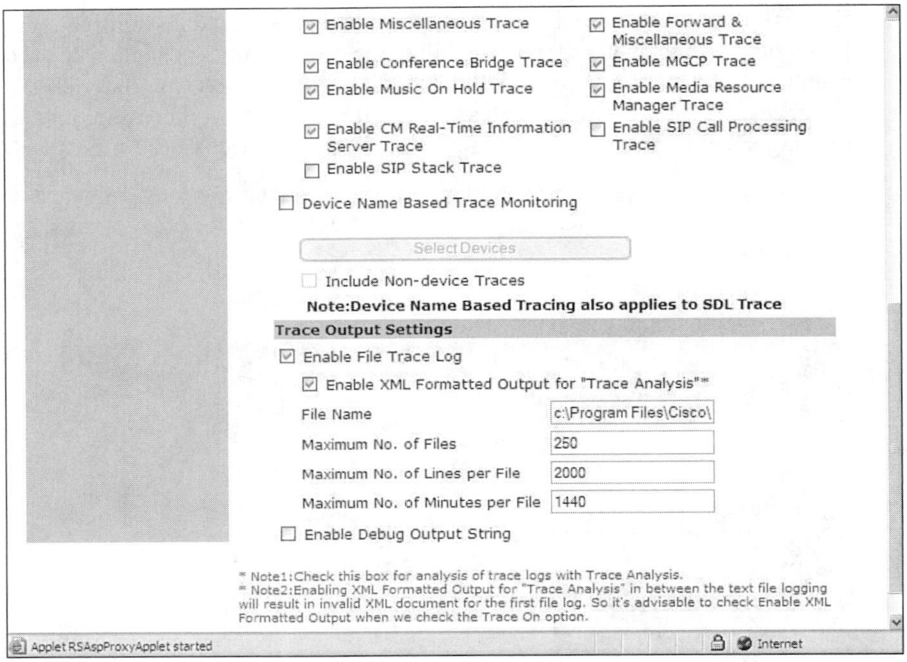

The files that are created are not the simplest to decipher and can contain an unmanageable amount of information. The next option, which is Analysis, helps present the trace information in a format that is easier to view than the raw format. In addition, when using this tool you can filter the trace results in order to more easily find the information for which you are looking.

The next option in this menu is the Q.931 Translator. This tool filters Q.931 messages and translates them into IOS equivalent messages.

The final menu option, Troubleshooting Trace Setting, allows you to quickly and easily set trace options for a variety of issues by simply selecting one or two check boxes.

Exploring CallManager Serviceability Tools

The Tools menu contains five options. The first is Service Activation. This interface allows you to activate and deactivate the various CallManager services. Each of these services was discussed in Chapter 2, "Preparing CallManager for Deployment." Caution should be taken when deactivating service. In some cases, such as with the Cisco IP Voice Media Streaming Application, the deactivation of a service can result in the removal of required resources.

The next option is Control Center. This option allows you to stop and start the various CallManager services. Figure 6-34 shows an example of this screen.

Figure 6-34 *Cisco CallManager Serviceability Control Center*

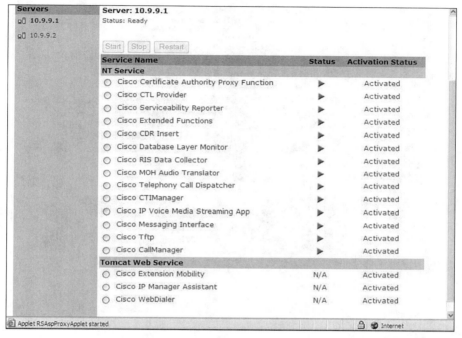

To stop, start, or reset a service, simply click the radio button that corresponds with the desired service and click the appropriate action (Stop, Start, or Reset) button.

NOTE   Stopping or restarting a service can result in temporary loss of service.

The next option in this menu is the Real-Time Monitoring Tool (RTMT). This is a very useful tool that administrators can use to monitor the current status of virtually any process and condition on the CallManager system. However, this interface is not accessible from this menu option. In earlier versions of CallManager it was, but with current versions it requires that the RTMT be installed in a client PC. This tool can be installed on a PC running Windows 98, XP, or 2000 from the plugins installation interface. You can also click on this menu option and a link for the plugins page displays.

The following eight figures (Figures 6-35 through 6-42) offer you a quick look at the information that can be retrieved using this interface. Unfortunately, truly appreciating and understanding this interface would take more space than can be provided in this text. For more information, you are encouraged to refer to the book *Cisco CallManager Best Practices* (ISBN 1-58705-139-7), which provides an excellent section on this tool.

The Summary screen offers an overview of the system resources and registered devices.

Figure 6-35 *RTMT—Summary*

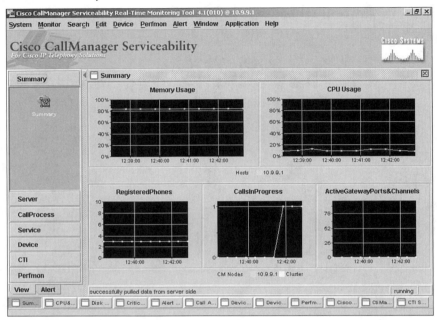

Figure 6-36 *RTMT—Server*

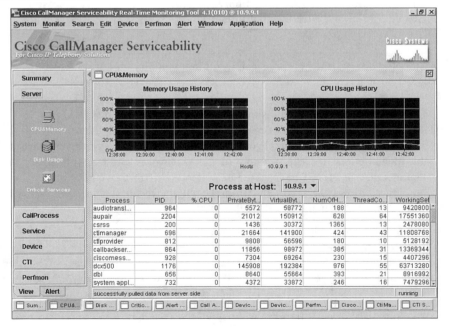

From the Server screen you can monitor the processes active on the CallManager and disk usage statistics.

Figure 6-37 *RTMT—CallProcess*

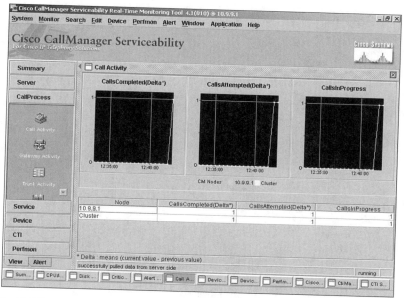

The CallProcess screen allows you to view call, gateway, and trunk activity and the SQL queue.

Figure 6-38 *RTMT—Service*

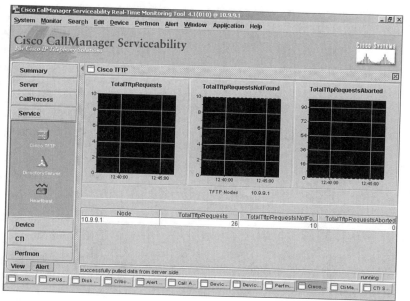

From the Service screen, information about the Trivial File Transport Protocol (TFPT) and DC services is viewable along with heartbeat information for these and the CallManager service.

Figure 6-39 *RTMT—Device*

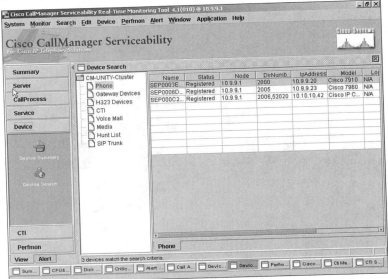

The Device screen allows you to search for information on a range of CallManager devices such as phones, gateways, hunt lists, and so on.

Figure 6-40 *RTMT—CTI*

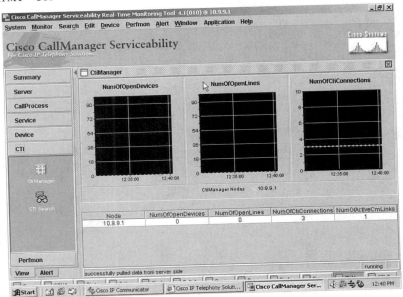

From the CTI screen, CTI manager information can be viewed.

Figure 6-41 *RTMT—Perfmon*

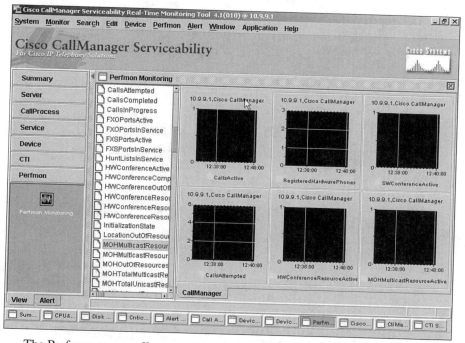

The Perfmon screen offers a real time graphical view of any performance monitor counter you choose. You select the counter to be displayed on this screen. From this screen you can also set up alerts based on any of these counters.

The Alert screen allows you to see all the configured alerts and modify them if desired. These alerts are used to create serviceability reports, which are discussed shortly.

The next option on this menu is the Quality Reporting Tool (QRT) viewer. The QRT allows users to report call quality issues directly from their phones. This is done by pressing the **QRT** softkey. After the key is pressed, callers are offered a number of options that help describe the issues they experienced. To allow callers this ability, a softkey template must be created and the QRT softkey assigned to it. Then apply the softkey template to the phones that will have this ability.

The QRT viewer allows you to view the issues that are reported using the QRT.

The last option on this screen is the Serviceability Reports Archive. This interface allows you to view reports that are created using the configuration information that is configured in RTMT. Figure 6-43 shows the Serviceability Reports Archive screen. From this screen you can see the reports that can be viewed.

Figure 6-42 *RTMT—Alert*

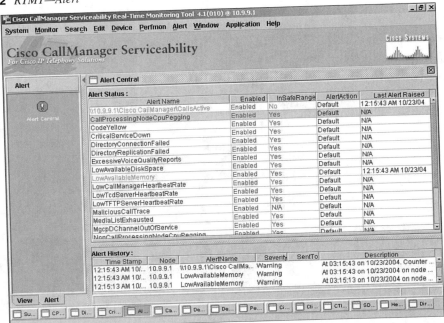

Figure 6-43 *Serviceability Report Archive*

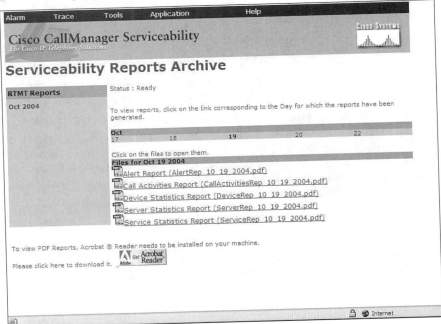

Summary

This chapter covered a lot of ground. It began by exploring the configuration required for features such as call park, Meet-Me conferences, and call pickup groups. Then the configuration of forced authorization codes and client matter codes was discussed. Next, configuration tasks required for the integration of Unity were explored. This included creating voice-mail ports and assigning them to line groups. The line groups were then assigned to a hunt list, and finally a hunt pilot was configured that pointed to the hunt list.

Next, the configuration of IP phone services was discussed. This section included the steps required to make an IP phone service available and how an administrator can subscribe a phone to a service. Following IP phone services Extension Mobility was explored and the features and configuration tasks were explained.

Media resources were then covered. This section included the features and functions of Transcoders, CFBs, MTP, MoH servers, and Annunciators. After explaining the configuration tasks for each of these, the chapter discussed the function of media resource groups and lists. The configuration tasks of adding media resources to groups, and then the groups to lists, were also covered.

SRST and AAR were discussed in the next section. You learned how SRST can help maintain system functionality for a remote site in the case of a WAN outage. You also learned how AAR can allow a call to successfully be routed over an alternate path if the call is rejected due to bandwidth limitations.

Finally, CallManager's serviceability tools were discussed in the last section of this chapter. In this section tools such as control center, QRT, RTMT, and Trace configuration were explored.

Unity Configuration

CHAPTER 7

Unity Predeployment Tasks

One of the most widely deployed phone system add-ons is voice-mail. Unity is the voice-mail solution of choice for CallManager, but Unity goes much further than most voice-mail solutions, because it offers a complete unified messaging solution. If your solution is going to be effective, proper configuration is essential, and the first step to proper configuration is verifying that the integration is correct and that all predeployment tasks have been completed. This chapter includes step-by-step instructions for completing predeployment tasks, such as verifying integration, defining system parameters and creating templates, distribution lists, and Class of Service (CoS).

Accessing and Navigating Unity Administrator

Most of the configurations discussed throughout the Unity portion of this book are accomplished through the Unity Administrator (UA), which is a web-based administration interface. Because this is the main administration interface, it is used for most administration tasks, and it is important that you become familiar with it. This section introduces you to the UA interface. Throughout the Unity portion of the book you will be instructed to access the administration interface and perform various tasks.

To access Unity Administrator, open Internet Explorer (5.5 or higher) and enter the server's name followed by /sa/web. If the server's name is DTWUNITY, for example, you enter DTWUNITY/sa/web in the address bar of Internet Explorer. Unlike when using CallManager, you should not be prompted for a username and password. You are authenticated based on your Window's Active Directory (AD) credentials. If you are logged in as a user that does not have an associated Unity subscriber with administrative rights, you will not have access to this interface. You need to log onto the network as a user that has Unity administrative rights.

NOTE   In Unity 4.0, it is recommended that Internet Explorer 6.0 or higher is used.

Unity Administrator is often referred to as System Administrator (SA). The term SA has been used for this interface for a number of years, whereas the UA term is relatively new. For this reason the term SA will be used throughout this book.

It is important that you understand that administrative rights for Unity are not associated with Windows rights. Having administrator rights for Windows does not automatically give you administrative rights for Unity. To access SA, your Windows account must have an associated Unity subscriber that has Unity administrative rights. During the installation, an administrator was selected. Use this account for now, and later we will discuss how to add administrative rights to subscribers.

After you are logged into SA, you see an interface similar to that shown in Figure 7-1. In Figure 7-1 each section of this interface has been labeled. The section labeled 1 is referred to as the navigation panel. This panel is used to access the various configuration screens. The section labeled 2 is referred to as the title strip, which contains icons that allow you to perform functions such as adding, deleting, and saving. The section labeled 3 is referred to as the page body. This is where most of the real work is done. From the page body you enter the specific configuration information for the object on which you are working.

Figure 7-1 *Unity Administrator Interface*

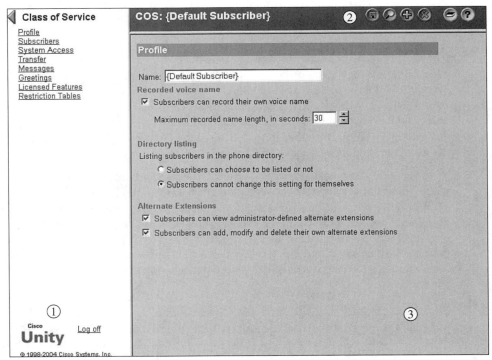

The following example should help you to better understand how this interface works; it is an example of changing the extension number that is associated with a subscriber. Each step includes a screen shot of the SA.

NOTE   Although a screen shot is provided here for almost every configuration task, that is not the general practice in this book. Step-by-step screen shots are important in this chapter to introduce you to the interface. However, throughout the rest of the book, screen shots are provided to help reinforce the topic being discussed and do not illustrate each step as they do in this example.

Step 1   Log on to SA by entering the server's name followed by **/Web/SA**. Figure 7-2 shows the main SA screen. Notice that the URL in the address bar is http://Server1/Web/SA. This means that the server name must be Server1. Note that there is no title strip in this figure.

Figure 7-2   *SA Main Screen*

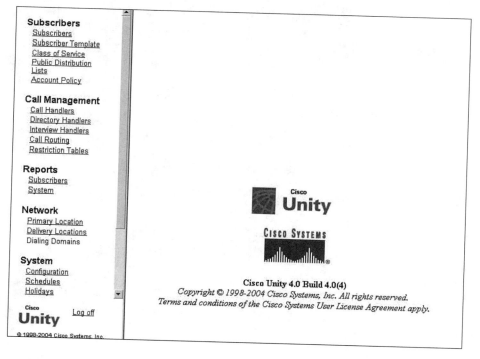

Note   If you are accessing SA using the Unity server's keyboard and screen, there is an icon on the desktop that is labeled System Administrator. Clicking this icon should open the System Administrator interface.

Step 2   From the navigation panel, click the **Subscribers** link, which is shown in Figure 7-2.

Step 3   Figure 7-3 shows that after the type of object you wish to configure is selected, the title strip displays and the page body changes. Also note that the navigation panel changes and presents you with all the options you can configure for that type of object. By looking in the navigation panel, you can see that we are in a Subscriber configuration, and by looking at the heading in the page body you can see that we are in the profile portion of the Subscriber configuration. For simplicity's sake, this screen is referred to as the **Subscribers>Profile** page. You will see many references of this type of syntax (called navigation syntax) throughout this portion of the book, so make sure you are comfortable with this concept.

Figure 7-3   *SA Subscriber Screen*

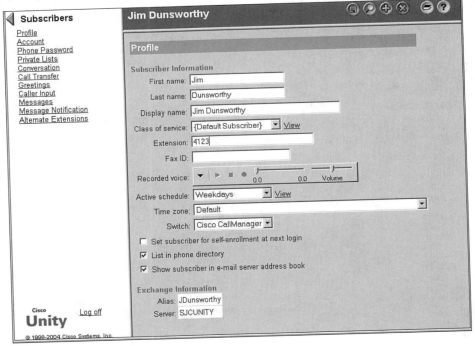

Note   In future step-by-step tasks, navigation syntax will be used to help you quickly understand at exactly which screen you should be. For example, if the navigation syntax were **Call Handlers>Call Transfer**, you would click Call Handlers from the main navigation menu and then select Call Transfer.

Step 4   In the page body, you see that the extension is 4123. To change the extension, simply change the number that displays in the extension field to **4321**. Figure 7-4 shows this. Although colors do not show in the screen captures of this book, you can see the colors on the screen if you follow these steps on a live system. The icon that looks like a floppy disk has changed colors. Previously it was grayed out, now it is blue. The disk displaying in blue means that changes have been made but not saved. The disk displaying in gray means that there is no new information that needs to be saved. You may also notice, in the title strip, there is an asterisk next to the Subscriber's name. This is another indication that there is unsaved data. Click the **disk** icon to save the change.

Figure 7-4   *Unity Subscriber Screen (Unsaved Data)*

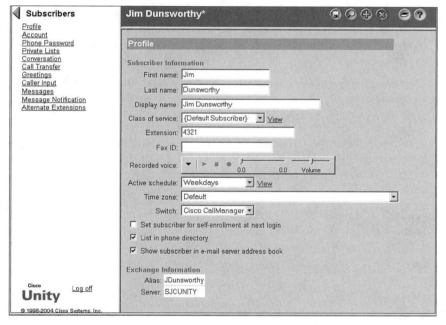

This example was fairly simple. Other Unity tasks will be more detailed. The goal of this example is to introduce you to the SA interface and some of the syntax that will be used in the step-by-step tasks.

Before moving on, let's look at the other icons that display in the title strip. In addition to the disk, there is a blue magnifying glass, a blue plus sign, a red X, a book framed by a yellow button, and a question mark framed by another yellow button. In addition, an icon of a running man displays when you run reports. A brief explanation of each follows:

- Disk (Save icon)—Displays in blue if there is unsaved data. Clicking this icon saves any unsaved data.

- Magnifying glass (Find icon)—Used to find items. Clicking this icon opens a search criteria window.

- Plus sign (Add icon)—Used to add a new object.

- ⊗ X (Delete icon)—Used to delete the current object.
- ⊖ Book (Help icon)—Opens an online documentation window.
- ⑦ Question mark (Field Help)—Displays a question mark next to each field. Clicking a question mark opens a help window that explains that field.
- Running Man (displays when reports are running) ⌨ (Run icon)—Clicking the icon causes the selected report to be queued.

NOTE   These icons are sometimes referred to as *sweet tarts*.

In the earlier example, you were introduced to navigation syntax. Let's look at one more example to make sure you are comfortable with the concept.

The navigation syntax for this example is **Subscribers>Class of Service>Transfer**. Figure 7-5 shows the main navigation menu. Class of Service is under the Subscribers heading. When you select **Class of Service**, the menu in the navigation panel changes to display a list of the configuration screens that deal with Class of Service. From this list, you can select Transfer as shown in Figure 7-6. To return to the main navigation menu click the blue arrow located in the upper-left corner of the navigation panel.

Figure 7-5   *Unity Main Screen*

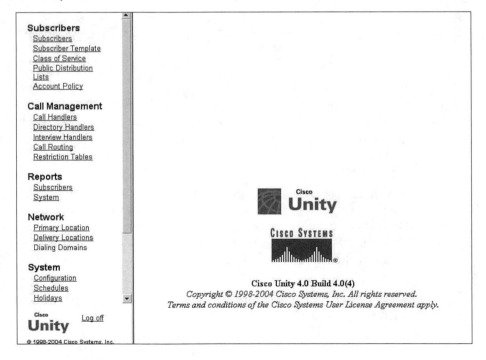

Figure 7-6   *Unity Sub-Menu Screen*

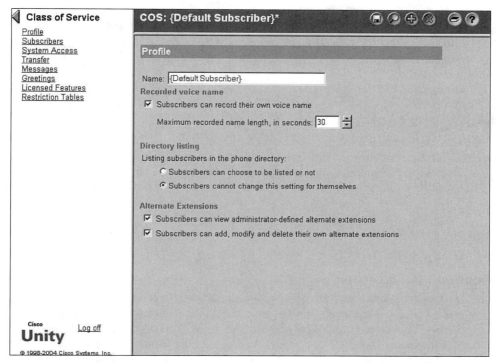

Now that you are familiar with the SA interface and the syntax that will be used in this portion of the book, let's start looking at the tasks that have to be accomplished first to ensure a properly configured system.

Integration Verification

Before Unity can be integrated with any system, you need to ensure that the all required PBX configuration is completed. The configuration tasks required on the PBX will be based on the type of PBX with which you are integrating. This book only addresses the configuration tasks required when integrating with a Cisco solution. If you are integrating with a traditional PBX, you need to refer to the installation guides and release notes that you can find at Cisco.com. A list of all integration guides can be found by searching **unity configuration guides** at Cisco.com.

At one time, more than 150 PBXs were supported and approved to work with Unity. That number has been drastically reduced. The main reason that Cisco acquired Activoice, which was the original developer of Unity, was so that Cisco could offer a feature-rich unified messaging solution, which would integrate well with CallManager. This does not mean that Cisco removed all support for traditional PBXs. There are times when CallManager will be integrated with an existing PBX. By allowing Unity to integrate with both CallManager and the existing PBX, Unity becomes a much more attractive solution to some customers. Cisco has since added support for other voice-over-IP (VoIP) solutions, such as Session Initialization Protocol (SIP). The following sections discuss tasks that should be completed to ensure that the Cisco IP-based solution with which Unity will integrate is configured and ready.

CallManager Integration

In this book it is expected that most Unity installations will be configured to operate with CallManager. Before Unity can communicate with CallManager, certain tasks must be accomplished on the CallManager and the Unity systems. In Chapter 6, "Configuring CallManager Features and Services," the CallManager side of the voice-mail configuration was discussed. You may need to refer back to that chapter to see how to configure the required components. Because the actual configuration steps have already been discussed, this section will focus on how to verify if all required configuration has been completed.

Voice-mail Port Configuration

Unity communicates with PBXs through a port. With traditional PBXs, the ports are most often analog lines. To enable this communication, a voice board is installed in the Unity server. The voice board usually has either four or 12 analog ports, which connect back to analog ports on the PBX. When Unity is integrated with CallManager, analog lines are not used, so a voice board is not required. Instead, virtual ports are configured on the CallManager. The only physical connectivity between the Unity server and the CallManager is Ethernet. When these ports are configured in Unity, a name and a Directory Number (DN) are assigned to them. The DN is significant only to the CallManager. Unity does not need to know what the DN is because Unity is concerned only with the name assigned to the port. Typically, the name looks something like Cisco-UM-VI1. This naming convention is only a suggestion; any name may be used.

The Unity Telephony Integration Manager (UTIM) is used to configure the voice-mail port names in Unity. The UTIM verifies that Unity can communicate with the port after you enter the name. If you are not sure of the name of the voice-mail port, you can find it by using the CallManager configuration interface as outlined in the steps that follow.

Step 1 Log on to the CCMADMIN interface.

Step 2 Select **Feature>Voice-mail>Cisco Voice-mail Port**.

Step 3 Click the **Find** button. On the left side of the screen all the voice-mail ports display. You are concerned with the prefix portion of the name. That is the portion that displays before the number. For example, if the name were CiscoUM-VI1, the prefix would be CiscoUM-VI.

Unity Telephony Integration Manager (CallManager)

The current integration settings can be found in the Unity's SA interface but can only be changed using UTIM. To view the integration settings, open SA and click on **Integration**. This can be found under the System heading on the left side. If there are multiple switch types, you can view the desired integration by clicking on the appropriate integration in the list on the left side of the integration page.

The configuration for the integration is accomplished using UTIM. When configuring UTIM, you enter information about the CallManager with which you are integrating Unity. It is a good idea to ensure that you have the following information available before running UTIM.

- **Integration Name**—This name is used to identify the integration. If the name is changed, make sure you use a name that makes it easy to identify the integration.

- **CallManager Cluster Name**—This name is used for reference only. Choose a name that helps to easily identify the cluster.

- **CallManager IP Addresses**—Unity needs to know the IP addresses of both the primary and secondary CallManagers with which it will be communicating.

- **TCP Port**—This is the TCP port number that Unity will use for connecting to CallManager. The default value is 2000. Leave it at the default.

- **Starting RTP Audio Port**—This is the first IP port number that is used for Real-time Transport Protocol (RTP) sessions. Leave this at the default.

- **MWI On/Off DNs**—Message Waiting Indicator (MWI) DNs are configured in CallManager. When these digits are dialed on behalf of a phone, the MWI lights, or goes on or off depending upon which DN is entered.

- **Number of Ports**—This is the number of ports for which you are licensed. If you are implement-ing a dual switch solution, this is the number of ports you wish to have communicate with CallManager.

- **Voice Mail Port Prefix Names**—This is the name of the voice mail port, not including any numbers at the end of the name. For instance, if the voice-mail ports were named CISCOUM1-VI1 through CISCOUM1-VI12, you would use CISCOUM1-VI as the prefix name.

- **Port Settings**—The voice mail ports can be set to perform multiple functions. Before you installed Unity you should have discussed what functions were to be handled by each port. The functions are as listed in Table 7-1.

Table 7-1   *Voice-mail Port Settings*

Parameter	Description
Enable	Allows the port to be used by Unity
Answer Calls	Allows the port to answer incoming calls
Message Notification	Allows the port to make outgoing calls for message notification purposes
Dialout MWI	Allows the port to be used to send MWIs
Telephony Record and Playback (TRAP) Connection	Allows the port to be used for recording and playing messages when a subscriber is using the web or an e-mail client

Note   If licensing for Audio Messaging Interchange Specification (AMIS) protocol networking is purchased for this system, an additional parameter of AMIS Delivery may be listed. This allows the port to send and receive AMIS messages. AMIS is discussed in more detail in Chapter 10: Implementing Unity Networking.

- **Trunk Access Codes**—Additional digits CallManager must dial when transferring a call to another PBX.

UTIM is part of the installation process. If the Unity server is already loaded, this information should already be configured. You can check and change the integration information by running UTIM. To run UTIM follow these steps:

Step 1   On the Unity Server, click **Start>Programs>Unity>Manage Integrations**.

Step 2   To show the CallManager Clusters, from the UTIM window click on the **CallManager integration**, which displays in the left column.

Step 3   Select the name of the CallManager cluster you wish to manage by clicking its name.

Note	If more than one CallManager cluster displays, make certain that you select the correct one. If configured properly, the name assigned to each cluster allows you to determine which one you want to access. If the name does not help you identify the cluster, you need to identify it by the IP address.

Step 4   A screen like that shown in Figure 7-7 displays. Notice that there are four tabs along the top right of the screen labeled Servers, MWI, Ports, and RTP.

Figure 7-7   *UTIM CallManager Screen*

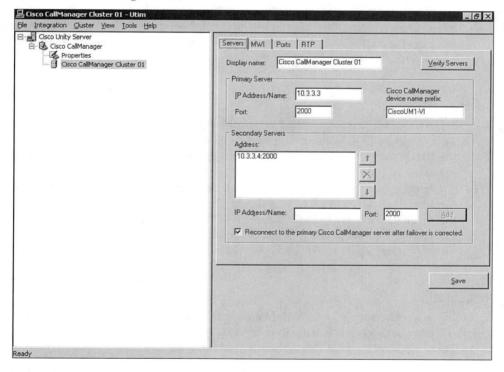

Step 5   Click the **Servers** tab to make certain the server parameters are brought to the front. From this screen you can change the Display name of the cluster, the IP address of the primary or secondary CallManager, the voice mail port device name prefix, and the TCP port. To change any of these settings simply enter the desired value.

Step 6   Click the **MWI** tab to change the MWI values.

Step 7 To change the functions that each voice mail port is allowed to perform, click the **Ports** tab and set each port. You may refer to Table 7-1 for an explanation of each function.

Step 8 If you need to change the starting RTP port number, you may do so by selecting the RTP tab and set a starting number. Leave this value at the default.

Step 9 After you have changed all the values you wish, click **Save**. When you save, you are prompted to restart Unity. Restarting Unity causes active calls to drop, so it is best to do this after hours. A restart is required for the changes to take effect.

Step 10 You can close the UTIM by clicking the **X** in the upper right corner.

After you have verified that the information is correct, CallManager and Unity should be able to communicate. The simplest way to check this is to dial the DN assigned to the first voice mail port. If you are dialing from a subscriber's phone, you should be asked to enter a password; otherwise, you should hear the opening greeting.

SIP Integration

As of Unity 4.0, SIP integration is supported. SIP is an open standard protocol that is used for call setup. SIP provides the same function in a SIP integration as Skinny Client Control Protocol (SCCP) does in a CallManager integration. The configuration required on the SIP proxy server is outside of the scope of this book. The next section describes the general configuration steps required on the SIP proxy server, however, you need to refer to "Cisco's SIP Integration Guide for Unity" which can be found at Cisco.com for more detailed information. Currently Unity is supported with SIP when using a Cisco SIP Proxy server. The configuration steps that follow are based upon the assumption that the Cisco SIP proxy server is being used.

SIP Configuration

If you are integrating with a SIP solution, it is assumed you have a solid understanding of SIP components and how the protocol works. With this understanding in mind, let's look at an overview of the steps required on the SIP server side.

Of course, before you can integrate Unity into a SIP solution, you must have a fully installed and functioning SIP solution. This includes the installation and setup of a Cisco SIP proxy server.

After the server is installed, the phones need to be configured so that calls are forwarded to the Unity system when the called party is on the phone or does not answer. You will set up the phone to forward to the SIP address of the Unity system. The format of this address is the same as all SIP addresses: host@server. The host portion of the address will be the line number used for Unity.

On the SIP gateway you need to configure an application session. This is done by configuring a VoIP dial-peer using the application session command.

On the SIP gateway you also need to disable the SIP media inactivity timer. This is done by issuing the following command at the gateway configuration prompt:

```
no timer receive-rtcp
```

Finally, you need to configure a VoIP dial peer on the gateway that enables a Dual Tone Multi-Frequency (DTMF) relay. The commands to do this are issued starting at the configuration prompt and are as follows:

```
Dial-peer voice <dial peer number> voip
Session protocol sipv2
Dtmf-relay rtp-ntme
```

After you have made certain that all of the SIP server configuration tasks are completed, you need to configure the Unity portion of the integration.

Unity Telephony Integration Manager (SIP)

Just as with a CallManager integration, UTIM is used to configure the integration parameters for a SIP integration. Before you run UTIM, you need to make sure that you have the information that will be entered in UTIM. The following is a list of the information that you will need:

- **Integration Name**—This name is used to identify the integration. If this name is changed, make sure you use a name that makes it easy to identify the integration.

- **Cluster Name**—This name is used for reference only. Choose a name that helps to easily identify the server. This is also referred to as the Display Name.

- **IP Addresses**—Unity needs to know the IP addresses of both the primary and secondary SIP proxy server with which it will be communicating.

- **Number of Ports**—These are the number of ports that will be used between The SIP server and Unity. This may be the same number of ports for which the system is licensed, unless you are using Unity in a dual switch integration environment.

- **Contact Line Number**—This is the number that is associated with Unity. Unity registers this name with the SIP proxy server.

- **Unity Port**—The TCP port number that Unity uses to connect to SIP server. Leave it at the default. Only change this number if you know that a different port is being used for SIP in your environment.

- **Preferred Codec**—The Codec that Unity first tries to use when placing outgoing calls.

- **Authentication Name and Password**—If SIP proxy authentication is being used, this is the user name and password Unity uses.

- **Port Settings**—The voice mail ports can be set to perform multiple functions. Before you installed Unity you should have decided what functions were being handled by each port. The functions are as listed in Table 7-2.

Table 7-2   *Voice-mail Port Settings*

Parameter	Description
Enabled	Allows the port to be used by Unity
Answer Calls	Allows the port to answer incoming calls
Message Notification	Allows the port to make outgoing calls for message notification purposes
TRAP Connection	Allows the port to be used for recording and playing messages when a subscriber is using the web or an e-mail client

Note   If licensing for AMIS networking is purchased for this system, an additional parameter of AMIS Delivery may be listed. This allows the port to send and receive AMIS messages. AMIS is discussed in more detail in Chapter 10.

- **Trunk Access Codes**—Additional digits must be dialed when transferring a call to another PBX.

When you have all of the information available, you can configure the SIP parameters for an existing integration or create a new integration using UTIM.

To add a new SIP integration, follow these steps:

Step 1   On the Unity Server, click **Start>Programs>Unity>Manage Integrations**.

Step 2   From the UTIM interface, select **Integration>New**.

Step 3   The Welcome to the Telephony Integration Setup Wizard window displays. Select **SIP** as the phone system type. Click **Next**.

Step 4   On the following screen, enter an Integration name and a Cluster name. The integration name should be something that helps you easily identify which phone system goes with this integration. The cluster name helps identify the specific SIP server in this integration. The cluster name appears as the display name when modifying this integration. After you have entered this information, click **Next**.

Step 5   On the next screen, enter the IP addresses for the primary and secondary SIP proxy server, and the port that will be used. Click **Next**.

Step 6   The next screen asks how many ports you wish to configure for this integration. If you are integrating only with a single SIP system, you should enter the total number of ports you have purchased. If you are integrating with multiple PBX systems, then enter only the number of ports you have decided to give to the SIP portion of the integration. Click **Next**.

Step 7   The following screen allows you to enter the Contact Line Name, Unity SIP port, Preferred Codec and the Preferred Transport Protocol. After entering this information, click **Next**.

Step 8   On the next screen you must enter the username and password for SIP authentication, if you are using it. If you are not using authentication, uncheck the box and click **Next**.

Step 9   If you have other integrations, the following screen asks what access code needs to be used to send calls to the other systems. Click **Next** after entering this information.

Step 10   The final screen shows a summary of what you have chosen. Click **Finish** to complete the configuration.

Step 11   You are now prompted to allow Unity to restart. Restarting Unity causes active calls to drop, so it is best done after hours. A restart is required for the changes to take effect.

To change an existing integration, follow these steps:

Step 1   On the Unity Server, click **Start>Programs>Unity>Manage Integrations**.

Step 2   From the UTIM window. Click on the SIP integration that will display in the left column to show the SIP Clusters.

Step 3   Click the name of the SIP cluster you wish to manage.

Step 4   A screen like that shown in Figure 7-8 displays. Notice that there are four tabs along the top-right side of the screen, Servers, SIP Info, Ports, and RTP.

Figure 7-8   *UTIM SIP Screen*

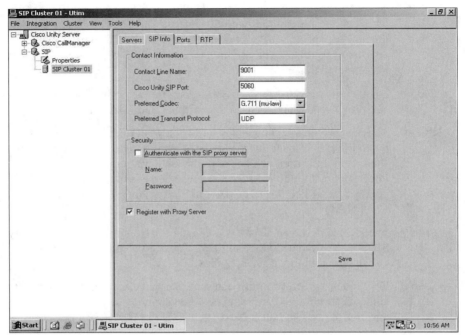

Step 5   Click the **Servers** tab to make certain that the server parameters are brought to the front. From this screen you can change the Display name of the cluster, the IP addresses of the primary or secondary SIP server, and the port number used. To change any of these settings, simply enter the desired value.

Step 6   You can change the Contact Line Name, SIP port, Preferred Codec and the Preferred Transport Protocol by clicking on the SIP Info tabs and changing the values. You can also change the SIP authentication settings from this screen.

Step 7   To change the functions that each voice mail port is allowed to perform, click the **Ports** tab and set each port as you desire. You may refer to Table 7-2 for an explanation of each function.

Step 8   If you need to change the starting RTP port number, you may do so by selecting the RTP tab and set a starting number. Leave this value at the default.

Step 9   After all changes are made, Click the **Save** button. After changes are saved, you are prompted to restart Unity, which will cause active calls to drop. It is best if this is done after hours. A restart is required for the changes to take effect.

Step 10 You can close the UTIM by clicking the **X** in the upper-right corner.

After you have verified that the information is correct, Unity should be able to communicate within the SIP environments. The simplest way to check this is to dial the DN assigned to the voice mail port. If you are dialing from a subscriber's phone, you should be asked to enter a password; otherwise, you should hear the opening greeting.

Now that you have verified that the Unity system is communicating with the phone system, you need to complete a number of predeployment configuration tasks. These tasks are discussed in the next section.

Defining System Configuration

Although it is possible to begin adding users now, you should first make sure that the system settings are appropriate for your environment. Often many are tempted to accept system defaults and assume they can go back and fix them later. In most cases, you can go back and change any setting you need, but it will almost always take you more time than it would have if you had set things up properly at the beginning.

NOTE	I once had a student who had a configuration issue that could have been avoided if the integrator had spent two minutes changing a few parameters before adding users. The integrator was not familiar with the system and assumed that, if necessary, the parameters could be changed later. To compound matters, the integrator then told the student how to fix the problem but not the easy way. The problem could have been fixed in about five minutes but instead took three days. The integrator was not invited to bid on any more projects. The old saying applies to such situations: An ounce of prevention is worth a pound of cure.

This section covers topics associated with system settings, such as schedules, languages, recording, and port settings. Because these settings affect all subscribers on the system, they can be thought of as global settings. If you log on to SA, you see the settings that are listed under the System heading in the navigation panel on the left side of the screen. The topics covered in this section include configuration, schedules, holidays, authentication, and ports. You may notice that licensing and integration also display under the System heading in SA. However, these are informational only and not configurable from the SA. They are not covered in the section.

NOTE	In some more recent versions of Unity, Short Message Peer-to-Peer (SMPP) support was added. This feature allows you to send message notifications to Short Message Service (SMS) devices, such as cell phones. More details on this feature can be found by searching **Setting Up Client SMS Applications** at Cisco.com.

Creating Schedules and Holidays

Just because something is the first thing in a list doesn't mean it is the first thing you do. You have probably already noticed that we have started the configuration process on the last five major headings in the navigation panel. The navigation menu was designed more for ease of use than as an ordered list of tasks. So, just as we did not begin at the first major area, we are not going to begin at the first area under System. Because you define a default schedule in the Configuration area, it would only make sense to have the schedules defined first. After defining schedules adding holidays is discussed.

Schedules are assigned to subscribers and call handlers and are used to define what hours Unity should consider opened and closed. Unity has the ability to play up to five different greetings. Two of these greetings depend on the schedule. The Standard greeting plays during open hours and the Closed greeting plays during closed hours.

A default schedule is defined and is assigned to all subscribers and call handlers when they are created. After an object is created, you may assign a different schedule to it. A total of 64 schedules may be defined.

Schedules are configured at the System>Schedules level of SA. Step-by-step instructions on how to perform the following Schedule-related tasks are as follows:

- Viewing/Changing an existing schedule
- Adding a new schedule
- Selecting a default schedule
- Deleting a schedule

View and Change a Schedule

To view and change existing schedules, use the steps that follow:

Step 1   From within SA, select **System>Schedules**.

Step 2   From the title strip, select the **Find** icon (magnifying glass). A list of schedules displays.

Step 3   Highlight the desired schedule and click **View**.

Note	The main part of the schedule screen is a grid that represents the seven days of the week, divided into half-hour increments. Check marks indicate the open hours.

Step 4   To modify the schedules, place check marks on the half hours that you want to be considered open. Remove the check marks from times to be considered closed.

Note	You may copy the open and closed hours of one day to another day, and to all weekdays and weekends by using the Copy Day's Schedule function at the bottom of the screen. Select the **source day** from the first drop-down list and the **destination day(s)** from the second drop-down list and click **Copy day's schedule**.

Step 5 At the top of the screen there is a check box labeled Observe Holidays. If this box is checked, this schedule is treated as if all hours are closed on holidays that are created in Unity.

Step 6 After all changes are made, click the **Save** icon in the title strip. The changes do not take effect until you have saved them.

Add a Schedule

To add a new schedule, similar steps are performed. The following are the required steps:

Step 1 From within SA, select **System>Schedules**.

Step 2 From the title strip, select the **Add** icon (blue plus sign). An Add a schedule window displays.

Step 3 Enter the name of the new schedule. You may choose to base the new schedule on an existing one. Doing this causes the new schedule to have the same open and closed hours as an existing one. Choose whether the new schedule should be based on an existing one or not and click the **Add** button.

Step 4 The new schedule displays.

Note	The main part of the schedule screen is a grid that represents the seven days of the week divided into half-hour increments. Check marks indicate the open hours.

To modify the schedules, place check marks on the half hours that you want to be considered open. Remove the check marks if you want that time to be considered closed.

Note	You may copy the open and closed hours of one day to another day, all weekdays or weekends by using the Copy Day's Schedule function at the bottom of the screen. Select the source day from the first drop-down list and the destination day(s) from the second drop-down list and click Copy day's schedule.

Step 5 At the top of the screen there is a check box labeled Observe Holidays. If this box is checked, this schedule is treated as if all hours are closed on holidays that are created in Unity.

Step 6 After all changes are made, click the **Save** icon in the title strip. The changes do not take effect until you have saved them.

Define a Default Schedule

The default system schedule that is selected during installation is the Weekdays schedule. The default schedule is changed at the System>Configuration>Settings level of SA. All the settings at this level are discussed in the next section. This section deals only with the default schedule portion of this level. To change the default schedule follow these steps:

Step 1 From within SA, select **System>Configuration>Settings**.

Step 2 The first field on this screen is Default Schedule. Select the schedule from the drop-down list.

Step 3 Click the **Save** icon.

To remove a schedule from Unity, follow these steps:

Step 1 From within SA select, **System>Schedules**.

Step 2 From the title strip, select the **Find** icon (magnifying glass). A list of schedules displays.

Step 3 Highlight the desired schedule, and click **View**.

Step 4 The selected schedule displays on the screen. Click the delete icon (red **X**) from the title strip.

Step 5 You are prompted to determine to which schedule you wish to reassign all objects that are currently using this schedule. Select a schedule from the drop-down list and click **Delete**.

Now that you have the schedules defined, the next logical thing to configure is the holiday schedule. Holidays are configured so that Unity knows which days the company will be closed. Unity plays the closed greeting all day on holidays.

Add a Holiday

To add holidays follow these steps:

Step 1   From within SA, select **System>Holidays**.

Step 2   The current list of holidays displays on the screen.

Step 3   To add a new holiday, click the **Add** icon (the plus sign).

Step 4   An Add a Holiday window displays. Select the date from the drop-down list and click **Add**.

Step 5   Repeat steps 3 and 4 for each holiday you wish to add.

NOTE   Note that you did not have to save these additions. Saving is required only when an object is changed. When an object is added, it is immediately written.

You have the option of copying holidays that were defined for one year to another year. This can be a great time saver, but you need to make sure that the holidays you are copying over are on the same date in the year to which you are copying them. To copy holidays from one year to another, simply click on the appropriately labeled button. This causes all the holidays from the earlier year to be copied. Remember to remove or change any incorrect dates.

Modify or Delete a Holiday

To change or delete a holiday follow these steps:

Step 1   From within SA, select **System>Holidays**.

Step 2   The current list of holidays displays.

Step 3   Click on the holiday you wish to change or delete. The fields in the Edit holiday for field should now show the date you selected.

Step 4   To change the holiday's date, edit the fields in the Edit holiday for area and click the **Save** icon.

Step 5   To delete this holiday, click the **Delete** icon. You are prompted to confirm the deletion. Click **OK**.

Now that you have all of the schedules and holidays configured, system settings should be done. The next section discusses a number of global system settings that should be defined before the system is put into production.

Defining Configuration Settings

Configuration settings are general Unity settings that define schedules, security, and languages, and a number of other things. All of these settings will be configured using the SA interface. This section is divided into subsections so that you can easily follow the settings shown here in the order in which they are presented in SA. If you go to the **System>Configuration** level in SA, you see the six selections that will be discussed in this section. Table 7-3 lists these topics and provides a brief description of each.

Table 7-3   *SA Configuration Settings Selections*

Topic	Description
Settings	General settings such as schedule, log files, and RSA settings
Software Versions	List of the version number of each Unity process
Recordings	Time limits for silence and clip length
Contacts	Name and number of those responsible for the system
Phone Languages	Phones languages that are available and loaded
GUI Languages	Languages available and loaded for the Unity Administrator pages

All the settings discussed throughout this section are configured under the System> Configuration level of the Unity Administrator pages.

Settings

The first configuration level under System>Configuration is Settings. From this level you configure items that deal with general settings within Unity. The following steps walk you through the settings screen. Figure 7-9 shows the screen that contains all the fields that will be discussed in these steps.

Step 1 From within SA, select **System>Configuration>Settings**.

Step 2 Select the schedule you wish to use as the default schedule from the drop-down list.

Step 3 If you want time to be expressed in 24-hour format (1900 hours instead of 7:00 pm), check the box labeled Use 24-hour time format for conversations and schedules.

Step 4 Next there is a box labeled Enable spelled name search. Typically you want other subscribers to spell by name, so this box should be checked. If you want to allow them only to dial by extension, uncheck this box.

Step 5 If you have implemented an RSA server for use with Unity, check the RSA Two Factor box. Typically this check box is unchecked.

Figure 7-9   *Settings Screen*

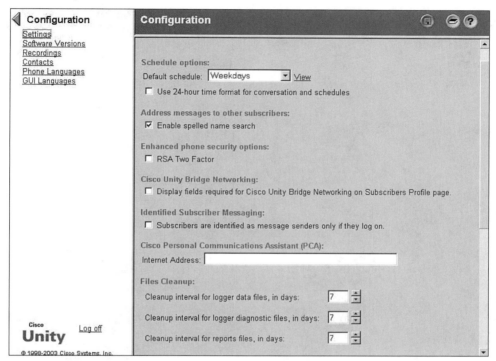

Step 6   The check box labeled Display fields required for Cisco Unity Bridge
Networking on Subscribers Profile page is only used if you are using a
bridge server to integrate with an Octel system. Typically this box is left
unchecked.

Step 7   If you want messages that are left by a subscriber to include the subscriber's
name or ID, leave the Subscribers are identified as message senders only if
they log on unchecked. If this box is checked, the subscriber leaving the
message will have to log in to be identified.

Step 8   Enter the URL used to access the Cisco Personal Communications
Assistant (CPCA) pages in the Internet Address field. Unity includes this
address in an e-mailed message notification. If CPCA is not being used,
leave this field blank.

Step 9   Set the number of days you want to keep log files in the cleanup interval
portion of the Files Cleanup field for each type of log.

The Settings screen contains four more areas. Three of these areas are not configurable and
are used to initiate replication or to view information. The last area allows you to configure
substitute objects. Figure 7-10 shows these areas.

Figure 7-10 *Settings Screen*

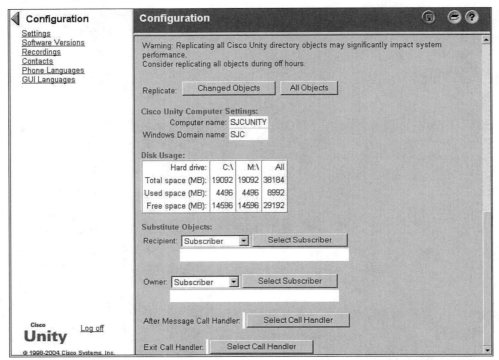

The first area is titled Replicate Cisco Unity Directory Objects. You can force a replication between AD and Unity to occur from here. When you select the Changed Objects or the All Objects button, Unity replicates with AD immediately. The button you select determines if you want to force a complete replication or only look for changed objects. This action should be performed only off hours.

The next area is titled Cisco Unity Computer Settings. This area displays the computer name of the Unity server and the Domain to which it belongs.

The third area on this screen is titled Disk Usage. This area displays the number and size of the logical hard drives in the Unity server.

The final area is titled Substitute Objects and contains four configurable parameters.

The Recipient parameter is used to define where messages should be delivered when they are left to a call handler or interview handler whose original recipient has been deleted. The Owner parameter is used to define which subscriber or public distribution list will become the owner of an object if the object's current owner is deleted.

The Recipient parameter and Owner parameter are configured in the same way, so the following steps show how to configure either.

Step 1 Select either **Subscriber** or **Public Distribution List** from the Recipient drop-down list.

Step 2 The button next to this field is labeled either **Select Subscriber** or **Select Distribution List** based on whether subscriber or public distribution list was selected. Click this button.

Step 3 If you are choosing a subscriber, a window displays that allows you to enter search criteria. Once entered, click the **Find** button and select the desired subscriber from the results listed in the Matching Subscribers box. If you are choosing a public distribution list, a window displays containing the lists. Select the desired public distribution list.

Step 4 Once you have selected the subscriber or distribution list, click the **Select** Button.

The last two parameters are similar in function and configuration. The first of the two deals with where a call is sent if the subscriber selected for the After Message Action of an object is deleted. The second defines where a call is sent when it exits a directory handler if the original destination object has been deleted. The following steps can be used to configure either of these parameters.

Step 1 Click the **Select Call Handler** button.

Step 2 A window displays that allows you to enter search criteria. Once entered, click the **Find** button and select the desired call handler from the results listed in the Matching Call Handlers box.

Step 3 . Click the **Select** button.

Software Versions

The second configuration level under System>Configuration is Software Settings. This area is strictly informational. The page is used to find the version of several Unity components and Windows version information. Because no configuration can be performed on this screen, let's move on to the next area.

Recordings

The third configuration level under System>Configuration is Recordings. The Recording page deals with time limits for silence and clip length settings. Figure 7-11 shows this screen and all its settings.

Figure 7-11 *Recordings*

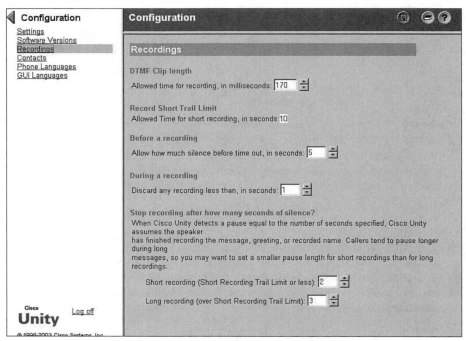

To set these configurations, follow these steps:

Step 1   From within SA select, **System>Configuration>Recordings**.

Step 2   Select the amount of time you want clipped off the end of a recording when the octothorpe (#) is pressed in the field labeled Allowed time for recording, in milliseconds. This is done so that the tone produced when the octothorpe (#) is pressed is not included in the messages. This value normally does not need to be changed unless the tone is being heard in messages or the ends of messages are being clipped off.

Note	The octothorpe is referred to by different names in different countries. For instance, it is called the pound in the U.S. and the hash in England.

Note	The next value, labeled Allowed Time for short recording, in seconds cannot be changed. This value determines how long a message must be before Unity considers it a long message. This is statically set to ten. In Step 5 you see how the value is used.

Step 3   Now, determine how long Unity will wait for someone to start talking by entering a value in the box labeled Allow how much silence before time out, in seconds. If the caller leaving a message does not begin talking within the amount of time set here, Unity assumes the caller is not going to leave a message.

Step 4   The field labeled Discard any recording less than, in seconds is used to prevent Unity from recording hang-ups. Typically, a value of one is sufficient for this field. Enter the desired value.

Step 5   The last two fields on this page determine how many seconds of silence Unity allows in a message. Two different values are set here. The first one, labeled Short recording, is the value used during the first ten seconds of the message. As discussed in the note following Step 2, a short recording is defined as ten. The second value is used when the message that is being recorded is longer than 10 seconds. Typically, these values can be left at default.

Step 6   Click the **Save** icon at the top of the page.

Contacts

The fourth configuration level under System>Configuration is Contacts. In the Contacts area, administration and support contact information is entered. This information helps others determine who is responsible for the system. Figure 7-12 shows this screen.

To enter this information go to System>Configuration>Contacts in SA and enter the appropriate names and numbers. When you are finished, click the Save icon.

Phone Languages

The fifth configuration level under System>Configuration is Phone Languages. This is where you determine which phones languages will be active on the Unity system. The phone language is the language that the Unity system uses when talking to a caller. One of the languages loaded must match the Windows operating system locale that was selected during the Windows install. Figure 7-13 shows this screen.

To configure the Phone Language settings follow these steps:

Step 1   From within SA, select **System>Configuration>Phone Languages**.

Figure 7-12 *Contacts*

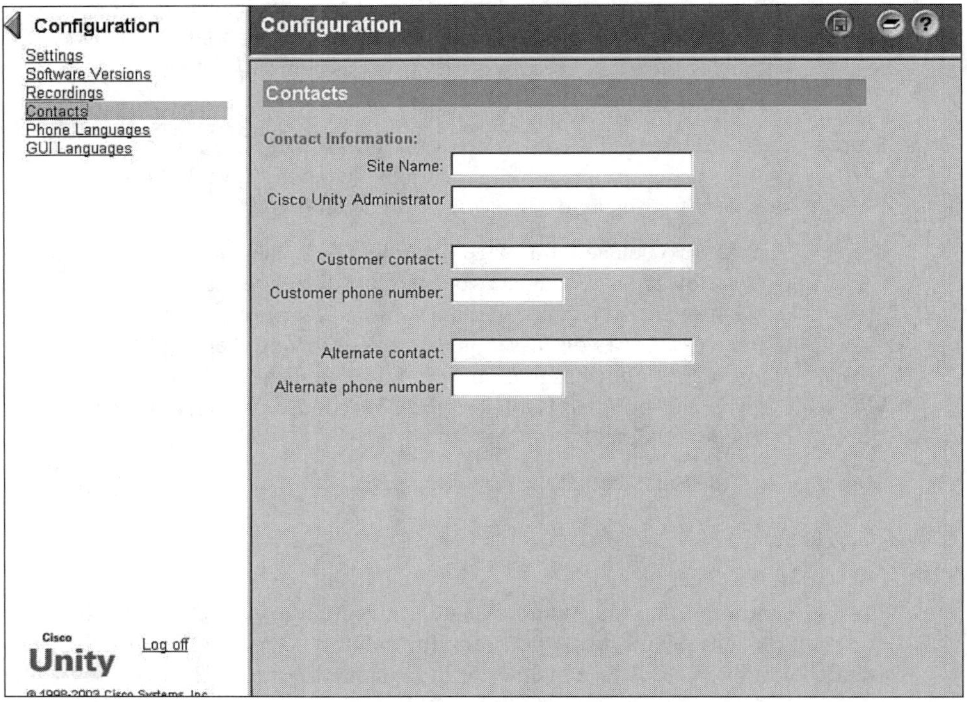

Step 2 The number of languages for which the system is licensed, and the number loaded, displays at the top of the page under the heading, License Counts. If the system is licensed for more than one language, add any of the languages listed in the field labeled Available. Highlight the desired language and click the **->** arrow. The language should now display in the loaded field.

Note Only languages that were chosen during the installation display are available. To add languages that do not display in the list, you must run the Cisco Unity Installation and Configuration Assistant (CUICA). Because running CUCIA causes some down time, it should be run during a planned off-hours period.

Step 3 From the drop-down list labeled Default Phone Language, select the language you want Unity to use by default for all objects.

Figure 7-13 *Phone Languages*

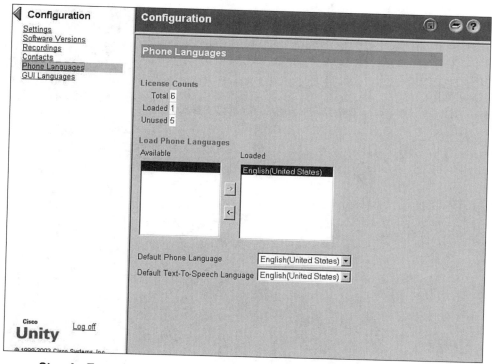

Step 4   From the drop-down list labeled Default Text-To-Speech Language,
select the language you want Unity to use by default when reading
e-mails to subscribers over the phone.

GUI Languages

The sixth, and last configuration level under System>Configuration is GUI Languages.
This is the language in which the SA will be displayed. Figure 7-14 shows this screen.

To access this configuration screen, go to System>Configuration>GUI LanguagesSettings
from within SA. You can move any language that displays in the Available list over to the
Loaded list by highlighting the desired language and clicking the **->** arrow.

Configuring Authentication Settings

The next area of the system for discussion is the authentication settings. This deals with the
authentication settings used when a subscriber logs into CPCA. If you have chosen to use
anonymous authentication for SA, these settings apply to SA and Status Monitor logins as well.
The configuration of these settings, which is outlined in the steps that follow, is fairly simple.

Figure 7-14 *GUI Languages*

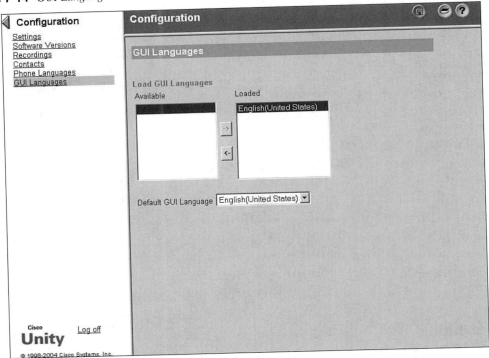

Step 1 From within SA, select **System>Authentication**.

Step 2 The screen shown in Figure 7-15 displays. The first configuration on this screen determines if the users' logon names are stored on their local PC and for how long. To have the logon name stored, check the box labeled Remember logons for: and enter the number of days you want it stored in the box to the right of the label. If you do not want the logon name stored on the client, make sure this box is unchecked. For security reasons it is recommended that you do not have the login names stored on the client.

Step 3 If you chose to have the logon name stored, the next field will be available for configuration. This field determines if the users' passwords are stored on their local PC and for how long. To have the password stored, check the box labeled Remember passwords for: and enter the number of days you want it stored in the box to the right of the label. If you do not want the password stored on the client, make sure this box is unchecked. For security reasons it is recommended that you do not have the passwords stored on the client.

Figure 7-15 *Authentication*

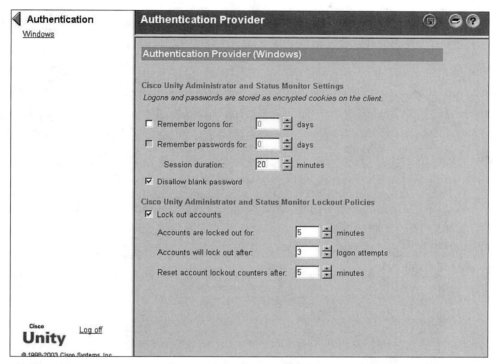

Step 4   The Session duration field allows you to set how long a subscriber remains logged into the interface if no activity has taken place. In other words, if the session is idle for the amount of minutes entered in this field, the subscriber is automatically logged out. The default is 20 minutes and in most cases should be adequate.

Step 5   The third configuration field on this page determines if blank passwords are allowed. To allow blank passwords, uncheck the box labeled Disallow blank password. Check this box if you do not want to allow blank passwords. For security reasons, it is recommended this field be checked so that blank logins cannot be used.

Step 6   The next check box is used to enable lockout polices. If you want to limit the number of times users can enter the incorrect password, this box should be checked. If this box is left unchecked, users are able to enter incorrect passwords an unlimited number of times.

Step 7   If lockout polices are enabled, limits must be set. Enter the number of minutes that a user will be locked out in the box labeled Accounts are locked out for. Enter the number of times users can enter incorrect passwords before they are locked out in the box labeled Accounts will lock out after. Enter the number of minutes in which Unity will reset the login attempts in the box labeled Reset account lockout counters after.

Step 8 Click the **Save** icon.

Configuring Ports

The last area of system configuration in this section is ports. As discussed previously, voice mail ports are used for communication between Unity and CallManager. These ports are created on CallManager. As shown earlier in this chapter, the Unity portion of configuration of these ports can be done using UTIM. However, these ports can also be modified from within SA. Regardless of how these ports are configured, the results are the same. Figure 7-16 shows the System>Ports screen. From this interface you can properly configure the ports according to their desired purpose. Table 7-4 lists the functions a port can be configured to perform.

Table 7-4   *Voice Mail Port Settings*

Parameter	Description
Extension	Should contain the extension number that is configured in CallManager for this port
Enabled	Allows the port to be used by Unity
Answer Calls	Allows the port to answer incoming calls
Message Notification	Allows the port to make outgoing calls for message notification purposes
Dialout MWI	Allows the port to be used to send MWI notifications
TRAP Connection	Allows the port to be used for recording and playing messages when a subscriber is using the web or an e-mail client

NOTE   If licensing for AMIS networking is purchased for this system, an additional parameter of AMIS Delivery may be listed. This allows the port to send and receive AMIS messages. AMIS is discussed in more detail in Chapter 10.

Before you start to configure the port, you should decide what functions will be needed and which ports will provide these functions. While making these decisions, keep in mind that outbound calls are sent from the higher numbered ports, and incoming calls are answered on the lower numbered ports. With this in mind, it makes sense to configure the higher numbered ports for functions such as MWI and message notification. This leaves the lower numbered ports available to answer incoming calls. It is recommended that approximately 75 percent of the ports should be configured to answer calls, whereas 25 percent should be configured for MWI and message notification. As you can see in Figure 7-16, other than the extensions, all values are enabled or disabled by checking and unchecking the appropriate box. To configure the ports, go to System>Ports in SA, enter the extension number and enable the desired function(s) for each port. Although it is not required to configure the extension number in these fields, it is recommended.

Figure 7-16 *Ports*

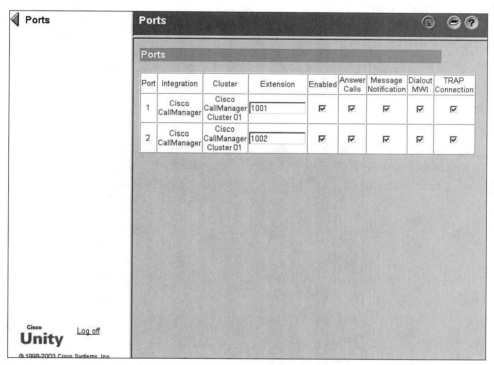

After the system configuration settings are completed, there are still a few more tasks to attend to before loading subscribers. The next section discusses how to configure system access rights and account policies.

Configuring System Access and Policies

Andrew Grove, the Chairman of Intel wrote a book called *Only the Paranoid Survive*. Although this may seem like an extreme title, there is much truth to it, especially when it comes to computers. Because Unity has the ability to access both voice-mail and e-mail, it is important to secure your system. Part of the securing process is setting up account polices and class of service (CoS). Account policies allow you to define parameters for subscribers' phone passwords. These parameters can prevent subscribers from using passwords that could be easily compromised. CoS defines the rights a subscriber has within the system, this includes how they can access Unity and the features they can use. Because these settings affect subscribers, it is best to configure them before adding subscribers.

Defining Account Polices

Account policies are basically about securing the subscribers' access to Unity. The link to Account Policy is located under the major heading of Subscribers. Two things are configured here, and the first is password restrictions. Password requirements are set here, including when a password expires, the required length of a password, and if the password must be unique when changed. In Figure 7-17 you can see the settings for this screen.

Figure 7-17 *Phone Password Restrictions*

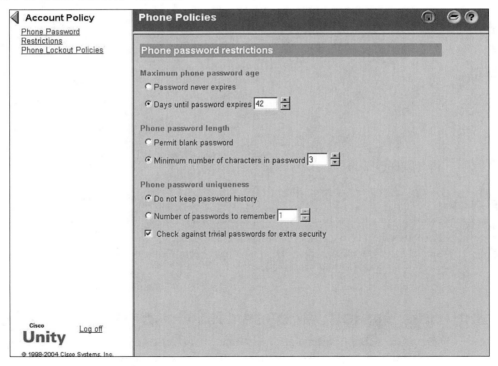

To configure phone password restrictions follow these steps:

Step 1 From within SA, select **Subscribers>Account Policy>Phone Password Restrictions**.

Step 2 First, set the length of time for which passwords are valid. Click the **Days until password expires** radio button and enter the number of days for which the password will be good. This determines how often subscribers have to change their passwords. If you have decided to allow the users to never have to change their passwords, click the **radio button** next to the phrase labeled Password never expires. It is recommended that you set passwords to expire.

Step 3 Click the radio button labeled **Minimum number of characters in password** and enter the desired number in the corresponding field. If you wish to permit blank passwords, click the radio button labeled **Permit blank passwords** instead. It is recommended that a password be required and that it be at least eight digits.

Step 4 Click the radio button labeled **Number of passwords to remember**. In the corresponding field, enter the number of previously used passwords you want Unity to keep in its history. The subscriber will not be able to use any previous password if it is still in Unity's history. If you do not want Unity to keep a history, click the radio button labeled **Do not keep password history**. This allows a subscriber to reuse the same password when the password expires. It is recommended that Unity keep at least three passwords in history.

Step 5 The last thing to configure is whether or not Unity should check against trivial passwords. Any of the following are considered trivial passwords:

> — Previous password
>
> — Password with all the same digits
>
> — Consecutive digits
>
> — The same as subscriber's extension
>
> — Password that spells the subscriber's name

Check the box labeled **Check against trivial passwords for extra security** if you want this feature to be active. It is recommended that this be checked.

Step 6 Click the **Save** icon.

The second area of configuration at this level is Phone Lockout Polices. These settings determine how many times a subscriber can enter the incorrect phone password before being locked out. The length of time a subscriber will be locked out of the account is also configured here. The steps that follow describe how to configure the settings that are shown in Figure 7-18.

Figure 7-18 *Phone Lockout Policies*

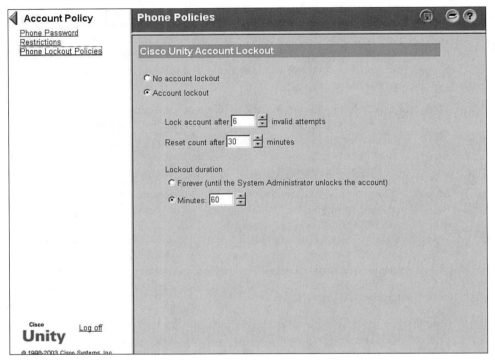

Step 1 From within SA, select **Subscribers>Account Policy>Phone Lockout Polices**.

Step 2 Check the radio button labeled **Account lockout**.

Step 3 Enter the number of times a subscriber can enter the incorrect password in the field labeled **Lock account after (field) invalid attempts**. If the radio button labeled No account lockout is checked, the account never locks regardless of how many times invalid passwords are entered. For security reasons, it is recommended that the **Lock account after (field) invalid attempts** radio button be selected.

Step 4 Enter the number of minutes Unity waits before resetting the attempts counter in the field labeled **Reset count after (field) minutes**.

Step 5 The last thing to configure on this screen is how long the account will be locked out if a subscriber exceeds the maximum invalid attempts. If you want the account to be locked until a system administrator unlocks it, click the radio button labeled **Forever**. You may also choose to have the account locked for a specified amount of time by clicking the radio button labeled **Minutes** and entering the number of minutes in the corresponding field.

Step 6   Click the **Save** Icon.

Now that account policies have been defined, CoS needs to be addressed.

Configuring Class of Service

Each subscriber in the system has an associated CoS, which is basically a list of rights and restrictions. The CoS defines how subscribers are allowed to access that system, and how they can use the system after they have accessed it. Because subscribers are assigned to a CoS when it is created, it is best to have all CoSs created before adding users.

The CoS in Unity components fit into eight categories. If you navigate to Subscribers> Class of Service in SA, you see the eight categories displayed as submenus under the Class of Service heading. The following is a list and brief description of each of these categories:

- **Profile**—Defines the name of the CoS and subscriber's name setting and directory listing
- **Subscribers**—Allows assignment of subscribers to CoS
- **System Access**—Defines the level of administrative access for a subscriber
- **Transfer**—Specifies if a subscriber can use Unity's holding and screening features
- **Messages**—Defines the message length and other message-related settings
- **Greetings**—Defines greeting length
- **Licensed Features**—Defines which licensed features the subscriber has
- **Restriction Tables**—Defines locations to which Unity can make calls on behalf of a subscriber. Restriction Tables would be used, for example, for Message Notification.

Before you configure CoS, it is best to record how many CoSs you need and how each will be configured. Typically, there are at least two CoSs: one for administrators and one for basic users. Unity has two default CoSs, so if you need only two, you can simply edit the defaults.

It is a good idea to leave the Default Administrator CoS alone. This is the CoS that allows administrative access. If you need a limited administrative access COS, it is best to create a new one.

The following tasks must be performed to add and edit a CoS. Each task is followed by step-by-step instructions.

Adding a CoS

Step 1 From within SA, select **Subscribers>Class of Service>Profile**.

Step 2 Click the **Add** icon (plus sign) in the title strip.

Step 3 A window displays, as shown in Figure 7-19, prompting you for a CoS name. From this screen, you may also choose to create the new class of service based on an existing one. This is useful if you need a new CoS that is very similar to an existing one. Enter a name and select the CoS you want to use as a base or select **New CoS**.

Figure 7-19 *Adding a CoS*

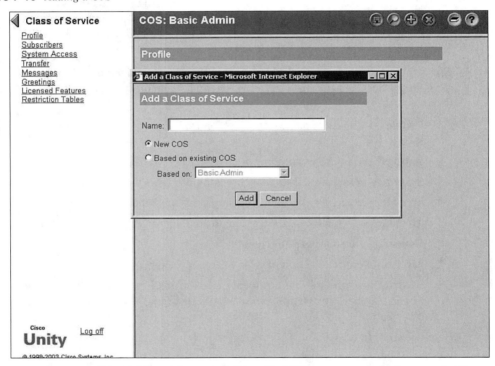

Step 4 Click **Add** and the new CoS is added. You are not required to save it. The saving action is required only when an object is modified, not when it is created.

Modifying a CoS

Modifying a CoS may require the configuration of all eight CoS categories or perhaps only one. For this reason, we will examine the configuration of each of these categories separately. However, before you can modify a CoS, you must first find it. To find the CoS you wish to modify, follow these steps:

Finding a CoS to Modify

Step 1 From within SA, select **Subscribers>Class of Service>Profile**.

Step 2 Click the **Find** icon. A list of CoSs displays.

Step 3 Select the CoS you want to modify and click **View**.

Modifying a CoS Profile

Now that the CoS has been found, the first configuration area is the CoS profile. The following steps are required to modify the profile of a CoS:

Step 1 From within SA, select **Subscribers>Class of Service>Profile**.

Step 2 As you can see in Figure 7-20, the first field is the name of the CoS. If you want to change it, enter the new name.

Figure 7-20 *CoS Profile*

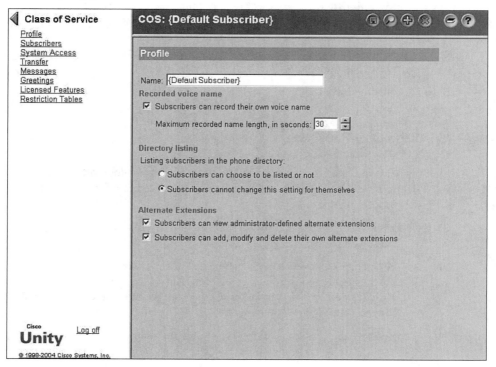

Step 3 Make sure the box labeled Subscribers can record their own voice name is checked. This allows subscribers to record their names for their mailbox.

Step 4 In the field **Maximum recorded name length, in seconds** field, enter the maximum length a recorded name can be. If you do not want the subscribers to be able to record their own voice names, uncheck the box labeled **Subscribers can record their own voice name**.

Step 5 The next setting allows subscribers to choose if they wish to be listed in the directory. If you do not want them to have this choice, click the radio button labeled **Subscribers cannot change this setting for themselves**. Otherwise, click the radio button labeled **Subscribers can choose to be listed or not**.

The next two settings determine if a subscriber is allowed to add or modify alternate extensions. Alternate extensions are used to associate a phone number other than the subscriber's extension to a subscriber's mailbox. This is typically used to associate a subscriber's cell phone number to the mailbox. When subscribers call from their cell phones, they are prompted to log in.

Step 6 To allow the subscriber to view alternate extensions that are defined by the administrator, select the radio button labeled Subscribers can view administrator-defined alternate extensions radio button. To allow subscribers to add and manage their own alternate extensions, select the **Subscribers can add, modify and delete their own alternate extensions** radio button.

Step 7 Click the **Save** icon.

Modifying CoS Subscribers

You can also modify which subscribers are assigned to a CoS. During the creation process, a subscriber is assigned to a CoS. The CoS they are assigned to is determined by the subscriber template that is used. If for any reason you need to move a subscriber to a different CoS, follow these steps:

Step 1 From within SA, select **Subscribers>Class of Service>Subscribers**. The screen shown is Figure 7-21 displays.

Step 2 As you can see, three actions can be performed. You can view the subscribers in this CoS, move (reassign) subscribers to a different CoS, or add (assign) subscribers to this CoS. Click the radio button associated with the action you wish to perform.

Figure 7-21 *CoS - Subscribers (View)*

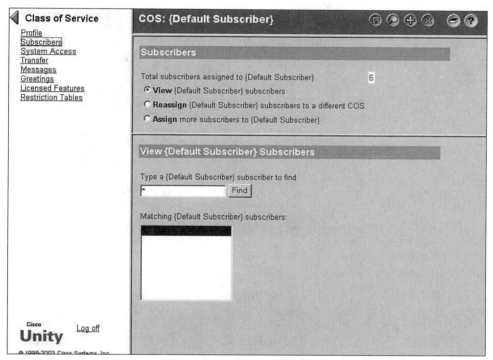

Step 3 To view subscribers in this CoS, click the radio button labeled **View** and click **Find**. You may enter search criteria in the field in front of Find to narrow your search. A list of subscribers that match the criteria are displayed.

Step 4 To move a subscriber from the current CoS to another CoS, click the radio button labeled **Reassign**. Figure 7-22 shows the screen that now displays is slightly different. Enter search criteria in the field in front of the Find button and click **Find**. From the list that displays, select the subscriber you wish to move. Now, from the drop-down list next to the Reassign button, select the CoS to which you want to move them. Click **Reassign**.

Step 5 To move a subscriber to the current CoS, click the radio button labeled **Assign**. Enter search criteria in the field in front of the Find button and click **Find**. From the list that displays, select the subscriber you wish to add. Click **Assign**.

Step 6 It is not necessary to save these changes, as they are saved automatically.

Figure 7-22 *CoS - Subscribers (Reassign)*

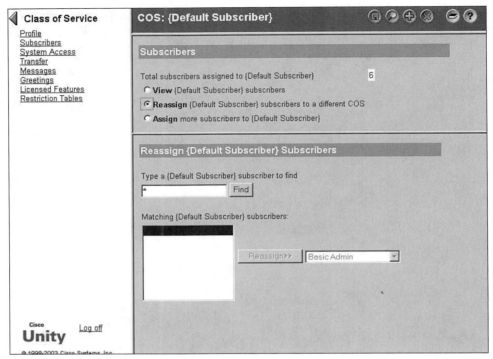

Modifying CoS System Access Settings

The CoS of subscribers determines the administrative level they have on the system. A number of rights can be granted. Table 7-5 shows these rights and what access can be assigned to them.

Table 7-5 *CoS Subscriber Rights*

	Enable	Read	Edit	Add	Delete
UA access	X				
CoS access		X	X	X	X
Directory Handlers access		X	X	X	X
Subscribers access		X	X	X	X
Unlock accounts	X				
Public distribution lists		X	X	X	X
Schedules/holidays	X				
Restriction tables access	X				

Table 7-5   *CoS Subscriber Rights (Continued)*

	Enable	Read	Edit	Add	Delete
Routing tables access	X				
Call handlers access	X				
Status monitor access	X				
Reports access	X				
Network access	X				
Diagnostic access	X				
Technician functions access (configuration, licensing, ports and switch pages)	X				

Figure 7-23 shows these fields as they display on the screen.

Figure 7-23   *CoS - System Access*

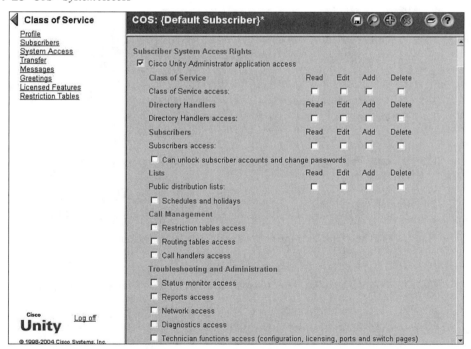

To assign system access rights to a CoS, follow these steps:

Step 1   From within SA, select **Subscribers>Class of Service>System Access**.

Step 2   Check the box labeled **Cisco Unity Administrator application access**.

Step 3   Check the appropriate boxes to assign the rights you want this CoS
to have.

Step 4   Click the **Save** icon.

Modifying CoS Transfer Settings

A CoS can define whether a subscriber can use the call screening and holding options or
not. To configure these options follow these steps:

Step 1   From within SA, select **Subscribers>Class of Service>Transfer**.

Step 2   To allow subscribers to determine if Unity announces who is calling
before they accept the call, check the box labeled **Subscribers can
change call screening options**.

Step 3   To allow subscribers to configure Unity to place an incoming call on hold
when they are already on the phone, check the box labeled **Subscribers
can change call holding options**.

Step 4   Click the **Save** icon.

Modifying CoS Message Settings

In the CoS message setting area, four things are defined:

1   The length of a message that a subscriber with this CoS can leave for another
subscriber.

2   Whether a subscriber can send messages to public distribution lists.

3   Whether messages that a subscriber deletes from the phone are moved to the deleted
items folder.

4   If, after listening to a message, a subscriber can have Unity dial the extension number
of another subscriber who left the message. This feature is called Live Reply.

Figure 7-24 shows the configuration screen for these settings.

To configure these settings follow these steps:

Step 1   From within SA, select **Subscribers>Class of Service>Messages**.

Step 2   In the **Maximum length of message subscribers can record, in
seconds** field, enter the maximum length in seconds of a message from a
subscriber with this class of service, to another subscriber.

Step 3   Check the box labeled **Subscribers can send messages to public
distribution lists** if you wish to allow subscribers with the CoS to send
messages to distribution lists.

Figure 7-24 *CoS - Message Settings*

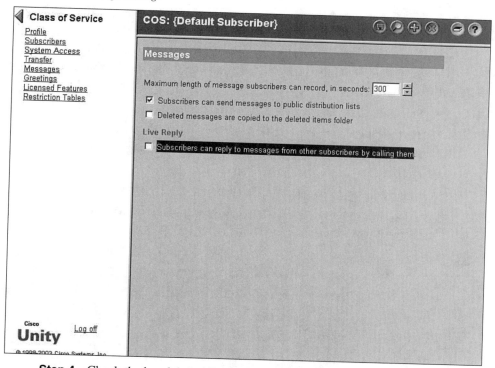

Step 4 Check the box labeled **Deleted messages are copied to the deleted items folder** to allow message that are deleted from the phone to be stored in the Deleted Items folder. Keep in mind that enabling this can have a negative impact on disk space.

Step 5 To allow subscribers to use the Live Reply feature, check the box labeled **Subscribers can reply to messages from other subscribers by calling them**.

Step 6 Click the **Save** icon.

Modifying CoS Greetings Settings

The greetings configuration for CoS defines the maximum length of a greeting. To configure these settings follow these steps:

Step 1 From within SA, select **Subscribers>Class of Service>Greetings**.

Step 2 Set the maximum number of seconds you want for a subscriber's greeting in the field labeled **Maximum greeting length, in seconds**.

Step 3 Click the **Save** icon.

Modifying COS Licensed Features Settings

The features to which a subscriber has access are, in part, determined by the licensed features configured in the CoS to which they are assigned.

The features that can be assigned to a subscriber are determined by the license that was purchased. The following is a list of the features that you may be able to assign through the CoS:

- **FaxMail**—fax management through the phone
- **Text-to-Speech**—e-mails to be heard over the phone
- **Unity Assistant**—subscriber's settings managed through the web
- **Unity Inbox**—voice-mail retrieved through the web

To configure these setting follow these steps:

Step 1   From within SA, select **Subscribers>Class of Service>Licensed Features**. The screen shown in Figure 7-25 displays.

Figure 7-25   *CoS - Licensed Features*

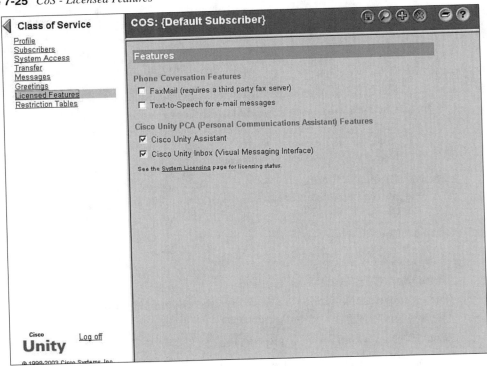

Step 2   Check the boxes of the features that you want subscribers of this CoS to have.

Step 3   Click the **Save** icon.

The last area to be configured in CoS is Restriction Tables. Because Restriction Tables deal with call management, they are covered in Chapter 9: Call Management.

Now that the CoS has been configured, we are almost ready to begin the process of adding subscribers, which is covered in Chapter 8: Subscriber Reference. However, before moving on, one last topic needs to be discussed—public distribution lists.

Creating and Managing Public Distribution Lists

The last thing discussed in this chapter is public distribution lists (PDLs). PDLs allow a single message to be sent to a group of people. Although subscribers can be added to PDLs manually, it is more efficient to add them during subscriber creation. This can be done because the template that is used during subscriber creation can contain the PDLs to which the subscriber is assigned. PDLs can contain both subscribers and other PDLs. For instance, you may have three groups, one for Detroit sales, one for New York sales, and one for Chicago sales. Each of these groups will contain subscribers from the associated location. You could then create a PDL called USSales and simply add the three sales PDLs, instead of having to add each subscriber again.

Creating Public Distribution Lists

To create and configure PDLs follow these steps:

Step 1   From within SA, select **Subscribers>Public Distribution Lists>Profile**. The screen shown in Figure 7-26 displays.

Step 2   If you wish to add a new PDL, click the **Add** icon (plus sign). Enter the name of the PDL in the window that displays. You can choose to create a completely new PDL, base it on an existing list, or import an Exchange group. Choose the appropriate option for this group and click **Add**.

Step 3   On the Profile screen, as shown in Figure 7-26, you see that the name and owner fields are populated. Each PDL must have an owner. By default, the owner will be the subscriber that created the PDL.

Step 4   You may record a name for this PDL by pressing the **Record** button on the media master control panel. The panel that has VCR-like buttons is the media master, and the record button is the round (red) button. The recorded name is played back when a subscriber dials the PDL by name.

Figure 7-26 *Public Distribution Lists*

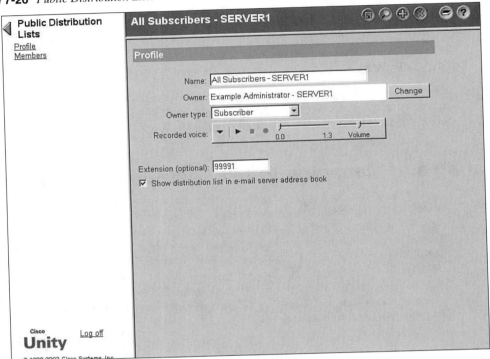

Note	It is a good idea to become familiar with the media master interface because you will be using it within SA when recording messages for objects, such as call handlers and subscribers. The first time you click the Play or Record button on the media master panel, the Phone Record and Playback Settings window displays. This window prompts you for the extension number of the phone you will use for recording and the name of the Unity server. This displays only the first time you use this interface from a particular PC.

As you can see in Figure 7-26, there are four buttons on this control panel. The first is an arrow that points down. When this button is clicked, you are presented with a menu that offers the following eight options:

— **Paste**—Allows you to paste audio that is in the clipboard into the current recording

- **Paste from file**—Allows you to paste an audio file into the current recording

- **Copy**—Allows you to copy the current recording to the clipboard

- **Copy to file**—Allows you to copy the current recording to a file

- **Playback Devices**—Allows you to choose to use either a phone or the sound card of the PC for playback

- **Record Devices**—Allows you to choose to use either a phone or the sound card of the PC for recording

- **Options**—Allows you to change the name of the server and the extension that you entered when the Phone Record and Playback Settings box appeared, the first time you used the media master on the PC.

- **About**—Displays version details for the media master

The next button is the play button (an arrow that points to the right). This arrow is blue if there is a recording already present for the object. To listen to the recording, click the Play button. The phone should ring, and the recording is played once the phone is answered.

The third button is the Stop button (square). To stop the recording, click this button.

The final button is the Record button (red circle). To record a message, click the Record button. The phone should ring. Answer the phone and record the message after the beep. In some cases an informational window displays in SA asking if you wish to overwrite the current recording before you can record the message.

Take a few minutes to get use to this interface, because you will find yourself using it often within SA.

Step 5 You may assign an extension by entering the desired extension number in the field labeled **Extension**. An extension is not required but is recommended. If a new extension is not assigned, a subscriber can send a message only by using the phone to dial the PDL by name.

Step 6 Check the box labeled **Show distribution list in e-mail server address book** if you want the PDL to display in the e-mail address book.

Step 7 Click the **Save** icon.

Managing PDL Members

As mentioned earlier, the easiest way to add a subscriber to a PDL is at the point of creation. If this is not done, or changes need to be made, they can be made manually from within SA. To view, add, or remove members from PDLs, follow these steps:

Step 1   Navigate to **Subscribers>Public Distribution Lists>Members** of the PDL you wish to manage. The screen shown in Figure 7-27 should display.

Step 2   You have the option of viewing, adding, or removing members from the PDL. Select an action by clicking the appropriate radio button at the top of the screen. If you choose to add members, you must select either **Selected subscriber** or **Public distribution lists** from the drop-down list.

Figure 7-27   *PDL Members*

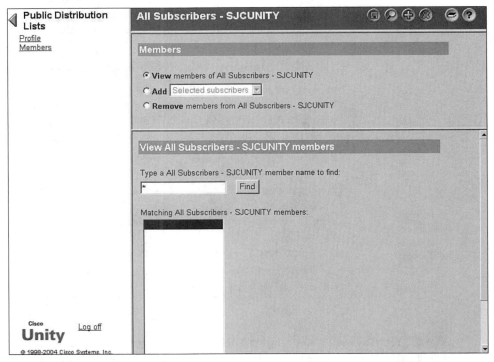

Step 3   Enter the search criteria for the subscriber (or public distribution list) you wish to manage in the field to the right of the Find button and click **Find**. If you are simply viewing, the PDL list displays. If you are adding or removing, a list displays with either an Add to list button or a Remove button. Select the subscriber you wish to manage and click the Add or Remove button.

Step 4   Click **Save**.

The settings that are configured in this chapter affect the entire system. Now that the system is step up, you must conduct tests to ensure the configurations you made are going to deliver the results you are anticipating. Take the time to test that the various settings you configured such as schedules, holidays and port function, just to name a few, are configured properly.

Summary

That's all there is to it. Well, not really. There is much more to this, but these steps complete the chapter. All the hard work you have done up to now is about to pay off. In this chapter you first learned how to verify a proper integration with CallManager. Then system configuration settings such as schedules, holidays, and languages were discussed. In addition, authentication and port settings were examined. The last portion of this chapter discussed how to configure account polices and class of service setting. In the next chapter, you start adding subscribers.

CHAPTER 8

Subscriber Reference

After a proper integration between Unity and CallManager is achieved and the predeployment tasks discussed in the previous chapter are completed, subscribers can be added. In this chapter, the different types of subscribers are examined, and the proper use for each. Then, the process for adding, importing, and managing subscribers is explored. Within the Managing Subscriber section, various administrative tasks are discussed, which range from how to reset a subscriber password, to how to grant a subscriber administrative access. Each task includes step-by-step instructions.

Defining Various Types of Subscribers

In Chapter 1, "Cisco CallManager and Unity Overview," you learned the various types of Unity subscribers. In this chapter you learn how to create and manage these subscribers. A brief review of the different types of subscribers follows:

Exchange

The Exchange subscriber is the most common subscriber found in a Unity deployment. As the name implies, this type of subscriber uses Exchange for its message store. Exchange subscribers may be either voice-mail only or unified messaging subscribers. Voice-mail only subscribers use the Exchange server as a place to store only their voice-mail messages. They are not able to retrieve their e-mail through Unity or their voice-mail through a PC. The unified messaging subscribers have both their e-mail and voice-mail stored on the same Exchange server and can access both types of messages from a phone or a PC.

These types of users may have many different ways to access Unity, such as through the Internet or over a phone. The user's CoS determines exactly what entry points they may use.

Domino

The Domino subscriber is used in environments that use Domino as their e-mail solution. Because a voice-mail only environment does not support Domino, these types of subscribers are unified messaging subscribers.

Domino subscribers have the same type of access to Unity as Exchange subscribers. This means they can access Unity using either a PC or phone.

Networked Subscribers

In addition to the Exchange and Domino subscribers, there is what is known as a Network subscriber, meaning that these types of subscribers are created only if some type of Unity networking is deployed. Because these users are directly related to Unity networking, they are discussed in Chapter 10, "Implementing Unity Networking."

Creating Exchange/Domino Subscribers

To add subscribers to the system, you can either create them from within Unity or import them into Unity. If the subscribers you wish to add exist on the mail store (Exchange or Domino), they can be imported. In fact, if Domino is being used, the subscriber must exist on the Domino system and then be imported into Unity. Subscribers may also be imported using a Comma Separated Value (CSV) file. This is an efficient way to add a number of subscribers. Exchange subscribers may be imported from Active Directory (AD) or the Exchange 5.5 directory. When a user is imported using a CSV file, a Windows domain and Exchange account can be automatically created for that subscriber.

NOTE   It is possible to configure Unity so that all subscribers must be imported. In this case, subscribers must exist in Exchange before they can be added (imported) into Unity. This is often done in an environment where different groups manage the Exchange and Unity. Setting up this requirement helps to keep Windows domain and Exchange accounts manageable.

The actual process of creating a single subscriber is, at the surface, a very simple task. However, when looked at closely, you see that each subscriber has more than 50 individual settings. The reason that creating a subscriber looks so simple is that it requires only a few pieces of information and a few keystrokes, but to ensure that the subscriber is properly configured requires much more work. Each time a subscriber is added, every setting must be given a value. So creating a subscriber requires the configuration of more than 50 settings, but at the same time a subscriber can be created with just a few keystrokes. How is this possible? The creation of a subscriber is based on what is known as a subscriber template. The values configured in the template are applied to the newly created subscriber. The next section discusses the use and creation of subscriber templates.

Creating Subscribers Templates

When you create or import subscribers, a large number of them have very similar attributes. Subscriber templates automatically allow you to assign the same settings to each subscriber during the creation process. The use of a subscriber template is not optional. Each time you add a subscriber, a template must be chosen. Two subscriber templates are created during the installation process. These are the default administrator and the default subscriber templates. As their names imply, they each have settings that are commonly found in administrative level subscribers and standard subscribers.

NOTE   Although you can use the default templates to create subscribers, it is best to confirm the settings of the default template's settings first. Do not take for granted that the default settings are the best settings for your deployment.

Before creating any subscriber templates, plan how each subscriber will use the system. Templates allow you to configure everything from the subscriber's time zone, to what happens to a call if a caller presses **4** while listening to the greeting. Because of their configuration, it is possible to find yourself creating many templates. Be careful not to get carried away. Remember, the templates are used to help assign settings to a group of subscribers that are going to have similar, not necessarily identical, attributes. In most cases, the template you create should apply to at least five subscribers. If you find that you are creating a large number of templates and applying each of them to a small number of subscribers, you may want to rethink your deployment strategy. Although each subscriber has unique settings, there will be a large number of settings that are the same for the majority of subscribers.

When determining how many subscriber templates you need, it is a good idea to try to organize subscribers into groups. These groups should begin at a very general level. The members in these groups require the same type of features and access to Unity. Let's assume you are implementing unified messaging, but only some of the users need to retrieve their e-mail from the phone. From this we can assume that there are at least three types of subscribers. One group, which is needed in all environments, is the administrator group. The other two types of subscribers are the subscribers that need access to text-to-speech and those that don't. There may be a requirement for additional groups, but this lets you determine the different templates you may need. A list of questions that you should consider when determining how many templates you need follows. These questions are directly related to the various settings you configure in the subscriber templates. In addition to answering these questions, you should go through the process of actually creating a test template so you become familiar with the settings that are configured.

1   How many CoSs are there?

Typically you will need at least one template for each CoS you have created.

2 How many schedules are there?

3 Are all subscribers in the same time zone?

4 Are all subscribers on the same phone switch?

5 Are multiple mailstores being used?

6 Will there be call accounting for Unity outbound calls?

7 How many billable departments are there?

Unity can create a report of each outbound call that it places and associate it to a billing ID.

8 Will all subscribers have the same password restrictions?

9 Will subscribers be allowed to control their own conversation flow? If not, how many base flows are needed?

This deals with things such as menu styles, time format, and message playback order.

10 Will all phones ring when dialed from Unity?

This refers to what happens when a subscriber's extension is dialed from within Unity. Typically, you want the phone to ring, but in some cases you may want to go directly to voice-mail or a different extension.

11 Will all phones ring the same number of times when transferred from Unity?

12 What greetings are enabled by default?

A subscriber may have five greetings: standard, closed, busy, internal, and alternate. You need to determine which greeting is enabled by default and if the same greetings are enabled for all subscribers.

13 While listening to a greeting, what options will a caller have? Will this be the same for all phones?

While listening to a greeting, the caller can be given a list of options such as To skip this message press <option number>, or To reach an operator press <option number>.

14 How long can messages be? Will this be the same for all phones?

15 How many public distribution lists are there?

16 Will message notification be used? How many groups will require this?

You may modify the two default templates, but they cannot be deleted. You can create up to 64 subscriber templates. Common logic and a well-designed plan will help determine how many you need.

Before moving on to the actual process of creating subscriber templates, it is important that you understand that these templates are significant only at the point of creation. This means the setting of a template affects the subscriber only when the subscriber is first created. If you create 50 users using a template, changes you make to that template after the subscribers are created do not affect the subscriber's settings. If you need to change certain settings on a large number of subscribers, use the Bulk edit utility. This utility is discussed in Chapter 11, "Exploring Unity Tools."

Figure 8-1 displays a split screen that shows the submenu for a subscriber and the submenu for a subscriber template. This figure shows that the submenus are very similar.

Figure 8-1   *Subscriber and Subscriber Template Submenus*

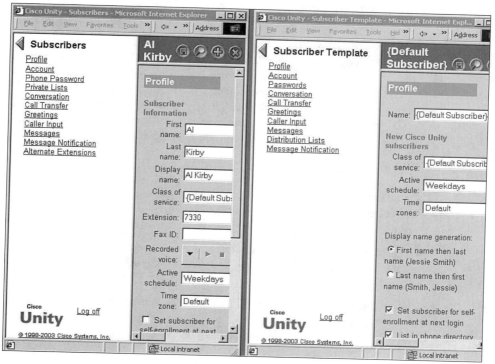

There are more than 50 configurable settings for each subscriber, so there must be at least that many settings for each subscriber template. It is important to understand the affect of each setting. The following is an overview of the types of settings each submenu contains.

- **Profile**—General settings, such as schedules and time zones, are set in this area. Information relating to the subscribers' names is also set here, such as how their Windows domain user names are generated.

- **Account**—This area allows you to set a billing ID for subscribers and determine if the subscriber's account will be available for use as soon as it is created or if an administrator will have to unlock it first.

- **Passwords**—This area allows you to configure default passwords and expiration settings.

- **Conversation**—The conversation area allows you to configure how the Unity system interacts with a subscriber. This includes things such as volume, menu style, time format, message playback order, and many other settings. If you allow the subscribers access to Cisco Personal Communication Assistant (CPCA), subscribers can change most of these settings themselves.

Note   The conversation settings are important to the success of the system, because allowing control over the settings makes the new system more acceptable to the end user. I was once asked to deliver some end user training for a company whose employees were very frustrated with the system. As it turned out, 90 percent of their concerns related to the conversation settings. After they learned to configure these settings themselves, the majority of the issues were resolved.

- **Call Transfer**—This area determines what action is taken when a subscriber's extension is dialed from within Unity. Most of the time, this occurs when an outside caller dials the extension from the auto attendant.

- **Greetings**—The greetings area configures which greetings are enabled, what action is allowed during the greeting, and what action is taken after the greeting.

- **Caller Input**—During a greeting, a caller has a number of choices, such as to skip the greeting by pressing #, or to reach an operator by pressing 0. The caller input settings determine what happens if a digit is pressed while the greeting is being played.

- **Messages**—The settings in this area determine how long messages can be, whether callers can edit messages, and the actions taken after taking a message. The extension to use for Message Waiting Indicator (MWI) is also configured here.

- **Distribution Lists**—The distribution lists to which the subscriber belongs are configured here.

- **Message Notification**—The devices used to notify a subscriber of a new message are configured in this area.

At this point you should have an idea of the different templates you need. Let's go through the process of creating and managing a template so you fully understand all of the settings that must be configured. We begin by adding a new template. The following are the steps required to add a new subscriber template.

Step 1 From within SA, select **Subscribers>Subscriber Template**.

Step 2 Click the **Add** icon in the title strip.

Step 3 A window such as the one in Figure 8-2 displays. Enter the name for the new Subscriber template.

Step 4 If there is an existing template similar to the one you are creating, click the **Based on existing Template** radio button, and choose the existing template from the drop-down list. Otherwise, click the **New Template** radio button and click **Add**.

Figure 8-2 *Subscribers>Subscriber Template (Adding)*

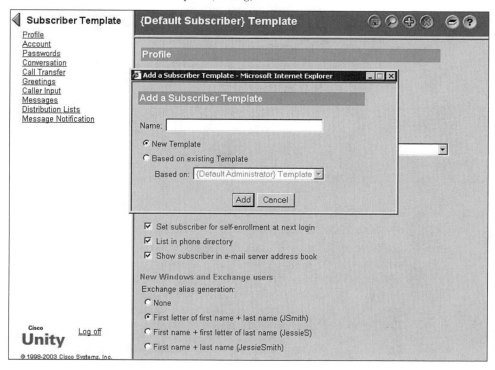

The creation of a template is the easy part. Now you need to configure the settings within each submenu. As Figure 8-1 shows, there are 10 submenus under subscriber templates. The configuration of settings in each submenu follows. Let's start by configuring the template's Profile settings. Figure 8-3 shows the Subscriber Template Profile page, and the following steps describe how to configure these settings.

Figure 8-3   *Subscribers>Subscriber Template>Profile*

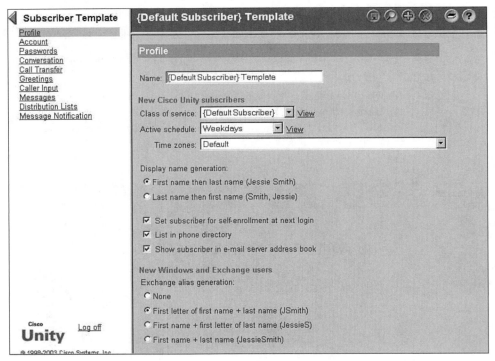

Configuring Subscriber Template Profile Settings

Step 1   From the previous steps, click **Profile** from the list on the left side of the screen and move on to the next step. Otherwise, from within SA, select **Subscribers>Subscriber Template**. If the name of the template you wish to manage does not display in the title strip, click the **Find** icon and select the desired subscriber template. Once the template is active, click **Profile** from the list on the left side of the screen.

Step 2   The name of the template displays in the **Name** field on this screen. This name is chosen when the template is created. You may change it here if you wish.

Step 3 Select the desired **Class of service**, **Active schedule**, and the **Time zones** from the appropriate drop-down lists.

Step 4 In a dual switch integration, choose the phone system that the subscriber's phone is on in the **Switch** field. This field displays only with a dual switch integration.

Step 5 Under the **Display name generation:** heading choose either **First name then last name** or **Last name then first name**. This setting should be similar to the existing names in Exchange.

Step 6 To force subscribers to record name and greeting and change their passwords on the next login, check the **Set subscriber for self-enrollment at next login** box. Subscribers can choose to be listed in the directory during the self-enrollment process, if the subscribers' CoS allows this option.

Step 7 To list subscribers in the auto attendant directory, check the **List in phone directory** box.

Step 8 Check the **Show subscriber in e-mail server address book** box if you want the subscriber's address to display in the outlook address book. If this box is unchecked, other subscribers cannot use the Outlook address book to address messages to the subscriber.

Step 9 Finally, you need to choose how to generate the Exchange alias. Use this when creating subscribers who do not already have Exchange accounts. An Exchange account is created when the subscriber is added, and the alias generated is based on this selection. If there are existing Exchange accounts, make sure that the format you choose matches the format of the existing Exchange aliases.

Step 10 Click the **Save** icon in the title strip.

Configuring Subscriber Template Account Settings

Next, configure Account information for the template.

Step 1 If you are continuing from the previous steps, click **Account** from the list on the left side of the screen and move on to the next step. Otherwise, from within SA, select **Subscribers>Subscriber Template**. If the name of the template you wish to manage does not appear in the title strip, click the **Find** icon and select the desired subscriber template. Once the template is active, click **Account** from the list on the left side of the screen.

Step 2 The **Cisco Unity account status Locked** check box allows you to lock the account at the point of creation. You may want the account locked at the point of creation so that the account cannot be used before the deployment is completed. Decide whether you want the accounts you create, using this template, to be locked upon creation and set the check box accordingly.

Step 3 The other setting for Account information is a billing ID. A billing ID determines which subscriber or department is billed for outbound calls placed by Unity. A billing ID is assigned to an individual mailbox or a group of mailboxes. If you want to assign the same billing ID for all subscribers using this template, enter it here. If you plan to have different billing IDs for each user or not use them at all, leave this field blank.

Step 4 Click the **Save** icon in the title strip.

Configuring Subscriber Template Passwords Settings

The Subscriber Template Passwords page allows you to define password specific settings. From this page you can set default passwords and phone password settings. Figure 8-4 shows how the settings are configured.

Figure 8-4 *Subscribers>Subscriber Template>Passwords*

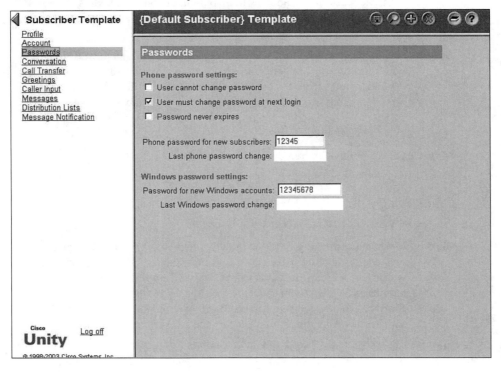

To configure these settings follow these steps.

Step 1   From the previous steps, click **Passwords** from the list on the left side of the screen and move on to the next step. Otherwise, from within SA, select **Subscribers>Subscriber Template**. If the name of the template you wish to manage does not display in the title strip, click the **Find** icon and select the desired subscriber template. Once the template is active, click **Passwords** from the list on the left side of the screen.

Step 2   Under the **Phone password settings:** heading there are three settings. These settings determine if the subscribers are able to change their passwords, whether subscribers must change their passwords on the next login, and if the password will expire. If you do not want the users to be able to change their passwords, check the **User cannot change password** box.

Step 3   You want to force subscribers to change their passwords on their first login. Check the **User must change password at next login** box to do so.

Step 4   To enhance security, it is a good idea to force subscribers to change their passwords on a regular basis. However, a password can be set never to expire. If you choose to **configure** the phone's password so it never expires, check the **Password never expires** box. If this box is left unchecked, the password expires based on the setting you make in Account Policy. Although you can set a password never to expire, this is not recommended.

Step 5   The subscribers' default password is determined by the passwords set in the template. In the **Phone password for new subscribers:** field enter the desired default phone password.

Step 6   The next field is not configurable. The **Last phone password change:** field displays the date on which the phone password was last changed.

Step 7   When new Exchange subscribers who do not have existing Windows domain accounts are added, Windows domain accounts are created for them. In the **Password for new Windows accounts:** field enter the Exchange password you want assigned to this account.

Step 8   The final field on this screen in not configurable. The **Last Windows password change:** field displays the date the last time the windows password was changed.

Step 9   Click the **Save** icon in the title strip.

Configuring Subscriber Template Conversation

The Subscriber template conversation settings allow you to configure how Unity interacts with a subscriber. This page has more configurable settings than any other page in Unity, so there are more configuration steps than the areas we have configured up to now. It is important to understand how these affect a subscriber's settings because the settings have a significant impact on the subscriber's satisfaction with the system. The following steps explain what affect the settings have and how to configure them. Figure 8-5 shows the fields in Steps 1–10.

Figure 8-5 *Subscribers>Subscriber Template>Conversation*

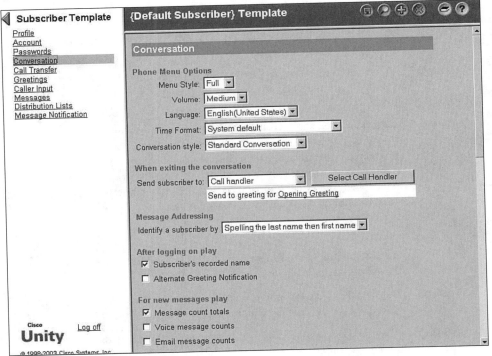

Step 1 From the previous steps, click **Conversation** from the list on the left side of the screen and move on to the next step. Otherwise, from within SA, select **Subscribers>Subscriber Template**. If the name of the template you wish to manage does not display in the title strip, click the **Find** icon and select the desired subscriber template. Once the template is active, click **Conversation** from the list on the left side of the screen.

Step 2 The first setting determines whether the subscriber hears full or brief menus. It is a good idea to set the menus to full for users who are new to the system because full menus explain more than brief menus. After users are familiar with the menus, you may want to change to a brief menu. Choose the desired menu style from the **Menu Style:** drop-down list.

Step 3 Select the volume at which the Unity conversation is played from the **Volume:** drop-down list. The choices are Quieter, Medium, and Louder. Medium should work for most users.

Step 4 If multiple languages are installed, you may select the language from the **Language:** drop-down list. This determines the language for the subscriber conversation.

Step 5 Select a time format different from the system default by selecting 12-hour or 24-hour format from the **Time Format:** drop-down list. If you leave this field set to System default, the format selected under Setting>Configuration> is used.

Step 6 The **Conversation style:** field determines which touch tones you use to do things such as save and delete messages. If you are migrating from another voice-mail system, it is a good idea to become familiar with these conversations and pick the one closest to previous voice-mail system conversations. There are three choices. The first one, Standard Conversation, is a good choice for locations where users are not familiar with a certain voice-mail menu format. The second conversation, Optional Conversation 1, is a good choice if users are familiar with an Octel-like menu system. The third choice, Hospitality Conversation, is only used when Unity's Hospitality and Property Management System is deployed.

Step 7 Under the **When exiting the conversation** heading you can configure where subscribers are sent when they end the subscriber conversation. A number of choices are available from the drop-down list, but configure this to send the subscriber to a call handler or hang up. Select the destination from the **Send subscriber to:** drop-down list.

Step 8 To configure how a subscriber is prompted to address messages to other subscribers, select one of the available choices: **Spelling the last name then first name**, **Spelling the first name then last name**, or **Enter the extension**. Select the desired format from the **Identify a subscriber by** drop-down list.

Step 9 When subscribers log onto the system, they may be greeted by hearing their recorded names, so they know they are logged into the correct account. To enable this greeting, check the **Subscriber's recorded name** box.

Step 10 An alternate greeting is used when a subscriber is out of the office for a long period of time, such as vacation. It is important that the subscriber remember to turn this greeting off when they return. Configure Unity to inform the subscriber if the alternate greeting is enabled when they log in by checking the **Alternate Greeting Notification** box. Starting with Unity 4.04, when a subscriber enables the alternate greeting they can automatically schedule a time for the alternate greeting to be disabled.

The next group of settings to configure in the conversation area deal with the type of messages played and their order. Figures 8-6 and 8-7 show the fields that are covered in these steps.

Figure 8-6   *Subscribers>Subscriber Template>Conversation (Continues)*

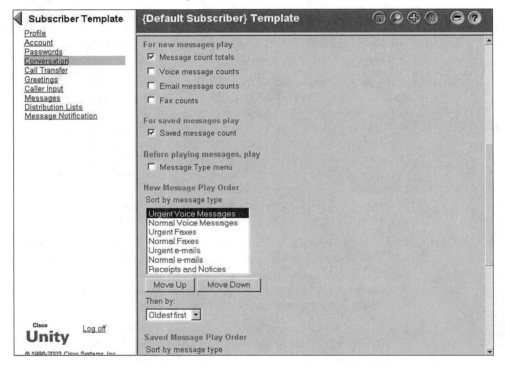

Step 11 To configure Unity to inform the subscriber of the total number of new messages and of the message count, check the box next to each type of message count you want the subscriber to hear. The choices are **Message count totals**, **Voice message counts**, **Email message counts** and **Fax counts**. It is best to offer only the message counts for the messages the subscriber is likely to retrieve using the phone. For example, if the subscriber retrieves only voice-mail using the phone, only **Voice message counts** is chosen.

Step 12 To announce the number of saved messages to the subscriber, check the
Saved message count box.

Figure 8-7 *Subscribers>Subscriber Template>Conversation (Continued)*

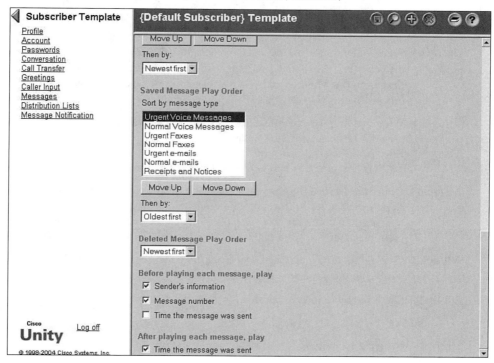

Step 13 To allow subscribers to determine the types of messages they wish to
hear, check the **Message Type menu** box. When this option is enabled,
the subscriber hears the following message: "Press 1 to hear voice
messages, Press 2 to hear e-mails, Press 3 to hear faxes, Press 4 to hear
receipts."

Step 14 Users can configure the order in which new messages are played. Under
the **New Message Play Order** heading is a list of the various types of
messages. The messages are played as they appear from top to bottom.
To change the order, highlight the type of message you wish to move and
then click the **Move Up** or **Move Down** button. Do this with all of the
message types until they are in the desired order.

Step 15 When playing new messages, the default behavior of Unity is to play the
oldest message first. To play the newest message first, choose **Newest
first** from the **Then by:** drop-down list. In most cases it is best to leave
this setting at **Oldest first**.

Step 16 Users can configure the order in which saved messages are played. Under the **Saved Message Play Order** heading is a list of the various types of messages. The messages are played as they appear from top to bottom. To change the order, highlight the type of message you wish to move and then click the **Move Up** or **Move Down** button. Do this with all of the message types until they are in the desired order.

Step 17 When playing saved messages, the default behavior of Unity is to play the newest message first. To play the oldest message first, choose **Oldest first** from the **Then by:** drop-down list. In most cases it is best to leave this setting at **Newest first**.

Step 18 When playing deleted messages, the default behavior of Unity is to play the newest message first. To play the oldest message first, choose **Oldest first** from the drop-down list below the **Deleted Message Play Order** heading. In most cases, it is best to leave this setting at **Newest first**.

Step 19 Under the **Before playing each message, play** heading you can choose to play the sender's information, message number, and time the message was sent. To configure what is played, check the box next to each of the messages that you want played.

Step 20 To play the time a message was sent after a message is played, check the **Time the message was sent** box.

Step 21 Click the **Save** icon in the title strip.

Configuring Subscriber Template Call Transfer

The subscribers' template call transfer settings determine what happens to a call when an outside caller attempts to reach a subscriber's phone from the auto-attendant. An outside caller may attempt to reach a subscriber by entering the subscriber's extension number or by using Unity's dial-by-name feature. When Unity finds a match for either the extension number or the name, it looks at the subscriber's call transfer settings to determine where to send the call. One would think that Unity would send the call to the PBX, so the call could be delivered to the phone. Although this is the most common action, it is not always desired. A number of circumstances dictate that the call not be sent to the phone.

If the call is sent to the phone, it can be transferred to the PBX in one of two ways. The first is called **Release to switch**. In this type of transfer, Unity sends the call to the PBX and is finished with that call. If the called party does not answer or the phone is busy, it is the responsibility of the PBX to forward the call back to Unity. You might think that if the PBX sent the call back to Unity, Unity would just loop the call back to the PBX because the call transfer settings dictate it. The reason it does not loop is because the call transfer settings do not affect calls that are forwarded to Unity from the PBX. If the transfer settings were applied to every call, unanswered and busy calls would loop forever.

The second type of transfer is called **Supervised transfer**. On a supervised transfer, Unity holds open the port used to transfer the call and tries to determine if the call is answered. When Unity determines that the call is answered, Unity releases the call and the port is closed. If Unity determines that the call is busy or is not answered within the number of rings defined for this transfer, Unity pulls the call back and plays the subscriber's greeting. Because Unity maintains control of the call during a supervised transfer, additional features can be implemented, such as holding options and call screening.

Figure 8-8 shows the call transfer setting page. The following steps describe how to configure the various settings and the effect they have on transferred calls.

Figure 8-8   *Subscribers>Subscriber Template>Call Transfer*

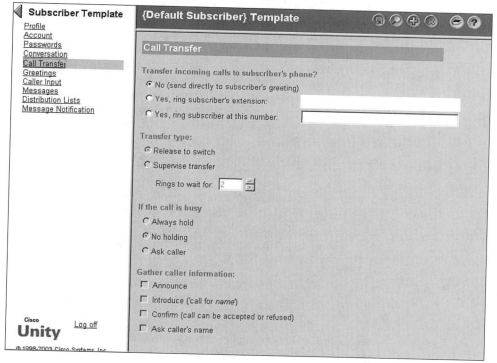

Step 1   From the previous steps, click **Call Transfer** from the list on the left side of the screen and move on to the next step. Otherwise, from within SA, select **Subscribers>Subscriber Template**. If the name of the template you wish to manage does not appear in the title strip, click the **Find** icon and select the desired subscriber template. Once the template is active, click **Call Transfer** from the list on the left side of the screen.

Step 2   To configure whether, and to which phone, a call will be sent, select the **Yes, ring subscriber's extension:** radio button. If you do not want the phone to ring and the call to be sent straight to the subscriber's greeting, select the **No (send directly to subscriber's greeting)** radio button. The call may also be sent to an extension other than the one associated with the subscriber by selecting the **Yes, ring subscriber at this number:** radio button. Set the transfer setting to send the call to the subscriber's extension. If **No (send directly to subscriber's greeting)** is selected, the remaining steps in this section do not apply.

Step 3 If the call is transferred to an extension, the type of transfer must be selected under the **Transfer type:** heading. If holding and screening options are desired, select the **Supervise transfer** radio button. If these features are not needed, select the **Release to switch** radio button. If **Release to switch** is selected, the remaining steps in this section do not apply.

Step 4 Unity has the ability to queue calls for subscribers if they are on the phone when a call is transferred from Unity. You must choose one of three options for Unity to know if the subscriber's extension is busy. The first choice, **Always hold** informs the caller that the extension is busy and places the caller on hold. The second option, **No holding**, prompts the caller to leave a message or dial another extension. The third choice, **Ask caller**, informs the caller that the extension is busy and offers the choice of holding, leaving a message, or dialing another extension. Select the desired action by clicking the associated radio button.

Note When implementing the option to allow the caller to hold, remember that this will hold a port open while the caller is on hold. If this option is offered to a number of subscribers, it could adversely affect Unity's ability to handle incoming calls.

Step 5 Unity has the ability to gather caller information for screening purposes on a supervised transfer. There are four options under the **Gather caller information:** heading. These options are as follows:

— Announce—Unity announces "transferring call" when the subscriber answers the call.

— Introduce—Unity announces whom the call is for when the subscriber answers the phone. This feature is used when more than one person receives calls on the same phone.

— Confirm—Unity asks the subscriber to press 1 to accept the call or press 2 to send the call to voice mail.

— Ask caller's name—Unity asks the callers to record their names and plays the recorded names to the subscriber when the phone is answered.

Select the options you wish to enable by selecting the radio button next to each option.

Step 6   Click the **Save** icon in the title strip.

Configuring Subscriber Template Greetings

The greetings setting of the template allows you to define what greetings are enabled and how they are configured. A subscriber can use up to five greetings, each played under different circumstances. Table 8-1 lists these greetings and the function of each.

Table 8-1   *Greetings*

Greeting	Function
Standard	Plays during open hours unless overridden by another greeting. If closed greeting is not enabled, standard plays after hours.
Closed	Plays during closed hours as defined in the schedule associated with the subscriber.
Busy	Plays when the call is transferred to Unity because the subscriber's extension was busy.
Internal	Plays when the caller is another subscriber on the system.
Alternate	When enabled, overrides all other greetings. This greeting plays all hours, all days until disabled.

Figure 8-9 shows the subscriber template greetings configuration screen. The following steps discuss the effects of these settings and how to configure them.

Step 1   After the previous steps, click **Greetings** from the list on the left side of the screen and move on to the next step. Otherwise, from within SA, select **Subscribers>Subscriber Template**. If the name of the template you wish to manage does not appear in the title strip, click the **Find** icon and select the desired subscriber template. Once the template is active, click **Greetings** from the list on the left side of the screen.

Step 2   From this screen you can enable and configure each of the five greetings. From the **Greeting:** drop-down list select the greeting you wish to configure. Start with the Standard greeting.

Step 3   Under the **Status:** heading, the greeting may be enabled or disabled. If the greeting is disabled it will not be used. The Standard greeting is enabled by default and cannot be disabled. If you are configuring a greeting other than the standard greeting, select the **Enabled** radio button to enable this type of greeting.

Figure 8-9 *Subscribers>Subscriber Template>Greetings*

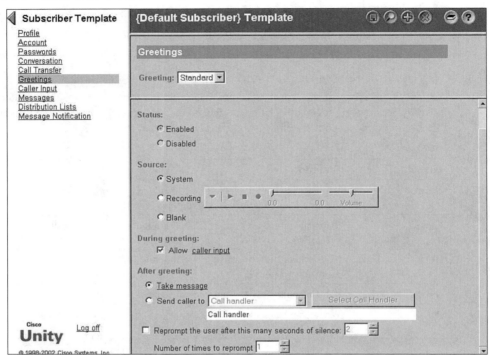

Step 4   Under the **Source:** heading, the source of the message is chosen. The three choices for the source are as follows:

— System—Plays the prerecorded greeting "Sorry <subscriber's name> is not available." If the subscriber has not yet recorded a name, the greeting "Sorry the subscriber at extension <subscriber's extension number> is not available" is played.

— Recording—Plays the greeting that the subscriber recorded.

— Blank—Plays no greeting and goes directly to the after greeting action.

Typically, **Recording** is chosen for this setting, so the subscribers can create their own greetings. Select the desired source by clicking the appropriate radio button.

Step 5   If **Recording** is chosen, you can use the media master control panel (the VCR-like panel next to the record label) to record a greeting. This interface also allows you to copy, cut, and paste the recording.

Step 6   To allow callers to try to reach another extension or select options during a greeting, check the **Allow <u>caller input</u>** box. Notice that caller input is underlined; this is a link to the caller input page. The caller input page is covered later in this section.

Step 7   After the greeting is played, the caller has the opportunity to leave a message. To enable this, click the **Take message** radio button. If you want a different action to take place, click the **Send caller to** radio button and select the desired destination from the drop-down list as follows:

— CVM Mailbox Reset—Sends the call to a conversation that allows the caller to reset the mailbox. This is only available when the Community Voice-mail (CVM) package is being used.

— Call Handler—Sends the call to the selected call handler.

— Caller System Transfer—Sends the callers to a prompt that allows them to enter another extension to which they would like to be transferred.

— Directory Handler—Sends the call to the directory handler you select.

— Greetings Administrator—Sends the call to a conversation that allows them to manage the greetings of call handlers that they own.

— Hang up—Disconnects the call.

— Hotel Checked Out—This option works in concert with Cisco Unity's Hospitality and Property Management Integration. It allows guests to archive their messages when checking out.

— Interview Handler—Sends the call to the interview handler you select.

— Sign-in—Sends the call to subscriber sign in.

— Subscriber—Sends the call to another subscriber's greeting or extension depending upon how it is configured.

— Subscriber System Transfer—Allows callers to transfer to another extension after they log in with subscriber credentials. They may then transfer to any number that their restriction table allows.

When choosing to send the call to a call handler, directory handler, interview handler, or another subscriber, you have to specify the specific handler or subscriber. A **Select** *type_of_object_you_selected* button becomes available to the right of the type of object you select.

For example, if you select the option to send the call to a subscriber, choose the **Select Subscriber** button. When you click this button, a search criteria window displays. Enter the appropriate criteria and click **Find**. Select the desired object from the list. If a subscriber or call handler is selected, you must also select whether the call should be sent to the greeting or the phone extension. To send the call to the extension, select **Attempt transfer for** from the **Conversation** drop-down list. To send the call to the subscriber's greeting select **Send to greeting for** from the **Conversation** drop-down list.

Note	The fact that you have to choose to send the call to the greeting, or attempt to transfer it, has caused many administrators hours of frustration and troubleshooting. Make sure that if you want the phone of the subscriber to whom the call is transferred to ring, you must select **Attempt transfer for**.

Step 8 If callers remains silent after being offered the opportunity to leave a message, they can be reprompted. To have a caller reprompted, select the **Reprompt the user after this many seconds of silence:** box and enter the number of seconds to wait for the caller to begin speaking. Then enter the number of times you want the caller to be reprompted; the maximum is 100.

Step 9 Click the **Save** icon in the title strip.

Configuring Subscriber Template Caller Input

When callers reach a greeting, a list of options is made available to them. Often the caller is given the option to dial another extension or reach an operator by pressing a certain digit. Adding options to a spoken greeting isn't enough; these options must also be configured under the Caller Input section of the template.

The following steps show how to configure the Caller Input settings, which are shown in Figure 8-10.

Step 1 From the previous steps, click **Caller Input** from the list on the left side of the screen and move on to the next step. Otherwise, from within SA, select **Subscribers>Subscriber Template**. If the name of the template you wish to manage does not appear in the title strip, click the **Find** icon and select the desired subscriber template. Once the template is active, click **Caller Input** from the list on the left side of the screen.

Step 2 The first setting that must be configured determines whether callers are able to reach a different extension when listening to a subscriber's greeting. This is commonly allowed because callers might rather try to reach someone else instead of leave a message. To allow a caller to enter another extension while listening to a greeting, check the **Allow callers to dial an extension during greeting** box.

Figure 8-10 *Subscribers>Subscriber Template>Caller Input>*

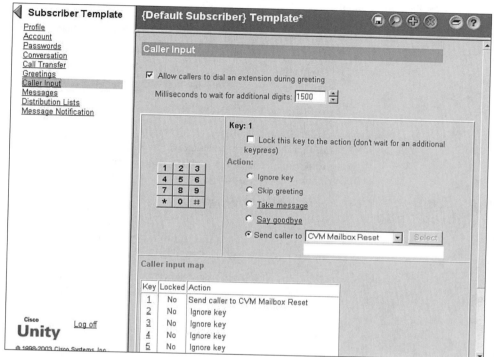

Step 3   If the option to allow callers to dial another extension during the greeting is enabled, an interdigit time out must also be configured. The **Milliseconds to wait for additional digits: setting** is the amount of time Unity waits before deciding the caller has finished pressing digits. The default value is 1500 milliseconds, which is a second and a half. Typically, this value is adequate. If, during a greeting, callers are transferred or receive error messages from Unity before they are finished dialing an extension, increase this value.

Step 4   From the dial pad on the screen you can configure the action that is taken when a digit is pressed. A button can be configured for five types of actions:

— Ignore key—No action is taken when digit is pressed.

— Skip greeting—The greeting is skipped and Unity proceeds to the after greeting action.

— Take message—The caller can press this key to cause Unity to take a message.

- Say goodbye—Unity plays a goodbye message and disconnects the call.

- Send caller to—This option allows selection of any of the following destinations:

  - CVM Mailbox Reset—Allows the caller to reset mailbox (available with Community Voice-mail package).

  - Call Handler—Sends the call to the selected call handler.

  - Caller System Transfer—Allows the caller to transfer to another extension after they log in with subscriber credentials. They may then transfer to any number their restriction table allows.

  - Directory Handler—Sends the call to the directory handler you select.

  - Easy Sign-In—Sends the call to a login process that asks for the password for this mailbox.

  - Greetings Administrator—Sends the call to a conversation that allows them to manage the greetings of call handlers that they own.

  - Hang up—Disconnects the call.

  - Hotel Checked Out— This option works in concert with Cisco Unity's Hospitality and Property Management Integration. It allows guests to archive their messages when checking out.

  - Interview Handler—Sends the call to the interview handler you select.

  - Sign-In—Sends the call to the subscriber sign in.

  - Subscriber—Sends the call to another subscriber's greeting or extension depending upon how it is configured.

Step 5 Click on the digit you wish to configure and then select the action by clicking on the appropriate radio button.

As with the Greetings settings, when choosing to send the call to a call handler, directory handler, interview handler or another subscriber, you have to specify the specific handler or subscriber.

Step 6 If the **Lock this key to the action (don't wait for an additional keypress)** field is checked, an extension that begins with this digit cannot be entered. Unity then transfers the call to the destination assigned to that key without waiting to see if the caller is going to enter other digits. Only enable this field on digits that are not leading digits for any extensions.

Step 7 After you have all the digits configured, click the **Save** icon in the title strip.

Configuring Subscriber Template Messages Settings

The subscriber template messages section allows you to configure caller message specific attributes, such as how long messages can be, what to do after the message, caller options, and MWI settings.

Figure 8-11 shows the various settings that are configured from this screen. The following steps show how to configure these settings and the effect on each setting.

Figure 8-11 *Subscribers>Subscriber Template>Messages*

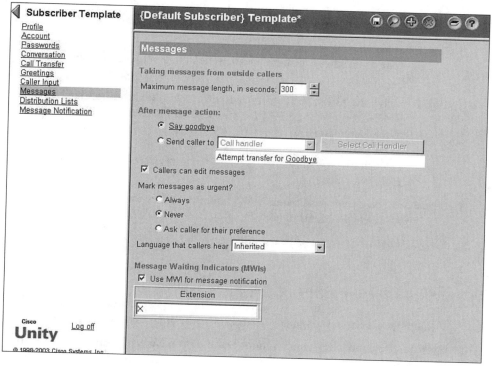

Step 1 From the previous steps, click **Messages** from the list on the left side of the screen and move on to the next step. Otherwise, from within SA, select **Subscribers>Subscriber Template**. If the name of the template you wish to manage does not appear in the title strip, click the **Find** icon and select the desired subscriber template. Once the template is active, click **Messages** from the list on the left side of the screen.

Step 2   To set the maximum length of a message that an outside caller can leave, enter the value in seconds in the **Maximum message length, in seconds** box. This setting applies only to messages left from outside callers. The limit for subscribers is set by the subscriber's CoS.

Step 3   After the message is recorded, select either the **Say goodbye** or the **Send Caller to** radio button. When choosing **Send Caller to** the destination must be chosen. The destinations are the same as those under the **Send caller to** drop-down list in the caller input section.

Step 4   If you wish to let callers listen to, and change or delete, the message they leave, check the **Callers can edit message** box.

Step 5   Allow the caller to label a message urgent by selecting the **Ask caller for their preference** radio button under the **Mark messages as urgent?** heading. To mark a message always urgent without asking the caller, select the **Always** radio button, or to never mark the message urgent select the **Never** radio button.

Step 6   Select the language in which Unity plays its prompt from the **Language that callers hear** drop-down list. When this field is set to **Inherited**, it uses the language used by the parent call handler.

Step 7   Under the **Message Waiting Indicators (MWIs)** heading, enable MWI by checking the **Use MWI for message notification** box. Entering an X in the **Extension** box causes the extension associated with the subscriber to be activated. If you place an extension number in this field, that extension's MWI is activated when users created from the template receive a voice mail.

Step 8   If you do not wish to use MWI, simply uncheck the **Use MWI for message notification** box.

Step 9   Click the **Save** icon in the title strip.

Configuring Subscriber Template Distribution Lists Settings

The most efficient way to add subscribers to a Public Distribution List is by adding them through the subscriber template. The following steps show how this is done.

Step 1   From the previous steps, click **Distribution Lists** from the list on the left side of the screen and move on to the next step. Otherwise, from within SA, select **Subscribers>Subscriber Template**. If the name of the template you wish to manage does not appear in the title strip, click the **Find** icon and select the desired subscriber template. Once the template is active, click **Distribution Lists** from the list on the left side of the screen.

Step 2 Figure 8-12 shows that the available **Public Distribution Lists** are displayed on the left side of the screen and the **New subscribers added to:** lists are on the right side. To move a list from one column to the other, highlight the desired list and select either the >> button or the << button.

Figure 8-12 *Subscribers>Subscriber Template>Distribution Lists*

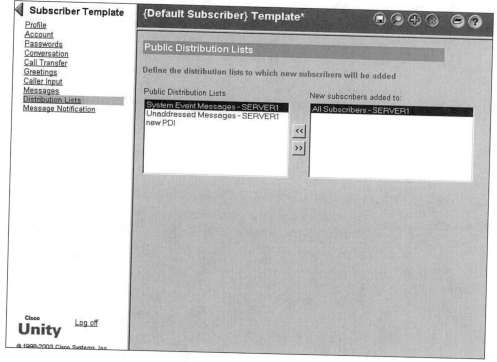

Step 3 Click the **Save** icon in the title strip.

Configuring Subscriber Template Message Notification Settings

Message notification allows a subscriber to be notified through a pager, phone or other external device when a new message arrives. This type of notification is very useful for subscribers who are seldom in the office, such as outside sales people or service technicians.

It may seem odd that you can set up message notification in the subscriber template. After all, you will not want to send a message to the same pager when any subscriber, who was created using this template, receives a new message. However, the subscriber template is an excellent place to create the same type of flow and generic notification settings for a large number of subscribers. After the subscribers are added, you can have them fill in the details such as the specific phone numbers using CPCA.

More than a dozen devices can be configured for message notification. This includes eight phones, four pagers, and a number of text-based devices. Message notification can be configured to notify the subscriber of any new voice mails, faxes, and e-mails. The settings on this screen determine what type of message triggers a notification and what device(s) are notified.

The following steps show how these settings are configured and the effect they produce.

Step 1 From the previous steps, click **Message Notification** from the list on the left side of the screen and move on to the next step. Otherwise, from within SA, select **Subscribers>Subscriber Template**. If the name of the template you wish to manage does not appear in the title strip, click the **Find** icon and select the desired subscriber template. Once the template is active, click **Message Notification** from the list on the left side of the screen.

Step 2 Figure 8-13 shows the first few settings that must be configured. First you must select which device you wish to configure. From the **Device:** drop-down list choose a device.

Figure 8-13 *Subscribers>Subscriber Template>Message Notification (Phone or Pager)*

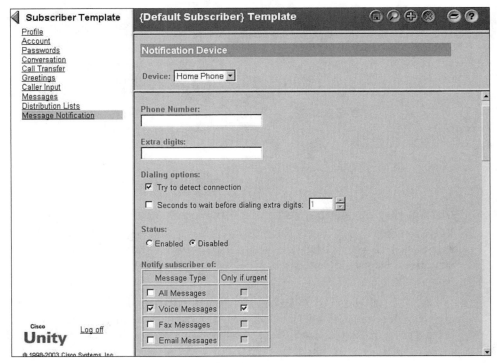

Step 3   The next few configuration fields vary slightly depending on whether you choose a phone or an e-mail as the notification device. If you choose a phone or a pager, enter the phone number of that device in the **Phone Number:** field. After dialing the phone number, enter any digits that still need to be dialed in the **Extra digits** field. Extra digits are typically needed for pagers that use PINs.

If you choose a device that will use an e-mail address as the delivery mechanism, such as a text pager or Text for Visual Messaging Interface (VMI), enter the e-mail address in the **To:** field. Then enter the pilot number for Unity in the **From:** field. Some cell phones will act as pagers and can call back the number that is in the **From:** field. Figure 8-14 shows these fields.

NOTE	VMI is the old name for CPCA inbox, which allows a subscriber to check messages from a webpage.

Figure 8-14   *Subscribers>Subscriber Template>Message Notification (E-Mail Device)*

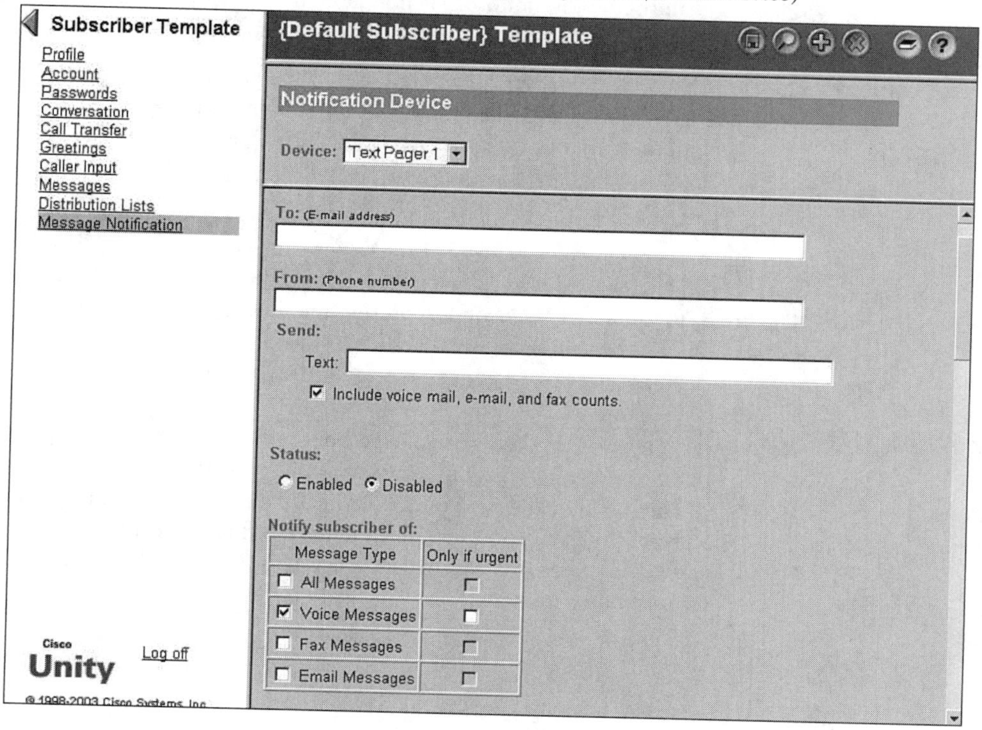

Step 4   When a phone is chosen as the notification device you can set it so that the extra digits are not sent until a connection is detected as seen in Figure 8-13. To enable this option, check the **Try to detect connection** box. If you want it to wait a specified number of seconds, instead of trying to detect a connection, check the **Seconds to wait before dialing extra digits:** box and enter the number of seconds to wait in the box to the right of that field. You may use the **Seconds to wait** option if Unity is having trouble detecting a connection due to various factors, such as poor line quality. In some cases you may need to use both the **Try to detect a connection** and **Seconds to wait** options. It may be necessary to set the parameters and then test these settings a few times before getting them to work properly with different paging companies.

Step 5   When a device that uses an e-mail address is selected, enter the text that you want to appear in the notification in the **Text:** field as seen in Figure 8-14. A message count can be included in this notification by checking the **Include voice-mail, e-mail, and fax counts** box.

Step 6   To enable this device to be used for message notification, you must select the **Enabled** radio button. It is not enough to simply configure the device—you must ensure that the Enable button is selected.

Step 7   Under the **Notify subscriber of:** heading, select the types of messages of which the subscriber should be notified. As shown in Figure 8-14, you can select all messages or only one type, such as voice-mail. You can further narrow it down by selecting only urgent messages.

Step 8   The next area of the screen shown in Figure 8-15 is a grid that represents the days of the week, with each day broken into half-hour segments. This grid is used to define at what hours of the day notifications are sent out. The boxes that have a check mark represent the time of day that notification will be sent. Edit the schedule as needed.

Note   You may copy the open/closed hours of one day to another day, and to all weekdays or weekends, by using the **Copy Day's Schedule** field under the grid. Select the **source day** from the first drop-down list and the **destination day(s)** from the second drop-down list and click **Copy day's schedule:** as shown in Figure 8-15.

Figure 8-15 *Subscribers>Subscriber Template>Message Notification*

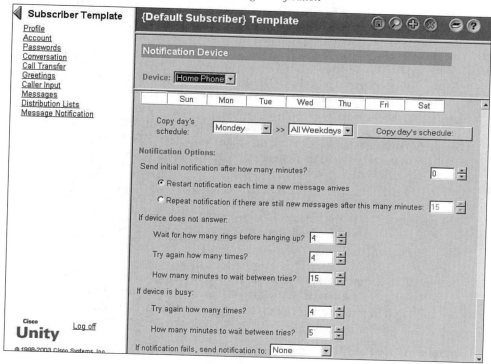

Step 9 The notification can be configured to be sent immediately or wait a specified number of minutes. If cascading notification is being deployed, some devices are configured to wait for a certain number of minutes before being notified. The term cascading notification means that notification is sent, and if the message has not been retrieved after a specified number of minutes, a different device is notified. If, after an additional amount of time, the message is still not retrieved, another device is notified. An example of cascading flow might look something like this:

1 First notification is sent to your pager.

2 You don't retrieve the message.

3 Ten minutes later a notification is sent to your cell phone.

4 You don't retrieve the message.

5 Ten minutes later a notification is sent to your boss's pager.

6 You're busted!

Step 10 Enter the number of minutes that Unity should wait before notifying this device in the **Send initial notification after how many minutes?** field. Unity only sends the notification if the message has not been retrieved after this amount of time.

Step 11 To have Unity send another notification to this device, only when a new message arrives, select the **Restart notification each time a new message arrives** radio button. To invoke what some refer to as the "nag factor," you can have the device notified every so many minutes until the message is retrieved by selecting the **Repeat notification if there are still new messages after this many minutes:** radio button. Enter the number of minutes in the field to the right of this label.

Note   If the device you are configuring is a text pager or Text for VMI, none of the following settings display. Simply click the **Save** icon in the title strip to complete this task.

Step 12 Under the **If device does not answer:** heading enter how many rings Unity should wait before hanging up, how many times Unity should try again, and how many minutes Unity should wait between tries in the appropriate fields.

Step 13 Under the **If device is busy:** heading enter how many times Unity should try again and how many minutes Unity should wait between tries in the appropriate fields.

Step 14 If the notification fails, you can specify another device to be notified by selecting the device from the **If notification fails, send notification to:** drop-down list.

Step 15 Click the **Save** icon in the title strip.

At this point you have completed creating a subscriber template. Make sure to take some time to figure out how many templates you will need, based on the information discussed at the beginning of this chapter. Add the templates to Unity using the preceding steps as a guide.

Now that the subscriber templates are created you can start to add subscribers. The next section explains how to add Exchange- and Domino-based subscribers. A lot of configuration is necessary to get to this point. However, the success of your deployment rests heavily upon a properly prepared foundation. Okay, enough of this foundation stuff, let's start adding subscribers!

Creating New Exchange Subscribers

Now that you have the subscriber templates created, the process of creating a user is fairly simple. To create a subscriber, enter a few pieces of information, click **Add** and the user is created. Because subscriber creation is based on one of the templates you created, all of the additional settings will be populated. There are times when you want to change the settings of a subscriber; the process for making the most common changes comes later in this chapter in the Managing Subscribers section.

This section focuses on the creation of Exchange-based subscribers. The next section discusses how to import existing Exchange and Notes subscribers.

The following steps show how to add a new Exchange-based subscriber to Unity.

Step 1   From within SA, select **Subscribers>Subscribers**.

Step 2   Click the **Add** icon (plus sign) in the title strip.

Step 3   A window such as that shown in Figure 8-16 displays. Select the **New Subscriber**: radio button and select **Exchange** from the drop-down list to the right of the label.

Figure 8-16   *Add Subscriber Window*

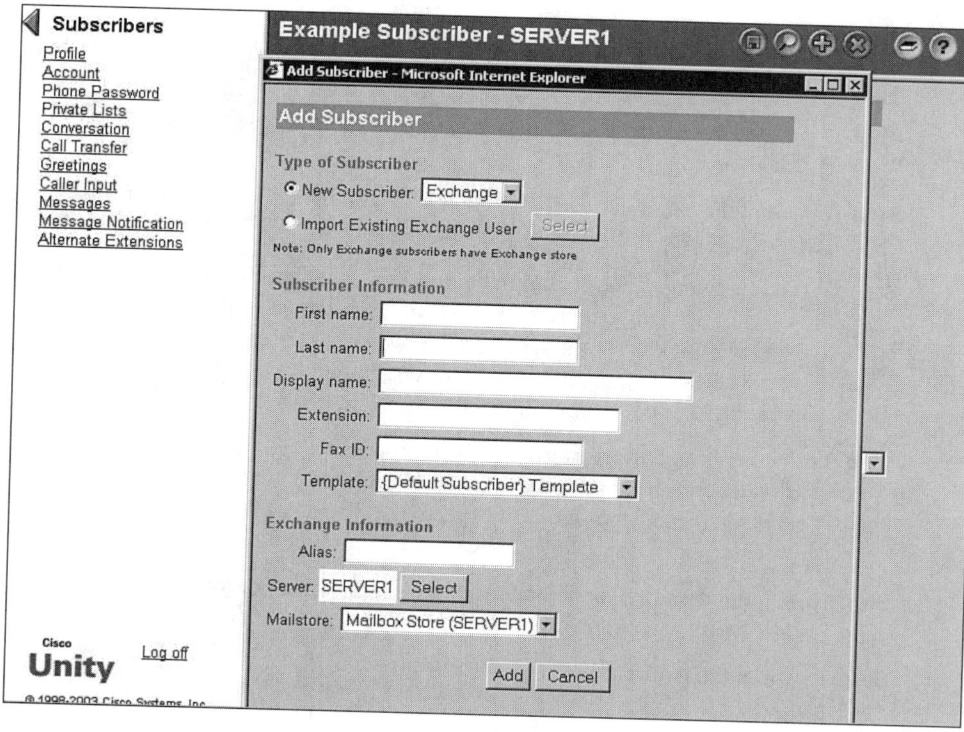

Note	If you have more than one Exchange server, click the **Select** button, which appears next to the name of the default Exchange server near the bottom of the page. A search criteria window opens. Click the **Find** button and select the Exchange server from the list provided. The reason you perform this step first is that if you fill in the other fields and then select a different Exchange server, all the information you entered disappears and you need to reenter it.

Step 4 Enter the first and last name of the new subscriber in the fields labeled as such. The display name is automatically generated. This is the name that is displayed in Exchange and the SA. If needed, you can edit this.

Step 5 An extension number must be assigned to every subscriber, and this should be the extension number that is assigned to the subscriber's phone. Enter the subscriber's extension number in the **Extension:** field. In rare cases the extension number in Unity is different than the actual extension assigned to the subscriber's phone, but this should be avoided. All extensions in Unity must be unique—that is each extension can only be assigned to one subscriber.

Step 6 In the **Fax ID:** field, enter the number that a caller dials to send a fax to this subscriber.

Step 7 Select the subscriber template that is used during the creation of this subscriber from the **Template:** drop-down list.

Step 8 The Exchange alias is automatically populated based on the settings you select in the Subscriber Template Profile screen, but this can be edited if needed. One of the options available was not to populate the Exchange Alias field automatically. If the aforementioned was selected, this field must be manually configured.

Step 9 As mentioned in the note at the beginning of these steps, you should have already chosen the desired Exchange server. Be aware that selecting a different Exchange server at this point will cause all of the information entered on this page to disappear and require reentering.

Step 10 If more than one mailstore is available, select the one you want from the **Mailstore:** drop-down list.

Step 11 Click the **Add** button.

Step 12 The information is processing, and it may take up to 15 seconds. During this time, an Exchange mailbox and Windows domain account is being created. The Unity specific information is being added to the SQL database. After the user is created, you return to the subscriber profile screen of the newly created subscriber.

NOTE   You do not have to click the Save icon when adding a user. That is because you only have to save when you are changing something. Whenever something new is added, it is written to the database automatically.

So, that is all there is to it. The subscriber you added is now ready for use. As you can see, adding a subscriber is a much simpler process than creating subscriber templates. Because you use a template during the creation process, the majority of the subscriber settings are automatically configured, which shows the value of the subscriber template. However, there are two types of subscriber configurations that are not configured using the subscriber template. These are Private lists and Alternate extensions. These settings are not part of the subscriber template because they are unique for each subscriber.

Private lists are lists of other subscribers with whom a subscriber can communicate when sending voice mail. Instead of having to add each subscriber as a recipient, the subscriber can select a private list as the recipient, and the voice mail will be sent to everyone in the list. Subscribers are encouraged to create their own private lists, but these lists can be created and managed using SA.

Alternate extensions are used for multiple purposes. When an alternate extension is added to a subscriber, Unity treats all calls to or from that extension as if they are to or from the subscriber's primary extension. Think of it as a way to associate multiple extensions to one mailbox. Imagine that a subscriber has multiple extensions on the system. When someone calls the subscriber and the call is not answered, the caller is forwarded to the same mailbox regardless of which of the subscriber's extensions the caller dialed. This feature is also used to allow subscribers easy message access when calling from an outside phone. When calling from the outside, a subscriber must press the asterisk (*) key and enter an extension number and password. By adding the phone number of phones that are commonly used to access voice-mail, such as a cell phone, this process is simplified. Because Unity recognizes the incoming caller ID as an alternate extension, the subscriber is simply being prompted for a password, just as if calling from an office phone.

Configuring private lists and alternate extensions are covered in the "Managing Subscribers" section of this chapter.

Importing Subscribers

When integrating Unity with an existing Exchange or Domino server, you can import the users from the existing mailstore. This can be done one at a time or in bulk by using the Unity Bulk Import Wizard. When importing a large number of users, use the Bulk Import Wizard. When importing only one or two users, SA can be used.

The following steps show how to import a single Exchange user. The steps for importing a Domino user are very similar.

Step 1   From within SA, select **Subscribers>Subscribers**.

Step 2   Click the **Add** icon.

Step 3   Select the **Import Existing Exchange User** radio button.

Step 4   Click the **Select** button. A search criteria window displays like that shown in Figure 8-17.

Figure 8-17   *Exchange User Search Screen*

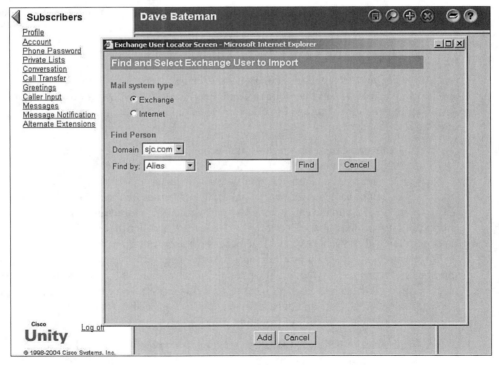

Step 5   Select the **Exchange** radio button.

Step 6   Ensure that the user's domain is in the **Domain** field.

Step 7   You can search for the user by the alias, first name, or last name. Select one of these choices from the **Find by:** drop-down list and enter the search criteria in the next field. Click **Find**.

Step 8   A list of users that match the search displays. Click the first name of the user you wish to import. An **Add Subscriber** window like that shown in Figure 8-18 displays.

Figure 8-18   *Importing an Exchange User*

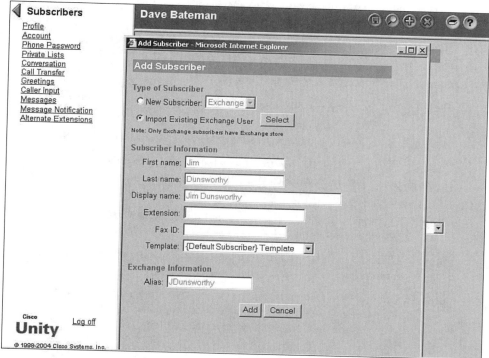

Step 9   Only the extension, Fax ID, and template fields are edited on this screen. All other fields are populated using the information imported from the mailstore account. Enter the Extension number in the **Extension:** field. If the subscriber has a Fax extension, enter it and select the subscriber template you wish to use from the **Template** drop-down list.

Step 10 Click **Add**.

As mentioned, subscribers can be added using the Bulk Import Wizard. This utility can import users from an existing mailstore or from a CSV file. When importing from a CSV file, Unity adds Exchange mailboxes and Windows domain accounts for the imported users if these accounts do not already exist. Because the accounts already exist when importing from an Exchange server, there is no need for Unity to create these. When importing from a Domino server, only Unity subscribers are created; no AD accounts are automatically created for these subscribers.

The import utility works in much the same way, regardless from which source you are importing. The following are the steps required when importing from a CSV file.

Step 1 Create a CSV file. There are more than 40 values that can be entered in the CSV file for each subscriber. Of these fields, only three are required: **First name:**, **Last name:**, and **Extension:**. The remaining fields are populated with the settings defined in the subscriber template you choose during the import.

Step 2 Using the start menu on the Unity server, click **Start>Programs>Unity>Cisco Unity Bulk Import**.

Step 3 The Import Wizard starts. Click **Next**.

Step 4 You are asked if you wish to import the users from a CSV file or AD. Choose **CSV** and click **Next**.

Step 5 You may accept the default for the log files location and click **Next**.

Step 6 The next page asks you to select what type of Subscriber you are importing. In most cases you will choose either Unified Messaging or Voice-mail only. Choose the desired type of subscriber and click **Next.**

Step 7 On the next screen, accept the default to create new mailboxes and Windows account. Click **Next**.

Step 8 Choose a template to use for the users you will import. Select the appropriate subscriber template and click **Next**.

Step 9 Choose a Domain and container in which to create the new users. Click **Browse**, highlight the appropriate container and click **OK**. You will return to the previous window; click **Next**.

Step 10 Select your server in the next window. Make sure you have highlighted your server before continuing. Click **Next**.

Step 11 Select the CSV file you wish to use. Click **Browse**. Locate the CSV file and click **Next**.

Step 12 The data is examined and you are presented with a summary of what was found. Click **Next**.

Step 13 Check the box of each subscriber you wish to import. You may also click **Select All**. Click **Next**.

Step 14 Confirm that you wish to import the data that is shown in the summary screen. Click **Add**.

Step 15 When the import is complete, you see a final summary screen. You may
view the output and error log from this screen.

Now that the subscribers are added, your system is ready for basic voice mail use. Users
can now configure their personal settings, such as passwords and greetings by dialing the
voice mail pilot number and going through subscriber self-enrollment.

Managing Subscribers

After subscribers are created, there may be some basic day-to-day administration required.
For the most part, as long as things don't change, the subscriber administration tasks should
be minimal. Then again, things don't tend to go unchanged for long. This section is a
collection of common subscriber administrative tasks. No task discussed in this section is
difficult and, if performed often, can be done without reference to this section. The goal
is to provide a quick reference for you when you are required to perform an unfamiliar
administrative task. Use this reference at least the first few times you perform any of these
tasks. Although they are not difficult, some can cause hours of troubleshooting if incorrectly
configured. The tasks are divided into four categories: subscriber access, call transfer and
greetings, message access and notification, and conversation management settings.

NOTE   The steps shown for each task are designed so they can stand on their own. That is, each
individual set of steps is not dependent upon other sets of steps. This is done intentionally
so the reader does not have to jump back and forth between multiple sections to complete
one task. This format does, however, require the repetition of the same steps in multiple
tasks. The text may seem repetitive, but in order to offer a task-independent reference, this
format is required.

Managing Subscriber Access

A subscriber can access Unity in a number of ways. This section covers administrative tasks
that are associated with subscriber access, such as passwords, CoS, and licensed features.

Unlocking a Subscriber's Account

Often subscribers lock themselves out of Unity by entering the incorrect password too
many times. These thresholds are configured on the subscriber>Account Policy>Phone
Password Restrictions> page.

There are two types of subscriber accounts that may become locked. Figure 8-19 shows the
account setting for a subscriber who is locked out of both types of access. The first is called
Unity account status: When this is locked, the subscribers cannot access their messages

from the phone. They still have access to Unity via CPCA and viewmail, if they have these features. The second type of account lock out is called **Unity GUI access status:** When this is locked, the subscribers cannot have access via CPCA or viewmail. This also prevents any subscriber that has access to SA, or status monitor, from accessing these interfaces.

Figure 8-19 *Locked Account*

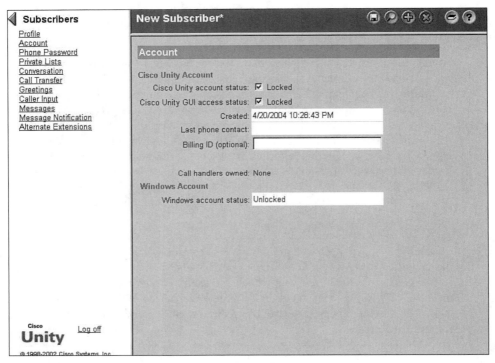

To unlock either of these accounts follow these steps.

Step 1   From within SA, select **Subscribers>Subscribers>**. Click the **Find** icon and search for the user you want to manage.

Step 2   Once the name of the desired subscriber appears in the title strip, select **Account** from the menu that appears on the left side of the screen.

Step 3   To allow the subscriber access to messages from a phone, uncheck the **Cisco Unity account status:** box.

Step 4   To allow the subscriber access to CPCA and viewmail, uncheck the **Cisco Unity GUI access status:** box. Remember, only subscribers who have a CoS that allows them access to these interfaces are able to access them regardless of what this setting is.

Step 5   Click the **Save** icon in the title strip.

Resetting Passwords

Another common issue is that subscribers forget their passwords. This phenomenon has baffled system administrators for years. However, with the average person having to keep track of numerous passwords, it is a common event.

Step 1 From within SA, select **Subscribers>Subscribers**. Click the **Find** icon and search for the user you want to manage.

Step 2 Once the name of the desired subscriber appears in the title strip, select **Phone Password** from the menu that appears on the left side of the screen.

Step 3 In the **Password:** field enter the new password.

Step 4 In the **Confirm password:** field enter the new password again.

Step 5 Click the **Save** icon.

Changing a Subscriber's Extension

Step 1 From within SA, select **Subscribers>Subscribers**. Click the **Find** icon and search for the user you want to manage.

Step 2 Once the name of the desired subscriber appears in the title strip, select **Profile** from the menu that appears on the left side of the screen.

Step 3 In the **Extension:** field enter the new extension number.

Step 4 Click the **Save** icon.

Changing a Subscriber's CoS

Many of the features that you want to give a subscriber are configured in the CoS. If you wish to give the feature to all subscribers in the CoS, you can simply edit their current CoS. However, if you want to grant certain features to only a subset of subscribers that share the same CoS, you need to create a new CoS based on the current CoS, edit the new CoS, and assign it to those subscribers. This section includes the steps required to add various features to CoS. The following steps show how to change a subscriber's CoS.

Step 1 From within SA, select **Subscribers>Subscribers**. Click the **Find** icon and search for the user you want to manage.

Step 2 Once the name of the desired subscriber appears in the title strip, select **Profile** from the menu that appears on the left side of the screen.

Step 3 In the **Class of service** field select the desired class of service from the drop-down list.

Step 4 Click the **Save** icon.

Granting Access to Licensed Features (FaxMail, Text-to-Speech, CPCA)

In order to allow subscribers to have access to various licensed features, you must grant them rights. These rights are granted based on the subscriber's CoS. If you wish to grant all the subscribers of a particular CoS these rights, you can simply edit their current CoS. However, if you do not want to grant these rights to all subscribers in a CoS, you need to create a new CoS, grant the rights to that CoS, and assign the new CoS to the selected subscribers.

To add access to the features of an exiting CoS, follow these steps:

Step 1   From within SA, select **Subscribers>Class of Service**.

Step 2   Click the **Find** icon and a list of CoS displays.

Step 3   Highlight the CoS you wish to edit and click **View**.

Step 4   Select **Licensed Features** from the left side of the screen.

Step 5   To allow subscribers to manage faxes using the phone, check the **FaxMail** box. This feature requires that your organization has a supported third party fax solution.

Step 6   To allow subscribers to listen to their e-mail over the phone, check the **Text-to-Speech for e-mail messages** box.

Step 7   To allow subscribers to configure their personal setting via a web browser, check the **Cisco Unity Assistant** box.

Step 8   To allow subscribers to check their voice mail via a web browser, check the **Cisco Unity Inbox** (Visual Messaging Interface) box.

NOTE   All of these features require a license for each subscriber who is assigned to the feature.

Granting Additional System Access Rights

Unity allows you to assign subscribers limited administrative rights that enable them to deal with certain administrative tasks. These rights are strictly Unity rights and do not correspond to any AD rights. By assigning limited rights to some subscribers, you can enable them to assist in various tasks such as unlocking accounts, changing passwords, and running reports. These rights are based on the subscribers' CoS. The following steps describe how to add administrative rights to an exiting CoS.

Step 1   From within SA, select **Subscribers>Class of Service**.

Step 2   Click the **Find** icon and a list of CoS displays.

Step 3   Highlight the CoS you wish to edit and click **View**.

Step 4 Select **System Access** from the left side of the screen.

Step 5 Figure 8-20 shows the various rights that may be assigned to a CoS. Based on what tasks you want the subscriber to perform, check the appropriate boxes. For the most part, these rights are self-explanatory. Keep in mind that when you grant one right, another right may be inherited. For example, when you enable the **Can unlock subscriber accounts and change passwords** the **Subscriber access>read** right is granted. Inherited rights are not automatically removed when you remove the parent right. You need to manually remove any inherited rights.

Figure 8-20 *Subscriber>CoS>System Access*

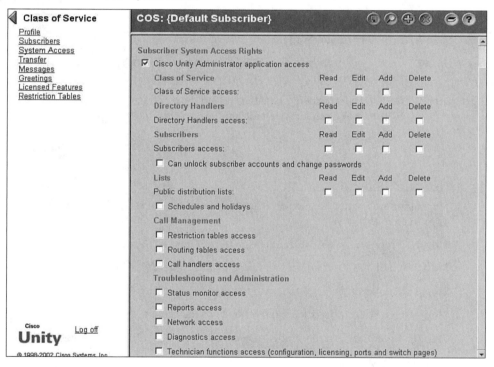

Step 6 Click the **Save** icon in the title strip.

Managing Call Transfer and Greetings

This section explores how to adjust subscriber settings that affect the outside caller's experience when they are transfers to a subscriber. This includes things such as call screening options and one-key transfer settings.

Allowing Screening and Hold Options

Using Unity's screening options, a subscriber can have Unity request the caller's name and play it to the subscriber before transferring the call. The subscriber can then choose to take the call or send it to voice-mail. Unity can also be configured so that subscribers can choose to have Unity ask callers to hold if they are on other calls. When either of these features is used, the voice mail port is held open until the call is transferred to a phone. It is best to use these options very sparingly to enable call screening and holding options. Refer to the following steps to configure these features.

Step 1   From within SA, select **Subscribers>Class of Service**.

Step 2   Click the **Find** icon and a list of CoS displays.

Step 3   Highlight the CoS you wish to edit and click **View**.

Step 4   Select **Transfer** from the left side of the screen.

Step 5   To allow subscribers to enable call-screening options, check the **Subscribers can change call screening options** box.

Step 6   To allow subscribers to enable call-holding options, check the **Subscribers can change call holding options** box.

Step 7   Click the **Save** icon in the title strip.

Changing Maximum Greeting Length

The maximum length a subscriber's greeting can be is determined by the CoS. Follow these steps to change this value:

Step 1   From within SA, select **Subscribers>Class of Service**.

Step 2   Click the **Find** icon and a list of CoS displays.

Step 3   Highlight the CoS you wish to edit and click **View**.

Step 4   Select **Greetings** from the left side of the screen.

Step 5   Enter the desired number of seconds in the **Maximum greeting length, in seconds:** field.

Step 6   Click the **Save** icon in the title strip.

Enabling and Disabling Greetings

A subscriber can have up to five greetings configured. You can refer back to Table 8-1 to review the available greetings. Both the subscriber and the administrator have the ability to enable or disable these greetings. The steps for doing this from with SA are as follows:

Step 1   From within SA, select **Subscribers>Subscribers**.

Step 2　Click the **Find** icon and enter search criteria that will match the subscriber account you plan to edit and click **Find**.

Step 3　Choose the subscriber from the list that displays.

Step 4　Select **Greetings** from the left side of the screen.

Step 5　Choose the greeting you wish to enable/disable from the **Greeting** drop-down list as shown in Figure 8-21.

Figure 8-21　*Subscribers>Subscribers>Greetings*

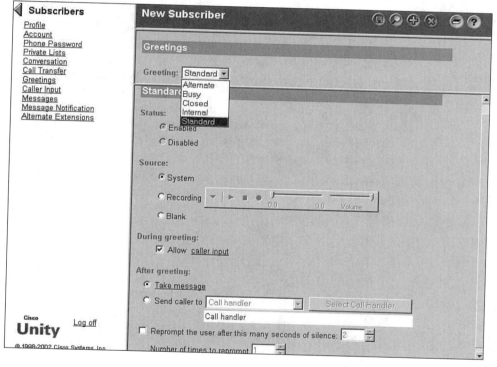

Step 6　Select either the **Enabled** or the **Disabled** radio button.

Step 7　Click the **Save** icon in the title strip.

Modifying Caller Input Options

Subscribers' greetings can include options that allow an outside caller to be transferred to another number by pressing a key on the dial pad. These are referred to as *one key transfers*. In order for these to work, the administrator must configure the caller input options, which is the same as configuring caller input for a subscriber template. The steps that follow show how to configure these options for a subscriber:

Step 1   From within SA, select **Subscribers>Subscribers**.

Step 2   Click the **Find** icon and enter search criteria that will match the subscriber account you plan to edit and click **Find**.

Step 3   Choose the subscriber from the list that displays.

Step 4   Select **Caller Input** from the left side of the screen.

Step 5   To allow callers to enter another extension while listening to a greeting, check the **Allow callers to dial an extension during greeting** box.

Step 6   If the option to allow callers to dial another extension during the greeting is enabled, an interdigit time out must also be configured. This is the amount of time Unity waits before deciding the caller has finished pressing digits. This setting is **Milliseconds to wait for additional digits**. The default value is 1500 milliseconds, which is a second and a half. Typically, this value is adequate. If, during a greeting, callers are transferred or receive error messages from Unity before they are finished dialing an extension, increase this value.

Step 7   From the dial pad on the screen, configure the action that will be taken when a digit is pressed. A button can be configured for the following five types of actions:

— Ignore Key—No action is taken when digit is pressed.

— Skip Greeting—The greeting is skipped and Unity proceeds to the after greeting action.

— Take Message—The caller can press this key to cause Unity to take a message.

— Say Goodbye—Unity plays a goodbye message and disconnects the call.

— Send caller to—With this option you are able to select any of the following destinations:

— CVM Mailbox Reset—Allows the caller to reset mailbox (Available with Community Voice-mail package).

— Call Handler—Sends the call to the selected call handler.

— Caller System Transfer—Sends callers to a prompt that allows them to enter another extension to which they want to be transferred.

— Directory Handler—Sends the call to the directory handler you select.

— Easy SignIn—Sends the call to a login process that asks for the password for this mailbox.

— Greetings Administrator—Sends the call to a conversation that allows them to manage the greetings of call handlers, which they own.

— Hang up—Disconnects the call.

— Hotel Checked Out—Used only with Unity's Hospitality and Property Management System.

— Interview Handler—Sends the call to the interview handler you select.

— Sign-in—Sends the call to subscriber sign in.

— Subscriber—Sends the call to another subscriber's greeting or extension depending upon how it is configured.

— Subscriber System Transfer—Allows the callers to transfer to another extension after they log in with subscriber credentials. They may then transfer to any number that their restriction table allows.

Step 8 Click on the digit you wish to configure and then select the action by clicking on the appropriate radio button.

Note	When you choose to send the call to a call handler, directory handler, interview handler, or another subscriber, you have to specify the specific handler or subscriber.

Step 9 If the **Lock this key to the action (don't wait for an additional keypress)** field is checked, an extension that begins with this digit cannot be entered. Unity then transfers the call to the destination assigned to that key without waiting to see if the caller is going to enter other digits. Only enable this field on digits that are not leading digits for any extensions.

Step 10 After you have all the digits configured as desired, click the **Save** icon in the title strip.

Managing Message Access, Notification, and Indication

Unity allows subscribers to manage their messages from both the phone and an e-mail client. In order to do this efficiently, Unity offers many features that impact how messages can be sent, received, and managed. This section discusses various settings that affect these features.

Allowing Subscribers to Send to Distribution Lists

You may choose to allow or disallow subscribers to send messages to public distribution lists. This setting is based on a subscriber's CoS. The following steps explain how to configure this:

Step 1   From within SA, select **Subscribers>Class of Service**.

Step 2   Click the **Find** icon and a list of CoS displays.

Step 3   Highlight the CoS you wish to edit and click **View**.

Step 4   Select **Messages** from the left side of the screen.

Step 5   To allow subscribers with this CoS to send messages to distribution lists, check the **Subscribers can send messages to public distribution lists** box. Uncheck this box if you do not want subscribers with this CoS to send messages to distribution lists.

Step 6   Click the **Save** icon in the title bar.

Allowing Messages Deleted from the Phone To Be Saved in the Deleted Items Folder

By default, when a subscriber deletes a message from the phone, the message is deleted completely from the system after the phone is hung up. However, you can configure Unity to store the message in a subscriber's deleted items folder. Subscribers can then retrieve messages they have deleted from the phone through Outlook or Unity Inbox (version 4.03 or later). The following steps explain how to enable this feature:

Step 1   From within SA, select **Subscribers>Class of Service**.

Step 2   Click the **Find** icon, and a list of CoS displays.

Step 3   Highlight the CoS you wish to edit and click **View**.

Step 4   Select **Messages** from the left side of the screen.

Step 5   Check the **Deleted messages are copied to the deleted items folder** box.

Step 6   Click the **Save** icon in the title bar.

Enabling Live Reply for a Subscriber

A feature called Live Reply allows subscribers to have Unity connect them with the extension of a subscriber, who left them a message, by pressing 44 at the end of listening to the message. This feature is granted based on the subscriber's CoS. To enable these features follow these steps:

Step 1 From within SA, select **Subscribers>Class of Service**.

Step 2 Click the **Find** icon, and a list of CoS displays.

Step 3 Highlight the CoS you wish to edit and click **View**.

Step 4 Select **Messages** from the left side of the screen.

Step 5 Check the **Subscribers can reply to messages from other subscribers by calling them** box.

Step 6 Click the **Save** icon in the title bar.

Creating Private Lists

Private lists are similar to public distribution lists but are private to the subscriber for whom they are created. Either the administrator or the subscriber can create these lists. The following steps show how to create these lists from SA:

Step 1 From within SA, select **Subscribers>Subscribers**.

Step 2 Click the **Find** icon and enter search criteria that will match the subscriber account you plan to edit and click **Find**.

Step 3 Choose the subscriber from the list that displays.

Step 4 Select **Private Lists** from the left side of the screen.

Step 5 Select an unused list number from the **Private Lists** drop-down list.

Step 6 Enter a name for the list in the **Name of list** field.

Step 7 Record a name for the list by clicking the **red dot** on the media master control panel. This should cause the phone to ring. Answer the phone and speak the name of the private list.

Step 8 Click the **Change Members** button. A search criteria window displays. Enter search criteria that match the members you wish to add to this list and press **Find**.

Step 9 A list of matching objects displays on the left side of the window. Highlight the objects you wish to add to the private list and click the **>>** button.

Note   You may choose multiple objects by holding the **Ctrl** key down as you click on the object's name.

Step 10 Once all desired members have been added, click the **Save** button.

Configuring Message Notification

Subscribers or the system administrator can configure message notification. If possible, encourage your users to control and configure their own message notification using CPCA. If it is necessary to configure message notification through the SA, the process is very similar to configuration through a subscriber template. The following steps describe how to configure message notification:

Step 1 From within SA, select **Subscribers>Subscribers**. Click the **Find** icon and search for the user you want to manage.

Step 2 Once the name of the desired subscriber appears in the title strip, select **Message Notification** from the menu that appears on the left side of the screen.

Step 3 First you must select which device you wish to configure. From the **Device** drop-down list choose a device.

Step 4 Depending on whether you choose a phone or an e-mail device as the notification device, the next few configuration fields vary slightly. If you choose a phone or a pager, enter the phone number of that device in the **Phone Number** field. After dialing the phone number, enter any digits that still need to be dialed in the **Extra digits** field. Extra digits are typically needed for pagers that use PINs.

Step 5 If you choose a device that will use an e-mail address as the delivery mechanism, such as a text pager or Text for VMI, enter the e-mail address in the **To** field. Then enter the pilot number for Unity in the **From** field. Some cell phones act as pagers and can call back the number that is in this field.

Step 6 When the notification device is a phone or pager, you can set it so that the extra digits are not sent until a connection is detected. To enable this option, check the **Try to detect connection** box. If you want it to wait a specified number of seconds instead of trying to detect a connection, check the **Seconds to wait before dialing extra digits** box and enter the number of seconds to wait in the box to the right of that field. You may use the **Seconds to wait** option if Unity is having trouble detecting a connection due to poor line quality. In some cases you may need to use both the **Try to detect a connection** and **Seconds to wait** options. It may be necessary to set the parameters and then test these settings a few times before getting them to work properly with different paging companies.

When a device that uses an e-mail address is selected, enter the text that you want to display in the notification in the **Text** field. A message count can be included in this notification by checking the **Include voice-mail, e-mail, and fax counts** box.

Step 7 To enable this device to be used for message notification, select the **Enabled** radio button. It is not enough to simply configure the device— you must ensure that the enable button is selected.

Step 8 Under the **Notify subscriber of** heading select the types of messages of which the subscriber should be notified. You can select all messages or only one type, such as voice mail. You can further narrow it down by selecting only urgent messages.

Step 9 The next area of the screen is a grid that represents the days of the week. Each day is broken down into half-hour segments. This grid is used to define what hours of the day notifications will be sent out. The boxes that have a check mark represent the time of day that notification will be sent. Edit the schedule as needed.

Note You may copy the open/closed hours of one day to another day, all weekdays or weekends, by using the **Copy Day's Schedule** function found below the grid. Select the **source day** from the first drop-down list and the **destination day(s)** from the second drop-down list and click **Copy day's schedule**.

Step 10 The notification can be configured to be sent immediately or held a specified number of minutes before being sent. If cascading notification is being deployed, some devices are configured to wait for a certain number of minutes before being notified. Cascading notification occurs when a notification is sent, and if the message has not been retrieved after a specified number of minutes, a different device is notified. If, after an additional amount of time, the message is still not retrieved, another device is notified.

Step 11 Enter the number of minutes that Unity should wait before notifying this device in the **Send initial notification after how many minutes** field. Unity sends the notification only if the message is not retrieved after this amount of time.

Step 12 To have Unity send another notification to this device, only when a new message arrives, select the **Restart notification each time a new message arrives** radio button. You can have the device notified every so many minutes until the message is retrieved by selecting the **Repeat notification if there are still new messages after this many minutes** radio button. If the **Repeat notification if there are still new messages after this many minutes** radio button is selected, enter the desired number of minutes in the field to the right of this label.

Note	If the device you are configuring is a text pager or Text for VMI, none of the following settings display. Simply click the **Save** icon in the title strip to complete this task.

Step 13 Under the **If the device does not answer** heading enter how many rings Unity should wait before hanging up, how many times Unity should try again, and how many minutes should elapse between tries in the appropriate fields.

Step 14 Under the **If device is busy** heading enter how many times Unity should try again and how many minutes should elapse between tries in the appropriate fields.

Step 15 If the notification fails, you can specify another device to be notified by selecting the device from the **If notification fails, send notification to** drop-down list.

Step 16 Click the **Save** icon in the title strip.

Adding Alternate Extensions

Alternate extensions are assigned to subscribers to provide easy message access when calling Unity from a number other than that associated with subscriber accounts. A maximum of nine alternate extensions can be configured for each subscriber. To configure alternate extensions for a subscriber, use the following steps:

Step 1 From within SA, select **Subscribers>Subscribers**.

Step 2 Click the **Find** icon and enter search criteria that match the subscriber account you plan to edit and click **Find**.

Step 3 Choose the subscriber from the list that displays.

Step 4 Select **Alternate Extensions** from the left side of the screen.

Step 5 Nine Extension fields appear. Enter the desired alternate extension(s) in the fields labeled 1 through 9. You can choose to configure as few as one or up to all nine alternate extensions.

Step 6 Click the **Save** icon in the title strip.

Step 7 The other field is simply a check box. This box is used when deleting alternate extensions. To delete an alternate extension, check the box next to the one you wish to delete and click the **Delete** button.

NOTE   In some versions of Unity, this page contains nine fields which allows you to add or delete up to nine alternate extensions at once.

Changing Maximum Outside Caller Message Length

Step 1   From within SA, select **Subscribers>Subscribers**.

Step 2   Click the **Find** icon and enter search criteria that match the subscriber account you plan to edit. Click **Find**.

Step 3   Choose the subscriber from the list that displays.

Step 4   Select **Messages** from the left side of the screen.

Step 5   Enter the maximum number of seconds that a message from an outside caller can be in the **Maximum message length, in seconds** field.

Step 6   Click the **Save** icon in the title strip.

Adjusting Urgent Message Marking

Step 1   From within SA, select **Subscribers>Subscribers**.

Step 2   Click the **Find** icon and enter search criteria that match the subscriber account you plan to edit and click **Find**.

Step 3   Choose the subscriber from the list that displays.

Step 4   Select **Messages** from the left side of the screen.

Step 5   Under the **Mark messages as urgent?** heading you have three choices. To mark all incoming messages urgent, click the **Always** radio button. To mark incoming messages never urgent, click the **Never** radio button. To allow the caller to determine if the messages should be marked urgent, click the **Ask caller for their preference** radio button.

Step 6   Click the **Save** icon in the title strip.

Enable MWI on Another Extension

There may be times you want an extension, other than the one associated with a subscriber, to activate MWI when a new message arrives. This might be desirable if a subscriber has phones in different physical locations with different extensions and wants to be able to receive MWI for a single voice mailbox on both phones.

Step 1   From within SA, select **Subscribers>Subscribers**.

Step 2   Click the **Find** icon and enter search criteria that match the subscriber account you plan to edit and click **Find**.

Step 3   Choose the subscriber from the list that displays.

Step 4   Select **Messages** from the left side of the screen.

Step 5   Click the **Add** button, which is at the bottom of the screen under the MWI Extension field.

Step 6   Enter the extension number on which you want to activate MWI in the new empty field that displays.

Step 7   Click the **Save** icon in the title strip.

Adding and Removing Subscribers from a Distribution List

To view, add or remove members from Public Distribution Lists (PDLs), follow these steps:

Step 1   From within SA, select **Subscribers>Public Distribution Lists**.

Step 2   Click the **Find** icon in the title strip. Enter your search criteria and select the **Find** button. A list of PDLs displays. Click the PDL from which you wish to add or remove subscribers.

Step 3   Select **Members** from the left side of the screen.

Step 4   You have the option to view, add, or remove members from the PDL. Select the action you want by clicking the appropriate radio button on the top part of the screen. If you choose to add members, you must select either **Selected subscriber** or **Public distribution lists** from the drop-down list.

Step 5   Enter the search criteria for the subscriber you wish to manage in the **Type a subscriber name to find** field and click **Find**.

Step 6   If you are simply viewing, the PDL list displays. If you are adding or removing, a list displays with either an **Add to list** or **Remove**. Select the subscriber you wish to manage and click the **Add** or **Remove** button.

Step 7   Click **Save**.

Conversation Management Settings

One area of configuration that can greatly impact end-user satisfaction is the conversation. These settings define how Unity communicates with the subscriber over the phone. If subscribers feel the voice-mail system is not offering them an efficient interface, they become very frustrated. Because there is no such thing as a typical user, Unity allows the conversation to be tailored to each end-user's needs. The subscribers can configure most of the conversation using CPCA. However, often the administrator is called upon to complete these tasks. The most common conversion configuration tasks are discussed in this section.

Changing Menus from Full to Brief

Step 1   From within SA, select **Subscribers>Subscribers**.

Step 2   Click the **Find** icon and enter search criteria that match the subscriber account you plan to edit and click **Find**.

Step 3   Choose the subscriber from the list that displays.

Step 4   Select **Conversation** from the left side of the screen.

Step 5   Using the **Menu Style** drop-down list select **Brief**.

Step 6   Click the **Save** icon in the title strip.

Change How a Subscriber Searches for Other Subscribers

Step 1   From within SA, select **Subscribers>Subscriber**.

Step 2   Click the **Find** icon and enter search criteria that match the subscriber account you plan to edit and click **Find**.

Step 3   Choose the subscriber from the list that displays.

Step 4   Select **Conversation** from the left side of the screen.

Step 5   From the **Identify a subscriber by** drop-down list select how a subscriber will be prompted to address messages to other subscribers. The available choices are **Spelling the last name then first**, **Spelling the first name then last** or **Enter the extension**.

Step 6   Click the **Save** icon from the title strip.

Change What Message Count Is Played to a Subscriber

Step 1   From within SA, select **Subscribers>Subscribers**.

Step 2   Click the **Find** icon and enter search criteria that match the subscriber account you plan to edit and click **Find**.

Step 3   Choose the subscriber from the list that displays.

Step 4   Select **Conversation** from the left side of the screen.

Step 5 The settings under the **For new messages play** heading determine what message counts Unity plays when a subscriber logs in. To play the total number of new messages in a subscriber's mailbox (this includes voice mail, e-mail and faxes), check the **Message count totals** box. Three other message count options are available. They are **Voice message counts**, **E-mail message counts**, and **Fax counts**. To break down the message count by the type of message or limit the count to a particular type of message, check the box next to the desired message count label.

Step 6 To have Unity announce the total number of saved messages, check the **Saved message count** box.

Step 7 Click the **Save** icon in the title strip.

Change the Order in Which Messages Are Played

Step 1 From within SA, select **Subscribers>Subscribers**.

Step 2 Click the **Find** icon and enter search criteria that match the subscriber account you plan to edit and click **Find**.

Step 3 Choose the subscriber from the list that displays.

Step 4 Select **Conversation** from the left side of the screen.

Step 5 You can configure the order in which new messages are played. Under the **New Message Play Order** heading is a list of the various types of messages. The messages are played as they appear from top to bottom. To change the order, highlight the type of message you wish to move and then click the **Move Up** or **Move Down** button. Do this with all of the message types until they are in the desired order.

Step 6 The default behavior of Unity is to play the oldest message first when playing new messages. To play the newest message first, choose **Newest first** from the **Then by:** drop-down list found below the **New Message Play Order** list. In most cases it is best to leave this setting at **Oldest first**.

Step 7 You can also configure the order in which saved messages are played. Under the **Saved Message Play Order** heading is a list of the various types of messages. The messages are played as they appear from top to bottom. To change the order, highlight the type of message you wish to move and then click the **Move Up** or **Move Down** button. Do this with all of the message types until they are in the desired order.

Step 8 The default behavior of Unity is to play the newest message first when playing saved messages. To play the oldest message first, choose **Oldest first** from the **Then by:** drop-down list found below the **Saved Message Play Order** list. In most cases, it is best to leave this setting at **Newest first**.

Step 9   After changing these settings to the desired order, click the **Save** icon in the title strip.

Change What Header Information Is Heard While Listening to Messages

Step 1   From within SA, select **Subscribers>Subscribers**.

Step 2   Click the **Find** icon and enter search criteria that match the subscriber account you plan to edit and click **Find**.

Step 3   Choose the subscriber from the list that displays.

Step 4   Select **Conversation** from the left side of the screen.

Step 5   Navigate to the **Before playing each message, play** heading near the bottom of the page. To have the sender's name played before the message is played, check the **Sender's Information** box.

Step 6   To have the number of the current messages played before the message, check the **Message number** box.

Step 7   To play the time the message was sent before the message is played, check the **Time message was sent** box under the **Before playing each message, play** heading.

Step 8   To play the time the message was sent after the message is played, check the **Time message was sent** box under the **After playing each message, play** heading.

Although this chapter has not listed every possible subscriber-related administrative task that you may need to perform, you should find that the more common tasks are covered. In future chapters you will build on what you have learned here and be able to apply this knowledge to other components found within Unity.

Summary

This chapter has explored all the predeployment subscriber-related tasks, and the more common subscriber-related administrative tasks. At this point you should understand the role subscriber templates play and how to create them. A large portion of this chapter is dedicated to the creation and configuration of these templates. This is because a smooth trouble-free deployment is heavily dependant upon the proper configuration of subscriber templates. Finally, you should feel comfortable with creating subscribers and most of the common day-to-day subscriber administrative tasks. At this point, your system should be ready to handle your company's voice mail needs, but because Unity is more than just voice mail, it is important to understand Unity's other capabilities. The next chapter explores the call handling capabilities of Unity.

CHAPTER 9

Call Management

As stated previously in this book, Unity is much more than just a voice-mail system. In addition to providing voice and unified messaging services, Unity can be configured as an auto attendant. An auto attendant is an application that answers incoming calls and plays a greeting to callers. The callers can then navigate through the voice prompts to reach desired destinations. This chapter discusses the components that make up an auto attendant and how to configure them properly.

Today it is nearly impossible to call a large company and not be greeted by one of these systems. There are many horror stories about these systems and for that reason some companies choose not to deploy them. Even if you are not going to deploy an auto attendant this chapter is useful, because it covers Unity's call handling capabilities. Although call handling functions are typically used within an auto attendant application, you may find other uses for them. With a solid understanding of the call handling capabilities that Unity offers, you can build a custom call handling system.

Understanding Call Flow

Have you ever bought one of those build-it-yourself desks or entertainment centers? It looks good in the store, and you figure it shouldn't be too hard to build. When you get home the first thing you do is find the instructions and put them in a nice safe place, just in case you need to refer to them later. Everyone knows that you don't use instructions the *first* time you try to build it. Eventually, we have a screwdriver in one hand, the instructions in the other and a look of total bewilderment on our faces. Don't let this happen to you when it comes to building a call handling application within Unity. It is best if you have a solid understanding of what you are going to build and understand the mechanics behind it.

This section discusses the mechanics behind Unity's call handling capabilities, so that once you have created the application, it looks and acts the way you expect, unlike many of the build-it-yourself projects I have created.

Call Flow Architecture

An outside caller's experience with Unity is very important because in some cases it is the first contact he has with your company. Just as you spend time determining how Unity will interface with the subscribers, you must spend time determining what type of conversation an outside caller will hear when calling. Unity has the ability to determine how a call flows through the system based on a number of things, including time-of-day, called number, calling number, and caller input. The job of the administrator is to determine the paths calls take and the criteria to determine actual call flow. In other words, how the call will be handled.

Let's start by looking at a simple automated attendant flow. One of the simplest types of auto attendant is one that asks callers to enter the extension of the parties with whom they wish to speak. If they don't know the number, they can hold for an operator. Typically within Unity, the caller is also given the option of entering the person's name using the letters on the telephone keypad. In the following example this option is not given.

When the caller reaches the auto attendant, an opening greeting is heard. A sample greeting is "Thank you for calling Bailey's Guard Dogs. If you know your party's extension, you may enter it now. Otherwise, please hold on the line for an operator." Let's look at three call flows that can occur within this auto attendant.

In the first path, a caller dials an extension and the called party answers. The flow looks like this:

1　During the greeting the caller enters a subscriber's extension.

2　The call is transferred to the subscriber's extension.

3　The called party answers.

In the second path, a caller dials an extension, but the called party does not answer the call. The flow looks like this:

1　During the greeting, the caller enters a subscriber's extension.

2　The call is transferred to the subscriber's extension.

3　The called party does not answer.

4　After a certain number of rings, the call is forwarded to Unity on behalf of the called party's extension.

5　Because the call is forwarded to Unity from a known subscriber's extension, Unity plays the subscriber's greeting.

The final path, which the call may take, occurs when the caller does not enter anything. The flow looks like this:

1　During the greeting, the caller enters nothing.

2　After a certain number of seconds, the call is transferred to the operator's extension number.

The preceding examples are very simplistic, but they are designed to help you understand the call flow architecture.

Although a standard auto attendant like this one may work for certain deployments, much more can be done by using call handlers. The following section begins to explore what call handlers are and how they are configured.

Call Handler Overview

Now that you understand how a standard auto attendant works, let's explore more advanced call handling capabilities.

At the core of Unity are call handling capability components appropriately called "call handlers." The job of a call handler is to route the call through the Unity system based on caller input. There are three types of call handlers. The first is a Standard or Generic Call Handler. Because this type of call handler has no predefined purpose, it is the most flexible. Most auto attendant applications contain more of these call handlers than any other. Later in this section, more discussion is devoted to the various functions this call handler can provide.

The second type of call handler is called a Directory Handler. A directory handler allows the caller to search for the desired party by spelling a name using the letters on the telephone keypad. This feature is sometimes referred to as dial-by-name. Unity includes a default directory handler, which normally contains all of the subscribers on the system. You can also create additional directory handlers and later in this section we will discuss how having them can be beneficial.

The third and final type of call handler is called an Interview Handler. An interview handler is used to request detailed information from the caller that may not be retrieved by asking only one question. An interview handler can be configured to ask the caller up to 20 questions and gives the caller time to answer between each question. An example of an interview handler is a class survey hotline. After students take a class, they are able to call a number and answer five questions. The answers are later transcribed and entered into the school's database.

An advanced feature that can be incorporated into an auto attendant is the ability to make certain static information available to callers without the need for human intervention. This feature is sometimes referred to as an audio text application. For example, you may allow callers to hear store hours or directions using the auto attendant. The audio text application is a number of call handlers configured so that the callers can navigate to the information they need without having to talk to a live person. Often this is not only a cost savings to the company but a time saver for the caller. Instead of having to wait on hold to find out when the store opens, the caller simply presses a few buttons to hear the store hours.

The term audio text has been defined in many different ways. It is often used when referring to an advanced auto attendant; however, in its purist sense audio text is much more than that. It is defined in the Cisco Press book *Cisco Unity Deployment and Solutions Guide* as follows: "audio text encompasses everything that you can do with a phone call in Unity other than leaving or retrieving messages."

Most advanced auto attendants include all three types of call handlers and an audio text application or two. Figure 9-1 shows a sample auto attendant menu, which includes each of these. Each box represents a call handler.

Figure 9-1 *Example Auto Attendant*

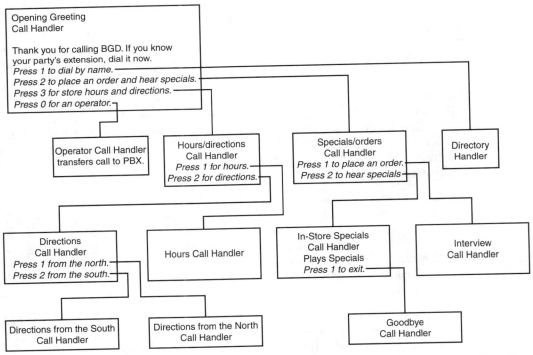

The menu starts at what is called the opening greeting call handler. Most outside calls entering the system begin at a standard call handler. By default there are three call handlers in Unity. The first is called the Opening Greeting and is the default entry point for outside calls. The opening greeting plays a greeting, which offers the caller the available choices. In this example, if callers press 0 or hold on the line, they are transferred to the second default call handler, the Operator Call Handler. Its job is to deliver the call to the PBX with instructions to forward the call onto the operator's extension. The third default call handler is the Goodbye Call Handler. This call handler politely ends a call. It gives the caller one last chance to dial an extension and then hangs up if an extension is not entered. In this example, if callers press 1 after hearing the in-store specials, they are sent to the goodbye call handler.

Let's take a look at an example of an audio text application. Assume a person who lives north of the store wants directions. Once she reaches the opening greeting, she presses 3 for store hours and directions. Then she presses 2 for directions, and finally she presses 1 because she wants directions from the north. The caller was able to obtain the information she needed without having to wait to speak with someone.

Callers also have the option of dialing by name if they don't know their party's extension. By pressing 1 from the opening greeting, callers are sent to the directory handler, where they may enter the name of the person they wish to reach.

This example also includes the use of an interview handler. If callers wish to place an order, they press 2 from the opening greeting. They are transferred to the specials/orders call handler from which they can press 1 to place an order. They are then transferred to an interview handler, which requests four pieces of information: name, customer number, the product being ordered, and shipping method. The questions are not shown in the figure; they are simply part of the interview handler.

After reviewing this example, you should have a good understanding of how the different types of call handlers work together and how they can be tied to one another. The next section provides a more detailed look at these components and how each is configured.

Creating Basic Call Routing Systems

Now that you have a basic understanding of the call handling capabilities of Unity, it's time to put some of that knowledge to work. The first thing to do is decide how advanced a call handling system you want to provide. As discussed earlier, Unity can be configured to offer a very simple call handling system or a much more advanced one. This section discusses what steps are required to create a very basic call handling system.

The goal of this section is to create the components needed for an auto attendant system that allows outside callers to enter a subscriber's extension number, dial by name, or reach the operator. By default these options are activated by using the opening greeting that comes with Unity. If these are the only features you require, very little configuration is needed. However, this section goes into greater detail, so the auto attendant provides the desired service, and so you will understand how to make changes as needed. Throughout this section each configuration setting is discussed so that you understand the impact each setting will have on the system.

Creating Call Handlers

Typically, calls are sent to the Unity system in one of two methods. With the first method, each subscriber has a Direct Inward Dial (DID) number. When an outside caller dials this number, the call is sent to the subscriber's phone. If the subscriber's phone is busy or is not answered, the call is forwarded to Unity, where the subscriber's greeting is played. When

DIDs are not available, calls are sent to the Unity system using the second method. With this method, a company may route calls to the main number on to Unity. A call handler, typically called Opening Greeting is the entry point for calls that enter the system by dialing the company's main number. In some cases there may be a need for multiple opening call handlers, such as for a company that wants a separate auto attendant for each division of the company. In such cases, the greeting the caller hears depends on the number dialed to reach the company. The steps for providing this functionality are covered in the "Creating Advanced Call Routing Systems" section. In this example we will assume that all incoming calls reach the same main greeting. Because all calls enter the system at a call handler, the first step is to create or modify a call handler. In most cases you modify the call handler named Opening Greeting. Let's look at the creation and configuration process for call handlers.

Logic tells us that before we can configure something, it must exist, hence before we can configure a call handler, one must be created. Three call handlers are created during the installation of Unity. In most environments, more need to be created. Let's begin with creating a call handler as outlined in the steps that follow:

Step 1 From within SA, select **Call Management>Call Handlers**.

Step 2 From the title strip, click the **Add** icon.

Step 3 A new Add a Call Handler window displays as shown in Figure 9-2. Enter a name for the new call handler.

Figure 9-2 *Add a Call Handler*

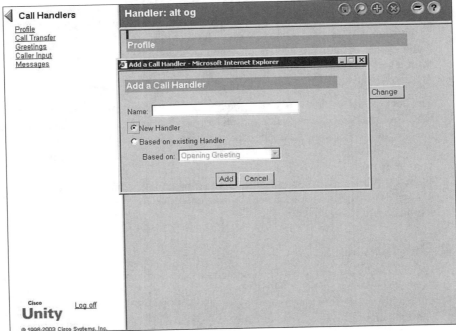

Step 4   Call handlers do not use templates to define their parameters. However, you can choose to create a new call handler based on an existing one. When you do this, the new call handler has all the attributes of the call handler on which it is based. To create the call handler with the same attributes as an existing call handler, select the **Based on existing Handler** radio button and select the existing call handler from the **Based on:** drop-down list. If you do not want the new call handler to copy the attributes of an existing call handler, select the **New handler** radio button.

Step 5   Click the **Add** button.

Step 6   Once the call handler is created, you need to configure it to accomplish the task you designed for it. The next section covers the configuration process.

Configuring Call Handlers

The creation of the call handler is simple. Many of the configuration steps are very similar to those you perform when you configure subscribers. The reason for this is that every subscriber has an associated call handler. Even though many of these steps seem identical, there are some subtle differences to highlight.

Each call handler has five configurable areas. Table 9-1 shows each of these areas and the types of parameters configured in each.

Table 9-1   *Call Handler Configurable Parameters*

Parameters	Details
Profile	General settings such as schedules and languages, recorded name for the call handler and the owner of the call handler are configured in this area.
Call Transfer	This area determines what action is taken when this call handler is reached. Unlike subscribers, you can configure the call handler to transfer the call differently based upon schedules assigned to the call handler.
Greetings	The greetings area is used to configure which greetings are enabled and what action is allowed during the greeting and what action is taken after the greeting.
Caller Input	Often during a greeting a caller is given a number of choices such as "press 1 for Sales, 2 for Support, or to reach an operator press 0." The caller input settings determine what action is taken if a digit is pressed during the greeting.
Messages	The settings in this area determine how long messages can be, whether callers can edit messages, and the action to be taken after receiving a message. Most importantly this is where you configure which subscriber receives the message.

The following steps take you though configuring each area shown in Table 9-1.

Profile Settings

Figure 9-3 shows the parameters that can be configured on the Profile page of a call handler. The following steps explain how to configure these parameters and the effect of each.

Figure 9-3 *Call Management>Call Handler>Profile*

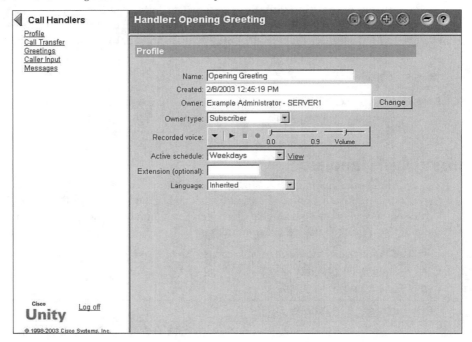

NOTE When a multiswitch integration is present an additional field will show on the page depicted in Figure 9-3. The field is Switch and allows you to specify which phone system the call handler uses.

Step 1 From within SA select **Call Management>Call Handlers**. Click the **Find** icon, enter the search criteria, and click **Find**. Select the desired call handler from the list and click the **View** button. Click the **Profile** link on the left side of the screen.

Step 2 The name of the call handler is shown in the **Name:** field. The name can be changed in this field if needed.

Step 3 The **Created:** field on this page shows when the call handler was created.

Step 4   Each call handler must have an owner. The current owner is shown in the **Owner:** field. An owner can be either a subscriber or a Public Distribution List (PDL). The owner of a call handler can be allowed to change the greeting of the call handler remotely. If you wish to allow a group of subscribers to change the greeting, you should select a PDL that contains those subscribers as the owner. In the **Owner type:** field select either a subscriber or PDL.

Step 5   If no owner exists, or if you want to change the owner, click the **Change** button. A search criteria window displays. Enter criteria and click the **Find** button. A list of subscribers displays. Highlight a subscriber in the list and click the **Select** button.

Step 6   Using the media master control panel, or **Recorded voice:** field, you can record a name for the call handler. This is not where you record the greeting. This is only the recorded name of the call handler. For instance, if you name the call handler "Store hours" you would record the words **store hours** here.

Step 7   From the **Active Schedule:** drop-down list select the schedule you want associated with this call handler. The call handler transfer setting uses this schedule to determine how and where the call is transferred.

Step 8   A call handler may have an extension number assigned to it. This **Extension:** field is optional but can be useful to outside callers. By entering the extension number from the opening greeting, a caller can jump right to this call handler. The caller would hear something like, In the future to come directly to this menu press 231, and 231 would be the extension number of the call handler. Keep in mind that all extension numbers in Unity must be unique. Enter the extension number if desired.

Note   Another good reason for adding an extension is to manage the greeting of this call handler remotely. Unity offers the ability to change the greeting of a call handler by dialing into the system from any phone. This feature is called Cisco Unity Greetings Administrator (CUGA). However, to use this feature the call handler you wish to change must have an extension assigned to it.

Step 9   The **Language:** drop-down list is used to set the language in which Unity prompts are played under this call handler. If **Inherited** displays in this field, whatever language was used in the previous call handler will continue to be used. Select the desired language from the drop-down list. When in doubt set it to **Inherited**.

Step 10   Click the **Save** icon in the title strip.

Call Transfer Settings

Call transfer settings determine how a call that reaches the call handler is treated. It determines whether the call is transferred to a phone and, if so, what type of transfer is used or if the greeting is played. To configure a call handler's call transfer settings follow these steps:

Step 1   From within SA, select **Call Management>Call Handlers**. Click the **Find** icon, enter the search criteria, and click **Find**. Select the desired call handler from the list and click the **View** button. Click the **Call Transfer** link on the left side of the screen.

Step 2   Figure 9-4 shows the Call Transfer page. At the top of the page is a **Transfer Rule applies to:** drop-down list. This field allows you to have a call handler transfer calls based on the schedule with which it is associated. For example, you could have a call handler transfer the call to a phone during open hours and go directly to a greeting during closed hours. Three types of transfer rules can be configured: Alternate, Closed, and Standard. The most common is Standard. This transfer rule applies during open hours. It also applies at all hours if no other transfer rule is enabled. If enabled, the Closed transfer rule applies during closed hours. If the Alternate transfer rule is enabled, it supersedes the other two transfer rules and is applied all hours on all days. Select the transfer rule from the drop-down list that you wish to configure.

Figure 9-4   *Call Management>Call Handlers>Call Transfer*

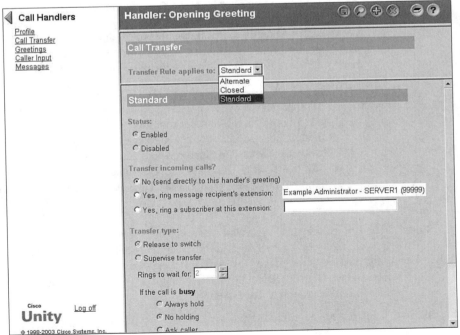

Step 3   To enable the rule you just selected, click the **Enabled** radio button. To disable this rule click the **Disabled** radio button.

Step 4   Depending on the use of the call handler, you may want to configure it to play the greeting or transfer to a phone. In the case of a call handler used to help guide a caller through the menu, click the **No (send directly to this handler's greeting)** radio button. The call handler can also be configured to transfer the call to a phone instead of playing a greeting. To transfer the call to the phone associated with the owner of the call handler, click the **Yes, ring message recipient's extension:** radio button. To transfer the call to some other phone number, click the **Yes, ring a subscriber at this extension:** radio button and enter the phone number in the field to the right of the label.

Step 5   If the call is to be transferred to an extension, the type of transfer must be selected under the **Transfer type:** heading. If holding and screening options are desired, the **Supervise transfer** radio button is selected. If these features are not needed, select the **Release to switch** radio button. If Release to switch is selected the following steps do not apply.

Step 6   In the **Rings To Wait for:** field, enter the number of rings that Unity waits before assuming the call will not be answered. Unity has the ability to queue calls if the number to which Unity transfers a call is busy. You must choose one of three options under the If call is busy heading:

— The first choice, **Always hold** informs the caller that the extension is busy and places the caller on hold.

— The second option, **No holding**, prompts the caller to leave a message or dial another extension.

— The third and final choice, **Ask caller,** informs the caller that the extension is busy and offers the choice of holding, leaving a message, or dialing another extension.

Step 7   Unity has the ability to gather caller information for screening purposes on a supervised transfer. There are four options under the Gather caller information heading. These options are as follows:

— **Announce**—Unity says "transferring call" when the subscriber answers the call.

— **Introduce**—Unity announces who the call is for when the subscriber answers the phone. This feature is used when more than one person receives calls on the same phone.

— **Confirm**—Asks the caller to press **1** to accept the call or **2** to send the call to voice mail.

— **Ask caller's name**—Unity asks callers to record their names and plays the name when subscribers answer their phones.

Step 8 Select the options you wish to enable by selecting the radio button next to each option.

Step 9 Click the **Save** icon in the title strip.

Configuring Call Handler Greetings Settings

Each call handler can have up to five different greetings, the same five that can be configured for a subscriber, Alternate, Busy, Closed, Internal and Standard. Chapter 8, "Subscriber Reference" discusses the function of each of these greetings. These greetings can be configured using SA and can be managed by the owner of the call handler using CUGA. This feature is discussed later. For now, let's look at the following steps that show how to configure these setting using SA.

Step 1 From within SA, select **Call Management>Call Handlers**. Click the **Find** icon and enter the search criteria and click **Find**. Select the desired call handler from the list and click the **View** button. Click the **Greetings** link on the left side of the screen.

Step 2 Figure 9-5 shows the call handler Greetings page. From this screen you can enable and configure each of the five greetings. From the drop-down list, select the greeting you wish to configure. Start with the **Standard** greeting.

Figure 9-5 *Call Management>Call Handler>Greetings*

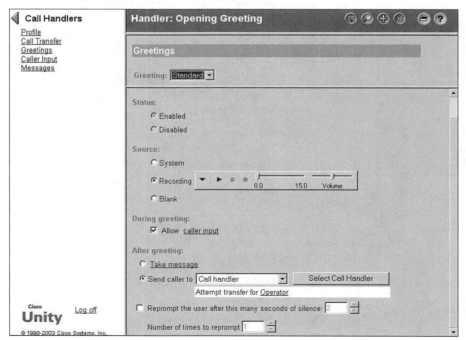

Step 3 Under the **Status** heading, the greeting may be enabled or disabled. If the greeting is disabled it will not be used. The Standard greeting is enabled by default and cannot be disabled. When configuring any greeting other than standard, you must select the **Enabled** radio button to enable this type of greeting.

Step 4 Under the **Source** heading, the source of the message is chosen. The three choices for the source are as follows:

— **System**—Plays the prerecorded greeting "Sorry <subscriber's name> is not available."

— **Recording**—Plays the greeting that the subscriber recorded.

— **Blank**—Plays no greeting and goes directly to the after-greeting action.

Typically **Recording** is chosen for this setting so that a custom greeting can be created for this call handler. Select the desired source by clicking the appropriately labeled radio button.

If Recording is chosen you can use the media master control panel (the VCR-like panel next to the record label) to record a greeting. This interface also allows you to copy, cut, and paste the recording.

Step 5 To allow callers to try to reach another extension or select options during a greeting, check the **Allow caller input** box. You will notice that the words caller input are underlined, this is a link to the caller input page, which is covered later in this section.

Step 6 Recall when you configured subscribers. In most cases, after the greeting was played, the caller was given the opportunity to leave a message by clicking the Take message radio button. Depending on the type of call handler and its function in the application, you may instead want to send the caller to another call handler. If you want a different action to take place, click the **Send Caller To** radio button and select the desired destination from the drop-down list. The available options in the drop-down list are as follows:

— **CVM Mailbox Reset**—Sends calls to a conversation that allows the caller to reset the mailbox. This is available only when the Community Voice Mail (CVM) package is being used.

— **Call Handler**—Sends calls to the selected call handler.

— **Caller System Transfer**—Sends callers to a prompt that allows them to enter another extension to which they would like to be transferred.

— **Directory Handler**—Sends calls to the directory handler you select.

— **Greetings Administrator**—Sends calls to a conversation that allows them to manage the greetings of call handlers.

— **Hang up**—Disconnects calls.

— **Hotel Checked Out**—This option works in concert with Cisco Unity's Hospitality and Property Management Integration. It allows guests to archive their messages when checking out.

— **Interview Handler**—Sends calls to the interview handler you select.

— **Sign-in**—Sends calls to subscriber sign in.

— **Subscriber**—Sends calls to another subscriber's greeting or extension depending upon how it is configured.

— **Subscriber System Transfer**—Allows callers to transfer to another extension after they login with subscriber credentials. They may then transfer to any number their restriction table allows.

When choosing to send the call to a call handler, directory handler, interview handler, or another subscriber, you will have to specify the specific handler or subscriber. The **Select <type of object you selected>** button becomes available to the right of the type of object you select. For example, if you select to send the call to a subscriber, choose the **Select Subscriber** button. When you click this button, a search criteria window displays. Enter the appropriate criteria and click **Find**. Select the desired object from the list. If a subscriber or call handler is selected, you must also select whether the call should be sent to the greeting or the phone. To send the call to the extension, select **Attempt transfer for** from the **Conversation** drop-down list. To send the call to the subscriber's greeting, select **Send to greeting for** from the **Conversation** drop-down list.

NOTE   The fact that you have to choose to send the call to the greeting or attempt to transfer has caused many administrators hours of frustration and troubleshooting. Make sure that if you want the phone of the subscriber to whom the call is transferred to ring, you must select **Attempt transfer for**.

Step 7   If the caller remains silent after being offered the opportunity to leave a message, he can be reprompted. To have the caller reprompted, select the **Reprompt the user after this many seconds of silence:** box and enter the number of seconds to wait for the caller to begin speaking. Then, enter the number of times you want the caller to be reprompted. The maximum is 100.

Step 8   Click the **Save** icon in the title strip.

Configuring Call Handler Caller Input Settings

Call handlers are often used to guide a caller through the menu. To do this, the greeting tells the caller what number to press to be transferred to a certain destination. The call handler input settings are used to configure the call handler to transfer the calls when a touchtone is heard.

The following steps show how to configure the Caller Input settings, which are shown in Figure 9-6.

Step 1   From within SA, select **Call Management>Call Handlers**. Click the **Find** icon, enter the search criteria, and click **Find**. Select the desired call handler from the list and click the **View** button. Click the **Caller Input** link on the left side of the screen. A screen similar to that shown in Figure 9-6 appears.

Figure 9-6   *Call Management>Call Handlers>Caller Input>*

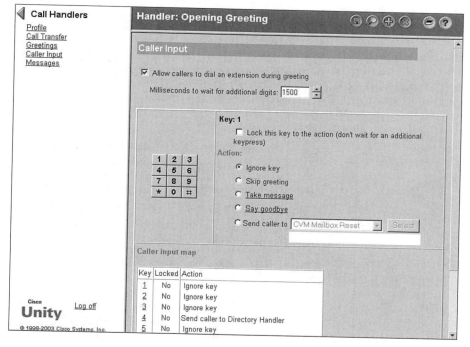

Step 2   The first configuration setting determines whether callers can try to reach a different extension when listening to a greeting. To allow a caller to enter an extension while listening to a greeting, check the **Allow callers to dial an extension during greeting** box.

Step 3 If the option to allow callers to dial another extension during the greeting is enabled, an interdigit time out must also be configured. The **Milliseconds to wait for additional digits:** setting is amount of time Unity waits before deciding the caller is finished pressing digits. The default value is 1500 milliseconds, which is a second and a half. Typically this value is adequate. If you get comments that callers are transferred or receive error messages from Unity before they have finished dialing an extension during a greeting, increase this value.

Step 4 From the dial pad on the screen you can configure the action to be taken when a digit is pressed. This is where the option in the spoken greeting is tied to the call handler. A button can be configured for five types of actions:

— **Ignore Key**—No action is taken when a digit is pressed.

— **Skip Greeting**—The greeting is skipped and Unity proceeds to the after greeting action.

— **Take Message**—The caller can press this key to cause Unity to take a message.

— **Say Goodbye**—Unity plays a goodbye message and disconnects the call.

— **Send caller to**—With this option select any of the following destinations:

  • **CVM Mailbox Reset**—Allows callers to reset mailbox (Available with Community Voice Mail package).

  • **Call Handler**—Sends calls to the selected call handler.

  • **Caller System Transfer**—Sends callers to a prompt that allows them to enter another extension to which they would like to be transferred.

  • **Directory Handler**—Sends calls to the directory handler you select.

  • **Greetings Administrator**—Sends calls to a conversation that allows the caller to manage the greetings of call handlers that they own.

  • **Hang up**—Disconnects calls.

  • **Hotel Checked Out**—Used only with Unity's Hospitality and Property Management System.

- **Interview Handler**—Sends calls to the interview handler you select.

- **Sign-in**—Sends calls to subscriber sign in.

- **Subscriber**—Sends calls to another subscriber's greeting or extension depending upon how it is configured.

- **Subscriber System Transfer**—Allows callers to transfer to another extension after they log in with subscriber credentials. They may then transfer to any number their restriction table allows.

Step 5   Click on the digit you wish to configure and then select the action by clicking on the appropriately labeled radio button. As with the Greetings settings, when choosing to send the call to a call handler, directory handler, interview handler or another subscriber, you will have to specify the specific handler or subscriber.

Note   If a subscriber or call handler is selected, you must also select whether the call should be sent to the greeting or the phone extension. To send the call to the extension, select **Attempt transfer for** from the **Conversation** drop-down list. To send the call to the greeting, select **Send to greeting for** from the **Conversation** drop-down list.

Step 6   If the **Lock this key to the action (don't wait for an additional keypress)** field is checked, an extension that begins with this digit cannot be entered. This option causes Unity to transfer the call to the destination assigned to that key without waiting to see if the caller is going to enter other digits. Only enable this field on digits that are not leading digits for any extensions.

Step 7   After you have all the digits configured as desired click the **Save** icon in the title strip.

Configuring Call Handler Messages Settings

Unlike subscribers, call handlers do not have mailboxes. Therefore, when allowing a call handler to take messages, you must select a subscriber to receive them. By default, the creator of the call handler will be the message recipient. From the call handler Messages page, you can configure the message recipient and other message-related settings.

Figure 9-7 shows the call handler Messages page. To configure the settings seen in this figure, follow these steps:

Step 1 From within SA, select **Call Management>Call Handlers**. Click the **Find** icon, enter the search criteria, and click **Find**. Select the desired call handler from the list and click the **View** button. Click the **Messages** link on the left side of the screen.

Step 2 Using the **Message Recipient** drop-down list you can choose to have the message recipient be either a subscriber or a PDL. Typically, messages are sent to a single subscriber. If you need to have multiple subscribers receive the message, create a PDL that contains the subscribers, and then select the PDL as the message recipient.

Step 3 Click the **Select** button. A search criteria window displays. Enter the search criteria and click the **Find** button. Highlight the desired subscriber/PDL from the list and click the **Select** button.

Step 4 The maximum length of a message a caller can leave is set by entering the desired value in seconds in the **Maximum message length, in seconds:** box. Enter the desired value.

Figure 9-7 *Call Management>Call Handler>Messages>*

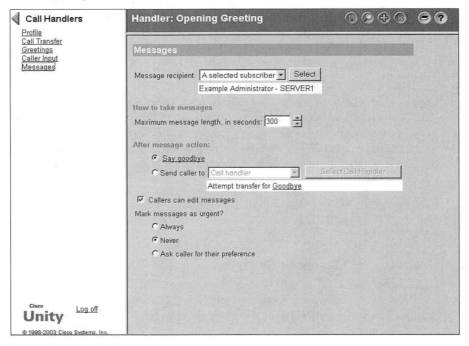

Step 5   Select the action to be taken after the message is recorded by selecting either the **Say goodbye** or the **Send caller to** radio buttons. When choosing **Send caller to,** the destination must be chosen. The destinations are the same as those listed under Send caller to in the caller input section.

Step 6   To let callers listen to, change, or delete the messages they leave, check the **Callers can edit messages** box.

Step 7   You may allow the caller to label a message as urgent by selecting the **Ask caller for their preference** radio button under the heading **Mark messages as urgent?** You may choose to always mark it urgent without asking the caller by setting the **Always** radio button or never have the message marked urgent by selecting the **Never** radio button.

Step 8   Click the **Save** icon in the title strip.

That is all there is to configuring a call handler. It is similar to configuring a subscriber because each subscriber has an associated call handler. Therefore, when you create a subscriber you are also creating a call handler for that subscriber. That is why the two tasks are so similar.

This section focused on the standard type of call handler. We briefly discussed the other two types of call handlers, the directory handler and the interview handler. In the next section, we take a closer look at the directory handler.

Configuring Directory Handlers

When callers dial the subscriber's name, they are sent to a directory handler. The directory handler "listens" to the keys that are pressed and, using the letters assigned to each key, looks for possible matches. Once the caller has finished entering digits, the directory handlers either plays the possible matches or routes the call directly to the matched subscriber. In earlier versions of Unity, there was only one directory handler, which made it impossible to search a selected group of subscribers for a match. In environments with multiple departments where each wants a separate auto attendant, multiple directory handlers are often requested. As of Unity version 4.0, it is possible to create multiple directory handlers that resolve this limitation.

By default, one directory handler exists called Directory Handler. For companies that do not need multiple directory handlers, just use the default. A directory handler is created using nearly the same steps used to create a new call handler, as shown in the steps that follow.

Configuring a directory handler involves four elements: Profile, Search Options, Match List Options, and Caller Input. The Profile is used to assign an owner, recorded voice, extension, and language. The Search Options define if and how the search is limited. The Match Options determines how Unity acts upon finding matches. The Caller Input in the directory handler determines timeout thresholds and reprompt settings, which is different than the caller input setting in standard call handlers.

Directory Handler Profile Settings

Figure 9-8 shows the settings found on the Profile page of a directory handler. The following steps explain these settings and how to configure each of them.

Figure 9-8   *Call Management>Directory Handler>Profile*

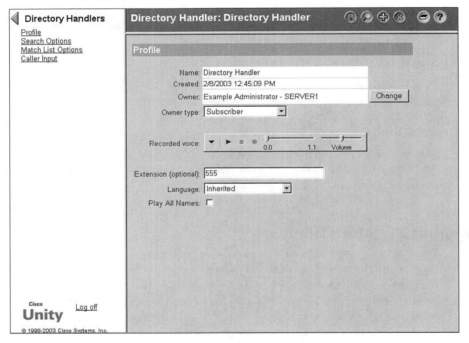

Step 1   From within SA select **Call Management>Directory Handlers.** Click the **Find** icon, enter the search criteria, and click **Find**. Select the desired call handler from the list and click the **View** button. Click the **Profile** link on the left side of the screen.

Step 2   The first two fields cannot be edited. They show the name of the directory handler and the date and time it was created.

Step 3   As with standard call handlers, directory handlers must have an owner. The owner can be a subscriber or a PDL. If you need to change the owner type, select the new type from the **Owner type:** drop-down list. To change the owner, click the **Change** button next to the current owner. A search criteria window displays. Enter the search criteria and click the **Find** button. Highlight the desired subscriber/PDL from the list and click the **Select** button.

Step 4   The **Recorded voice:** media master control panel is used to create a recorded name for this directory handler.

Step 5   Although optional, you may add an extension to a directory handler by entering a unique extension number in the **Extension (optional):** field. By giving the directory an extension, a caller can jump to the directory handler from anywhere in the system's menu by entering the extension.

Step 6   The **Language:** drop-down list is used to set the language in which Unity prompts are played under this call handler. If **Inherited** displays in this field, whatever language was used in the previous call handler will be continued to be used. Select the desired language from the drop-down list. When in doubt set it to **Inherited**.

Step 7   If you check the **Play All Names:** box, Unity plays all the names in the directory instead of having the caller spell the name using the phone keypad. If more than five subscribers are in the directory, Unity offers the caller the choice of spelling the name. If more than 50 subscribers are in the directory, Unity will not play all the names and the caller must spell the name. Unless you have a very small directory, leave this box unchecked.

Step 8   Click the **Save** icon in the title strip.

Directory Handler Search Options Settings

In larger companies that are using a single Unity system for multiple divisions, more than one directory handler is often needed. In current versions of Unity, multiple directory handlers may be created. When creating a directory handler you can configure the search options so that Unity searches only a selected group of subscribers' names.

Figure 9-9 shows the directory handler Search Options page. Following are the steps that are required to configure these options.

Step 1   From within SA, select **Call Management>Directory Handlers.** Click the **Find** icon, enter the search criteria, and click **Find**. Select the desired call handler from the list and click the **View** button. Click the **Search Options** link on the left side of the screen.

Figure 9-9 *Call Management>Directory Handlers>Search Options*

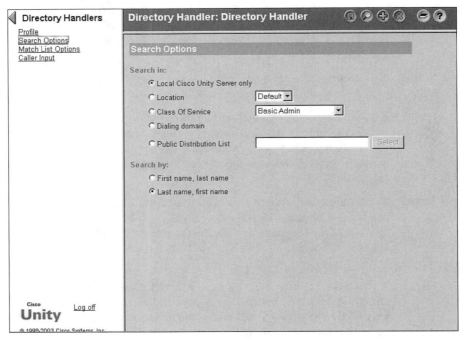

Unity can limit its search by searching only the subscribers that match the criteria selected under the heading **Search in**. The options under this heading are as follows:

— Local Cisco Unity Server Only

The directory handler searches only subscribers associated with the Unity server on which the call came in.

— Location

The directory handler searches only subscribers associated with the primary and local delivery locations for this Unity server.

— Class Of Service

The directory handler searches only subscribers associated with the selected Class of Service (CoS) on the local Cisco Unity server.

— Dialing Domain

Expands directory handler searches to include subscribers associated with other Unity servers within a dialing domain. Dial Domains will be discussed in further detail in Chapter 10,

"Implementing Unity Networking." If you have subscribers with the same name in multiple locations, it is better not to have the directory handler search based on the dialing domain. Instead, use Local Cisco Unity Server Only, a PDL or CoS.

— Public Distribution List

The directory handler searches only subscribers associated with the selected PDL. Subscribers in the PDL that do not have recorded names will not be presented when the matches are played.

Note	A PDL is an easy way to configure a directory handler to search a specific group of subscribers. Simply create a new PDL, add the subscribers to it, and create a directory handler that uses that PDL.

Step 2   Select which of these options you want the directory handler to use by clicking the radio button next to the desired option. If Location or Class of Service is chosen, use the drop-down list to choose the specific object. If Public Distribution List is selected, click the **Select** button. A window displays that allows you to choose the domain you want to search. Select the domain from the drop-down list and click the **Find** button. A list of PDLs displays; click the correct one.

Step 3   The outside caller will be asked to enter either the first name first or the last name first. To configure Unity to request the first name, select the **First name, last name** radio button. To have Unity request the last name first, select the **Last name, first name** radio button.

Step 4   Click the **Save** icon in the title strip.

Directory Handler Match List Options Settings

Once the directory handler has found a match or possibly multiple matches, it will present those matches to the caller based on the settings configured under Match List Options. Figure 9-10 shows these settings. The following steps explain the settings and how to configure them.

Step 1   From within SA, select **Call Management>Directory Handlers**. Click the **Find** icon, enter the search criteria and click **Find**. Select the desired call handler from the list and click the **View** button. Click the **Match List Options** link on the left side of the screen.

Figure 9-10 *Call Management>Directory Handlers>Match List Options*

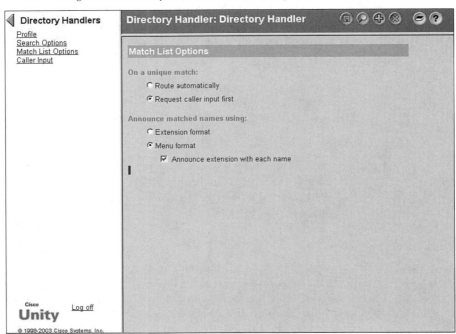

Step 2 If the directory handler finds only one match, you can configure it to send the call directly to the subscriber, or play the subscriber's name and ask callers to confirm that they want to be connected with this subscriber. Allow the caller to confirm the transfer. To have the directory handler transfer the call without caller verification, select the **Route automatically** radio button. To have the directory handler ask the caller for verification, select the **Request caller input first** radio button.

Step 3 When the directory handler finds multiple matches, Unity plays the list of subscribers and asks the caller to select the subscriber by entering the subscriber's extension, or by pressing a single digit. To configure the directory handler to announce the extensions, and ask the caller to enter the desired extension, click the **Extension format** radio button. The prompt that the caller hears is something like, "For Roger Robert press 602, for John Roberts press 610...." To have the directory handler announce the subscribers' names and have the caller press a single digit to transfer, select the **Menu format** radio button. The prompt that the caller hears is something like, "For Roger Robert press 1, for John

Roberts press 2...." If the **Announce extension with each name** box is checked, the caller hears the matching names and their extension but still presses a single digit to transfer.

Step 4 Click the **Save** icon in the title strip.

Directory Handler Caller Input Settings

Timeouts must be set within a directory handler so that it can determine when the caller has finished entering digits. If no timeouts are configured, the caller has to press the pound key (#) when finished entering digits. Timeouts also tell the directory handler how long to wait for the caller to begin entering digits. Figure 9-11 shows the timeout views that can be configured. The following steps explain how to configure these values and the effect each will have.

Step 1 From within SA, select **Call Management>Directory Handlers**. Click the **Find** icon, enter the search criteria, and click **Find**. Select the desired call handler from the list and click the **View** button. Click the **Caller Input** link on the left side of the screen.

Figure 9-11 *Call Management>Directory Handlers>Caller Input*

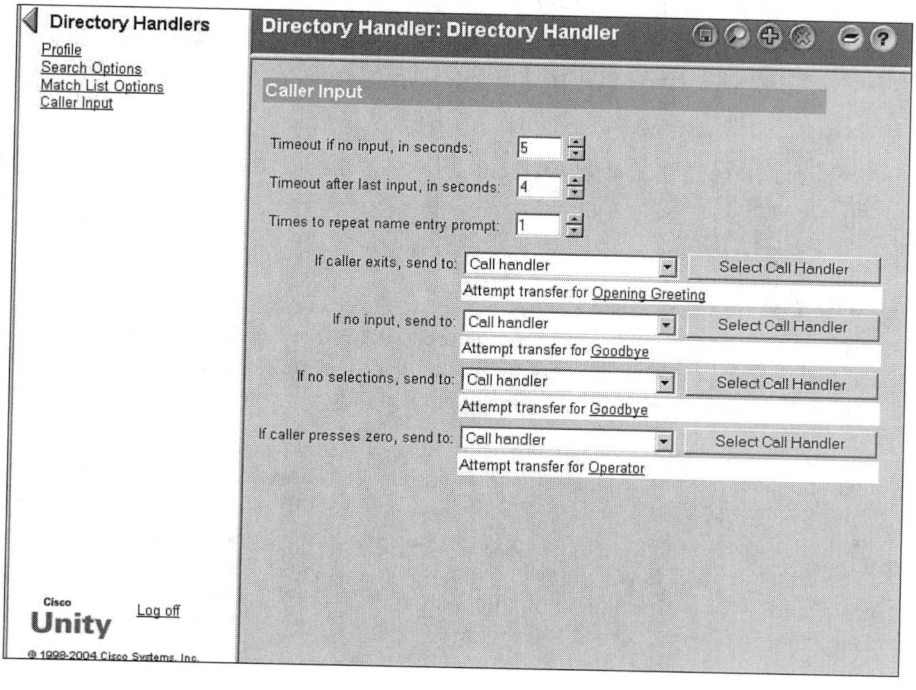

Step 2   The **Timeout if no input, in seconds:** field is the number of seconds the directory waits for the caller to begin entering digits. Enter the desired time in the field.

Step 3   The **Timeout after last input, in seconds:** field is the number of seconds the directory handler waits after a digit is pressed. If no more digits are pressed within this time, the directory handler assumes the caller has finished entering digits and searches for a match.

Step 4   If the caller enters nothing within the allotted time, the directory handler can reprompt them. Enter the number of times an outside caller will be reprompted in the **Times to repeat name entry prompt:** field.

Step 5   When a caller leaves the directory handler, the call must be sent somewhere. Select the type of destination to which the call will be sent from the **If caller exits, send to:** drop-down list.

Step 6   In the **If no input, send to:** drop-down list, select the destination to which the caller is sent when no number is entered.

Step 7   In the **If no selection, send to:** drop-down list, enter the destination to which the call is sent if the caller enters a name but does not select anything from the resulting menu.

Step 8   In the **If caller presses zero, send to:** drop-down list, select the destination to which the call is sent if the caller presses 0.

Step 9   Click the **Save** icon in the title strip.

Now that you understand how to configure the components that make up an auto attendant, let's move on and create one.

Configuring Auto Attendant

The components needed for a basic auto attendant are simple. The previous sections explained how to create and configure call handlers and directory handlers. Now we are going to discuss how to create a basic auto attendant.

First, you need to sketch on paper the flow of the auto attendant you are planning. Having a map expedites the actual configuration process, just as using a map on a trip helps avoid being delayed or lost. The auto attendant we will create in this section is very basic. It will allow an outside caller to enter the extension of a subscriber, dial-by-name, or reach an operator. Later we will create a more advanced auto attendant. The flow chart in Figure 9-12 is an example of a flow chart that is created before actually configuring anything in SA.

Figure 9-12 *Auto Attendant Flow Chart*

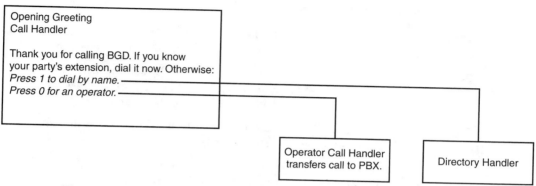

There are only three objects required for this auto attendant: two standard call handlers and one directory handler. All of these objects are automatically created when Unity is installed, so you only need to configure a few things.

Because the detailed steps for any of the configurations that you need to perform were covered in the previous sections, we will just look at the summary of the steps required. If you are uncertain of how to perform the specific steps, refer to the previous section in this chapter for more details.

The configuration process should begin at the lowest level of the menu you are creating, in our example, the operator call handler or the directory handler. You don't start at the highest level because those objects will point to objects in lower levels, which must first exist. Let's start with the operator call handler.

The Operator call handler already exists, so you won't need to create it. This handler determines what happens to a call when a caller presses 0 while in the auto attendant. Only a few things need to be verified/configured as follows:

Step 1   From within SA, select **Call Management>Call Handlers**. Click the **Find** icon, enter the search criteria, and click **Find**. Select the Operator call handler from the list and click the **View** button.

Step 2   On the Profile page, verify that the extension number assigned to the Operator call handler is 0.

Step 3   On the Call Transfer page select the standard transfer rule. Click the **Yes, ring a subscriber at this extension:** radio button and enter the extension number in the field to the right of this label. When callers press 0 from within the auto attendant, they will be transferred to the extension you entered here.

Step 4   All other settings can be left at default. Click the **Save** icon in the title strip.

Because the default directory handler will list all the subscribers we have added, there is no need to edit the handler.

The Opening Greeting call handler is the last handler that should be configured because all other handlers are beneath it. The following are the settings that must be configured/verified.

Step 1 From within SA select **Call Management>Call Handlers,** click the **Find** icon, enter the search criteria, and click **Find**. Select the Opening Greeting call handler from the list and click the **View** button.

Step 2 On the Call Transfer page, select the standard transfer rule. Verify the **No, (send directly to this handler's greeting)** radio button has been selected.

Step 3 From the Greetings page, record the desired greeting using the media master control panel. This greeting should reflect all options a caller has. In the example shown in Figure 9-12, the greeting would be "Thank you for calling BGD. If you know your party's extension dial it now. Otherwise: Press 1 to dial by name or Press 0 for an Operator."

Step 4 On the Caller Input page, configure the keys so that they are in line with the recorded greeting. For this example, key number 1 is configured to "send caller to directory handler" and key 0 is configured to "send caller to Attempt transfer for Operator."

Step 5 No other settings for this call handler should need to be changed. Click the **Save** icon in the title strip.

That's all there is to it. Pretty easy isn't it? Now that you have mastered the basic auto attendant we will move onto creating a more advanced system.

Creating Advanced Call Routing Systems

A basic auto attendant is useful for some companies, but Unity has the ability to offer more advanced services. This section discusses some of these features but mainly covers the components and concepts that are needed to create an advanced auto attendant. An advanced auto attendant can allow a caller to navigate through a menu and retrieve pre-recorded information. An example given earlier in this chapter allowed the caller to get directions without having to wait to speak with someone. Later in this section the steps required to build an auto attendant with some of the more advanced features are discussed. First, let's look at one more type of call handler, the Interview call handler.

Using Interview Handlers

The interview call handler is used when you need to have the caller answer a number of specific questions. You can use an interview call handler to allow a caller to request a catalog or a similar task. The interview handler asks questions such as name, street address, city, zip code, and so on.

To create an Interview handler follow these steps:

Step 1   From within SA, select **Call Management>Interview Handlers**.

Step 2   From the title strip click the **Add** icon.

Step 3   In the **Add an Interview Handler window** enter a name for the new Interview handler.

Step 4   Interview handlers do not use templates to define their parameters. However, you can choose to create a new interview handler based on an existing one. When you do this, the new interview handler has all of the attributes of the one that you based it on. To create the interview handler with the same attributes of an existing one, select the **Based on existing Interview Handler** radio button and select the existing interview handler from the **Based on:** drop-down list. If you do not want the new interview handler to copy the attributes of an existing interview handler, select the **New Interview Handler** radio button.

Step 5   Click the **Add** button.

Once the interview handler is created it must be configured. To configure the interview handler's Profile settings, follow the steps for the settings shown in Figure 9-13.

Step 1   From within SA select **Call Management>Interview Handlers**. Click the **Find** icon, enter the search criteria, and click **Find**. Select the desired Interview handler from the list and click the **View** button. Click the **Profile** link on the left side of the screen.

Step 2   The name of the Interview handler is shown in the **Name:** field. The name can be changed in this field if needed.

Step 3   Each Interview handler must have an owner. The current owner is shown in the **Owner:** field. If you want to change the owner, click the **Change** button. A search criteria window displays. Enter criteria and click the **Find** button. A list of subscribers displays. Highlight a subscriber in the list and click the **Select** button.

Step 4   The **Created:** field shows the date and time the Interview handler was created.

Step 5   Using the **Recorded voice:** media master control panel, you can record a name for the interview handler. This is not where you record the greeting. This is only the recorded name of the interview handler.

Figure 9-13 *Call Management>Interview Handlers>Profile*

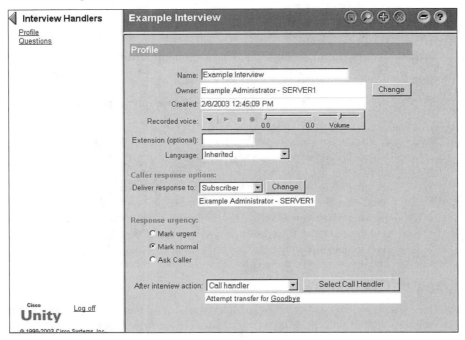

Step 6 In the **Extension (optional):** field, an interview handler may have an extension number assigned to it. Although optional, it can be useful to outside callers. By entering the extension number from the opening greeting, a caller can jump right to this interview handler. Enter the extension number if desired.

Step 7 The **Language** drop-down list is used to set the language in which Unity prompts are played under this Interview handler. If **Inherited** displays in this field, whatever language was used in the previous call handler will continue to be used. Select the desired language from the drop-down list. When in doubt set it to **Inherited**.

Step 8 The responses can be delivered to either a subscriber or a PDL. Select either subscriber or distribution list from the **Deliver response to:** drop-down list. Click the **Change** button. A search criteria window displays. Enter the search criteria and click the **Find** button. Highlight the desired subscriber/PDL from the list and click the **Select** button.

Step 9 You may allow the caller to label a message urgent by selecting the **Ask Caller** radio button under the heading **Response Urgency:**. You may choose to always mark it urgent without asking the caller by selecting the **Mark Urgent** radio button, or not have the message marked urgent by selecting the **Mark Normal** radio button.

Step 10 In the **After interview action:** field, choose the destination to which the call will be sent after the caller has answered all the questions.

Step 11 Click the **Save** icon in the title strip.

Step 12 Next, the questions need to be configured for the Interview handler. Figure 9-14 shows this configuration page. The following steps explain how these settings are configured.

Figure 9-14 *Call Management>Interview Handlers>Questions*

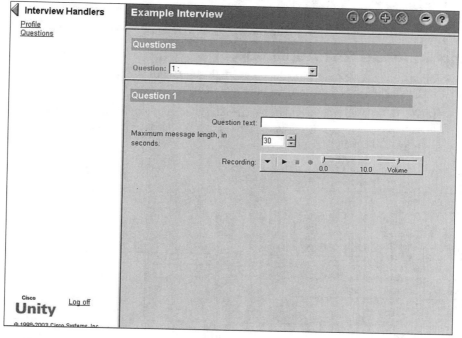

Step 13 From within SA, select **Call Management>Interview Handlers**. Click the **Find** icon, enter the search criteria, and click **Find**. Select the desired Interview handler from the list and click the **View** button. Click the **Questions** link on the left side of the screen.

Step 14 From the **Question:** drop-down list select the number **1**.

Step 15 In the **Question text:** field, type the question that the caller will be asked. This text is just for reference. You still need to record the actual question the caller will hear in Step 5.

Step 16 In the **Maximum message length, in seconds:** field, enter the maximum number of seconds a caller's response can be.

Step 17 Using the **Recording:** media master control panel, record the question.

Note	When recording a question, it is a good idea to notify callers that they may press the pound key (#) when finished with each response. This way the callers don't have to wait for the silence timeout, which sometimes causes issues in noisy environments.

Step 18 Click the **Save** icon in the title strip.

You have now learned how to create each type of object that will be needed for an advanced auto attendant. Now let's review the steps required to build one.

Creating an Audio Text Application

In this section we take a look at an example auto attendant and the steps required to build it. This exercise brings together what you have learned so far in this chapter.

Figure 9-15 shows the flow chart of the advanced auto attendant that we looked at earlier in this chapter. The section starts an exploration of the steps required to build the advanced auto attendant.

Figure 9-15 *Sample Advanced Auto Attendant*

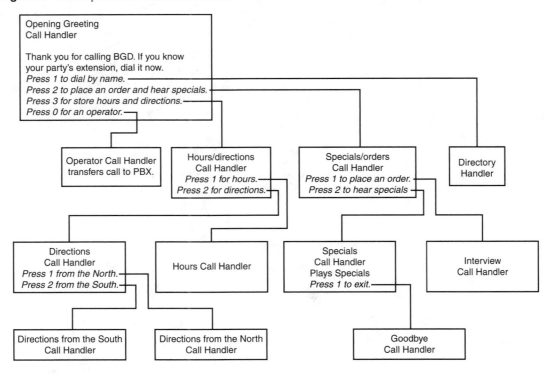

When building an auto attendant, remember that it is best to start at the bottom. Of course, before you start any configuration within SA, you should have the design on paper. In Figure 9-15 you see that there are three call handlers at the lowest level of the menu. One is the Goodbye Call Handler, which is a default call handler, so no configuration is required. The other two are the call handlers that offer directions to a caller. These are standard call handlers, which are created using the steps in the previous section called "Creating Basic Call Routing Systems." These call handlers can be viewed as the last call handlers in the auto attendant. Once these call handlers are created and you make sure the proper greeting has been recorded, you can move up to the next level.

The next level up has four call handlers. Three of them are standard call handlers and the fourth is an interview handler. You can start with any call handler at the same level. We will start with the interview handler. The interview handler is created using the steps found in section "Using Interview Handlers" found earlier in this chapter. Keep in mind that before creating this handler you should have the list of questions created and know to whom the responses are going to be delivered.

Next, let's build the three standard call handlers. They are: the Hours call handler, which states the store hours, the Specials call handler, which plays this week's store specials, and the Directions call handler, which asks from which direction the caller is coming. These call handlers are created just like any standard call handler. Please note that because the Directions and Specials call handlers allow callers to press a single digit to transfer elsewhere, the caller input page must be configured to reflect this.

The next level up has four call handlers. Three of them are standard call handlers, and the third is a directory handler. In this example, there is only one directory handler, so the default can be used. If you need multiple directory handlers, you can use the steps in the previous section titled "Configuring Directory Handlers." The Operator call handler shown in this example is created during the installation process, so it already exists. It does need to be configured the same way it was configured in the "Configuring Auto Attendant" section of this chapter.

The other two call handlers, the Hours/Directions and the Specials/Orders, are standard call handlers and are created the same way the others were created. These call handlers are used to help navigate the caller through the system. Their only real purpose is to prompt the caller for input to determine where the call is transferred.

The top level of the menu is the Opening Greeting. Because an Opening Greeting call handler already exists, just rerecord the greeting and configure the caller input page to link to the call handlers. This is described in the "Configuring Call Handler Caller Input Settings" section of this chapter.

This is a high-level overview of the configuration task required to create an advanced auto attendant. This section, in combination with previous instructions, should have you well on your way to being able to create an auto attendant of which Alexander Graham Bell would be proud.

Remotely Managing Call Handlers

Unity offers the ability to allow owners of call handlers to remotely manage and change the greeting of the call handler. This is a popular feature, and is fairly easy to configure.

First, the call handler being changed remotely must have an assigned extension number. Second, the person capable of making the greeting must be the owner of the call handler. After these two tasks are completed, you need to configure a way for a user to access the remote greeting administrator, known as CUGA.

One of the best ways to do this is to create a call handler that transfers the caller to CUGA. The following steps outline how this can be done.

Step 1 Create a call handler called **CUGA** (or any name you choose).

Step 2 Assign an extension number far outside the range that a normal caller would ever dial. For instance, if the company uses 4 digit extensions in the 3000 range, you could pick 5434632. This should ensure that the number is not dialed by accident. Keep in mind that this extension is only dialed from within Unity, so it does not need to exist in CallManager.

Step 3 On the Call Transfer page, enable the Alternate rule under the **Transfer Rule applies to:** heading and set the **Transfer incoming calls?** to **No, (send directly to this handler's greeting)**.

Step 4 On the greetings page, set the recording source to **Blank**. Set the **After greeting:** action to **Send caller to:** and select Greetings Administrator.

Step 5 Click the **Save** icon in the title strip.

Let the subscribers who are going to need access to CUGA know what the extension of this call handler is. They can then dial the Unity pilot number from any phone and enter this extension. They will be prompted for their ID and PIN, and then they can remotely manage the call handlers they own.

Configuring Call Routing

Often Unity is deployed in an environment that requires multiple opening greetings, for example, when Unity is providing service for multiple departments or locations. This can be accomplished by creating call routing rules. Unity checks each incoming call against the call routing rules. The first rule in the list that matches the criteria of the incoming call is used to route the call. These rules route calls based on the following criteria:

- If the call is internal or external
- The Port the call came in on
- The Trunk the call came in on
- The Dialed Number

- The Calling Number
- The Schedule (time of day)

After looking at this information, the call routing rules determine the language the caller hears and the destination to which the call will be sent.

There are two types of call routing rules: Direct Calls rules and Forwarded Calls rules.

Figure 9-16 shows the configuration page for Direct Calls rules. The following steps show how to create and configure a call routing rule.

Figure 9-16 *Call Management>Call Routing>Direct Calls*

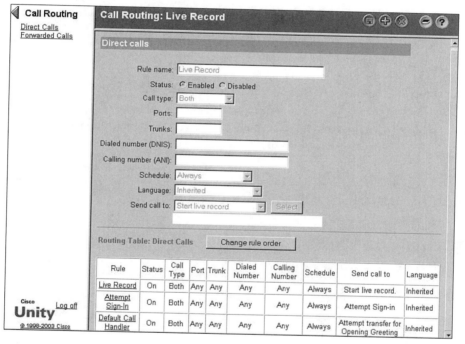

Creating and Configuring a Call Routing Rule

Step 1   From within SA, select **Call Management>Call Routing**.

Step 2   Select either **Direct Calls** or **Forwarded Calls** from the left side of the screen.

Step 3   Click the **Add** icon in the title strip.

Step 4   Enter a name for the new rule.

Step 5   Click the **Add** button.

Note	Because you are adding something new to the database, you do not have to save it. This, however, can cause problems. As soon as you add a rule, it becomes active. The problem is that every call that comes in will match this rule. When a new rule is created, it sends matched calls to the directory handler. Therefore, because every call will match this rule, every call will go to the directory handler until you edit or disable the new rule. As you add a new rule, disable it until it is completely configured and ready for use. With this in mind, it is best to configure these rules off-hours.

Step 6   The name on the rule displays in the **Rule name:** field. It may be edited if needed.

Step 7   To disable the rule, select the **Disabled** radio button. To enable the rule select the **Enabled** radio button.

Note	It is not possible to disable the default rules from this screen.

Step 8   The rule may apply to internal, external, or both types of call. Select the type of call to which the rule should apply from the **Call type:** drop-down list.

Step 9   The port through which a call enters is used to determine if the rule is applied. This could be used in a dual switch environment to limit the rule to affect only calls coming from one of the PBXs. If you want the rule to apply to all calls regardless of the port they came in on, leave the **Ports:** field blank. If you are configuring a forwarded calls rule, this field does not appear.

Step 10   The trunk on which the call came in is also used to determine if the rule will apply. If you want the rule to apply to all calls regardless of the trunk, leave the **Trunks:** field blank. If you are configuring a forwarded calls rule, this field does not appear.

Step 11 By using the dialed number to route a call, you can send calls to a different opening greeting based on the number the caller dialed. This is useful for companies that have multiple departments with different main numbers. Enter the dialed number in the **Dialed number (DNIS):** field. The pattern for the dialed number can contain the digits 0 through 9 and the asterisk (*). The * is a wildcard that matches any digit and any number of digits. For instance, to match any number that begins with 555, you enter 555*. Leave this field blank to have the rule match regardless of the dialed number.

Note	It is important to realize that the wildcards used in Unity differ from those used in CallManager. In Unity an asterisk (*) stands for any digit and any number of digits, whereas in CallManager an exclamation point (!) is the wildcard that matches any digit and any number of digits.

Step 12 Calls can also be routed based on the calling number. You can configure it so that all calls from a certain area code are routed to a specific call handler. The pattern for the calling number can contain the digits 0 through 9 and the *. The * is a wildcard that matches any digit and any number of digits. For instance to match any number that begins with 555, you enter 555*. Enter the calling number pattern in the **Calling number (ANI):** field.

Step 13 The rule will be active during open hours of the schedule assigned to it. Select the desired schedule using the **Schedule:** drop-down list.

Step 14 Using the **Language:** drop-down list, select the language in which Unity prompts will be played for calls that match this rule.

Step 15 Once you have determined the criteria that will match this rule, you must assign a destination for the call. Using the **Send call to:** drop-down list select a destination. The available destinations are the same as those found under caller input for a call handler. They are as follows:

— **Attempt Forward**—Forwards call to an extension of a subscriber

— **Attempt Sign-in**—Sends the call to the login prompt

— **CVM Mailbox Reset**—Allows caller to reset mailbox (available with Community Voice-Mail package)

- **Call Handler**—Sends the call to the selected call handler

- **Caller System Transfer**—Sends callers to a prompt that allows them to enter another extension to which they would like to be transferred.

- **Directory Handler**—Sends call to the directory handler you select

- **Greetings Administrator**—Sends call to a conversation that allows the caller to manage the greetings of call handlers, which they own.

- **Hotel Checked Out**—Used only with Unity's Hospitality and Property Management System

- **Interview Handler**—Sends call to the interview handler you select

- **Sign-in**—Sends call to subscriber sign-in

- **Start Live Record**—Starts recording call in subscriber's mailbox. This feature is not supported on all phone systems.

- **Subscriber**—Sends call to another subscriber's greeting or extension depending upon how it is configured

- **Subscriber System Transfer**—Allows callers to transfer to another extension after they log in with subscriber credentials. They may then transfer to any number their restriction table allows.

When choosing to send the call to a call handler, directory handler, interview handler, or another subscriber, you have to specify the specific handler or subscriber.

NOTE	If a subscriber or call handler is selected, you must also select whether the call should be sent to the greeting or the phone. To send the call to the phone, select **Attempt transfer for** from the **Conversation** drop-down list. To send the call to the greeting, select **Send to greeting for** from the **Conversation** drop-down list.

Step 16 Click the **Save** icon in the title strip.

Step 17 The rule that has just been added displays at the top of the routing table. Because Unity sends the call to the first match in the table, the order in which the rules display is important. Change the order by clicking the **Change rule order** button. The window shown in Figure 9-17 displays.

Figure 9-17 *Direct Calls Rules Reorganization*

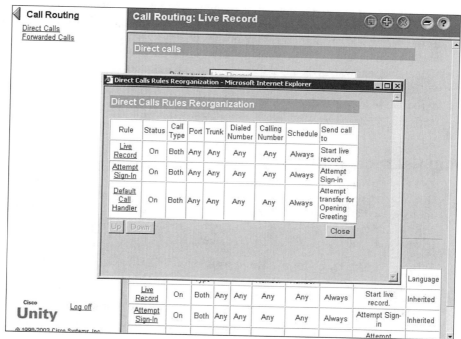

To change the order, click on the name of the rule you wish to move and then click Up or Down to move it to the desired level in the list.

NOTE   You cannot move the last rule in this list using this interface. This last rule should send calls to the opening greeting. Think of this as an "if all else fails" route.

Based on the previous steps, you should now be able to route calls based on incoming call criteria. For instance, if you wanted all calls that entered the system by dialing 5551122 to be sent to a call handler called "BGD greeting," you would create a rule that has 5551122 in the **Dialed number (DNIS):** field and select the call handler named "BGD greeting" in the **Send call to:** field. Using these rules you can configure Unity to handle a number of call routing tasks.

WARNING   A word of caution should be added pertaining to call routing. More than once, I have had students call telling me that during work, suddenly all the calls went straight to the directory handler (or some other unlikely destination). My first question is, "Did you touch the call routing table?" The common answer is, "Well, yes but I didn't save anything." Remember that when you add a rule, it is automatically active. Once the student removed or disabled the rule, everything started working properly again. It is a good idea to add rules during off hours, or at the very least, slow calling times.

Managing Restriction Tables

This chapter focuses mainly on how call handlers can provide call routing and management. One other area of call management needs to be addressed. As you know, Unity has the ability to enable some fairly advanced call routing capabilities at both the call handler level and the subscriber level. This is one of Unity's great strengths, but as with any strength, if exploited it can cause unexpected repercussions.

Subscribers have the ability to have Unity make outbound calls for them for three purposes: message notification, call transfer setting, and fax forwarding. Because Unity is not bound by the same calling rights and restrictions as the caller may have on his phone, the subscriber could configure any of these to dial to locations they are not allowed. This opens up the possibly of unexpected long-distance charges and possible toll fraud.

To prevent this, the CoS to which the subscriber is assigned has a Restriction Table for each of the three types of calls. Let's take a look at how restriction tables are created and configured.

When you look at the default restriction tables, you see that a number of patterns already exist which block various types of calls. Here are two examples: 91???????*, which matches on long distance numbers assuming 9 is an outside line access code; and 9011???????*, which matches international numbers dialed from the US. The following steps show how to create your own restriction tables.

To create a new restriction table, follow these steps.

Step 1   From within SA, select **Call Management>Restriction Tables**.

Step 2   From the title strip, click the **Add** icon.

Step 3   In the **Add a Restriction Table** window enter a name for the new Restriction Table.

Step 4   Restriction tables do not use templates to define their parameters. However, you can choose to create a new restriction table based on an existing one. When you do this, the new restriction table has all the attributes of the one on which you based it. To create the restriction table with the same attributes as an existing one, select the **Based on existing Restriction Table** radio button and select the existing restriction table from the **Based on:** drop-down list. If you do not want the new restriction table to copy the attributes of an existing restriction table, select the **New Restriction Table** radio button.

Step 5   Click the **Add** button.

Figure 9-18 shows the Restriction Tables configuration page. The following steps show how these settings are configured.

Step 1   From within SA, select **Call Management>Restriction Tables**. Click the **Find** icon, enter the search criteria, and click **Find**. Select the desired Restriction Table from the list and click the **View** button.

Step 2   The name of the restriction table is in the **Restriction Table name:** field. The name may be changed here.

Step 3   The **Minimum digits allowed:** field determines the minimum number of digits that must exist in a string in order for this restriction table to apply. If there are fewer digits, the call is not permitted. For example, if this value is set to four, then three-digit numbers would not be permitted.

Figure 9-18   *Call Management>Restriction Tables*

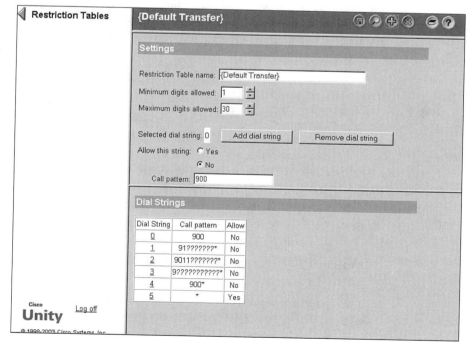

Step 4   The **Maximum digits allowed:** field determines the maximum number of digits that must exist in a string in order for this restriction table to apply. If there are a greater number of digits, the call is restricted.

Step 5   The **Selected dial string:** field identifies which of the dial strings listed in the Dial Strings section of the page is the one being edited. To add a new string, click the **Add dial string** button. To remove the current dial string, click the **Remove dial string** button.

Step 6   A dial string can be blocked or permitted based on the **Allow this string:** selection. If **Yes** is selected, the dial string is permitted, and if **No** is selected, the dial string is blocked.

Step 7   The dial string that you want to allow is entered in the **Call pattern:** field. The pattern that you enter here are similar to the patterns discussed in the CallManager section of this book. The wildcards that are used are the question mark (?), which stands for any single digit and the asterisk (*), which matches any number of digits. For example, the call pattern 50? would match 500, 501, 502, 503, 504, 505, 506, 507, 508 and 509. The call pattern 54* would match any dial string that begins with 54. Enter the call pattern you wish to block or permit.

Step 8   The order of the dial strings is very important. Cisco Unity sequentially compares a phone number to the call pattern in the restriction table, starting with Dial String 0. If the number does not match this string, it is compared to the next string. When a match is found, Unity either permits or restricts the number depending on how the string is configured. Once the pattern is entered and configured, click the **Save** icon in the title strip.

Step 9   Remember, that for these restriction tables to be active, they must be assigned in the subscriber's CoS. To assign a restriction table to a CoS, navigate to **Subscribers>Class of Service** and find the CoS for which you want to configure restrictions tables. Click **Restriction Tables** from the list on the left side of the screen. Now simply assign the desired restriction table to each of the three types of calls. The following is a list of the three types of calls Unity may place on behalf of a subscriber.

— **Outcalling**—Restricts numbers that Unity will allow for message delivery

— **Transfers**—Restricts numbers that Unity will allow for call transfer settings

— **Fax**—Restricts numbers that Unity will allow for fax dial strings

Summary

In this chapter you learned how to create both basic and advanced auto attendant systems. The three types of call handlers discussed in this chapter were the Standard Call Handler, the Directory Call Handler, and the Interview Call Handler. At this point you should be comfortable with creating and configuring these three types of call handlers and using them to create an auto attendant.

In addition, this chapter discussed the steps necessary to implement call routing and restrictions tables. Using these features you are now able to route calls based on incoming call criteria and prevent Unity from sending calls to destinations that have been blocked.

CHAPTER 10

Implementing Unity Networking

Some companies need to connect Unity with their existing voice-mail system. This is a common request during a migration period. Often customers choose to test the new system by deploying a pilot group of users. These users still need to be able to send and forward voice mail to users on the existing voice-mail server. This is where Unity networking comes in. Unity networking gives companies the ability to nearly seamlessly integrate Unity with an existing voice-mail server. Not only does Unity networking allow you to connect with a traditional voice-mail server, it also allows multiple Unity servers to be connected together and act as a single system.

This chapter discusses the various components of Unity networking and explores the types of networking that are available. Throughout this chapter you will become familiar with the features that Unity networking offers, and by the end, you will be able to determine the proper type of networking needed within a given environment.

Unity Networking Overview

Unity networking is a rather broad term that is easily misunderstood. The term networking can mean anything from connecting a few PCs together to the art of making contacts with other professional people. Because the word networking has taken on many meanings in today's world, it is understandable that assumptions about its meaning are sometimes incorrect. In short, Unity networking is the ability to interconnect a Unity server with another voice-mail system. That, of course, is the short answer. Networking allows connections with other voice-mail systems and creation of an environment that allows the two systems to appear to be functioning as one.

Just as there are multiple ways to integrate Unity with a PBX, there are multiple ways to network. When integrating Unity with a PBX, the method used is dictated by the PBX. When networking, the same is true. There are basically five different types of networking. The type of networking that should be used is determined by capabilities of the voice-mail system with which you are networking. The following list briefly describes the different types of networking.

- Digital

  Digital Networking allows you to network multiple Unity systems that share a single directory.

- SMTP

  Simple Mail Transfer Protocol (SMTP) networking allows you to connect Unity with other Unity systems that do not share a common directory but do have some type of IP connectivity.

- AMIS

  Audio Messaging Interchange Specification (AMIS) allows Unity to be connected to a non-Unity voice-mail system across analog lines.

- VPIM

  Voice Profile for Internet Mail (VPIM) allows Unity to be connected to a non-Unity voice-mail system across the Internet or a private IP network.

- Bridge

  Bridge networking allows Unity to be connected to an Octel voice-mail system. The bridge solution is unique in that it requires an additional server to act as the bridge server.

Each of these types of networking requires specific configuration procedures that are typically completed by an integrator. It is not possible to go over these procedures step-by-step in a book of this focus. However, the following sections explain in more detail each type of networking and its various required components.

Networking Components

Although the configuration tasks for each type of networking are specific to the type of system to which Unity is connecting, they all share various components. This section provides an overview of the components that are found in each type. Each component is discussed in more detail in the individual networking sections.

Locations

Locations are objects that are stored in SQL and Active Directories (AD). By default each Unity server has a primary location to which subscribers of that server belong as members. The location information is used to determine how to route the voice mail. Delivery locations can also be created that contain information about other voice-mail servers to which Unity is networked. The information contained within the location includes server's domain name or phone number, the location Dial ID, search options, the recorded name, and addressing options. If a message is sent to a subscriber who belongs to a delivery location, Unity uses the location information to determine how to route the call. The simplest way to think of a location is as an object that defines the route Unity will use to connect to other servers.

Message Addressing

Messages can be addressed using blind addressing, by creating external network subscribers, or by using a combination of the two methods. When blind addressing is used, subscribers on networked systems cannot be searched from a directory handler. In this case, the only way that a message can be addressed to a user on a networked voice-mail server is if the sender knows both the user's extension and the Dial ID of the delivery location associated with the networked server.

Network Subscribers

If you want users on a networked voice-mail server to be listed in the Unity directory, a network subscriber must be created for each user. Network subscribers have no real access to Unity. Network subscribers do not have mailboxes within the Unity system; their mailboxes reside in the voice-mail server to which Unity is networked. Each type of networking has its own type of subscriber as discussed later.

NOTE   Network subscribers do not need to be created when Unity servers are networked together using Digital Networking.

Voice Connector

The Voice Connector (VC) is used to ensure that a voice-mail message is formatted properly so that when it reaches the other voice-mail system, it is recognized as voice mail. In some cases, without the use of VC, messages are delivered but cannot be recognized as voice mail. In other cases, messages fail to be delivered at all. The VC is installed on the Exchange server and is used whenever a voice mail is sent to or received from another voice-mail system.

Schema Extensions

The schema of the Active Directory, of which Unity is a part, must be extended in order to add networking-specific attributes when using Exchange 2000 or Exchange 2003. Although the schema is extended before Unity is loaded, the networking-specific attributes may not be added. When running the schema extension utility, you must choose which type of networking to use. If Digital or AMIS networking is used, the core schema extensions that were created before Unity was installed will be adequate. If Bridge or VPIM networking is used, the schema may need to be extended further.

Although the previously mentioned components play a part in Unity networking, the manner in which these components are implemented depends on which type of networking is deployed. The next two sections break Unity networking into two broad categories. These are Unity-to-Unity Networking and Unity-to-Legacy (traditional) Voice-Mail Networking.

Unity-to-Unity Networking Overview

Companies that have multiple Unity servers may need or want to network the Unity servers together. There are multiple benefits to this. These benefits offer both the subscriber and the outside caller additional functionality. Subscribers will now be able to easily send, forward, and reply to messages from subscribers on other Unity servers. Networking also offers the ability to add subscribers on a different Unity server to local distribution and private lists. Depending on how the search options are configured, the outside caller may be able to search for subscribers who are on other Unity servers.

Unity-to-Unity networking is accomplished by using either Digital Networking or SMTP networking. The type of networking is determined by whether the Unity systems share the same directory or not.

If the Unity servers share the same directory, Digital Networking should be used. Because the Unity servers share the same directory, it is easy to have these systems communicate and determine the delivery location of subscribers. Digital Networking is considered a standard feature. That is, it is included as a feature starting with the base voice-mail system.

If the Unity servers do not share the same directory, SMTP networking must be used. SMTP networking is based on the same principles and concepts that are used to deliver e-mail all over the world. Because the Unity systems do not share a common directory, this type of networking requires more work on behalf of the administrator to make the system function as seamlessly as possible.

NOTE There are plans to remove the support for SMTP networking in versions beyond Unity 4.04. When support for SMTP is removed VPIM will be used to provide the same functionality.

Unity-to-Legacy Voice-Mail Networking Overview

In a perfect world there would be only one voice-mail solution, and that solution would be Unity. That statement might be considered slightly biased, but the idea of there being only one type of voice-mail system would make connecting systems together easier. But we do not live in a homogeneous world, so we must create ways to allow dissimilar systems to communicate with one another. The technology that is deployed to allow Unity systems to communicate with non-Unity voice-mail systems is based on standards that have been used to connect voice-mail systems together for years.

Typically, three types of networking are used to connect Unity and non-Unity systems. They are VPIM, AMIS, and Bridge. Each is described in greater detail in the following sections, but a brief description of each follows:

- VPIM

    Allows messaging between Cisco Unity and other voice messaging systems using some type of IP connection. The other voice messaging system must support VPIM version 2 protocol. Messages are sent over an IP network using the VPIM messaging format.

- AMIS

  Allows messaging between Cisco Unity and other voice messaging systems over an analog connection. The other voice-mail system must support AMIS, which is an industry-standard protocol.

- Bridge

  Bridge networking allows messaging between Cisco Unity and Octel systems. This solution requires an additional server known as a bridge server. Messaging between Cisco Unity and the Bridge is done by using a digital protocol that is based on the VPIM protocol and is sent over an IP connection. Messaging between the Octel servers and the Bridge is done by using the Octel analog networking protocol. Cisco Unity and the Octel systems maintain separate voice-mail directories.

Now that you have a basic understanding of the different types of networking and when each is used, you can better understand the next section, which takes a closer look at each type and explains how the networking components are used.

Unity Networking Configuration

Most tasks discussed so far are considered administrative. However, the implementation of Unity networking can prove to be very involved and should only be attempted by someone with a solid understanding of Unity, and the remote voice-mail system with which Unity will be integrated. Explaining the specific integration steps for each type of networking is outside of the scope of this book, however, it is important that you understand each type of networking so you can properly manage a networked system.

The following sections will help you become familiar with the specific components and requirements of each type of networking. We will start by looking at networking Unity to other Unity systems.

Defining Digital Networking

Cisco Unity Digital Networking is the feature that allows subscribers associated with one Cisco Unity server to exchange voice messages with subscribers associated with other Cisco Unity servers. One requirement of Digital Networking is that all Cisco Unity servers connected to a network share a single, global directory.

Digital Networking also allows calls to be transferred from the automated attendant or directory assistance to subscribers who are associated with the other Unity server.

Subscriber information is stored in SQL on the Unity server with which the subscriber is associated. Some of this information is replicated to the global directory. This information includes things such as distribution lists, locations, and certain subscriber information. Because this information is stored in the directory, the other Unity servers have access to it, which provides the means for Digital Networking. A process running on each Unity server scans the directory for information that relates to other Unity servers and adds it to its database. This allows subscribers on one Unity server to address messages to subscribers on the other Unity server.

The directory in which Cisco Unity stores data is specified when Cisco Unity is set up. When integrating with Dominos, you specify through which Dominos server Unity (the partner Dominos server) communicates to the other servers. When using exchange, each server is part of the same directory, which allows this information to be shared.

Now that you have a basic understanding of what Digital Networking provides, take a closer look at the components required. The setup of Digital Networking is rather easy. You must first verify that your environment meets the minimum requirements for Digital Networking that are outlined in the following list:

- Dominos Requirements

    — Partner Dominos servers must be in the same notes domain.

    — All Unity servers must monitor the primary Domino directory for the domain names.nsf.

- Exchange Requirements (one of the following conditions must be met)

    — All Unity servers must be in the same Exchange 2000 or Exchange 2003 organization.

    — All unity servers must be in the same Exchange 5.5 organization.

    — Site connectors and Directory replication must be configured for all Exchange 5.5 servers that are not in the same site.

- General Requirements

    — All Unity servers must be version 3.1(2) or later.

    — When using Exchange in a mixed mode environment, all Unity partner servers must be Exchange 2000 or Exchange 2003.

    — No additional license is required for Digital Networking.

Once you have confirmed that the preceding requirements have been met, very little further configuration is required. However, before moving forward, you need to have a good understanding of your existing dial plan and that of any other Unity server with which you plan to network.

Because Digital Networking allows multiple Unity servers to share the same directories, overlapping extensions can cause problems. By fully examining existing dial plans, you can avoid these problems. Because all extensions within a Unity system must be unique, a component known as dialing domains can be implemented to allow environments with overlapping extensions to participate in Digital Networking. An example is shown in Figure 10-1.

Figure 10-1 *Dialing Domains*

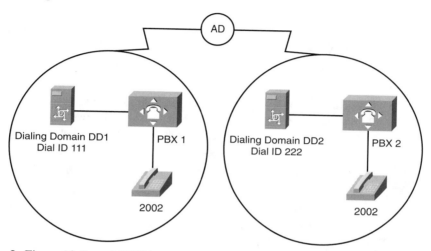

In Figure 10-2, each PBX has a phone with the extension of 2002 attached. Unity searches its local server first and allows the subscriber attached to the local PBX to be reached by subscribers on that server. Hence, if a caller wishes to reach the 2002 on the other PBX dials 2002, Unity sends the call to the 2002 in its local directory, which is not what is desired. By putting each Unity server in its own dialing domain and assigning unique dial IDs, a caller could reach the 2002 in the other dialing domain by preceding the extension number with the dial ID. In this example, if a caller on Unity 1 wishes to reach the extension 2002 on Unity 2, she dials 2222002, which is the dial ID of dialing domain 2 followed by the extension number of 2002. In this example, dialing domains can be used to limit the search when overlapping extensions exist. Dialing domains can also be used to enlarge the search capabilities of Unity. How to broaden Unity searches is described next.

Figure 10-2 *Dialing Domain Example*

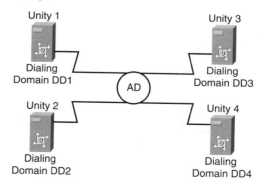

Because Digital Networking allows subscribers from one Unity server to be searched from another Unity server's auto attendant, you must decide how broad you will allow these searches to be. There are three choices when determining how broad the search may be. The available search parameters are as follows:

- This Server

  This limits the directory search to the subscribers associated with the server itself.

- Dialing Domain

  Dialing domains are used to expand the directory search to include other Unity servers. When choosing this type of search, Unity first searches its local directory. If no match is found in the local directory, the search expands to other servers in the same dialing domain as the local server.

- Global Catalog (referred to in the pull-down list as Global Directory)

  This search option allows all servers that are part of the global directory to be searched. Unity begins by searching the local server, then expands to the dialing domain (if one exists), and finally searches all other servers in the Global Address List (GAL).

The searching parameters are defined in the primary location of the Unity server. Each Unity server has a Primary location that is created during the installation and cannot be deleted. This location can and should be modified when networking is implemented.

A Primary Location consists of two areas. The first is the profile. Within the profile the following are defined:

- Display Name

  This is the name of the location. By default the name of the default location is default. It is recommended that you change this name to represent the physical location of this server. For instance, if the server is located in Detroit, you might name the location DTW (Detroit airport code).

- Dial ID

  A Dial ID is used to differentiate between locations. Each location must have a unique ID. It is recommended that the fixed length IDs be used throughout the network for Dial IDs. Dial IDs must also be unique. Make certain that the Dial IDs do not overlap with existing extensions.

- Recorded Name

  A name that represents the location must be recorded here. For instance, if the location is named Detroit, record the name Detroit in this field. Subscribers will hear this name when they dial by name and match the location.

- Dialing Domain

  In the example in Figure 10-1, you see how dialing domains are used to address overlapping extension issues. Dialing domains are also used to increase Unity searches to other servers while still preventing all servers from being searched. Figure 10-2 shows an environment with four Unity servers. All these servers belong to the same AD. Applying the same dialing domain to servers 1 and 2, limits Unity's search to these two servers when a search is initiated by a call on either of these systems.

  Dialing domains are created based on dial plans that exist within the telephony infrastructure. If a particular company has many PBXs interconnected to one another via trunking, they may all have one dial plan and thus need only one dialing domain. However, there are times when multiple dialing domains may be needed. It is best to start with one dialing domain and then expand from there if needed.

- SMTP Information

  This field is required for SMTP and VPIM networking and is discussed in those sections.

The second area is the Addressing Options. In this area you configure where the Unity searches for matches. Two types of searches must be configured:

- Subscriber Searches

  This parameter defines where Unity searches when a subscriber addresses a message from a phone. It also defines the search parameter used when adding subscribers to a public or private distribution list.

- Blind Addressing

  Blind addressing allows a subscriber to send a message to another subscriber by entering the Dial ID of the delivery location and the other subscriber's extension. For instance, if another subscriber location Dial ID is 222 and their extension is 2002 then the subscriber sending the message enters 2222002 from the telephone to address the message. The **Blind Addressing Allowed locations:** field determines where Unity will search for valid IDs when addressing messages using blind addressing.

Figures 10-3 and 10-4 show the location configuration screens within SA.

Once primary locations are configured on each server, Digital Networking for all intents and purposes is functioning. For Digital Networking to work, not only must the primary location be configured, but the server must know about all its delivery locations. When implementing Digital Networking, there is no need to configure the delivery locations as location information is stored in AD; the other server's primary location is learned and added as a delivery location. If you look at the Delivery locations defined on the Unity server, you see that the locations created on all of the Unity servers within the common directory are present. When primary location information is changed, it can take up to 15 minutes for this information to replicate to the other servers.

Figure 10-3 *Network>Primary Location>Profile*

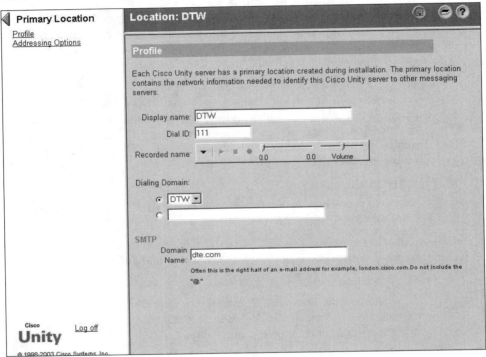

Now that you understand the components required for Digital Networking, let's explore the example shown in Figure 10-5.

In this example, four Unity servers are running Exchange on-box. They all belong to the same AD forest, Unity 1 and 2 service subscribers on PBX 1, and Unity 3 and 4 service subscribers on PBX 2. Overlapping extensions exist on the PBXs. To allow Digital Networking to work, the following needs to be configured.

Configure the primary location on each Unity server, making sure the following requirements are met:

- Each has a Display name that represents its geographical location.
- Each has a unique Dial ID that does not overlap with existing extensions.

In order to deal with the overlapping extensions, make certain that Unity 1 and 2 are in the same dial domain and that Unity 3 and 4 are in the same dialing domain. For instance, Unity 1 and 2 may be in a dialing domain called UNDOM12, and Unity 3 and 4 may be in a dialing domain called UNDOM34.

Figure 10-4 *Network>Primary Location>Addressing Options*

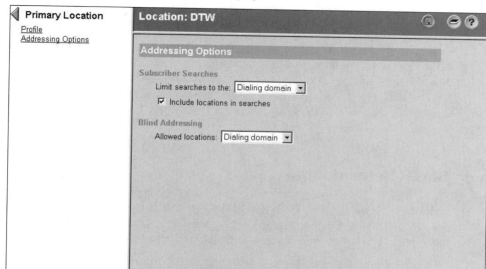

Figure 10-5 *Digital Networking Overview*

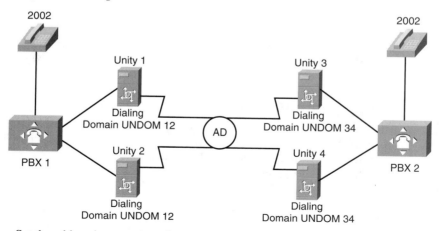

Set the addressing search options to be the dialing domain for both Subscriber Searches and Blind Addressing.

The above configuration allows subscribers to search for other subscribers that are on the same PBX from a directory handler. They may also address messages to subscribers on the other PBX by entering the Location Dial ID of the other Unity server followed by the extension number.

This section examined the requirements for networking Unity together with other Unity servers using Digital Networking. Digital Networking requires all Unity servers to be part of the same directory. Other means of networking are required to network Unity servers that do not share a common directory. The next section explores how this is accomplished using SMTP Networking. For more information on SMTP networking, refer to the SMTP networking section in Cisco's Networking in Cisco Unity Guide, found at Cisco.com by searching "SMTP Networking."

Defining SMTP Networking

SMTP networking allows subscribers on one Unity server to send and receive messages with subscribers on another Unity server that is connected via an IP network. This differs from Digital Networking in that the Unity servers are not part of the same AD forest. The following is a list of environments in which SMTP networking is the proper solution:

- Each Unity/Exchange server is in a separate AD forest.
- Exchange 5.5 is used and each server is in a different organization.

NOTE   As of Unity 4.04 SMTP networking works only with Exchange. Digital Networking is the only supported type of networking in environments where Notes is the mailstore. In future versions of Unity, the networking options for Notes may be expanded.

Another feature of SMTP networking allows subscribers and callers to leave voice-mail messages for individuals who do not have a mailbox on any connected Exchange server. This is accomplished by creating Internet Subscribers. This concept is discussed later in this section.

SMTP Networking Components

The components that make up SMTP networking are similar to those required when implementing Digital Networking. Locations need to be configured and addressing options must be chosen. In addition to these, a component called a Voice Connector must be configured. The following sections explore each of the required components.

SMTP Connectivity

Since SMTP is the transport used to send messages between Unity servers, you must make sure that SMTP is correctly configured on the Exchange bridgehead server. This task must be done by the Exchange engineer. If your organization is currently using Exchange to send e-mail across the Internet, this is most likely already functioning properly.

Voice Connector

When sending a voice message across SMTP, the Unity attributes can be stripped, which results in the message arriving at the other side simply as an e-mail message with a WAV attachment. This poses a problem because the arrival of the message will not cause an Message Waiting Indicator (MWI) to activate, and the subscriber will not be able to retrieve the message from the phone. A component called the Voice Connector is used to resolve this issue. The Voice Connector is installed on the Exchange Bridgehead server and is registered to handle all messages with the VOICE address type. The Voice Connector allows the message to be safely transported to the other Exchange server with all Unity attributes intact. The Voice Connector must also be loaded on the remote Exchange server.

Locations

As with Digital Networking, the Primary location is used to define Dial IDs and search options. In addition, the Primary Location also includes the SMTP domain name of the server. This information is not needed for Digital Networking.

In addition to Primary locations, Delivery location must also be configured. In Digital Networking these locations are automatically learned since all Unity servers use the same directory; this is not the case in SMTP Networking so you must manually create a Delivery location for each remote Unity server.

Addressing Options

When a subscriber addresses a message to a subscriber on the remote Unity server, two types of addressing are used: Subscriber Searches and Blind Addressing. With the first type, Subscriber Searches, the subscriber can simply dial by name. For this to work, however, an Internet subscriber must be configured for each subscriber on all remote Unity servers. Configuration of Internet Subscribers is discussed next. The second type, Blind Addressing, allows a subscriber to send a message to another subscriber on a remote Unity server by entering the Dial ID of the delivery location and the other subscriber's extension. For instance, if the other subscriber's location Dial ID is 222 and the extension is 2002, the subscriber sending the message enters 2222002 to address the message. This option requires less administrative work. Keep in mind that Unity does not check to see if the remote extension is valid or to whom it belongs. This can cause subscribers to accidentally misaddress messages.

Internet Subscriber

Internet Subscribers can be used for a number of purposes. The most common use is to allow subscribers of a remote Unity server to appear in the directory when using SMTP networking. Because all Unity servers within an SMTP networking environment do not share a common directory, only the subscribers associated with the local Unity server are searchable. If an Internet Subscriber is created for each remote Unity subscriber, subscribers of a remote Unity server can appear in the local directory.

Internet subscribers can also be used to allow individuals who are not subscribers on any Unity server to appear in the directory and receive voice mail. How can this be, if they don't have a mailbox? When an Internet subscriber is created for them, their SMTP e-mail address is entered. This can be any normal e-mail address. When a message is left for them, it is routed to their e-mail server, and they receive it as an e-mail with a WAV attachment. They can then play the message using most any media player.

Another common use for an Internet subscriber is to allow a phone that does not have a voice-mail account to appear in the directory, so that callers may search for the phone from within a directory handler. When used in this fashion, the Internet subscriber account setting is configured so that a message cannot be left if the phone goes unanswered.

Now that the components of SMTP networking have been discussed, let's examine a high-level overview of how the components work together. Figure 10-6 shows a simple SMTP networking solution.

Figure 10-6 *Dialing Domains*

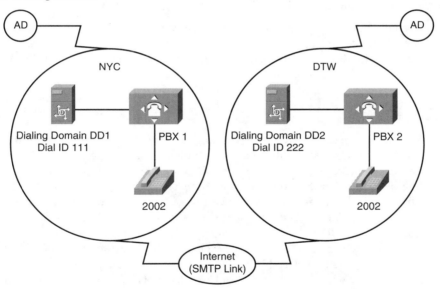

This figure shows two locations with a Unity server, each in its own AD. Each location is connected to the Internet. In order to allow the subscribers in DTW to send voice messages to subscribers in NYC, the following is required:

- SMTP connectivity between both sites must be verified.
- Primary location on each Unity server must be configured.
- Delivery locations for each remote Unity server must be configured on each Unity server.

- VC is loaded on the Exchange Bridgehead server at both sites.
- Internet subscribers must be configured if the remote subscribers are to be listed in the directory.

Table 10-1 shows sample location information for each Unity server.

Table 10-1   *Unity Server Location Information*

DTW	Primary	Remote
Name	Detroit	New York
Dial ID	222	111
Dialing Domain	None	None
SMTP Domain	Detroit.com	New_York.com
NYC	**Primary**	**Remote**
Name	New York	Detroit
Dial ID	111	222
Dialing Domain	None	None
SMTP Domain	New_York.com	Detroit.com

The goal of this chapter is to provide you with a solid overview of the concepts and components that are used with Unity Networking. As you have noticed, step-by-step instructions are not included, as the tasks required to accomplish Unity networking are outside the scope of this text. However, because Internet Subscribers may be used even if networking is not deployed, the steps required to create them need to be addressed. The following section provides step-by-step instructions on how to create Internet Subscribers.

There are two ways to create Internet Subscribers. The first is to import them from a Comma Separated Value (CSV) file. The steps for importing them are very similar to those used when importing Exchange subscribers from a CSV file. The second way to create Internet Subscribers is to manually add them one at a time from within UA. This is the method that is described here.

Step 1   From within SA select **Subscribers>Subscribers**.

Step 2   Click the **add** icon (plus sign) in the title strip.

Step 3   A window such as that in Figure 10-7 displays. Select the **New Subscriber:** radio button and select **Internet** from the drop-down menu to the right of the label.

Step 4   Enter the first and last name of the new subscriber in the fields labeled as such. The display name will be automatically generated. This is the name that is displayed within SA. If needed, this can be edited.

Figure 10-7 *Add Subscriber Window*

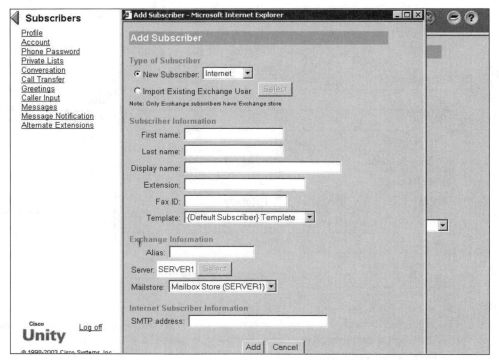

Step 5 An extension number is an optional setting for Internet subscribers. However, if an extension number is not entered, the subscriber will not be listed in the directory. Enter the subscriber extension number in the **Extension:** field. All extensions in Unity must be unique, that is, each extension can be assigned only to one subscriber.

Step 6 In the **Fax ID:** field, enter the number that a caller dials to send a fax to this subscriber. This information is not required.

Step 7 Select the subscriber template that will be used during the creation of this subscriber from the **Template:** drop-down list.

Step 8 The Exchange alias is automatically populated but can be edited if needed.

Step 9 If more than one mailstore is available, select the desired mailstore from the **Mailstore:** drop-down list.

Step 10 In the **SMTP address:** field enter the e-mail address to which the voice-mail message will be delivered.

Step 11 Click the **Add** button.

Step 12 You are informed that the information is being processed. This may take up to 15 seconds. During this time an account is being created. The

Unity-specific information is being added to the SQL database. Once the user is created, you are returned to the subscriber profile screen of the newly created subscriber.

Now that you understand the concepts and components needed to network Unity systems with other Unity systems, next you learn the concepts and components that allow Unity to network with non-Unity voice-mail systems.

Unity to Non-Unity Networking Concepts

Unity has the ability to connect to other voice-mail systems, which allows subscribers to send messages to users on the other systems. The exact features available within a networked solution vary, based on the type of networking that is deployed. The goal of this section is to introduce you to the three types of networking that are used to connect Unity to other voice-mail systems: AMIS, VPIM, and Bridge Networking.

The required networking tasks are quite involved. They should only be attempted by an individual who is trained on Unity networking tasks and has experience and a solid understanding of the other voice-mail system to which Unity will be networked. It is best to leave this to someone who has proven experience in this area. If you are up to this task, you need to refer to the networking integration guides available on Cisco.com, as this section does not describe the actual integration process, only concepts.

Defining AMIS Networking

AMIS networking allows Unity to network with non-Unity voice-mail systems that also support AMIS. As with all types of networking, the goal is to allow users on both systems to exchange voice mails with one another as if they were using the same system.

AMIS networking is a licensed Unity feature that must be purchased from Cisco. In most cases the other voice-mail system will also require a license, which is purchased from that voice-mail system's manufacturer.

Unity sends the messages to the other voice-mail servers via analog lines. To do this, Unity must have analog lines at its disposal. In most cases, a voice board is installed in the Unity server. The voice board has a number of analog ports (normally 4 or 12) and these ports are used to send messages to the other voice-mail system.

Because the messages are sent via analog lines the transmission speed of these messages is not very fast. In short, it will take the message duration time, plus setup and tear down time to transmit the message. If sending a single message to multiple recipients, the time it takes to deliver each message is multiplied. For example, if you wish to send a two-minute message to five people, it will take at least 10 minutes to deliver the messages.

In order to implement AMIS networking, a few components must be configured in Unity. This section provides a high-level overview of these components.

A mailbox called UAMIS must be created in the Exchange server. This mailbox is used to store all messages sent to and from the remote voice-mail system while they are being processed and waiting delivery. Because the transmission mechanism is not that efficient, it is possible the messages may queue up in this mailbox for some time. Therefore, you need to make sure the storage limits for this mailbox are adequate to accommodate a large number of queued messages. Be sure to review this mailbox's limits and increase them as needed. If this mailbox becomes full, it will cause inbound and outbound AMIS messages to fail.

The ports used to deliver AMIS messages must be configured. It is possible to use more than one port for message transport functions. You can also configure schedules that will allow AMIS message delivery to occur only at certain times of the day. This leaves the ports available for other functions if required.

The Voice Connector must be installed on the Exchange server. The Voice Connector is used to format the outbound message and deliver it to the UAMIS mailbox.

The primary location and delivery locations must be configured. A delivery location must be configured for each remote system. The delivery location will include the remote systems AMIS Node ID and the delivery phone number.

If you want the remote system user to appear in Unity's directory, you must create AMIS subscribers. These subscribers are contacts in AD. Because they do not have a mailbox on the Unity system, these subscribers have virtually no direct access to the Unity system.

When an AMIS subscriber is created, a special e-mail address is associated with that subscriber. This address contains the information that Unity needs to determine where the message is to be delivered. Because this address is associated with the Dial ID of the location to which the subscriber belongs, it is necessary to update this information if the Dial ID is changed. A utility called the Extension Address Utility can be run, which will update this information.

This section provided you with a brief overview of the components required to implement AMIS networking. However, only the Unity side of the configuration was discussed. The remote side also needs to be configured. Make sure only a qualified engineer performs this implementation. For additional information on AMIS networking, refer to the AMIS sections of the *Networking in Cisco Unity Guide* that is found on Cisco.com along with a number of other excellent AMIS documents.

Defining VPIM Networking

VPIM Networking allows Unity to send and receive messages from a non-Unity voice-mail server via an IP connection. The goal of this networking is the same as any type of Unity Networking, to allow users on both systems to easily exchange voice-mails.

VPIM is an industry standard protocol that allows for the exchange of voice, fax, and text messages between voice messaging systems over an IP network. This protocol is based on the SMTP and Multi-Purpose Internet Mail Extension (MIME) protocols.

Once VPIM networking is implemented, companies can send, receive, forward, and reply to messages between different systems. Because VPIM uses SMTP as its transport, it is not susceptible to the delays that are often associated with AMIS Networking. There is a possibility that transport costs may be less than those of AMIS, as toll charges may not be incurred.

The VPIM specification defines how the messages are transferred and the required format of the messages. VPIM is a Unity-licensed feature that must be purchased from Cisco. Remember that the remote voice-mail system may also require licensing for VPIM. This must be purchased from the manufacturer of that voice-mail system.

As with any type of networking, a number of components must be configured when implementing VPIM. The following is an overview of the required components.

Because VPIM uses SMTP as its transport mechanism, connectivity to an SMTP server must be configured. This means the Exchange server used with Unity must be able to send and receive e-mail to and from the mail server of the remote voice-mail system.

The AD schema must be extended to allow for specific VPIM attributes. The schema is extended during the installation on Unity but if the VPIM option was not selected (it is not by default), then the required attributes do not exist. In this case, the schema extension utility must be run again with the VPIM option selected. As of Unity 4.04, VPIM is only supported with Exchange 2000 and Exchange 2003.

The Voice Connector must be installed. It handles all VPIM messages. The Voice Connector is responsible for properly formatting the message so it can be delivered to the other system. To do this, it transforms outbound messages from Messaging Application Programming Interface (MAPI) (Exchange's native format) to MIME. VPIM checks the delivery location to determine if it must convert that message to G.726 and does so if needed. The Voice Connector also handles inbound messages by converting them from MIME to MAPI.

You must configure the Primary location and create delivery locations. A delivery location must be configured for each remote system. The delivery location includes the SMTP domain name of the remote system. If multiple Unity servers exist within the same AD forest, delivery locations only need to be configured on one Unity system. The search options must also be configured with the location.

If you want the user on the remote system to appear in Unity's directory, you must create VPIM subscribers. These subscribers will be contacts in AD. Because they do not have a mailbox on the Unity system, they have virtually no direct access to the Unity system.

When a VPIM subscriber is created, a special e-mail address is associated with that subscriber, as with AMIS subscribers. This address contains the information that Unity needs to determine where the message is delivered. Because this address is associated to the Dial ID of the location to which the subscriber belongs, it is necessary to update this information if the Dial ID is changed. To update this information, run a utility called the Extension Address Utility.

In addition to the configuration of these components, the remote system must be configured for VPIM. It is recommended that only a qualified engineer perform this type of networking. For additional information on the VPIM protocol, check out http://www.ema.org/vpim. There are also a number of VPIM networking documents on Cisco.com.

Defining Bridge Networking

Bridge networking is used to connect Unity to Octel voice-mail systems. This solution is unique, but the overall goal is the same: to provide a way for users on both systems to easily and effectively utilize all the features of each system.

Bridge networking is unique because it is the only type of networking that requires an additional server. The server, referred to as a Bridge server, is a gateway between Unity and Octel. This solution uses two protocols to accomplish its job. A Digital Networking protocol based on VPIM with proprietary extension is used to communicate between Unity and the Bridge server. Octel's Analog networking protocol is used to communicate between the Bridge server and the Octel system.

Figure 10-8 shows an overview of how the Bridge server is connected to the voice-mail systems. The connectivity used between the Unity's Exchange server and the Bridge is IP, so an Ethernet connection is required on the Bridge server. The Octel system communicates with the Bridge server via analog lines that are connected to the PBX. A Brooktrout voice board must be installed in the Bridge server for this connectivity.

As with the other types of networking mentioned in this section, Bridge networking is a licensed feature of Unity. If multiple Unity systems networked together are required to network with an Octel system, a single Unity server is used to communicate with the Bridge server. In addition to requiring licensing on Unity, the Octel server must be licensed for Octel's analog networking.

For Bridge networking to work, certain components must be configured on the Unity system. Let's look at the required components.

As with VPIM networking, the AD schema must be extended. This is done by running a schema extension utility that is included with Unity. This is the same utility used when Unity was first installed, but this time the Bridge networking option must be chosen.

The Voice Connector must be installed. The Voice Connector is used to transform the out-bound messages to VPIM and handle inbound VPIM messages.

A mailbox called UOmni must be created on the Exchange server. Unlike the UAMIS mailbox, this mailbox is not used to queue messages but to handle administrative messages that are received from the Bridge server.

Locations must be configured. The primary location must be customized and delivery locations created for each Octel system with which Unity will be communicating. Delivery locations need to be created only on the Unity server that communicates with the Bridge server. Search options must also be defined within the location.

Figure 10-8 *Bridge Server*

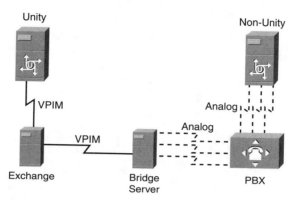

If you wish to have users who have mailboxes on the Octel system to appear in the directory of Unity, Bridge subscribers must be created for each of these users. Subscribers are created in three different ways. They can be manually created on the Unity server, created on the Bridge server, or they can automatically be created using usage-based NameNet emulation. Because Bridge subscribers do not have a mailbox on the Exchange server and are only contacts in AD, they have no access to the Unity server.

This section has outlined the components required for Bridge networking and provided a summary of its application. For more information, you are encouraged to read the various Unity Bridge release notes and installation guides found on Cisco.com.

Summary

This chapter explored the various types of networking Unity can use to connect with other voice-mail systems. Unity can easily integrate with other Unity systems that share the same directory by implementing Digital Networking. The SMTP networking section explained how Unity is configured to connect other Unity systems that do not share a common directory. This chapter also explored the three types of networking used to connect Unity to non-Unity systems. Now that you have a high-level overview of the different types of networking and the environments for which each is designed, you can determine the type of networking required for a given deployment. Be sure to refer to the various networking integration guides and white papers available at Cisco.com for additional information on these topics.

CHAPTER 11

Exploring Unity Tools

This book covers many of the day-to-day configuration tasks that must be performed to create and maintain an efficient unified messaging solution. Most of these tasks are accomplished using the SA web-based interface. The beauty of this interface is that you can access it from nearly any system that has connectivity to the Unity system, providing the system runs Internet Explorer (IE). However, because it is a web-based application, SA does have its drawbacks. It is not overly responsive and is often incapable of performing certain tasks.

Over the years the developers of the Unity application have created a number of tools that help make the job of the integrator and administrator much easier. These tools assist in a wide range of tasks that range from bulk editing to integration monitoring. As of Unity 4.0, these tools are available from the desktop of the Unity server by clicking the icon labeled Unity Tools Depot. Many of these tools work with previous versions of Unity but may have to be installed manually.

In addition to tools, Unity can produce reports designed to monitor the system and extract other useful data. This chapter explores the Tools Depot, reports, and also examines ways that these tools can help keep the system running smoothly.

Using Unity Web-Based Tools

Many of the tools explored in this chapter must be run from the Unity server console; however, reports and limited monitoring are accomplished via IE.

From SA you can run a number of reports that allow valuable information to be gathered and presented in a web page or stored in a comma separated value (CSV) file for later manipulation. An IE-based monitoring tool called Status Monitor is also available. Through this interface you can monitor the current status of Unity. Confusion often surrounds the IE-based Status Monitor utility because there is an exe application with a very similar name. To reduce the confusion, the IE-based Status Monitor is often referred to as "Status Monitor (HTML)."

This section explores the various reports that can be run from SA and also examines the monitoring capabilities of Status Monitor (HTML). Let's start by taking a look at the monitoring capabilities.

Monitoring

The Status Monitor (HTML) allows you to view the current status of the system, ports, reports, and disk drives via a web browser. This utility is useful because you can access it from any PC on a network with IP connectivity to Unity and IE. Accessing Status Monitor (HTML) is quite simple. If you are logged on at the Unity console, simply click the **Status Monitor icon** on the desktop. Be aware that by default, Status Monitor will overtake the last active web page you have open. So if you have SA open when you start Status Monitor, it will cause your SA session to disappear. To prevent this, open Status Monitor by right clicking on the **Unity icon** in the system tray next to the clock. When you right click on this icon, a menu of options displays. One of these is **Launch Status Monitor**. Clicking on this selection causes Status Monitor to begin in a new window.

Figure 11-1 is the Status Monitor (HTML) screen. This figure shows five icons at the top of the page. Clicking the icons shows the status of the various processes. When Status Monitor (HTML) is opened, the system status screen displays.

Figure 11-1 *Status Monitor*

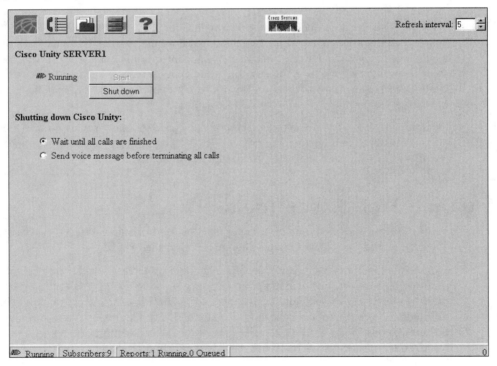

The following list explains each of the icons and outlines the information each screen presents.

Figure 11-2 *System Status Icon*

When the icon shown in Figure 11-2 is selected the System Status screen displays.

Figure 11-3 *System Status Screen*

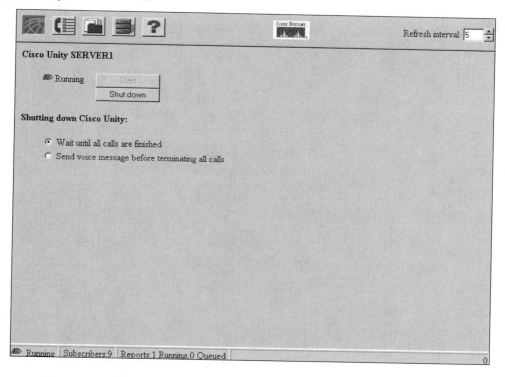

Figure 11-3 shows the System Status screen. This screen displays whether Unity is currently running and allows you to shut down Unity. If you wish to shut the system down from this screen, you must first select whether or not you wish to send out a notification. If you wish to notify active users of the system shutdown before shutting down the system, click the **Send voice message before terminating all calls** radio button. This causes a message to be played on all active ports informing the caller that the system is going to disconnect them and shut down. If you would rather wait for all calls to complete before the system shuts down, then click the **Wait until all calls are finished** radio button. After you have chosen one of the radio buttons, simply click on the **Shut down** icon to shut the system down. If the system is shut down, you can start the system up by clicking the **Start** button.

Figure 11-4 *Ports Status Icon*

By clicking on the Ports Status icon shown in Figure 11-4, you can view the current status of each port.

Figure 11-5 *Ports Status Screen*

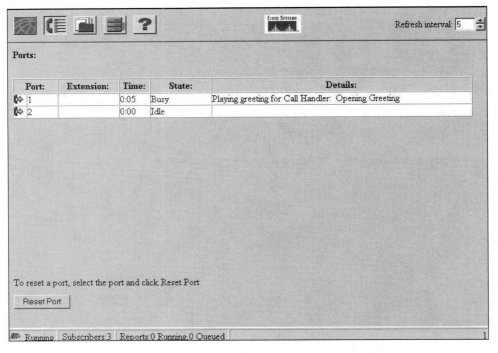

Figure 11-5 shows the port status screen. By default this screen refreshes itself every five seconds. The screen displays the port number and extension of each port, the state of each port, and any available details. For instance, the details portion may show which call handler is being played. From this screen you can reset the port by highlighting the port and pressing the **Reset Port** button.

TIP	You can use the status monitor to check for ports that are locked up. By monitoring the time field, you can easily see if a port has been active an inordinate amount of time.

Figure 11-6 *Reports Status Icon*

By clicking on the Reports Status icon shown in Figure 11-6, you can view the status of the reports that are queued.

Figure 11-7 *Reports Status Screen*

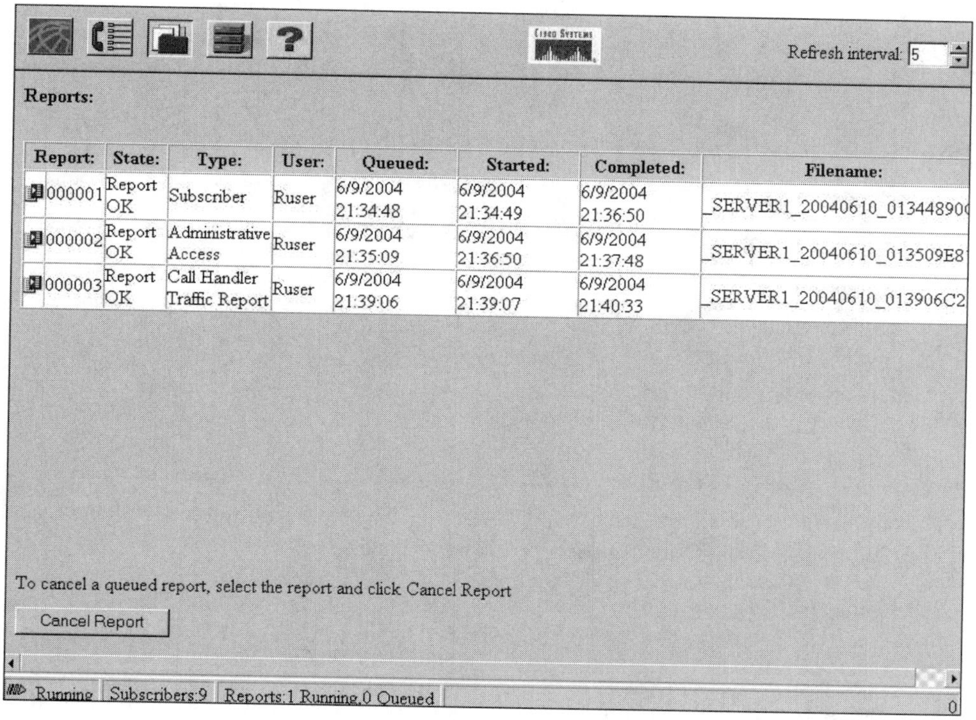

Reports:

Report:	State:	Type:	User:	Queued:	Started:	Completed:	Filename:
000001	Report OK	Subscriber	Ruser	6/9/2004 21:34:48	6/9/2004 21:34:49	6/9/2004 21:36:50	_SERVER1_20040610_01344890(
000002	Report OK	Administrative Access	Ruser	6/9/2004 21:35:09	6/9/2004 21:36:50	6/9/2004 21:37:48	_SERVER1_20040610_013509E8
000003	Report OK	Call Handler Traffic Report	Ruser	6/9/2004 21:39:06	6/9/2004 21:39:07	6/9/2004 21:40:33	_SERVER1_20040610_013906C2

Refresh interval: 5

To cancel a queued report, select the report and click Cancel Report

Cancel Report

Running | Subscribers:9 | Reports:1 Running,0 Queued   0

Figure 11-7 shows the reports status screen. For each report that is run, this screen displays the type of report that is queued along with information such as when it was queued, started, and finished.

Figure 11-8 *Disk Drive Status Icon*

Information about the disk drives in the system can be viewed by clicking on the Disk Drive Status icon shown in Figure 11-8.

Figure 11-9 *Disk Drive Status Screen*

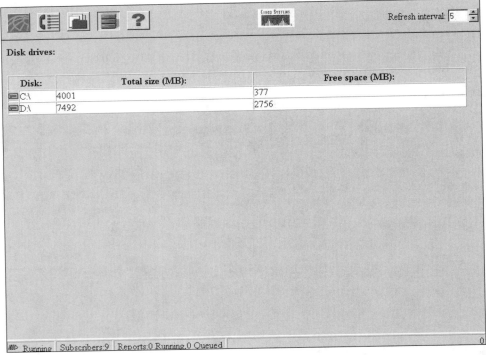

Figure 11-9 shows the disk drive status screen. This screen shows the total amount of space and the available space for each drive on the system.

Figure 11-10 *Help Icon*

When the Help icon in Figure 11-10 is clicked, a new window displays that contains online help for the Status Monitor (HTML) interface.

The status monitor allows you access to very rudimentary monitoring on Unity. A later section in this chapter explores more advanced utilities that offer more detailed monitoring capabilities, but exploring the reporting capabilities of Unity comes first.

Reports

Unity offers the ability to run a number of reports for the SA interface. The reports are separated into two categories—subscriber and system.

As the name implies, subscriber reports deal with subscriber-related information, and the system reports deliver information related to system issues. This section explores the information that can be obtained from each report and the various times and reasons you may want to run certain reports.

Before various reports are explored, a few basic concepts regarding reports need to be covered. One of the most common questions regarding reports is: How do you schedule reports to run? The short answer is: You don't. As of Unity 4.04, all reports run from SA must be run interactively, that is, you must run them manually.

When running reports, you have the choice of saving them as HTML pages or CSV. When saving them as HTML pages, there is a 220 MB limit to the size of the report. Most often reports are saved as CSV files, so that the data can be imported into a spreadsheet application and manipulated. When the report is complete, it is delivered to the e-mail account of the person that ran the report. In addition, reports can be found in the Commserver\Reports folder of the Unity server.

Some types of reports require a date range input; they use the information stored in the log files to create the report. When running these reports, you can only select a date within the number of days for which the Unity server was configured to store log files. Other reports do not require a date range, because they report on the system at the point in time when the report is run.

Subscriber Reports

Now let's look at the subscriber reports. There are six different types of subscriber-related reports that can be run:

- Subscribers
- Subscriber Message Activity
- Distribution Lists
- Failed Login
- Transfer Call Billing
- Outcall Billing

Each report is discussed in detail in the sections that follow.

Subscribers

This report provides the following information for selected subscribers: first and last name, Exchange alias, location, Windows domain, billing ID, class of service, extensions, and inbox size.

Subscriber Message Activity

Useful for providing information useful to help troubleshoot voice-mail problems, this report shows detailed information for a selected subscriber. The information found in this report determines if the problems subscribers are running into are self-created. The report shows each action that has taken place within a mailbox. When running this report you must select a subscriber, and a date and time range. The following details are provided for each message: date and time action was taken, source of the message, response action, number of new messages, sender's name and Dual Tone Multifrequency (DTMF), date and message arrival, dialout number, dialout result.

Distribution Lists

This report provides a list of all distribution lists and the members of each list. Run this report for all distribution lists, or select a single list. The details in each report include: list creation date, list alias, number of subscribers, distribution list name, owner, and members (optional).

Failed Login

If subscribers are often locked out of their accounts, and they insist they have not entered an incorrect password, this report can be very helpful. This report lists all failed logins and the caller ID of the device from which the unsuccessful login occurred. This can help determine if someone is trying to gain unauthorized access to the system. The information included in this report is subscriber, alias, Caller ID, subscriber DTMF, date and time, maximum failures exceeded, and failure number.

The report also includes the following information for each failed SA login: user name, computer, user domain, event ID, date and time and failure number. This information can be used to determine if someone is trying to gain unauthorized administrative access.

Transfer Call Billing

When Unity transfers a call from a subscriber account or call handler, the PBX simply records it as a call made by Unity. Some companies need to know which subscriber or call handler requested the transfer, so the call can be billed back to the proper department. This report shows all outbound calls made by Unity on behalf of a subscriber or call handler. The information in this report includes: name, extension, billing ID, date, time, dialed number, and transfer result.

This report requires you to select an object for which to run this report. The valid object choices are subscriber, distribution list, billing ID, or call handler. You must also select a date and time range. You may run this report on all subscribers at one time if you wish.

OutCall Billing

This report is very similar to the Transfer Call Billing reports except that it reports on all message notification calls. The report includes the following information: name, extension, billing ID, time, dialed number, call time, and delivery device.

The report requires that you select an object in which to run this report. The valid object choices are subscriber, distribution list, billing ID, or call handler. You must also select a date, and time range. You may run this report on all subscribers at one time if you wish.

System Reports

In addition to Subscriber reports, you can run System reports. These reports can be used to help monitor the status and health of the system. A list and explanation of the various System reports follows:

- Administrative Access
- Event Log
- Port Usage
- System Configuration
- Unresolved References
- Call Handler Traffic
- Audio Messaging Interchange Specification (AMIS) Out-Traffic and AMIS In-Traffic

The following sections describe each system report in more detail.

Administrative Access

Use this report to track all changes made within SA. In a properly configured system, administrators are required to use their own login to access SA. By doing this, it is possible to track the action of each administrator, which proves helpful when determining who made certain changes and why. The report includes the following information: administrative action, administrator's first and last name, administrator's Exchange alias, date and time of action, property changed and new value.

Event Log

This report is generated from the information found in the Windows application log. Choose to create the report based on all application data or only Unity data. The following information is included in this report: date and time, type of event, source, message, and computer and additional information. Although information found in the report can be obtained from the Windows event viewer, the report format is sometimes more convenient, such as when you want to send the information to another person for review.

Port Usage

Use this report to determine if the ports on the system are running close to capacity. A more advanced tool called Port Analyzer, which is discussed in the next section, can deliver more detail, but this report is helpful because it can be run from any PC on the system. The information in this report includes: port number, unit of time, date range, time, ports, number of calls, length of calls, average length of calls, utilization, average calls per hour, and average calls per day.

System Configuration

This report provides information about the server and software. The following data is included in this report: serial number, Original Equipment Manufacturers (OEM) code, product, number of voice ports, languages, available license, total license, leading silence, trailing silence, minimum length of recording, domain name, hard drive space, and other system settings.

Print this report and keep it as a paper backup in case you are unable to access the system and need this information.

Unresolved References

All Call Handlers are associated with a subscriber account. If the subscriber account is deleted and the associated call handlers are not removed or re-associated with other subscribers, problems may occur. This report lists all call handlers that are associated with subscribers who no longer exist. The data in this report includes: handler name, handler ID, handler type, owner, and message recipient.

Call Handler Traffic

After a system is up and running, check to see if the call handlers you created are being used. The Call Handler Traffic report shows how many times a call handler was accessed and how calls exited the call handler. Use this information to determine if the call handler flow is working as expected. The information detailed in this report is start time, total calls, exit method, key, DTMF ID, invalid DTMF ID, after greeting action, and hang ups.

Audio Messaging Interchange Specification (AMIS) Out-Traffic and AMIS In-Traffic

If AMIS networking is implemented, in-bound and out-bound traffic reports can be generated. The reports show detailed information about each AMIS message sent or received. The following information is included in these reports: date and time, importance, sender/recipients' extension, target number, start time, duration, status, port number, total successes, and total failures.

In total, 14 different reports can be run, however, the process for running each report is very similar. It would be a waste of paper and time to detail the steps required to run each report. However, the generic steps for running a report are described in this section. Refer to these steps the first time or two you need to run a report, but you will soon find that the process is rather simple and intuitive.

Step 1   From within SA, select the type of report you want to run by selecting either **Reports>Subscribers>** or **Reports>System. Reports> Subscribers>** is used in this example.

Step 2   From the menu on the right side of the screen, shown in Figure 11-11, select the report you want to run. In this example the Subscriber report is selected.

Figure 11-11 *Reports>Subscribers Reports>Subscribers*

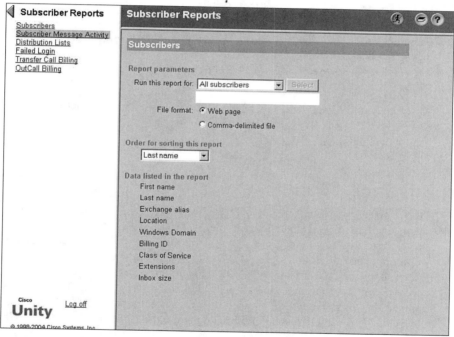

Step 3   After the type of report is selected, choose the criteria that the report will use to gather data. The specific criteria needed vary based on the report. For example, you may need to select which subscribers this report should include.

Step 4   Choose the file format in which the report will be saved. CSV format is the most flexible because you can easily import this data into other programs.

Step 5   Depending on the type of report, you might need to enter a date and time range. If required, enter this information. Some reports rely on the system's log files to gather information. Because these logs are kept only for a specified number of days (which is configured on the

System>Configuration>Settings page within SA), you might not be able to select a date that is beyond this range. By default, log files are stored for seven days.

Step 6 After all the criteria are entered, click the **run** icon, which is the icon of a man running, located in the title strip.

Step 7 A window displays informing you that the report is queued.

Step 8 After the report is complete, an e-mail is sent to the person who started the report. You can check the status of all reports from within Status Monitor (HTML).

WARNING Running reports can create a draw on the system, so it is recommended that they be run only during nonpeak hours.

Now that you understand the tools that are available via a browser, let's look at some of the more advanced tools. These tools are often more powerful than those just discussed, so use caution when implementing them.

Using Advanced Tools

Over the years many advanced tools have been developed that aid administrators and engineers in the management and troubleshooting of the Unity systems. These tools are divided into five major categories: Administration, Audio Management, Diagnostic, Reporting, and Integration tools. As of Unity 4.0, clicking on the icon labeled Cisco Unity Tools Depot can access these tools. This icon opens a common interface that allows you access to both the tools and some excellent help files for each tool. Figure 11-12 shows this application. There are two sections to this interface, the left side is a list of the tools and the right side is used to display information about the highlighted tool.

To run any of the tools in the Tools Depot, you must double click it. If you click the tool just once, the online help displays in the right side of the window. By using online documentation that comes with these tools, you should be able to understand how to use the tools. This chapter introduces you to the various tools by offering an overview of each tool. Some of the tools are very useful and you will use them quite often, whereas you might never touch others. The high number of tools makes it impossible to provide a step-by-step guide on how to run each one. However, as mentioned earlier, each of these tools includes an excellent online help screen that can assist you.

Take a few minutes for a quick review of what tools are available and how they function. A quick review now can help you save time when resolving issues because you will know what tools are at your disposal.

Figure 11-12 *Cisco Unity Tools Main Screen*

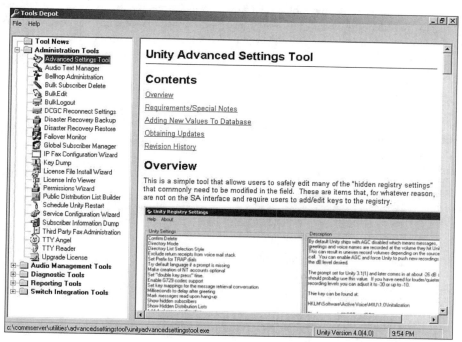

NOTE   The tools available to you may vary depending on the version of Unity running. If any of the listed tools are not available on your system, they may be downloaded from www.ciscounitytools.com. However, be certain to read the "Requirements/Special Notes" section of the online help for each of these tools, which lists the required version of Unity for that specific tool.

Also note that many of these tools must be run on box (on the Unity server), whereas others are recommended to run off box (on a system other than the Unity server). Because these recommendations and requirements change as the utilities are improved, check the help file for the current recommendations on each tool.

Administration Tools

As of the writing of this book, there were more than 25 administration-based tools. The exact number of tools that are available vary slightly depending on the version of Unity. These tools assist in tasks ranging from common administration tasks to very specialized tasks. Because they are listed in alphabetical order in the Tools Depot, the tools are presented in the same order here.

NOTE   Some of these tools may not appear in the Tools Depot due to the version of Unity running. This is true not only for older versions of Unity but also for some of the newer versions. In some cases tools have been removed or moved in later versions of Unity.

- Advanced Settings Tool
- Audio Text Manager
- Bellhop Administration
- Bulk Import Exchange
- Bulk Subscriber Delete
- Bulk Edit
- Bulk Logout
- DCGC Reconnect Settings
- Disaster Recovery Backup
- Disaster Recovery Restore
- Failover Monitor
- Global Subscriber Manager
- IP Fax Configuration Wizard
- Key Dump
- License File Install Wizard
- License Info Viewer
- Message Store Manager
- Migrate Subscriber Data
- Permissions Wizard
- Public Distribution List Builder
- Schedule Unity Restart
- Service Configuration Wizard
- Subscriber Information Dump
- Third Party Fax Administration
- TTY Angel
- TTY Reader
- Upgrade License

The sections that follow describe each of the tools in more detail.

Advanced Settings Tools

A number of Unity's settings are stored in the Windows registry and are hidden. Issues arise from time-to-time that require adjustments to these settings. As you may know, editing registry settings on any Windows system can result in disaster if done incorrectly. The Advanced Settings Tool offers a friendly, safe interface from which to adjust these settings. Tasks you can accomplish using this tool are varied, but a few examples follow:

- Enable optional conversation
- Set maximum recording time higher than 20 minutes
- Check to see if the mailbox is full before taking messages

Audio Text Manager

The main purpose of this tool is to make the task of creating and managing Audio Text Applications easier. Audio Text Manager can also be used for many common administrative tasks and as a troubleshooting aid. From within this tool, you can manage call handlers and subscribers. Most tasks that you commonly perform from within SA can be performed here.

This interface allows you to see a tree view of the Call Handlers and Subscribers, where you can see how the call handlers and subscribers are connected through one key dialing. A grid view is also available from within this interface, which displays a list of Call Handlers and Subscribers.

Many administrators find this tool a more efficient interface for managing existing Subscribers and Call Handlers. Although many of the common tasks normally accomplished in SA can be performed here, certain tasks cannot. This is easily remedied as the interface has a hyperlink that takes you directly to the selected object within SA when you need to complete such a task.

This tool can save hours of administration time once you fully understand its capabilities. If you use only one of the advanced tools, make it this one. However, as you explore the rest of the tools, I am sure you will find many others that will also be useful.

Bellhop Administration

When the Cisco Unity Bellhop service is installed, this tool allows hotel staff to easily view a list of guests and their checked in/out status and to reset passwords and perform other common administrative tasks.

Bulk Import Exchange

This tool is also called Cisco Unity Bulk Import tool which was discussed in Chapter 8, "Subscriber Reference." This tool allows you to import a large number of users from either a CSV file or an existing Exchange server. Refer to Chapter 8 for more information on this tool.

Bulk Subscriber Delete

The Bulk Subscriber Delete tool allows you to easily delete a large number of subscribers at one time. This tool is significantly faster than using SA and deleting subscribers one at a time.

It is a wizard that allows you to remove the subscriber only from Unity and leave the directory and mailstore account, or remove the directory and mailstore account and the subscriber information.

Bulk Edit

Bulk Edit allows you to edit the attributes of a large number of subscribers or call handlers at once.

NOTE	I know a person who went to each subscriber's account and manually changed the transfer rule to ring the phone first. She had to do this because her integrator used the default subscriber template, which sends all subscriber calls directly to voice mail without ringing the phone first. It took more than three days to accomplish this task using SA. When I showed her how to accomplish this task in a matter of minutes using the bulk edit tool, she was very pleased but also somewhat frustrated with her integrator.

This tool is fairly intuitive and allows you to change many attributes ranging from transfer settings to editing and adding alternate extensions. After using it, the tool will soon become one of your favorites. Keep in mind that the tool saves you time even if you only need to change the same attributes on a few objects. The tool lets you complete tasks in a number of minutes rather than hours.

Bulk Logout

Bulk Logout allows you to force the logout of a number of users from Exchange 5.5. This may be necessary if you are moving users from one Exchange server to another. Although this tool can be used with Exchange 2000/2003, it is more often needed with Exchange 5.5.

DCGC Reconnect Settings

The tool allows you to view or change the current settings for Unity's Domain Controller (DC) and Global Catalog (GC) server reconnect feature. It is recommended that you leave this setting set to default.

Disaster Recovery Backup

Often referred to as DIRT, or DIsaster Recovery Tool, this tool can back up all Unity-specific data. The tool can also be used for migration. The data is backed up from one server and restored to another; however, the Unity versions must be the same on both servers. Data is restored using the next tool, Disaster Recovery Restore. Current versions of the Disaster Recovery Backup can also back up subscriber messages. This should be done only in small voice-mail-only environments, because it can require a large amount of disk space for the backup.

NOTE	It is recommended that all deployments have an approved backup solution for their primary means of backup.

Disaster Recovery Restore

This tool is used to restore the backup data that was made using the Disaster Recovery Backup tool. To do this, Unity must first be installed and running on the server. Remember that these two tools only back up Unity-specific data and not the entire system.

Failover Monitor

Failover Monitor allows you to view the current status of the failover configuration. You can also use this tool to force failover. This is useful if you wish to perform maintenance on the primary server.

Global Subscriber Manager

Managing subscribers can become difficult in larger environments where there is more than one Unity server or a large number of subscribers. The Global Subscriber Manager tool helps make managing such environments easier. This interface allows administrators to access subscribers through a single interface, regardless of the server on which they are located. Imagine having five servers, each with 500 subscribers. Keeping track of which server each subscriber is on could be quite a job. This interface allows you to search all servers for the subscriber you want to manage. There are two ways to find subscribers. The first way is by starting the tool where a tree view displays. The servers and dialing domains in the Unity network display on the left side of the screen. Click on a server and you can display the subscribers of that server on the right side of the screen. Click on the subscriber you want to manage and the SA interface opens and brings you directly to this subscriber. The second way is to search for a subscriber by pressing F2. A search criteria box displays, which allows you to search based on any of the following: Alias, Display Name, First Name, Last Name, DTMF ID, and Subscriber type.

Using this interface you can also do more advanced tasks such as move, delete, or import subscribers. The import feature of this utility allows you to import AD users. Although useful, if you need to import a large number of users, the Cisco Unity Bulk Import utility is a more efficient tool. The delete feature of this tool assists in cleanly removing a subscriber. When you right click on a subscriber, a menu displays and one of the options is delete. Click this and a Delete Object Wizard walks you through cleanly removing the user. You may also move a subscriber from one Unity server to another, as long as the servers are on the same dialing domain. To do this, right click on the subscriber and choose move from the menu that displays. A move wizard walks you through the move process. The move, delete, and import features require at least Unity 4.0 (1).

IP Fax Configuration Wizard

Unity has the ability to process faxes that are delivered to a queue mailbox. The Unity service monitors a single mailbox for inbound fax messages and then tries to determine the intended recipient by looking at the subject line of the fax. If the service is unable to determine for whom the message was intended, it sends the message to a single mailbox for undeliverable or unaddressed faxed messages. This tool walks you through the setup of the IP FAX configuration.

Key Dump

In Unity 3.x and 2.x, a physical device known as a dongle was used for licensing purposes. This device attaches to either a parallel or USB port. It contains the licensing information for that server. This device is sometimes referred to as a key. The Key Dump utility can be used to display license information. The information includes, serial number, version number, number of licensed ports, languages and subscribers, and networking features. To retrieve similar information in Unity 4.x, use the License Info Viewer tool.

License File Install Wizard

Each Unity system must have a license file properly installed. This license file determines how many subscribers and for what features the system is licensed. The license is loaded during the installation of the system. This utility can be used when adding new licenses. When you run this utility, you are given the opportunity to select a license file(s). Make sure you select all license files; this includes any that may have been previously loaded on the system.

License Info Viewer

The License Info Viewer shows the current license on the server. This tool is used with Unity 4.x and later. The information includes, serial number, version number, number of licensed ports, languages, and subscribers, and networking features. To retrieve similar information in Unity 3.x and 2.x, use the Key Dump tool.

Message Store Manager

Many routine tasks can take up an administrator's valuable time. This utility allows an administrator to perform a number of these tasks from within a single interface. In addition, once configured, these tasks can be set to run automatically using Microsoft's tasks scheduler. The tasks that can be performed using this tool are as follows:

- Detailed CSV file of subscribers accounts
- Move messages
- Delete messages
- Restore Messages that are in the Deleted Items folder
- Set Mailbox Limits
- Hide mailbox from address list

Migrate Subscriber Data

This tool allows you to associate an existing subscriber account to a mailstore account. This is useful when migrating from voice mail only to unified messaging. It can also be used to migrate Bridge subscribers to Exchange subscribers.

Permissions Wizard

The Permissions wizard is run during the installation of Unity and is used to set the proper permission on the accounts used by Unity. Normally this does not need to be run again, however, it has been known to resolve issues created by someone changing the rights on accounts after the installation. Before running this tool, make sure the AD users, which are used by Unity, already exist. These accounts include installation, administration, directory service, and message store accounts. After these accounts are created, the permissions wizard walks you through, selecting each account for the proper role and assigning the proper permissions to the accounts.

Public Distribution List Builder

This tool enables an administrator to quickly and easily add subscribers to new or existing Public Distribution Lists (PDLs). You can search for subscribers based on Class of Service

(CoS), extension range, CSV file, their home mail server, or the switch with which they are associated. You can select all the subscribers who match certain criteria or pick them from the list that displays.

Schedule Unity Restart

As with most systems running Windows, occasionally the system needs to be rebooted and that time is almost never opportune. When you are lucky, the system will need to be rebooted but not necessarily immediately. If so, the Schedule Unity Restart tool comes in handy. Using this tool, Unity can be set to reboot at a given time. You can configure it to reboot the server, restart Unity, or restart only certain Unity services.

NOTE   Although highly unlikely, it is always possible that a server will not come back up after a reboot. For this reason, it is always recommended that a complete backup be done on a regular basis.

Service Configuration Wizard

This wizard runs during the installation process. Its job is to associate accounts to certain Unity processes. These are the same accounts to which the Permissions wizard assigns rights. If someone changes or deletes these accounts, it may become necessary to run this wizard again.

Subscriber Information Dump

This tool allows an administrator to create a CSV file that contains many subscriber attributes. The attributes sent to the CSV range from the subscriber alias to the transfer type. Most of the subscriber attributes you can see within SA can be exported using this tool.

Third Party Fax Administration

Unity has the ability to work with a number of Fax servers that integrate with Exchange. This tool is used to configure Unity to integrate with the Fax server.

TTY Angel

The TTY Angel tool can be used to create WAV files that can be played to TTY devices. Type in text and the tool converts it to a WAV file. This produces a WAV file that can be understood by any TTY device that supports the Baudot protocol.

TTY Reader

This tool can pull text that is represented by Baudot TTY tones, out of a WAV file. This allows for the ability to read a message left by TTY/TDD devices without having to run it through such a device.

Upgrade License

Use this tool when upgrading licensing on a Unity 3.x or 2.x systems. When upgrading this version, you receive a file in the e-mail, which must be installed using this utility. To complete this process choose the upgrade option from within this interface and select the location of the file. The file is then used to upgrade the licensed features.

Audio Management Tools

Because Unity is responsible for handling many audio-related tasks, such as recording messages and greetings, it may be necessary to modify some of its audio handling functions. The following tools assist in doing this.

- AudioStat
- Codec Checker
- Set Prompt Speed
- Set Record Format
- Set Volume
- Set WAV Format
- WaveGain

The sections that follow discuss the audio-related tools included within the Tools Depot.

AudioStat

When Unity is deployed in a Voice Over IP (VoIP) environment, it becomes susceptible to the same issues that sometimes occur within any VoIP environment. In an IP Telephony environment, Unity is susceptible to the same voice quality issues as IP Phones. The AudioStat tool can help troubleshoot these issues by displaying real time information about the audio driver. The following are three viewable screens within this tool.

- **Global**—Displays information relating to the incoming and outgoing packets.
- **Device**—Displays all audio recording devices and their current status.
- **Record Log**—After a recording is complete, writes the information to a log. A summary of all recordings can be viewed there.

Codec Checker

The prompts and greetings used in Unity can be recorded at a number of codecs. The most popular are the G.711 or G.729 codec. Over the course of time, with various upgrades and system changes, it is possible that an environment may end up with a mixture of codecs. The Codec Checker tool checks each prompt and greeting and displays the following information about each recording: codec, file name and location, sample rate, date of last modification, and the file size. This information can be saved to a CSV file.

Set Prompt Speed

From time-to-time customers may request that the Unity prompts either slow down or speed up. This tool allows you to change the speed of Unity prompts. Make sure to back up existing prompts before using this tool.

Set Record Format

This utility allows you to change the default codec that Unity uses to record all recordings. Any codec that is installed on the server can be selected. The default for record format is 8Kb MuLaw. Remember that the format selected is used for *all* recordings, so make sure that you are happy with the quality before selecting it.

Set Volume

In Unity 3.1(1), Automatic Gain Control (AGC) was introduced. It is used to normalize the volume of all recordings. However, prior to 3.1(1), depending upon the volume of the incoming stream there were issues with varying volume levels. If you have upgraded from a version earlier than 3.1, it is possible that some of the older recordings will be at varying volume levels. This tool allows you to quickly set all recordings at the same volume level. By default, -26dB is used and it is strongly recommended that you use the default. Running the conversion process several times may cause the recordings to become distorted.

Set WAV Format

As mentioned earlier, Unity can use G.711 or G.729 codecs for recording. If the codec is changed, you may want to convert all existing greetings to the new codec. The Set WAV Format tool allows you to do this. Select the greeting you wish to change and the desired codec. This tool offers you the option of saving the original greetings to a backup location. You are encouraged to do this.

NOTE   Some people argue that converting all greetings to the same codec is not necessary because Unity has the ability to transcode between G.711 and G.729 on the fly. Keep in mind, however, that each time Unity must transcode, it takes CPU cycles away from other processes.

WaveGain

In earlier versions of Unity, before 3.1(1), it was sometimes necessary to change the recording and play-volume of the system. These are registry settings, so in order to change them you had to edit the registry. These settings would take effect when the server was rebooted. The WaveGain tool allows you to change the volume-level settings on the fly, which allows you to determine the proper setting before making the changes in the registry. Because changes made using WaveGain are active only until the next reboot, make sure that you also change it in the registry. The registry settings can be set using the Advanced Settings Tool found in the Tools depot.

Diagnostic Tools

As with any system, there are times when you need to troubleshoot issues occurring within the Unity system. Troubleshooting is more of an art than a science, and often the hardest part of fixing a problem is finding the problem, or more accurately, the cause of the problem. The Tools Depot includes some excellent diagnostic tools that assist in many troubleshooting exercises. The following are the diagnostic tools available from within the Tools Depot.

- CUPID
- DataLink Explorer
- DBWalker
- Directory Access Diagnostics
- DOH Prop Test
- Event Monitoring Service
- Grant Unity Access
- Remote Serviceability Kit Configuration
- SysCheck
- Unity Diagnostic Tool (UDT)
- Unity Diagnostic Viewer (UDV)

The sections that follow describe these tools in more detail.

CUPID

Cisco Unified Performance Information and Diagnostics (CUPID) is used to monitor Windows performance counters. The data that is collected is written to a CSV file that can be imported later into a spreadsheet for analysis. Although the information you obtain using this utility is the same information that you see in the performance monitor, this tool has many added benefits. An XML configuration file is used to determine what counters this tool reads. The counters are then read every few seconds based on the time interval you define. You can define the maximum size of a log file. After reaching the defined size, a new file is created and automatically named based on the time and date.

DataLink Explorer

The data stored in Unity is in an SQL database. The Cisco Unity DataLink Explorer is an interface that allows you to view the tables in the database and offers definitions for the various tables and columns. This tool can be helpful when trying to determine the exact purpose of an object.

DBWalker

DBWalker can "walk" through the database and check for errors and inconsistencies. You can configure the tool to check for errors or to fix certain errors automatically when found. It is a good idea not to allow the automatic correction of errors on the first run, so that you can explore them and determine how they occurred. After the tool runs, it creates a report that shows the results and lists all errors and warnings found. Run this tool before backing up the data in preparation for an upgrade.

Directory Access Diagnostics

This tool, which is also known as DAD, is used when you experience errors when trying to import AD users into Unity. Errors may occur when the account used for services to enable importing does not have the proper rights. DAD is used as a test to determine if the proper rights have been granted to allow the import to the user.

DOH Prop Test

WARNING This is a low-level database editor and requires the user to have an extensive understanding of the database structure.

Because this tool is so powerful, it is password protected. If a Terminal Access Controller (TAC) engineer needs you to access this tool, they will supply the password.

This tool can be used without a password, but it will operate in a read-only mode.

Event Monitoring Service

When certain events occur, an entry is written to the Windows event log. You can configure the Event Monitoring Service to monitor the event log and alert an administrator when specified events occur.

Grant Unity Access

When individuals log into SA, the AD account they use to log into the domain determines what rights they will have within SA. This account is associated with a subscriber account that has administrator access in Unity. If the AD account has somehow lost this association, the Grant Unity Access tool is used to re-associate the AD account to the subscriber. This is a command line utility that is run from a DOS prompt. The following is the syntax used and shows an example for each:

- GrantUnityAccess–u <Domain>\<UserAlias> -s <UnitySubscriberAlias>
- GrantUnityAccess–u DTW\Jsmith -s Jsmith

This example would associate the AD account, Jsmith in the DTW domain to the Unity subscriber Jsmith.

This Utility is also used to associate multiple AD accounts with a single Unity subscriber.

Remote Serviceability Kit Configuration

This tool allows you to add Simple Network Management Protocol (SNMP), Syslog, and Cisco Discovery Protocol (CDP) support to a Unity server.

SysCheck

Run the Syscheck tool to test to see if the account Unity is using has the proper rights to create Unity subscribers. This tool can also check to see if Unity is properly configured to communicate with the mailstore. This tool reports any issues it finds and offers possible resolutions.

Unity Diagnostic Tool (UDT)

When troubleshooting problems within a Unity environment, it may be necessary to enable trace files. Trace files record detailed information of each Unity action. The exact information logged is based on the traces that you enable. Typically, you enable traces on the request of a TAC. This tool allows you to enable traces and gather log files. This information is sent to a TAC for analysis; however, you may also use the Unity Diagnostic Viewer to view this information.

Unity Diagnostic Viewer (UDV)

This tool is used to analyze the log's output from the Unity Diagnostic Tool. It allows you to filter out unneeded data and view only what is important to you.

NOTE	Because filtering large amounts of data can burden the processor, it is recommended that you load and run this tool on a PC other than the Unity server.

Reporting Tools

After the system is up and running, it is important to monitor the system. As you learned earlier, Unity has a number of reports that can be run from within the SA. As good as these reports are, sometimes more detailed information is needed. The Tools Depot includes a number of tools that are able to offer more detailed information. The following are the Reporting tools available within the Tools Depot.

- Bridge Traffic Analyzer
- Event Notification Utility
- Gather Unity System Information
- Port Usage Analyzer

The sections that follow briefly describe each tool.

Bridge Traffic Analyzer

If you have implemented Bridge networking, you want the ability to monitor the amount of traffic that is being sent through the server. The Bridge Traffic Analyzer does just that. This tool has the ability to produce reports on port usage, number of messages passing through message queues, length of time messages were in the queue, and the number of messages delivered.

Event Notification Utility

The Event Monitoring Service tool has replaced the Event Notification Utility. The Event Monitoring Service is discussed in the diagnostic tools section of this chapter.

Gather Unity System Information

When a TAC is assisting you in troubleshooting an issue, certain information needs to be sent to the TAC. This tool facilitates the gathering of this information by creating a cabinet (CAB) file that contains the following information about the system:

- Application and System Event logs (5 days)
- System information
- All services, startup options, and associated accounts

Port Usage Analyzer

As mentioned in the reports section of the book there is a tool that can deliver more detailed information about Port Usage reports. The Port Usage Analyzer is that tool. This tool can deliver information on the following:

- **Port availability**—This information can be displayed by the day, or by the hour sections.
- **Call Distribution**—This displays the types of calls each port handled.
- **Port Time Use**—This displays the amount of time each port spent handling each type of call.
- **Call Traffic**—This displays how many of each type of call each port handled for each minute of the day. This report can display by the day or by the hour.

Switch Integration Tools

From time-to-time it may be necessary to view or edit the way the switch is communicating with Unity. The Switch Integration Tools, available with the Tools Depot, are discussed in this section as follows:

- Call Viewer
- Edit Switch Utility
- Integration Monitor
- Learn Tones
- Port Status Monitor
- Restrict Dial
- Unity Telephone Integration Manager

The following sections briefly describe each of these tools.

Call Viewer

Call Viewer creates a single line summary of each inbound call to Unity. The information displayed includes the time the call arrived, the origin of the call, reason, trunk ID, port ID, dialed number, calling number, and forwarding station. This information can be helpful when troubleshooting various issues.

Edit Switch Utility

This tool allows you to view and, if needed, edit switch integration information. The settings configured with this tool include things such as message waiting indicator (MWI) information and outgoing call access codes, incoming ring times, and many other integration values. This tool is only used under the supervision of a TAC.

Integration Monitor

The Integration Monitor tool is very similar to the Call Viewer tool, but it can only be used with Simplified Message Desk Interface (SMDI) and DTMF integration. This tool displays the time, packet number, port number, origin, reason, trunk number, calling number, and forwarding extension. This tool does not work in a CallManager integration.

Learn Tones

When Unity is integrated with a traditional PBX, it needs to understand the tones sent from the PBX. Unity comes with the ability to understand a variety of phones systems; however, if you experience problems with transfers, message notification or MWIs, you may need to run the Learn Tones tool. This tool will relearn the tones that the PBX sends.

NOTE	When running the Learn Tones tool, Unity must be shut down. After the tool is started, it runs automatically.

Port Status Monitor

The Port Status Monitor allows you to view all events taking place on any port in real time, and to create a log of these events. You may select any or all ports. You can save the information compiled by this program into a CSV file. This file contains the following five columns: Port, Date, Time, Trace and Info.

Restrict Dial

Some traditional PBXs are scheduled to reboot each day. During this time, it is necessary to have Unity not send MWI or message notifications to the PBX. The Restrict Dial tool allows you to define this schedule.

Unity Telephone Integration Manager

This tool allows you to edit the integration settings configured during the installation of the system and add additional integrations. This tool is often referred to as Unity Telephony Integration Manager (UTIM) and was covered in great detail earlier in this book. Please refer to Chapter 7, "Unity Predeployment Tasks" for more details on this tool.

Summary

This chapter focused on the monitoring and reporting tools for Unity. Two types of reports are run from within SA, Subscriber and System reports. Another web-based tool, Status Monitor, shows the status of the system, the ports, queued reports, and disk drives.

Included with Unity are additional tools that are accessed from the Unity Tools Depot icon on the server's desktop. These tools offer detailed information on many Unity processes. They are divided into five categories: administration, audio management, diagnostic, reporting, and switch integration.

After reading this chapter you should feel comfortable running the various web-based reports and be able to monitor the Unity system using the web-based Status Monitor interface. Furthermore, you should be aware of the various tools available within the Tool Depot and be able to determine which tool might help in a given situation.

PART III

Leveraging the Power of CallManager and Unity

CHAPTER 12

Maximizing the Capabilities of Unity and CallManager

This book has examined the configuration tasks required for the most commonly used features and functions of CallManager and Unity. Unfortunately it is not possible to include all features in every conceivable configuration in a book of this size. This chapter introduces you to a few of the more advanced features available in each application. In addition, this chapter encourages you to take what you have learned in this book and create innovative solutions for unique issues by offering a few examples of what others have done.

The first section discusses a number of the newer and more advanced features found in CallManager. These features include administrative access, time of day routing, Attendant Console, IP Manager Assistant (IPMA) and hunt lists. The next section discusses how Unity is configured to provide a few enhanced call-handling features such as call screening and call queuing. The final section of this chapter shows you how the features of both CallManager and Unity is configured to work together to offer a number of advanced features.

Advanced CallManager Features

As CallManager evolves as a product, new features are added and existing features are enhanced. Some features that are added as the product grows are not necessarily unique to CallManager. However, there are some features that are unique to CallManager and others that are enhanced by CallManager. This section takes a look at some of the new and enhanced features of CallManager.

Configuring MLA

Once logged into CCMAdmin, you can configure nearly every aspect of CallManager. This ability can prove disastrous in the wrong hands. Often administrators want the ability to hand certain configuration tasks over to the assistant administrators but may not want them to have full access to all administrator functions. This can be done by enabling and configuring Multi-Level Access (MLA) for CallManager.

MLA allows you to configure and create different administrative accounts, each with their own level of access. In CallManager 4.0 and later, this is installed but not enabled by default. Previous to CallManager 4.0, MLA had to be downloaded from the software center on Cisco.com and installed before it could be used.

MLA offers the ability to allow varying degrees of access and administration rights to others. This is accomplished by configuring users, user groups, and functional groups.

Before MLA can be used, it must be enabled. The steps that follow show how to enable MLA in CallManager 4.0 and later.

Adding a Functional Group

Step 1   From within CCMAdmin, select **User>Access Rights>Configure MLA Parameters**.

Step 2   Change the **Enable MultiLevelAdmin** parameter to **True**.

Step 3   Two new fields display. Enter the password for the new CCMAdmin administrator (CCMAdministrator) in both of these fields.

Note	Once MLA is enabled, you need to use the account called CCMAdministrator to log into CCMAdmin with full access.

Step 4   Click the **Update** button.

Step 5   A window displays informing you to close the browser and log back on using CCMAdministrator and the password you just entered. Click **OK**.

Step 6   Another window displays informing you that you must restart webserver on all CallManager servers in the cluster. Click **OK**.

Step 7   Close the browser.

Step 8   From Window's services, restart the worldwide web publishing service.

Once MLA is enabled, functional and user groups must be configured. Before looking at how to configure these components, let's explore the function of each.

Functional groups determine to which administrative menus users have access. Figure 12-1 shows a portion of the configuration screen for a functional group.

Figure 12-1 *Functional Groups Configuration*

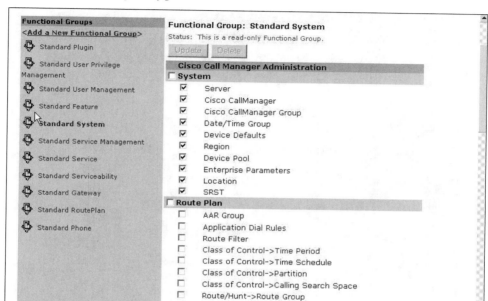

Each menu selection that is available in CCMAdmin is listed in the functional group; the menu selections that are checked determine to which menus the functional groups allow access. Figure 12-1 shows that the functional group allows access to all the System menus but not the Route Plan menus.

User groups assemble users together and determine the rights of these users to functional groups. Each user group contains all the functional groups and is granted no access, full access, or read-only access to each. Figure 12-2 shows the configuration screen for User Groups.

The first step to configuring MLA is to determine how many different levels of access are required. Once this is determined, you can start to create the functional groups. However, let's first take a closer look at the functional groups that are created by default when CallManager is installed. You may find that the functional groups you need are already created.

Each of the default functional groups and the selected menus of each are listed in Table 12-1.

Figure 12-2 *User Group Configuration*

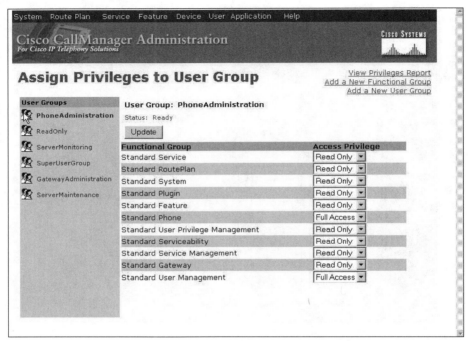

NOTE   Depending on the version of CallManager you are running, the default functional groups
           may vary slightly.

Table 12-1 *Default Functional Groups*

Functional Groups	Menu Selections
Standard Plugin	Application>
	Install Plugins
	Update Plugin URL
Standard User Privilege Management	User>
	Access Rights>
	Functional Groups
	User Groups
	Assign Privileges to User Groups
	Configure MLA Parameters

Table 12-1 *Default Functional Groups (Continued)*

Functional Groups	Menu Selections

Standard User Management	User>
	    Add a New User
	    Global Directory

Standard Feature	Feature>
	    Client Matter Code
	    Forced Authorization Code
	    Call Park
	    Call Pickup
	    Cisco IP Phone Services
	    Meet-Me Number/Pattern
	    Voice-Mail>
	        Cisco Voice-Mail Port
	        Cisco Voice-Mail Port Wizard
	        Message Waiting
	        Voice-Mail Pilot
	        Voice-Mail Profile

Standard System	System>
	    Server
	    Cisco CallManager
	    Cisco CallManager Group
	    Date/Time Group
	    Device Defaults
	    Region
	    Device Pool
	    Enterprise Parameters
	    Location
	    SRST
	Application>
	    Cisco CallManager Administration

Standard Service Management	Tools>
	    Service Activation
	    Control Center

continues

Table 12-1 *Default Functional Groups (Continued)*

Functional Groups	Menu Selections

Standard Service	Service>
	    Cisco IPMA Configuration Wizard
	    Cisco CM Attendant Console>
	        Pilot Point
	        Hunt Group
	        Cisco CM Attendant Console User
	        Cisco CM Attendant Console Server
	    Media Resource>
	        Annunciator
	        Conference Bridge
	        Media Termination Point
	        Music On Hold Audio Source
	        Music On Hold Server
	        Transcoder
	        Media Resource Group
	        Media Resource Group List
	    Service Parameters

Standard Serviceability	Application>
	    Cisco CallManager Serviceability>
	        Alarm>
	            Configuration
	            Definitions
	        Trace>
	            Configuration
	            Analysis
	            Collection
	            Q931 Translator
	            TroubleShooting Trace Settings
	        Tools>
	            Real-Time Monitoring Tool
	            QRT Viewer
	            Serviceability Report Archive

Standard Gateway	Device>
	    Gateway
	    Gatekeeper
	    Trunk

Table 12-1   *Default Functional Groups (Continued)*

Functional Groups	Menu Selections

Standard Route Plan	Route Plan>
	    AAR Group
	    Application Dial Rules
	    Route Filter
	    Class of Control>
	       Partition
	       Calling Search Space
	    Route Filter
	    Route/Hunt>
	       Route Pattern
	       Line Group
	       Route Group
	       Route List
	       Hunt List
	       Hunt Pilot
	    Translation Pattern
	    External Route Plan Wizard
	    Route Plan Report

Standard Phone	Device>
	    CTI Route Point
	    Phone
	    Device Settings>
	       Device Profile Default
	       Device Profile
	       Firmware Load Information
	       Phone Button Template
	       Softkey Template

If you determine that you need to add a functional group, the following steps can walk you through this process.

Adding a Functional Group

Step 1   From within CCMAdmin, select **User>Access Rights>Functional Group**.

Step 2   Click the **Add a New Functional Group** link.

Step 3 In the **Functional Group Name** field, enter a name for the new group.

Step 4 Check the box of each menu item this group will contain. To add all menu items listed under a major heading, select the major heading. For example, to add all the menu items listed under System, check the box next to **System**.

Step 5 Once all the desired menu items have been selected, click the **Insert** button.

It is important to remember that functional groups do not determine if access is allowed to the menu items they contain. Functional groups are simply used to define to which menu items privileges or restrictions will be assigned within a user group.

After you have created all the functional groups needed, user groups must be configured. Each user group contains a list of all functional groups and determines the privileges of each of these groups.

Before creating user groups, take a look at the default groups that are created. You may find that these groups are sufficient. Table 12-2 lists all the default user groups and the privileges of each.

NOTE Depending on the version of CallManager you have, the default user groups may vary slightly.

Table 12-2 *Default User Groups*

User Group	Functional Groups	Privileges
PhoneAdministration	Standard Service	Read Only
	Standard RoutePlan	Read Only
	Standard System	Read Only
	Standard Plugin	Read Only
	Standard Feature	Read Only
	Standard Phone	Full Access
	Standard User Privilege Management	Read Only
	Standard Serviceability	Read Only
	Standard Service Management	Read Only
	Standard Gateway	Read Only
	Standard User Management	Full Access
Read Only	Standard Service	Read Only
	Standard RoutePlan	Read Only
	Standard System	Read Only

Table 12-2   *Default User Groups (Continued)*

User Group	Functional Groups	Privileges
Read Only	Standard Plugin	Read Only
	Standard Feature	Read Only
	Standard Phone	Read Only
	Standard User Privilege Management	Read Only
	Standard Serviceability	Read Only
	Standard Service Management	Read Only
	Standard Gateway	Read Only
	Standard User Management	Read Only
ServerMonitoring	Standard Service	Read Only
	Standard RoutePlan	Read Only
	Standard System	Read Only
	Standard Plugin	Read Only
	Standard Feature	Read Only
	Standard Phone	Read Only
	Standard User Privilege Management	Read Only
	Standard Serviceability	Full Access
	Standard Service Management	Read Only
	Standard Gateway	Read Only
	Standard User Management	Read Only
SuperUserGroup	Standard Service	Full Access
	Standard RoutePlan	Full Access
	Standard System	Full Access
	Standard Plugin	Full Access
	Standard Feature	Full Access
	Standard Phone	Full Access
	Standard User Privilege Management	Full Access
	Standard Serviceability	Full Access
	Standard Service Management	Full Access
	Standard Gateway	Full Access
	Standard User Management	Full Access

continues

Table 12-2 *Default User Groups (Continued)*

User Group	Functional Groups	Privileges
GatewayAdministration	Standard Service	Read Only
	Standard RoutePlan	Full Access
	Standard System	Read Only
	Standard Plugin	Read Only
	Standard Feature	Read Only
	Standard Phone	Read Only
	Standard User Privilege Management	Read Only
	Standard Serviceability	Read Only
	Standard Service Management	Read Only
	Standard Gateway	Full Access
	Standard User Management	Read Only
ServerMaintenance	Standard Service	Full Access
	Standard RoutePlan	Read Only
	Standard System	Full Access
	Standard Plugin	Full Access
	Standard Feature	Full Access
	Standard Phone	Read Only
	Standard User Privilege Management	Read Only
	Standard Serviceability	Read Only
	Standard Service Management	Full Access
	Standard Gateway	Read Only
	Standard User Management	Read Only

If you determine that an additional user group is required, the following steps walk you through the process of adding one.

Adding a User Group

Step 1 From within CCMAdmin, select **User>Access Rights>User Group**.

Step 2 Click the **Add a New User Group** link.

Step 3 A new screen displays. Enter the name for the new group in the **User Group Name** field.

Step 4 Click the **Insert** button.

Step 5 At this point the user group is created but no privileges are assigned. To assign privileges to this group, click the **Assign Privileges** link.

Step 6 A screen listing all the functional groups displays. From the **Access Privileges** drop-down list next to each Functional group, select the desired privilege. You may choose from the following three privileges for each group:

— No Access—Allows no access to the menus contained in this functional group.

— Read Only—Allows information in the menus contained in this functional group to be viewed but not added to, deleted, or edited.

— Full Access—Allows information in the menus contained in this functional group to be added to or edited.

Step 7 Click the **Update** button.

Now that the functional and user groups have been configured, you need to add users to the user groups. The users you want with administrative access to CallManager must have user accounts created on CallManager. The steps to add users are covered in the "Creating Users" section in Chapter 6, "Configuring CallManager Features and Services."

To add users to user groups use the following steps:

Step 1 From within CCMAdmin, select **User>Access Rights>User Group**.

Step 2 Select the group to which you are adding users from the list of groups on the left side of the screen.

Step 3 Click the **Add a User to Group** link.

Step 4 Enter a portion of the user's name in the **User Search** field and click the **Search** button.

Step 5 Check the box next to each user being added to the group and click **Add Selected**.

Attendant Console

In the past, some traditional PBXs had large attendant stations that allowed an operator to view the status of a large number of lines. Because the largest number of lines that can be displayed on any Cisco IP phone is 34, (7960 with two 7914s attached) it may not be possible to monitor every line. The solution to this is an application called Attendant Console. Attendant Console is an application that runs on a PC and allows monitoring and easy access to all lines on the system. Figure 12-3 shows this application.

Attendant Console offers the user many features such as line monitoring, drag and drop transfers, speed dial just to name a few. This section focuses more on the tasks required to configure Attendant Console than its features. Make sure that all users of this application are properly trained on its many features and functions. Also, make certain all users of this application have read the Attendant Consoles users guide, which can be found on Cisco.com by searching for "Attendant Console User Guide."

Figure 12-3 *Attendant Console*

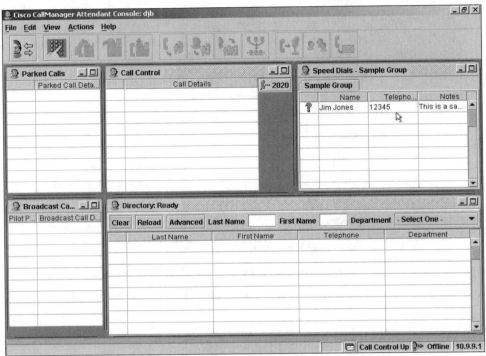

A number of tasks must be completed in order for Attendant Console to function properly. This section walks you through each of the required tasks. Let's start by creating Attendant Console users.

An Attendant Console user must be created for each user who will use this application. To create an Attendant Console user, follow these steps:

Step 1   From within CCMAdmin, select **Service>Cisco CM Attendant Console>Cisco CM Attendant Console User**.

Step 2   Click the **Add a New Attendant Console User** link.

Step 3   Enter the user ID for this user in the **User ID** field.

Step 4   Enter the password for this user in the **Password** and **Confirm** fields.

Step 5   Click the **Insert** button.

Add additional Attendant Console users as needed.

Now a pilot point and hunt List need to be created. A pilot point is a virtual number that is used to route the call to an available member of a hunt group. A hunt group is a list of directory numbers (DN)s or users.

To create pilot points, follow these steps:

Step 1 From within CCMAdmin, select **Service>Cisco CM Attendant Console>Pilot Point**.

Step 2 Click the **Add a New Pilot Point** link.

Step 3 In the **Pilot Name** field, enter a name for this pilot point.

Step 4 Select the desired Device Pool from the drop-down list.

Step 5 Select the appropriate Partition and Calling Search Space (CSS) from the drop-down list.

Step 6 Enter the number for the pilot point in the **Pilot Number** field. Make sure that this number is unique and that it is not shared with any other line or pattern.

Step 7 The **Route Calls to:** field has two choices that determine which member of the hunt group receives the call. Select **First Available Hunt Group Member**, if you want the calls to be sent to the first available member of the hunt group. Select **Longest Idle Hunt Group Member**, if you want the calls evenly distributed to all of the members of the hunt group.

Step 8 If locations are being used in your environment, select the appropriate one from the **Locations** drop-down list.

Step 9 Click the **Insert** button. The status line will read Insert complete once the pilot number is added.

Once the Pilot Point is added, you need to create a hunt group and assign members to it. The following steps show how this is done:

Step 1 From within CCMAdmin, select **Services>Cisco CM Attendant Console>Hunt Group**. A screen similar to that shown in Figure 12-4 displays.

Step 2 Select the pilot point for this hunt group from the list of pilot points on the left side of the screen.

Step 3 Members of a hunt group can either be directory numbers or Attendant Console users. To add an Attendant Console user click the **Add Member** button. Then select a name from the **User Name** drop-down list and a line number from the **Line Number** drop-down list and click **Update**.

Figure 12-4 *Hunt Group Configuration*

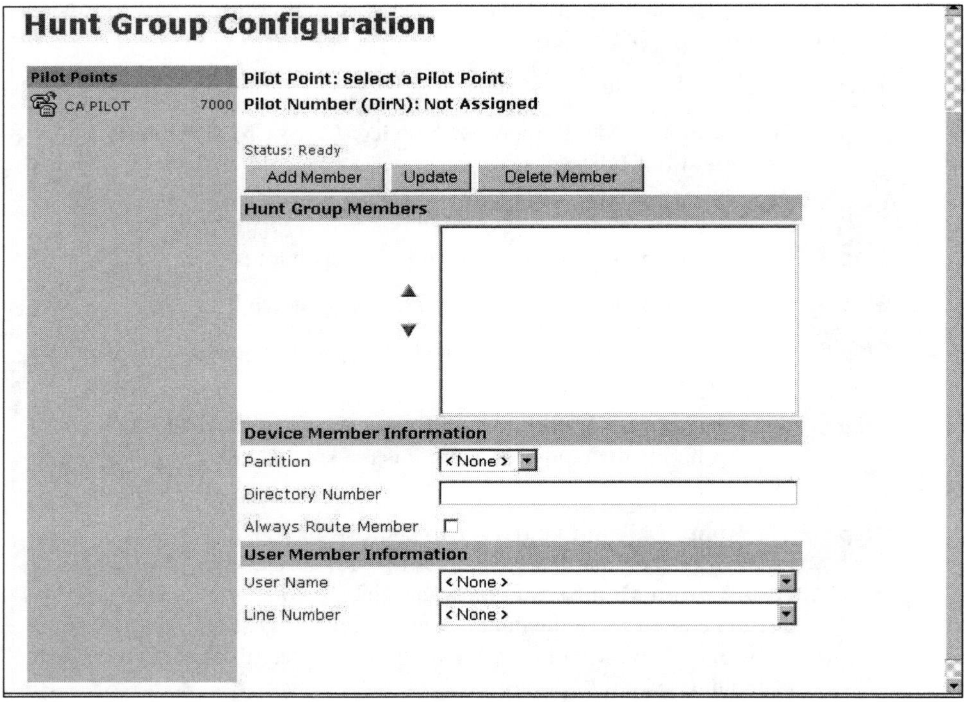

Step 4   To add a directory number, click the **Add Member** button. Then select the partition of the directory number and enter the DN in the **Directory Number** field. If the Always Route Member check box is selected, the call will always be sent to this destination. This is used when the final number on a hunt group points to voice mail or an auto attendant.

Step 5   Repeat Step 3 until all members have been added.

Step 6   Click the **Update** button.

Once the Attendant Console (ac) users, pilot points and hunt groups are configured, the ac user must be created. The ac user is created in the same way as a CallManager user. After the ac user is created it must associated with the pilot point and phones to be used with Attendant Console. The following Steps guide you through this process.

Step 1   From within CCMAdmin, select **User>Add a New User**.

Step 2   Enter **Attendant** as the first name and **Console** as the last name in the appropriate fields.

Step 3   In the **User ID** field enter **ac**. You must use ac for this user's ID.

Step 4   Enter **12345** in the **User Password** field and the **Confirm Password** field.

Step 5   Enter a PIN of your choice in the **PIN** field and confirm it by entering it again in the **Confirm PIN** field.

Step 6   Enter the telephone number of the user in the **Telephone Number** field.

Step 7   Check the **Enable CTI Applications Use** box.

Step 8   To allow the CTI application to control all CTI devices, check the **CTI Super Provider** box. If this box is checked, the Enable CTI Applications Use box should also be checked.

Note   Depending on your version of CallManager the CTI Super Provider box may not be available. In this case, just check the **Enable CTI Applications Use** box.

Step 9   Check the **Call Park Retrieval Allowed** box.

Step 10   Click the **Insert** button to add this user.

Step 11   Select the **Device Association** link.

Step 12   Enter search criteria in the search field that will return the pilot number and phones that are to be associated with the Attendant Console and click the **Select Devices** button.

Step 13   Check the box next to the pilot point and phones that are to be associated to the Attendant Console and click **Update Selected**.

Step 14   If there are other phones to associate to the Attendant Console, repeat Steps 12 and 13.

Because the Attendant Console is an application that runs on the user's PC, it must be loaded. To load the application on the PC, follow these steps:

Step 1   Log into CCMAdmin from the user's PC.

Step 2   From within CCMAdmin, select **Application>Install Plugins**.

Step 3   Select the Cisco **CallManager Attendant Console** plugin. When asked whether to run the program or save it, select **Run** and click **OK**.

Step 4   If a security warning pops up, click **Yes**.

Step 5   Click **Next** on the CallManager Attendant Console Installation Wizard.

Step 6   Click the **I accept the license agreement** radio button and click **Next**.

Step 7   Accept the default installation directory and click **Next**.

Step 8   The installation is ready to begin. Click **Next** to start the installation.

Step 9   Once the installation is complete, click **Finish**.

The application is complete. The first time users log in, the CallManager IP addresses and their phone extensions must be entered. They will be asked for a user ID and password. This is the Attendant User ID and password, not the CallManager user ID.

The Attendant Console is now configured and installed. Another application that is similar but used by managers and assistants is called IP Manager Assistant (IPMA). The next section introduces you to this application.

IPMA

IPMA allows assistants to monitor and manage calls for their managers. IPMA is configured in two different ways. The first is called proxy-line mode, which allows the manager to create filters that determine which calls are automatically diverted to the assistant and which calls are allowed through. To work, the incoming call must be intercepted, which is done by the use of CSS and Partitions. Running the IPMA Configuration Wizard configures CSS and Partitions and assigns them to the appropriate devices. Although the proxy-line mode offers more features than shared line, it also requires more configuration within CallManager and more administration on the part of the manager.

The other IPMA mode is called shared-line mode, which allows a subset of the features found in the proxy-line mode. However, in most cases, the features found in the shared-line mode are sufficient. This section takes a closer look at the configuration tasks required to implement shared-line mode.

The basic idea behind shared-line mode is that the manager's line displays on the assistant's phone as a shared line. This, coupled with the IPMA application, which is similar to the Attendant Console, allows the assistant to easily manage calls for the manager.

The manager has the same features that most users have plus the following three, which are configured as softkeys on the phone:

- DND—Do not disturb. Turns the ringer off.
- ImmDiv—Immediate Divert. Causes all calls to be diverted to a chosen destination.
- TransferToVM—Transfer to voice mail. Sends the call directly to voice mail.

The assistant must log into the IPMA console to manage the manager's phone. Figure 12-5 shows this interface. It looks very similar to Attendant Console and offers many of the same functions.

The configuration of IPMA can be quite involved and requires a solid understanding of many CallManager components. The steps provided in this section walk you through the bare minimum of configurations that are required. Because there are additional optional configurations that you may want to explore, you are encouraged to review the IPMA section of the CallManager administration guide, which can be found on Cisco.com. To find this document search "IPMA administration guide" at Cisco.com.

Figure 12-5 *IPMA Console*

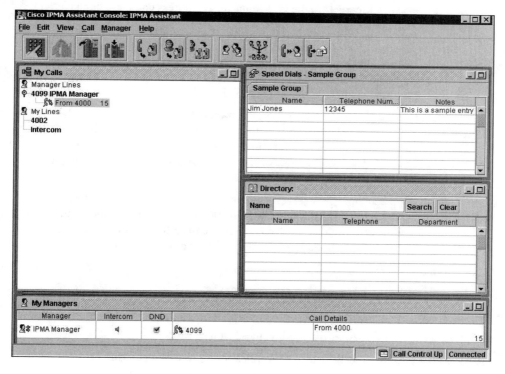

Set IPMA Service Parameters

You must set the IP address of the primary CTI Manager and Cisco IPMA Server before IPMA will function. To do so, follow these steps:

NOTE   The IPMA service must be activated before any configuration can be done. This service is activated from the CallManager's service activation page.

Step 1   From within CCMAdmin, select **Service>Service Parameters**.

Step 2   Select the CallManager on which IPMA is active from the **Server** drop-down list.

Step 3   Select the **Cisco IP Manager Assistant** from the **Service** drop-down list.

Step 4   A new screen displays. In the **CTI Manager (Primary) IP Address** field enter the address of the CallManager that is to be used as the primary CTI manager. It is best to select a lower utilized subscriber for the CTI manager. A window displays informing you that the Tomcat Service must be restarted before the CTI Manager IP address change will take effect. Click **OK**.

Step 5   If a backup CTI manager is configured, enter that IP address in the **CTI Manager (Backup) IP Address** field. A window displays informing you that the Tomcat Service must be restarted before the CTI Manager IP address change will take effect. Click **OK**.

Step 6   In the **Cisco IPMA Server (Primary) IP Address** field, enter the address of the CallManager that is to be used as the primary IPMA server. A window displays informing you that the Tomcat Service must be restarted before the IPMA server IP address change will take effect. Click **OK**.

Step 7   If a backup IPMA server is going to be used, enter that IP address in the **Cisco IPMA server (Backup) IP Address** field. A window displays informing you that the Tomcat Service must be restarted before the IPMA server IP address change will take effect. Click **OK**.

Step 8   Select **Update** to save your changes.

Restart IPMA Service

To restart the IPMA service, follow these steps:

Step 1   Access the Tomcat Web Application browser by entering **http://**IPMAServer_IP_Address**/manager/list** in a browser.

Step 2   When prompted, enter the administrator user name and password.

Step 3   Click the **Stop** and then the **Start** link next to the Cisco IP Manager Assistant.

Step 4   Close the Tomcat Web Application window.

Configure Manager and Assistant

The next step is to configure managers and assistants. The steps in this section are based on the following assumptions:

- Users for the managers and assistants are already created.
- CTI Application use is selected for all assistants and manager's user configurations.

- The manager and assistant have 7960 or 7970 phones, and they are associated with the user.
- A shared line has been configured on the manager and assistant's phone.

The following steps show how to create and configure managers and assistants:

Step 1 From within CCMAdmin select **User>Global Directory**.

Step 2 Enter the name of the user to be configured as the manager in the search field. Click **Search**.

Step 3 Select the name for the manager from the list that displays.

Step 4 Click on the **Cisco IPMA** link.

Step 5 In the screen that displays, click the **Continue** button to configure this user as a manager.

Step 6 A screen similar to that shown in Figure 12-6 displays. On the next screen check the **Automatic Configuration** check box.

Step 7 Check the **Uses Shared Lines** check box.

Figure 12-6 *Manager Configuration*

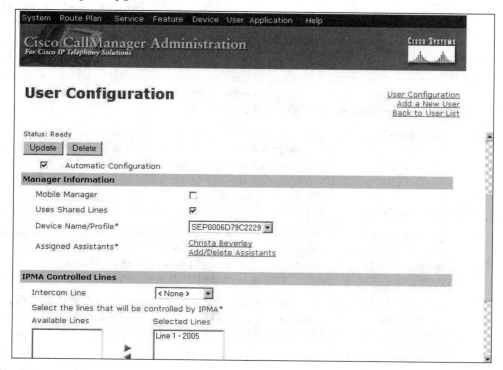

Step 8 In the list of **Available Lines**, highlight the line that is shared with the assistant and click the arrow that points toward the **Selected Lines**.

Step 9 Click the **Add/Delete Assistants** link. Enter the name of the user to be assigned as this person's assistant in the search field and click the **Search** button.

Step 10 Check the check box next to the name of the assistant. Click **Insert and Close**.

Step 11 Click the **Update** button.

Install Assistant Console Application

The following steps walk you through the process of loading the IPMA Assistant Console.

Step 1 From a browser on the PC on which the Assistant Console is to be loaded, enter **http://***IPMAServer_IP_Address***/ma/Install/ IPMAConsoleInstall.jsp**. This URL is case sensitive.

Step 2 Click **Yes** if a security warning pops up.

Step 3 Close the window once the installation is complete.

To access the application, click on the **IPMA** icon on the desktop. Enter the user name and password of the assistant.

These steps are the bare minimum that are required to configure IPMA Shared-line mode. Refer to the IPMA section of the CallManager administration guide, which can be found on Cisco.com for more details on other configuration options. To find this document search "IPMA administration guide" at Cisco.com.

In addition to the administrative guide, you will want to download the latest copy of the IPMA user's guide from Cisco.com and provide each user of this application with a copy. It is also a good idea to provide some hands-on training for both the managers and the assistants.

Time of Day Routing

The ability to route calls based on time of day is a feature that is available in CallManager 4.1 and later. This added function allows certain calls to be allowed and restricted based on time of day. It works in concert with CSS and partitions, which allows you to apply certain time-of-day routing rules to one group of users and other rules to other groups.

In the simplest terms, the way this works is that a time frame is assigned to a partition. During that time frame, the partition is accessible by any device that has a CSS that includes the partition. Outside that time frame, no device has access to the partition.

To configure time of day routing Time Periods and Time Schedules must be created. Time Periods define a time range and days to which it applies. Time schedules are groups of time periods. Time schedules are then assigned to the partitions. By using time schedules you are able to assign more than one time period to a partition.

Let's take a look at how these two components are configured. Because time schedules contain time periods, time periods must be configured first.

Creating a Time Period

The following steps explain how to configure a Time Period.

Step 1   From within CCMAdmin, select **Route Plan>Class of Control>Time Period**.

Step 2   Click the **Add a New Time Period** link.

Step 3   A screen similar to that shown in Figure 12-7 displays.

Figure 12-7   *Time Period Configuration*

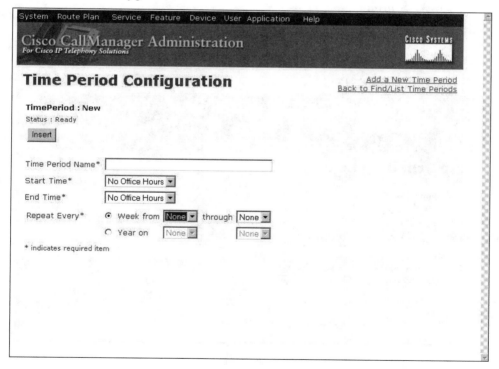

Step 4   Enter the name of this time period in the **Time Period Name** field.

Step 5   From the **Start Time** and **End Time** drop-down lists select the time range for this time period.

Step 6   You can choose to apply this time range to days of the week or a specific date. To apply it to days of the week, select the **Week from** radio button. Select the day range by selecting the beginning day from the first drop-down list and the end day of the range from the second drop-down list.

Step 7   To select a specific date instead of a weekday range, select the **Year on** radio button. Select the month from the first drop-down list and the date from the second drop-down list.

Step 8   Click the **Insert** button.

Repeat these steps to add all the time periods that are required. Once all are created, they need to be assigned to a time schedule.

Create a Time Schedule

Step 1   From within CCMAdmin, select **Route Plan>Class of Control>Time Schedule**.

Step 2   Click the **Add a New Time Schedule** link.

Step 3   A screen similar to that shown in Figure 12-8 displays.

Figure 12-8   *Time Schedule Configuration*

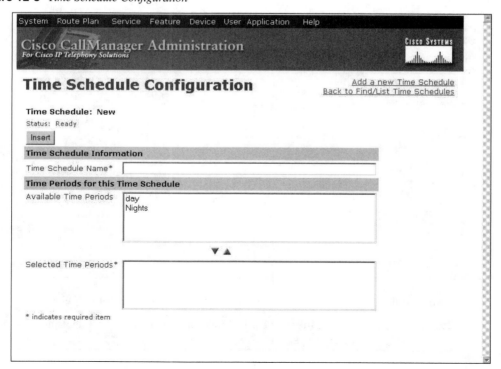

Step 4 Enter the name of the time schedule in the **Time Schedule Name** field.

Step 5 Select a time period from the **Available Time Periods** box, and click the **down arrow** to add it to the **Selected Time Periods** box.

Step 6 Once all the desired time periods are listed in the Selected Time Period box, click the **Insert** button.

After the time schedule is created, it needs to be assigned to a partition, as explained in the section that follows.

Assign a Time Schedule to a Partition

Step 1 From within CCMAdmin, select **Route Plan>Class of Control>Partition**.

Step 2 Enter search criteria to limit the partition results in the search field, and click the **Find** button.

Step 3 Click on the partition to which you want to assign a time schedule.

Step 4 From the **Time Schedule** drop-down list, select the desired time schedule.

Step 5 You can choose to apply the time schedule based on the time zone of the device that is placing the call or another time zone of your choosing. To base it on the time zone of the calling device, select the **Originating Device** radio button. To select another time zone, select the **Specific Time Zone** radio button and select the desired time zone from the drop-down list.

Step 6 Click the **Update** button.

Once a time schedule is applied to a partition, time of day routing is active for any pattern to which that the partition is assigned.

Hunt List

Often it is desirable to have an unanswered call roll from one directory number to another. To do this a hunt list is created. A hunt list is a list of directory numbers that a call is routed through until it is answered. Make sure that you don't confuse this with hunt groups, which are specific to the Attendant Console.

A hunt list is actually made up of three components as follows:

- Line Groups—A list of directory numbers
- Hunt Lists—A list of Line Groups
- Hunt Pilot—A pilot number that points to a hunt list

A hunt list works when a call is placed to the number assigned to the hunt pilot, for example, if an outside caller calls the main number. The hunt pilot points to the hunt list, which in turn sends the call to a member of the line group. The member to which the call is sent depends on how the line group is set up.

The following are the steps required to configure a hunt list. These components must be created in this order: Line Group, Hunt List and then Hunt Pilot.

Creating a Line Group

The following steps show how to create a line group.

Step 1   From within CCMAdmin, select **Route Plan>Route/Hunt>Line Group**.

Step 2   Click the **Add a New Line Group** link.

Step 3   A screen similar to that shown in Figure 12-9 displays. Enter a descriptive name for this line group in the **Line Group Name** field.

Step 4   The RNA Reversion Timeout determines how long a line will ring before it is sent to the next member of the group. RNA stands for Ring No Answer. This value is set in seconds not rings. Enter the number of seconds you want each line in the group to ring.

Figure 12-9 *Line Group Configuration*

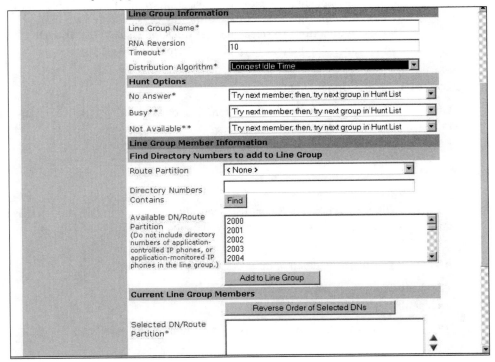

Step 5   The next field determines how the call is distributed to the members of the line group. The available options are as follows:

- Top Down—Rings the first idle member on the line group regardless of all other factors

- Circular—Rings the member of the group that follows the member that had received the last call

- Longest Idle Time—Extends the call only to idle members starting with the member that has been idle the longest

- Broadcast—Sends the call to all idle members

Step 6   Select the desired distribution method from the **Distribution Algorithm** drop-down list.

The next three fields determine what happens when a member of the group does not answer, is busy, or the line is not available. The available options are as follows:

- Try next member; then, try next group in hunt list—Tries all the idle members of the group. If none answer, the call is sent to the next line group in the hunt list.

- Try next member; but do not go to next group—Tries all the idle members of the group. If none answer, the call is not sent to the next line group in the hunt list.

- Skip remaining members, and go directly to next group—If the member that the call is extended to does not answer, the call is sent to the next group.

- Stop hunting—Tries to sends the call to the first idle member of the line group. If the call is not answered, it will not send it to another member and stops hunting.

Step 7   Select the desired setting for each of the three conditions (No Answer, Busy, or Not Available) from the drop-down list.

Step 8   Select a partition from the **Route Partition** drop-down list if one is required for this line group.

Step 9   To limit the numbers that display in the Available DN/Route Partition box, enter search criteria in the **Directory Numbers Contains** field. For example, if you want to add lines 2020, 2030, 2040, and 2050 to a line group, you can enter 20[2-5]0 in this field. Remember that the wildcard [] matches a single number in a range.

Step 10   In the **Available DN/Route Partition** box, highlight a line you wish to add to this line group and click the **Add to Line Group** button. Repeat this step until all desired lines display in the **Selected DN/Route Partition** box.

Step 11 To adjust the order in which the lines display in the group, highlight a line and use the **up** and **down arrow** to the right of the Selected DN/Route Partition box.

Step 12 To remove a member from the Line Group, highlight the member and click the **down arrow** beneath the Available DN/Route Partition box. This moves the line to the Removed DN/Route Partition box.

Step 13 Click the **Insert** button to add this line group.

Once the line groups are added, they need to be assigned to hunt lists. The following steps guide you through this process.

Creating Hunt List

Step 1 From within CCMAdmin, select **Route Plan>Route/Hunt>Hunt List**.

Step 2 Click the **Add a New Hunt List** link.

Step 3 Enter a name for this line group in the **Hunt List Name** field.

Step 4 Enter a description in the **Description** field.

Step 5 Select the CallManager group to which this hunt list will register from the **Cisco CallManager Group** drop-down list.

Step 6 Click the **Insert** button. A window displays stating that you must add a least one Line Group. Click **OK**.

Step 7 A screen similar to that shown in Figure 12-10 displays. The **Enable this Hunt List** check box determines if the hunt list is active or not. Check this box to activate the hunt list.

Step 8 To add a line group to this hunt list click the **Add Line Group** button. A new screen displays. From the drop-down list, select the line group you wish to add and click **Insert**. A window displays stating that the line group has been added and the hunt list must be reset. Click **OK**.

Step 9 Repeat Step 8 to add all desired line groups to this hunt list.

Step 10 To adjust the order in which the line groups display in the hunt list, highlight a line group and use the **up and down arrows** to the right of the Selected Groups box.

Step 11 To remove a line group from the hunt list, highlight the line group and click the down arrow beneath the **Selected Groups** box. This moves the line to the Removed Group box.

Step 12 Click the **Update** button to save changes made to this hunt list. A window displays stating that hunt list must be reset for changes to take effect. Click **OK**.

Figure 12-10 *Hunt List Configuration*

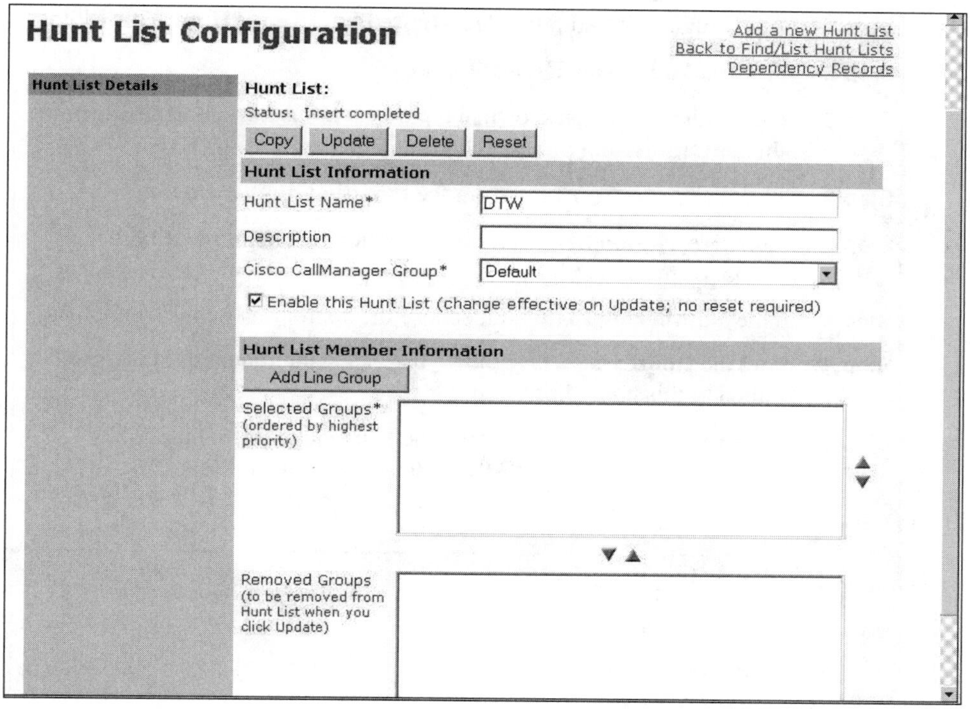

Step 13 Click the **Reset** button. A window displays informing you that you are about to reset the hunt list, which will cause CallManager to reject calls to this hunt list during the process. Click **OK**.

Note	Because resetting a hunt list can cause calls to be rejected, it is recommended that you do this during off hours.

Step 14 A window displays stating that the hunt list is being reset. Click **OK**.

Once the line groups and hunt lists are created, hunt pilots need to be created which send calls to the hunt lists.

Creating Hunt Pilots

Creating hunt pilots is the same as creating route patterns. Most of the parameters configured when creating a Hunt Pilot have already been discussed, in the "Creating Basic Patterns" section of Chapter 4, "Implementing a Dial Plan."

To create a Hunt Pilot follow these steps.

Step 1   From within CCMAdmin, select **Route Plan>Route/Hunt>Hunt Pilot**.

Step 2   Click the **Add a New Hunt Pilot** link.

Step 3   A screen similar to that shown in Figure 12-11 displays. Enter a directory number for this hunt pilot in the **Hunt Pilot** field.

Step 4   Select the desired partition from the **Partition** drop-down list.

Step 5   In the **Description** field, enter a description that helps identify the purpose of this hunt pilot.

Step 6   In the **Numbering Plan** field, choose the appropriate numbering plan.

Step 7   From the **Route Filter** drop-down list, select the route filter that is to be applied to this hunt pilot.

Step 8   Determine the precedence level to be assigned to this hunt pilot by selecting it from the **MLPP Precedence** drop-down list.

Figure 12-11   *Hunt Pilot Configuration*

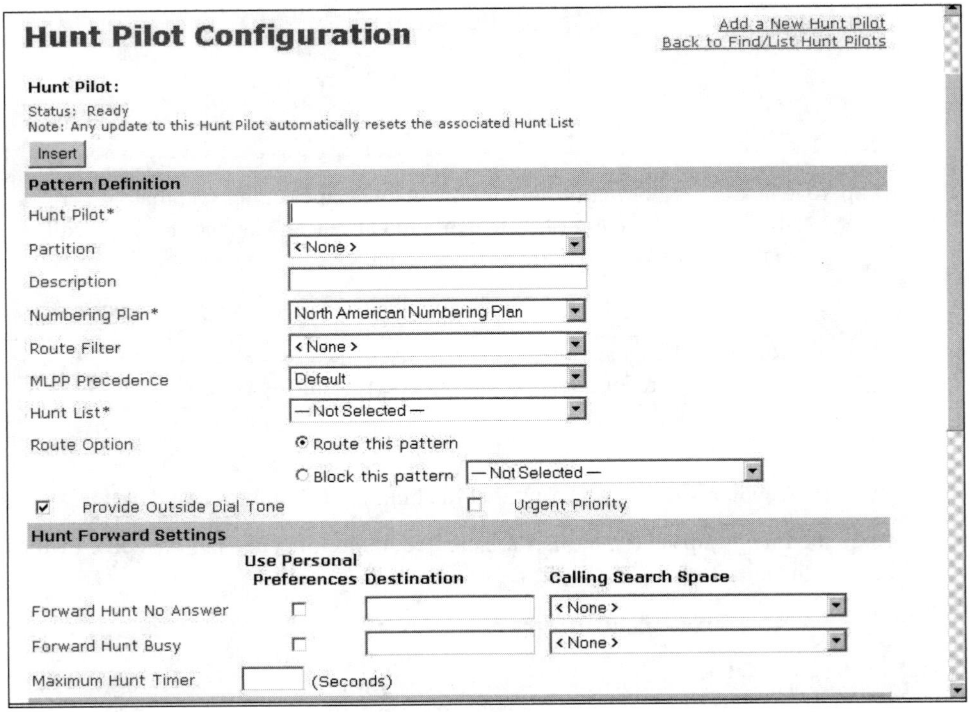

Step 9   From the **Hunt List** drop-down list, select the **hunt list** to which calls to the directory number assigned to this hunt pilot should be sent.

Step 10   To allow calls that match this hunt pilot to be routed, select the **Route this pattern** radio button.

Step 11   If you wish to have a secondary dial tone played after the first digit is dialed, check **Provide Outside Dial Tone**.

Step 12   If you wish to route a call as soon as it matches this route pattern, check the **Urgent Priority** box. Take caution when selecting this option. It could cause patterns that are similar to fail. For instance if the hunt pilot pattern was 5246 and another pattern was 524XXXX, when someone tried to dial 5426000, the call would match the 5426 hunt pilot and ignore the 000 if the hunt pilot was set to urgent priority.

Step 13   In the **Forward Hunt No Answer** field, enter the directory number to which you want calls to be sent if no member of the Line Groups answers the call. Also enter a CSS from the **Calling Search Space** drop-down list if one is needed.

Step 14   In the **Forward Hunt Busy** field enter the directory number to which you want calls to be sent if all destinations of the hunt list are busy. Also enter a CSS from the **Calling Search Space** drop-down list if one is needed.

Step 15   To limit how long the hunt pilot number rings, you can enter a value in the **Maximum Hunt Timer** field. This value is set in seconds, not number of rings.

Step 16   If you wish to affect caller ID information, configure the fields found under the Calling Party Transformations heading. The first field is labeled **Use Calling Party's External Phone Number Mask**. This field determines if the mask configured on the directory number is used for calls that are routed through this hunt pilot.

Step 17   In the **Calling Party Transform Mask field**, enter any mask you wish to affect the caller ID.

Step 18   In the **Prefix Digits** (Outgoing Calls) field, enter any digits that you want added to the front of the caller ID.

Step 19   The Calling Line ID Presentation field determines if caller ID information is to be blocked for outbound calls that match this hunt pilot. To block caller ID, select **Restricted** from the drop-down list. To allow caller ID, select **Allowed** from the drop-down list.

Step 20   The Calling Name Presentation field determines if caller name information is to be blocked for outbound calls that match this hunt pilot. To block calling name ID, select **Restricted** from the drop-down list. To allow calling name ID, select **Allowed** from the drop-down list.

Step 21 The Connected Line ID Presentation field determines if the connected party's ID information is to display on the calling party's phone. To block the connected party's ID, select **Restricted** from the drop-down list. To allow the connected party's ID, select **Allowed** from the drop-down list.

Step 22 The Connected Name Presentation field determines if the connected party's name information is displayed on the calling party's phone. To block the connected party's name, select **Restricted** from the drop-down list. To allow the connected party's name, select **Allowed** from the drop-down list.

Step 23 From the Discard Digits drop-down list, select the digit discard instruction that should be applied to calls that match this hunt pilot.

Step 24 In the **Called Party Transform Mask** field, enter the mask you want to use for calls that match this hunt pilot. If no mask is to be used, leave this field empty.

Step 25 In the **Prefix Digits** (Outgoing Calls) field, enter any digits that you want added to the front of a dialed number before it is sent to the hunt list.

Step 26 Click **Insert** to add the Hunt Pilot.

Once the Hunt Pilot is created the configuration for hunt lists is completed.

Now that you are familiar with some of the features in CallManager that help solve specific business needs, let's move on to a few features in Unity that can also add enhanced call handling capabilities.

Advanced Unity Features

Unity has a number of advanced features that are not always utilized. The job of Unity is to provide voice mail, auto attendant, and unified messaging services, which it does quite well. However, it can also provide other services that are not always thought of as being a function of a voice-mail system. This section explores a couple of these features. Although all the configuration tasks required to implement these features have been discussed in previous chapters, this chapter allows you to take a closer look at how you can use the features within Unity for some additional functionality.

Enabling Call Queuing

One of the underutilized features Unity provides is that of call queuing. Unity's queuing capabilities let callers decide if they want to be placed on hold or transferred to voice mail if the number they are trying to reach is busy. Although this can be a handy feature, remember that a caller who chooses to hold a voice mail port will be consumed for the entire time that the call is on hold. Therefore, this feature should be used only in environments in which an ample number of voice-mail ports exist. Furthermore, this feature is normally configured for only a small number of subscribers.

To configure call queuing, follow these steps.

Step 1   From within UA, select **Subscribers>Subscribers**.

Step 2   Click the **Find** icon, enter search criteria that will narrow the search results, and click the **Find** button.

Step 3   Select the subscriber for whom you are enabling call queuing.

Step 4   Click the **Call Transfer** link.

Step 5   Make sure that the Transfer incoming calls to subscriber's phone field is set to **Yes, ring subscriber's extension** or **Yes, ring subscriber at this number**.

Step 6   Select the **Supervise Transfer** radio button.

Step 7   Set the **Rings to wait for** value to a value that is less than that set in CallManager for this subscriber. Keep in mind that the value in CallManager is in seconds, whereas the value in Unity is in number of rings.

Step 8   Select the **Ask Caller** radio button under the **If the call is busy** options.

Step 9   Click the **Save** icon.

Once this is done, callers, who try to reach this extension through Unity and find the extension busy, are given the opportunity to be placed on hold or leave a message. Unity informs them of how many callers are ahead of them and then, every 30 seconds, offers them an opportunity to leave a message. If callers want to stay on hold instead of leaving a message, they must press "1" each time they are asked if they wish to continuing holding.

Configuring Destination Call Screening

Unity also provides the option to screen calls before they are transferred. The idea of allowing a called party to screen calls is often associated with avoiding phone calls. However, it is possible to use this feature to add functionality to a system.

Call screening can allow the recipient of a call to not only find out who the incoming call is coming from but also who it is intended for. For instance, in a warehouse with multiple workers and only a single phone, it may be helpful for the person answering to know whom the call is for before the call is connected. This way if the intended recipient of the call is not in, the call can be directed to that person's voice mail by pressing **2** saving time for the person answering. For this to work, a voice-mail box must be created for each person.

The following summary of steps indicates what must be done to configure this.

Step 1   Create a subscriber for each user with a unique extension that is different than the one assigned to the phone that they share. Apply the following Call Transfer settings to each of these subscribers.

— Ring the extension of the shared phone by selecting **Yes, ring subscriber at this number** and entering the extension number.

— Supervise Transfer with a ring value less than that set in CallManager.

— Under the Gather Caller Information heading, check Introduce and Confirm.

Once this is configured, all calls transferred from Unity to the shared phone will announce whom the call is for and allow the person who answered the call to press **1** to accept the call or **2** to send the call to voice mail.

This is only a small sampling of some of the advanced features of Unity. Additional features are discussed in the Cisco Press book "Cisco Unity Deployment and Solutions Guide."

Unique Solutions

From time to time a client wants a feature that isn't available or wishes an existing feature had an enhancement or two. In these cases, find out the true functionality that the customer is seeking and see if you can offer that functionality by leveraging the features found in both CallManager and Unity. This section offers a few examples of real-world requests and how each was solved.

This section does not offer a step-by-step solution but rather introduces you to a few unique solutions with the hope that it will encourage you to go beyond what you have learned in this book and create your own solutions with CallManager and Unity.

Configuring Unity as a Meet-Me Conference Manager

CallManager's Meet-Me conferences offer the ability to allow multiple people to dial into a conference call. However, Meet-Me does not have any way to announce who has joined the conference or offer the option of disallowing certain individuals from joining. Of course, using CSS and partitions, devices can be blocked from Meet-Me numbers but this is often impractical.

By using CSS, partitions and call handlers, this functionality can be added to a CallManager and Unity environment. The steps that follow outline the tasks that are required.

Step 1   Create a MEETME_PT partition and a MEETME_CSS CSS that contains the MEETME_PT partition.

Step 2   Assign the MEETME_PT partition to the Meet-Me numbers.

Step 3   Assign the MEETME_CSS CSS to all voice-mail ports and to the phones that will initiate the conference. At least one phone must have this CSS or another CSS that allows access to the MEETME_PT partition. The Meet-Me conference can only be initiated from a phone that has access to the MEETME_PT partition.

Step 4   Create a call handler for each Meet-Me number and assign it the same extension number as the Meet-Me conference. Set the call handler to ring the extension of the Meet-Me conference. This is the same number that is entered for this call handler's extension. Also, set up the call handler to do a Supervise Transfer with a ring value less than that set in CallManager. Under the **Gather Caller Information** section of the call handler heading, check **Confirm** and **Ask Caller's Name**.

The result is that the phone allowed to initiate a Meet-Me conference will do so. All other participants then dial into Unity and enter the Meet-Me number. You may want to change the opening greeting so that outside callers know to enter the Meet-Me number. When the caller dials the Meet-Me number, Unity sends the call to the call handler with the same extension as the Meet-Me number. The call handler then asks the callers to record their names. The call is then forwarded to the conference and the caller's name is played. Unity then instructs participants in the conference to press 1 to accept the call or 2 to send the call to voice mail. You may want to set the greeting for the call handlers to say something like, "I'm sorry, but you are not authorized to enter this conference call" and then have the call handler send the caller back to the opening greeting.

NOTE   Be aware of two things. First, you must create a call handler for each Meet-Me pattern that exists in CallManager. Second, any member of the conference will be able to allow and disallow callers into the conference by pressing **1** or **2**.

Directed Call Pickup

Directed call pickup is a feature that is found on a number of phone systems. This feature allows a user to answer a specific ringing phone. Although CallManager does allow you to pick up a ringing phone from a group, if two phones in the same group are ringing, you are not able to select which specific phone you want to answer.

This feature can be mimicked with CallManager. Adding the feature is a simple rather than advanced task. However, many people ask how this can be done, so it has been included in this book. All you need to do is place each phone in its own Call Pickup Group.

It is good to have the group number contain the extension number of the line to which it is assigned. For instance, if the line number is 2005, the group number could be 52005. To answer a call coming in on 2005 from a phone that does not have the 2005 line, press the GPickup softkey and then 52005.

Sometimes simplicity is a beautiful thing.

Managing Multi-Location Overlapping Extensions

This section examines an actual problem faced by a client who failed to plan properly for the future. As mentioned early in this book, poor planning, or the entire lack of planning, causes failed deployments. As the saying goes, "He who fails to plan is planning to fail."

This client's problem was that the company had overlapping and duplicate extension numbers at multiple locations. All the phones were registered to a single cluster and all voice-mail boxes were on the same Unity system. That by itself can cause problems, but the main issue was that all incoming calls from each location were routed over the wide-area network (WAN) to the Unity auto attendant. Therefore, when an outside caller dialed the Memphis office, the call was routed to the Unity that resided in New York. The outside caller would then enter 324 to be transferred to extension 324. The problem was that there was a 324 in both Memphis and New York, so it was unclear to which location the call would be sent.

In order to solve this problem, you need to call upon the CSS and partitions again. The resolution of a number of issues requires the use of CSS and partitions.

The NYC_PT partition must be assigned the New York 324 and the Memphis_PT partition to the Memphis 324. Indeed, all of the directory numbers in NYC must be assigned a partition other than the one that the Memphis directory numbers have. In most cases this is desirable even if this issue does not exist. To make this work use two hunt lists: one to direct calls to voice-mail ports that have a CSS with access to the lines in NYC_PT but not Memphis_PT; the other to direct calls to voice-mail ports that have a CSS with access to the lines in Memphis_PT but not NYC_PT. All incoming calls from Memphis are directed to the hunt list that points to the ports that have access to Memphis_PT. All NYC incoming calls are directed to the hunt list that points to the ports that have access to NYC_PT.

Although this is by no means the ideal solution, it solved the immediate problem, which gave the company time to rework their entire dial plan. The major drawback to this solution is that the voice-mail ports must be dedicated to specific sites instead of being shared.

Summary

This chapter introduced you to some of the new and more advanced features of CallManager and showed how the features within CallManager and Unity are used to provide more functionality.

The tasks required to configure MLA, Attendant Console, IPMA, time of day routing, and hunt lists in CallManager were explained and step-by-step procedures provided for each. The steps to enable call queuing and destination call screening in Unity were discussed. Finally, you learned how issues such as Meet-Me conference limitations and overlapping extensions are resolved.

At this point you should feel comfortable with the majority of the day-to-day configuration and administration tasks that a CallManager and Unity deployment require. Because you will not have to perform all these tasks on a daily basis, you can refer to this book when confronted with an unfamiliar task.

Additional Reference Resources

A large number of concepts and technologies have been discussed throughout this book. The presentation of these topics was designed to help you understand how to configure various components and how each component fits into a Cisco IP communications solution. However, you may have found places in the book where you wish you had more detail. Because the size of the book is limited, this appendix has been added to outline a list of additional references.

The appendix has two sections; the first is a list of concepts and components in alphabetical order. After each item, a pointer to additional documentation discusses each topic in further detail. The second section is a list of additional interesting reading. This section lists Cisco Press books that deal with this technology and a brief description of each.

Additional References

Have you ever wanted information on a topic and been told that you could find it on the web? It's like asking someone for the best way to get somewhere and being told the best way is to drive. Although driving may be the best way, you were probably hoping for a little more detail. That is what this section offers you. Instead of just referring you to Cisco.com for more details, each topic offers a specific link or book from which you can find more information. The hope is that this will save you time and allow you to gain a better understanding of a given topic.

However, don't stop here. Always continue to increase your knowledge. A favorite quote of a friend of mine seems to become truer with each passing year. Alvin Toffler writes that the illiterate of the future "will not be those who cannot read and write, but those who cannot learn, unlearn, and relearn."

Automatic Alternate Routing

Understanding Route Plans found in Cisco CallManager System Guide, Release 4.0(1)

http://www.cisco.com/en/US/products/sw/voicesw/ps556/products_ administration_guide_chapter09186a00801ec5a4.html#1056007

Audio Message Interface Standard (AMIS) Networking

Networking in Cisco Unity Guide (With Microsoft Exchange), Release 4.0(4)—AMIS Networking section

http://www.cisco.com/en/US/products/sw/voicesw/ps2237/products_ installation_and_configuration_guide_chapter09186a008022cd8e.html

Annunciators

Annunciator section in Cisco CallManager System Guide

http://www.cisco.com/en/US/products/sw/voicesw/ps556/ products_administration_guide_chapter09186a00801ec5b9.html

Audio Text Application

Cisco Unity Deployment and Solutions Guide: Chapter 18—Audio-Text Application

Cisco Press 2004 ISBN: 1-58705-118-4

Bulk Administration Tool (BAT)

Bulk Administration Tool User Guide

http://www.cisco.com/en/US/products/sw/voicesw/ps556/products_ user_guide_book09186a0080212686.html

Bridge Networking

Cisco Unity Bridge Networking Guide

http://www.cisco.com/en/US/products/sw/voicesw/ps2237/products_ installation_and_configuration_guide_book09186a008022ffac.html

Call Handlers

Cisco Unity Fundamentals: Chapter 5—Cisco Unified Communication System Customization

Cisco Press 2004 ISBN: 1-58705-098-6

Calling Search Space (CSS)

Cisco CallManager Fundamentals: A Cisco AVVID Solution

Cisco Press 2001 ISBN: 1-58705-008-0

Dial Plan

Dial Plan section of Cisco IP Telephony Solution Reference Network Design (SRND) for Cisco CallManager 4.0

http://www.cisco.com/en/US/products/sw/voicesw/ps556/products_ implementation_design_guide_chapter09186a00802c37f9.html

Digital Networking

Digital Networking section of Networking in Cisco Unity Guide (With Microsoft Exchange), Release 4.0(4)

http://www.cisco.com/en/US/products/sw/voicesw/ps2237/products_ installation_and_configuration_guide_chapter09186a008022cd84.html

Emergency Responder

Cisco Emergency Responder User's Guide

http://www.cisco.com/en/US/products/sw/voicesw/ps842/products_ user_guide_chapter09186a0080315d34.html

Extension Mobility

Cisco CallManager Extension Mobility section of Cisco CallManager Features and Services Guide

http://www.cisco.com/en/US/products/sw/voicesw/ps556/products_ administration_guide_chapter09186a00802e225c.html

Gatekeeper

Configuring an Anonymous Device Gatekeeper with Cisco CallManager Versions 3.3 and 4.1

http://www.cisco.com/en/US/products/sw/voicesw/ps556/products_ configuration_example09186a0080169445.shtml

Understanding H.323 Gatekeepers

http://www.cisco.com/en/US/tech/tk652/tk701/technologies_tech_ note09186a00800c5e0d.shtml

H.323

H.323 Tutorial

http://www.iec.org/online/tutorials/h323/

Inter-Cluster Trunks (ICT)

Understanding Cisco CallManager Trunk Types section of Cisco CallManager System Guide

http://www.cisco.com/en/US/products/sw/voicesw/ps556/products_ administration_guide_chapter09186a00801ec5ce.html

IP Phone Services

Developing Cisco IP Phone Services

2002 Cisco Press ISBN: 1-58705-060-9

IP Manager Assistant (IPMA)

Cisco IP Manager Assistant User Guide for Cisco CallManager

http://www.cisco.com/en/US/products/sw/voicesw/ps5015/products_
user_guide_book09186a0080312d23.html

Locations

Cisco CallManager Best Practices, pages 60–65

Cisco Press June 28, 2004 ISBN : 1-58705-139-7

Media Resource Management

Media Resource Management section of Cisco CallManager System
Guide

http://www.cisco.com/en/US/products/sw/voicesw/ps556/products_
administration_guide_chapter09186a00801ec5bc.html

Media Gateway Control Protocol (MGCP)

Understanding MGCP Interactions with Cisco CallManager

http://www.cisco.com/en/US/tech/tk652/tk701/technologies_
tech_note09186a00801da84e.shtml

Multi-Level Access (MLA)

Cisco CallManager Best Practices: Chapter 9—Using Multilevel
Administration

Cisco Press 2004 ISBN : 1-58705-139-7

Multi-Level Precedence and Preemption MLPP

Multilevel Precedence and Preemption section of Cisco CallManager
Features and Services Guide

http://www.cisco.com/en/US/products/sw/voicesw/ps556/products_
administration_guide_chapter09186a00801ed11e.html

Music on Hold (MOH)

Music on Hold section of Cisco IP Telephony Solution Reference Network
Design (SRND) for Cisco CallManager 4.0

http://www.cisco.com/en/US/products/sw/voicesw/ps556/products_
implementation_design_guide_chapter09186a00802c37af.html

Media Termination Points (MTP)

Media Termination Points section of the Cisco CallManager System Guide

http://www.cisco.com/en/US/products/sw/voicesw/ps556/products_
administration_guide_chapter09186a00801ec5be.html

Partitions

Cisco CallManager Fundamentals: A Cisco AVVID Solution

Cisco Press 2001 ISBN: 1-58705-008-0

Patterns

Cisco CallManager Fundamentals: A Cisco AVVID Solution

Cisco Press 2001 ISBN: 1-58705-008-0

Phone Models

http://www.cisco.com/en/US/products/hw/phones/ps379/prod_
models_home.html

Quality of Service (QoS)

Cisco QoS Exam Certification Guide, Second Edition

Cisco Press 2004 ISBN: 1-58720-124-0

Restriction Tables

Restriction Tables section of Cisco Unity System Administration
Guide (With Microsoft Exchange)

http://www.cisco.com/en/US/products/sw/voicesw/ps2237/products_
administration_guide_chapter09186a008022cb4f.html

Route Filters

Cisco CallManager Fundamentals: A Cisco AVVID Solution:
Chapter 2—Call Routing

Cisco Press 2001 ISBN: 1-58705-008-0

Security Concerns (CallManager and Unity)

Cisco CallManager Best Practices: Chapter 6—Securing the Environment

Cisco Press 2004 ISBN: 1-58705-139-7

Serviceability Tools

Cisco CallManager Best Practices: Chapter 13—Using Real-Time Monitoring Tool

Cisco Press 2004 ISBN: 1-58705-139-7

Session Initiation Protocol (SIP)

IP Telephony/Voice over IP (VoIP)—Understanding Packet Voice Protocols

http://www.cisco.com/en/US/tech/tk652/tk701/technologies_white_paper09186a008009294d.shtml

Simple Mail Transfer Protocol (SMTP) Networking

SMTP Networking section Networking in the Cisco Unity Guide (With Microsoft Exchange)

http://www.cisco.com/en/US/products/sw/voicesw/ps2237/products_installation_and_configuration_guide_chapter09186a008022cdbc.html

Survivable Remote Site Telephony (SRST)

Ensuring IP Telephony High Availability in the Branch Office

http://www.cisco.com/en/US/products/sw/voicesw/ps2169/products_white_paper09186a008009264e.shtml

Spanning Tree Protocol (STP)

Understanding and Configuring Spanning Tree Protocol (STP) on Catalyst Switches

http://www.cisco.com/en/US/tech/tk389/tk621/technologies_configuration_example09186a008009467c.shtml

Tool for Auto-Register Phones Support (TAPS)

Working with the Tool for Auto-Registered Phones Support Bulk Administration Tool User Guide

http://www.cisco.com/en/US/products/sw/voicesw/ps556/products_user_guide_chapter09186a00801ecedc.html

Voice Profile for Internet Mail (VPIM) Networking

Networking in Cisco Unity Guide (With Microsoft Exchange)

VPIM Networking

http://www.cisco.com/en/US/products/sw/voicesw/ps2237/products_installation_and_configuration_guide_chapter09186a008022cda1.html

Interesting Reading

Have you read any good books lately—aside from the one in your hands that is? Well, I have, and they are listed below. This is by no means a list of all the great Cisco Press books on the subject of IP telephony. It is simply a list of a few books I have in my library that I have found helpful. It doesn't matter how long you have been doing something or how many times you have done it, there is always more to learn. So if you are planning to grow your Cisco IP telephony library, I suggest the following books.

Voice Over IP Fundamentals

ISBN: 1-57870-168-6; Published: Mar 27, 2000

Whether you come from a voice background and are trying to learn the data side or you come from a data background and are trying to ramp up on voice, this book is an excellent resource.

It offers a comparison of traditional voice systems to VoIP, which helps the reader gain a solid understanding of how the Public Switched Telephone Network (PSTN) works and how VoIP fits into modern solutions.

An excellent explanation of many of the traditional telephony signaling protocols and PSTN services are covered in the first portion of the book.

This book includes an IP primer, which can be a great help to anyone who is new to this data world. It helps one to understand the basics of the OSI model and routing protocols.

Many more topics are covered in this book such as VoIP protocols, dial plans, and QoS. A great deal of information is packed into this book, which is less than 400 pages. It is a great book for anyone who is either new to, or has experience with, this industry.

Cisco CallManager Fundamentals: A Cisco AVVID Solution

ISBN: 1-58705-008-0; Published: Jul 31, 2001

Don't be fooled by the title. Although this book does cover the fundamentals of CallManager, it goes into excellent detail on many of the key aspects. Although written in 2001, much of the information is still valuable today.

Regardless of whether you are new to CallManager or have experience working with it, you are sure to learn something while reading this book.

The book offers a glance inside the CallManager to see how it really works. It shows how decisions are made within the system so you understand why it does what it does.

Troubleshooting Cisco IP Telephony

ISBN: 1-58705-075-7; Published: Dec 11, 2002

If your job responsibilities require you to troubleshoot CallManager issues, this book will be indispensable to you.

The book begins by offering a proven methodology for troubleshooting. It goes on to cover nearly every component found in a Cisco IP telephony environment and offers recommendations for proper deployment of Cisco IP telephony.

Time is spent explaining troubleshooting techniques for each component within the system, from phones to gateways, to SQL and beyond. The book includes a section on trace files, which are one of the most helpful and often difficult-to-understand tools for troubleshooting.

After looking at this book and seeing the wealth of information within it, you are sure to want a copy for yourself.

Cisco CallManager Best Practices: A Cisco AVVID Solution

ISBN: 1-58705-139-7; Published: Jun 28, 2004

The name says it all. This book offers solid, proven best practices for a CallManager deployment. The subjects cover best practices for everything from planning through installing, to securing the system and so much more.

If you have ever found yourself asking, "I wonder what the best way to . . . is?" then this book is for you.

Integrating Voice and Data Networks

ISBN: 1-57870-196-1; Published: Oct 20, 2000

Everything you ever wanted to know about voice over data networks is in this book. It goes into great detail on so many areas that it's hard to cover them all in just a few paragraphs.

Although the title may suggest a focus solely on voice over data, rest assured it is not. Ample time is spent in the text to explain traditional voice concepts so you can understand what must be done to integrate this technology with a data network.

This is one of those books you will find yourself referring to time and again—one of those books you are glad you added to your library. Many will find this book an excellent reference when they require an in-depth understanding of many VoIP concepts.

Cisco Unity Fundamentals

ISBN: 1-58705-098-6; Published: Jul 6, 2004

This book offers a detailed explanation of most of the components and concepts found within a Unity system. Because it focuses on Unity, the book can offer a detailed explanation for many of the concepts that *Configuring CallManager and Unity* introduced.

In addition to covering administrative topics, the book explains many of the engineering portions of Unity, such as the hardware and software architecture.

Although this book is not marketed as a "test guide," it is an excellent book to read if you wish to take the Cisco UCSE exam, as it covers many of the topics that you need to understand to pass this test.

Cisco Unity Deployment and Solutions Guide

ISBN: 1-58705-118-4; Published: Aug 3, 2004

Many people have a limited view of Unity, which they display by saying, "It's just voice-mail." As I have stated, time and again, Unity is so much more. If you need any proof of this, next time you are at a bookstore pick up a copy of this book and leaf through it.

You shouldn't have much trouble finding it among the other books as this is one of the larger. I feel that the size speaks volumes (please excuse the pun) as to how complex Unity can be.

The topics covered in this book range from design through installation to managing and beyond. It is touted as the definitive guide to Unity, which is no understatement.

This book is written by some of the most respected names in the Unity world. If you wish for an exhaustive resource that covers the inner workings of Unity, look no further.

INDEX

B

C

D

R

S

T

U

V

W

SEARCH THOUSANDS OF BOOKS FROM LEADING PUBLISHERS

Safari® Bookshelf is a searchable electronic reference library for IT professionals that features thousands of titles from technical publishers, including Cisco Press.

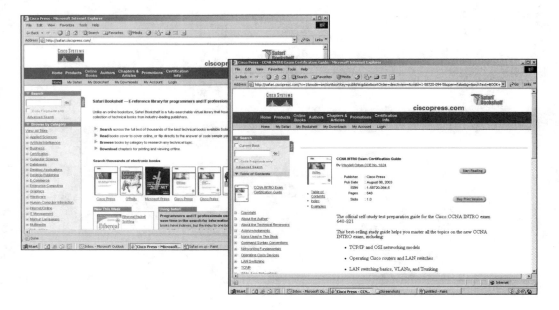

With Safari Bookshelf you can

- **Search** the full text of thousands of technical books, including more than 130 Cisco Press titles from authors such as Wendell Odom, Jeff Doyle, Bill Parkhurst, Sam Halabi, and Dave Hucaby.

- **Read** the books on My Bookshelf from cover to cover, or just flip to the information you need.

- **Browse** books by category to research any technical topic.

- **Download** chapters for printing and viewing offline.

With a customized library, you'll have access to your books when and where you need them—and all you need is a user name and password.

TRY SAFARI BOOKSHELF FREE FOR 14 DAYS!

You can sign up to get a 10-slot Bookshelf free for the first 14 days.
Visit **http://safari.ciscopress.com** to register.